H. LEVITSKY

KIEV

a short guide

MISTETSTVO PUBLISHERS
KIEV

PROGRESS PUBLISHERS
MOSCOW

1980

Генрих Юзефович Левицкий

КИЕВ
Краткий путеводитель

На английском языке

Редакция литературы по спорту и туризму

Translated from the Russian by *Angelia Graf* and *Christopher English*
Editors of the Russian text *Es. Umantseva, V. Ostroumov*
Editor of the English text *G. Pavlov*
Designed by *N. Nesterenko*
Art Editor *Y. Malikov*
Lay out by *G. Kalintseva*
Maps by *L. Cheltsova*

Updated to March 1, 1979

Л $\frac{20904-031}{014(01)-80}$ 91–80 1905040100

Contents

Kreshchatik Street, Kiev's main thoroughfare

COME TO KIEV

As you take your first steps in our city from an airplane ramp or an express train, Kiev welcomes you and presages many interesting meetings and discoveries during your stay.
Kiev is the capital of the Ukrainian Soviet Socialist Republic, one of the fifteen equal Soviet constituent republics and a founding member of the United Nations Organisation. The nature and tempo of life in the city fully accords with its status as a political, administrative, economic, scientific and cultural centre. Located in Kiev are the Central Committee of the Communist Party of the Ukraine, the Supreme Soviet of the Ukrainian SSR, the Council of Ministers of the Ukrainian SSR, the Ukrainian Republican Trade Union Council, the Central Committee of the Leninist Young Communist League of the Ukraine, various ministries, departments and societies, and a whole number of foreign consulates. A considerable portion of the republic's industrial might is concentrated in Kiev, which has well-developed machine-building, precision electrical instruments and light industries. The capital is also the seat of the Academy of Sciences of the Ukrainian SSR; dozens of research and design organisations, the republican boards of artistic unions, 18 institutions of higher learning, seven theatres, a radio and television centre, publishing houses and film studios, several major

libraries and museums housing precious collections, and extensive sports facilities.
Kiev's history spans fifteen centuries, full of dramatic events and heroic deeds. For centuries it was the gold-domed capital city of Kievan Rus, the cradle of the fraternal Russian, Ukrainian and Byelorussian peoples. Here outstanding philosophers, artists, architects, poets, scholars and revolutionaries dreamed of a radiant life to come.
On more than one occasion the city was razed to the ground by foreign invaders, but again and again it rose from its ashes. Its architectural monuments, the pride of the nation, are now famous throughout the world.
Kiev has a vivid revolutionary past. In bronze and granite the city has perpetuated the memory of the Decembrists, Russian revolutionaries from the nobility who started the first armed uprising in Russia against tsarist autocracy in December 1825; of the heroes of the 1905 Revolution; of the Kiev workers, ardent fighters in the October (1917) and January (1918) armed uprisings, who bravely followed the Russian proletariat in raising the banner of the Great October Socialist Revolution.
Kiev is one of the Soviet hero cities. Its courage and valour played an outstanding role in the Soviet people's Great Patriotic War against the nazi invaders.
Kiev is a city of lively housing estates on the picturesque hills

and plains bordering the Dnieper. It now extends more than fifty kilometres along both banks of the river. Woods, parks and public gardens make up over half its area of nearly 80,000 hectares.

The flag of Kiev bears two Orders of Lenin and a Gold Star medal, testimony of the city's working people's great services to the socialist state.

The monument in Honour of the Great October Socialist Revolution

ХАЙ ЖИВЕ ЛЕНІНІЗМ!

The building of the Supreme Soviet of the Ukrainian SSR

The building of the Executive Committee of the city Soviet of People's Deputies

Kreshchatik celebrates

The Rusanovka Canal ▶

The Ukrainian Trade Union Council building *The Dnieper's left bank*

The monument to Taras Shevchenko

The Hotel Kiev ▶

КИЇВ

THE GATEWAYS TO KIEV

BORISPOL AIRPORT

(35 km southeast of Kiev along Kharkov Highway; scheduled buses, route taxis)

This major international airport is named after the ancient town of Borispol, which lies nearby. Airlines from socialist countries, like LOT, MALEV, Interflug, Balkan, CSA and JAT, have flights to Borispol and planes from Moscow headed for Montreal, Paris and Zürich and vice versa make transit stops here. Liners manned by Borispol crews fly to seventeen countries, to cities such as Budapest, Warsaw, Berlin, Prague, Sofia, Vienna and London. Kiev also has uninterrupted aerial communication with the Soviet Union's largest industrial and cultural centres. Passengers are served by the comfortable TU-124, TU-134, TU-154, YAK-40, IL-62 and other liners.

The airport is equipped with the most up-to-date engineering radio-technical and meteorological systems and can thus receive all existing kinds of planes.

The modern-style terminal building, which is both functional and attractive, is the pride of Kiev architects. Its spacious rooms

contain service sectors, an extensive network of communications and information services, lounges, make-and-mend service shops, restaurants, cafeterias, bars and various kinds of kiosks. The right wing of the building houses an international sector, where Intourist premises, rooms for members of the diplomatic corps and the offices of airlines from the socialist countries are located.

Besides Borispol Airport, Kiev is served by the Zhulyany air terminal, which is mainly used for intra-republican flights. The two airports receive and see off over five million passengers a year.

The staff of the international sector of the Central Agency for Aerial Communications will help foreign passengers with their travel documents and tickets for all of Aeroflot's international and national flights and for all planes leaving Soviet airports.

Borispol Airport, International Sector—tel. 267243

Zhulyany Airport, International Sector—tel. 712460

Central Agency for Aerial Communications, International Sector—tel. 744223

The Bus Terminal platforms

THE CENTRAL BUS TERMINAL

(3 Moskovskaya Ploshchad; trolleybuses 1, 11, 12 to the city centre)

The Central Bus Terminal, an important junction of bus routes from all regions of the Soviet Ukraine and a large number of cities in the Russian Federation, the Byelorussian SSR and the Moldavian SSR, has more than 400 incoming and outgoing buses a day.

There are altogether five inter-city bus terminals in Kiev.

The city's bus stations have 68 inter-city routes with an overall length of more than 24,000 kilometres, as well as 100 suburban and inner-city routes. The inter-city routes are served by the Kiev, Lybid, Darnichanka and Zhovtnevy bus lines. You can also tour the Ukraine's historic and other sights aboard the comfortable express buses.

Express tourist buses also link Kiev and the Hungarian People's Republic, the German Democratic Republic, the People's Republic of Bulgaria, the Polish People's

The Railway Station

Republic and the Czechoslovak Socialist Republic.

Rationally distributed among the Central Bus Terminal's three storeys are booking offices, a waiting room, restaurant and hotel. The interiors are decorated with views of Kiev done in mosaics in a folk art style.

Controller's office—tel. 634127, 637180

Central taxi bureau—tel. 082

THE RAILWAY STATION

(Vokzalnaya Ploshchad; Vokzalnaya Metro station)

Kiev is a major national and international transport junction. In spring and summer, at the height of the tourist season, about half a million travellers arrive at the Kiev railway station every day. It serves as a point of departure, transit stop and final destination for special, international and long-distance trains. The capital of the Ukraine has railway connections with the most distant areas of the Soviet Union and many countries of Europe and Asia. From here you can travel direct to Warsaw, Berlin, Sofia, Prague, Budapest, Bucharest, Belgrade, Vienna, Paris, Stockholm, Rome, Athens, Istanbul and Ulan Bator. The Kiev branch of Intourist arranges the travel documents for international trains and carriages.

The station building itself, which was erected in 1932 and occupies a prominent place in the

city's architecture, has been reconstructed several times to keep up with the rapid growth of railway transport. The huge lobby is conveniently connected by passages and stairways with the waiting-rooms on the first and second floors, with the cloakrooms and platforms, the restaurant and the gallery built over the tracks, and holding about a thousand persons. Near the central entrance to the station you will find an excursion office of the Kiev Travel and Excursion Bureau. A short distance away is the suburban train station, from where you can leave on an interesting trip to the picturesque environs of Kiev.

Information—tel. 005

The berths of the river station

The Vokzalnaya Metro station

THE RIVER STATION

(Pochtovaya Ploshchad; Pochtovaya Ploshchad Metro station)

The Kiev River Port is one of the largest on the Dnieper. Each year this modern concern handles large numbers of passengers and millions of tons of various freight.

A genuine revolution occurred in transport on the river with the appearance of high-speed hydrofoil boats. The Kiev River Station, commissioned in 1961, serves long-distance passengers on such vessels. The first two storeys are given over to administrative and auxiliary premises, booking-offices and cloakrooms. On the third and fourth floors are waiting-rooms, a hotel and a restaurant. Particularly noteworthy in the interior decoration are the ornamental panels "From the Varangians to the Greeks", "Bogdan Khmelnitsky's Arrival in Kiev", "The Establishment of Soviet Power in the Ukraine", "Industry on the Dnieper", "Relaxing on the Dnieper". The suburban pavilions, from which one can depart

The excursion ship Yevgeny Vuchetich

on an interesting tour of the Dnieper's nearby coves, share the main station's platform.

The comfortable four-deck motor ships *Yevgeny Vuchetich* and *Sovietskaya Rossiya*, each accommodating 360 passengers, make cruises along the Dnieper through the central and southern Ukraine. The ships have one, two and three berth cabins with air conditioners and all that is needed for a comfortable journey.

River Passenger Transport Agency—tel. 361268, 367111.

THE LANDMARKS OF THE ANCIENT CITY

THE GOLDEN GATES

(corner of Vladimirskaya and Yaroslavov Val Streets; trolleybuses 4 and 12 from the Bus Terminal, trolleybus 2 from the Railway Station, bus 71 from the River Station)

Kiev's Golden Gates date from the 11th century. Surrounded by a picturesque public garden, they, like other monuments of the past, are carefully protected by the state. It is from here that tourists usually begin their rounds of Kiev of the times of Prince Yaroslav the Wise, under whom Kievan Rus reached the height of its flowering and might.

The Golden Gates were a monumental structure, 7.5 metres wide, with a 12-metre-high and approximately 25-metre-long passage, which served both as the main entrance to the central part of the capital's citadel and a mighty defensive barrier. Their dual purpose, by analogy with the Golden Gates of Constantinople, and perhaps also the fact that the grand entranceway's oaken doors were reinforced with copper and decorated with precious metals were what gave the gates their name. Judging from chronicles, the Golden Gates were a rectangular, two-tiered structure with Church of the Annunciation over the entrance. Their walls were built of natural stone—granite, quartzite and slate—and plinths of large, flat bricks laid in pink mortar. The alternation of brown-red and grey-green stone with strips of pink mortar, and the decorative, semi-circular niches in the wall gave the building a particularly attractive appearance. The Golden Gates were damaged during the Mongol-Tatar invasion of 1240, but continued to serve as the entrance to the city until the mid-seventeenth century. In order to preserve them, the remnants of the ancient monument were covered with earth in 1750. In the 1830's they were excavated by the Kiev archeologist K. Lokhvitsky, and somewhat later measures were taken in consultation with the architect A. Beretti to conserve the ruins. Today all that is left of the Golden Gates are fragments of the two parallel walls, which give an idea of stone-laying techniques in Ancient Rus. Projects have now been drawn up to restore this architectural monument.

The Golden Gates. 11th century

THE ST. SOPHIA MUSEUM

(24 Vladimirskaya Ulitsa; trolleybuses 2, 4, 12; buses 20, 38, 68, 71)

In 1934 this unique complex of 11-18th-century buildings acquired the status of a State Museum of Architecture and History by decision of the government of the Soviet Ukraine. A magnificent example of ancient Russian and Ukrainian architecture, it covers an area of five hectares in the centre of Kiev.

The crowning glory of the en-

A bird's-eye view of the St. Sophia museum

ST.SOPHIA CATHEDRAL, STATE MUSEUM OF ARCHITECTURE AND HISTORY

1. St. Sophia Cathedral
2. Belltower
3. Metropolitan's residence
4. Refectory
5. Monks' cells
6. Seminary
7. Consistory
8. South entrance tower
9. West gateway (Zaborovsky Gate)

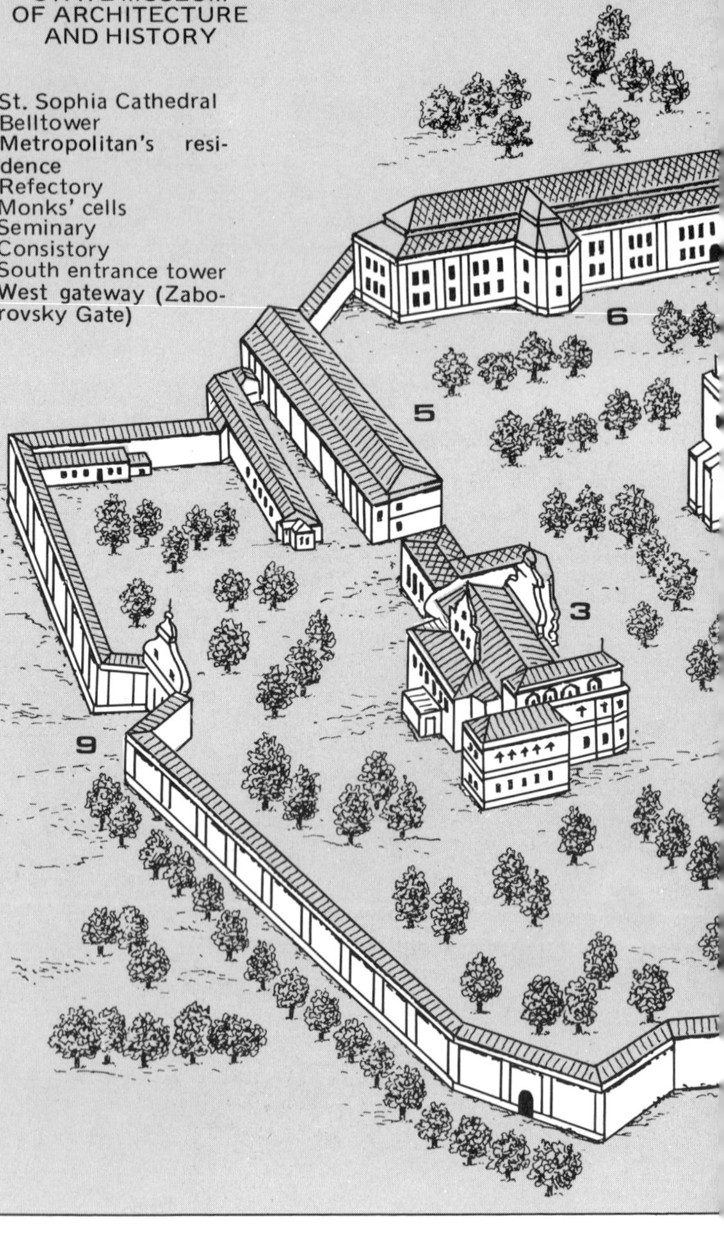

1
2
4
7
8

The St. Sophia Cathedral, an 11th-18th centuries architectural monument

semble is the St. Sophia Cathedral. The foundations of this multi-domed, five-naved church with its open gallery were laid by Prince Yaroslav the Wise in honour of his victory over the Pechenegs, and it was then erected by unknown masters in 1037. The Cathedral stood out among the other buildings of "Yaroslav's Town" for its particular grandeur. As Russia's main metropolitan church, it was to symbolise the wisdom of Christian dogma and affirm feudal princely power. At the same time the Cathedral was the centre of the ancient Russian state's social and cultural life. It witnessed the ceremony of the princes' "seating" on the throne, the debating of the Kiev *veche* (popular assembly), receptions of West European sovereigns, dynastic rituals, the beginnings of chronicle writing, the founding of the first Russian library, and popular festivities. In the course of its existence, St. Sophia underwent many enemy attacks, partial destruction and reconstruction, but retained its original appearance up to the 17th century, as some sketches by the Dutch artist Abraham van Westervelt dating from 1651 testify. Major repairs undertaken in the late 17th and in 18th centuries radically changed the Cathedral's external appearance. Six cupolas were added to the original thirteen, and the contours of the main domes were changed to give them the pear-shaped form characteristic of Ukrainian architecture of the period. It was also at this time that second storeys were built over the Cathedral's external galleries. In 1889 St. Sophia's west façade was entirely rebuilt, a narthex was added, and the 18th-century baroque pediment was replaced by an arched one. This is the form in which the Cathedral has come down to us.

As you cross the Cathedral's threshold, you are immediately overcome by its grandeur and splendour. Its majestic size (length—37 metres; width—55; height from the floor to the top of the central cupola—29), severe inner proportions and monumental wall decorations (260 square metres of mosaics and about 3,000 square metres of frescoes) dating from the 11th century overwhelm you with their perfection "before you can even see and grasp all the details and understand all that the creators of this masterpiece of architecture and painting wanted to say", as the prominent Soviet historian B. Grekov once said. The mosaics of Christ the Pantocrator, the Mother of God (Orante), the Annunciation, Deisus and Eucharist never fail to captivate visitors. Equally famous are the frescoes depicting ancient sporting contests, hunting scenes, performing jesters and so on. There is also a mural of the numerous family of Prince Yaroslav the Wise. You may be interested to know that the Grand Prince's daughters became queens of Norway, France and Hungary, that Yaroslav himself was married to a daughter of the Swedish king Olaf, that his sister married the Polish king Cazimir I, that his sons Svyatoslav and Vsevolod married Byzantine princesses and that the famous Norwe-

The main entrance to the St. Sophia Museum

"Christ the Pantocrator". 11th-century mosaic

gian Vikings Olaf the Saint, Magnus the Good and Harold the Hard Ruler as well as the English king's sons and the heir to the Hungarian throne Andrei I found political asylum at Yaroslav's court. The court thus had truly extensive dynastic ties, and this contributed to enhancing the international prestige of the ancient Russian state.

For a long time the St. Sophia Cathedral served as the burial place of the Kiev princes. It was here that Yaroslav the Wise, Vsevolod Yaroslavich, Rostislav Vsevolodovich, Vladimir Monomakh and other Kiev rulers were buried. But only the marble sarcophagus of Yaroslav the Wise, an object of great historic and artistic value, has been preserved to this day.

On your tour of the Cathedral, do not fail to have a look at its south side-chapels, which made their appearance after the 17th- and 18th-century reconstructions and now house a collection of 12th-century mosaics and frescoes, which were carefully removed by Soviet restorers from the walls of St. Michael's Cathedral (sometimes called the Golden Heads) which could not be saved from destruction.

On the territory of the museum there are quite a number of 18th-century buildings, which form an ensemble characteristic of Ukrainian monasterial architecture of the period. The 76-metre-high, four-tiered belfry, with a gilt, pear-shaped cupola, which now towers over the whole group of structures making up the museum complex, was frequently reconstructed and repaired after it was built between 1699 and 1706. In 1709 at the foot of the belfry the inhabitants of Kiev triumphantly greeted the victors of the Battle of Poltava, headed by Peter the Great, who had routed the troops of the Swedish king Charles XII, and so it is also called the Triumphal Tower. To its south lies the monastery refectory, to the southwest, the consistory, to the north, the seminary

and monks' cells, while opposite the main entrance to the St. Sophia Cathedral is the Metropolitan's residence. The entire compound is surrounded by a stone wall, which had three entrances in the 18th century: under the belfry, under the south entrance tower and through the west gateway, or so-called Zaborowsky Gates, named after the Kiev Metropolitan Rafail Zaborowsky, under whom many churches were built in the city.

The St. Sophia Cathedral is a State Museum of Architecture and History, affiliated to which are the churches of St. Cyril and St. Andrew in Kiev, the Sudak fortress in the Crimea and the Chernigov preserve. All these monuments attract an incessant flow of tourists, but the St. Sophia Cathedral remains the most important, most prized and most popular among them, with about two million Soviet and foreign visitors a year.

St. Sophia Cathedral Museum—tel. 296152

"Bear hunting". 11th-century fresco

THE KIEV-PECHERY LAVRA

(21 Ulitsa Yanvarskovo Vosstaniya; trolleybus 20)

In 1926 this unique group of 11-18th century buildings acquired the status of a State Historical and Cultural Museum by decision of the government of the Soviet Ukraine. The complex covers an area of 28 hectares; forty of its one hundred stone structures are valuable specimens of 11-12th and 17-18th-century architecture and art. The Church of Our Saviour in Berestovo, the Trinity Gateway Church, All Saints Church, the Church of the Exaltation of the Cross and the Near and Far Caves are open to the public.

The museum embraces the territory of the former monastery, first mention of which is found in the famous chronicle *Povesti Vremennykh Let* (The Tale of Bygone Years) among the entries for the year 1051. The origins of the monastery, which is called by the Byzantine name of Lavra, are linked with the spread of Christianity in Russia. In ancient times it was a leading cultural centre, where the chroniclers Nestor, Nikon and Iakov lived and worked, as well as the painter Alipi and the physicians Agapit and Damiant, who made a notable mark in the history of Ancient Rus. The monastery buildings, like the whole of Kiev, were subjected to destruction on more than one occasion, but with the passage of time they again rose from their ruins and ashes, resurrected by talented artisans. The monastery acquired its final architectural form in the second half of the 17th and early 18th centuries, a time of economic, political and cultural growth stimulated by the Ukraine's reunification with Russia.

The Kiev-Pechery Lavra's main shrine was the Cathedral of the Dormition, which was built and decorated in 1073-1089. This six-pillared, single-cupola, stone church was notable for its luxuriance and wealth of decorations, and as an annalist testifies, it was "like onto the heavens". Particularly impressive were the gorgeous, multi-tiered iconostasis, the carved and gilt interior and the inlaid marble floor. After being ruined during the Mongol-Tatar invasions, the cathedral was restored in 1470. Its interior and exterior decorations were subsequently destroyed in a 1718 fire; the cathedral was then rebuilt between 1722 and 1729 under the supervision of the Russian master I. Kalandin into a large, two-tiered church with seven cupolas and rich interior and exterior decorations. In the 1760's the monastery's talented serf architect Stepan Kovnir added figured pediments over the cathedral's top cornice, while the sculptor Iosif Belinsky contributed stucco ornamentations. The Cathedral of the Dormition with its wealth of artistic treasures was destroyed during the Great Patriotic War. Only an insignificant part of it remains, but this is enough to give one a general idea of what this outstanding architectural monument was like.

The main entrance to the monastery is surmounted by the harmoniously proportioned and richly ornamented Trinity Gateway Church, which was built in 1108. Following the 1718 fire, the church was somewhat reconstructed in the 1730's, and in 1731 it was finely decorated by the talented master Vasily Stefanovich. Wave-like pediments were added to the small, four-pillared church and the drum of its single cupola was effectively decorated with stucco ornaments and coloured ceramic rosettes, characteristic of the Ukrainian baroque style. The murals on the façades and interior walls of the church were executed in the first half of the 18th century by masters of the monastery's icon-painting school. The emerald green of the walls combined with the gilt lace of the cornices strikes a forceful major chord against the background of the severe fortification walls.

The Trinity Gateway Church, a priceless specimen of ancient Russian architecture, has remained well preserved to this day.

The museum also includes the Church of Our Saviour in Berestovo, built in the late 11th and early 12th centuries in the village of Berestovo, which served as the Kiev princes' out-of-town residence. It was a large, six-pillared church with three apses, which was girt by a meander brick frieze and crowned by a drum with a semi-spherical cupola. The church is decorated with a profusion of frescoes. The genre scene, "Christ Appears to His Disciples on Lake Tiberias" is notable for its dynamic composition and free style of painting, and the frescoes of the Annunciation and the Nativity are quite expressive. The 17th-century fresco portrait of the Kiev Metropolitan Pyotr Mogila by a Ukrainian artist is outstanding for its depth of characterisation. It is under Pyotr Mogila that the church, also destroyed during the Mongol-Tatar invasions, was rebuilt in 1644. The Greek masters he invited for the purpose were

The Lavra's Great Belfry dates from the 18th century

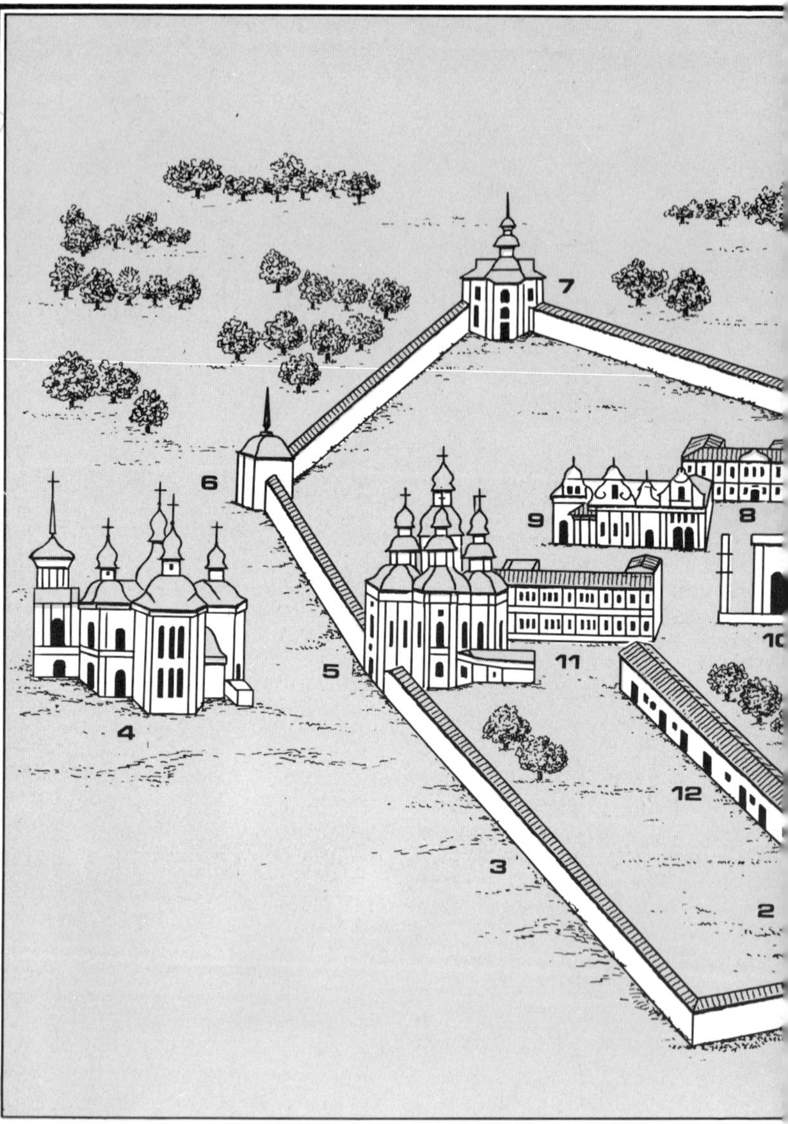

KIEV-PECHERY LAVRA

1. Trinity Gateway Church 2. St. Nicholas Church 3. Fortress Walls 4. Church of Our Saviour in Berestovo 5. All Saints Church 6. Malyarnaya Tower 7. Onufri Tower 8. Lavra Printing house 9. Kovnir Building 10. Church of the Dormition (ruins) 11. Economic Building 12. Monks' cells 13. Great

Belfry 14. Monks' cells 15. Kushnik Tower 16. Governor-General's residence 17. Clock Tower 18. Metropolitan's residence 19. Refectory (nearby are the graves of I. Iskra and V. Kochubei) 20. Belltower in the Near Caves 21. Church of the Exaltation of the Cross 22. Church of the Conception of St. Anne 23. Belltower in the Far Caves 24. Church of the Nativity of the Mother of God.

The All Saints Church and the Economic Building. 17th-19th centuries

The Church of the Nativity of the Mother of God. 17th century

The Church of Our Saviour in Berestovo. 11th-19th centuries

able to splendidly harmonise their new paintings with the church's internal architecture. In ancient times the church served as the family sepulchre of the Monomakhovichi princes, and the son of Vladimir Monomakh, the Kiev Prince Yuri Dolgoruky, who is known in history as the founder of Moscow, was buried here in 1157.

The monastery's Great Belfry soars high above all its other buildings. With its height of 96.52 metres, it used to be the tallest tower structure in Russia. Completed in 1744 under the direction of the famous St. Petersburg architect Johann Shedel, the Belfry is an octagon-shaped, four-tiered tower with a gilt cupola. The first tier is built in the style of rustic masonry. The second is decorated with 32 Roman-Doric columns, arranged in groups of four between eight windows. The third is surrounded by 16 Ionic columns in sets of two between eight arches. The third tier housed the tower's 13 bells, the largest of which weighed over 27 tons. Another bell weighing about 16.5 tons was cast in 1732 by the well-known Russian master Ivan Motorin, the author of the "Tsar Bell" in the Moscow Kremlin. Only three small bells have been preserved. The fourth tier of the Belfry is decorated with light Roman Corinthian semicolumns arranged in groups. The 18th-century clock on a special platform of the fourth tier under the cupola was replaced by a new one in 1903, modelled by Moscow artisans after the Kremlin clock. Each

The interior of the St. Sophia Cathedral

The Trinity Gateway Church. 12th-18th centuries

A view of the Vydubechi Monastery and the Bereznyaki housing estate

"The Descent of the Holy Spirit". Detail of the St. Cyril Church paintings by M. Vrubel

The St. Andrew Church. 18th century

quarter of an hour the chimes play a musical scale, and the hours are marked by a corresponding number of bell tolls. The local serf craftsmen Stepan Kovnir, Iosif Rubashevsky, Ivan Gorokh and others took part in the construction of the Belfry.

On the north side of the monastery is the long, 18th-century economic building, where the monastery's economic and administrative offices were located. Beyond it rises the All Saints Church, which was a watch-tower on the wall that girdles the entire territory of the monastery. The All Saints Church is one of the finest examples of the Ukrainian baroque style.

Not far from the remaining part of the Cathedral of the Dormition stands the building which formerly housed the monastery press. Next to it is Kovnir Building. Erected in the 18th century by Stepan Kovnir, it successfully combined the monastery bakery and bookshop, which were put up at different periods. The structure is now a unified architectural whole embellished with pediments. The Kovnir building now houses a museum.

From the viewing platform of the Upper Lavra one can get a good look at the Lower Lavra, whose territory contains caves that have become known as the Near and Far Caves. These ancient caves are first referred to in the *Povesti Vremennykh Let* annals under the year 1051. From the 1060's the churches built aboveground became the centre of the monastery's religious life and the caves turned into a burial site. For nearly six hundred years they served as the monastery cemetery, where the monks, members of the high clergy and feudal princes were interred in special niches, which are marked by tiny windows in the walls of the labyrinths. The caves are the resting place of the chronicler Nestor, the icon-painter Alipi, the physician Agapit and others whose names have come down in history. Specific climatic conditions and the composition of the caves' soil helped mummify the bodies of the dead. The enterprising monks then gave them out to be "sacred relics", created an aura of holiness around the caves and made them into a place of pilgrimage by the faithful. This in turn prompted the clergy to reconstruct the caves from time to time; gradually spacious corridors were built here and the individual side branches were united into a single main circular passageway. Particular importance was attached to the caves' religious decoration: icons and crosses were set up in them and underground churches built, some of which are of high artistic value.

The Far Caves are 280.5 metres and the Near Caves 228 metres long. They lie at a depth of 5 to 15 metres. The corridors are up to 1.5 metres wide and have an average height of two metres. The labyrinths, which are included among the monastery complex of historical monuments, are open to visitors.

The territory of the Kiev-Pechery Museum also includes several museums on the history of art.

The Mariinsky Palace

The monument to Bogdan Khmelnitsky, the outstanding 17th-century general and statesman

THE VYDUBECHI MONASTERY

(A ten minutes' walk along the Naberezhno-Pecherskaya Road from the Paton Bridge, or take trolleybus 15 to the Botanichesky Sad stop)

This group of 11-18th-century architectural monuments lies in a little amphitheatre among the high hills along the Dnieper. Legend has it that it was right across from here that the wooden idol of Perun which was thrown into the Dnieper after the adoption of Christianity was washed ashore. The place's name, Vydubechi, is accordingly derived from the old Russian verb for surfacing, emerging. The monastery itself was founded by Prince Yaroslav the Wise near a crossing over the Dnieper. In 1070 Yaroslav's son Vsevolod laid the foundations here for the Church of St. Michael, one of the outstanding buildings of the time. It was a large, eight-pillared, domed-cross church, richly decorated with frescoes, but only its western part has come down to us. The monastery acquired its present appearance in the late 17th and early 18th centuries with the building of the Cathedral of St. George, an excellent example of a five-cupola, domed-cross church with a cosy refectory and a three-tiered belfry. It is in the Vydubechi Monastery that its Father Superior Silvestr re-edited the ancient *Povesti Vremennykh Let* annals in 1116. The so-called "Kiev Chronicle" was written here.

The supporting half-arches of the printing house in the Kiev-Pechery Lavra

On the grounds of the Vydubechi Monastery

ASKOLD'S GRAVE

(A ten minutes' walk from the Hotel Dnipro along Petrovskaya Alleya)

According to chronicles and popular tradition, the Princes Askold and Dir became established in Kiev in 862, and that part of the city that had sprung up in the Ugorsk area, in the neighbourhood of present-day Pechersk, began to play the leading role in the life of the city. The Ugorsk area became Askold's fortified residence. It lay farther downstream than the older settlements of Upper Kiev and Podol, in the vicinity of a convenient ford over the Dnieper. Askold evidently regarded this to be of decisive significance for the city's assuming a leading position in the development of commercial ties with the Byzantine empire.

In 882 fighting vessels of the Novgorod Prince Oleg drew up along the bank below Ugorsk. Askold and Dir were killed in the ensuing battle. After becoming master of the city, Oleg moved the princely residence to Starokievskaya (old Kiev) Hill, which most advantageously combined good defence possibilities with proximity to a protected harbour and the main routes connecting the city to the west and south, and declared: "This will be the mother of Russian cities." Oleg laid the groundwork for uniting the East Slav tribes into the single ancient state of Kievan Rus.

In 1810 a church was built according to a design by the well-known architect A. Melensky on the hill overlooking the Dnieper where Askold is said to be buried. The church, a choice specimen of early 19th-century architecture, was later made into a rotonda with a classical colonnade. In 1935 a second storey was added to the building and a park laid around it.

The "Askold's Grave" park

ST. CYRIL CHURCH

(103 Ulitsa Frunze; trolleybus 18)

This fine architectural and artistic monument dates from the 12-19th centuries. In 1146 the Olgovichi princes, who fought long and persistently for the possession of Kiev, founded their own monastery on its northern boundary, where access to the city was most convenient. On a high hill in the centre of the compound they built a monumental stone church dedicated to Saint Cyril. It was a triple-naved, six-pillared domed-cross church with one semispherical cupola. In ancient times it served as a princely sepulchre. One of the heroes of the *Lay of Igor's Host* epic, the Kiev Prince Svyatoslav Vsevolodovich, was interred here in 1194. Up until the mid-17th century, the church and the entire monastery were often subjected to destruction and pillage. The church's appearance was considerably changed as a result of restoration work undertaken in the late 17th and early 18th centuries during which four new octagon cupolas decorated with stucco star-shaped rosettes were added to it. Of particular interest is the church's interior, with its well-preserved monumental wall-paintings—over 800 square metres of 12th-century frescoes, a 17th-century tempera portrait of the monastery's Father Superior and 19th-century oil paintings, among which the compositions of the renowned Russian artist Mikhail Vrubel hold pride of place.

The St. Cyril Church is now a branch of the St. Sophia Museum and houses an exhibition telling about its history, the scholarly research and restoration work that have been done on it and paintings by Vrubel and other 19th-century artists. On Saturdays and Sundays recordings are played here of 16-18th century choral music.

The museum is open from 10 a.m. to 6 p.m. daily except Friday.

The St. Cyril Church. 12th-19th centuries

ST. ANDREW CHURCH

(23 Andreyevsky Spusk; a three minutes' walk from Bogdan Khmelnitsky Square)

For over two centuries now this outstanding creation of the architect Bartolomeo Rastrelli has delighted all who see it with its exquisite forms, majestic design and original location. The distinctive domed-cross five-cupola church (length 32, width 23, and height 42.6 metres, foundation depth up to 15 metres) stands on a steep projection of Starokievskaya Hill, which rises nearly 90 metres above the Dnieper. When you look at it from the streets of the ancient Podol district, it seems to be floating in the air. From

The St. Andrew Church

Vladimirskaya Street lying on a hill, the contours of the church with its Corinthian columns, white pilasters and turquoise and gold cupolas stand out in bold relief against the background of the light-toned expanses beyond the Dnieper.

Rastrelli's design was carried out by his assistant, the Moscow architect I. Michurin. The church's interior is also magnificent, with its fine three-tiered gilt iconostasis, carved ornamentation and sculptures, pulpit and altar canopy. The paintings in the iconostasis were executed by first-rate artists of the time, the Russian A. Antropov and the Ukrainian D. Levitsky. Equally worthy of attention are the paintings "Prince Vladimir Selects a Faith" by an unknown artist and "Apostle Andrew's Sermon on the Banks of the Dnieper" by the local painter G. Borispolets. The church was repaired on several occasions following its consecration in 1767, but did not undergo any substantial alterations. Between 1974 and 1978 it was completely restored, and is now a branch of the St. Sophia Museum. It contains an exhibition devoted to the history of the church and the work of Rastrelli. Here on Saturdays and Sundays one can listen to recordings of 18th-century Russian and Ukrainian choral music.

The museum is open from 10 a.m. to 6 p.m. daily except Thursday.

Tel. 295861

THE MARIINSKY PALACE

(5 Ulitsa Kirova; trolleybus 20, bus 62)

The Mariinsky, or Tsar's, Palace is a fine monument of 18-19th-century architecture, based on a plan by Rastrelli according to which the palace in the village of Perovo near Moscow was also built. Erected in 1755, the Mariinsky Palace with its wings and church premises had a stone first floor and a wooden upper storey, but lost its original appearance during a 1819 fire. It was not until in 1870 that the building was reconstructed. The design by architect K. Mayevsky retained the famous Rastrelli's stylistic peculiarities, and it is in this form that the two-storey baroque stone palace has come down to us. The front façade is 65.3 metres long, the side facing the park—119 metres, the width of the central block is 20 metres and its height—about 16. The palace's paired white semi-columns and turquoise outer walls with their stucco mouldings blend beautifully with the greenery of the adjacent park. The Russian tsars frequently stayed at the Mariinsky Palace and it was the residence of the military governors of Kiev, including the great Russian general Mikhail Kutuzov. In 1917 the revolutionary committee which directed the preparations for the armed October uprising in Kiev had its headquarters in the palace; the Kiev Committee of the Bolshevik Party and the Council of People's Commissars also used the premises for some time following the establishment of Soviet power in the Ukraine. During the years of nazi occupation the Mariinsky Palace was destroyed. After the war it was restored basically to its former state according to a design by the architect P. Alyoshin, and is now protected by the state as an architectural monument. It is the site of official receptions for the city's most honoured guests and of governmental functions on the occasion of important dates and events in the life of the Soviet state.

ST. VLADIMIR CATHEDRAL

(20 Bulvar Tarasa Shevchenko; Universitet metro station)

This functioning church, consecrated in 1896 in honour of the 900th anniversary of Russia's adoption of Christianity is another fine piece of architecture. The first plan of the church, drawn up in 1853 by the St. Petersburg architect I. Shtrom, was not carried out on account of the great construction costs. The foundations for the cathedral were finally laid in 1862 according to Shtrom's design, substantially modified by A. Beretti. Later the prominent Kiev architects R. Berngard, V. Nikolayev and K. Mayevsky and the engineer D. Birkin also took part in its construction. All this led to a certain disharmony in the building's appearance. The triple-naved, eight-pillared, domed-cross cathedral is crowned by seven cupolas and rises to a height of 49 metres. The main façade, which is nearly 30 metres wide, is adorned by a richly ornamented double-leaved doorway with relief bronze sculptures of Princess Olga and Prince Vladimir against a blue enamel background. The cathedral's frescoes were executed by the major Russian artists V. Vasnetsov, M. Vrubel, M. Nesterov, P. Svedomsky, V. Kotarbinsky and others under the direction of Kiev University art professor A. Prakhov.

St. Vladimir Cathedral

The monument to Prince Vladimir Svyatoslavich (Detail)

THE MONUMENT TO PRINCE VLADIMIR SVYATOSLAVICH

(Vladimirskaya Gorka Park; a five minutes' walk from Ploshchad Leninskovo Komsomola)

The monument to the outstanding statesman of Kievan Rus, Prince Vladimir Svyatoslavich, was unveiled on September 23, 1853. The 20.4-metre-high monument was erected according to a design by the Russian sculptor Vasily Demut-Malinovsky and the architect Konstantin Ton on one of the most picturesque terraces of Vladimir Hill, which towers 70 metres above the Dnieper. The bronze figure of the prince, which is 4.5 metres high and weighs about 6 tons, is the work of professor P. Clodt. St. Vladimir is dressed in the garb of an ancient Russian warrior, with a princely mantle on his shoulders. He holds a large cross in his right hand, and the dynastic Crown of Monomakh in his left. His expressive face is turned toward the mighty Dnieper. The monument's octagonal base, faced in cast-iron slabs, bears the ancient coat-of-arms of Kiev, a bronze bas-relief depicting the Kievans' adoption of Christianity and profuse mouldings of flowers. The monument looks splendid from any angle and adds much to the city's silhouette. It is an important part of the city's architectural and artistic aspect.

THE MONUMENT TO BOGDAN KHMELNITSKY

(Ploshchad Bogdana Khmelnitskovo; trolleybuses 2, 4, 12, buses 20, 38, 68, 71)

The monument to Bogdan Khmelnitsky, a Ukrainian national hero, statesman and military leader, was unveiled on May 15, 1888. It was erected according to a design by the sculptor M. Mikeshin and the architect V. Nikolayev with funds raised by the population. The monument stands on the historic site where the inhabitants of Kiev welcomed

The Monument to Bogdan Khmelnitsky (Detail)

Khmelnitsky after his troops' victory over the Polish invaders. The bronze horseman on the granite pedestal is a most expressive figure: checking his steed in full gallop, Bogdan Khmelnitsky points to the north with his hetman's mace, in the direction of Moscow. This energetic gesture symbolises the Ukrainian people's desire to be forever reunited in a single state with its fraternal Russian people. The monument is one of the city's notable sights.

THE EVER-PRESENT PAST

It is not too long ago that Kiev archeologists finished studying the 5-8th century materials they unearthed during excavations on Zamkovaya, Starokievskaya and Detinseva Hills and in the Podol district. The most important result of these digs was the discovery of an ancient settlement, whose moat and ramparts defended the northeastern projection of Starokievskaya Hill. In it specialists saw actual traits of "Kii town", about which the chronicler Nestor relates the following ancient legend in the *Povesti Vremennykh Let* annals:

"There were three brothers: one was named Kii, the second Shchek, and the third Khoriv, and their sister Lybed. Kii ruled on the hill which is now called Borichev, and Shchek sat on the hill which is now called Shchekovitsa, and Khoriv on the third, which after him was called Khorevitsa, and they founded a city and called it by the name of Kiev (Russian for Kii's.—*Tr.*) in the name of their eldest brother."

There is a legend telling of the visit of Kii, prince of the East Slavs, to Constantinople and his reception there by the Byzantine emperor. Studies of indirect written sources have shown that this visit might have taken place in the

530s, during the reign of the emperor Justinian I. One would naturally expect that Prince Kii set out for Byzantium after his city was founded on Starokievskaya Hill, and materials obtained from archeological digs have confirmed that Kiev arose in the last decades of the 5th century AD. Thus science has thrown new light on the legend and the chronicler's question: "Whence did the Russian land take its origin and who were the first princes in Kiev?" The city of Kiev will mark its 1500th anniversary in May 1982.

Ancient Kiev has given us priceless frescoes, architectural monuments, and a wealth of eloquent museum relics. Many of its street names—Vladimir, Decimal, Golden Gates, Yaroslav's Ramparts, Igor—seem to be taken from the pages of ancient chronicles and together with the very stones of their buildings evoke the images and deeds of distant ancestors—statesmen and simple artisans, brave warriors and talented architects. Everywhere one finds reminders of important dates, striking events, vivid personalities:

—The glorious campaigns of

A view of the Dnieper from Vladimir Hill

the warriors of Prince Oleg, whose rule saw the unification of the ancient Russian lands and Kiev's establishment as the capital city of a mighty state. The princes Igor and Svyatoslav actually put an end to the incessant incursions of nomad tribes.

—In 988 Prince Vladimir Svyatoslavich adopted Christianity and took drastic steps to unite all the Slav principalities into a single state. His possessions stretched from the Baltic and the Carpathians to the Black Sea and the Volga. According to Karl Marx, this period (980-1015) was the "culminating point" in the history of the ancient Russian state, the time of its greatest political might. Kiev became a major centre of commerce, crafts and culture. Its boundaries and population expanded. Extensive construction work went on in the city simultaneously with the erection of new defence works. "Vladimir's Town" became one of the largest and richest cities in Europe.

—After his brilliant victory over the Pechenegs, who had forced their way through to the city, Yaroslav the Wise (1019-1054) erected the new "City of Great Kiev" on the battlesite, to the southwest of "Vladimir's Town". At this time Kievan Rus came to be one of the most powerful states in the world arena. The written language spread, and the city's first cultural and political figures appeared. Foreign merchants and envoys were struck by the luxury and magnificence of

"Yaroslav's city" with its Golden Gates and St. Sophia Cathedral, the chief metropolitan church of Kievan Rus.

—In the 12th century the chronicler Nestor wrote his immortal *Povesti Vremennykh Let* and an unknown author composed *The Lay of Igor's Host*, that pearl of ancient Russian literature.

...Ancient Kiev went through a period of great flourishing, as well as long years of decline. The feudal division of Kievan Rus into apanage principalities, internecine wars, nomad raids and devastating fires led to the city's loss of its position as the political centre of

A mosaic on the façade of the Rovesnik Cinema depicting the founders of Kiev

Yaroslav the Wise. Stained glass work from the Historical Museum

all Russia, although nominally it remained the state's capital. Its inhabitants had only just managed to raise it from its ruins when the Mongol-Tatar hordes of Khan Batu again razed it to the ground. The charred walls of churches and houses could still be seen in Kiev until the end of the 14th century. A few decades of revival were again followed by a period of desolation after the Crimean Khan Mengli-Girei looted and burnt the city together with its finest monuments in 1482.

Many more foreign conquerors hankered after the keys to Kiev, which are now on display in the historical museum. But the capital city, like the whole of Russia, always fought stubbornly against its invaders.

Kiev played a leading role dur-

A reconstructed model of Kiev in the 10th-13th centuries

The 19th-century keys to the gates of the Kiev-Pechery fortress. Historical Museum

The monument to Grigory Skovo-roda, 18th-century Ukrainian educator, philosopher and poet

In the early 18th century this was the study building of the Kiev Academy

ing the Ukraine's war of liberation against its Polish invaders, during its struggle to reunite with Russia. After his victory in the battle of Zholtiye Vody and Korsun, the Hetman Bogdan Khmelnitsky declared Kiev his capital. In January 1654, welcoming the decision of the Pereyaslav Rada (Council) on the Ukraine's reunification with Russia, the inhabitants of Kiev took an oath of loyalty to their friendship with the fraternal Russian people.

An active role in the liberation movement was played by the Kiev Brotherhood, a national religious association set up at the Kiev Bratsky Monastery in the Podol district at the beginning of the 17th century. The Brotherhood had a school and was one of the centres of the city's political and cultural life. Its members were Zaporozhye Cossacks headed by the Hetman P. Sagaidachny. In 1632 through the merger of the Kiev Brotherhood and the Kiev-Pechery Lavra schools the Kiev-Mogilyansky Collegium was formed. It was transformed into the Kiev Academy by Peter I in 1701. The Academy's graduates included many prominent public leaders and cultural figures who did much to strengthen the ties uniting the Ukrainian, Russian and Byelorussian peoples.

The Ukraine's reunification with Russia had a decisive effect on its economic and cultural development as a whole and that of Kiev in particular. The second half of the 17th and the 18th centuries saw the rebirth of architecture and the growth of national culture and art in the city.

The monument to the outstanding Ukrainian writer Ivan Kotlyarevsky

A plaque commemorating the Decembrists

The monument to the great Russian poet Alexander Pushkin

By the end of the 18th century Kiev already had a population of 30,000. It had considerably grown in area, but in view of its peculiar historical development it lacked territorial integrity and, as in the past, was basically made up of the separate Starokievsky, Pechersk and Podol districts. This period saw the appearance of wooden buildings in the Khreshchataya Valley (present-day Kreshchatik), between whose forest-covered slopes flowed a small stream.

It was only at the beginning of the 19th century that the first draft of Kiev's general development plan was drawn up by the city's chief architect, A. Melensky. His plan was in the main implemented in subsequent years.

Between 1806 and 1811 the great Russian general Mikhail Kutuzov was the Governor-General of Kiev. In connection with the Russo-Turkish War, extensive fortification work was carried out in the city under his supervision. Civilian construction was also in full swing: an arcade of shops was begun in the Podol district, and an invalids' home in Pechersk; the candles lighting the city streets were replaced by oil lamps; and the first gymnasium and girls' school were opened in town, as well as a trade school in the Podol

The main block of Taras Shevchenko University

Taras Shevchenko's house-museum

district and several parochial schools.

In the 1820's Kiev became one of the centres of the struggle against the tsarist autocracy by the Decembrists, members of the revolutionary nobility. Congresses of the leaders of their Southern Society, founded in the Ukraine, and talks between representatives of the Southern and Northern societies on a joint armed uprising against tsarism were held in the city. The Decembrists gathered in the Contract House in the Podol district, using the yearly fairs here as a pretext for their coming to Kiev. Another of the Decembrists' frequent meeting-places was the house on Alexandrovskaya Street (presently 14 Kirov St.) belonging

to the hero of the 1812 Patriotic War General N. Raevsky whose family was closely connected with the Decembrist movement. One of the friends of the family was the great Russian poet Alexander Pushkin who had been exiled by the tsarist government to the Ukraine at the time.

After the mid-19th century the city was embellished by many remarkable neo-classical buildings designed by the architects V. and A. Beretti, A. Schille, A. Melensky and others. The most notable of them, which greatly influenced the further development of the city's architecture, was the University building, the work of V. Beretti.

A pleiad of brilliant Russian scientists and cultural figures is linked with Kiev University. Among its honorary members were the scientists Dmitry Mendeleyev, Ilya Mechnikov and Nikolai Pirogov and the writers Ivan Goncharov, Lev Tolstoy, and Ivan Turgenev. The prominent scientists A. Bakh, D. Zabolotny, N. Strazhesko and Y. Tarle, the playwright A. Korneichuk and the poet M. Rylsky studied here at different times.

The magnificent Ukrainian poet, artist and revolutionary and democratic thinker Taras Shevchenko dreamed of teaching at the University. He was taken on here in 1847 as a drawing instructor, but never started work on account of his arrest together with all the other members of the illegal Cyril and Methodius Society,

The early 20th-century building of the former Catholic church

The Polytechnic Institute

Kreshchatik in the latter half of the 19th century

НОТАРІУСЪ
С.Б.ШЕНФЕЛЬДЪ
ПЕРАТОРСКАГО УНИВЕРСИТЕТА Св. ВЛАДИМІРА
АПТЕКА А.МАРЦИНЧИКА

which fought against serfdom. He was banished from Kiev under strict surveillance as a soldier in the Orenburg Corps and prohibited from writing or drawing. The poet loved Kiev and wrote many splendid works there. While in exile he wrote: "...Most often of all I soothe my aged imagination with pictures of gold-domed, garden-cloaked and poplar-crowned Kiev."

Many events in Shevchenko's life and work are connected with Kiev, and its inhabitants lovingly preserve the memory of the great bard. There are now two Shevchenko museums in the city and the University has also been named after him. Across from it, where a statue of Nicholas I once stood, is a monument to the poet.

In second half of the 19th century the first large works of engineering began to appear in the city on the Dnieper. One of them was the suspension bridge over the river, which was built in 1853. Its history is a particle of Kiev's: in 1912 the first electric tram crossed it, in 1920 it was blown up by retreating White Poles, in 1925 it was rebuilt according to a design by the Kiev professor Y. Paton, during the Great Patriotic War it was blown up for the second time, and in 1965 it was replaced by the Metro bridge.

Toward the end of the 19th century the city was becoming a developed industrial centre. By then it had railway connections with Moscow, Kursk and Odessa and its first large industrial enterprises, the present-day Bolshevik and Leninskaya Kuznitsa factories, had sprung up. The first electric station, the first water pipes

Modern buildings on the Dnieper's left bank

and the first electric tram in Russia and second in Europe, which linked Kreshchatik with the Podol district, also made their appearance in Kiev at this time.

In 1898 the first Polytechnic Institute in Russia was founded in Kiev on public initiative and with public funds. The great Russian chemist Dmitry Mendeleyev took an active part in the establishment of this major educational institution.

At the beginning of the 20th century more than half the buildings in Kiev were still wooden; at that time the city's population had already passed the 500,000 mark. As in the other cities of tsarist Russia, only the central part of town was relatively comfortable and well laid out, but the architecture of many public and residential buildings on the city's main thoroughfares, where the local bourgeoisie lived, was characterised by modernistic trends and a mixture of styles.

On the one hand were the fashionable restaurants and stores, banks and rented houses along Kreshchatik street, which became the centre of the city's business life; on the other was the gloomy poverty of the working districts on the outskirts, which had neither water pipes nor sewer systems and where starvation and epidemics took the lives of whole families. These were the faces of Kiev during the rapid development of capitalism in Russia and the Ukraine, in the hard years before the revolution.

On the eve of the First Russian Revolution the city's proletariat already had considerable experience in the class struggle, largely

"The 1905 Sappers' Uprising in Kiev". A drawing on display at the Historical Museum

thanks to the work of Marxist groups, whose active members included the prominent revolutionaries P. Zaporozhets, L. Ketskhoveli, A. Lunacharsky and Y. Melnikov. The Kiev League of Struggle for the Emancipation of the Working Class and the newspaper *Iskra* support-groups played an important part in the working class movement. The Ulyanov family had close connections with the city's Party underground. In 1903-1904 Lenin's mother Maria Alexandrovna and his sisters Anna and Maria lived on Laboratory Street (presently 12 Ulyanovs St.), while his brother Dmitry resided in the centre at what is now 30 Pushkin St. His family kept Vladimir Lenin posted on all the events in the Ukraine's revolutionary struggle.

On October 18, 1905, the blood of the working people was shed on Duma Square (now October Revolution Square) when the police, gendarmes and Cossacks broke up a meeting numbering many thousands, killing and wounding over 500 persons. At the height of the revolutionary movement in the city there arose the Kiev Soviet of Workers' Deputies.

In November 1905 insurgent sappers commanded by second lieutenant B. Zhadanovsky left their barracks arms in hand. Along the way from Pechersk their ranks were joined by workers from the Arsenal and Southern Russian Engineering factory and the Main Railway Workshops, and students. Soldiers and workers, who until then had been on opposite sides of the barricades, marched side by side for the first time. A massacre

The memorial plaque on the wall of the house where Dmitry Ulyanov lived in 1903 and 1904

occurred on Galitskaya Square (now Victory Square), in which hundreds of workers and soldiers were killed and wounded. This insurrection is on a par with the uprising on the battleship *Potemkin*, the revolutionary actions of soldiers and sailors in Sebastopol and other such events.

The heroic traditions of the Kiev proletariat were established in the revolutionary battles of 1905. During the subsequent years of reaction and the First World War it continued to carry on an organised struggle against the autocracy, growing experienced and mature as it prepared for the decisive battles to come. Its traditions manifested themselves to their full extent in October 1917 and January 1918...

The ever-present past... If you gaze carefully at today's city, you will at every step see landmarks from its history.

THE BANNER OF REVOLUTION

HEROES OF ARSENAL SQUARE

(Arsenalnaya Metro station)

The streets leading to this small square in the centre of Pechersk District were once the site of selfless fighting by the Kiev proletariat for Soviet power.

On the Moscow Street (Ulitsa Moskovskaya) side, the square is lined by the immense stone wall of one of the shops of the Arsenal Factory, one of the oldest industrial enterprises in Kiev. Pocked with bullet marks, this wall is a silent but eloquent witness to those distant, stormy events.

The victorious October Revolution in Petrograd touched off mighty echoes here. On October 29, 1917, the revolutionary Arsenal workers and the soldiers of the Third Airpark formed the vanguard of Kiev's October armed uprising. After three days of stubborn fighting, power came into the hands of the Soviets. But the nationalist bourgeois Central Rada took advantage of this victory to promote its policy of breaking away from Soviet Russia and inciting a fratricidal war. Dealing the insurgents a treacherous blow in the back, the Central Rada established a bloody dictatorship. But in spite of its great losses, the proletariat of Kiev rallied under the leadership of the Bolshevik Revolutionary Committee and prepared for new battles...

In 1923 the cannon from which the Arsenal workers fired the first shot at the troops of the

"The Arsenal Workers at the Barricades". High relief sculpture

counter-revolutionary Central Rada was set up on a red granite pedestal in the centre of the square.

In 1961 a high-relief sculpture by M. Korotkevich and N. Kovtun, depicting "The Arsenal Workers at the Barricades", was affixed to the bullet-scarred factory wall, which it was decided to leave untouched. Next to it is the entrance to the People's Museum of the legendary Arsenal factory.

The commemorative plaque on the wall of the house where the Ulyanov family lived

THE MONUMENT TO THE HEROES OF THE GREAT OCTOBER SOCIALIST REVOLUTION

(Sovietskaya Ploshchad; trolleybus 20)

This monument was erected in 1927 over the common grave of the revolutionary workers and soldiers who died the death of the brave in the fighting for Soviet power between October 29 and 31, 1917. Like many others, it was destroyed by the nazi invaders during the last war. It was restored in 1949.

A red granite bowl rests on a black marble slab. The monument's surroundings are equally symbolic: nearby, is the building which served as the headquarters for the Kiev Revolutionary Committee, headed by the ardent Leninist revolutionary A. Ivanov, and the white building of the Ukrainian Supreme Soviet, flying the State Flag of the Ukrainian Soviet Socialist Republic. In the vicinity is a viewing platform with a panorama of today's Kiev.

THE MONUMENT TO THE HEROES OF THE JANUARY ARMED UPRISING

(Sovietski Park; trolleybus 20)

This majestic bronze figure of a worker with a banner in his hand atop a labradorite pedestal personifies the fighters who bravely stood up against the nationalist bourgeois Central Rada in January 1918.

...The First All-Ukrainian Congress of the Soviets of Workers' and Soldiers' Deputies, held in Kharkov in December 1917, was a turning-point in the Kiev proletariat's struggle for Soviet power. The congress proclaimed the Ukraine a Soviet republic and solemnly declared the establishment of an indissoluble union between the Soviet Ukraine and Soviet Russia.

On the order of the Central Executive Committee of the Ukraine, revolutionary troops, actively supported by units from Soviet Russia, set out from Kharkov onto Kiev shortly after the Congress.

On January 15, 1918, when the revolutionary troops were already approaching the city, an armed uprising began in Kiev under the leadership of the Revolutionary Committee. As in October 1917, its focal point was the Arsenal factory; workers from many of the city's districts came to the aid of their Arsenal brethren. The Central Rada was forced to withdraw its most reliable troops from the front and send them in to suppress the uprising. Hard battles were fought for lite-

Heroes of the Arsenal Square

Soviet Square

М
АРСЕНА

ВІЧНА СЛАВА
УЧАСНИКАМ СІЧНЕВОГО
ЗБРОЙНОГО ПОВСТАННЯ
1918 РОКУ В КИЄВІ,
ЯКІ ЗАГИНУЛИ В БОРОТЬБІ
ЗА ВЛАДУ РАД

ally every street. The Arsenal cted as a true bastion in the fighting; its defenders repulsed wave fter wave of attacking counter-evolutionaries, their superiors in trength. But their ranks eventually began to thin and their ammunition to run out. On January 21 the blood-thirsty counter-revolutionaries burst onto the territory of the Arsenal factory and massacred the insurgents. Many workers were hacked up and tortured o death on the spot and three undred were executed by a firing quad.

But the counter-revolutionaries id not enjoy their victory for ong. The uprising facilitated the evolutionary troops' successful dvance on Kiev. On January 22, Soviet units commanded by Yuri Kotsyubinsky, the son of the outtanding Ukrainian writer Mikhail Kotsyubinsky, occupied the Darnitsa district and the bridges over the Dnieper. Red Cossack detachments commanded by Vitay Primakov entered the Kurenevka district. There they routed the Central Rada troops, the remnants of which fled. On January 26, 1918, Soviet power was established in Kiev, and on January 30 the ntire city turned out for the uneral of the heroes of the anuary armed uprising.

On Soviet holidays workers with their families use to come to he streets named after the Arsenal heroes Andrei Ivanov, Nikolai Gaitsan, Alexander Anishchenko and Prokop Aistov and lay flowers t the foot of the monuments to heir fathers and grandfathers who ought for their future in the revoutionary battles of 1917 and 1918.

'he monument to the participants n the January armed uprising of 918

The monument to the heroes of the January armed uprising was unveiled in 1967.

OCTOBER REVOLUTION SQUARE

(Ploshchad Oktyabrskoi Revolyutsii Metro station)

This square, where the City Duma (assembly) once stood, has witnessed a lot: the flowing blood of workers in 1905, the revolutionary tread of the Red Guard detachments in October 1917, the resounding hoofbeats of the Red Cavalry in January 1918; in November 1943 when Kiev was liberated from the nazis, the Soviet tanks filed by here in a triumphant procession; and it is here that the hitlerites guilty of exterminating thousands of Kiev citizens were executed in accordance with wartime laws as retribution for their butchery.

In 1977 Kiev celebrated the 60th anniversary of the Great October Revolution on the unrecognisably renovated square. It was then that the Monument in Honour of the Great October Socialist Revolution by sculptors V. Borodai, V. Znoba and I. Znoba and architects A. Malinovsky and N. Skibitsky was unveiled.

The monument's red granite pylon in the form of a symbolic unfurled banner, the majestic figure of Lenin and the courageous features of the revolutionary fighters—a worker, a peasant in a soldier's great coat, a woman com-

October Revolution Square during an arts festival

missar and a sailor—look impressive both in the sunny daylight and under their special evening illumination. The glittering streams of the monument's waterfall fountain, the geometric shapes of the flower-beds, which take up an area of 540 square metres, the dark-grey, polished granite slabs which cover its centre, accessible to pedestrians, and the green terraces and steps of its main approach are all conceived in an integral architectural and artistic style.

The monument, which is located in the city centre, is surrounded by the buildings of the October Palace of Culture, the highrise Moskva Hotel, the Tchaikovsky Conservatoire, the Central Post Office and the Ukrainian Trade Union council. The square is, as it were, the heart of Kiev; here one feels with particular intensity the rhythm of this large modern city.

KIEV IN THE TWENTIETH CENTURY

In the centre of the capital of the Soviet Ukraine, at the convergence of the city's three main thoroughfares—Kreshchatik, Taras Shevchenko Boulevard (Bulvar Tarasa Shevchenko) and Red Army Street (Ulitsa Krasnoarmeiskaya)—rises a monument to the founder of the Communist Party and the world's first socialist state, Vladimir Ilyich Lenin. The red granite figure of this leader conveys fiery impulse and a passionate appeal to his contemporaries and descendants. Inscribed in gold letters on the statue's pedestal are Lenin's words: "Given united action by the Great-Russian and Ukrainian proletarians, a free Ukraine is *possible*; without such unity, it is out of the question."

The working people of the Ukraine were among those who initiated the formation of the Union of Soviet Socialist Republics in 1922. Under the leadership of the Communist Party and in collaboration with the other peoples of the Soviet Union they successfully coped with the most difficult tasks of socialist industrialisation, collectivisation in agriculture and cultural development and were also able to realise their age-old dream of reuniting all the Ukrainian lands into a single Soviet state.

The Ukraine has become a flourishing republic with a mighty industry, highly developed agriculture and advanced science and culture. It contributes greatly to implementing plans for communist construction in the Soviet Union, to strengthening the unity of the socialist community and developing friendly ties and cooperation among all peoples.

The Ukraine's economy—an integral part of the country's

The monument to Vasily Bozhenko, hero of the 1918-1920 Civil War

single economic complex—is developing according to the laws of socialist division of labour and Lenin's precepts as to the brotherhood of all nations. The Ukrainian people's enormous social and economic achievements have been recorded in its Constitution, which was drawn up with regard to national developmental peculiarities in the letter and spirit of the Fundamental Law of the USSR, the manifesto of a mature socialist society.

...The city on the Dnieper went through a lot during the hard years of the Civil War. Foreign interventionists, White Guard hordes and nationalist bourgeois counter-revolutionaries tried to get a hold on the Ukrainian land and its chief city of Kiev. But underground fighters, led by Communist-Leninists, and workers' detachments defended the gains of Soviet power. Their selfless efforts together with the powerful attacks of the Red cavalrymen led by Vasily Bozhenko, Vitaly Primakov, Nikolai Shchors and Yuri Kotsyubinsky brought the city its long-desired freedom.

...The October Revolution opened up unprecedented possibilities for development to Kiev and all the other cities of the Soviet Union. Planned rehabilitation and construction of residential, public and industrial buildings was begun under socialist conditions. Between 1921 and 1925 alone, 25,000 of Kiev's workers moved into new apartments from the basements and hovels where they used to live.

The 1930s were a time of particularly energetic development for the capital of the Soviet Ukraine. The volume of capital investments in the municipal economy markedly increased and the town's

The monument to Vitaly Primakov, hero of the 1918-1920 Civil War

industrial potential showed rapid growth.

The Soviet people's creative labour was interrupted by the treacherous attack of nazi Germany on the Soviet Union. On June 22, 1941, the first bombs fell on Kiev and many other of the country's towns and villages.

In the very first days of the war, 200,000 of Kiev's inhabitants entered the ranks of the defenders of their socialist homeland. About half the members of the city's Party organisation joined the Red Army. All of Kiev's enterprises were urgently put on a war footing and volunteer corps, communist regiments and avengers' battalions were formed. On July 2, 1941, 160,000 of the city's inhabitants worked on the construction of defence works on the approaches to Kiev.

On July 10 and 11 the front reached the city and its heroic defence lasted for over two and a half months. The nazi command twice issued orders for its troops to parade along Kreshchatik, but their schemes were foiled by the courage of the Soviet soldiers and volunteer corps. The defence of Kiev played an important part in frustrating Hitler's plan for a "Blitzkrieg".

A stubborn struggle against the nazi invaders, in which the Party underground operated with success, began in occupied Kiev. The patriots disrupted all the invaders' attempts to organise the work of the city's enterprises and arrange the supply of their troops.

The enemy marked its stay in Kiev with bloody atrocities. During the years of the city's occupation the nazis tortured, shot, hung and gassed 200,000 of its citizens.

But the hour of liberation came, and on November 6, 1943, the red flag was again raised over Kiev.

The soldiers of the First Ukrainian Front who liberated Kiev found a scene of fearful destruction. Kreshchatik lay in ruins and the city seemed dead. The occupationists had destroyed 42 per cent of Kiev's housing and put more than a thousand of its enterprises out of commission. The city's museum and library collections had been looted and the nazi barbarians had shipped home many artistic treasures from the cathedrals of St. Sophia and the Dormition.

On the day after liberation, the whistle of the Leninskaya Kuznitsa factory sounded over Kiev, and all the remaining enterprises in the city followed its example. Armed with pickaxes and spades, the population began to clear the ruins; they worked over two and a half million man-hours overtime in the ashes of Kreshchatik alone.

The historic Letter of the Working People of the Capital of the Soviet Ukraine to the Russian People, whose text was adopted by the Kievans right after the city's liberation, reads in part: "We publicly confirm that the Ukraine's freedom and happiness lies in its indissoluble union with the Russian people and all the fraternal Soviet peoples. We publicly swear to strengthen this sacred and salutary union. And we bequeath our oath to our children and descendants for all times."

The city's rebirth became the concern of the whole Soviet Union. Machinery and equipment, building materials and provisions reached Kiev day and night from Moscow, Sverdlovsk, Gorky, Tash-

The monument to Vladimir Ilyich Lenin

ЛЕНІН

The monument to the heroic crew of the armoured train Tarashchanets, who were killed in 1919

The monument to Nikolai Shchors, hero of the 1918-1920 Civil War

kent, Ufa and all the fraternal Soviet republics. The solicitude shown by the Communist Party and the state, the collaboration and mutual assistance of all the peoples of the Land of the Soviets and the heroic efforts of the inhabitants of Kiev were the sources of renewal thanks to which the city's grave wounds were quickly healed and it became even richer and more beautiful than before the war.

During the years of postwar construction the city's housing facilities quadrupled and its population more than doubled.

Today Kiev puts out twenty times more industrial produce than before the Great Patriotic War. It makes automatic machine-tools, river boats, excavators, airliners, computer technology, artificial diamonds, motorcycles, television sets, cameras and silk fabrics. The articles its industry manufactures are exported to over sixty countries.

At present there are more than 80 institutions under the Ukrainian Academy of Sciences in Kiev. Science has become an important branch of the Ukrainian capital's economy, in which nearly one out of ten working inhabitants is involved. Particularly productive are the well-known groups of scientists employed at the Yevgeny Paton Electrical Welding Institute, the Cybernetics Institute of the Ukrainian Academy of Sciences, the Institute of Material, and others who do much to accelerate scientific and technological progress.

An unprecedented amount of work has been done in the postwar period to gasify Kiev, develop public transport and the town's park territory. But most impressive of all are perhaps the rate and

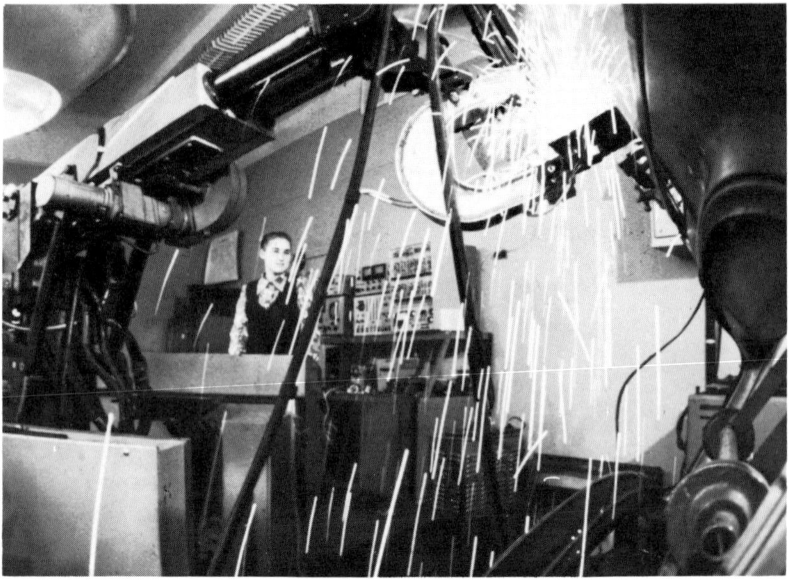

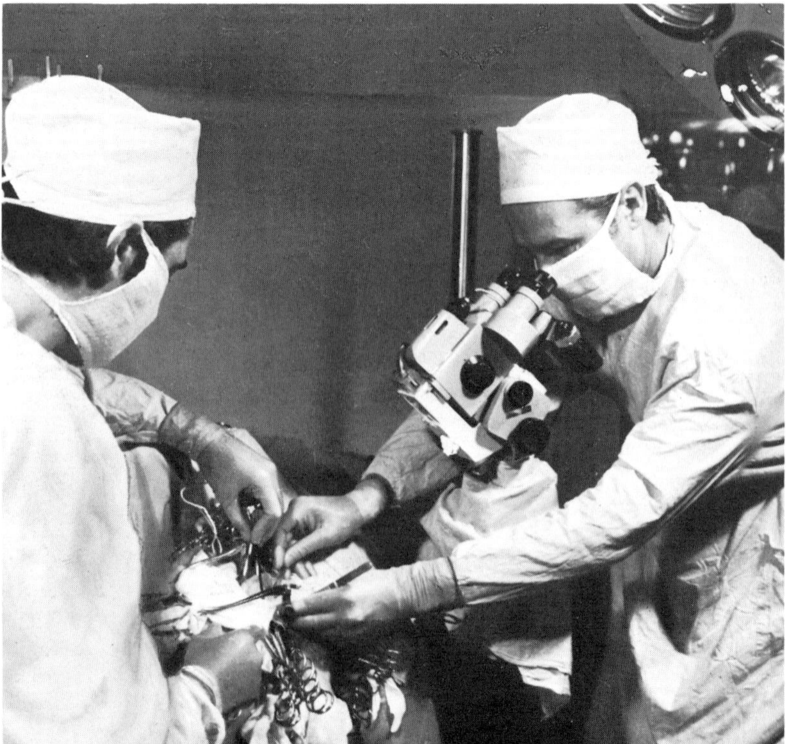

An automatic electric welder of car bodies designed at the Yevgeny Paton Institute

scope of housing construction in the city. During the tenth five-year-plan period alone 6.6 million square metres of housing will have been commissioned in Kiev.

The basic principles of the third Master Plan for the capital of the Soviet Ukraine, which covers the period up to the year 2000, are the even distribution of the population over the city's territory and the combination of urban comfort and natural beauty. The Dnieper with its islets, lakes and coves, which are left untouched in the midst of the new housing developments, is be-

In the operating-theatre of the Institute of Neurosurgery

An atomic reactor at the Nuclear Research Institute

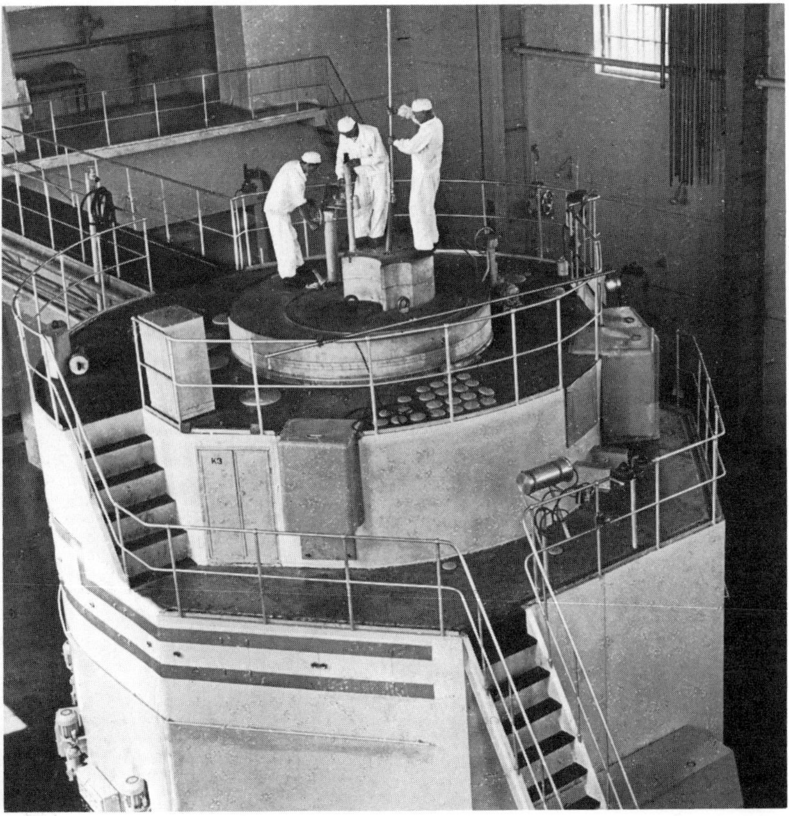

The Moskovsky Bridge built during the ninth five-year-plan period

coming the architectural and compositional pivot of the city's building projects. Bereznyaki, Rusanovka bordered by a man-made canal, Hydropark, Voskresenka, Obolon, Nikolskaya Borshchagovka, Nivki, Vinogradar, Teremki and other new residential districts surround today's Kiev in a white stone ring. Eighty per cent of its present buildings are new.

Every fifteen minutes a baby is born and every twenty minutes a new apartment is finished in Kiev. The comparison is symbolic. Its humane essence is particularly clear if one recalls what an enormous response the Kievans' "All the best for our children! " movement aroused in the republic and the country at large.

In 1976 the City Party Committee, the City Soviet of People's Deputies, the City Trade Union Council and the City YCL Committee drew up a comprehensive

programme of organisational, ideological, educational, social and economic measures to further improve educational, health and other services for children over the 1977-1980 period. By the end of the tenth five-year-plan period about 200 new Young Pioneer camps and clubs for adolescents, 150 school workshops, 19 children's stadiums, five music schools and many other facilities for children will have been built in Kiev.

In the first three years of the tenth five-year-plan period alone oven 100 preschool institutions were built, fifty per cent more than during the entire preceding five-year period. The Kievans' initiative is thus finding actual embodiment.

The city has made great progress in the fields of public education and health protection, which, as everyone knows, are free in the Soviet Union.

Today nearly 200,000 young people are enrolled in Kiev's 18 higher and 40 specialised secondary educational establishments. The material and technical facilities of the hundreds of general education and trade schools, technical colleges and institutes are expanding every year.

Kiev boasts nearly 30,000 medical workers employed in approximately 200 medical, prophylactic and health-building institutions. The municipal health services get scientific and practical help from the city's 22 research organisations. The state allotted 32,000,000 rubles for the construction of medical establishments in Kiev during the tenth five-year period.

Foreign visitors to the city are invariably interested in the basic aspects of the Soviet health care system: prophylaxis, complete checkups of health centres, first aid, etc. The ambulance service of Dijon, France, for instance, is quite aptly named after Kiev, for the Ukrainian capital's experience in organising first aid services has been borrowed here.

In 1958 the first Institute of Gerontology and Experimental Pathology in the Soviet Union and

the world was set up in Kiev. Here a group of scientists from the USSR Academy of Medical Sciences studies the biological foundations of aging and environmental factors that influence longevity. The Institute's policlinic department now keeps tabs on over one hundred Kiev centenarians.

The year 1980 marks two important anniversaries in the life of the Soviet people. Thousands of Kiev's leading workers reached their Tenth Five-Year-plan targets ahead of schedule in honour of the 110th anniversary of the birth of Vladimir Ilyich Lenin and the 35th anniversary of the Soviet people's victory in the Great Patriotic War of 1941-45. At the same time the celebrations provide an opportunity to review the work that the city has done in the last few years. Kiev has built many fine works of engineering and also public buildings. Among them are the new lines of the city's Metro, the large Moskovsky Bridge, the Ukrainian Trade Union Council building, the new

During the "Days of the Twin-Cities" of Bratislava and Tampere

The Economic Achievements Exhibition of the Ukrainian SSR

building of the Kiev branch of the Central Lenin Museum, new cinemas-cum-concert halls, policlinics, schools, sport complexes, libraries and museums.

Kiev's international cultural ties have become varied and intensive in recent years. Days devoted to its twin-cities of Bratislava, Cracow, Leipzig, Kyoto, Tampere, Toulouse and Florence are regularly held in the city. At this time various exhibitions are on display illustrating the development of the twin-cities and the life, work and art of their inhabitants, visiting foreign artists give performances at Kiev theatres and concert halls and the best foreign films are shown in cinemas.

Kievans look to the future with optimism.

A movement with its vanguard of nearly 200,000 Communists in the city Party organisation is presently gathering momentum in Kiev to trasform the Ukrainian capital into a city of highly productive labour, great culture and exemplary public order.

WAR MEMORIALS IN THE HERO-CITY

THE PARK OF ETERNAL GLORY

(trolleybus 20)

The memorial complex of the Park of Eternal Glory in honour of the Soviet soldiers who fell during the Great Patriotic War was erected in 1957.

In the centre of the memorial, resting on the edge of a hill overlooking the Dnieper, is the tomb of the unknown soldier. An Eternal Flame burns at the foot of a 26-metre-high granite obelisk, surrounded by a bronze wreath and an abundance of live flowers. Nearby is the necropolis of the heroes who gave their lives for the freedom and independence of their Soviet homeland; the names of 34 fightingmen killed in the battles against the nazi invaders during the defence and liberation of Kiev gleam in the reflection of the Eternal Flame on the marble gravestones. Among those who are buried here are one of the organis-

ers of the city's defence in 1941, Hero of the Soviet Union and commander of the Southwest Front, Colonel-General Mikhail Kirponos, and Hero of the Soviet Union, Sergeant-Major of the Guards Nikifor Sholudenko, whose tank was the first to break through into the burning city on November 6, 1943.

The war brought them together here forever, soldiers, officers and generals, on the banks of the ancient Dnieper in the capital of the Soviet Ukraine. They have now entered the world of legend and become heroes for all time, Captain of the Guards Yuri Novikov and Major-General Anton Pilipenko, Hero of the Soviet Union, Sergeant-Major of the Guards Nikolai Gogichaishvili and Hero of the Soviet Union, Major Ivan Leonov, Colonel Ivan Eliseyev and Major Pyotr Lusta, Hero of the Soviet Union, People's Hero of

The Park of Eternal Glory

The monument to the Hero of the Soviet Union Mikhail Kirponos, one of the commanders in the 1941 defence of Kiev

Yugoslavia Andrei Vitruk and Hero of the Soviet Union, Captain of the Guards Nikolai Avdeyev. The grateful inhabitants of Kiev and the whole Ukrainian people honour the memory of these and many other sons of the multinational Soviet Union.

On national holidays the salvos of military salutes and the anthems of the Soviet Union and the Ukrainian SSR resound in the Park of Eternal Glory and marshals and generals, war veterans and former partisans and underground fighters bow their heads here before the ashes of the dead. Komsomol members and Young Pioneers stand in the guard of honour at the heroes' graves, and flowers always lie next to the Eternal Flame.

Here in the Park of Eternal Glory one recalls the fine words of the outstanding Soviet Ukrainian writer and film director Alexander Dovzhenko: "May Kiev never forget the heroes of the Dnieper! May poets sing their glory through the ages over the goodly course of a good many long years, how they ascended Vladimir Hill from all corners of the Soviet Union, how they reddened the white sands of its ancient banks with their blood!"

GOLOSEYEVSKY PARK

(trolleybuses 4, 11, 12)

Here on the wooded Goloseyevsky Heights, which occupy key positions on the immediate approaches to the city, the citizens of Kiev first met the enemy, the invading nazi hordes, face to face in July 1941. Volunteer corps fighters and Soviet soldiers engaged in battle here on the defensive lines prepared beforehand by the city's inhabitants, and bitter fighting took place here in August.

The courage of the defenders of Kiev, who fought selflessly on the Goloseyevsky Heights, foiled the enemy's publicly ennounced intention to hold a parade of the nazi troops on Kreshchatik Street in the presence of the Führer. The Fifth Airborne Brigade under the command of Hero of the Soviet Union Colonel A. Rodimtsev and the Komsomol volunteer regiment particularly distinguished themselves in the battles here. Between August 1 and 16, 1941, over 30,000 of Hitler's soldiers were killed or wounded on the Goloseyevsky lines, and the enemy's frontal attack on the city proved a dismal failure.

On May 8, 1965, when the Soviet people celebrated the twentieth anniversary of their victory in the Great Patriotic War, an Obelisk of Glory was ceremonially unveiled on one of the Goloseyevsky hills. Carved on the red granite rectangle are the words: "This obelisk was erected by the Soviet Ukraine as a token of love, respect and gratitude to you, the Heroes, soldiers and commanders of the Soviet Army, the sailors of the Dnieper military flotilla, the volunteer corps fighters and partisans, who gave their blood and lives in defending Kiev from the nazi hordes between July and September 1941."

The war trenches have long since grown over in the Goloseyevsky forest, and the trunks of trees have closed around the splinters of lethal metal. Properly speaking, this is no longer a forest, but a recreation park. It has been named after the famous Soviet Ukrainian poet and translator Maxim Rylsky, who wrote a cycle of marvellous philosophical and lyrical poems entitled *Goloseyevsky Autumn*. Here in the park is the poet's house, which has now been made into a museum. Nearby are the blocks of the agricultural Academy, the buildings of the Ukrainian Economic Achievements Exhibition and the Kiev centre of international youth tourism "Mir".

Goloseyevsky Park with its picturesque thickets and lakes, numerous entertainment facilities and sports grounds has become a favourite recreation place of the visitors and inhabitants of Kiev alike, the site of art festivals and popular festivities.

There are always many people here, and live flowers surround the Obelisk of Glory at any time of year. Here the Hero City's veterans review the yearly parade of Octobrians, the youngest generation of Soviet patriots, when Victory Day is celebrated in May.

The monument to the workers of Kiev machine-tool plant who were killed at the fronts of the Great Patriotic War

THE MONUMENT TO ARMY GENERAL VATUTIN

(Sovietsky Park; trolleybus 20)

The name of Hero of the Soviet Union, commander of the First Ukrainian Front, Army General Nikolai Vatutin is linked with one of the most impressive pages in the history of the Great Patriotic War, the liberation of the capital of the Soviet Ukraine from the nazi occupationists on November 6, 1943. The battles of Stalingrad and on the Kursk Bulge added to Vatutin's experience in military command, which he brilliantly applied in the battle for the Dnieper.

Before advancing on Kiev, where Vatutin had studied and worked until the war, the commander of the Front said at a meeting in his headquarters: "The Hitlerites try to frighten us by claiming they have bound the Dnieper in concrete and iron and turned it into an inaccessible 'Eastern Rampart'. But we are convinced that our valorous soldiers will force the river on their first attempt and seize the bridgeheads on the right bank. We have been accounted the great honour of liberating the capital of the Soviet Ukraine from nazi servitude. Kiev awaits us, comrades! "

The course of the offensive operation confirmed these words of his. Masterfully executing a daring manoeuvre, the soldiers of the First Ukrainian Front forced the Desna and the Dnieper in a lightning spurt, overcame the enemy's fierce resistance in street fighting and took the city by storm. The red flag was raised over the building of the Central Committee of the Ukrainian Communist Party at 12:30 a.m. on November 6, 1943, and Kiev became Soviet once again on the eve of the 26th anniversary of the Great October Revolution.

At a city-wide meeting on November 27, 1943, General Va-

tutin addressed the following words to the citizens of Kiev: "We know what bleak days of privation and grief you had to endure during these two years. But the Soviet people have never submitted to anyone, nor will they ever. Glory to the heroes of the Battle of Kiev! The hour of our victory is near! "

About 2,500 officers and soldiers were awarded the high title of Hero of the Soviet Union for the forcing of the Dnieper and liberation of Kiev, and thousands received Orders and medals. Among them were representatives of almost all the nationalities and peoples of the Soviet Union and soldiers in the First Czechoslovak Independent Brigade commanded by Ludvik Svoboda. Sixty-five Red Army units and formations were given the honorary appellation of "Kiev".

"To Hero of the Soviet Union General Vatutin from the Ukrainian people" is inscribed in gold on the pedestal of the monument erected on the commander's grave in 1947.

The Soviet general Nikolai Vatutin died in Kiev on April 15, 1944, after being gravely wounded.

The granite statue of the hero is the work of the well-known Soviet sculptor Yevgeny Vuchetich.

The bas-reliefs on the monument to General Nikolai Vatutin

The memorial honouring the soldiers of the First Czechoslovak Independent Brigade who took part in the liberation of Kiev in 1943

THE MONUMENT TO THE TANK CREWS WHO TOOK PART IN THE LIBERATION OF KIEV

(Zavod Bolshevik Metro station)

The monument was unveiled on November 3, 1968, as a token of the people of Kiev's eternal gratitude to the Guards of the Third Tank Army, who liberated the city from the nazi invaders.

...On a November night in 1943 when a crimson glow blazed over Kiev, a Guards tank company with a landing party of sub-machine gunners burst through here in the area of Brest-Litovsk Avenue (Brest-Litovsky Prospekt) to head off the retreating nazi forces. A Battle ensued in the course of which the commander's T-34 tank was put out of action but its crew continued to fight, knocking out three enemy tanks and devastating a column of enemy vehicles...

One of the famous T-34 tanks, a fighting machine of legendary fame which inspired terror in the nazis, has now been erected on a pedestal in memory of the exploits not only of the heroes of the battle front but also of the heroes of the home, the workers, engineers and scientists from all the fraternal Soviet republics who tirelessly forged this victorious

The monument to the Soviet civilians and war-prisoners who were murdered in 1941-1943

The Eternal Flame

The Obelisk of Glory honouring the participants in Kiev's heroic defence of July-September 1941

The Mound of Immortality, a monument to those who fell in the Great Patriotic War

The monument to Hero of the Soviet Union, General Nikolai Vatutin

ГЕНЕРАЛОВІ
ВАТУТІНУ
ВІД
УКРАЇНСЬКОГО
НАРОДУ

СЛАВА

The monument to the heroic Soviet tank crews who took part in the 1943 Battle for Kiev

weapon. A group of Ukrainian automatic welding experts headed by the outstanding scientist Yevgeny Paton, who were evacuated from Kiev to the Urals in 1941, did much to make the armour-plating on Soviet tanks invulnerable. The so-called "Paton seam" proved its worth in all the major tank engagements of the Great Patriotic War.

The museum dedicated to Kiev's liberation from the nazi invaders in 1943

THE MOUND OF IMMORTALITY

(Park Pobedy; a ten minutes' walk from the Darnitsa Metro station)

This distinctive memorial to those who fell in the Great Patriotic War was opened on June 21, 1967, in the centre of the new Victory Park, laid out by the inhabitants of Kiev together with envoys from the Hero Cities of Moscow, Leningrad, Odessa, Sebastopol and Volgograd.

The Mound contains earth brought here from the soldiers' graves in many villages and towns of Russia, the Ukraine and Byelorussia.

A broad avenue leads up to the Mound of Immortality, built in the shape of a relief five-pointed star whose contours are deliminated by granite blocks. The star is always radiant with live flowers.

THE MEMORIAL COMPLEX DEDICATED TO THE 68,000 VICTIMS OF NAZISM

(Darnitsa Woods; special bus)

Sixty-eight thousand Soviet civilians, soldiers and officers were tortured to death by the nazis between 1941 and 1943 in the Darnitsa concentration camp. The present memorial complex was opened on the site of the former death camp on November 3, 1968.

The entrance to the memorial symbolically incorporates part of the barbed-wire and chain-link fence which once surrounded the territory of the camp. The avenue leading to the complex's main monument is covered with granite slabs. A stone lying at its edge bears the inscription: "The martyrs' last path. Exhausted, famished and bloody, they walked

The monument of the Soviet civilians and war-prisoners who were tortured to death by the nazis in the Darnitsa concentration camp

The monument to the Polytechnic Institute's students and teachers who were killed during the Great Patriotic War

this trail to be shot, carrying in their hearts hatred for the enemy and faith in our victory."

At the end of the avenue in the midst of a small clearing surrounded by pines, is a hill whose top is crowned by a granite sculpture depicting a group of uncowed Soviet soldiers supporting one another. The epitaph on the nearby tombstone calls on the living to remember the tragedy of the past war.

BABI YAR

(Ulitsa Demyana Korotchenko; trolleybus 16)

The whole world knows of the tragedy of Babi Yar, like that of Khatyn, Lidice and Oswiecim. Here the nazis committed one of their most bestial crimes.

The occupation of Kiev lasted 779 days, throughout which period mass executions went on in Babi Yar. The nazi invaders mercilessly exterminated members of the Soviet underground and partisans, captured Soviet soldiers and officers, as well as thousands of civilians, among them many children, women and old people.

The monument which rises over the former Babi Yar in the park of the Syrets housing estate serves as an eternal reminder of this tragedy. The inscription on it reads: "Over ONE HUNDRED THOUSAND citizens of Kiev and prisoners-of-war were shot here by the nazi invaders between 1941 and 1943."

The monument's composition symbolises the courage and unbroken spirit of the Soviet people. The central avenue leads up to a raised platform on which eleven bronze figures stand arrested in motion. In front is a Communist member of the underground, boldly looking death in the face with eyes filled with resoluteness and confidence in the triumph of the just cause. A soldier stands with tightly clenched fists next to a sailor shielding an old woman. A young boy who refused to bow his head before the nazis falls into the death pit. Crowning the group is the figure of a young mother, a symbol of life's triumph over death.

The monument to the Soviet civilians and war prisoners who died at the hands of the nazis in Babi Yar

THE MONUMENT TO THE BRAVE FOOTBALLERS OF THE KIEV DYNAMO TEAM

(Dynamo Stadium; a three minutes' walk from the Hotel Dnipro)

The monitor Zheleznyakov, a monument to the sailors of the Dnieper flotilla who displayed heroism during the Great Patriotic War

The exploit of the Kiev footballers who were shot by the nazis has been immortalised in a monument unveiled at the Dynamo Stadium on June 19, 1971.

...One of the Dynamo soccer team's favourite players, Makar Goncharenko, was wounded in the fighting in the Goloseyevsky forest during the city's defence and thus ended up on occupied territory. On learning that besides Goncharenko a few more of the famous Kiev Dynamo players were left in the city, the nazis decided to arrange a match be-

The monument to the Kiev Dynamo footballers who were shot by the nazis tween them and the Luftwaffe team, one of their army's best, which included professional players.

"We well realised," reminisced Goncharenko, one of the participants in the "death match", "that this would be no simple match. They tried to intimidate us by warning that we'd be hung on the goal if we won. The referee entered the dressing-room before the start of the game. He was dressed not in traditional garb, but in Gestapo uniform. He ordered: 'We have a single greeting—Heil Hitler! Don't you forget it.' The teams drew up in the centre of the field. The Germans raised their arms in their habitual salute. Our lads thrice gave the traditional cry of Soviet players. This was already a direct manifestation, but for the time being it, as well as our red football jerseys, were forgiven, for everything would be settled during the game. The match got off to a difficult start. The Luftwaffe players knew that we, emaciated and famished, had little strength, and had not trained for a long time to boot. The first half ended

with the Germans leading by a score of 3:2. We conferred during the break. The referee wouldn't let us get anywhere near the penalty area: he declared it to be 'offside', and that was that. We knew we could expect reprisals if we won. But we had to win without fail. So we'd shoot for the goal from a distance. That's what we decided, and that's how we began the second half."

The Dynamo team won that memorable game with a score of 5:3. One of the goals was made by Goncharenko. The enraged nazis threw the Kiev players into a concentration camp, where Goncharenko was able to escape death only by a miracle.

...The 4.3-metre-high monument is situated near the entrance to the stadium's stands. The figures of the courageous participants in the "death match" who were executed by the Hitlerites, Ivan Kuzmenko, Nikolai Trusevich, Alexei Klimenko and Nikolai Korotkikh, seem to rise out of the mighty granite block. The monument is surrounded by a green lawn suggesting a soccer field, and four birches.

THE SEASONS IN KIEV

The city on the Dnieper is beautiful at any time of the year. In spring it is filled with a riot of chestnut blossoms, in summertime its streets and squares are shaded by the thick green crowns of trees. Autumn decks parks and gardens in a captivating array of crimsons and golds, which in winter give way to the lacy white patterns of hoar-frost and snow.

Kiev has a mild, moderate continental climate. The average yearly temperature of the air is +7.2°C. The average temperature of the warmest month, July, is +19.5°C, while that of the coldest, January, is —5.8°C. On the hottest days of the year the thermometer can rise to +40°C, and on the coldest it may drop to —34°C. An average 600 mm of precipitation a year falls in the Kiev region, but the amount can exceed 900 mm.

In May the city celebrates the "Kiev Spring" arts festival, when companies from all the fraternal Soviet republics perform on the stages of theatres and Palaces of Culture, in the parks or simply in the street, and Kiev becomes filled with multilingual speech, a polyphony of music and a colourful assemblage of national costumes.

The summer is the peak of the tourist season, a time of mass recreation along the Dnieper, of tours by theatre and variety groups from other republics of the Soviet Union and many foreign countries.

Kiev is resplendent in autumn, with bunches of flaming rowanberries hanging from the branches of still leafy trees and masses of shiny brown chestnuts.

In winter Kiev's streets and parks are covered with a soft layer of snow, the ice-hummocks on the Dnieper sparkle in the sun and

The Ukraina Palace of Culture

The "Kiev Spring" arts festival

thousands of lovers of ice fishing patiently sit by holes in the river's frozen surface. The Ice Stadium is the site of exciting sports encounters, and the air is filled with the ringing of troika bells and the delicious smell of *blini* during the traditional "Goloseyevskaya Shrovetide" holiday.

Modern-day Kiev covers an area of over 80,000 hectares, more than half of which is taken up by woods, public gardens, parks and tree-lined boulevards. There is about 20 square metres of greenery for each inhabitant, much more than in many European capitals. Kiev is justly called one of the world's greenest cities, with its 66 parks, 39 boulevards and more than 170 public gardens. To this must be added its three wooded parks, which embrace 38 mass recreation zones. These scenic spots draw campers and groups of relaxing Kievans and tourists.

The capital's green zone is an object of particular concern and pride on the part of its inhabitants. Back in 1937, a scientifically-grounded verdurization programme was elaborated in Kiev. It provided for the formation of a system of parks and gardens embracing absolutely all the city's districts, their even distribution over its entire territory and func-

Taras Shevchenko Boulevard

tional differentiation (health-building, mass recreation, sports and other areas), the transformation of forests into wooded parks and the creation of a closed outer ring of forests and an inner ring of parks around the core of the city.

The programme began to be carried out mainly after the war when the Victory, Peoples' Friendship, Partisan Glory, Grushki and International parks were formed. The largest of them is the Peoples' Friendship Park, with an area of 520 hectares. It was laid out on the left bank of the Dnieper in 1972, in honour of the 50th anniversary of the formation of the Union of Soviet Socialist Republics, and successfully combines cultivated landscapes and expanses of virgin nature. In the near future two more parks of

The fountain in the Golden Gates garden

A road junction in the Nikolskaya Borshchagovka housing estate ▶

The Dnieper's embankment in summer

The Dnieper on a calm day

Spring comes to Kiev

In the Golo-seyevsky Park

The Mlyn Restaurant in the Hydropark

Environmental protection is a particular concern of Kievans

The bridge over the Venetsiansky strait in the Hydropark

approximately the same size will appear on the left bank of the Desenka next to the Troeshchina residential district and on the right bank of the Dnieper near the Obolon housing estate.

All the old parks along the high right bank of the Dnieper—the Vladimir Hill, Young Pioneer, First of May and Soviet parks—as well as the green slopes of the Dnieper and Askold's Grave, have merged into the Central Recreation Park, which has an area of over 260 hectares. Much work has been done to improve the park, including the laying of a road which links Petrovskaya Avenue (Petrovskaya Alleya) with the Dnieper Descent (Dneprovsky Spusk), Park of Eternal Glory and Embankment Highway (Naberezhnoe Shosse). Imposing historical and cultural monuments, viewing and concert platforms, amusement parks and pavilions, cinemas, restaurants and cafés are to be found on the Central Park's

picturesque terraces. Adjoining the Park Road is 4,000-seat open-air theatre (Zelyony Teatr), which harmoniously blends in with the surrounding terrain, stands of greenery, the remains of an ancient bastion of the Pechersk fortress and park architecture elements.

The Fiftieth Anniversary of the October Revolution Park, laid on the territory of a former settlement which was destroyed during the war, is very popular among Kiev's inhabitants. It lies on an island washed by the waters of the Dnieper and the Venetsiansky (Venetian) and Rusanovka straits and is connected with the city by a Metro line. Avenues lead from the Metro station to the beaches and recreation areas. The city's Master Plan provides for the creation of three zones in this 260-hectare hydropark: a zone of cultural and sports facilities, an amusement-park zone and a mass recreation zone. Cafés, a restau-

Relaxing on the Dnieper

The traditional "Farewell Winter" festival

The Vitaly Primakov Park in autumn

A winter park

rant and vending stands have been built here.

Kiev's system of verdant zones begins in the forests of Kiev Region and forms a nearly uninterrupted circular belt of protective wooded parks along the city boundaries. It extends in wedges into the built-up areas of town and merges with the green expanses of local parks, gardens and boulevards. Green zones break up Kiev's territory into separate districts. By late 1980 the amount of verdure in the city will have nearly doubled and there will consequently be 38 square metres of greenery for every inhabitant.

Much attention is also devoted in Kiev to protecting the city's air and water. No new enterprises are planned within the city limits, except for those essential to satisfy the population's needs. During the last few years about 60 per cent of the city's industrial enterprises and workshops have been moved outside its boundaries.

Suburban health resort zones superbly complement the city centre's water and park preserves. Such places as Pushcha-Voditsa, Koncha-Zaspa and Vorzel, which have a great number of health and holiday homes, are famous for their salubrious forests and air, ponds and lakes.

The protection of Kiev's environment is a matter of both state and public concern. This is why Kiev now has an integral area of greenery, which makes for healthy natural surroundings for its inhabitants and a unique architectural landscape; this, too, is why it is beautiful in all seasons.

CULTURAL TREASURES

Kiev is one of the Soviet Union's major cultural centres. Statistics show that every evening upwards of 5,000 persons attend the city's seven theatres (three of which have the high title of Academic), nearly 50,000 persons fill the premises of its 116 Palaces and Houses of Culture and clubs, and 115,000 persons go to its 77 cinemas. (Open to Kievans and visitors to the city are a large number of state museums and about 1,300 libraries with a total collection of 65,000,000 books. More than 110,000 Kiev working people are members of amateur art groups of various kinds.

The city's museum collections are rich and varied. The *Kiev Branch of the Central Lenin Museum* (57 Vladimirskaya Ulitsa; tel. 240291; closed Monday) is a major centre for popularising the ideas of Marxism-Leninism. The museum's more than 7,000 exhibits tell not only of the life and activities of the great Lenin, but also of the history of the Party he founded, the heroic accomplishments of the Soviet people, the development of the world communist and national liberation movement, the struggle of the world's peoples for peace, democracy and socialism and the ultimate triumph of the immortal ideas of Marxism-Leninism.

The *Ukrainian Museum of the History of the Great Patriotic War of 1941-1945* (8 Ulitsa Chekistov; tel. 936071; closed Monday) was opened in 1974 to perpetuate the memory of the Soviet people's feat of arms. Its 20 rooms hold

The Lenin Museum

more than 6,000 exhibits, including the battle standards of military units and partisan detachments, photographs and personal effects of Soviet Army soldiers and officers and specimens of the weapons used. In chronological order the displays describe how the Soviet people, led by the Communist Party, won a victory of world-wide historic importance over nazism, defended the freedom and independence of its socialist homeland and saved the peoples of Europe from enslavement.

The *Historical Museum of the Ukrainian SSR* (2, Vladimirskaya Ulitsa; tel. 294864; closed Monday) has a fund of over 450,000 items exhibited over an area of 32,000 square metres. During the years of Soviet power the museum has become a real treasury of historical relics. Visitors are invariably attracted to its dioramas of "The Heroic January 1918 Uprising of Kiev's Workers and Soldiers", "The Storming of the Perekop Isthmus", "The Construction of the Dnieper Hydroelectric Power Station", "Ancient Kiev", "The Fraternal Meeting of the Don and Zaporozhye Cossacks" and so on.

The *Museum of Historical Treasures of the Ukrainian SSR* (21 Ulitsa Yanvarskovo Vosstaniya; tel. 976032; closed Tuesday) is a branch of the Historical Museum. It is housed in nine rooms of a building erected in the 18th century by the talented Ukrainian serf architect Stepan Kovnir. The museum has a unique collection of artifacts dating from the 6th century BC to the 19th century

The Museum of the Great Patriotic War of 1941-1945

AD. Among the items on display are many highly artistic platinum, gold and silver objects decorated with precious stones, and the famous gold pectoral ornament of a Scythian ruler, a priceless find by Ukrainian archeologists. There are also collections of West European and Russian medals, and Ancient Greek, Roman, Byzantine, Polish, Austrian, Italian, Spanish, French, German, Dutch, English, American, Chinese, Japanese and Egyptian coins.

The *Ukrainian Fine Arts Museum* (6 Ulitsa Kirova; tel. 296462; closed Friday) is one of Kiev's leading art museums. It has some of the finest examples of Ukrainian painting, sculpture, drawings and other fine arts from the 12th century to the present, split into two sections covering the pre-revolutionary and Soviet periods.

The *State Museum of Decorative Ukrainian Folk Arts* (21 Ulitsa Yanvarskovo Vosstaniya; tel. 976540; closed Tuesday) was opened in 1954. It has over 50,000 unique specimens of folk art from the 15th century to the present—wood carvings, fine embroidery, weaving, ceramics, clothing, glass, porcelain and pottery.

There are about 200,000 exhibits in the repositories of the

The open-air exhibition grounds of the Museum of the Great Patriotic War

Museum of Theatrical, Musical and Film Arts of the Ukrainian SSR (21 Ulitsa Yanvarskovo Vosstaniya; tel. 977652; closed Tuesday), among which are the manuscripts of prominent artistic figures, photographic materials, posters, programmes, scores, costumes, props, sketches of sets and trappings by outstanding theatre artists, and paintings, sculptures and drawings.

Many of the exhibits at the *Kiev Museum of Russian Art* (9 Ulitsa Repina; tel. 246107; closed Thursday) testify to the strong links between Ukrainian and Russian culture. The museum has 35 rooms whose displays of paintings by outstanding Russian artists of the past and present reflect the basic stages in the development of Russian art from the 12th century to the present.

The works of the finest foreign artists are assembled at the *Kiev Museum of Western and Eastern*

The Historical Museum of the Ukrainian SSR

A room in the Historical Museum of the Ukrainian SSR ▶

Art (15 Ulitsa Repina; tel. 246162; closed Wednesday). The origins of the museum's collections date back to the late 1870's, when the local connoisseurs of Western and Eastern art B. and V. Khanenko began to buy outstanding works in Paris, Rome, Florence, Berlin, Vienna and Warsaw and at antique fairs in Moscow, St. Petersburg and Kiev. As a result they amassed a valuable collection of West European paintings and sculptures, antique sculptures, terracotta and glass, Italian majolica, antique furniture, tapestries, enamels, silver, coins, fabrics and works of Eastern art. These formed the basis for the museum, which was founded in 1919, and it has become a true treasure-house of art.

The *Taras Shevchenko Museum* (12 Bulvar Tarasa Shevchenko;

Detail of the pectoral ornament on display at the Museum of Historical Treasures of the Ukrainian SSR

The Ukrainian Fine Arts Museum

tel. 242523; closed Monday) is very popular among both residents of Kiev and visitors. Its 24 rooms contain documents relating to the life and work of the great Ukrainian poet, manuscripts of his works, rare photographs, lifetime and nearly all succeeding editions of his works and original paintings and drawings.

There is a large collection of materials dealing with the poet's life in Kiev at the *Taras Shevchenko Literary and Memorial House-Museum* (8a Pereulok Tarasa Shevchenko; tel. 293511; closed Friday).

Lovers of books and students of their history might like to visit the *State Museum of Books and Printing of the Ukrainian SSR* (21 Ulitsa Yanvarskovo Vosstaniya; tel. 976449; closed Tuesday), located in Kiev's first printing house, which was founded in 1615. Its over 3,000 exhibits trace the origins of the Slavs' written language, the appearance of the first manuscript books, the development of printing in the Ukraine since its inception and the establishment and flowering of Soviet publishing.

The following museums are also of interest:

The "*Kosoi kaponir*" *historical, revolutionary and architectural monument and museum* (24

Gospitalnaya Ulitsa; tel. 675791; closed Monday);

The *Museum of Folk Arhitecture and Ethnography of the Ukrainian SSR* (Pirogovo Village; tel. 662406; closed Wednesday);

The *Literary-Memorial Museum of the Ukrainian poetess Lesya Ukrainka* (97 Ulitsa Saksaganskovo; tel. 214235; closed Thursday);

The *Literary-Museum of the Ukrainian poet Maxim Rylsky* (7 Ulitsa Maksima Rylskovo, tel. 631210; closed Friday);

The *Literary-Memorial House-Museum of the Ukrainian Playwright Alexander Korneichuk* (Plyuty Village; tel. 614358; closed Monday);

The *Central Natural History Museum of the Ukrainian Aca-*

N. Burachek. "The Road to the Collective Farm". The Museum of Ukrainian Fine Arts

The Museum of Russian Art

Exhibits from the Museum of Decorative Ukrainian Folk Art

The Museum of Folk Architecture and Ethnography of the Ukrainian SSR

Madonna and Child by G. Bellini at the Museum of Western and Eastern Art

The Taras Shevchenko Opera and Ballet Theatre

The Ivan Franko Ukrainian Drama Theatre

In the opera studio of the Tchaikovsky Conservatoire

At the Museum of Books and Printing of the Ukrainian SSR

demy of Sciences (15 Ulitsa Lenina; closed Wednesday);

The *Central Literary and Art Archives Museum of the Ukrainian SSR* (22a Ulitsa Vladimirskaya; tel. 294481; closed Saturday and Sunday).

The *Taras Shevchenko Opera and Ballet Theatre of the Ukrainian SSR* (50 Vladimirskaya Ulitsa; tel. 247144, 245509) occupies a leading place in the Ukrainian capital's theatrical life. During its history of more than a century the theatre has witnessed vivid episodes in the struggle of progressive cultural figures for a democratic art. In their day the world-famous Fyodor Chaliapin, Leonid Sobinov, Antonina Nezhdanova and Valeria Barsova sang here, as did Ukrainian operatic stars Maria Litvinenko-Volgemut and Ivan Patorzhinsky. The

The monument to the outstanding Ukrainian poetess Lesya Ukrainka

The monument to the great Ukrainian writer Ivan Franko

theatre's present company, which includes the invariably popular singers People's Artists of the USSR Yevgenia Miroshnichenko, Dmitry Gnatyuk, Anatoly Mokrenko and Anatoly Solovyanenko and many brilliant ballet dancers is also widely known. The Kiev productions of Y. Meitus's opera "The Young Guard", K. Dankevich's "Bogdan Khmelnitsky", G. Maiboroda's "Milana" and "Arsenal", M. Skorulsky's ballet "Forest Song" and many others became landmarks in the development of Ukrainian musical theatre art. Productions of Russian and Ukrainian classics are a popular part of the theatre's repertoire. For its outstanding services in developing culture and art, the theatre has been awarded the Order of Lenin and of the Red Banner of Labour.

The *Ukrainian Theatre* (3 Ploshchad Ivana Franko; tel. 29591) bears the name of the celebrated Ukrainian writer Ivan Franko. It has staged nearly all the works of the Soviet Ukrainian dramatist Alexander Korneichuk and its current repertoire includes Ukrainian, Russian and foreign classical and modern plays.

The *Russian Drama Theatre*, named after the Ukrainian poetess Lesya Ukrainka, (5 Ulitsa Lenina; tel. 249063) is the city's oldest company. It often puts on the best plays from the fraternal Soviet republics and abroad, and its stagings of plays by Pushkin, Ostrovsky, Gorky, Naidyonov, Chekhov, Tolstoy, Trenyov, Ivanov, Pogodin and Lavrenyov have been notable events in Kiev's theatrical life.

Boxes at the Opera and Ballet Theatre

The Kiev ballet is applauded all over the world

A show of the Kiev Music Hall

You might also like to see:

The *Operette Theatre* (53/3 Krasnoarmeiskaya Ulitsa; tel. 272241);

The *Leninist Komsomol Theatre for Young Spectators* (15/17 Ulitsa Rozy Luxembourg; tel. 935475);

The *Puppet Theatre* (13 Ulitsa Shota Rustaveli; tel. 251059);

The *Kiev State Philharmonic Society* (2 Vladimirsky Spusk; tel. 296251);

The *Opera Studio of the Tchaikovsky Conservatoire* (11 Ulitsa Kreshchatik; tel. 291242);

The *Circus* (1 Ploshchad Pobedy; tel. 740120);

The *Ukraina Palace of Culture* (103 Krasnoarmeiskaya Ulitsa; tel. 683308);

The *Oktyabrsky Palace of Culture* (1 Ulitsa Oktyabrskoi Revolyutsii; tel. 297492).

The Operetta Theatre

For information on the current work and plans of members of Kiev's intelligentsia visit:

The *Club of the Ukrainian Writers' Union* (2 Ulitsa Ordzhonikidze; tel. 934586);

The *Artists' Club* (1-5 Ulitsa Artyoma; tel. 791481);

The *Cinema Club* (6 Ulitsa Saksaganskovo; tel. 275225);

The *Architects' Club* (7 Novopushkinskaya Ulitsa; tel. 249227);

The *Actors' Club* (13 Ulitsa Shota Rustaveli; tel. 251069);

The *Scientists' Club* (45 Vladimirskaya Ulitsa; tel. 244236).

SPORTING KIEV

A P.E. class in a kindergarten

◀ *Olympic champion sprinter Valery Borzov*

Prominent figure-skaters Irina Moiseyeva and Andrei Minenkov performing in Kiev

A rhythmic gymnastics class at a sports school

The Sports Palace

Every fourth inhabitant of this city of more than two million people regularly engages in some form of sport or physical fitness activity. They are able to pursue their sporting hobbies in the city's 830 physical fitness groups set up at factories, building sites, educational and other establishments. These groups are affiliated to sports societies and organisations.

Physical fitness activities are usually best organised in those establishments where the managers themselves regularly engage in sport. For example, Academician Boris Paton, President of the Ukrainian Academy of Sciences; general aircraft designer Oleg Antonov; Victor Glushkov, director of the Institute of Cybernetics of the Ukrainian Academy of Sciences to name but a few, are all enthusiastic sportsmen.

Every four years USSR Games are held, and as part of this Kiev also holds its own city games. The 1978 Kiev Games involved the participation of more than 800,000 people, with contests in nearly 40 different sports.

Close attention is given in Kiev to the task of ensuring the fitness of the population. More than 200 sports grounds have been laid in residential areas, particularly in the new estates. Every year multi-sport competitions are held: the Youth Games for children and teenagers, and the Health Games for adults. The highlights of these are the football and ice-hockey contests held in the residential areas.

Emphasis is also placed here on the development of sport for children. Right from infancy children are placed under the su-

A bird's-eye view of the Central Stadium

pervision of doctors and sports consultants. The majority of the city's tots attend pre-school establishments where physical education is a high priority and is directed towards the child's all-round development, and improving its fitness. In these establishments children are taught to swim, ski, skate and ride a bicycle.

An important stage in children's physical education begins at school. At present there are more than 50 sports schools in the city, providing coaching for more than 20,000 boys and girls. The curricula of general schools make provisions for compulsory gym classes, athletics and other sports.

A total of almost 3,000 full-time P.E. teachers are employed in Kiev to further the development of physical education and sport amongst the city's inhabitants.

Kiev has impressive material and technical facilities for the development of physical fitness activities and sport, including 21 stadiums, 22 swimming pools, 420 gymnasiums, an indoor athletics arena, an ice stadium, a Palace of Sports and thousands of playgrounds. Coming years will see a notable increase in the number of such sports facilities. Funds for their construction are allocated not only by the state, but also by trade unions, enterprises and establishments.

All this taken together constitutes a firm foundation for the development of sport. In 1978 alone 17 residents of Kiev won the title of world champion, 25 that of European champion, 80 that of USSR champion, and 71 became Masters of Sport (international

Kiev fans

class), all of whom form part of the city's pool of potential Olympic material.

The Soviet Union's first Olympic team, which took part in the Helsinki Games in 1952, included 13 residents of Kiev. The first of our citizens to win an Olympic gold was the gymnast Nina Bocharova.

Citizens of Kiev were prominent in all the following Olympics, and their representation in the national team constantly grew in size. Thus, at the 17th Games there were 20 team-members from Kiev, at 19th—27, and at the 21st—54.

Kiev is proud to be playing host to competitors and guests to the 1980 Olympics. An enormous programme of preparatory work has been carried out for this honourable occasion. Practically all the city's stadiums have been modernised and a large number of new sports facilities have been constructed.

A major undertaking has been the reconstruction of the Central Stadium, where the Olympic football preliminary rounds will be played. This stadium was built shortly before the last war and has been reconstructed on a number of occasions since. This giant sports centre has been thoroughly reconstructed for the 1980 Olympics in accordance with modern requirements. The football field has been completely relaid. A new draining system and underground heating make it possible to maintain the field in excellent repair regardless of the whims of the

Merited Masters of Sport of the USSR, world, European and USSR champions Nadezhda Tishchenko and Margarita Kukharenko

A sports parade on Kreshchatik

The Spartak women's handball team, many-times USSR champion and holder of the European Champions' Cup

spartak

УЧАСТНИК
42
ЕМПИ

When a favourite team plays

The Dynamo Stadium pool

The Kiev Sokol ice-hockey team in action

G 521

Along the vast expanses of the Dnieper

weather. The lighting in the stadium has been greatly improved. The old 35-metre floodlight masts have been replaced by masts 82 metres high. These are fitted with powerful floodlights, whose candlepower meets the IOC requirements and makes possible high quality colour TV coverage. The lower level of the stands has been changed and placed on a concrete foundation. The central pavilion has also been thoroughly reconstructed, and now houses changing rooms, judges' rooms and service premises. The pavilion has acquired two more storeys, and all

Oleg Blokhin, the Kiev Dynamo soccer team's famous forward

Participants in a track-and-field meet between the USA, USSR and Bulgaria in Kiev

the changing rooms have small swimming pools. Rooms have been equipped for officials, such as representatives from the IOC and the FIFA. The pavilion contains medical rooms and massage rooms.

A considerable area of the new pavilion at the Central Stadium is taken up by a press centre. The journalists who will come here to cover the Olympic preliminaries will not experience the least inconveniences. Here, in the information centre, they will be able to receive the most varied information about the competitors, and about events at the other Olympic centres. Photographers will be

Merited Master of Sport of the USSR Irina Deryugina, world champion in rhythmic gymnastics, after a successful performance

The Stroitel basketball team during a USSR championship match

Merited Master of Sport of the USSR, Olympic champion Yuri Sedykh

A relay-race

able to have their films developed in the laboratories housed in pavilion. Comfortable commentators' cabins have been fitted for radio and TV correspondents. A modern communications centre is attached to the press centre. The journalists will have at their disposal bars and cafés.

The Dynamo stadium has also been considerably modernised, along with the Spartak, Lokomotiv, and Army Sports Club stadiums, which will provide excellent training facilities for the Olympic contestants.

A sports centre has been set up for the Olympians in the Kiev suburb of Koncha-Zaspa, in a pine forest on the banks of the Dnieper. Here the competitors will find all they need for the purposes of leisure and training: comfortable hotel rooms with all conveniences, saunas, a medical centre, gymnasiums, a pool, and open-air sports grounds. The sports centre is linked to the city by a speedway, the journey to the stadium taking no more than 20 minutes.

The city's guests will find it interesting to visit Kiev's other sports facilities, such as the Kiev Palace of Sport. In a matter of minutes its hall can be converted into an ice rink, into basketball courts or into a concert stage.

The Kiev fencing school has produced many famous masters

A rowing contest in Matveyevsky Cove

Kiev can boast of many more remarkable sports areas. Along the broad blue expanses of the Dnieper the visitor will see fragile canoes, powerful hydrofoils and graceful, white-sailed yachts. The triumphs of Kiev oarsmen and yachtsmen are widely known. This is one of the reasons for the growing popularity of the smooth waters of the Matveyevsky creek and the Rusanovka canal as a venue for major regattas.

The inhabitants of Kiev have done their best to ensure a hospitable welcome for the Olympians, coaches, journalists and tourists, to supply all their needs throughout the Olympic events, and give them every possible opportunity for sightseeing and leisure. New luxury hotels are rising in the Ukrainian capital for this purpose, to be ready to receive their first guests by the opening of the 1980 Olympics.

Special medical establishments are set aside for Olympians and visitors. Several new service stations and carparks are to be made

The Kiev racecourse

available to tourists who come by car. An extensive cultural programme has also been planned. All the best theatres in Kiev as well as the Ukraine's leading orchestras, song and dance companies will give performances during the period of the Olympic Games.

The development of sport in Kiev is such that we can be sure of seeing a large number of its residents participating in the 1980 contests. The Soviet Olympic team will include track and field athletes, swimmers, footballers, wrestlers, basketball and handball players, scullers, canoeists, fencers and exponents of many other sports. There are 218 Kiev athletes in the country's Olympic reserve.

KIEV IN 24 HOURS

We invite those of our foreign guests whose stay in Kiev is brief to choose amongst the following Intourist coach tours:

1. Kiev—capital of the Ukrainian SSR
2. The city's architectural and historical monuments
3. Sporting Kiev
4. Kiev's construction sites

TOUR NO. 1

This tour will acquaint our guests with the history of Kiev from its very origins, showing them round the celebrated landmarks of the Ukrainian capital's revolutionary past, of its war experiences and peace-time achievements, they will see for themselves how its present-day inhabitants live, what their aspirations and plans for the future are. The tour starts on Vladimir Hill, which overlooks the city's left bank and the Dnieper plain. From here it proceeds through the territory of ancient Kiev, along its central thoroughfares, where the theatres, concert halls, museums, institutes, cultural centres, sports facilities, major hotels and shopping centres are to be found. The visitors will also see the buildings which house the republic's supreme organs of power and the Hero City's numerous monuments. From here they will cross the Dnieper into the new housing estates and visit the sweeping leisure zone on the islands in the Dnieper.

The route of the tour is as follows: Vladimir Hill—Bogdan Khmelnitsky Square—St. Sophia Cathedral—the Golden Gates—Taras Shevchenko Opera and Ballet Theatre—Presidium of the Ukrainian Academy of Sciences—Taras Shevchenko University—Central Stadium—Red Army St.—Kreshchatik St.—Monument to Lenin—Leninist Komsomol Square—the Philharmonic building—CPSU Library—Dnipro Hotel—Monument to G. Petrovsky—Kirov St.—Council of Ministers of the Ukrainian SSR—Supreme Soviet of the Ukrainian SSR—Soviet Square—Monument to N. Vatutin—Monument to the Heroes of October—Monument to the Arsenal Revolutionary Workers—January Uprising St.—Park of Eternal Glory—Monument to the Unknown Soldier—N. Ostrovsky Young Pioneer and Schoolchildren's Palace—Park of Askold's Grave—Metro Bridge—Hydropark—Rusanovka housing estate—Slavutich Hotel—Y. Paton Bridge—V. Primakov Park—Park Road—Kreshchatik St.

TOUR NO. 2

This tour includes visits to two of the most famous architectural complexes of the city, ranging from the 11th to the 18th century—the St. Sophia State Architectural Historical Museum and the Kiev-Pechery Lavra.

The tour takes the following route: Bogdan Khmelnitsky Square—St. Sophia Museum—Kalinin Square—October Revolution Square—Kreshchatik St.—Kirov St.—January Uprising St.—Kiev-Pechery Lavra (Trinity Gate Church—Lavra Great Belfry—Cathedral of the Dormition—Church of the Saviour in Berestovo—Kovnir Building—Museum of Historical Treasures—Refectory—Museum of Ukrainian Folk Art—Near or Far Caves)—Kreshchatik St.

TOUR NO. 3

This tour will take our foreign guests around the city's major sports facilities, including the Central Stadium, venue for the preliminary rounds of the 1980 Olympic football tournament. The guests will be told about the development of sport in the Ukraine, about the achievements of Ukrainian athletes, about the facilities available for Soviet citizens' sporting and leisure pastimes and about the training of athletes.

The tour will take the following route: Central Stadium—Rus Hotel—Palace of Sports—Red Army St.—Monument to Lenin—Institute of Physical Education—Ukraina Palace of Culture—40 Years of October Avenue—New Complex of Shevchenko University—Racecourse—Ice Stadium—Exhibition of Economic Achievements of the Ukrainian SSR—Goloseyevsky Park—Science Avenue—Friendship of Peoples' Boulevard—Y. Paton Bridge—Bereznyaki housing estate—Indoor Athletics Arena—Rusanovka housing estate—Hydropark—Metro Bridge—Dnieper Embankment—Vladimirsky Spusk (Hill)—Dynamo Stadium.

TOUR NO. 4

On the Observation Platform of the Young Pioneer Park, which gives a panoramic view of the new town, the visitors will be given an interesting account of the history of Kiev's growth, and about the Master Plan for the city's future development, which reaches right up to the year 2000. This tour will take in new housing estates on both sides of the Dnieper, familiarising the visitor with modern building and town planning methods, with the special features of the city's landscape and its natural environment. During the tour they will see the new TV centre with its 387-metre tower and will visit Babi Yar, the site of a memorial to the victims of the nazi invasion.

The tour takes the following route:

Leninist Komsomol Square—Young Pioneer Park Observation Platform—Vladimirsky Spusk—Pochtovaya Square—Dnieper Embankment—Y. Paton Bridge—Rusanovka Embankment—Levoberezhnaya (Letf Bank) Metro station—Komsomolskaya Metro station—Moscow Bridge—M. Zalka St.—Vinogradar housing estate—Babi Yar Memorial Complex.

INTOURIST WELCOMES YOU TO KIEV

The Kiev branch of Intourist, USSR Company for Foreign Travel, invites foreign visitors to Kiev to stay in the modern luxury hotels Dnipro, Lybid, Rus and those who come by car in the Prolisok motel and camping site.

Intourist organises:
—individual and group tours of the city, to museums and exhibitions;
—hikes along the Dnieper;
—visits to concerts and theatres;
—excursions to the town of Cherkassy;
—excursions by boat and bus to the town of Kanev visiting the grave of the great Ukrainian poet Taras Shevchenko;
—excursions to the town of Chernigov visiting architectural landmarks of the 11th to 18th centuries and the house-museum of the Ukrainian writer M. Kotsyubinsky;
—trips out of town, picnics in the country;
—visits to restaurants specialising in Ukrainian cuisine and wines: Khata Karasya, Vitryak, Natalka, Verkhovina, Dubki, Kureni, Mlyn;
—visits to the Finnish baths, bowling alley.

Intourist offers for hire chauffeur-driven Volga cars, as well as self-drive Volgas and Zhigulis.

Intourist sells:
—tours to the cities of the Soviet Union;
—plane, train and boat tickets;
—petrol and oil coupons.

Intourist will organise international phone calls.

For the information of our guests: the hotels Dnipro (Ploshchad Leninskovo Komsomola), Lybid (Ploshchad Pobedy) and Rus (21, Ulitsa Kuibysheva) all have bars open daily from 8 p.m. to 2 a.m.

Dear visitors to Kiev, we ask you to phone the following numbers to find about additional services provided by these hotels:
Dnipro—290989
Lybid—742066
Intourist—245976; 255397
Prolisok—440093

We hope you thoroughly enjoy your stay in our city and come away with the best impressions.

INTOURBUREAU OFFERS ITS SERVICES

Every year Kiev is visited by large numbers of foreign tourists who come through the USSR Central Council of Trade Unions in accordance with programmes based on agreements with the trade union organisations of socialist countries as well as travel firms and public organisations of capitalist countries working under the auspices of trade unions. These guests are attended to by the Intourbureau of the Kiev City Council for Tourism and Excursions.

Intourbureau accommodates its guests in comfortable hotels, for the most part situated on the picturesque left bank of the Dnieper and linked to the centre by the Metro and other forms of transport.

The guests have at their service the Yunost, Gorishche and Kazbek restaurants; here they will be able to order their own national dishes as well as those of Ukrainian cuisine.

The production complex of the Kiev City Council for Tourism and Excursions offers its guests a range of souvenirs—badges, pennants, sew-on badges and many others, decorated with sporting and Ukrainian symbols.

We ask you to address all enquiries to the address:

5 Friendship of Peoples Boulevard (Bulvar Druzhby Narodov), Druzhba Hotel, tel. 687550.

SPUTNIK AT YOUR SERVICE

The emblem of the Soviet young people's travel organisation—a sputnik soaring above the earth—is well-known all over the world.

The Ukrainian branches of Sputnik are working hard to develop tourism amongst young people, and at present have more than 40 regional and city bureaux of international young people's tourism, as well as its international youth centres—Sputnik in Gurzuf, Verkhovina in Uzhgorod, and Mir in Kiev.

Every new year brings an increase in the volume and scope of international young people's tourism. At the present time Sputnik is cooperating with 400 youth, student, trade union and tourist organisations of 70 countries. The majority of its tourist exchanges are with the socialist countries. Tourist organisations of capitalist countries are also to be found amongst Sputnik's traditional partners.

Sputnik's Mir youth tourist centre in Kiev is situated next to the Goloseyevsky Park named after M. Rylsky. When its high-rise hotel block is put into operation it will be able to accommodate 800 tourists at a time. The guests will have at their convenience single, double and triple rooms, luxury suites, two restaurants, cafés, a bar and a modern sauna complete with pool. An interesting and varied programme will be laid on for their stay in the Mir centre, including evenings of international friendship, meetings with leading Soviet athletes, round-table discussions and debates, lectures in foreign languages, improvised concerts and film festivals.

Sputnik arranges:

—accommodation in tourist class hotels;
—coach, rail and car transport;
—a 50 per cent reduction on rail travel;
—a 30 per cent reduction on air travel for the period between October 1 and April 25;
—reductions on tickets to museums, art galleries and lecture halls;
—qualified interpreter-guides.

The programme for foreign tourists' stay in our country which has been carefully prepared and worked out by the Sputnik travel bureau acquaints our guests with the life of the Soviet people in all its breadth and variety.

Sputnik is always glad to welcome old and new friends!

Address all enquiries to the address: Kiev 25, 4 Ulitsa Chkalova, tel. 245084; telex 132164.

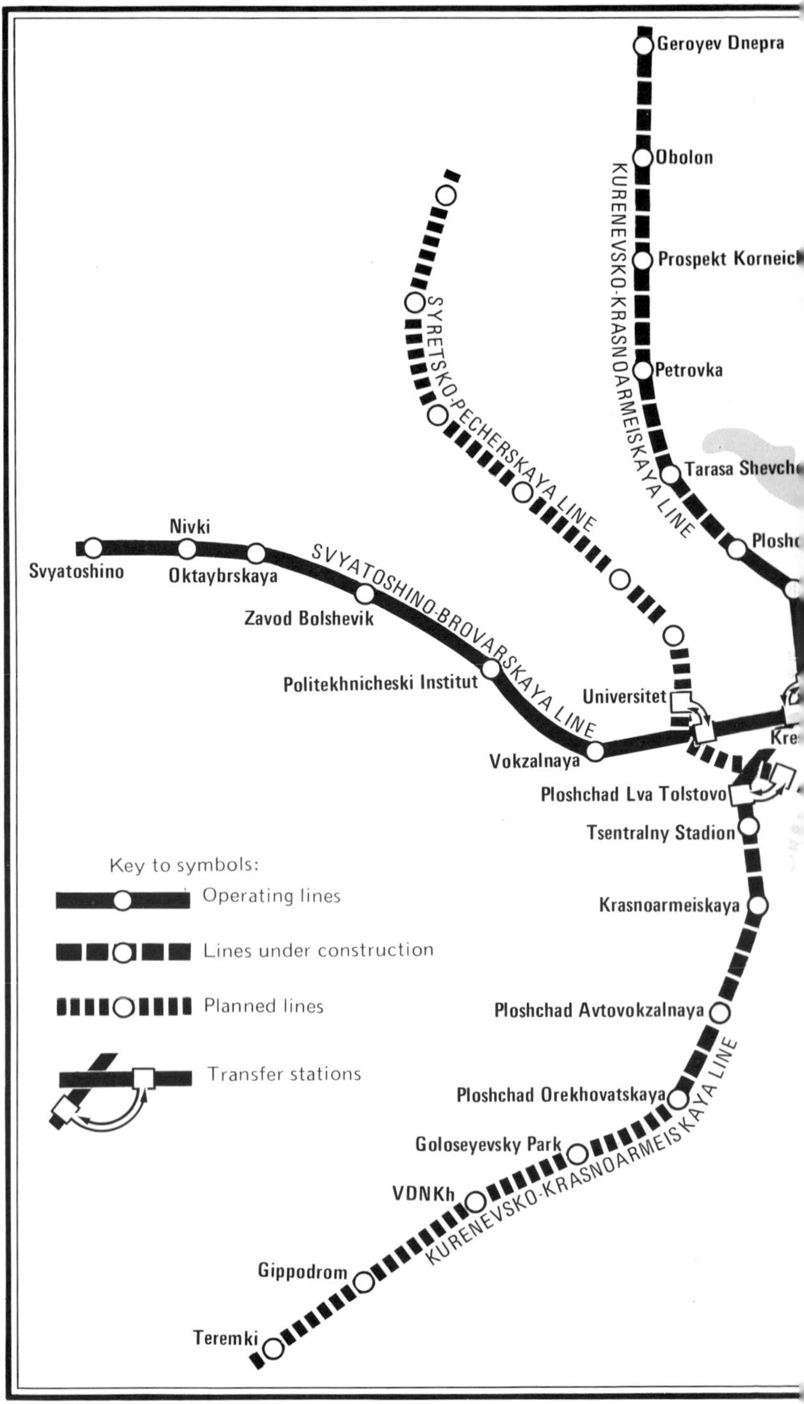
Geroyev Dnepra
Obolon
Prospekt Korneic
Petrovka
Tarasa Shevch
Plosh
KURENEVSKO-KRASNOARMEISKAYA LINE
SYRETSKO-PECHERSKAYA LINE
Svyatoshino
Nivki
Oktaybrskaya
Zavod Bolshevik
SVYATOSHINO-BROVARSKAYA LINE
Politekhnicheski Institut
Universitet
Vokzalnaya
Kre
Ploshchad Lva Tolstovo
Tsentralny Stadion
Krasnoarmeiskaya
Ploshchad Avtovokzalnaya
Ploshchad Orekhovatskaya
Goloseyevsky Park
VDNKh
KURENEVSKO-KRASNOARMEISKAYA LINE
Gippodrom
Teremki
Key to symbols:
Operating lines
Lines under construction
Planned lines
Transfer stations

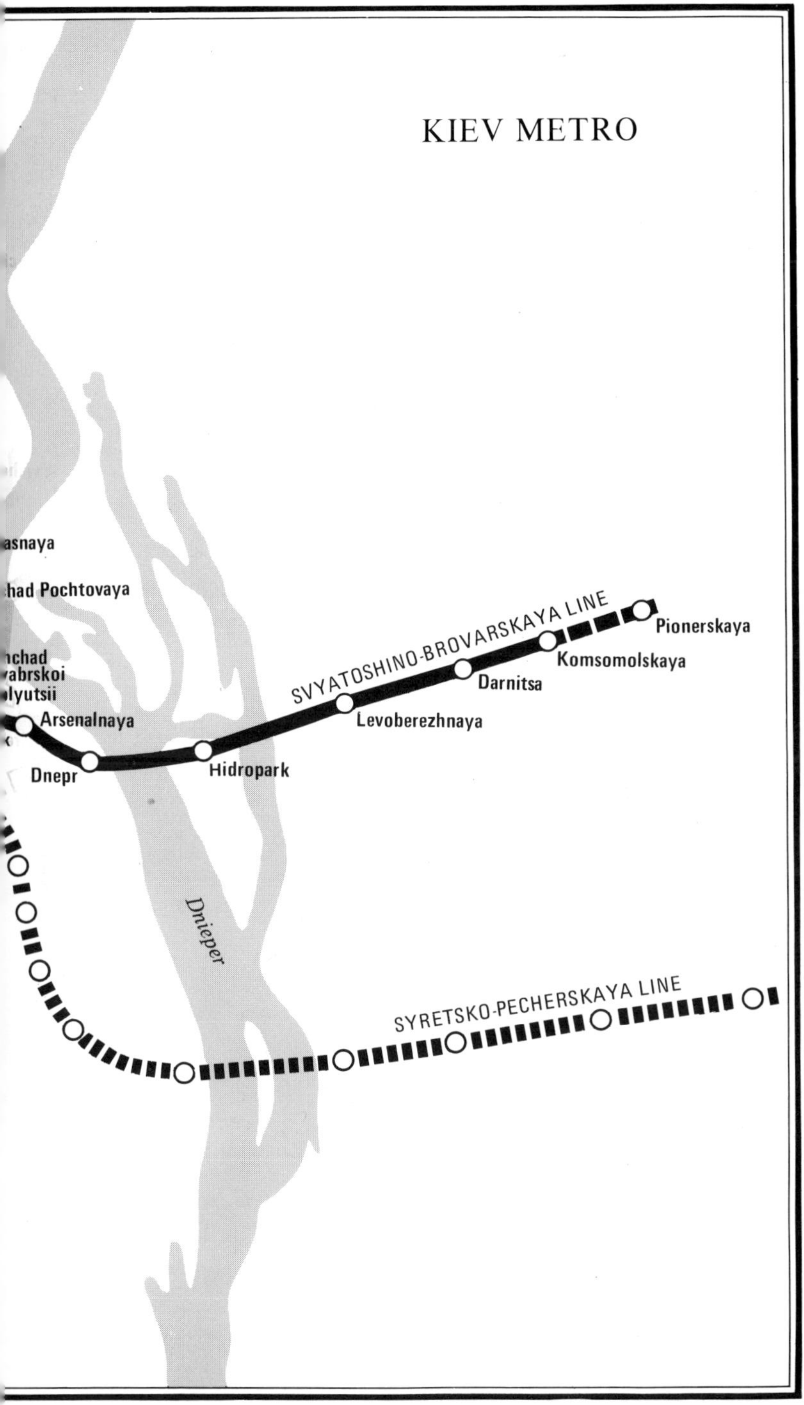

KIEV METRO
asnaya
had Pochtovaya
nchad
abrskoi
lyutsii
Arsenalnaya
Dnepr
Hidropark
Levoberezhnaya
Darnitsa
Komsomolskaya
Pionerskaya
SVYATOSHINO-BROVARSKAYA LINE
Dnieper
SYRETSKO-PECHERSKAYA LINE

SOUVENIRS TO BUY

Guests to Kiev will find a wide range of souvenirs in the city's shops to satisfy everyone's taste.

Amongst the goods available for purchase are gold jewellery, silver and cupro-nickel cutlery, crystal ware, exquisite necklaces, pendants, earrings, rings with precious stones such as diamonds, sapphires and emeralds.

Ukrainian embroidery enjoys great popularity. Whatever the current fashion, embroidery never goes out of style. Embroidered tablecloths, napkins, Ukrainian towels, curtains, shirts, blouses, skirts, bedspreads and carpets are brightly decorated with Ukrainian motifs.

Our guests' attention is always drawn by Ukrainian ceramic wares. Pots, bowls, and clay figurines never fail to delight connoisseurs of this original form of applied art.

Ukrainian wood carvings provide another sort of unusual souvenir, illustrating another area of folk art. The visitor will find a great variety of boxes, plates, and statuettes decorated with detailed ornament.

The famous Kosov inlaid souvenirs represent a marvellous combination of different types of wood and metal, horn, mother-of-pearl and beadwork.

The shops also offer Soviet-made radio and photographic wares which are outstanding for their high quality and reliability; fur garments from silver fox, astrakhan, polar fox, mink, musquash and sable; confectionary and liqueurs, and caviar.

Guests will find all these goods and souvenirs in the Kashtan department store on 24/26 Bulvar Lesi Ukrainki, tel. 956127, in kiosks in the hotels Dnipro, Lybid, Rus and the Prolisok motel, at Borispol Airport, in the St. Sophia museum and the Kiev-Pechery Lavra as well as in art shops. These are situated at the following addresses: 12 Ulitsa Lenina; 27 Ulitsa Lenina; 41 Krasnoarmeyskaya Ulitsa; 17 Ulitsa Entuziastov.

A visit to one of these salons will be sure to leave the foreign guest to our city impressed by the artistry and talent of the Ukrainian people, and the souvenirs he acquires will serve as a permanent reminder of his pleasant stay in the capital of the Soviet Ukraine.

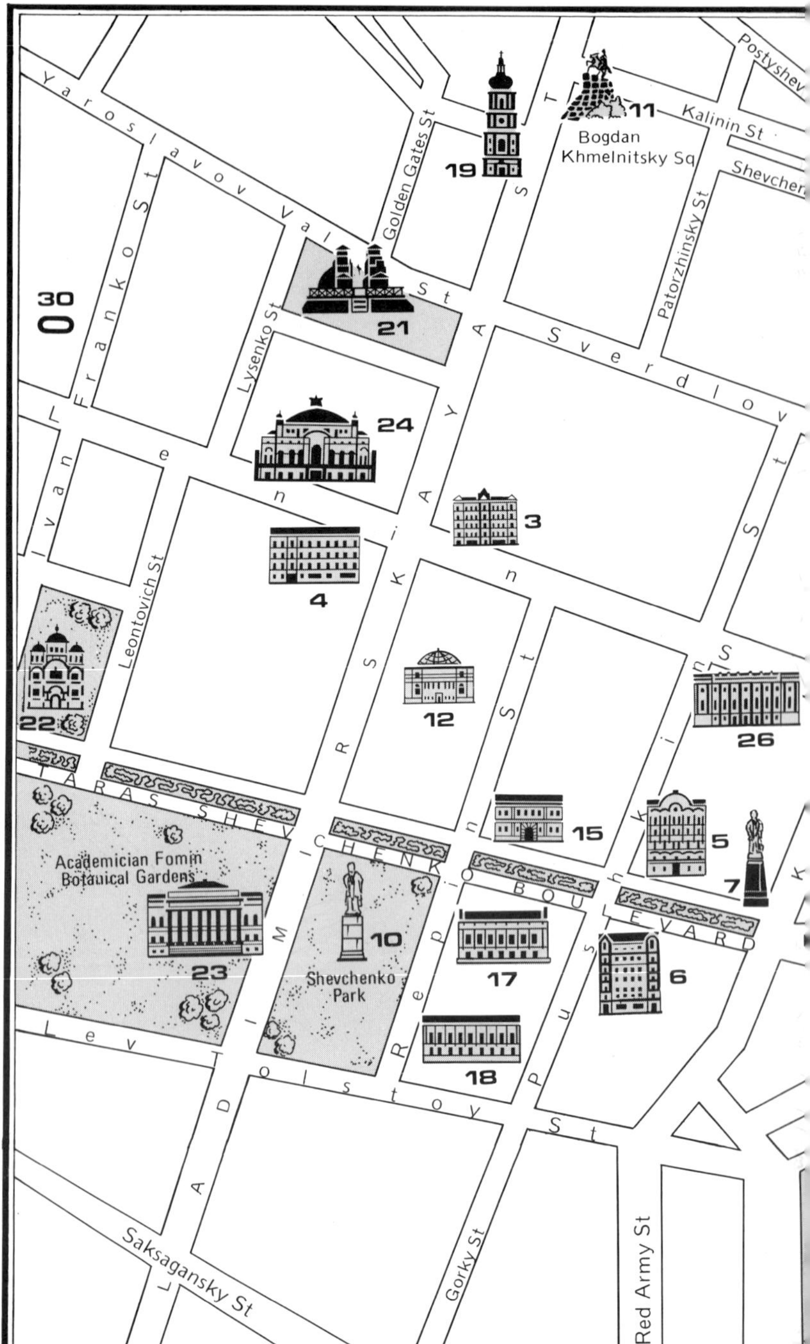
30
0
Yaroslavov Val St
Golden Gates St
Bogdan Khmelnitsky Sq
Kalinin St
Postyshev
Shevchen
Patorzhinsky St
Sverdlov St
Lysenko St
Ivan Franko St
Lenin St
Leontovich St
Vladimirskaya St
Kreshchatik
Pushkin St
Taras Shevchenko Boulevard
Academician Fomin Botauical Gardens
Shevchenko Park
Repin St
Lev Tolstoy St
Saksagansky St
Gorky St
Red Army St
3
4
5
6
7
10
11
12
15
17
18
19
21
22
23
24
26

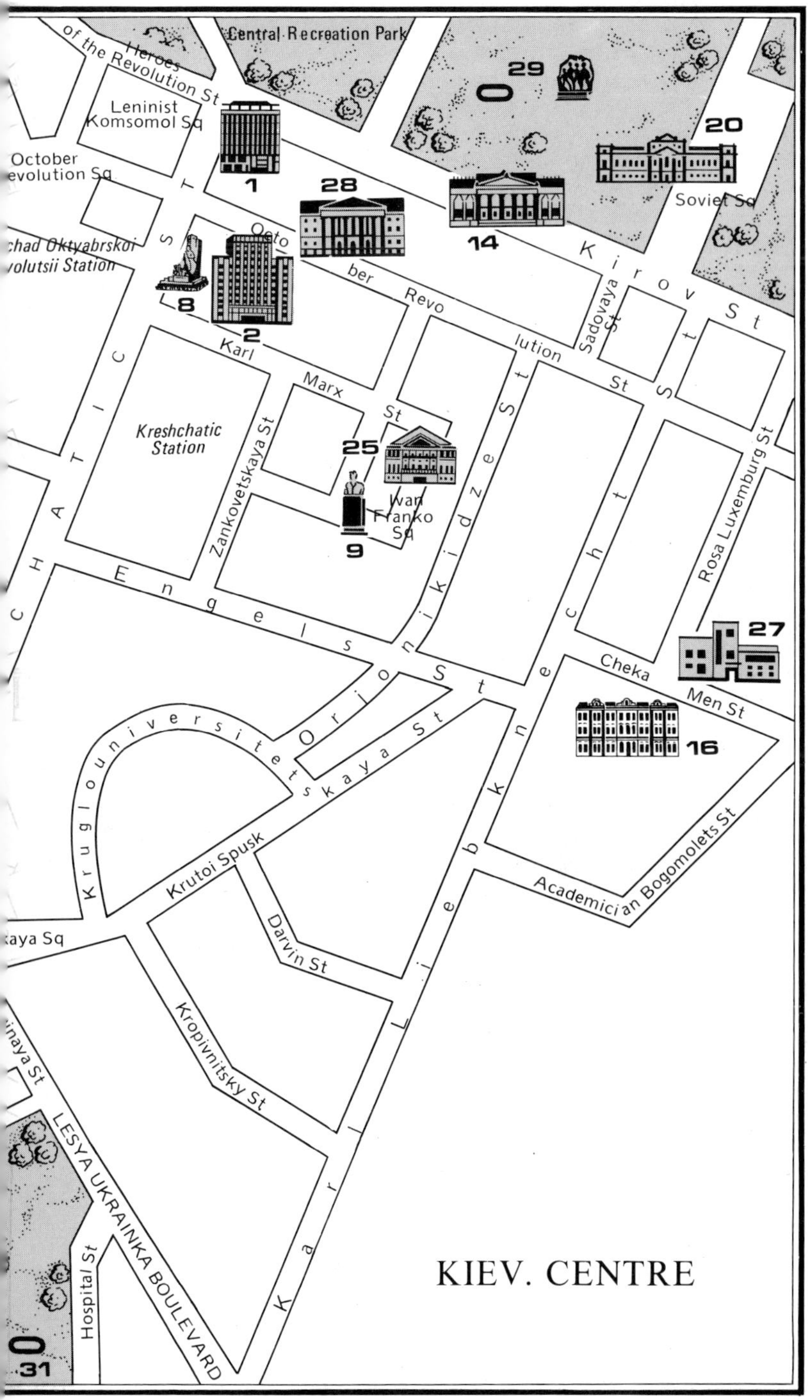
Central Recreation Park
Heroes of the Revolution St
Leninist Komsomol Sq
October evolution Sq
chad Oktyabrskoi volutsii Station
Kreshchatic Station
Kreshchatic St
October Revolution St
Karl Marx St
Zankovetskaya St
Ivan Franko Sq
Engels St
Ordzhonikidze St
Kirov St
Sadovaya St
Soviet Sq
Liebknecht St
Rosa Luxemburg St
Cheka Men St
Academician Bogomolets St
Kruglouniversitetskaya St
Krutoi Spusk
Darvin St
Kropivnitsky St
Karl Liebknecht St
LESYA UKRAINKA BOULEVARD
Hospital St
aya Sq
inaya St
1
2
8
9
14
16
20
25
27
28
29
31

KIEV. CENTRE

KIEV
(City Centre)

Hotels

1. Dnepr
2. Moskva
3. Intourist
4. Teatralnaya
5. Leningradskaya
6. Ukraina

Monuments

7. Monument to V. I. Lenin
8. Monument in honour of the Great October Socialist Revolution
9. Monument to Ivan Franko
10. Monument to Taras Shevchenko
11. Monument to Bogdan Khmelnitsky

Museum

12. Kiev branch of the Central Lenin Museum
13. Taras Shevchenko House-Museum
14. Museum of Ukrainian Fine Arts of the Ukrainian SSR
15. Shevchenko Museum
16. Museum of the History of the Great Patriotic War of 1941-1945
17. Museum of Russian Art
18. Museum of Western and Eastern Art

Historical and Architectural Monuments

19. St. Sophia Cathedral Museum
20. Mariinsky Palace
21. Golden Gates
22. St. Vladimir Cathedral
23. Shevchenko University

Teatres and Concert Halls

24. Shevchenko Opera and Ballet Theatre
25. Ivan Franko Ukrainian Drama Theatre
26. Lesya Ukrainka Russian Drama Theatre
27. Leninist Komsomol Theatre for Young Spectators
28. Oktyabrsky Palace of Culture

Sports Facilities

29. Dynamo Stadium and monument to the Dynamo soccer players who were shot by the nazis
30. Cycling Track
31. Central Stadium
32. Sports Palace

Request to Readers

Progress Publishers would be glad to have your opinion of this book, its translation and design and any suggestions you may have for future publications.
Please send all your comments to 17, Zubovsky Boulevard, Moscow, USSR.

ИБ № 7588

Редактор русского текста *В. В. Остроумов*

Контрольный редактор *Г. А. Павлов*

Художник *Н. В. Нестеренко*

Художественный редактор *Я. А. Маликов*

Технический редактор *Г. Н. Калинцева*

Сдано в набор 18.4.1979г. Подписано в печать 11.7. 1979г.
Формат 84 × 108 1/32 Бумага офсетная мелованная Гарнитура «Столетие»
Печать офстная Условн.печ.л. 10,08 Уч.–изд.л. 11,32
Тираж 110 000 экз. Заказ № 005 Цена 1 руб. 90 коп. Изд. № 28798

Издательство «Прогресс» Государственного комитета СССР по делам издательств, полиграфии и книжной торговли.
Москва, 119021, Зубовский бульвар, 17

«Ланд ог Фольк» Дания

Genetics and Biotechnology of Bacilli

Academic Press Rapid Manuscript Reproduction

Proceedings of the Second International Conference
on the Genetics and Biotechnology of Bacilli
Held at Stanford University, Stanford, California
July 6–8, 1983

Genetics and Biotechnology of Bacilli

Edited by

A. T. GANESAN
Department of Genetics
Stanford University Medical School
Stanford, California

JAMES A. HOCH
Department of Cellular Biology
Research Institute of Scripps Clinic
La Jolla, California

1984

ACADEMIC PRESS, INC.
(Harcourt Brace Jovanovich, Publishers)
Orlando San Diego New York London
Toronto Montreal Sydney Tokyo

ACADEMIC PRESS, INC.
Orlando, Florida 32887

United Kingdom Edition published by
ACADEMIC PRESS, INC. (LONDON) LTD.
24/28 Oval Road, London NW1 7DX

Library of Congress Cataloging in Publication Data

International Conference on Genetics and Biotechnology of Bacilli (2nd : 1983 : Stanford University)
Genetics and biotechnology of bacilli.

"Proceedings of the Second International Conference on Genetics and Biotechnology of Bacilli, held at Stanford University, Stanford, California, July 6-8, 1983."
Includes index.
1. Bacillus subtilis--Congresses. 2. Bacillus thuringiensis--Congresses. 3. Bacterial genetics--Congresses. 4. Biotechnology--Congresses. I. Ganesan, A. T. II. Hoch, James A. III. Title.
QR82.B3I58 1983 589.9'5 84-45263
ISBN 0-12-274160-9 (alk. paper)

PRINTED IN THE UNITED STATES OF AMERICA

84 85 86 87 9 8 7 6 5 4 3 2 1

Contents

Session II: Secretion

Session III: Transcription

Session IV: Cloning

Focus Sessions

Contributors

Numbers in parentheses indicate the pages on which the authors' contributions begin.

Hannah Alexander[1] (223), *Department of Molecular Biology and Microbiology, Schools of Medicine, Veterinary Medicine, and Dental Medicine, Tufts University and Sackler School of Graduate Biomedical Sciences, Boston, Massachusetts 02111*

Juan-Carlos Alonso (413), *Max-Planck-Institut für Molekulare Genetik, D-1000 Berlin 33, Federal Republic of Germany*

Hiroyuki Anaguchi (333), *Department of Applied Biochemistry, Hiroshima University, Fukuyama 720, Japan*

Amil G. Anderson (19), *Department of Microbiology and Immunology, University of North Carolina School of Medicine, Chapel Hill, North Carolina 27514*

Linda Anderson (413), *Department of Microbiology, University of North Carolina, Chapel Hill, North Carolina 27514*

Tadahiko Ando (413), *Department of Microbiology, Riken Institute, Saitama 351, Japan*

Maryvonne Arnaud (113), *Institut Pasteur, 75724 Paris Cedex 15, France*

Arthur I. Aronson (359), *Department of Biological Sciences, Purdue University, West Lafayette, Indiana 47907*

Elisabeth Aubert (113), *Institut Pasteur, 75724 Paris Cedex 15, France*

Hitoshi Ayaki (333), *Department of Applied Biochemistry, Hiroshima University, Fukuyama 720, Japan*

R. R. Azizbekyan (345), *Institute of Genetics and Selection of Industrial Microorganisms, VNII Genetica, Moscow 113545, USSR*

Carl D. B. Banner (163), *Department of Molecular Genetics, Genex Corporation, Gaithersburg, Maryland 20877*

Marjorie H. Barnes (413), *Department of Pharmacology, University of Massachusetts Medical School, Worcester, Massachusetts 01605*

William Beckman (359), *Department of Biological Sciences, Purdue University, West Lafayette, Indiana 47907*

Kenneth F. Bott (19), *Department of Microbiology and Immunology, University of North Carolina School of Medicine, Chapel Hill, North Carolina 27514*

[1]Present address: Department of Molecular Biology, Research Institute of Scripps Clinic, La Jolla, California 92037.

Allan M. Campbell (3), *Department of Biology, Stanford University, Stanford, California 94305*

Bruce C. Carlton (387), *Department of Molecular and Population Genetics, University of Georgia, Athens, Georgia 30602*

Glenn H. Chambliss (407), *Department of Bacteriology, University of Wisconsin, Madison, Wisconsin 53706*

Ellson Y. Chen (173), *Molecular Biology Department, Genentech, Inc., South San Francisco, California 94080*

G. G. Chestukhina (345), *Institute of Genetics and Selection of Industrial Microorganisms, VNII Genetica, Moscow 113545, USSR*

V. G. Debabov (345), *Institute of Genetics and Selection of Industrial Microorganisms, VNII Genetica, Moscow 113545, USSR*

Aline I. Desmyter (235), *Department of Microbiology, Ohio State University, Columbus, Ohio 43210*

Roy H. Doi (209), *Department of Biochemistry and Biophysics, University of California, Davis, California 95616*

Eugenie Dubnau (407), *Department of Microbiology, Public Health Research Institute, New York, New York 10016*

E. J. Duvall (275), *Department of Biological Sciences, University of Maryland, Baltimore County, Catonsville, Maryland 21228*

Manuel Espinosa[2] (413), *Department of Biology, Brookhaven National Laboratory, Upton, New York 11973*

Stanley Falkow (9), *Department of Medical Microbiology, Stanford University Medical School, Stanford, California 94305*

Eugenio Ferrari (173, 323), *Biocatalysis Department, Genentech, Inc., South San Francisco, California 94080*

Franco Ferrari (323), *Syntro Corporation, San Diego, California 92121*

David Filpula (163), *Department of DNA Chemistry, Genex Corporation, Gaithersburg, Maryland 20877*

Agnès Fouet (113), *Institut Pasteur, 75724 Paris Cedex 15, France*

Allessandro Galizzi (407), *Department of Genetics and Microbiology, University of Pavia, 27100 Pavia, Italy*

Philippe Gay (141), *Laboratoire Genetique et Membranes, Institut Jacques Monod, CNRS et Université Paris 7, 75251 Paris Cedex 05, France*

Michael S. Gilmore (265), *Institut für Genetik und Mikrobiologie, D-8700 Würzburg, Federal Republic of Germany*

Werner Goebel (265), *Institut für Genetik und Mikrobiologie, D-8700 Würzburg, Federal Republic of Germany*

David S. Goldfarb[3] (209), *Department of Biochemistry and Biophysics, University of California, Davis, California 95616*

[2]Present address: Instituto de Inmunologia y Biologia Microbiana, C.S.I.C., Madrid-6, Spain.

[3]Present address: Department of Structural Biology, Stanford University Medical School, Stanford, California 94305.

José M. González, Jr. (387), *Department of Molecular and Population Genetics, University of Georgia, Athens, Georgia 30602*

Christopher J. Green (35), *SRI International, Menlo Park, California 94025*

Donald M. Green (413), *Department of Biochemistry, University of New Hampshire, Durham, New Hampshire 03824*

M. Ya. Haykinson (297), *Institute of Genetics and Selection of Industrial Microorganisms, VNII Genetica, Moscow 113545, USSR*

A. P. Healey[4] (67), *Department of Biochemistry, University of Sydney, New South Wales 2006, Australia*

Dennis J. Henner (173, 249), *Molecular Biology Department, Genentech, Inc., South San Francisco, California 94080*

Hirohiko Hirochika (333), *Institute for Plant Virus Research, Tsukuba Science City, Ibaraki 305, Japan*

Hideo Hirokawa (403), *Life Sciences Institute, Sophia University, Tokyo 102, Japan*

James A. Hoch (323), *Department of Cellular Biology, BCR2, Research Institute of Scripps Clinic, La Jolla, California 92037*

Philippe Hoet (403), *University of Louvain, 1200 Brussels, Belgium*

T. P. Iismaa (67), *Department of Biochemistry, University of Sydney, New South Wales 2006, Australia*

Charles Johnson (407), *The Biological Laboratories, Harvard University, Cambridge, Massachusetts 02138*

L. Kääriäinen (153), *Recombinant DNA-Laboratory, University of Helsinki, 00380 Helsinki 38, Finland*

N. Kalkkinen (153), *Recombinant DNA-Laboratory, University of Helsinki, 00380 Helsinki 38, Finland*

Muriel Kauffmann (309), *Transgene S.A., 67000 Strasbourg, France*

Fujio Kawamura[5] (333), *Institute of Applied Microbiology, University of Tokyo, Tokyo 113, Japan*

André Klier (113), *Institut Pasteur, 75724 Paris Cedex 15, France*

Yasuo Kobayashi (333), *Department of Applied Biochemistry, Hiroshima University, Fukuyama 720, Japan*

Ronald Korn[6] (79), *Department of Molecular, Cellular and Developmental Biology, University of Colorado, Boulder, Colorado 80309*

Jürgen Kreft (265), *Institut für Genetik und Mikrobiologie, D-8700 Würzburg, Federal Republic of Germany*

J. W. Kronstad (375), *Department of Microbiology and Immunology, SC-42, University of Washington, Seattle, Washington 98195*

[4]Present address: Queensland Institute of Medical Research, Brisbane 4006, Australia.

[5]Present address: Department of Biochemistry and Biophysics, University of California, Davis, California 95616.

[6]Present address: Albert Einstein College of Medicine, Bronx, New York 10461.

J. Oliver Lampen (129), *Waksman Institute of Microbiology, Rutgers–The State University of New Jersey, Piscataway, New Jersey 08854*

Jose M. Lazaro (195), *Centro de Biología Molecular (CSIC-UAM), Universidad Autónoma, Canto Blanco, Madrid-34, Spain*

Jean-Pierre Lecocq (309), *Transgene S.A., 67000 Strasbourg, France*

Dominique Le Coq (113, 141), *Institut Jacques Monod, 75251 Paris Cedex 05, France*

Stuart F. J. LeGrice[7] (223), *Department of Molecular Biology and Microbiology, Schools of Medicine, Veterinary Medicine and Dental Medicine, Tufts University and Sackler School of Graduate Biomedical Sciences, Boston, Massachusetts 02111*

P. Lehtovaara[8] (153), *Recombinant DNA-Laboratory, University of Helsinki, 00380 Helsinki 38, Finland*

P. S. Lovett (275), *Department of Biological Sciences, University of Maryland, Baltimore County, Catonsville, Maryland 21228*

K. Lundström[9] (153), *Recombinant DNA-Laboratory, University of Helsinki, 00380 Helsinki 38, Finland*

Robert Marrero (403), *Department of Molecular, Cellular and Developmental Biology, University of Colorado, Boulder, Colorado 80309*

Timothy McKenzie (79), *Department of Molecular, Cellular and Developmental Biology, University of Colorado, Boulder, Colorado 80309*

Rafael P. Mellado (195), *Centro de Biología Molecular (CSIC-UAM), Universidad Autónoma, Canto Blanco, Madrid-34, Spain*

Peter S. F. Mézes (129), *Waksman Institute of Microbiology, Rutgers–The State University of New Jersey, Piscataway, New Jersey 08854.*

Stephan Miller[10] (223), *Department of Molecular Biology and Microbiology, Schools of Medicine, Veterinary Medicine, and Dental Medicine, Tufts University and Sackler School of Graduate Biomedical Sciences, Boston, Massachusetts 02111*

Scott A. Minnich (359), *Department of Biological Sciences, Purdue University, West Lafayette, Indiana 47907*

Sumi Mizumoto (51), *Cancer Research Institute, Kanazawa University, Kanazawa 920, Japan*

S. Mongkolsuk (275), *Department of Biological Sciences, University of Maryland, Baltimore County, Catonsville, Maryland 21228*

Shigeki Moriya (51), *Cancer Research Institute, Kanazawa University, Kanazawa 920, Japan*

[7]Present address: Institute for Biology, F. Hoffmann–La Roche & Co., A.G., CH-4002 Basel, Switzerland.

[8]Present address: Biotechnical Laboratory, Recombinant-DNA-Group, SF-02150 Espoo 15, Finland

[9]Present address: Research Laboratories of the Finnish State Alcohol Company ALKO Ltd., SF-00101 Helsinki, Finland.

[10]Present address: Department of Microbiology, Harvard School of Public Health, Boston, Massachusetts 02115.

Bodo Müller (265), *Institut für Genetik und Mikrobiologie, D-8700 Würzburg, Federal Republic of Germany*

Akira Nakayama (181), *Institute of Biological Sciences, University of Tsukuba, Sakura 305, Japan*

Masanao Oda (333), *Department of Applied Biochemistry, Hiroshima University, Fukuyama 720, Japan*

Naotake Ogasawara (51), *Cancer Research Institute, Kanazawa University, Kanazawa 920, Japan*

Kazutaka Ohmura (181), *Institute of Biological Sciences, University of Tsukuba, Sakura 305, Japan*

Masaji Okamoto (333), *Department of Applied Biochemistry, Hiroshima University, Fukuyama 720, Japan*

George Ordal (413), *Department of Biochemistry, University of Illinois, Urbana, Illinois 61801*

G. R. Ostroff[11] (285), *Department of Pharmacology, University of Massachusetts Medical School, Worcester, Massachusetts 01605*

Kiyotaka Otozai (181), *Institute of Biological Sciences, University of Tsukuba, Sakura 305, Japan*

I. Palva (153), *Recombinant DNA-Laboratory, University of Helsinki, 00380 Helsinki 38, Finland*

J. J. Pène (285), *School of Life and Health Sciences, University of Delaware, Newark, Delaware 19716*

John B. Perkins (103), *Department of Cellular and Developmental Biology, The Biological Laboratories, Harvard University, Cambridge, Massachusetts 02138*

R. Pettersson (153), *Recombinant DNA-Laboratory, University of Helsinki, 00380 Helsinki 38, Finland*

Chester W. Price (209, 407), *Department of Biochemistry and Biophysics, University of California, Davis, California 95616*

P. M. Rabinovich (297), *Institute of Genetics and Selection of Industrial Microorganisms, VNII Genetica, Moscow 113545, USSR*

Benny Rådén (403), *Department of Bacteriology, Karolinska Institutet, S-104 01 Stockholm, Sweden*

Georges Rapoport (113), *Institut Pasteur, 75724 Paris Cedex 15, France*

Pascal Ratet[12] (141), *Laboratoire Genetique et Membranes, Institut Jacques Monod, CNRS et Université Paris 7, 75251 Paris Cedex 05, France*

John N. Reeve (235), *Department of Microbiology, Ohio State University, Columbus, Ohio 43210*

Bernard E. Reilly (403), *Department of Microbiology and Dentistry, University of Minnesota, Minneapolis, Minnesota 55455*

[11]Present address: Genzyme Corporation, Microbiology Research Center, Boston, Massachusetts 02111.

[12]Present address: Institut de Microbiologie, Université Paris-Sud, 91405 Orsay Cedex, France.

Hans J. Rhaese (407) , *Department of Biology, University of Frankfurt, Frankfurt 6000, Federal Republic of Germany*
Craig S. Rhodes (163), *Department of Molecular Genetics, Genex Corporation, Gaithersburg, Maryland 20877*
Jacqueline B. Rice (235), *Department of Microbiology, Ohio State University, Columbus, Ohio 43210*
Huiga Saito (333). *Institute of Applied Microbiology, University of Tokyo, Tokyo 113, Japan*
Margarita Salas (195), *Centro de Biología Molecular (CSIC-UAM), Universidad Autónoma. Canto Blanco, Madrid-34, Spain*
Kathleen Sandman (103), *Department of Cellular and Developmental Biology, The Biological Laboratories, Harvard University, Cambridge, Massachusetts 02138*
M. Sarvas (153), *National Public Health Institute, 00280 Helsinki 28, Finland*
H. E. Schnepf (375), *Department of Microbiology and Immunology, SC-42, University of Washington, Seattle, Washington 98195*
Hidenori Shimotsu[13] (333), *Institute of Applied Microbiology, University of Tokyo, Tokyo 113, Japan*
M. Sibakov (153), *Recombinant DNA-Laboratory, University of Helsinki, 00380 Helsinki 38, Finland*
M. T. Smith (67), *Department of Biochemistry, University of Sydney, New South Wales 2006, Australia*
Jose M. Sogo[14] (195), *Centro de Biología Molecular (CSIC-UAM), Universidad Autónoma, Canto Blanco, Madrid-34, Spain*
Abraham L. Sonenshein (223), *Department of Molecular Biology and Microbiology, Schools of Medicine, Veterinary Medicine and Dental Medicine, Tufts University and Sackler School of Graduate Biomedical Sciences, Boston, Massachusetts 02111*
Denis Speck (309), *Transgene S.A., 67000 Strasbourg, France*
Jean Spence[15] (323), *Syntro Corporation, San Diego, California 92121*
Mark L. Stahl (173), *Biocatalysis Department, Genentech, Inc., South San Francisco, California 94080*
Michel Steinmetz (141), *Laboratoire Genetique et Membranes, Institut Jacques Monod, CNRS et Université Paris 7, 75251 Paris Cedex 05, France*
A. I. Stepanov (297), *Institute of Genetics and Selection of Industrial Microorganisms, VNII Genetica, Moscow 113545, USSR*
V. M. Stepanov (345), *Institute of Genetics and Selection of Industrial Microorganisms, VNII Genetica, Moscow 113545, USSR*
Charles Stewart (403), *Department of Biology, Rice University, Houston, Texas 77001*

[13]Present address: Genentech, Inc., South San Francisco, California 94080.
[14]Present address: ETH, Institut für Zellbiologie, Hönggerburg, CH-8093 Zürich, Switzerland.
[15]Present address: Department of Biology, University of Utah, Salt Lake City, Utah 84112.

George C. Stewart[16] (19), *Department of Microbiology and Immunology, University of North Carolina School of Medicine, Chapel Hill, North Carolina 27514*

Noboru Sueoka (79), *Department of Molecular, Cellular and Developmental Biology, University of Colorado, Boulder, Colorado 80309*

K. Takkinen (153), *Recombinant DNA-Laboratory, University of Helsinki, 00380 Helsinki 38, Finland*

Gakuzo Tamura (181), *Department of Agricultural Chemistry, University of Tokyo, Tokyo 113, Japan*

Teruo Tanaka (79), *Department of Molecular, Cellular and Developmental Biology, University of Colorado, Boulder, Colorado 80309*

Leo D. Thompson (163), *Department of Molecular Genetics, Genex Corporation, Gaithersburg, Maryland 20877*

Donald J. Tipper (407), *Department of Molecular Genetics and Microbiology, University of Massachusetts, Worcester, Massachusetts 01605*

Kathleen Trach (323), *Department of Cellular Biology, BCR2, Research Institute of Scripps Clinic, La Jolla, California 92037*

Thomas Trautner (403), *Max-Planck-Institut für Molekulare Genetik, D-1000 Berlin 33, Federal Republic of Germany*

I. Ulmanen (153), *Recombinant DNA-Laboratory, University of Helsinki, 00380 Helsinki 38, Finland*

N. Vasantha (163), *Department of Molecular Genetics, Genex Corporation, Gaithersburg, Maryland 20877*

Gerard Venema (413), *Department of Genetics, Groningen University, Haren, The Netherlands 9751 NN*

Michael Vodkin (407), *Pathology Division, U.S. Army Research Institute of Infectious Disease, Fort Detrick, Frederick, Maryland 21701*

Barbara S. Vold (35), *SRI International, Menlo Park, California 94025*

Michael A. Von Tersch (407), *Department of Molecular and Population Genetics, University of Georgia, Athens, Georgia 30602*

R. G. Wake (67), *Department of Biochemistry, University of Sydney, New South Wales 2006, Australia*

Wu Wang (129), *Waksman Institute of Microbiology, Rutgers–The State University of New Jersey, Piscataway, New Jersey 08854*

Gerhard Weidinger[17] (265), *Institut für Genetik und Mikrobiologie, D-8700 Würzburg, Federal Republic of Germany*

A. S. Weiss (67), *Department of Biochemistry, University of Sydney, New South Wales 2006, Australia*

James A. Wells (173), *Biocatalysis Department, Genentech, Inc., South San Francisco, California 94080*

[16]Present address: Department of Microbiology, University of Kansas, Lawrence, Kansas 66045.

[17]Present address: Institut für Physiologische Chemie, D-8700 Würzburg, Federal Republic of Germany.

H. R. Whiteley (375), *Department of Microbiology and Immunology, SC-42, University of Washington, Seattle, Washington 98195*

D. M. Williams (275), *Department of Biological Sciences, University of Maryland, Baltimore County, Catonsville, Maryland 21228*

Scott Winston (79), *Department of Molecular, Cellular and Developmental Biology, University of Colorado, Boulder, Colorado 80309*

H. C. Wong[18] (375), *Department of Microbiology and Immunology, SC-42, University of Washington, Seattle, Washington 98195*

Sui-Lam Wong (209), *Department of Biochemistry and Biophysics, University of California, Davis, California 95616*

Hidetoshi Yamada (333), *Department of Applied Biochemistry, Hiroshima University, Fukuyama 720, Japan*

Kunio Yamane (181), *Institute of Biological Sciences, University of Tsukuba, Sakura 305, Japan*

Makari Yamasaki (181), *Department of Agricultural Chemistry, University of Tokyo, Tokyo 113, Japan*

Hisato Yamazaki (181), *Institute of Biological Sciences, University of Tsukuba, Sakura 305, Japan*

Yue-Qin Yang (129), *Waksman Institute of Microbiology, Rutgers–The State University of New Jersey, Piscataway, New Jersey 08854*

Daniel G. Yansura (249), *Department of Vaccine Development, Genentech, Inc., South San Francisco, California 94080*

Ronald Yasbin (413), *Department of Microbiology, University of Rochester, Rochester, New York 14642*

Yu. V. Yomantas (297), *Institute of Genetics and Selection of Industrial Microorganisms, VNII Genetica, Moscow 113545, USSR*

Hiroshi Yoshikawa (51), *Cancer Research Institute, Kanazawa University, Kanazawa 920, Japan*

Michael Young (89), *Department of Botany and Microbiology, University College of Wales, Aberystwyth, Dyfed SY23 3DA, United Kingdom*

Philip Youngman (103), *Department of Cellular and Developmental Biology, The Biological Laboratories, Harvard University, Cambridge, Massachusetts 02138*

Mark M. Zukowski[19] (309), *Transgene S.A., 67000 Strasbourg, France*

[18]Present address: Cetus Corp., Emeryville, California 94608.

[19]Present address: Amgen, 1900 Oak Terrace Lane, Thousand Oaks, California 91320.

Preface

The Second International Conference on the Genetics and Biotechnology of Bacilli was held at Stanford University on July 6–8, 1983. Over 280 scientists representing 17 countries gathered to exchange ideas about advances made in this field since the previous conference in 1981. The conference was made possible by the generous financial support of the Syntro Corporation of San Diego, California, and was sponsored by the Syntro Corporation and the Stanford Medical School.

Dr. Dominick Purpura, Dean of Stanford Medical School, and Dr. Thomas Parmeter, President of the Syntro Corporation, opened the conference with welcoming addresses. These were followed by keynote speeches by Dr. Allan M. Campbell, Professor of Biology at Stanford University, and Dr. Stanley Falkow, Professor of Medical Microbiology at Stanford Medical School. There were six main sessions: biotechnology, chromosomal organization, secretion, transcription, cloning, and synthesis of sporulation associated products. These sessions were chaired by Drs. William Phillips, Frank E. Young, J. O. Lampen, Janice Pero, J. A. Hoch, and A. I. Aronson, respectively. In addition to the main sessions, topics that were covered in detail during the previous conference were included in three focus sessions: general genetics, phages, and spores. These sessions were chaired, respectively, by Drs. R. E. Yasbin, T. A. Trautner, and D. J. Tipper, who also summarized the proceedings in this volume. During the three-day conference, about 30 posters were presented.

The contributions to this volume reflect the impressive sophistication that has been achieved in various facets of Bacillus biology, especially in identification of promoters, cloning of foreign genes, and selection of expressed gene products. It is clear from the proceedings that the Bacilli will become the most useful organisms for biotechnological applications.

The articles in this volume were organized and prepared for publication by Ms. Marsha Shearer. Ms. JoAnn Katheiser helped with various aspects of the conference organization at Stanford.

Opening Session

OPENING ADDRESS

THE INTEGRATED PROPHAGE: IMPLICATIONS AND PERSPECTIVES

Allan M. Campbell

Department of Biology
Stanford University
Stanford, California

Right now, in 1983, is a wonderful time to be doing research in biology. The technical advances in molecular genetics in the last few years have made it possible to pose questions and obtain answers at a level that we could hardly dream of achieving a few years ago. These successes have brought with them some attendant problems, and I want to touch on one of them this morning. I'm not going to dwell on the familiar and, in my opinion, frequently exaggerated problems connected with the commercialization of science and its possible corrupting influence on the basic research enterprise. Suffice it to say that, while conflicts of interests involving financial gain make juicy headlines, personal ambition remains a much more potent force in diverting research scientists away from the disinterested pursuit of truth and the free dissemination of knowledge. A more serious concern is the effect that the rapid rate of progress has had on the goals of research scientists and on their communication of these goals to others, where the "others" may include nonscientists, scientists in related disciplines and even in some cases the individual's own students who may become enthusiastically occupied in the pursuit of answers to questions that they themselves never thought to ask. Most important of all, the scientist himself, surrounded by new laboratory toys and buffeted by new information and unanticipated results from his own research and those of his colleagues, should not lose sight of the long-range objectives with which he started. So both for

ISBN 0-12-274160-9

our own good and the good of others, it behooves each of us to formulate, as explicitly as possible, what those were and are.

Prokaryotic genetists have a special problem in this regard. Most of the molecular technology in current use has its roots and studies on prokaryotes. When we point with pride at our past achievements, we may generate the impression that the important objectives have in fact been achieved, inviting outsiders, both scientists and non-scientists, to ask, "What have you done for us lately?" I think we can all agree that long-range objectives should be shelved when the questions actually have been solved. I would like to respond to this challenge by example. What I'd like to do is to try to define the major theme of my own work over the past 20 years and to indicate some of the questions that I consider to be of current, rather than historical, interest to the general biologist. Now I'll apologize in advance for being somewhat specific in talking about bacteriophage lambda to an audience of Bacillus workers, but I think for purposes of illustration it's best for me to stick to material with which I am familiar, and I'm sure that many of you could pick similar examples from many other areas of prokaryotic genetics.

The genesis of my own outlook on temperate viruses goes back to work of Lwoff in the early 1950's and that's work, incidently, which began with the study of a lysogenic strain of Bacillus megaterium. The actual reasons I started working on temperate viruses are a different story and I'm not going to burden you with that here. In a review written in 1953, Lwoff pointed out that temperate phage stand at a crossroads between cellular and viral heredity. Once they have joined the cellular genome, viruses may be regarded operationally as part of that genome. A geneticist studying that genome after the fact has no criteria to distinguish genes of viral origin from genes of cellular origin. I encountered Lwoff's review at an impressionable age and responded by taking the equivalence of viral and host genes quite literally, probably more so than Lwoff himself did. I set out a few years later exploring the consequences of the idea that once a phage becomes a prophage, its relationship with the rest of the host genome is in no way different from the relationship of normal elements of the host genome to one another. One result of that approach is ancient history by now, and that's some of what Ganesan was referring to in his introduction. It was shown that the lambda prophage is physically inserted into the continuity of the bacterial chromosome. The phosphodiester bonds that connect the viral DNA to the rest of the chromosome are just like those connecting one bacterial gene to another. This idea seems so obvious now it's hard to imagine alternatives, but such was not always the case. The example of lambda integration provided the direct framework for understanding the relationship of the chromosome to other bacterial elements, such as conjugative plasmids, and played a less definable part in understanding the insertion of other viruses, such as retroviruses. O.K., that was then. Several labs, including my own, continue to study lambda insertion and other aspects of lambda biology in 1983. Are the current studies providing any information or insights of more than parochial interest? Are we just cleaning up the details of a classical system? With techniques which are now available, wouldn't students of other organisms learn more by direct investigation than by model systems like lambda? So I want to discuss a few aspects of lambda biology which I consider to be of current interest.

Lambda insertion in itself I consider to be of general interest now, because it constitutes, at the moment, the best understood example of controlled DNA rearrangement. By making two separate enzymes, the integrase and the excisionase, where the latter is required only for excision of the virus and not for its insertion into the chromosome, the phage can regulate not only the rate of insertion into the chromosome, but also the direction of that reaction. The differential control of integrase and excisionase required to achieve this result is effective by regulation both of transcriptional initiation and of posttranscriptional processing. The major control circuitry that coordinates this reaction with the life cycle of the virus has become clear during the last few years. Some of these studies have revealed previously unknown mechanisms such as the control of RNA processing by a downstream site sensitive to RNase III. This is a process that has been dubbed retroregulation. In fact, lambda integrase control provides results of special interest to students both of initiation and termination of transcription. However, I think the feature of lambda retroregulation of most general interest lies not in its molecular mechanism, but in its relationship to the insertion event. The RNase III processing site is so located that it lies downstream from the integrase gene in an infected phage particle, and when the phage inserts its DNA into the chromosome to become a prophage the site is separated from the integrase gene thus rendering the message insensitive to processing. Thus an induced lysogenic bacterium makes integrase, wherease an infected cell destined to lyse does not, even though the integrase gene is transcribed from the same promoter in both cells. The state of DNA rearrangement thus feeds back on the activity of the very genes that caused the rearrangement. In some sense you could say the DNA molecule knows what state it's in and responds accordingly to external signals for the expression of genes that effect the integrated state and can change it. Models like this for controlled DNA rearrangement seem most important to those of us who imagine the controlled rearrangements play a major rather than an incidental role in other biological systems, most especially in the regulation of gene expression during differentiation of multicellular organisms or in chromosomal evolution. The few known examples, such as immunoglobin specification in vertebrates or the control of mating-type specificity in yeast, generally exhibit either less precision in the rearrangement process or less determinism in its control than is the case in lambda insertion. The clear message from lambda insertion is that such imprecision and uncertainty are now inherent in the biochemistry of rearrangement mechanisms. If precisely controlled rearrangements play no part in terminal differentiation of specialized cells, the reason is not lack of means but must be the availability of more efficient alternatives.

I have occasionally mentioned another implication to evolutionists. Controlled DNA rearrangements provide a plausible mechanism for a type of Lamarckian inheritance where germinal DNA can change in response to a specific selective agent in the environment. If such strategies are rarely used, it must be because their adaptive value is slight, but not because some rule or taboo forbids their occurrence. You can of course avoid this last issue altogether by viewing lambda insertion as a mechanism characteristic of viruses and other selfish DNA elements, as distinguished by normal cellular processes. Some biologists seem to take that position, at least implicitly. I think that means that 30 years after Lwoff's insights, not everyone has taken the lesson of his work to heart as literally as I did.

A second focus of recent lambda work has been the study of operator-promoter function, which is exemplified most beautifully by the work of Mark Ptashne's group on the p_R promter and its regulation. In that case, admiration for the state-of-the-art virtuoso molecular biology that's been done should not obscure the fact that the major interest of that system rests on the nature and function of the promoter rather than on the molecular interaction per se. The world is full of operators, promoters and DNA binding proteins. The p_R promoter is of special interest because of its key element of the bistable switch that channels the infected cell in the direction either of lysogeny or of viral development. The manner in which regulatory proteins interact to generate a switch with the appropriate responsiveness, coordination and specificity provides a paradigm that must have many counterparts.

The last area I want to mention is the evolution of extrachromosomal elements. We've known for a long time now that phage, plasmids and, more recently, transposons, not only can move around from cell to cell, from one chromosomal location to another, but also that they can pick up chromosomal genes, incorporate them into their own structure and later deposit them in new locations. Much that has been said and written in the last few years, especially by those who have only become recently aware of this situation, might suggest that all this traffic obscures any boundaries between chromosomal DNA and extrachromosomal DNA, or even between the chromosomal DNA of different bacterial species, leaving us with one panmictic melting pot. My own viewpoint is somewhat different. Even among genes whose primary effect is on the phenotype of the host, there are some genes, such as the antibiotic resistance gene found on plasmids and transposons, which frequently move from one host to another, which are adapted to functioning in the context of different host genomes and which frequently form new associations of natural importance when they move. Other operons' genes, such as those of the biosynthetic operons, are typically chromosomal genes. Means do exist for their intercellular transfer, and such transfer may occasionally produce new combinations of adaptive value, but the total impact of that transfer is too small to impede the differentiation of bacterial populations into distinct species with separate gene pools. A corollary to that is that within a bacterial species the genes of chromosomal and extrachromosomal elements are not drawn from a common pool either.

Now you may note that this conclusion departs from my original simplistic view on the equivalence of viral and host genes. Viral genes and host genes may be equivalent to the extent that either virus or host may occasionally borrow genes from the other and incorporate them into its own circuitry. We presume that viruses originated in this manner. However, I believe that successful events of this type must be very rare. Existing viruses such as lambda appear to be of considerable antiquity and to be composed of genes that have evolved over a long period of function as viral genes. I think that conclusion can be drawn from comparative studies of lambda-related phage and defective relics of lambda-related phage found in various bacterial strains. I think one could also draw the same conclusion from other material: defective subtilis phage, bacterial plasmids and such.

So I started out by indicating that scientists should formulate and try to communicate explicitly the purpose of their work and the major themes of their work and I have tried to set an example by reducing my own efforts to variations on a simple theme. I'd encourage each of you to do likewise, but I would include one caveat. When you try to boil everything you've done down to a single sentence, that is an excellent way to become conscience of your own insignificance. But, I think you should bear in mind that, in the long run, a single sentence is about all that anyone else is going to remember anyhow.

OPENING REMARKS

SCATOLOGY AND BIOTECHNOLOGY

Stanley Falkow

Department of Medical Microbiology
Stanford Medical Center
Stanford, California

It was kind of the Symposium organizers to extend me the invitation to talk with you about "any subject I wished". I admit to a good deal of skepticism about the relevance of any science I have done as it relates to the central theme of this meeting. But, Dr. Ganesan hoped my remarks would be of a general and personal bent. Given the title of my talk, I mean no disrespect when I tell you it is the presence of Allan Campbell on the program that encouraged me to talk to you in a general way about my past experiences with medically important organisms. It is a well guarded secret that Allan enticed me into microbial genetics in 1955 at the University of Michigan and he encouraged me to look at the genetics of medically important microbes.

I had always loved bacteriology and was fascinated by the stories of plaques and pestilence. Consequently I worked my way through the University of Maine as a neophyte medical microbiologist and a diener in the autopsy room. When I arrived at Ann Arbor to begin my graduate work, I was prepared to devote myself to the study of anthrax or some other suitable infectious agent. However, the powers that be assigned me to assist a new faculty member, Allan Campbell, in teaching a course in General Bacteriology. I shall never forget the first time I saw Allan. He was sitting in front of a Warburg apparatus with his head bobbing back and forth as he took readings. Anyway, he quickly introduced me to a variety of new subjects that I had only heard about in a vague way. Once I did try to read some papers about the genetics of E. coli but I could never get by the jargon.

ISBN 0-12-274160-9

In any event, neither Allan nor I stayed very long at Michigan and I returned to the hospital laboratory full time for two years. However, Allan had planted the seed of genetics and molecular biology (even though there was no Journal of Molecular Biology then) into my head and eventually I ended up as a predoctoral student at Brown University. There I had the good fortune to work with Professor C. A. Stuart, a marvelous bacteriologist who had done an enormous amount of work on the typhoid Bacillus and a group of enteric organisms now named Providentia stuartii. At the same time Seymour Lederberg arrived as a Professsor at Brown to begin teaching bacteriophage genetics and to take over the teaching of General Bacteriology.

It was the best of both worlds for me, but not without difficulties. Stuart did not believe in genes and Lederberg felt that aseptic technique meant that if you worked with a large enough population of cells, a few contaminating bacteria didn't make any difference. Anyway, I began to happily work on the typhoid Bacillus and with the help of L. S. Brown and Sam Formal at the Walter Reed Army Institute of Research we began to transfer E. coli genes into S. typi. It was astounding! There they were, lactose-fermenting typhoid! (Stuart would sneak in every night and pick these Lac^+ cells, convinced that they were S. typhi contaminated somehow with E. coli cells.)

Subsequently, Lou Baron sent me a naturally-occurring lac^+ strain of S. typhi and after a time we found that the lac gene was on an extrachromosomal element. The biggest shock of my young career came, however, when I presented this work at the Mecca of bacterial genetics, Cold Spring Harbor, in the summer of 1960. After my talk I received a critique from a group of established microbial geneticists and biochemists. Now I hope what they told me wasn't colored by the fact that I fell off the stage during the talk, but that's a possibility. Anyway, the work they said was interesting, but who cared about typhoid anymore? Afterall, if I wanted to work on extrachromosomal elements there was F-lac in E. coli K12. What I was doing wasn't really basic science.

Well, I took the advice of these older and wiser men and began to work on F-lac. Well, E. coli K12 is a nice enough microorganism but it had little personality; it had even given up its ancestral home, the large intestine, for the more comfortable environment of the laboratory. I missed my stool specimens! So back I went to medical microbiology in 1963 and began to work on bacillary dysentery with Sam Formal. Two things were wrong. First, while one could generate a simple genetic map of Shigella, trying to map genes that were important in virulence was extraordinarily difficult. The available genetic tools were just not powerful enough for us to get a "handle" on pathogenicity as a genetic marker. The second thing that was wrong was that I contracted bacillary dysentery. I no longer missed the stool specimens quite so much!

Fortunately for me, R-plasmids came along and they occupied a good deal of my time. They seemed a good compromise. They were medically relevant and involved medically important organisms and much of the research employed the use of E. coli K12. If the work entailed the use of E. coli K12 (I suppose like Bacillus subtilis), it must be basic science. It was a meeting in London in 1968 that put me back into thinking about the genetics of microbial pathogenicity. Two things happened. First I saw Allan Campbell again who asked me why I had stopped working on the genetics of bacterial pathogenicity. Second, I met H. Williams-Smith who had done quite simple, yet elegant, experiments to show that E. coli enterotoxins and adherence factors were essential for the development of bacterial diarrhea in pigs. Best of all these bacterial factors were found on bacterial plasmids. Back to the stools again!

The work on the plasmids encoding E. coli enterotoxins (Ent) and the E. coli adherence factors progressed well primarily through the efforts of Carlton Gyles, a veterinarian at the University of Geulph, and Magdelene So, who was then a graduate student in my laboratory at the University of Washington. Most of our initial work concerned the characterization of these plasmids but, because of the large size of the plasmids we did not have a way to really examine the toxin or adherence genes in any detail. Our whole world changed, so to speak, in the Fall of 1972 during a plasmid meeting in Hawaii. During the course of this conference there was a late evening snack attended by Stanley Cohen, Herb Boyer, Charlie Brinton and me. It was over sandwiches and beer that I heard some of the first strategies to clone bacterial genes. A few days later, when I left, Herb Boyer promised to let me know how the experiments came out. We agreed that if they looked good I would send Maggie So to his lab to try to isolate the genes for the E. coli entertoxin. About three months later Boyer called. In June of 1973, Magdelene went to San Francisco to learn what is now called molecular cloning. After her return to Seattle she isolated the structural gene for the heat-stable enterotoxin (ST) by recombinant DNA methods. It was now possible to look at the determinants of bacterial pathogenicity in detail.

Of course this revolution in research possibilities has not just affected our capacity to examine problems in medical microbiology. The impact of recombinant DNA technology, nucleotide sequencing, transposon mutagenesis and all the other wonders that have become available to biologists over the past ten years is what this current meeting is all about. If the "new" biotechnology has had its impact on medical microbiology, it has had no less impact on those of you interested in the Bacilli. In addition, meetings such as this one also reflect yet another impact on academic scientists and that is the "new" partnership between academia and industry. This has been dealt with so many times that it would be superfluous for me to discuss it here in any detail. It has become a fact of life and, by and large, academic standards have not suffered, the established pharmaceutical industry has been revitalized, and new entrepreneurial ventures have been launched across the world. At one time it was common for scientists applying for a grant to put in fanciful practical applications of their basic research into the Significance section of research grants. Now some of these fanciful notions have become, or are about to become, market-place realities. By the same token it has been remarkable to see the application of molecular biology to the diagnosis of disease and the new emphasis of "drug" companies on the development of vaccines rather than antibiotics. I confess that antibiotics always seemed the antithesis of good medicine. The idea is to prevent disease not be able to cure it once it developed. Antibiotics were never all that good as a prophylactic measure thanks to the R-plasmids as well as the laws of genetics. Hence vaccines make good sense and the importance of recombinant DNA methods and other aspects of biotechnology have now made vaccines a realistic goal once again. Simply stated now that one can understand better the precise mechanisms by which viruses, bacteria, protozoa and fungi cause infection and disease, it has become easier to design strategies to prevent them. In those instances where one knew how to prevent disease but was limited because of the cultivation of an infectious agent, we now see cloned derivatives in E. coli, Bacillus subtilis or yeast cells becoming the shortcut to success.

One of the most interesting aspects of the "new" biotechnology is the role that computers play in the analysis of data. My own involvement has been with regard to the determinants of bacterial pathogenicity, particulary bacterial toxins, but I know this cuts across all areas of biology. It is rare indeed to walk into any laboratory involved in recombinant DNA research and not see at least one communications terminal. That it is possible to enter DNA sequences into a computer and instantly receive back a complete restriction map as well as the translation of the sequences into polypeptide sequences is one thing. However, the data base of other available DNA sequences and protein sequences provides a means of obtaining other "hidden" data as well as experimental strategies. For example, when the polypeptide sequence of the E. coli heat-stable enterotoxin (ST) was published, insofar as anyone knew, it was unique to microorganisms. Not so. Several enterprising individuals ran the sequence through a data base of known protein sequences and came up with the surprising fact that there was a strong relationship to the Conotoxins of molluscs and some rare sea snakes! Moreover, the mode of action of some of these toxins had been worked out and provided an important clue to understanding how the ST toxin worked precisely in humans. Then, on the basis of shared homologies among different ST molecules and their shared homology with the "discovered" venoms, it was possible to synthesize a polypeptide fragment corresponding to the probable active site of the toxin and show that this peptide subunit was, indeed, toxic. Moreover while ST itself was considered to be nonimmunogenic, it has been possible to conjugate the toxin fragment in such a way to engender an antibody response and to devise a means to immunize against the disease associated with the ST-producing bacteria in livestock. To me this is still astounding. Most graduate students who deal with molecular cloning seem to take these wonders for granted. I watch with considerable fascination as my students enter in a DNA sequence and, after answering the appropriate inquiries from the computer, generate a primary peptide sequence, a model for the secondary structure of the protein and then identify likely functional sites on the polypeptide. One cannot help but think that as the data base for sequences increases, as it is, and we gain more and more experience with the translation of computer-generated data into experimental reality, that there will be seen even more in the way of a biotechnological revolution.

Despite all of my enthusiasm for biotechnology, there are several facets that I find disturbing; presumably many of you have your own pet concerns. One of mine revolves around the fact that organisms like E. coli K12 and, yes, Bacillus subtilis, are becoming even more ingrained in the lore of basic science. There is a danger, I think, that we will ignore the ecology and natural history of microbial populations for the sake of a limited number of genes of a particular academic or economic importance. It is essential that we develop vaccines and other strategies to prevent infectious diseases, but I would be saddened to think we do so at the expense of understanding the role and interactions of the microorganisms that make up the normal flora of humans and other animals. I suppose it is back to the stool specimens once again!

Medical Microbiology has become something more than just a subject that medical students need to pass on their way to become practicing physicians. Textbooks of Medical Microbiology need no longer be divided into separate sections dealing with "basic science" and medically important microorganisms as if the two were mutually exculusive. The course that many people called "bugs and drugs" now contains basic science too.

Finally, it may be useful to consider some of the things with which biotechnology cannot help us. When you study infectious diseases it soon becomes clear that the United States and the Western world, in general, is not what you call average. People in these parts of the world have the luxury of living beyond childhood. In the U.S. and most of Europe we really worry more about degenerative diseases. Many individuals still die from infection, of course, but the kinds of infection they die from are usually hospital-acquired infection because these patients have been immunocompromised. In most of the world (dare I say the real world?) people die daily from a variety of infectious agents we now ignore. The world's leading cause of death is malaria; the tenth leading killer is leprosy. Thus, it can be understood why the major goal of the World Health Organization is clean water for all by the year 2000.

In line with my theme of scatology and biotechnology, you should realize that the third leading cause of death worldwide is diarrheal disease. Generally this occurs in the first year of life. There could be a profound impact on the world's public health if we could provide more toilets and latrines. One does not need biotechnology to achieve this end. If this is not fundamental enough for you, consider one other problem. Even if, by some stretch of the imagination, it were possible to clone toilets, most of the world squats when defecating! The simple fact of the matter therefore is that the concept that toilets can immeasurably aid the public health is based on the concept that everyone knows how to use a toilet properly! Thus if you take a perfectly good toilet and put it into many villages of the world, it will be noted that most individuals will not sit on the seat, rather they will precariously squat over the toilet seat. This clearly defeats one of the primary goals of toilet use.

Now in a fundamental experiment a number of health workers tried to solve this problem. I suppose it is really fundamental biotechnology in one sense of the word. They set up some new toilets and latrines in a part of New Guinea - it was a lovely setting overlooking the bay - but the inhabitants of this village still squatted over the toilet seats. So the answer to this biotechnological problem was to supply instructions in the native "pidgin" language written on a sign placed by the toilets. I reproduce these instructions here:

Putnim as
Stret lang hul
Na Pek

To translate, "Putnim" means place; "as", posterior; "Stret lang hul", straight over the hole; and "Na pek". The translation of "Na Pek" is difficult...well I suppose one could translate this as "let it slide". I am happy to say that this experimental approach worked. With this simple solution of an intricate problem as an example, I bring my remarks to an end. Biotechnology can do some remarkable things for us, but there are still rather straightforward matters in the world that require our attention as well. We might well serve human-kind better if we were to consider, at least recognize, that many of the world's problems cannot, nor need not, be approached through biotechnology but by the application of common sense.

Session I:
Chromosomal Organization

GENETIC MAPPING OF CLONED RIBOSOMAL RNA GENES[1]

Kenneth F. Bott
George C. Stewart[2]
Amil G. Anderson

Department of Microbiology and Immunology
University of North Carolina School of Medicine
Chapel Hill, North Carolina

I. INTRODUCTION

For the last several years one of the major projects of our laboratory has been to characterize the ribosomal operons of Bacillus subtilis. We have collected numerous cloned fragments representing portions of the 10 operons (Wilson et al., 1981; Stewart et al., 1982) and tried to establish their genetic position, their general structure and some details about them that would be helpful in making comparisons with other more thoroughly characterized species. This brief review summarizes our current knowledge of this project.

It has now been established by several independent researchers that B. subtilis contains 10 copies of the ribosomal RNA genes (Kobayashi and Osawa, 1982; Loughney et al., 1982; Stewart et al., 1982). Considering that the genomes of B. subtilis and Escherichia coli are about the same size this is a little unusual since E. coli normally has only seven copies and it can get along reasonably well without all of those (Ellwood and Nomura, 1980).

[1]*This project was supported by grant PCM 8022015 from the National Science Foundation and National Research Science Award GM 07900 to G.C.S.*
[2]*Present address: Department of Microbiology, University of Kansas, Lawrence, Kansas.*

ISBN 0-12-274160-9

As in E. coli, the rRNA genes of B. subtilis are arranged in transcriptional units (operons ?) in the order 16S, 23S, 5S (Colli et al., 1971; Zingales and Colli, 1977). However, there are two major differences immediately apparent in this Gram-positive system. Most of the B. subtilis operons are clustered in one specific portion of the chromosome. In fact, several of them are very close together and it is possible they may be in the same operon as one single transcriptional unit. In addition, there are probably just two (certainly no more than three) of the operons that contain genes for tRNA species (ile and ala) in the spacer region between the segments that transcribe the mature 16S and the 23S RNA species. Currently this is the sole difference observed **within** the operons studied; either they have a 1.1 kb or 1.3 kb EcoRI spacer fragment as shown by Loughney et al. (1982). Of course, the flanking sequences vary considerably since they may contain unique DNA or tRNA genes, etc. In E. coli it is more common to find one or more tRNA genes in the spacer regions between each of the 16S and 23S RNA genes (Nomura and Post, 1980).

II. METHODS

The principal technique we have used to locate the various rRNA genes on the chromosome is that originally described by Haldenwang et al. (1980). This method uses as a cloning vehicle a bifunctional plasmid vector which cannot replicate in B. subtilis for one restriction fragment of DNA derived from a region immediately adjacent to an RNA coding region. We have had our best success to date with the vector pJH101 constructed by Ferrari et al. (1983). The cloned DNA fragment, which is first shown by hybridization to light up a single band in restriction enzyme digested chromosomal DNA, provides homology with the B. subtilis chromosome such that integration of the plasmid by a Campbell-type of insertion causes an antibiotic marker from the plasmid to be integrated. We verify that the restriction digested band is changed in size showing insertion, and then the antibiotic resistance determinant is mapped by conventional genetic transduction with the phage PBS1 (Henner and Hoch, 1980; Wilson et al., 1981).

We still consider it odd that in identical types of experiments using a cloned DNA fragment from **within** the transcriptional unit for 16S or 23S, we have never seen integration of plasmids. (Theoretically, we expected that such a construction might be a useful cloning vector since it should be able to integrate into any of the 10 operons.)

The lack of recombination within operons is also supported by experiments of T. Trautner (personal communication) showing that a plasmid bearing a DNA fragment from a portion of one ribosomal RNA gene will not mediate "facilitation" (i.e. the uptake of the plasmid DNA by competent cells is **not** enhanced by ribosomal RNA gene fragments from homology inside the cell as it is with most other DNA fragments tested.)

Our studies have been aided considerably by two other sources. One has been the very cooperative exchange of unpublished data with H. Yoshikawa's lab; the other is the strikingly informative data provided by the EM study of Chow and Davidson (1973). Especially in the Ori C region, this pool of data has enabled us to relate restriction fragment sizes and cloned molecules with specific regions of the chromosome.

Several of the operons that are near the SP02 attachment site seem to be so closely clustered that we cannot tell their precise relationship to each other by genetic studies alone, but by piecing together data from several published sources and some hybridization studies we have been able to make an educated guess as to how they are arranged.

III. RESULTS

Figure 1 illustrates diagramatically the approximate genetic positions of the ribosomal RNA operons that have been mapped. The subsequent discussion will help to justify it.

Since the published literature already contains well documented descriptions of the locations and characterization of operons rrnO and rrnA (Ogasawara et al., 1983), I will only review them briefly.

A new observation reported here is the location and mapping of two previously undetected operons which we have termed rrnB and rrnC in the region near map position 270 (9:00) on the chromosome. Operon rrnB has been characterized extensively. Since we have determined the sequence of its promoters and that for the spacer region between the genes for mature ribosomal RNA species (Stewart et al., in press), plus much of that for the 16S and 23S RNA transcriptional units, we can predict some aspects of ribosomal RNA processing that must be necessary in B. subtilis. Recently, B. Vold and C. Green have shown that the 3' end of this operon contains the genes for 21 contiguous tRNA species, each different (these proceedings).

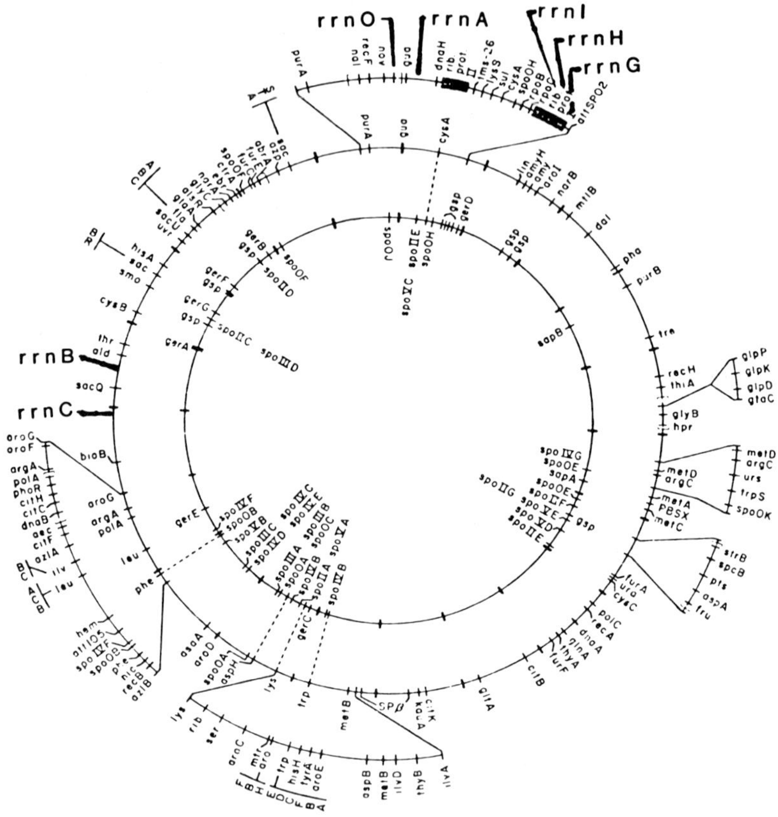

Figure 1. Genetic map of B. subtilis showing the approximate loci of the ribosomal RNA operons that have been mapped.

The major cluster of RNA genes suggested previously to reside close to the attachment site for phage SP02 has been confirmed by hybridization data. Our results show a different restriction pattern between a lysogen and a non-lysogen for phage SP02. In addition, as shown below, we can associate several cloned operons with this genetic region.

Figure 2 illustrates that the largest SalI restriction fragment in digests of chromosomal DNA to which ribosomal RNA probes hybridize is larger in an SP02 lysogen than a non-lysogen. The largest BglI band in DNA from a lysogen is smaller. None of the other band sizes differ when DNA from the lysogen and a non-lysogen is digested by these two

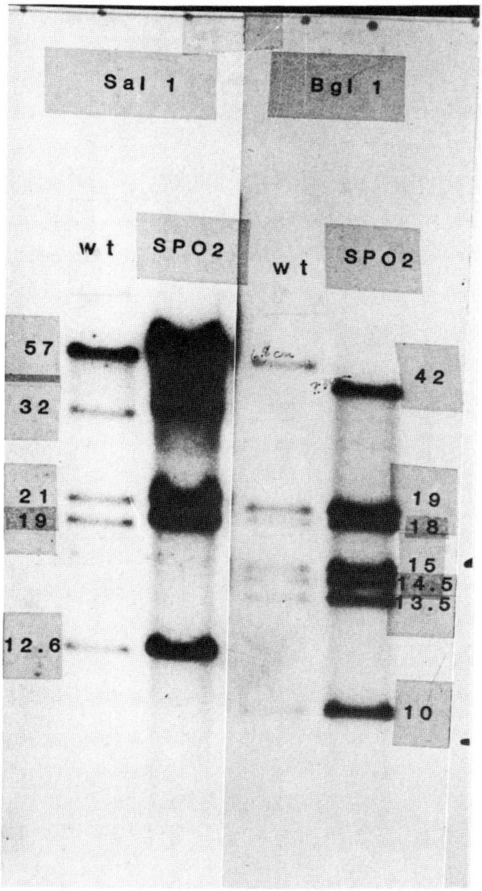

Figure 2. SalI and BglI restriction enzyme digest of DNA from B. subtilis 168 lysogen (SPO2) and nonlysogen (wt). Neither of these enzymes cleave within the coding region for ribosomal RNA. Probed with p14B8, an intact operon. Only the highest molecular weight bands are modified by lysogenization.

enzymes. These results confirm that one or more of the ribosomal operons must be close to the attachment site for phage SPO2.

Chow and Davidson (1973) examined a large number of heteroduplexed molecules in the EM. They saw clusters of single-stranded loops separated by regular double-stranded stems, each 5 kb in size. Since these structures were competed away by ribosomal RNA those authors were the first to show that the various rRNA transcriptional units of B.

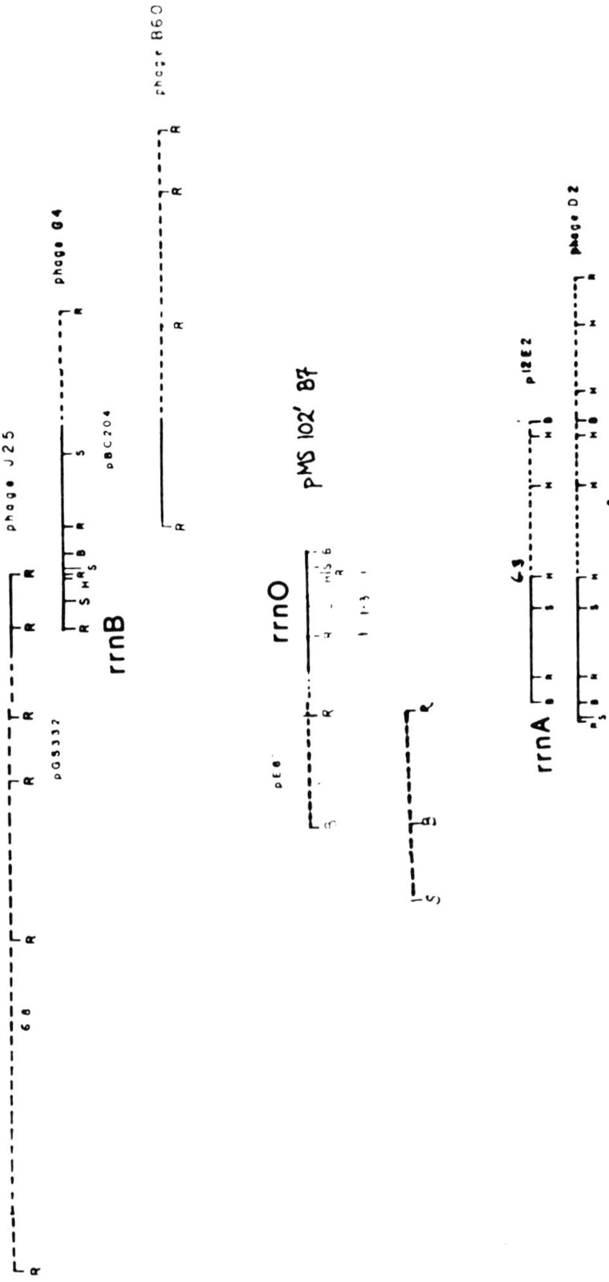
phage J25
pGS227
pGS332
rrnB
pBC204
phage G4
phage B60
rrnO
pMS 102' B7
rrnA
p12E2
phage D2
6.8
4.9
9.1

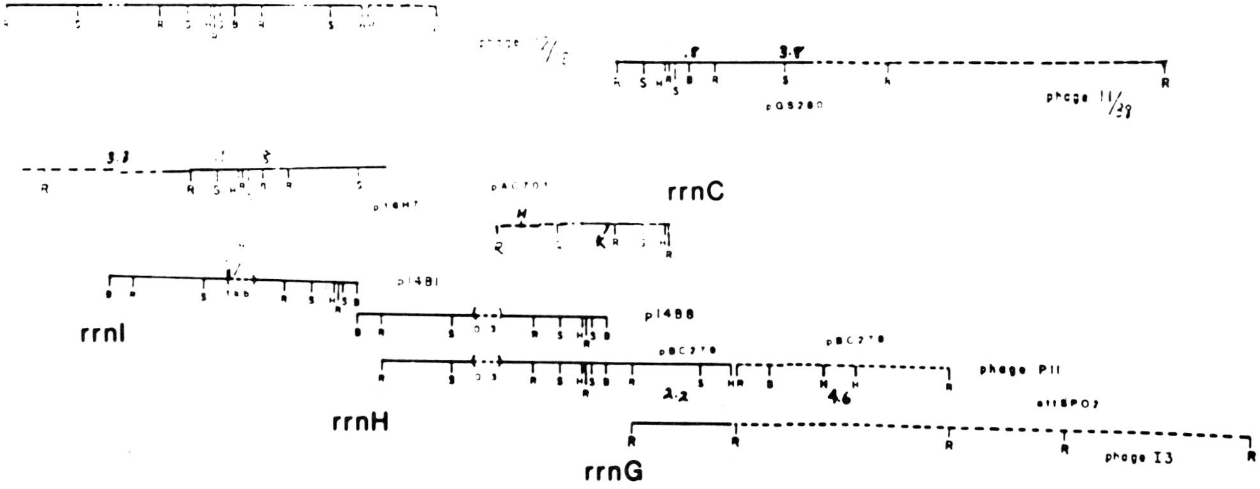

Figure 3. Collection of clones. Fragments designated as subclones have been used for genetic mapping or nick-translated for use as hybridization probes as described in the text.

Table 1. Proposed Linkage Groups of Adjacent rRNA[a]

```
A =  -----(0.6)-----
B =  -----(0.1)-----
C =  -----(15)-----
D =  -----(55)-----(1)-----(0.3)-----

E = C + D : and is adjacent to attSPO2

-----(15)-----(55)-----(1)-----(0.3)-----(6.2)attSPO2
```

----- represents 5 kb region of repeated DNA presumably coding for rRNA; numbers between parentheses represent size in kb of spacer DNA between operons, measured as single stranded loops in EM

[a]*Chow and Davidson, 1973; single operons not detected*

subtilis might actually be **physically** close. Their study suggested that the "linkage groups" could be placed into 4 or 5 major categories shown in Table 1 as A to D and E.

They also showed that the attachment site for phage SPO2 was 6.2 kb from the doublet that contained the 0.3 kb spacer. In fact the aggregate of their observations suggested strongly that linkage groups C and D were contiguous, thus the large linkage arrangement shown as E was very probable. Several of the clones we have analyzed contain fragments with spacers exactly as they described.

In the case of operons <u>rrnO</u> and <u>rrnA</u>, the entire DNA between them has been predicted by overlapping hybridization, and much of it cloned by Yoshikawa (Ogasawara et al, 1983; personal communication) so that we are certain the spacer Chow and Davidson described as 15 kb must correspond to that doublet. This spacer includes the genes for <u>guaA</u>, <u>ts8132</u> and one or two <u>rec</u> genes (Trowsdale et al., 1979). We have independently confirmed the genetic locus of <u>rrnO</u> by subcloning fragment E6' (a fragment to the left of the 5' end of the <u>rrnO</u>) from plasmid B7 provided by H. Yoshikawa, and then mapped its position between <u>gauA</u> and <u>purA</u>.

The collection of cloned DNA used in our studies is shown in Figure 3. This figure has been updated and modified from previous editions (Stewart et al., 1982) in light of direct sequence analysis.

Now that we know the DNA sequence of the plasmid p14B8 spacer region from Peter Zuber's dissertation (University of Virginia, 1982) we can be sure that this clone is the one

Table 2. Transduction Data

	ω % cotransduction with PBS1	kb[a]
cysA - *rrnG*	45	50
guaA - *rrnG*	23	90
aroG - *rrnC*	33	70
thr5 - *rrnC*	5.5	157
aroG - *rrnB*	21.5	98
thr5 - *rrnB*	38	61

Proposed Chromosomal Order:

```
                                                            pBC278
                                        cysA      (22)       cat
-----I-------------------------I---------------I---^--- rrnG
   guaA                 (40)                     attSPO2

                    pGS332
        thr           cat                             aroG
-------I-------------I---------------------I----- rrnB
             (62)              (78.5)

                              pAC701
        thr                     cat             aroG
-------I---------------------I------------I----- rrnC
              (94.5)                 (67)
```

Number in parentheses = t = map units as 100% - cotransduction frequency

[a]Size in kb calculated as suggested by Henner and Hoch (1980) using data from transduction with PBS1 $[C=1-t+t(\ln t)]$

with the 0.3 kb spacer. This exact fragment is found in phage P11 isolated from the Hoch collection (Ferrari et al., 1981), and that phage overlaps by hybridization with Charon phage I-3 which extends 10 kb beyond the ribosomal operon. Fragment pBC278 is a subclone from this region that maps genetically near the cysA gene, at a distance consistent with the map location indicated (see Table 2).

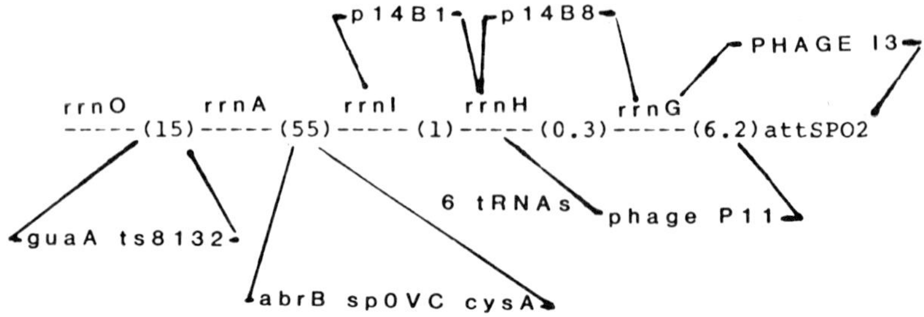

Figure 4. Linkage group E (Table 1) with known genetic loci and designated clones representing the region from attSPO2 to rrnO.

Assuming that the EM data is correct, phage I-3 should contain the attachment site for SPO2. Confirming studies are currently in progress.

One other observation of related interest is that both Peter Zuber's dissertation and the work of Wawrousek and Hansen (1983) have determined the nucleotide sequence of the spacer between operons in plasmid p14B1 and have shown it to contain six tRNA genes (asn, thr, gly, arg, pro, ala). The sequence data suggests that this spacer is the one Chow and Davidson refer to as the 1 kb spacer.

The 55 kb spacer must contain the abrB locus, all of the Losick clones (Haldenwang et al., 1980) and the cysA gene. Since this region of the chromosome is well characterized genetically (Smith and Smith, 1973; Trowsdale et al., 1979; Henner and Hoch, 1980; Wilson et al., 1981; Ogasawara et al, 1983), we are now reasonably certain that those linkage groups suggested by Chow and Davidson are arranged as shown in Figure 4 and that there are 3 ribosomal operons directly to the cysA side of the SPO2 attachment site.

The genetic data, the clone structures, the EM data and the restriction fragment sizes to which clones hybridize (see Table 3), confirm the same picture for the region all the way from SPO2 to the rrnO operon. It is currently uncertain whether there are also ribosomal operons distal to the SPO2 attachment site; there are still a few pieces missing from our puzzle.

Both the operons rrnB and rrnC map in the region between thr5 and aroG (Table 2). The genetic evidence, as well as the restriction digest patterns of clones originally isolated, clearly establishes that they are separate operons and that they must be at least 70 kb apart.

Table 3. BglI Restriction Enzyme Pattern of B. subtilis DNA

kb	Clone	Operon	tRNA	Position
42[a]	pBC278	rrnG, rrnH, rrnI	6[b]	10
19	phage 11/38		c	not assigned
18	pE6'	rrnO	ile, ala	0.4
15	p12E2	rrnA	ile, ala	4
14.5	phage B60		c	not assigned
13.5	pGS332	rrnB	21[d]	274
10	pAC701	rrnC	?	272

[a]*This band in DNA from SPO2 is larger.*

[b]*asn, thr, gly, arg, pro, ala - Spacer region from p14B1 sequenced by P. Zuber (see also Wawrousek and Hansen, 1983).*

[c]*Believed to contain tRNA (actual species unknown) because it hybridizes to bulk labeled tRNA and to the spacer DNA fragment from p14B1 (unpublished).*

[d]*val, thr, lys, leu, gly, leu, arg, pro, ala, met, ile, ser, fmet, asp, phe, his, gly, ile, asn, ser, glu (each different isoaccepting species) sequenced by C. Green and B. Vold.*

Operon rrnC is represented by a Rapoport cosmid clone formerly called cos7 that was kindly supplied by I. Mahler. Plasmid pAC701, subcloned from the cosmid representing a unique fragment to the 5' end of the operon, was used to map rrnC. Since the cosmid contains only the front half of rrnC we cannot yet tell whether rrnC is part of a tandem array. Even though lysates of cells containing this plasmid do make excessive amounts of low molecular weight RNA, this cosmid is in itself odd since the 5' end region of rrnC is completely stable as a clone when most promoter regions are usually unstable if cloned without special vectors.

Since the entire rrnB operon has been cloned we are sure that it is a single isolated operon, not part of a cluster. Clones containing the promoter region at the 5' end of rrnB are unstable in E. coli unless a special vector possessing a transcriptional terminator is used. This operon was derived from 2 separate Charon 28 clones from the Hoch Library (phages J25 and G4) and, as shown in Figure 3, they share a common 1.1 kb EcoRI spacer fragment. The DNA sequence of

```
                                                        50                                                        100
CTTTAATGCTCCCCTTGTGGTCATCAGTATTTAGTTCGTTTCACATACAAGAAAACGAAAAAAACAACAAGATCACATGACTGATGTATATGTTC   rrn B

                                                        150                                                       200
TTTTAAGAAACTTATATGATACACACGCTTTAGAAATCATGGCGAGGATTATAGTTTATTTGTTTTATAGATTTTTTTTAAAAAACTATTGCAATAAATA   rrn B

                                                        250                                                       300
AATACAGGTGTTTATATTATTAAACGTCGCTGATGCACAGCGGACACAACTAGATGCTTCAAAACAACTTGAAAAAAGTTGTTGACAAAAAAGAAGCTGAA   rrn B
          P1

                                                        350                                                       400
TGTTATATTAGTAAAGCTGCTTCATTGAGAAGTAACGAAATGATCTTTGAAAACTAAACAAGACAAAACGTACCTGTTAATTCAGTTTTTAAAAATCGCA   rrn B
   P2                                                    STEM

                                                        450                                                       500
CTGCGATGTGCGTATCATCAAACAGGGCCTGCACGACGCAGGTCACACAGGTGTCGCCGCAGGATGCGGTGAACTTAACCTGTGATCCATTTATCGGAGA   rrn B
                                                                                                  m16s

                                                        550                                                       600
GTTTGATCTTGGCTCAGGACGAACGCTGGCGGCGTGCCTAATACATGCAAGTCGAGCGGACAGGTGGGAGCTTGCTCGATGTTAGCGGCGGACGGGTGAG   rrn B

                                                        650                                                       700
TAACACGTGGGTAACCTGCCTGTAAGACTGGGATAACTCCGGGAAACCGGGGCTAATACCGGATGGTTGTTTGAACCGCATGGTTCAAACATAAAAGGTG   rrn B

                                                        750                                                       800
GCTTCGGCTACCACTTACAGATGGACCCGCGGCGCATTAGCTAGTTGGTGAGGTAACGGCTCACCAAGGCAACGATGCGTAGCCGACCTGAGAGGGTGAT   rrn B
```

Figure 5. Nucleotide sequence of operon rrnB promoter region.

both of these fragments identified the 2 as belonging to the same operon (Bott and Hollis, 1982; L.M. Anderson, unpublished).

Phage J25 generates a pin-point plaque morphology when plated on E. coli DP50. A 1.9 kb EcoRI fragment contains the sequences corresponding to the 5' terminus of 16S RNA and approximately 1.2 kb of DNA upstream of the rRNA determinant. Attempts to subclone this fragment into the RI site of pBR322 failed. However, we were able to insert this fragment into the RI site of the plasmid pKM-1 which contains the lambda phage tRI ρ-dependent transcription terminator (McKenney et al., 1981). This is consistent with the expected strong promoter activity of an rRNA gene set and the requirement for terminators of comparable strength to clone strong promoters (Gentz et al., 1981). The resulting plasmid, pGS227 was found to contain the 1.9 kb fragment and also the adjacent 1.1 kb EcoRI fragment. The 1.9 kb fragment could be stably cloned into plasmid pKM-1 only in one orientation.

The DNA sequence of this region, shown in Figure 5, suggests that this operon contains two tandem promoter regions (P1 and P2) not unlike those found in E. coli. There are 92 base pairs between the two "-10 regions" of the promoters. The second is 180 bp upstream from the start site for mature 16S RNA. Both possess -10 and -35 region sequences typical of E. coli and B. subtilis promoters. The -35 and -10 regions are the optimal 17 nucleotides apart and, especially in the case of P1, have the stretches of T's and A's upstream of the -35 region which are characteristic of promoters which efficiently use RNA polymerase associated with σ^{55} (Moran et al., 1982).

Comparison of this sequence data with that obtained for the <u>rrnO</u> operon, which is located near the origin of replication (Ogasawara et al., 1983), shows that the two do not differ significantly in the spacing or the location of the promoter sequences even though they are physically separated by one fourth of the chromosome. This observation also suggests that the promoter region of <u>rrnO</u> can probably not be significant as an origin of replication.

Although there is still not much information available regarding the transcription or initial processing events of the rRNA gene sets of Gram-positive species, a potential 29 base pair stem structure necessary for processing of the mature 16S RNA sequence can also be predicted from this analysis as shown in Figure 6.

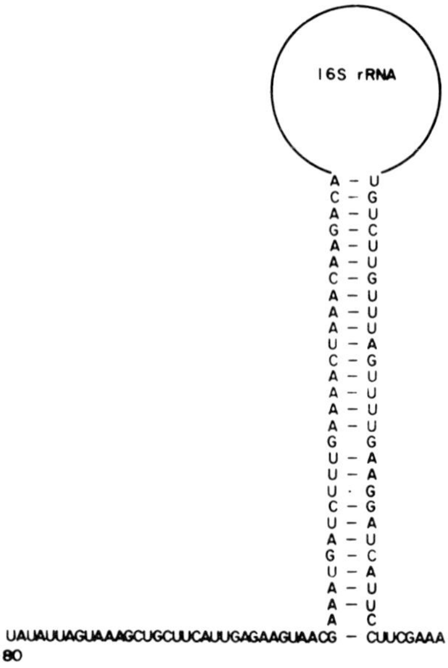

Figure 6. Secondary structure of RNA predicted from nucleic acid sequence adjacent to the coding region for mature 16S RNA.

IV. CONCLUSIONS

Seven of the 10 ribosomal RNA operons have been assigned a genetic locus on the map of B. subtilis. One cluster near the attachment site of SPO2 contains three closely situated repeats of the ribosomal transcription unit. These have tentatively been designated as rrnG, rrnH and rrnI in order to leave three unassigned letters for operons not yet mapped and maintain some semblence of alphabetic order. At least one of the missing operons must be represented by phage clone 11/38 from the collection shown in Figure 3. That operon is known to contain a region of DNA at its 3' end which hybridizes to labeled tRNA (see Table 3), and may represent a second major cluster of tRNA genes. In order to maintain consistency of observations with the EM study of Chow and Davidson, we expect that 2 of the unmapped operons represent a doublet with a spacer of 0.1 kb. The genetic and physical data of other researchers encourage us to postulate that one or more of the unidentified operons could be positioned to the right of the attachment site for phage SPO2, but at this time that is only speculation.

ACKNOWLEDGMENTS

We wish to thank M. F. Lampe, F. E. Wilson, K. T. Rogers and N. Harris for valuable discussion, technical assistance and enthusiastic criticism.

REFERENCES

Bott, K.F. and Hollis, M.A. (1982). In Molecular Cloning and Gene Regulation in Bacilli (A.T. Ganesan, S. Chang and J.A. Hoch, eds.) p. 3, Academic Press, New York.

Colli, W., Smith, and Oishi, M. (1971). **J. Mol. Biol. 56,** 117.

Chow, L.T. and Davidson, N. (1973). **J. Mol. Biol. 75**, 265.

Elwood, M. and Nomura, M. (1980). **J. Bacteriol. 143**, 1077.

Ferrari, E., Henner, D.J. and Hoch, J.A. (1981). **J. Bacteriol. 146**, 430.

Ferrari, F.A., Nguyen, A., Lang, D.L. and Hoch, J.A. (1983). **J. Bacteriol. 154**, 1513.

Gentz, R., Langer, A., Chang, A.C.Y., Cohen, S.N. and Bujard, H. (1981). **Proc. Natl. Acad. Sci. USA 78**, 4936.

Haldenwang, W.G., Banner, C.D.B., Ollington, J.F., Losick, R., Hoch, J.A., O'Connor, M.B. and Sonenshein, A.L. (1980). **J. Bacteriol. 142**, 90.

Henner, D.J. and Hoch, J.A. (1980). **Microbiol. Rev. 44**, 57.

Kobayashi, H. and Osawa, S. (1982). **FEBS Letts. 141**, 161.

Loughney, K., Lund, K.E. and Dahlberg, J.E. (1982). **Nucl. Acids Res. 10.**, 1607.

McKenney, K., Shimatake, H., Court, D., Schmeissner, U., Brady, C. and Rosenberg, M. (1981). In Gene Amplification and Analysis, Vol. II (J.G. Chirikjian and S. Takis, eds.) p. 384, Elsevier/North Holland, New York.

Moran, C.P., Jr., Lang, N., LeGrice, S.F.J., Lee, G., Stephens, M., Sonenshein, A.L., Pero, J. and Losick, R. (1982). **Molec. Gen. Genet. 186**, 339.

Nomura, M. and Post, L.E. (1980). In Ribosomes: Structure, Function and Genetics, (G. Chambliss, G.R. Craven, J. Davies, K. Davis, L. Kahan, and M. Nomura, eds.) p. 672, University Park Press, Baltimore.

Ogasawara, N., Seiki, M. and Yoshikawa, H. (1983). **J. Bacteriol. 154**, 50.

Stewart, G.C., Wilson, F.E. and Bott, K.F. (1982). **Gene 19,** 153.

Smith, I. and Smith, H. (1973). **J. Bacteriol. 114,** 1138.

Trowsdale, J., Chen, S.M.H. and Hoch, J.A. (1979). **Molec. Gen. Genet. 173**, 61.

Wawrousek, E.F. and Hansen, J.N. (1983). **J. Biol. Chem. 258**, 291.
Wilson, F.E., Hoch, J. and Bott, K.F. (1981). **J. Bacteriol. 148**, 624.
Zingales, B. and Coli, W. (1977). **Biochem. Biophys. Acta 474**, 562.

TRANSFER RNA GENE ORGANIZATION IN BACILLUS SUBTILIS[1]

Barbara S. Vold
Christopher J. Green

SRI International
Menlo Park, California

I. INTRODUCTION

Due to recent efforts in sequencing tRNA genes from Bacillus subtilis, a great deal of information about tRNA gene organization of this organism has been acquired in a relatively short period of time. One of the most interesting aspects of tRNA gene organization in B. subtilis to come from these studies is the extensive clustering of some tRNA genes.

Studies on the organization of tRNA genes in Escherichia coli have recently been reviewed by Ozeki (1980). There are approximately 50 to 60 genes reported for E. coli tRNAs representing about 35 different tRNA species. These tRNA genes tend to map in four regions, but they do not occur in large clusters and the numbers of tRNA genes associated in one group range between 1 and 7. Often, tRNA genes in one group are redundant and duplicate genes found in tandem. As in other prokaryotes, these groups of genes are usually co-transcribed forming a multimeric precursor.

B. subtilis tRNA gene organization has not been as well studied. What we know about B. subtilis tRNA gene organization comes from studies utilizing RNA-DNA hybridization, a few limited studies mapping suppressors, and recent studies sequencing tRNA genes.

[1]*This work was supported by Public Health Services Research Grant GM 29231 from the National Institutes of Health.*

ISBN 0-12-274160-9

A. Mapping of tRNA Genes in B. subtilis

One type of experiment to locate the position of tRNA and rRNAs on the B. subtilis chromosome was density transfer experiments in which newly replicated DNA made during spore outgrowth was separated from total chromosomal DNA and hybridized to radioactively labeled tRNA and rRNAs (Oishi et al., 1966; Smith et al., 1968). These studies estimated that the majority of tRNA and 5S RNA, and 16 and 23S RNAs were located in two regions of the chromosome, the predominate area being near the origin of replication. More recent hybridization experiments utilizing Southern blots of EcoRI digests of total B. subtilis DNA with rRNA and tRNA probes support the suggestion that tRNA genes are clustered in a few regions of the genome. These hybridization studies indicated the presence of six major EcoRI restriction fragments containing tRNA (Wawrousek and Hansen, 1983), however, it is not known where these areas might be located on the genetic map.

Other locations for tRNA genes were suggested from the mapping of suppressor mutations (Henner and Steinberg, 1979a; Lipsky et al., 1981). Although the biochemical mechanism involved in these suppressor mutations has not been clarified, two suppressor mutations have been mapped and they are likely to represent the location of tRNA genes. Both mutations map at position 10 (on a map from 0-100).

A third method has been to study the tRNA genes associated with rRNA operons of known map position. One such study has located the position of two rRNA gene sets on either side of the origin of replication with spacer tRNA genes between the 16 and 23S rRNA genes (Ogasawara et al., 1983). Another group of tRNA genes has been found at the 3'-side of an rRNA gene set designated as rrnB by Ken Bott (Stewart et al., 1982). It has been mapped to be in the area between argA and thr (G. Stewart, M. Lampe and K. Bott, unpublished observations). The tRNA genes in this area have been sequenced and are described in Section II. A summary of the areas where tRNA genes have been located on the B. subtilis chromosome is given in Figure 1.

B. Association of tRNA genes with rRNA Gene Sets and Existence as Independent Transcriptional Units

In prokaryotes, tRNA genes have been found in association with rRNA genes either occurring as spacers between the 16 and 23S rRNA genes in the region between two rRNA gene sets or at the promoter-distal end of an rRNA operon.

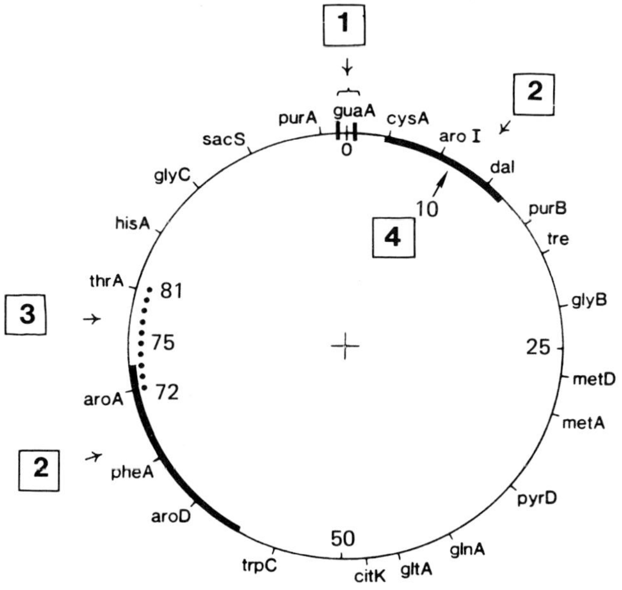

Figure 1. Areas where tRNA genes have been located on the B. subtilis chromosome. Map positions from 0 to 100 are shown inside the circle. Numbers in squares refer to the following: 1) two rRNA gene sets on either side of the origin of replication with spacer tRNA genes between 16 and 23S genes (Loughney et al., 1982; Ogasawara et al., 1983); 2) areas rich in 4S, 5S, 16S and 23S RNAs (Oishi et al., 1966; Smith et al., 1968); 3) tRNAs at the 3'-end of the rRNA gene set, rrnB (Green and Vold, 1983); and 4) suppressor mutations, sup3 (Henner and Steinberg, 1979a) and sup4 (Lipsky et al., 1981).

In E. coli all seven rRNA operons have spacer tRNAs between the 16 and 23S rRNA genes. Three have $tRNA^{Ala}$ and $tRNA^{Ile}$ as spacer tRNAs and four have $tRNA^{Glu}$ as a spacer (Ozeki, 1980). In B. subtilis, however, it is unusual for tRNAs to occur in this spacer region. Of the 10 rRNA gene sets of B. subtilis, only two contain spacer tRNAs (Osagawara et al., 1983). These spacer tRNAs represent sequences for $tRNA^{Ala}$ and $tRNA^{Ile}$. The other rRNA gene sets do not have any tRNA in the spacer region. Thus in this respect the organization of tRNA genes in B. subtilis is very different from that in E. coli.

The majority of tRNA genes are found in close association with rRNA genes according to the hybridization studies of Wawrousek and Hansen (1983) which showed that all six major EcoRI restriction fragments which hybridized to tRNA also hybridized to rRNA. Sequences of regions containing tRNA genes also indicate a close association with rRNA gene sets. Data on the tRNA gene regions, the sequences of which have been published, are shown in Table 1.*

In E. coli the largest tRNA cluster, which contains seven tRNA genes, exists as a separate operon with its own promoter and terminator and is apparently not linked to rRNA operons (Nakajima et al., 1981). B. subtilis also contains at least one cluster of four tRNA genes that appears to be a separate transcriptional unit (Yamada, 1983).

C. Number of tRNA Genes in B. subtilis

With respect to the numbers of tRNA genes, Smith et al. (1968) estimated about 40, Oishi et al. (1966) estimated about 35 and Jeng and Doi (1975) have reported 23 to 39 tRNA genes detectable when tRNA from exponentially growing cells were used as a probe, but 33 to 60 tRNA genes were estimated when tRNA from stage III cells was used as the probe. Sequences of 35 tRNA genes in B. subtilis have already been reported (refer to Table 1) and there are still some areas for which the sequence has not been completed.

One interesting question about B. subtilis tRNAs is whether or not different tRNA species might be transcribed at different growth stages. Based on their hybridization data, Jeng and Doi (1975) suggested that tRNA species with unique primary sequences exist in sporulating cells. However, Henner and Steinberg (1979b) analyzed tRNAs from cells at various growth stages using two-dimensional gel electrophoresis and concluded that there were minimal changes in the species of tRNAs. Also RPC-5 column chromatography comparison of tRNAs from vegetative cells and spores indicated a few possibilities for the existence of unique tRNAs at different growth stages (Vold and Minatogawa, 1972; Vold, 1973). Only two sets of isoaccepting tRNAs which change in relative amounts in B. subtilis have been sequenced, and in both cases, the change in chromatographic properties were due to posttranscriptional modifications (Vold et al., 1982; Menichi et al., 1980). However, expression of unique tRNA genes at certain stages of sporulation remains an open question until more sequence data is available.

**Note added in proof: Since this chapter was written, another cluster of 16 tRNA genes has been sequenced by Wawrousek <u>et al</u>. (1984), J. Biol. Chem. 259, 3694-3702.*

Table 1

tRNA Genes	Association with rRNA Genes	References
ile, ala	Spacer between 16S and 23S rRNA genes	Loughney et al., 1982 Ogasawara et al., 1983
asn, thr, gly, arg, pro, ala	Between 2 rRNA gene sets	Zuber, 1982 Wawrousek and Hansen, 1983
lys, glu, asp, phe	None known	Yamada et al., 1983
21 tRNA genes (see Figure 2)	Promoter-distal to an rRNA gene set	Green and Vold, 1983

II. SEQUENCE ANALYSIS OF A CLUSTER OF 21 tRNA GENES IN BACILLUS SUBTILIS

A. Origin of DNA and Sequence of tRNA Region

The sequence analysis has been described for a 4.5 kb EcoRI restriction fragment of DNA from B. subtilis cloned by Bott and designated rrnB (Stewart et al., 1982). It hybridized to 23 and 5S rRNA. It is probably identical to the largest EcoRI restriction fragment hybridizing to 23S rRNA and tRNA designated by Wawrousek and Hansen (1983) as trrnE. In our laboratory, the 4.5 kb fragment was reduced to a 3 kb piece by cleavage at a single SmaI restriction site in the 23S gene. This 3 kb piece contained approximately 500 bp of the 23 and 5S gene. Sequence analysis involved cloning into an M13 phage and sequencing of the cloned DNA by Sanger's dideoxynucleotide chain termination method (Green and Vold, 1983). The sequence of the region containing tRNA genes is shown in Figure 2.

B. Species of tRNAs Which Are Represented

Although this region contains 21 tRNA genes, none of the tRNA genes are repeated; when isoaccepting species are found they have different anticodons. The only classes of tRNAs that are not represented are those for cysteine, glutamine, tryptophan, and tryosine. The cloverleaf representation of the tRNA genes is shown in Figure 3. Of the 21 tRNA genes in this cluster, 9 are known from the published tRNA sequence:

$tRNA^{Ala}_{UGC}$, $tRNA^{Arg}_{ACG}$, $tRNA^{Gly}_{UCC}$, $tRNA^{Lys}_{UUU}$, $tRNA^{Met}_{CAU}$, $tRNA^{fMet}_{CAU}$,

$tRNA^{Phe}_{GAA}$, $tRNA^{Thr}_{UGU}$, and $tRNA^{Val}_{UAC}$

(Gauss and Sprinzl, 1983). The sequences of the tRNA genes in regions reported by others (refer to Table 1) match ours with the following exceptions: 1) a base pair in the stem of the GTψC loop of

$tRNA^{Ile}_{GAU}$; 2) two base pairs in $tRNA^{Asn}_{GUU}$, one in the stem

of the GTψC loop and one in the aminoacyl stem; and 3) a $tRNA^{Thr}$ which has a significantly different structure with a different anticodon.

The $tRNA^{Leu}_{CAG}$ gene reported here is unusual in that the sequence contains an A at the 5' end of the anticodon loop. This was confirmed by sequencing both strands of the DNA fragment containing this gene. All prokaryotic tRNAs and tRNA gene sequences so far reported contain only a pyrimidine at this site. A purine had been found in this position only in tRNAs of chloroplast and mitochondria (Gauss and Sprinzl, 1983).

C. Presence of a G at the 5'-End of the Gene for Histidine tRNA

All known $tRNA^{His}$ sequences have an extra nucleotide at the 5' end of the molecule, usually a G (Gauss and Sprinzle, 1983). In Drosophila melanogaster and Schizosaccharomyces pombe this nucleotide is added to the $tRNA^{His}$ posttranscriptionally and is not encoded in the gene (Cooley et al., 1982). No other prokaryotic $tRNA^{His}$ gene sequences have been published. The B. subtilis $tRNA^{His}$ gene that we have sequenced contains an extra G at the 5' end. None of the other 20 tRNA genes in this cluster or the 14 B. subtilis tRNA genes in other clusters (Wawrousek and Hansen, 1983; Loughney et al., 1982; Yamada, 1983) have a G before the normal coding sequence. Therefore, we believe that this is evidence that B. subtilis $tRNA^{His}$ has an additional G residue at the 5' end and that this residue is encoded in its gene and is not a posttranscriptional modification.

D. One of the Genes with a Methionine Anticodon Might Be an Isoleucine Acceptor

The assignments of amino acid accepting categories shown in Figure 3 were based on the anticodon except for one tRNA with a methionine anticodon. Three of the tRNA genes found in this cluster appear to code for the methionine anticodon CAU. The $tRNA^{fMet}$ gene codes for an RNA identical to that of the known $tRNA^{fMet}$ (Yamada et al., 1980). The tenth tRNA gene in the cluster differs from the reported sequence of $tRNA^{Met}$ of B. subtilis (Yamada and Ishirura, 1980) by an extra T in the dihydrouridine loop. This extra nucleotide increases the homology of this predicted B. subtilis $tRNA^{Met}$ with the known E. coli $tRNA^{Met}$ (Cory and Marker, 1970) and appears to give a definite band on our sequencing gels. The eleventh tRNA gene in this cluster also has a CAU anticodon but RPC-5 studies of B. subtilis tRNAs indicate the presence of only two species that can be aminoacylated with methio-

```
CCGGGATGGACGCACCGCTGGTGTACCAGTTGTTCTGCCAAGGGCATCGCTGGGTAGCTATGTGCGGACGGGATAAGTGCTGAAAGCATCTAAGCATGAA 0100

GCCCCCCTCAAGATGAGATTTCCCATTCCGCAAGAAGTAAGATCCCTGAAAGATGATCAGGTTGATAGGTCTGAGGTGGAAGTGTGGCAACACATGGAGC 0200
            23S
TGACAGATACTAATCGATCGAGGACTTAACCATATTTTTGAATGATGTCACACCTGTTATCTAGTTTTGAGAGAACACTCTCAATTTGTTTGGTGGCGAT 0300

AGCGAAGAGGTCACACCCGTTCCCATACCGAACACGGAAGTTAAGCTCTTCAGCGCCGATGGTAGTCGGGGGTTTCCCCCTGTGAGAGTAGGACGCCGCC 0400
                                          5S
AAGCAATTGCACGTTAGTGCAATATGGAGGATTAGCTCAGCTGGGAGAGCATCTGCCTTACAAGCAGAGGGTCGGCGGTTCGAGCCCGTCATCCTCCACC 0500
                                                      tRNA(Val,UAC)
ATTTTTCATTATACATATCGGTTTTACATATATGCCGGTGTAGCTCAATTGGTAGAGCAACTGACTTGTAATCAGTAGGTTGGGGGTTCAAGTCCTCTTG 0600
                                                      tRNA(Thr,UGU)
CCGGCACCACTTTTATATGATATAATATTCAAGTCTATTGTAAGAAGAGCCATTAGCTCAGTTGGTAGAGCATCTGACTTTTAATCAGAGGGTCGAAGGT 0700
            P                                                           tRNA(Lys,UUU)
TCGAGTCCTTCATGGCTCACCATTTACATGTTGCGGATGTGGCGGAATTGGCAGACGCGCTAGAATCAGGCTCTAGTGTCTTTACAGACGTGGGGGTTCA 0800
                                                           tRNA(Leu,CAG)
AGTCCCTTCATCCGCACCATTTCTGCGGAAGTAGTTCAGTGGTAGAACACCACCTTGCCAAGGTGGGGGTCGCGGGTTCGAATCCCGTCTTCCGCTCCAA 0900
                                                      tRNA(Gly,GCC)
CTATACCATCCACGCCGGGGTGGTGGAATTGGCAGACACACAGGACTTAAAATCCTGCGGTAGGTGACTACCGTGCCGGTTCAAGTCCGGCCCTCGGCAT 1000
                                                 tRNA(Leu,UAA)
TAAGTTTTGCGCCCGTAGCTCAATTGGATAGAGCGTTTGACTACGGATCAAAAGGTTAGGGGTTCGACTCCTCTCGGGCGCGCCATGATCTATATGAAAT 1100
                                          tRNA(Arg,ACG)
CGGGAAGTAGCTCAGCTTGGTAGAGCACATGGTTTGGGACCATGGGGTCGCAGGTTCGAATCCTGTCTTCCCGACCATTCTTGGGGCCTTAGCTCAGCTG 1200
                                      tRNA(Pro,UGG)
GGAGAGCGCCTGCTTTGCACGCAGGAGGTCAGCGGTTCGATCCCGCTAGGCTCCACTTGATTTCAAAAATATTTGGCGGTGTAGCTCAGCTGGCTAGAGC 1300
               tRNA(Ala,UGC)
GTACGGTTCATACCCGTGAGGTCGGGGGTTCGATCCCCTCCGCCGCTACCAATGGACCTTTAGCTCAGTTGGTTAGAGCAGACGGCTCATAACCGTCCGG 1400
        tRNA(Met,CAU)                                                                 tRNA(Ile,NAU)
TCGTAGGTTCGAGTCCTACAAGGTCCACCACTATACGGAGGAATACCCAAGTCTGGCTGAAGGGATCGGTCTTGAAAACCGACAGGGTGTCAAAGCCCGC 1500
                                                                           tRNA(Ser,UGA)
```

```
GGGGGTTCGAATCCCTCTTCCTCCGCCATACATATTCCTAATCATCGCGGGGTGGAGCAGTTCGGTAGCTCGTCGGGCTCATAACCCGAAGGTCGCAGGT 1600
                                                            tRNA(fMet,CAU)

TCAAATCCTGCCCCCGCAACCAAATTTTAAAATGGTCCGGTAGTTCAGTTGGTTAGAATGCCTGCCTGTCACGCAGGAGGTCGCGGGTTCGAGTCCCGTC 1700
                                                                   tRNA(Asp,GUC)

CGGACCGCCATTTAAATACTTAGGCTCGGTAGCTCAGTTGGTAGAGCAACGGACTGAAAATCCGTGTGTCGGCGGTTCGATTCCGTCCCGAGCCACCATT 1800
                                                      tRNA(Phe,GAA)

TATCAATATGCTTTGGCGGTTGTGGCGAAGTGGTTAACGCACCAGATTGTGGCTCTGGCATTCGTGGGTTCGATTCCCATCAATCGCCCCAAATAAAAAT 1900
                                             tRNA(His,GUG)

TGCGGGTGTAGTTTAGTGGTAAAACCTCAGCCTTCCAAGCTGATGTCGTGGGTTCGATTCCCATCACCCGCTCCATTTCTATATCGTCATGGGCCTGTAG 2000
                                 tRNA(Gly,UCC)

CTCAGCTGGTTAGAGCGCACGCCTGATAAGCGTGAGGTCGATGGTTCGAGTCCATTCAGGCCCACCATGACTTTTGTTCCACAGTAGCTCAGTGGTAGAG 2100
                    tRNA(Ile,GAU)

CTATCGGCTGTTAACCGATCGGTCGCAGGTTCGAATCCTGCCTGTGGAGCCAAATGGAGAAGTACTCAAGTGGCTGAAGAGGCGCCCCTGCTAAGGGTGT 2200
        tRNA(Asn,GUU)

AGGTCGTGTAAGCGGCGCGAGGGTTCAAATCCCTCCTTCTCCGCCATATGATTACAGATATCATAATTATCGGCCCGTTGGTCAAGCGGTTAAGACACCG 2300
              tRNA(Ser,GCU)

CCCTTTCACGGCGGTAACACGGGTTCGAATCCCGTACGGGTCATCCCAGAAGCCTTGCATATCCTGCAAGGTTTTTTGTTTTTATAAATCATGTATATG 2400
tRNA(Glu,UUC)                                                TERM

TCTTAGATTTTGTTCTTTATTTTAAAAACAGACTACAAAAATCTCCATATATTTCGTTTTTCTTCAGAAAATGAAGTTAATTGTCTATAAGTATAAGCCG 2500

TTTCAGGGAAAGGGCTTTTTTTTATTTCTTCGA
```

Figure 2. The nucleotide sequence of the cluster of 21 tRNA genes distal to an rRNA operon. The rRNA, tRNA, possible internal promoter and the terminator sequences are underlined. From Green and Vold (1983).

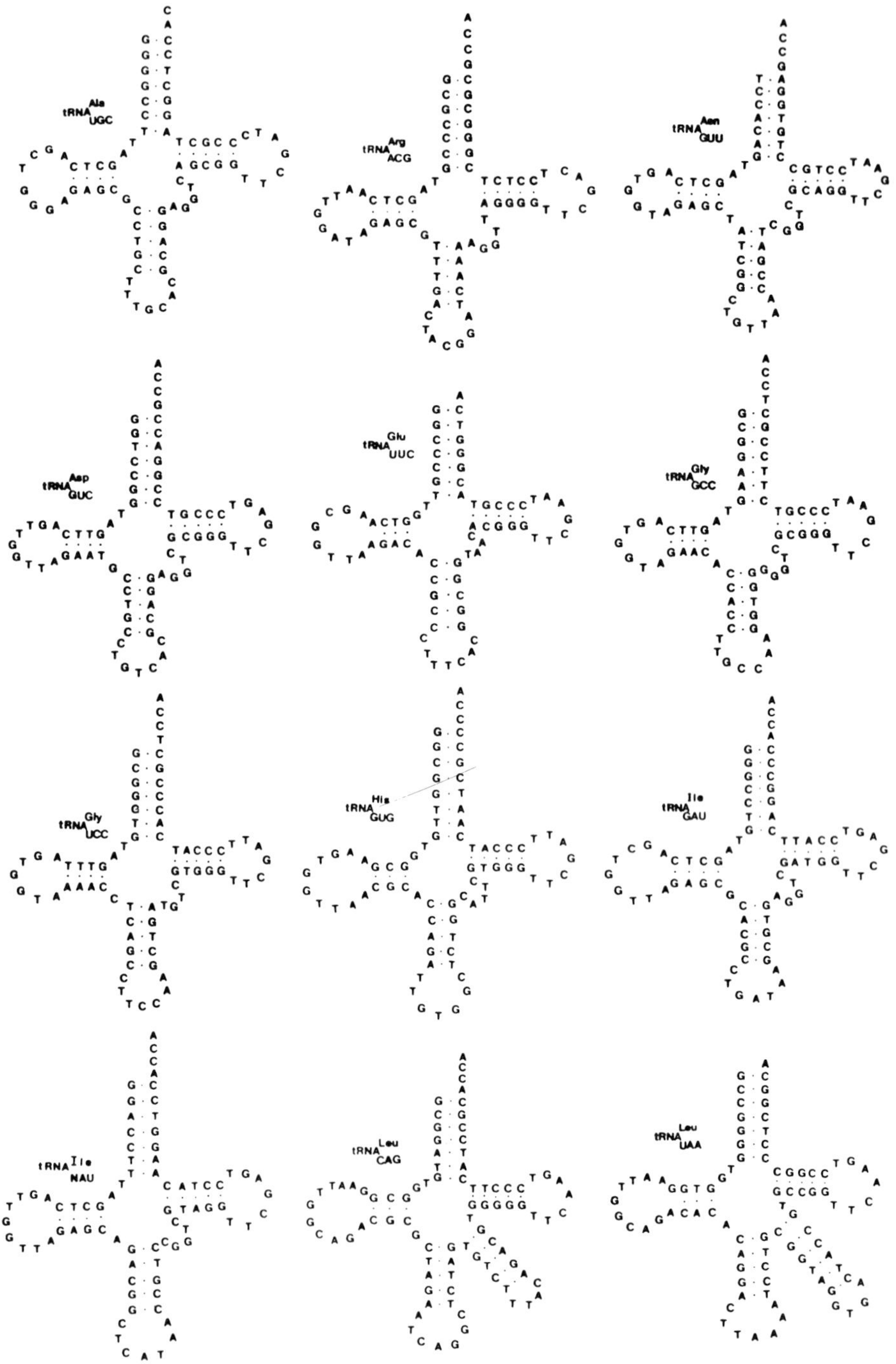
tRNA Ala UGC
tRNA Arg ACG
tRNA Asn GUU
tRNA Asp GUC
tRNA Glu UUC
tRNA Gly GCC
tRNA Gly UCC
tRNA His GUG
tRNA Ile GAU
tRNA Ile NAU
tRNA Leu CAG
tRNA Leu UAA

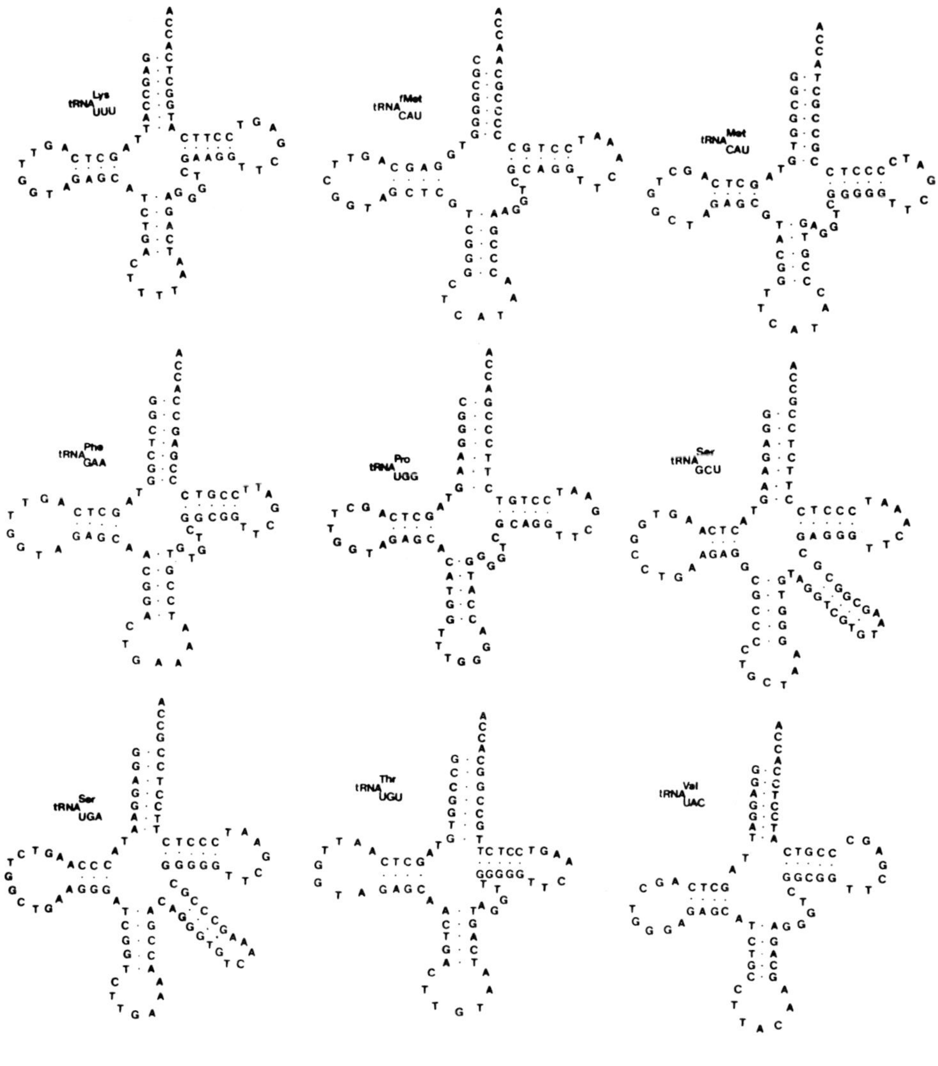

Figure 3. The secondary structures of the tRNA genes in this gene cluster. The genes for $tRNA^{Ala}_{UGC}$, $tRNA^{Glu}_{UUC}$, and $tRNA^{Leu}_{UAA}$ do not have CCA 3'-ends encoded in the gene sequence. $tRNA^{Ile}_{NAU}$ has a methionine anticodon (CAU), but, as described in the text, the C in the wobble position of its anticodon may be posttranscriptionally modified to recognize AUA codons. From Green and Vold (1983).

nine (Vold and Minotogawa, 1972). No other tRNAs for Met for fMet were observed by Yamada and Ishikura during the purification for sequence analysis of the methionine tRNAs from B. subtilis cells harvested in late logarithmic stage (Yamada and Ishikura, personal communication). The presence of an A-U base pair in the third position of the aminoacyl stem of this predicted tRNA may rule out its being recognized by a methionyl-tRNA synthetase (Schulman, 1979). Phage T4, E. coli and spinach chloroplasts have an unknown modified nucleoside in the wobble position of the anticodon of a $tRNA^{Ile}_{NAU}$ that may have originated from a C in the original transcript and may allow it to recognize AUA codons (Fukada and Abelson, 1980; Kuchino et al., 1980; Kashdan and Dudock, 1982; and Francis and Dudock, 1982). By analogy with these other examples and because of the extensive homology with the $tRNA^{Ile}_{GAU}$ gene, we conclude that the eleventh tRNA gene in this cluster is actually a gene for a $tRNA^{Ile}_{NAU}$ and not a methionine isoacceptor.

E. Presence or Absence of the 3'-Terminal CCA Sequence in tRNA Genes

In E. coli all tRNA genes have the 3'-terminal CCA sequence encoded in the genes whereas eukaryotic tRNA genes tend not to encode the CCA end. In B. subtilis, tRNA genes with and without the CCA end can be found. In the sequence in Figure 2, three out of the 21 tRNA genes, $tRNA^{Ala}_{UGC}$, $tRNA^{Glu}_{UUC}$, and $tRNA^{Leu}_{UAA}$, did not have the 3'-terminal CCA. Although it is much more common for tRNA genes to encode the CCA end than not, the other two clusters of tRNA genes which have been sequenced also contain some genes which lack the CCA end: $tRNA^{Asn}_{GUU}$ and $tRNA^{Tgr}_{GGU}$ (Wawrousek and Hansen, 1983) and $tRNA^{Glu}_{UUC}$ and $tRNA^{Phe}_{GAA}$ (Yamada et al., 1983). It is also interesting to note that the same tRNA genes in different clusters are not always without their CCA end.

F. Spacer Regions Between the Structural Genes for tRNA

The first tRNA gene, $tRNA^{Val}$, begins 21 bases downstream from the end of the 5S rRNA gene. The spacing between the 21 tRNA genes varies from 2 to 37 bases. The spacer regions on either side of the structural genes for both $tRNA^{Thr}_{UGU}$ and $tRNA^{Lys}_{UUU}$ have six-base sequences that could pair causing the CCA ends of these tRNAs to loop out. This type of tRNA precursor structure has been found in E. coli and B. subtilis and may create recognition sites for processing enzymes (Nakajima et al., 1981; Rossi and Landy, 1979; and Loughney et al., 1982). One common characteristic that the spacer regions share is that they are AT rich.

G. Putative Internal Promoter

Although these tRNA genes are probably all transcribed as part of the transcriptional unit from the rRNA gene set preceding them, inside the largest spacer region, between the second ($tRNA^{Thr}_{UGU}$) and third ($tRNA^{Lys}_{UUU}$) genes, there is a perfect consensus sequence (TATAAT) for a pribnow box (-10 region) for an RNA polymerase promoter (Figure 2). Upstream of this site, separated by 17 bases, is a corresponding -35 region that conserves the most important part of the -35 consensus sequence (TTGNNN) (Rosenberg and Court, 1979). It is interesting to note that this possible -35 region is inside the $tRNA^{Thr}_{UGU}$ gene and that the first two T residues in the -35 sequence results in the tRNA having two suboptimal U-G pairs at this junction of the aminoacyl and GTψC stems (Figure 3). The transcription start site for this predicted promoter is just upstream of the $tRNA^{Lys}_{UUU}$ gene. This promoter would presumably be recognized by the major, σ^{55}-containing, RNA polymerase found in both vegetative and sporulating cells (Losick and Pero, 1981: Doi, 1982). B. subtilis contains at least four different holoenzymes for RNA polymerase activity during vegetative growth and at least one new holoenzyme during sporulation (Johnson et al., 1983). The multiple forms are characterized by different sigma factors, and recognize different base sequences in the -35 and -10 regions of the promoter. However, relatively few promoters for the sporulating and minor RNA polymerases have been analyzed so that sequence information on their consensus recognition sites is incomplete. This tRNA gene cluster does not contain any other presently known -10 and -35 sequence combinations for these other RNA polymerases (Johnson et al., 1983). However, there may be some sites that approximate these known minor promoter sequences. As more polymerase recognition sequences are found, other promoter sites may be discovered on this sequence. The putative RNA polymerase promoter between the second and third tRNA genes may serve to increase the relative rates of transcription of the 19 downstream tRNA genes compared to the

$tRNA^{Val}_{UAC}$, $tRNA^{Thr}_{UGU}$, and rRNA genes lying upstream from

this promoter. In addition, it may serve to relieve the last 19 tRNA genes from the same type of regulation controlling the rRNA promoter. The possible discovery of other RNA polymerase recognition sites controlling the expression of these genes may answer the questions of the importance of any specific tRNA species to the process of sporulation.

H. Terminator

Immediately following the last tRNA gene, $tRNA^{Glu}_{UUC}$, there

is a 12 base-pair hairpin loop with a long stretch of Ts at the 3' end, characteristic of an RNA polymerase terminator site (Rosenberg and Court, 1979) (Figure 4). Such terminator structures have also been found in the other B. subtilis gene clusters (Wawrousek and Hansen, 1983; Yamada et al., 1983). The sequencing was continued for approximately 150 bases beyond this termination site without encountering any further tRNA genes or obvious RNA polymerase recognition sites. One base down from the 5S gene, there begins a seven base-paired hairpin loop (Figure 4). This loop does not have the stretch of T residues that are characteristic of terminator hairpins found in E. coli (Rosenberg and Court, 1979). Hairpin loops have been shown to occur in the spacer regions in E. coli (Nakajima et al, 1981) and B. subtilis (Yamada et al., 1983) tRNA gene clusters and may play a role in the processing of this primary transcript (Young and Steitz, 1978).

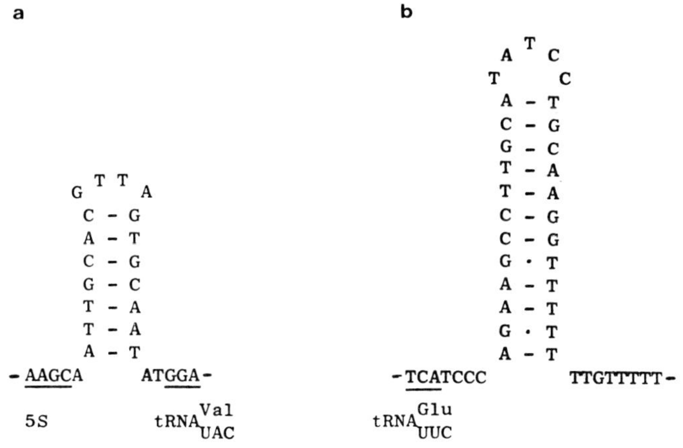

Figure 4. Possible loop structures. (a) The first hairpin loop in this gene cluster is found immediately before the first tRNA gene. (b) A possible RNA polymerase terminator hairpin possessing the stretch of T residues characteristic of prokaryotic terminators is found immediately following the last tRNA gene.

ACKNOWLEDGMENT

We are indebted to Ken Bott for providing us with the pBC204 plasmid.

REFERENCES

Cooley, L., Appel, B. and Söll, D. (1982). **Proc. Natl. Acad. Sci. USA 79**, 6475.
Cory, S. and Marker, K. (1970). **Eur. J. Biochem. 12**, 177.
Doi, R. (1982). **Arch. Biochem. Biophys. 214**, 772.
Francis, M.A. and Dudock, B. (1982). **J. Biol. Chem. 257**, 11195.
Fukada, K. and Abelson, J. (1980). **J. Mol. Biol. 139**, 377.
Gauss, D. and Sprinzl, M. (1983). **Nucl. Acids Res. 11**, r1.
Green, C.J. and Vold, B.S. (1983). **Nucl. Acids Res.**, in press.
Henner, D. and Steinberg, W. (1979a). **J. Bacteriol. 139**, 668.
Henner, D. and Steinberg, W. (1979b). **J. Bacteriol. 140**, 555.
Jeng, Y.-H. and Doi, R.H. (1975). **J. Bacteriol. 121**, 950.
Johnson, W.C., Moran, C.P. and Losick, R. (1983). **Nature 302**, 800.
Kashdan, M. and Dudock, B. (1982). **J. Biol. Chem. 257**, 11191.

Kuchino, Y., Watanabe, S., Harada, F. and Nishimura, S. (1980). **Biochemistry 19**, 2085.
Lipsky, R.H., Rosenthal, R. and Zahler, S.A. (1981). **J. Bacteriol. 148**, 1012.
Losick, R. and Pero, J. (1981). **Cell 25**, 582.
Loughney, K., Lund, E. and Dahlberg, J.E. (1982). **Nucl. Acids Res. 10**, 1607.
Menichi, B., Arnold, H.H., Heyman, T., Dirheimer, G. and Keith, G. (1980). **Biochem. Biophys. Res. Commun. 95**, 461.
Nakajima, N., Ozeki, H. and Shimura, Y. (1981). **Cell 23**, 239.
Ogawawara, N., Seiki, M. and Yoshikawa, H. (1983). **J. Bacteriol. 154**, 50.
Oishi, M., Oishi, A. and Sueoka, N. (1966). **Proc. Natl. Acad. Sci. USA 55**, 1095.
Ozeki, H. (1980). In Genetics and Evolution of RNA Polymerase, tRNA and Ribosomes (S. Osawa, H. Ozeki, H. Uchida and T. Yura, eds.) p. 173, Elsevier/North Holland Biomedical Press, New York.
Rosenberg, M. and Court, D. (1979). **Ann. Rev. Genet. 13**, 319.
Rosse, J.J. and Landy, A. (1979). **Cell 16**, 523.
Schulman, L. (1979). In Transfer RNA: Structure, Properties and Recognition (P.R. Schimmel, D. Söll and J.N. Abelson, eds.) p. 311, Cold Spring Harbor Laboratory, Cold Spring Harbor, NY.
Smith, I., Dubnau, D., Morrell, P. and Marmur, J. (1968). **J. Mol. Biol. 33**, 123.
Stewart, G., Wilson, F. and Bott, K. (1982). **Gene 19**, 153.
Vold, B.S. and Minatogawa, S. (1972). In Spores, V (H.O. Halvorson, R. Hanson and L.L. Campbell, eds.) p. 254, American Society for Microbiology, Washington, DC.
Vold, B.S. (1979). **J. Bacteriol. 113**, 825.
Vold, B.S., Keith, D.E., Jr., Buck, M., McCloskey, J.A. and Pang, H. (1982). **Nucl. Acids Res. 10**, 3125.
Wawrousek, E.F. and Hansen, J.N. (1983). **J. Biol. Chem. 258**, 291.
Yamada, Y., Kuchino, Y. and Ishikura, H. (1980). **J. Biochem. 87**, 1261.
Yamada, Y. and Ishikura, H. (1980). **Nucl. Acids Res. 8**, 4517.
Yamada, Y., Ohki, M. and Ishikura, H. (1983). **Nucl. Acids Res.**, in press.
Young, R. and Steitz, J. (1978). **Proc. Natl. Acad. Sci. USA 75**, 3593.
Zuber, P. (1982). Ph.D. Thesis, Microbiology Department, University of Virginia.

STRUCTURE AND FUNCTION OF THE REGION OF THE REPLICATION ORIGIN OF THE BACILLUS SUBTILIS CHROMOSOME[1]

Naotake Ogasawara
Shigeki Moriya
Sumi Mizumoto
Hiroshi Yoshikawa

Cancer Research Institute
Kanazawa University
Takaramachi, Kanazawa
Japan

I. INTRODUCTION

The chromosome of Bacillus subtilis replicates from a genetically fixed site and proceeds bidirectionally. In both bacterial plasmids and the Escherichia coli chromosome, functions essential for autonomous replication are known to be located in the small region of the replication origin. In contrast, vigorous attempts for identifying the autonomously replicating function of the B. subtilis chromosome have been unsuccessful. The failure to isolate an autonomously replicating unit from the chromosome may be due to unknown technical problems. Alternatively, the region of the replication origin of the chromosome may be so elaborately organized that it does not allow us to localize a functional unit by conventional cloning methods.

Based on these facts we decided to analyze the structure and function of the origin region of a fairly large size. During the last two years we have constructed a detailed physical and genetic map of the origin region covering some 45 kbp including sequencing of some 2000 bp (Ogasawara et

[1]*This work was supported by a Grant-in-Aid for Special Project Research, for Cooperative Research and for Scientific Research from the Ministry of Education, Science and Culture, Japan.*

ISBN 0-12-274160-9

al., 1983a; 1983b). Unexpectedly two ribosomal RNA operons were found in this region. Promoters for these operons showed a strong inhibitory effect on replication of a composite plasmid, both in E. coli and B. subtilis (Seiki et al., 1982). In addition, one of these operons, rrnO, nearest the origin had characteristic sequences different from other operons in the promoter and leader regions and affected transcription and processing of this operon (Ogasawara et al., 1983a). These results suggested involvement of the operon in replication.

In this report, we summarize these results with discussion on a possible role of the rRNA operons in the initiation of replication.

II. RESULTS

A. Physical and Genetic Map of the Origin Region

We reported that the first replicating DNA fragment B7 (BamH1-7) contained two tandem promoters. These promoters showed strong inhibitory effects on plasmid replication when they were inserted into a shuttle vector, thus designated as sar sequences (suppressor for autonomous replication) (Seiki et al., 1982).

In collaboration with Dr. Seror-Laurent's group, these promoters were found to be tandem promoters for a ribosomal RNA (rRNA) operon (Henckes et al., 1982). Based on this finding, we reexamined the structure of the origin region of the chromosome using an rRNA gene set (rDNA), gua and dnats8132, as probes for genetic markers. Figure 1 shows a physical (restriction enzyme cleavage map) and a genetic map of the region of the replication origin. Unexpectedly, two rRNA gene sets, rrnO and rrnA, were found in this region. The origin markers guaA and dnats8132 are located on the physical map for the first time. Recent observation by K. Bott's group showed that the genes for two subunits of DNA gyrase, nalA and novA, were located in the E6 fragment (reported at this meeting).

The origin region of some 45 kbp, containing the two rRNA gene sets, was cloned in Charon 28 vector using two cloned fragments, E6' and E3' located proximal to rrnO and rrnA, respectively, as probes for plaque hybridization. Most of the EcoRI subfragments in this region have been recloned in pBR vectors except for E4 and E5.

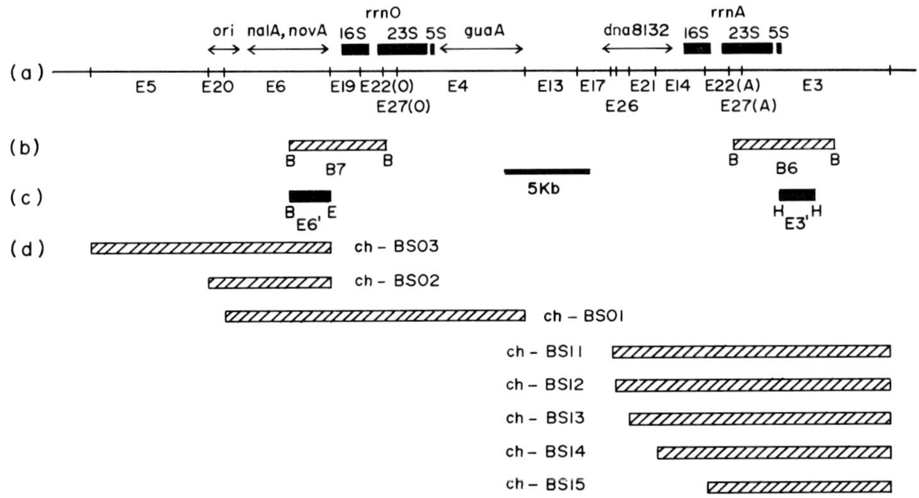

Figure 1. Physical and genetic map of the replication origin region. [A] A map of cleavage sites by EcoRI is shown. Exact locations of rRNA operons are indicated. Locations of other genetic markers including ori (the site of initiation) are approximate within the region indicated by <———>. [B] BamHI fragments originally cloned in a shuttle vector pMS102' (see Figure 8). [C] Sub-fragments of the BamHI fragments recloned in pBR322 that were used as the probes for plaque hybridization. [D] Fragments cloned in Charon 28.

B. Structure and Function of rRNA Operons

The two rRNA gene sets in the origin region, especially the one nearest the origin, may play an important role in initiation of replication. It was, therefore, of interest to determine the structure and transcription of these gene sets. Complete nucleotide sequences of the two gene sets were determined except for the central portion of the 16S and 23S rRNA structural genes whose sequences are essentially the same as those of other gene sets judging from the restriction map (Bott et al., 1981).

Figure 2 shows that the organization of the two sets is essentially the same but differs from other gene sets in the spacer region between 16S and 23S rRNA genes. Two spacer tRNA genes, $tRNA^{Ile}$ and $tRNA^{Ala}$, were found only in these gene sets (Loughney et al., 1982). The gene sets start from two tandem promoters and end with a typical termination signal. The sequence of the termination signal is identical

	Promoter 1		promoter 2	leader sequence	16S RNA	spacer 1	$tRNA^{Ile}$
rrnO	35	62	35	173	-	100	77
rrnA	36	48	35	111	-	(99)	(77)

	spacer 2	$tRNA^{Ala}$	spacer 3	23S RNA	spacer 4	5S RNA	termination signal
rrnO	11	76	83	-	55	116	42
rrnA	(11)	(76)	(83)	-	132	116	39

Figure 2. Sequence organization of the rrnO and rrnA operons. Number of nucleotide pairs is shown for each structural unit. Numbers in parenthesis are deduced because the fine restriction map of this region is identical in rrnO and rrnA.

to that of the precursor molecule of 5S RNA reported previously (Sogin and Pace, 1976). Therefore, we concluded that each of these gene sets constituted a single transcriptional unit, an operon. A putative transcript of rrnO is shown in Figure 3 in a possible secondary structure suitable for processing.

Examination of the DNA sequence revealed remarkable differences between the two operons in the promoter, leader and spacer regions. First, the first promoter of the tandem promoters (P1) of rrnO differs both in the -35 region and number of base pairs between the -35 region and the Pribnow box. The difference is more revealing when it is compared with other promoters known so far in B. subtilis. Figure 4 shows that the recognition sequence of B. subtilis promoters are highly conserved in sequence and number of base pairs. The P1 of rrnO is an exception case. Second, a remarkably inverted repeated sequence is found immediately downstream of the Pribnow box of rrnO. Interestingly, a part of the

Figure 3. Secondary structure of a putative transcript of the rrnO operon. Sequence of the transcript is deduced from the DNA sequence. A possible site of initiation of transcription was determined by S1 mapping (see Figure 5). Arrows indicate possible sites for endonucleolytic cleavage during processing. Dotted lines indicate ends of the structural genes.

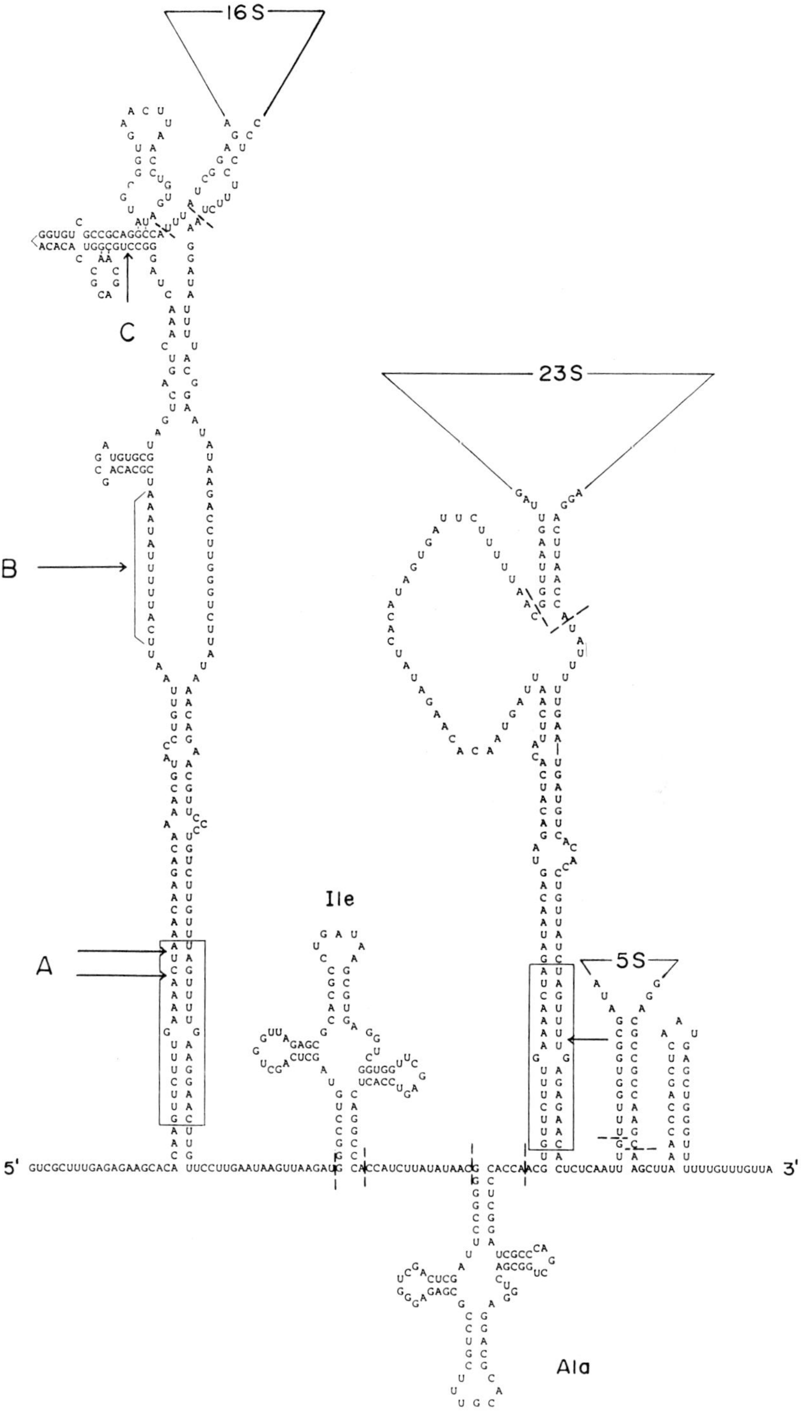
16S
C
B
23S
Ile
A
5S
5'
3'
Ala

rrnO P1	CGCTTTTTTGTGTCATAACCC	TTTACA	GTCATAAAAATTATGG	TATAAT	CATTTCT	GTTGTCT	TTTT
rrnO P2	AAAAACTTTTTCAAAAAAGTA	TTGACC	TAGTTAACTAAAAATGT	TACTAT	TAAGTA	GTCGCTT	TGAG
rrnA P1	TCATTTAATTGATATTATGTA	TTGACT	TAGACAACTGAAGGTCT	TATTCT	AATATAC	GTCGCTG	ATGA
rrnA P2	AAAGAAAATGCTAAAAAGTTG	TTGACA	GTAGCGGCGGTAAATGT	TATGAT	AATAAA	GTCGCTT	AAAC
rrnB P1	AGATTTTTTTTAAAAAACTA	TTGCAA	TAAATAAATACAGGTCT	TATATT	ATTAAAC	GTCGCTG	ATGC
rrnB P2	AAAACAACTTGAAAAAAGTTG	TTGACA	AAAAAGAACGTGAATGT	TATATT	AGTAAA	GCTGCTT	CATT
rrnT2	AAAAGTTTTTAAAAAAGGTTA	TTGACT	TTGAAGAAGTGACATTG	TATACT	AATAAA	GTTGCTT	TAAC
tRNA	AAAAAAGTTA	TTGCCA	CTTCTATTTGTTCGTGA	TATTAT	AAATCTC	GTTGTTA	CGGA
veg	TTGATATAATTTAAATTTTAT	TTGACA	AAAATGGGCTCGTGTTG	TACAAT	AAATGTACTGAGGTGGATGC		
tms	CTTGCACTTCATGAAGTCTCC	TTGAAA	TCAGAAGATATTTAGGA	TATATT	TTTCTATGGATAAAAAGGAT		
spoOF	GCAGTATTGTATGTATTCTGT	TTGATT	TTCCTATTTCCTTTAAT	TATAAT	AGTCTACTTTACGACATTT		
SPO1 early	AAAAATTTGCAAAAAGTTG	TTGACT	TTATCTACAAGGTGTGG	CATAAT	AATCTTAACAACAGCAGGAC		
consensus sequence		$TTGAC^{T}_{A}$		$TA^{TTT}_{CAA}T$		$GT^{C}_{T}G^{C}_{T}T^{T}_{Pu}$	

Figure 4. Nucleotide sequence of promoter-proximal region of various genes in B. subtilis. P1 and P2 indicate the first and the second promoter of the two tandemly repeated promoters in each rRNA gene set. References for sequence data are: rrnA (Ogasawara et al., 1983a), rrnO (Seiki et al., 1982), rrnB (K. Bott, personal communication), rrnT2 (Wawrousek and Hansen, 1983), tRNA (Yamada et al., 1983), veg and tms (Moran et al., 1982), spoOF (Shimotsu et al., 1983) and SPO1 early genes (Lee et al., 1980).

repeat appears at exactly the same number of base pairs down stream of the P2 promoter of the same operon. Third, the leader region of rrnO contains a 65 bp addition immediately before the start of the 16S rRNA structural gene. These characteristic features in the sequence of rrnO may have specific regulatory functions in transcription of the operon.

In order to test this possibility, transcription of rrnO and rrnA was studied in vivo using the S1 mapping method. Fragments containing promoters and leader sequences of rrnO and rrnA were cloned and used as hybridization probes to detect specific transcripts from these operons (Figure 5). Figure 5 shows that the P2 promoter is used predominantly in rrnO, while both P1 and P2 promoters are used in rrnA with a slight preference for the P1 promoter. In addition to these intact transcripts, discrete species of processed molecules were identified in both operons. Judging from the size of the processed molecule, two major cleavage sites were determined in both operons, two sites in one stem structure (site a) and multiple sites in a loop region (site b) flanking the 16S rRNA structural gene (Figure 3). In addition to these processed species common to the two operons, the third and minor processed molecule was found only in rrnO. The cleavage site (site C) was located near the 5' end of the 65 bp unique sequence which can be constructed into a fairly stable secondary structure (Figure 3). The processed molecule would give rise to a 16S rRNA with an additional 60 bp at the 5' end. It should be noted that this unusual species was synthesized during germination and not detected in exponentially growing cells under the present experimental conditions. Furthermore, this molecule was more stable against rifampicin treatment than other processed species which decreased rapidly during the incubation with rifampicin. These unique properties of the rrnO operon in transcription and processing suggest that the operon plays some additional roles other than the synthesis of rRNAs and tRNAs. It is tempting to assume that the operon is involved in initiation of chromosomal replication.

C. Reexamination of the Site of Initiation of Chromosomal Replication

We previously determined the site of initiation of replication by measuring the order of synthesis of restriction enzyme fragments during synchronous replication by germinating spores. It is now possible to determine the initiation site by a more sensitive method, that of determining the sites of synthesis of the first Okazaki fragments using cloned DNA fragments of the origin region as hybridization probes.

Spores of a thymine-requiring mutant of B. subtilis CRK2000 (leu8, trpC, thyAB) were germinated in a synthetic medium, GM11, in the absence of thymine for 2 hours. Replication was initiated synchronously by adding ^{3}H-thymidine of a high specific activity in the presence of 100 μM 6-hydroxyphenylazouracil (6HPU) for a short period of time. During a 2 minute incubation, accumulation of a small amount of labeled short strands of less than 1000 bp occurred. These fragments were hybridized with various cloned fragments of 1 to 2 kbp fixed on nitrocellulose paper and put together into the same hybridization mixture. The results shown in Figure 6 show that the highest peak of hybridization is observed near the junction between the E20 and E6 fragments. Thus, the initiation site is clearly located within the 3 kbp region. No complete EcoRI fragments were labeled during this early synthesis period. The present result is inconsistent with previously reported data in

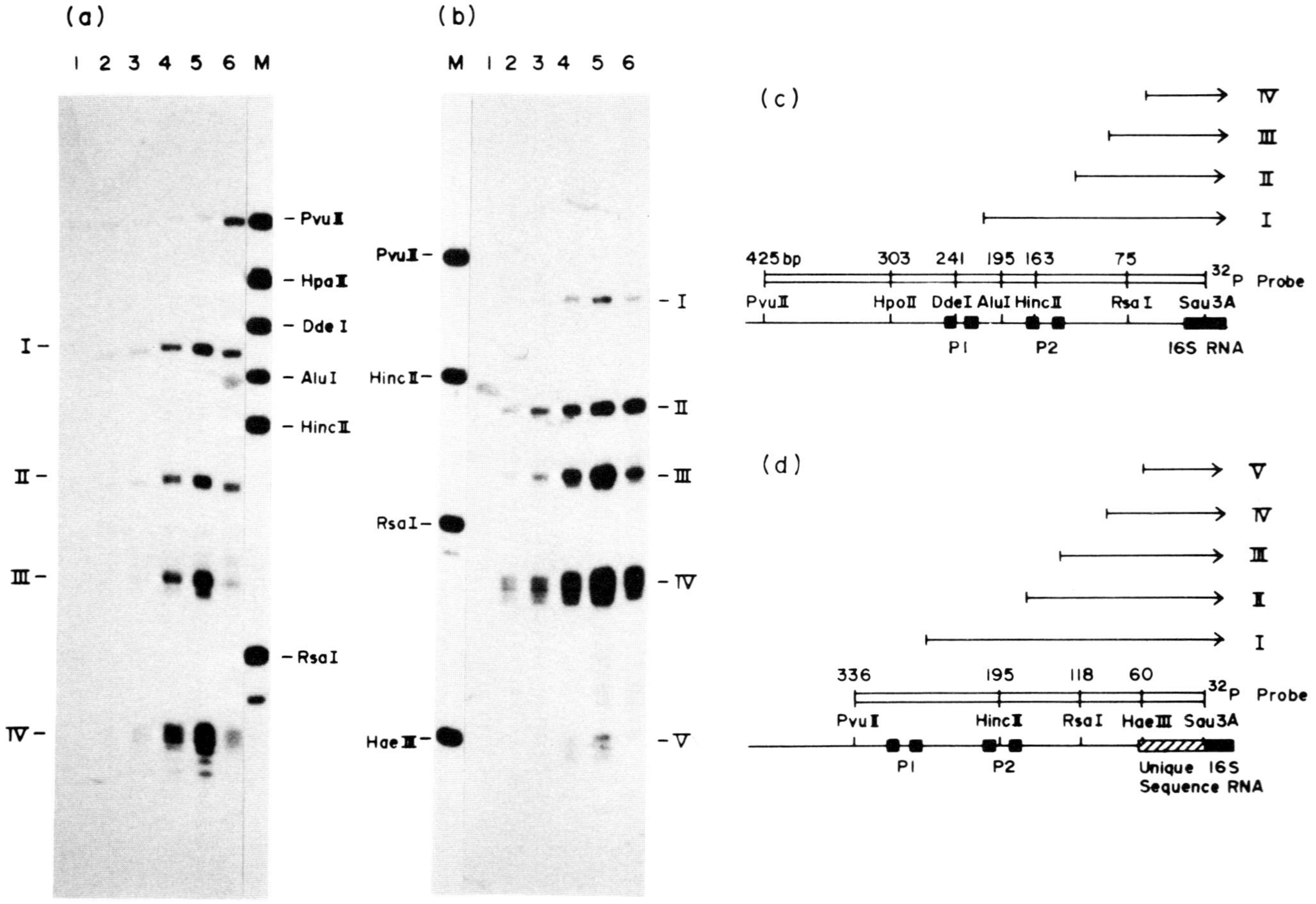

(a)
1 2 3 4 5 6 M
- PvuII
- HpaII
- Dde I
- AluI
- HincII
- RsaI
I -
II -
III -
IV -
(b)
M 1 2 3 4 5 6
PvuII -
HincII -
RsaI -
HaeIII -
- I
- II
- III
- IV
- V
(c)
IV
III
II
I
425 bp
303
241
195
163
75
^{32}P Probe
PvuII
HpoII
DdeI
AluI
HincII
RsaI
Sau3A
P1
P2
16S RNA
(d)
V
IV
III
II
I
336
195
118
60
^{32}P Probe
PvuII
HincII
RsaI
HaeIII
Sau3A
P1
P2
Unique Sequence
16S RNA

which the E19 fragment was the first to be replicated (Ogasawara et al., 1979). This discrepancy may be because of technical problems involved in analysis of labeled fragments by fluorography. Since the present method of determination of sites of the Okazaki fragment is more reliable and sensitive in analyzing the very early event of replication, we concluded that the actual synthesis of DNA strands begins at the junction between E20 and E6, the site which is some 5 kbp away from the rrnO operon.

D. Attempts at Isolating the Autonomously Replicating Fragment from the Origin Region of the Chromosome

For the isolation of functional oriB (replication origin of the B. subtilis chromosome), it is essential to construct a vector plasmid suitable for searching for the ori function. We reported previously on an ori-searching plasmid, pNO2, derived from a composite plasmid between pBR322 and pUB110 (Figure 7) (Seiki et al., 1981). A segment of

---

Figure 5. Identification of in vivo transcripts from rrnO and rrnA operons by S1 mapping. Total RNA was isolated from spores, germinating spores or exponentially growing cells and S1 mapping was performed as described previously (Ogasawara et al., 1983a). For germinating spores, spores of B. subtilis CRK2000 (leu8, trpC, thyAB), 10^8 spores/ml, were germinated in a synthetic medium, GM11 (Sueoka and Quinn, 1968), for various times and then killed in an ethanol-phenol mixture. For exponentially growing cells, B. subtilis CRK2000 was grown in a synthetic medium to Klett unit 120. RNA was isolated and used for the S1 mapping procedure with ^{32}P-labeled probes. Portions of ^{32}P-labeled probe DNA which are protected from S1 nuclease by RNA transcripts were separated in a 4% polyacrylamide gel containing 7 M urea. Autoradiograms are shown in [A] (rrnA probe) and [B] (rrnO probe). Lanes 1 to 5, transcripts from germinating spores for 0, 15, 30, 45 and 60 minutes, respectively; lane 6, transcripts from exponentially growing cells; lane M, restriction enzyme fragments of ^{32}P-labeled probes used as size markers. [C] and [D] describe maps of the probe. [C] Promoter-proximal region and part of the 16S rRNA gene of rrnA. [D] Promoter-proximal region of rrnO. Restriction enzyme cleavge sites and number of base pairs from the ^{32}P-labeled 5'-terminal residue are shown on each DNA probe. I-V correspond to protected fragments shown in [A] and [B].

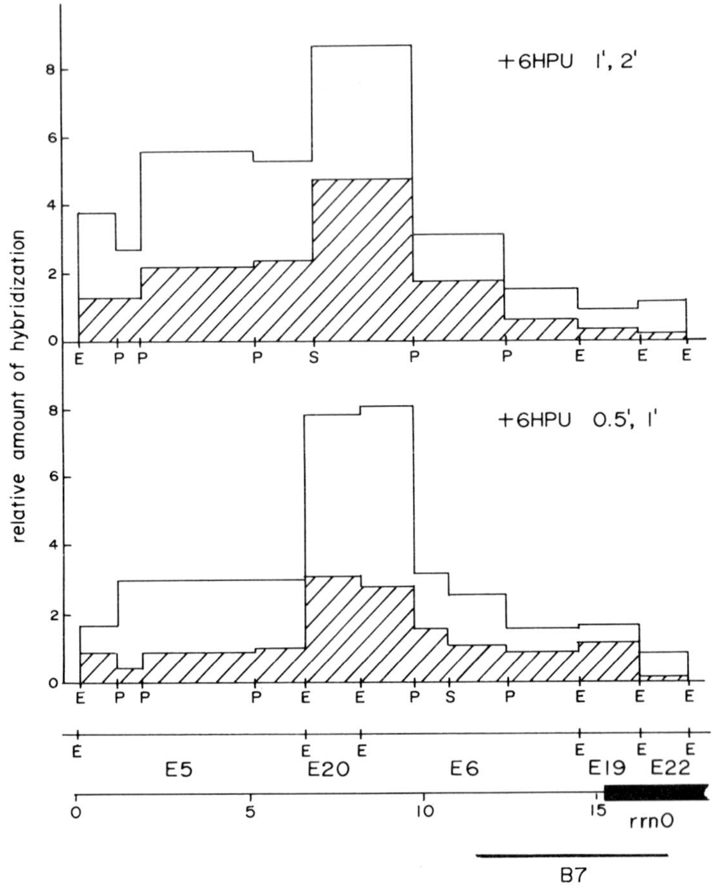

Figure 6. Location of the site of synthesis of the first Okazaki fragments. Spores of a thymine-requiring mutant B. subtilis CRK2000 (leu8, trpC, thyAB) were germinated as described in Figure 5 for 2 hours in the absence of thymine. DNA synthesis was initiated by adding ^{3}H-thymidine in the presence of 100 μM 6HPU for the time indicated. DNA was isolated, heat denatured and separated in a 5 to 10% sucrose gradient. Restriction enzyme fragments shown in the figure were blotted on nitrocellulose paper disks separately and mixed together in a hybridization buffer. ^{3}H-thymidine-labeled Okazaki fragments were hybridized with the mixture of these blotted paper disks. Radioactivity of each disk was measured to determine the amount of Okazaki fragments hybridized to each fragment. Restriction enzyme cleavage sites are: E, EcoRI; P, PstI; and S, SalI. Map locations of rrnO and the B7 fragment are shown at the bottom.

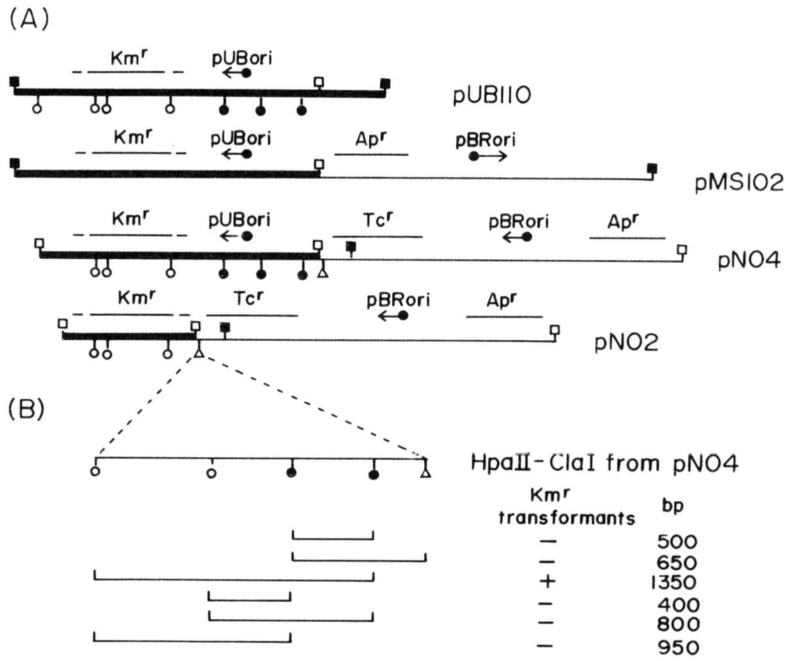

Figure 7. Structure of the ori searching vector pNO2 and the essential region for the replication pUB110 plasmid. [A] Genetic and restriction sites of pUB110, two shuttle vectors, pMS102' and pNO4, and an ori searching vector, pNO2, are shown. Restriction enzyme cleavage sites are: BamHI, ■ ; EcoRI, □ ; TaqI, ● ; HpaII, ○ ; and ClaI, Δ . [B] A HpaII-ClaI fragment was isolated from pNO4. Various fragments obtained by partial digestion with TaqI were inserted into the ClaI site of pNO2 to test for transformation of Km^r in B. subtilis. Only a 1350 bp fragment is active for the transformation.

1.5 kpb containing the origin of pUB plasmid was deleted in pNO2 from the pUB portion so that no transformation occurs in B. subtilis by the protoplast transformation method. Using this plasmid, a region essential for replication of pUB110 plasmid was determined. A 1.6 kbp ClaI-HpaII fragment containing the replication origin was cloned. Subfragments obtained by TaqI digestion were inserted into the ClaI site of pNO2 to test the ori function by assaying transformation for the Km^r marker. Figure 7 shows that a 1350 bp fragment is required for autonomous replication. The requirement of a relatively large size for replication

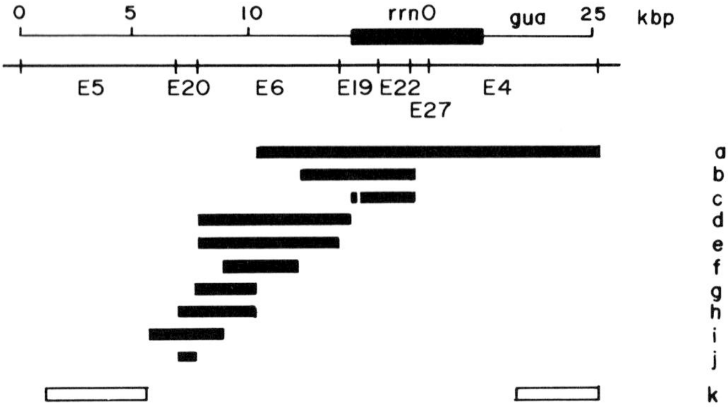

Figure 8. Map of fragments tested for the oriB function. Black squares indicate fragments cloned in Charon 28 (a) or in pNO2 (b to j). Open squares (k) indicate regions which could not be subcloned in pBR vectors.

suggests that an involvement of a dna gene or a binding site in the ori function, in addition to DNA sequence, is essential for replication.

Using this ori-searching plasmid, fragments cloned from the origin region of the chromosome were tested for the oriB function. No Km^r transformants were obtained when each fragment in Figure 8 was inserted into the BamH1 site of pNO2, cloned in E. coli and used for transformation of B. subtilis. In addition, a 15 kbp fragment containing the region from E6 through E4, including a complete set of rrnO, was self-circularized and tested for autonomous replication using the guaA marker as a selection marker. No transformants were obtained using $guaA^-$ - $recE^-$ cells as the recipient.

III. DISCUSSION

Discovery of an rRNA operon in the first replicating DNA fragment, B7, led us to construct for the first time a physical and genetic map of the replication origin region of the B. subtilis chromosome (Ogasawara et al., 1983b). Characteristic of this region is the presence of two rRNA operons, rrnO and rrnA. These two operons differ from other rRNA gene sets in B. subtilis in that 1) a single gene set constitutes a single transcriptional unit and 2) it contains two spacer tRNA genes between 16S and 23S rRNA genes.

We had assumed that the operon rrnO is located very close to or overlapping the replication origin because the 5.7 kbp B7 fragment which carries the 5' half of the operon is the first to be replicated. Reexamination of the site of initiation of replication by a more sensitive method, however, revealed that the first Okazaki fragments were synthesized at the junction of the E20 and E6 fragments. This site is some 5 kbp upstream of the first promoter for the rrnO operon. Recent observation by K. Bott's group (reported at this meeting) showed that genes for two subunits of DNA gyrase, nalA and novA, are located in the E6 fragment. Judging from the size of the fragment and molecular weight of the enzyme, no other genes seemed to be present between the site of initiation and the rrnO operon. Thus, gene organization of the origin region is oriB (initiation site) - novA - nalA - rrnO. No precise information on the other side of the initiation site is available. This gene organization may be fortuitous or may have a special biological function in initiation of replication.

Considering the distance between the site of initiation and the rrnO operon, it is unlikely that rrnO is directly involved in initiation. However, a regulatory role of the rrnO in initiation should be considered because its two tandem promoters show strong inhibition upon replication of a composite plasmid, both in E. coli and B. subtilis, when the promoters are inserted into the plasmid. The promoters are termed sar sequence for suppressor for autonomous replication (Seiki et al., 1982). The sar function of rrnO promoters is conditional in E. coli (Seiki et al., 1981). Thus, the plasmid can replicate and be maintained in the cell under selective pressure favorable for the plasmid, while it is removed rapidly from the cell when this pressure is removed. On the other hand, the effect is absolute in B. subtilis cells and no stable transformants were obtained under any conditions. The inhibition acts in cis but not in trans to the same coexisting plasmids, but without the insertion.

A similar cis-inhibitory effect by the rrnO promoters may affect initiation and replication from the chromosomal origin. It is tempting to assume that initiation of chromosomal replication is negatively controlled by transcription of the rrnO operon. Once in every cell cycle, transcription of rrnO or binding of RNA polymerase to the promoters may be blocked by alteration of the secondary structure of the promoter region to permit the the initiation to take place. In this respect, unique features in the sequence of the promoters and proximal region in rrnO attracts our attention. Indeed, this is the first demonstration that sequences of promoters and leader regions of an rRNA operon differ markedly from other multiple rRNA gene sets in one organism. Repeated sequences downstream of P1 and P2 promoters may play a role in conversion of the secondary structure of this region.

Isolation of a functional oriB fragment has been unsuccessful. It is essential to obtain a vector plasmid suitable for searching of origin functions. We found that the plasmid pNO2 which has been used in our laboratory is appropriate for this purpose. Using this plasmid, a region essential for autonomous replication of pUB110 was successfully identified. It should be noted that a fairly large size of some 1.4 kbp is required for replication. This suggests that the region codes for a protein required for replication, or alternatively, a partition (or membrane binding) function is located in this region. The membrane binding is reported to be required for replication of this plasmid (Winston and Sueoka, 1980).

The chromosomal origin is also bound to the membrane that is affected by mutation in the dnaB gene which also affects binding of pUB110 plasmid to the membrane (Winston et al., 1980). Both DNA sequences essential for initiation and membrane binding may be required for autonomous replication of the chromosome. If these two sites are located separately on the chromosome it may not be possible to isolate the functional origin in a single continuous fragment using pNO2 as a vector. Construction of vector plasmids in which conventional ori function and membrane binding function can be determined separately is now underway.

ACKNOWLEDGMENTS

We express our appreciation to Drs. K. Bott and B.S. Vold for communicating nucleotide sequence data before publication. We thank Drs. S. Murakami and K. Yamaguchi and other colleagues in our laboratory for discussion and Mrs. K. Terada and Mrs. K. Koshimura for their help.

REFERENCES

Bott, K.F., Wilson, F.E. and Stewart, G.C. (1981). In Sporulation and Germination (H.S. Levinson, A.L. Sonenshein and D.J. Tipper, eds.) p. 119, American Society for Microbiology, Washington, DC.

Henckes, G., Vannier, F., Seiki, M., Ogasawara, N., Yoshikawa, H. and Seror-Laurent, S.J. (1982). **Nature (London) 299**, 268.

Lee, G., Talkington, C. and Pero, J. (1980). **Molec. Gen. Genet. 180**, 57.

Loughney, K., Lund, E. and Dahlberg, J.E. (1982). **Nucl. Acids Res. 10**, 1607.

Moran, C.P., Jr., Lang, N., LeGrice, S.F.J., Lee, G., Stephens, M., Sonenshein, A.L., Pero, J. and Losick, R. (1982). **Molec. Gen. Genet. 186**, 339.

Ogasawara, N., Moriya, S. and Yoshikawa, H. (1983a). **Nucl. Acids Res.**, submitted.

Ogasawara, N., Seiki, M. and Yoshikawa, H. (1983b). **J. Bacteriol. 154**, 50.

Ogasawara, N., Seiki, M. and Yoshikawa, H. (1979). **Nature (London) 281**, 3480.

Seiki, M., Ogasawara, N. and Yoshikawa, H. (1981). **Molec. Gen. Genet. 183**, 220.

Seiki, M., Ogasawara, N., and Yoshikawa, H. (1982). **Proc. Natl. Acad. Sci. USA 80**, 658.

Shimotsu, H., Kawamura, F., Kobayashi, Y. and Saito, H. (1983). **Proc. Natl. Acad. Sci. USA 80**, 658.

Sogin, M.L. and Pace, N.R. (1976). **J. Biol. Chem. 251**, 3480.

Sueoka, N. and Quinn, W.G. (1968). **Cold Spring Harbor Symp. Quant. Biol. 33**, 695.

Wawrousek, E.F. and Hansen, J.N. (1983). **J. Biol. Chem. 258**, 291.

Winston, S. and Sueoka, N. (1980). **Proc. Natl. Acad. Sci. USA 77**, 2834.

Yamada, Y., Ohki, M. and Ishikura, H. (1983). **Nucl. Acids Res. 11**, 3037.

MAPPING AND CLONING DNA FROM THE REPLICATION TERMINUS REGION OF THE BACILLUS SUBTILIS CHROMOSOME AND THE MANNER OF REPLICATION FORK APPROACH AT TERMINATION[1]

R. G. Wake
A. S. Weiss
T. P. Iismaa
M. T. Smith
A. P. Healy

Department of Biochemistry
University of Sydney
N.S.W., Australia

I. INTRODUCTION

The replication terminus region of the Bacillus subtilis chromosome can be radioactively labeled during sporulation (Adams and Wake, 1980; Sargent, 1980). The labeled region comprises a discrete collection of restriction fragments that replicate in a defined order during the final stages of a round of replication (Weiss et al., 1981; Sargent and Monteiro, 1982; Weiss et al., 1982).

We summarize here the progress that has been made in further characterizing the terminus region and its replication. Analysis of the DNA labeled during sporulation has allowed the construction of a restriction map spanning the replication terminus, and information on the possible locations of citK and gltA within the map has been obtained. In conjunction with previous data, the map provides information on the manner of replication fork approach during the final stages of replication. Finally, terminus labeled DNA has been used to identify cosmid-cloned DNA from the terminus

[1]*This work was supported by grants awarded through the Australian Research Grants Scheme and the University of Sydney Cancer Fund.*

ISBN 0-12-274160-9

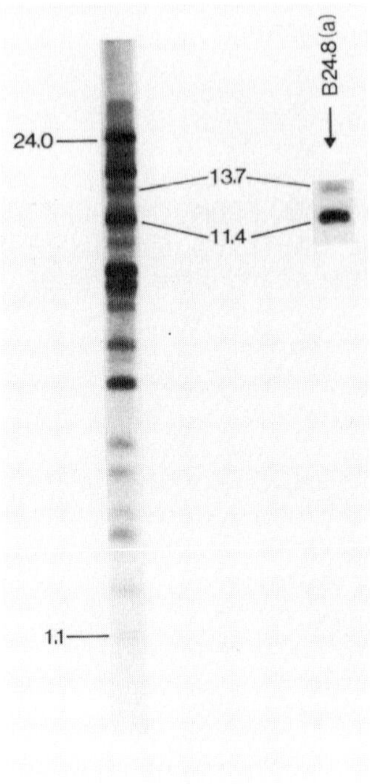

Figure 1. Radioactive BamHI and SalI (double-digest) fragments derived from 5 minute terminus-labeled DNA. The small inset on the right shows the fragments derived from the BamHI single-digest fragment of 24.8 kb (B24.8a). All sizes are in kb.

region and the cloned DNA, in turn, has provided direct confirmation of at least part of the map referred to above.

II. A RESTRICTION MAP OF 150 kb OF DNA SPANNING THE REPLICATION TERMINUS

Most of the mapping has been based on data obtained using highly purified DNA from B. subtilis dna-1 labeled during sporulation with ^{3}H-thymine for 5 minutes immediately prior to termination of replication. Figure 1 shows a fluorography of the separated BamHI + SalI (double digest) fragments in such DNA. The fragments cover the range 1.1 to 24.0 kb. Taking into account multiple copies of some fragment sizes (identified in other experiments) it could be calculated that 250 kb of DNA (ca. 5% of the chromosome of

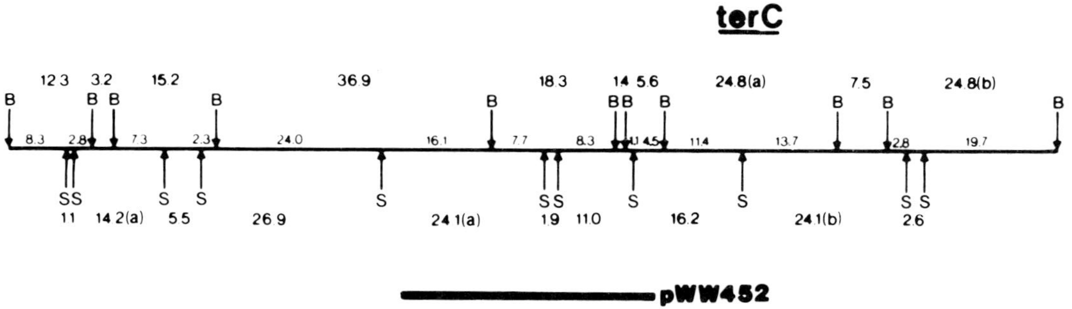

Figure 2. A restriction map of the replication terminus region of the *B. subtilis* chromosome. The lower heavy line shows the cloned region present in the recombinant cosmid pWW452.

4,500 kb) was labeled during the 5 minute period. The mapping procedure utilized the assignment of double-digest fragments to their BamHI and SalI parents. If parental (primary) fragments from each of the single digests were found to share a unique double-digest fragment, then those parental fragments were presumed to overlap. The assignments were achieved by the approach outlined by Parker and Seed (1980) and the experimental data will be described elsewhere (A. Weiss and R. Wake, submitted for publication). Data from 2.5 minute-labeled DNA was used to resolve some of the multiple assignments (of which there are only a few) but replication order of the fragments was not used in the map construction. With this overall approach the vast majority of double-digest fragments could be assigned to BamHI and SalI parents and more than half could be assembled into a unique map. This is shown in Figure 2. That it was possible to construct such a map argues for the validity of the assignment used. All of the major primary fragments are accounted for in the map. A tentative extension of the map to 300 kb, which relies on more complex data from 10 minute-labeled DNA, has been made (Weiss, 1983).

III. CHROMOSOME LOCATION OF THE MAPPED REGION

The portion of the chromosome covered by the map presented in Figure 2 contains the very latest replicating restriction fragments. On the genetic map of B. subtilis

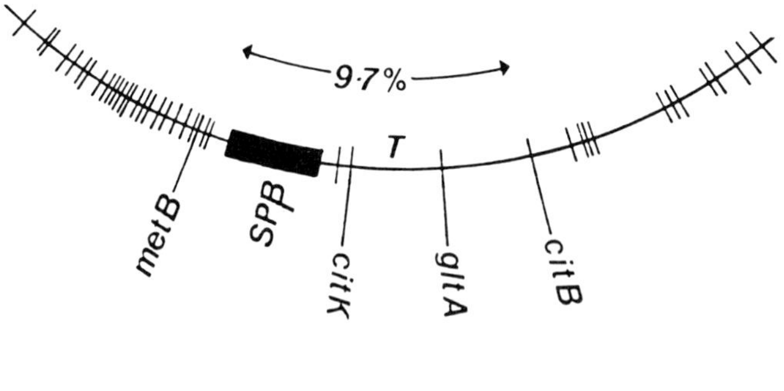

Figure 3. A genetic map of the terminus region of the B. subtilis chromosome based on the data of Henner and Hoch (1980). Only selected genes near the terminus (T) are identified. The terminus is considered to lie within the citK-gltA region. The distance between metB and citB corresponds to approximately 9.7% of the chromosome.

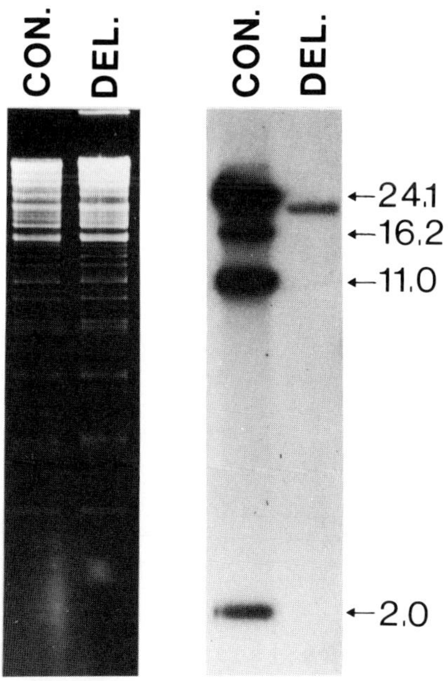

Figure 4. Southern transfer and hybridization of SalI digested DNA from the B. subtilis strains <u>*dna-1*</u> *(control) and CU1694 (deletion) with* ^{32}*P-labeled (nick-translated) pWW452 DNA. The lanes to the left show all fragments (stained with ethidium bromide), the lanes to the right show the hybridizing fragments (detected by fluorography). Sizes are in kb.*

the replication terminus is considered to lie in the vicinity of <u>citK</u> and <u>gltA</u> (Henner and Hoch, 1980; see Figure 3). These markers are separated by approximately 90 kb (calculated from the data of Rosenthal et al., 1979; Weiss et al., 1983). The prophage SPβ is located at a site less than half this distance to the left of <u>citK</u>. It has been established that the region mapped in Figure 2 overlaps at least part of the region of the chromosome extending from within SPβ, through <u>citK</u> and <u>gltA</u>. Figure 4 shows that DNA from a strain deleted in this region (CU1694 from S.A. Zahler) shows little hybridization with that portion of the map cloned in the recombinant cosmid, pWW452 (Weiss et al., 1983, see also Figure 2). The possible significance of the very low level of hybridization to a fragment in the deletion strain not in common with the control is being investigated, as are the precise limits of the overall deletion.

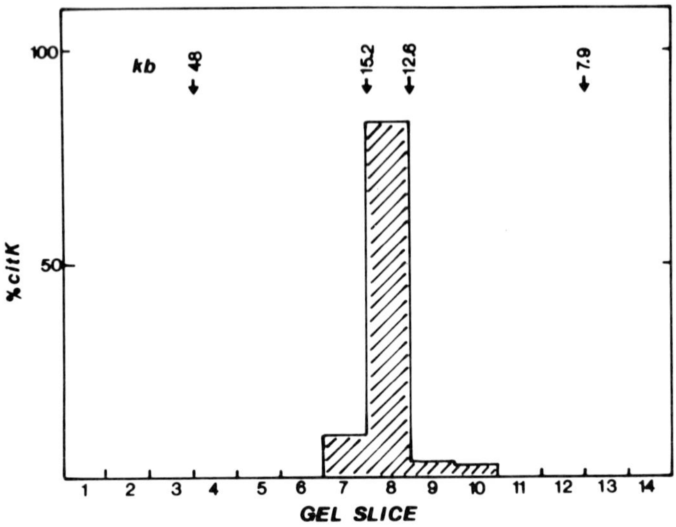

Figure 5. Assignment of citK activity to a size region within a SalI digest of B. subtilis dna-1 DNA. After electrophoresis of the digest in Sea Plaque agarose, consecutive slices (0.5 mm) were melted and citK activity measured by transformation. Samples of the same melted slices were used for size estimations, thus fraction 8 covered the range 12.6 to 15.2 kb.

To provide information on the possible locations of citK and gltA we have examined size fractionated SalI and BamHI digests of B. subtilis dna-1 DNA for these marker activities. After separation of a digest by electrophoresis in low gelling temperature agarose, consecutive gel slices were melted and assayed for citK or gltA by transformation. Figure 5 shows the result of a typical analysis of a SalI digest for citK. From a number of such experiments it has been extablished that citK resides in a SalI fragment of 14.3 ± 0.3 kb, and gltA in a BamHI fragment of 25.6 ± 1.1 kb. citK activity was almost completely destroyed by BamHI; some residual gltA activity remained after SalI cleavage, however, we did not determine the precise size of the fragment with which this activity is associated. On the basis of these data, potential candidates within the map for citK and gltA are S14.2(a) and B24.8(a), respectively. (S, B and D refer to SalI, BamHI and BamHI + SalI, respectively; thus S14.2(a) identifies a particular SalI fragment of 14.2 kb). Additional evidence, suggesting that B24.8(a) does indeed contain gltA, comes from the finding that cloned gltA (provided by A. Sonenshein) hybridizes heavily to BamHI, SalI and BamHI + SalI double-digest fragments of approximately 25, 24 and 13.4 kb, respectively. These could correspond to the B24.8(a), S24.1(b) and D13.7 fragments, respectively shown in the map. Thus, it is highly likely that gltA resides in D13.7 in the right hand portion of the map in Figure 2. If citK does reside in S14.2(a) in the left portion of the map the latter would have the same orientation (left to right) as the genetic map in Figure 3. However, it is possible that citK resides in an unidentified SalI fragment of ca. 14 kb to the right of terC. In this case the orientations of the maps in Figures 2 and 3 would be opposite.

IV. REPLICATION FORK APPROACH AT TERMINATION

The replication order of SalI fragments as termination is approached has been established to be (S14.2, S5.5), (S26.9, S24.1, S11.0), (S16.2, S1.9?) (Weiss et al., 1981). It was not clear if S1.9 should be included in the second or third (last replicating) group, and it was suggested that S16.2 was possibly the last to replicate. Fragments corresponding to all of these occur in the left two-thirds portion of the 150 kb map shown in Figure 2 and it appears that replication of this portion is achieved by the movement of a fork from left to right with a block or impediment of replication (referred to as terC) within or just to the right of S16.2, and certainly within the overlapping B24.8(a). (The precise limits of terC are yet to be established.) It can be seen from Figure 1 that D13.7 is labeled lightly in comparison with the adjacent D11.4 during the 5 minute period prior to termination. All fragments to the right of terC in the map are minor ones in terms of level of labeling. The simplest way to explain the two levels of labeling (high to the left of terC and low to the right) is by the approach of two forks at terC (see Figure 6, top section), with the leftward moving one (smaller arrow) arriving earlier (by less than 5 minutes). Alternatively, the leftward fork might continue to progress very slowly up to terC throughout the final 5 minutes. From the 'major' fragment composition of 2.5 and 1.0 minute-labeled DNA (A.S. Weiss and R.G. Wake, submitted for publication) it is clear that the rightward fork (large arrow) traversed distances of approximately 80 and 20 to 30 kb, respectively, immediately to the left of terC. Two such forks would complete the whole chromosome of 4,500 kb in approximately 70 minutes.

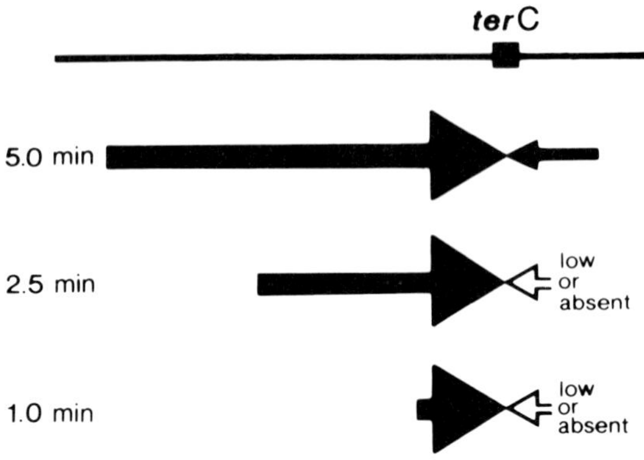

Figure 6. A possible model for replication fork movement leading to termination of chromosome replication in B. subtilis. In the 5 minute period prior to termination (top section) the leftward moving fork (smaller arrow) arrives at terC before the rightward moving fork (large arrow). Alternatively, the leftward fork might continue to move at a relatively slow rate so that the approaching forks arrive at terC at about the same time. In either situation, the extent of rightward fork travel is much greater than leftward travel and this is reflected in the two levels of labeling observed in the experimental approach used here. During the 2.5 minute (middle section) and 1.0 minute (bottom section) prior to termination the extent of rightward movement is proportionately less, and the leftward fork movement is either completely absent or less than in the 5 minute situation.

This is of the expected order, within a factor of two, for the time taken to complete a single round of replication during vegetative growth.

Recently, O'Sullivan and Anagnostopoulos (1982) have investigated replication fork approach at termination. They examined the process in a merodiploid strain containing a long nontandem duplication of the chromosome which shifted the citK-gltA region so that it was no longer diametrically opposite the origin. They concluded that there is a preferred site for termination, through which a replication fork either does not pass or passes extremely slowly. This is consistent with the present data. However, they located this site to the right of gltA, not to the left as suggested on the genetic map of the chromosome (Henner and Hoch, 1980). The results summarized here do not allow a firm

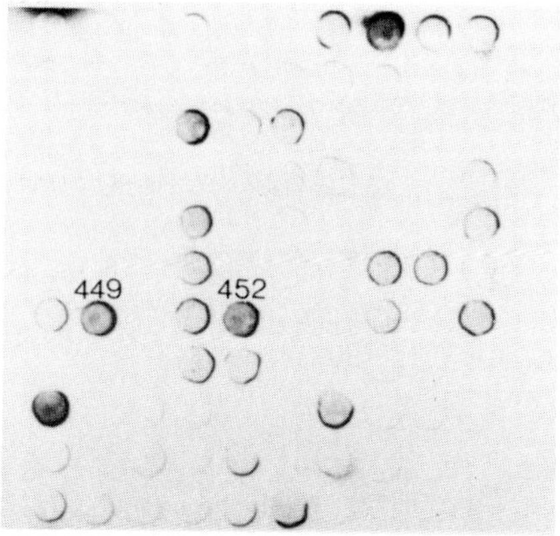

Figure 7. Screening of some of the E. coli cosmid clones for B. subtilis terminus region DNA inserts. 10 minute ^{3}H-thymine terminus-labeled DNA was used as the probe for hybridization and radioactivity was detected by fluorography. The clones containing the recombinant cosmids pWW449 and pWW452 are identified.

conclusion with respect to the precise limits of terC and its position relative to gltA, but terC and gltA are probably very close to one another.

V. CLONING DNA FROM THE TERMINUS REGION

DNA from the B. subtilis 168 prototroph, SB19, was partially cleaved with MboI and fragments in the size range 33 to 49 kb were cloned into the BamHI site of the Escherichia coli cosmid, pHC79. Four hundred and ninety (490) clones harboring recombinant cosmids containing B. subtilis inserts were screened for terminus region sequences by hybridization to 10 minute terminus-labeled DNA (see Figure 7). So far, the DNA inserts from about 20 positive clones have been found to yield collections of restriction fragments that are potential candidates for having arisen from either the 150 kb region mapped in Figure 2 or in an extension within the more tentative map of 300 kb referred to earlier. Several of these particular cosmids have been examined in detail and they can afford confirmation of regions of the map and have enabled us to get closer to cloning and examining the fragment containing terC. The maps of two cosmids containing overlapping inserts

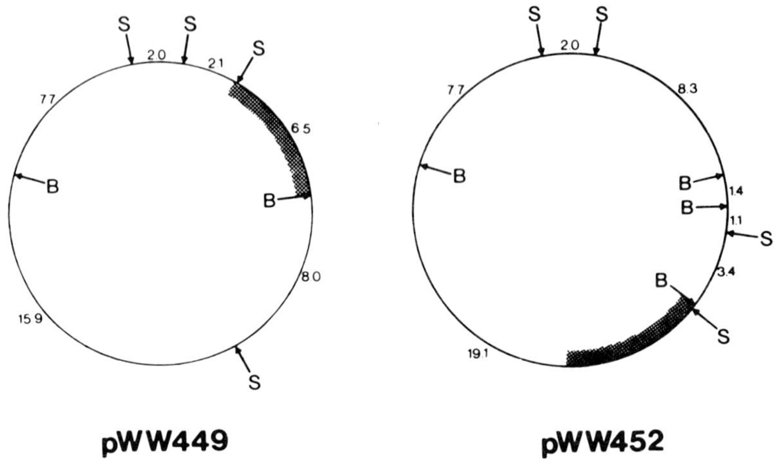

Figure 8. Restriction maps of two recombinant cosmids containing B. subtilis DNA inserts originating from the terminus region of the chromosome. The shaded regions represent the vector pHC79. B = BamHI, S = SalI. Taken from Weiss et al. (1983).

originating from the region just to the left of terC, pWW449 and pWW452, are shown in Figure 8. pWW452 contains B. subtilis DNA which extends into the latest replicating SalI fragment, S16.2 (see Figure 2). It is noteworthy that, whilst several recombinant cosmids containing DNA from regions very close to and on both sides of terC have been obtained (manuscript in preparation), the terC region itself has not been cloned. There are several possible reasons for this. One is that some special feature of this region prevents its maintenance within a plasmid replicating in E. coli. However, subcloned portions of two of the recombinant cosmids have provided specific probes for D11.4 and D13.7 and an effort is being made to clone these fragments by other approaches. The close proximity of gltA to terC (see previous sections) might also account for an unusual feature of the kinetics of transformation of this marker. When competent cells of a gltA strain of B. subtilis were mixed with wild-type DNA the rate of appearance of Glt^+ transformants, measured by plating on a selective medium at various times, was unusually slow. Transformants appeared only after a lag of 30 to 60 minutes at 37°C; this was not the case with other terminus markers examined - ilvA, citK, citB. Although we have not ruled out the possibility that this unexpected behavior of gltA transformation is the result of slow phenotypic expression, experiments utilizing deoxyribonuclease treatment have shown that the effect is not the result of slow DNA uptake.

VI. GENERAL COMMENTS

Termination of bacterial chromosome replication is an important aspect of cell division, and B. subtilis has a number of attributes that make it a favorable system for studying the division process. The information summarized here provides a foundation for more detailed studies of the molecular features and interactions of the replication fork movement and fusion at termination, and the coordination of replication with division.

In the map of the terminus presented, the linkage across terC needs to be confirmed by an independent approach, and work aimed at achieving this is in progress. Further work is also needed to establish definitively the location of terminus genetic markers and the consequent orientation of the restriction map relative to the genetic map. Also, the information on the manner of fork movement at termination which has emerged refers strictly to the process as it occurs during the last round of replication prior to sporulation. Whilst the terC region identified here with the sporulation approach to terminus labeling has been shown to be located in the same general region as would be expected for the vegetative situation, the question arises: Is the manner of replication fork approach in the two situations the same ? Cloned terminus DNA is currently being used to answer this question.

REFERENCES

Adams, R.T. and Wake, R.G. (1980). **J. Bacteriol. 143,** 1036.
Henner, D.J. and Hoch, J.A. (1980). **Microbiol. Rev. 44,** 57.
O'Sullivan, M.A. and Anagnostopoulos, C. (1982). **J. Bacteriol. 151,** 135.
Parker, R.C. and Seed, B. (1980). In Methods in Enzymology, Vol. 65 (L. Grossman and K. Moldave, eds.) p. 358, Academic Press, New York.
Rosenthal, R., Toye, P.A., Korman, R.Z. and Zahler, S.A. (1979). **Genetics 92,** 721.
Sargent, M. (1980). **J. Bacteriol. 143,** 1033.

Sargent, M.G. and Monteiro, M.J. (1982). In Molecular Cloning and Gene Regulation in Bacilli (A.T. Ganesan, S. Chang and J.A. Hoch, eds.) p. 181, Academic Press, New York.

Weiss, A.S. (1983). Ph.D. Thesis, University of Sydney, Australia.

Weiss, A.S., Hariharan, I.K. and Wake, R.G. (1981). **Nature 293**, 673.

Weiss, A.S., Hariharan, I.K., Adams, R.T. and Wake, R.G. (1982). In Molecular Cloning and Gene Regulation in Bacilli (A.T. Ganesan, S. Chang and J.A. Hoch, eds.) p. 197, Academic Press, New York.

Weiss, A.S., Smith, M.T., Iismaa, T.P. and Wake, R.G. (1983). **Gene**, in press.

TWO TYPES OF BINDING OF pUB110 TO BACILLUS SUBTILIS MEMBRANE[1]

Noboru Sueoka
Ronald Korn
Timothy McKenzie
Teruo Tanaka
Scott Winston

Department of Molecular, Cellular, and Developmental Biology
University of Colorado
Boulder, Colorado

I. INTRODUCTION

Membrane binding of the Bacillus subtilis chromosome is a necessary step for its initiation of replication at the origin (Winston and Sueoka, 1980a). In this paper, we present the results of our work on the nature of membrane binding of plasmids pUB110 and pSL103 in B. subtilis. A Staphylococcus aureus plasmid, pUB110, and its derivative, pSL103, can replicate efficiently and stably in B. subtilis with a copy number of 30 to 50 per cell (Gryczan et al., 1978; Keggins et al., 1978). pSL103 (8.0 kb) is a chimeric plasmid which consists of pUB110 (4.5 kb) and a trpC$^+$-containing DNA fragment (3.5 kb) from Bacillus pumilus (Keggins et al., 1978). We have previously shown that at the nonpermissive temperature (45°C), pSL103 cannot replicate in an initiation mutant dna-1 (dnaBI) (Winston and Sueoka, 1980b), whereas it can replicate in another initiation mutant, dnaB-19 (dnaBII) (Shivakumar and Dubnau, 1978; Winston and Sueoka, 1980b). These two mutations map closely but in distinct positions (Imada et al., 1980) and in both mutants the initiation of chromosomal replication of

[1]*This work was supported by a National Science Foundation grant, PCM80-11549 and a Public Health Service grant from the National Institutes of Health, GM 28133.*

ISBN 0-12-274160-9

B. subtilis stops at 45°C (Karamata and Gross, 1970; White and Sueoka, 1973). We have shown that at the nonpermissive temperature these plasmids in the dna-1 mutant detach from the membrane, both in vivo and in vitro, whereas they do not detach from the membrane of the dnaB-19 either in vivo or in vitro. This indicates that membrane attachment is a necessary condition for the initiation of these plasmids. Our studies on the membrane binding of these plasmids show that there are two entirely different types of specific membrane binding (type-I and type-II). Based on the various properties of these bindings so far obtained, we present a working model in which the two types of membrane binding represent two of the sequential steps for the initiation of pUB110 replication (see Figure 4).

II. TYPE-I BINDING

Both pSL103 and pUB110 in exponentially growing B. subtilis are found mostly in the membrane fraction (60 to 90%) isolated by either a high salt condition or a low salt condition (Winston and Sueoka, 1980a). These results also establish the fact that the membrane-chromosomal origin (oriC) complex and membrane-plasmid complex prepared from the cell are high salt resistant. Further studies showed that both membrane-oriC and membrane-pSL103 complexes disintegrate at the nonpermissive temperature in the dna-1 (dnaBI) mutant, but in the dna-B19 (dnaBII) mutant only the membrane-oriC complex, not the membrane-pSL103 complex, disintegrates (Winston and Sueoka, 1980b). These results show that the initiation of replication of both the chromosome and the plasmid is dependent upon their binding to the membrane. The products of both initiation genes (dnaBI and dnaBII) are essential for the initiation of replication and the membrane binding of the chromosome, whereas only the dnaBI gene product is necessary for the plasmid. This type of membrane binding which is so far formed only in vivo is termed type-I membrane binding and the membrane-replicon complex is termed type-I complex.

III. TYPE-II BINDING

In constrast to type-I binding, type-II binding was discovered by in vitro binding of pSL103 to the isolated membrane fraction of B. subtilis (Korn et al., 1983). The binding requires heat treatment (45°C for 15 minutes) without magnesium. Competition experiments with various non-radioactive DNAs have shown that the binding is specific for pUB110 or the pUB110 moiety of pSL103 (Korn et al., 1983). The binding is site specific, i.e., only certain areas of pUB110 are responsible for the binding (Figure 1) (Tanaka and Sueoka, 1983).

We have recently sequenced the four binding areas of pUB110 (MacKenzie et al., in preparation). The result indicates that the actual binding sites in these areas are much smaller. For example, the binding of MboI fragment F (250 bp) is destroyed by HinfI at the position 76, whereas a ThaI cut at 186 does not destroy binding (Figure 2). There are several other examples of this kind represented in Figure 1. Our sequence comparison between these binding areas by the aid of the computer led to the finding that a 7-mer sequence, "TCAGCAA" and its one base variants exists in unusually high frequencies in these areas (Table 1). The locations of these sequences and their directions do not give us a completely consistent picture which explains the overall results shown in Figure 1. The ambiguity may be resolved if another sequence in their vicinities is required for the binding. We are also approaching this problem by performing footprinting analysis of partial digests of the membrane-bound fragments by DNase I.

Thus far we know the following characteristics of the Type-II membrane-DNA complex of pUB110 or pSL103. 1) The type-II complex is salt sensitive (optimal concentration, 0.06 M KCl; Tanaka and Sueoka, 1983) in contrast to the type-I complex which is resistant to 5 M CsCl (Sueoka and Hammers, 1974). 2) Copy number of type-II binding (number of plasmid-bound per cell equivalent of membrane) saturates at approximately 30 (Korn et al., 1983), which is comparable to the in vivo copy number of pUB110 of 30 to 50 per cell (Gryczan et al., 1978). 3) Type-II binding occurs equally well to the membrane from cells with or without harboring pUB110 (Korn et al., 1983). 4) Unlike type-I binding, the functional product of the dnaBI gene is not necessary for the type-II binding (Tanaka and Sueoka, 1983).

IV. REPLICATION ORIGIN OF pUB110

Electron microscopic studies of replicative intermediates of pUB110 by Scheer-Abramowitz et al. (1981) showed that the origin of replication of pUB110 starts around the 9 o'clock area of the restriction map (Figure 1), and the replication proceeds counterclockwise as indicated in Figure 1. Our DNA sequencing covers this origin area; only

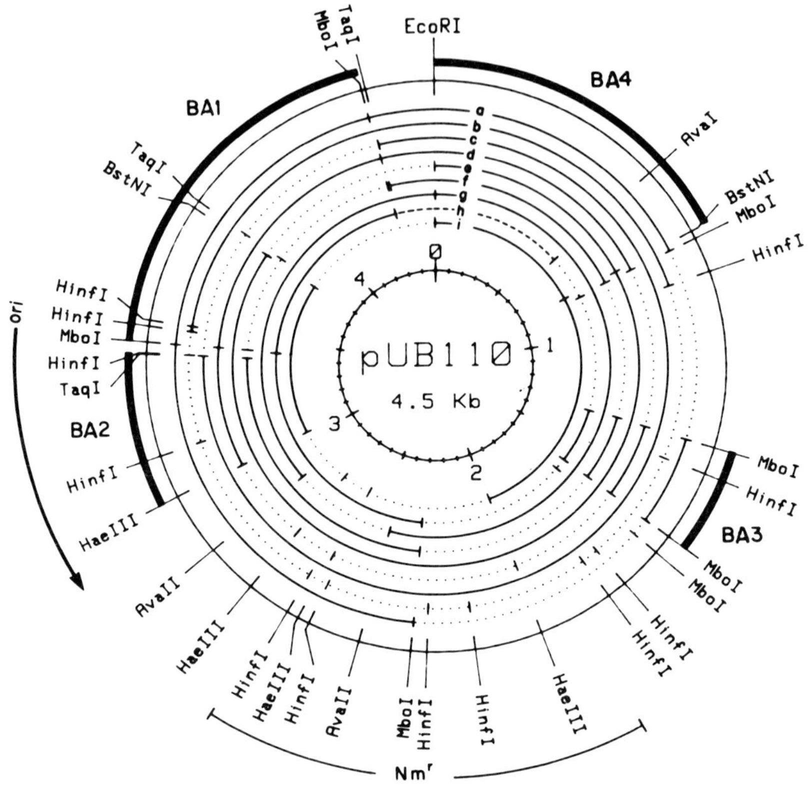

Figure 1. Membrane-binding map of restriction fragments of pUB110 (Tanaka and Sueoka, 1983). The solid and dotted lines in the concentric circles represent DNA fragments bound and not bound, respectively, to the membrane, and the broken line designates a fragment which bound, but less efficiently. The thick arcs outside the concentric circles depict the four membrane-bound areas that were found from the binding studies. Detailed descriptions of the bindings areas (BA1 to BA4) have been reported by Tanaka and Sueoka (1983). The restriction enzyme(s) used for the experiment for each of the concentric, solid or dotted line is: a, MboI; b, HinfI; c, TaqI; d, MboI and HaeIII; e, EcoRI and BstNI; f, TaqI and MboI; g, EcoRI and AvaII; h, MboI and AvaII; i, EcoRI, BstNI and HaeIII.

```
                                                                    AluI          HinfI
     MboI
1    GATCACTCAAAAAATCTCACTTTAAACCCTTGCCAATTTTTATTTTGTCCGTTTTGTCTAGCTTACCGAAAGCCAGACTCAGCAAGAATAAAATTTTTAT
     CTAGTGAGTTTTTTAGAGTGAAATTTGGGAACGGTTAAAAATAAAACAGGCAAAACAGATCGAATGGCTTTCGGTCTGAGTCGTTCTTATTTTAAAAATA   100

                       RsaI                                                                 ThaI
101  TGTCTTTCGGTTTTCTAGTGTACGACAAACCACTCAAAATAAAAAAGATACAAGAGAGGTCTCTCGTATCTTTTAATTCACAATCGCGCCCGATTGCTGA
     ACAGAAAGCCAAAAGATCACATGCTGTTTGGTGAGTTTTATTTTTTCTATGTTCTCTCCAGAGAGCATAGAAAATTAAGTGTTAGCGCGGGCTAACGACT   200

                         AluI
                                                               MboI
201  ACAGATTAATAATAGATTTTAGCTTTTTATTTGTTGAAAAAAGCTAATCAAATTGTCGGGATC
     TGTCTAATTATTATCTAAAATCGAAAAATAAACAACTTTTTTCGATTAGTTTAACAGCCCTAG
```

Figure 2. Nucleotide sequence of MboI-F fragment of pUB110. The MboI-F fragment occupies the area between 1.3 Kb and 1.6 Kb and it corresponds to binding area 3 (BA3) (Figure 1). The entire fragment loses the type-II binding ability by the cut at the HinfI site. By the ThaI cut the larger fragment retains type-II binding, whereas the smaller fragment does not bind to the membrane. The orientation of the sequence corresponds to the clockwise direction in the map shown in Figure 1.

Table 1. A 7-mer Sequence "TCAGCAA" and Its One-Base Variants in the Type-II Membrane-Binding Areas of pUB110

Sequence[a]	*Binding Area*[b]	*Position*[c]	*Strand*[d]
TCAGCAC	*BA1*	*481*	*CC*
TCAGCAA	*BA1*	*689*	*C*
TCAGCAC	*BA1*	*830*	*C*
TCAACAA	*BA2*	*14*	*C*
TCATCAA	*BA2*	*131*	*CC*
TCGGCAA	*BA2*	*304*	*CC*
TCAGCAA	*BA3*	*79*	*C*
TCAGCAA	*BA3*	*200*	*CC*
TCAACAA	*BA3*	*237*	*CC*
TCAGGAA	*BA3*	*309*	*CC*
TGAGCAA	*BA4*	*865*	*CC*

[a]*Sequence: These sequences are shown in the 5'-to-3' direction.*

[b]*Binding areas: These areas correspond to those shown in Figure 1.*

[c]*Position: Nucleotide positions from the left end of each area which corresponds to counterclockwise direction on the map in Figure 1.*

[d]*Strand: C, the strand with clockwise 5'-to-3' direction. CC, the opposite strand with counterclockwise 5'-to-3' direction.*

one potential starting site of transcription by RNA polymerase is recognized (Figure 3). Moreover, judged from the sequence, the transcript seems untranslatable; the ribosome binding sequence does not apparently exist when compared with other cases known in B. subtilis (Murray and Rabinowitz, 1982; Moran et al., 1982), and a number of initiation codons are clustered within the area between +1 and +30, which is not a normal situation for translation start (Figure 3). this area is, therefore, the logical candidate for the primer starting site for the initiation of replication in pUB110. It is interesting to note that the origin area is flanked by two type-II binding areas (BA1 and BA2; Figure 1). Since one (dnaBI) of two initiation genes (dnaBI and dnaBII; Imada et al., 1980) of B. subtilis, dnaBI, is necessary for the initiation of pUB110 also (Winston and Sueoka, 1980a), the mode of initiation of pUB110 replication should have some common feature with the mode of the initiation of B. subtilis chromosome replication.

V. DISCUSSION

The in vivo significance of the type-II binding is not clear at the moment, although the sequence specificity of the binding strongly suggests that the type-II binding is likely to be important. Currently, the model which we entertain to explain the roles of the two types of membrane binding on the initiation of replication is presented in Figure 4. It assumes that the type-I and type-II bindings represent two of the critical steps toward the initiation (Figure 4). According to this model, the plasmid first binds to a binding location on the membrane by the type-II binding sites of the plasmid, then the initiation complex will be built at or around the replication origin before initiation and replication start at the origin. The initiation complex constitutes the type-I binding. According to this model, the host-plasmid specificity resides in type-II binding, because without the type-II binding the plasmid cannot form the initiation complex (type-I binding) and therefore no initiation can start at the origin.

Other properties of plasmids such as copy number and stability of a plasmid may also be related to the capacity of holding the plasmid on the membrane and efficiency of type-II membrane binding. Currently, however, there is no evidence for supporting these possibilities. It is interesting to note that the copy number of pUB110 or pSL103 is comparable to the capacity of the membrane to accomodate these plasmids by type-II binding (Korn et al., 1983). The discovery of type-II binding as a different type of binding from type-I binding is also important in that the study of the membrane binding of replicons now can be focused individually on these two types of binding.

The plasmid binding site within the membrane envelope is not clear at the moment; the major alternative possibilities are either the binding sites distribute throughout the membrane envelope or the sites are confined to specific areas within the membrane envelope, e.g. the nucleoid-membrane attachment site.

```
      Hae III
  1   GGCCCGTTTGTTGAACTACTCTTTAATAAAATAATTTTTCCGTTCCCAATTCCACATTGCAATAATAGAAAATCCATCTTCATCGGCTTTTTCGTCATCA   100
      CCGGGCAAACAACTTGATGAGAAATTATTTTATTAAAAAGGCAAGGGTTAAGGTGTAACGTTATTATCTTTTAGGTAGAAGTAGCCGAAAAAGCAGTAGT

         Hinf I
101   TCTGTATGAATCAAATCGCTTTCTTCTGTGTCATCAAGGTTTAATTTTTTATGTATTTCTTTTAACAAACCACCATAGGAGATTAACCTTTTACGGTGTA   200
      AGACATACTTAGTTTAGCGAAAGAAGACACAGTAGTTCCAAATTAAAAAATACATAAAGAAAATTGTTTGGTGGTATCCTCTAATTGGAAAATGCCACAT

201   AACCTTCCTCCAAATCAGACAAACGTTTCAAATTCTTTTCTTCATCATCGGTCATAAAATCCGTATCCTTTACAGGATATTTTGCAGTTTCGGTCAATTG   300   BA2
      TTGGAAGGAGGTTTAGTCTGTTTGCAAAGTTTAAGAAAAGAAGTAGTAGCCAGTATTTTAGGCATAGGAAATGTCCTATAAAACGTCAAAGCCAGTTAAC

                                         Hinf I
                                     Taq I                           Mbo I                                     Hi
301   CCGATTGTATATCCGATTTATATTTATTTTTCGGTCGAATCATTTGAACTTTTACATTTGGATCTTTAAGTCTAATTTCATTGCCTTTTTCCAAAATTGA   400
      GGCTAACATATAGGCTAAATATAAATAAAAAGCCAGCTTAGTAAACTTGAAAATGTAAACCTAGAAATTCAGATTAAAGTAACGGAAAAAGGTTTTAACT

      nf I        Hinf I
401   ATCCATTGTTTTTGATTCACGTAGTTTTCTGTTATTCTAAAATAAGTTGGTTCCACACATACCATTACATGCATGTGCTGATTATAAGAATTATCTTTAT   500   ori ↑
      TAGGTAACAAAAACTAAGTGCATCAAAAGACAATAAGATTTTATTCAACCAAGGTGTGTATGGTAATGTACGTACACGACTAATATTCTTAATAGAAATA
                                                                  Initiation codons       "-10"

501   TATTTATTGTCACATCCGTTGCACGCATAAAACCAACAAGATTTTTATTAATTTTTTTATATTGCATCATTCGGCGAAATCCTTGAGCCATATCTGTCAA   600
      ATAAATAACAGTGTAGGCAACGTGCGTATTTTGGTTGTTCTAAAAATAATTAAAAAAATATAACGTAGTAAGCCGCTTTAGGAACTCGGTATAGACAGTT
         "-35"

601   ACTCTTATTTAATTCTTCGCCATCATAAACATTTTTAACTGTTAATGTGAGAAACAACCAACGAACTGTTGGCTTTTGTTTAATAACTTCAGCAACAACC   700
      TGAGAATAAATTAAGAAGCGGTAGTATTTGTAAAAATTGACAATTACACTCTTTGTTGGTTGCTTGACAACCGAAAACAAATTATTGAAGTCGTTGTTGG

                                                                     BSTN I                  Taq I
701   TTTTGTGACTGAATGCCATGTTTCATTGCTCTCCTCCAGTTGCACATTGGACAAAGCCTGGATTTGCAAAACCACACTCGATACCACTTTCTTTCGCCTG   800   BA1
      AAAACACTGACTTACGGTACAAAGTAACGAGAGGAGGTCAACGTGTAACCTGTTTCGGACCTAAACGTTTTGGTGTGAGCTATGGTGAAAGAAAGCGGAC

801   TTTCACGATTTTGTTTATACTCTAATATTTCAGCACAATCTTTTACTCTTTCAGCCTTTTTAAATTCAAGAATATGCAGAAGTTCAAAGTAATCAACATT   900
      AAAGTGCTAAAACAAATATGAGATTATAAAGTCGTGTTAGAAAATGAGAAAGTCGGAAAAATTTAAGTTCTTATACGTCTTCAAGTTTCATTAGTTGTAA

                          Nco I
901   AGCGATTTTCTTTTCTCTCCATGGTCTCACTTTTCCACTT                                                              1000
      TCGCTAAAAGAAAAGAGAGGTACCAGAGTGAAAAGGTGAA
```

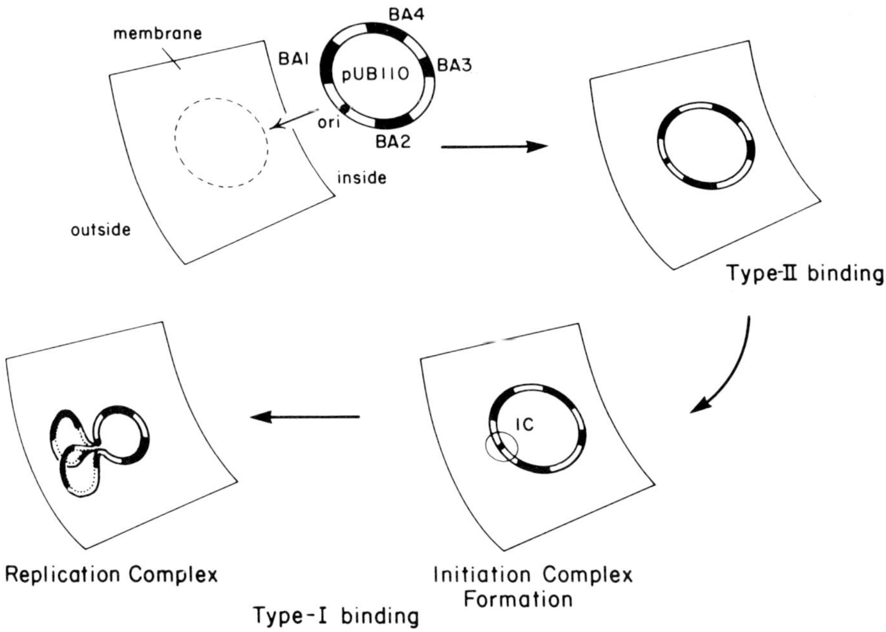

Figure 4. Successive membrane-binding model of pUB110 in B. subtilis. Step 1: pUB110 binds to the receptor area in the membrane by type-II binding sites of the plasmid. Step 2: Initiation complex is formed around the origin (type-I binding). Step 3: Replication complex is formed and the replication proceeds (type-I binding). BA1 to BA4: The type-II binding areas of pUB110.

Figure 3. Nucleotide sequence of the area covering the replication origin of pUB110. The examination of all sequences of promoters and ribosomal binding sites in B. subtilis compiled by Murray and Rabinowitz (1982) and by Moran et al. (1982) in relation to initiation codons led us to conclude that the "-10" and "-35" sequences shown in this figure are the best and most likely only candidate for transcriptional start in this area and that the location and direction of the transcriptional start from the promoter fits to the origin location and direction of replication previously proposed by Scheer-Abramowitz et al. (1981).

REFERENCES

Gryczan, T.J., Contente, S. and Dubnau, D. (1978). **J. Bacteriol. 134**, 318.

Imada, S., Carroll, L.E. and Sueoka, N. (1980). **Genetics 94**, 809.

Karamata, K. and Gross, J.D. (1970). **Molec. Gen. Genet. 108**, 277.

Keggins, K., Lovett, P. and Duvall, E.J. (1978). **Proc. Natl. Acad. Sci. USA 75**, 1423.

Korn, R.S., Winston, S., Tanaka, T. and Sueoka, N. (1983). **Proc. Natl. Acad. Sci. USA 80**, 574.

Moran, C.P., Lang, N., LeGrice, S.F.J., Lee, G., Stephens, M., Sonnenshein, A.L., Pero, J. and Losick, R. (1982). **Molec. Gen. Genet. 186**, 339.

Murray, C.L. and Rabinowitz, J.C. (1982). In Molecular Cloning and Gene Regulation in Bacilli (A.T. Ganesan, S. Chang and J.A. Hoch, eds.) p. 271, Academic Press, New York.

Scheer-Abramowitz, J., Gryczan, T.J. and Dubnau, D. (1981). **Plasmid 6**, 67.

Sueoka, N. and Hammers, J. (1974). **Proc. Natl. Acad. Sci. USA 71**, 4787.

Tanaka, T. and Sueoka, N. (1983). **J. Bacteriol. 154**, 1184.

White, K. and Sueoka, N. (1973). **Genetics 73**, 185.

Winston, S. and Sueoka, N. (1980a). **J. Bacteriol. 142**, 339.

Winston, S. and Sueoka, N. (1980b). **Proc. Natl. Acad. Sci. USA 77**, 2834.

GENE AMPLIFICATION IN BACILLUS SUBTILIS: THE ESTABLISHMENT OF MULTIPLE TANDEMLY-REPEATED COPIES OF A HETEROLOGOUS DNA SEGMENT IN THE BACTERIAL CHROMOSOME[1]

Michael Young

Department of Botany and Microbiology
University College of Wales
Aberystwyth, Dyfed
United Kingdom

I. INTRODUCTION

Gene amplification is of widespread occurrence in eukaryotic organisms (Schimke, 1982). It is often connected with a need to satisy a demand for elevated quantities of a specific gene product. For example, mammalian cells amplify DNA sequences containing the structural gene for dihydrofolate reductase when grown in the presence of methotrexate, an antifolate drug that is an inhibitor of the enzyme (Alt et al., 1978). Gene amplification may also occur at certain times during development (see, for example, Spradling and Mahowald, 1981; Glover et al., 1982; Chisholm, 1982). The multigene families that occur in eukaryotes are presumably the relics of gene amplification events that occurred in the evolutionary past (Hood et al., 1975).

The phenomenon of gene amplification in eukaryotic organisms is now very well documented, and Roberts et al. (1983) have recently obtained evidence concerning the mechanism by which multiple copies of a gene can arise. Although comparatively little is known about gene amplification in prokaryotes (but see Chandler et al., 1979; Vasseghi and Claverys, 1983), it would be unjustified to regard this phenomenon as the sole prerogative of eukaryotes. The existence of

[1]*The financial support of the SERC is gratefully acknowledged and I thank the Royal Society for a travel grant enabling attendance of this meeting.*

ISBN 0-12-274160-9

multiple copies of the ribosomal RNA genes in many prokaryotic organisms is well established. In Bacillus subtilis there appear to be about ten copies per chromosome (Stewart et al., 1982; Loughney et al., 1982). Interestingly, most of these copies lie close to the origin of replication of the chromosome (Stewart et al., 1982); the dichotomous replication that occurs in rapidly growing bacteria provides an additional physiological dimension to the amplification of these genes. It seems clear, however, that in the well studied prokaryotes, such as Escherichia coli and B. subtilis, single copies of most genes are to be found in the chromosome. In other prokaryotic organisms about which little is known the possibility that gene amplification occurs should not be ruled out. Perhaps some of the difficulties that are encountered in attempting to obtain mutant strains in certain bacterial species may arise from the presence of multiple copies of the genes in which mutations are being sought.

The familiar multicopy antibiotic-resistant plasmids of prokaryotes provide a convenient method for the amplification of cloned genes in these organisms. However, the phenomenon of plasmid instability has hampered many attempts to use B. subtilis as a host for obtaining the expression of foreign genes. Strains of B. subtilis showing chromosomal rearrangements have been described (see, for example, Schneider and Anagnostopoulos, 1981) but as a general rule the chromosome of this organism is a relatively stable genetic entity. It therefore seemed worthwhile to explore the possibility of using the chromosome itself as the "vector" for molecular cloning in B. subtilis. A necessary prerequisite for this has been the development of procedures for amplifying the gene(s) of interest. Apart from the obvious disadvantage that cloned DNA cannot readily be extracted from the host organism in a purified form, a further unexpected complication has arisen because it has not always proved possible to excise and and reisolate the sequences of interest once they have been amplified in situ. However, the possibility that cloned sequences may enjoy enhanced stability once they have become inserted into the chromosome, together with the prospect that it may prove possible to maintain them in the absence of positive selection pressure, encouraged us to explore these ideas in the experiments described below.

II. CONSTRUCTION OF STRAINS CL104 AND SA108

Strains CL104 and SA108 are derivatives of B. subtilis 168 that contain the chloramphenicol-resistance (Cm^r) determinant of the Staphylococcus aureus plasmid, pC194, integrated into the chromosome. They were obtained as follows. The plasmid p1949 is a chimeric molecule comprising pMB9 (Tc^r) and pC194 (Cm^r) that have been ligated together in a way that has resulted in the inactivation of the pC194 replicon (Haldewang et al., 1980). As a result, the plasmid cannot replicate in B. subtilis, although the Cm^r determinant can be expressed in this host. Resistance to both chloramphenicol and tetracycline is conferred on E. coli, a host in which the plasmid replicates normally. Maintenance of p1949 in B. subtilis therefore depends either on the insertion of a replication origin into the plasmid, or on the integration of the plasmid into a resident replicon. The insertion of a fragment of B. subtilis chromosomal DNA into the plasmid serves to direct integration of the recombinant molecule into the region of the chromosome from which the fragment originated (Haldenwang et al., 1980; Wilson et al. 1981). If the DNA is presented to competent cells as supercoiled plasmid molecules, the integration probably occurs by a Campbell recombination mechanism, whereas if the DNA is presented as a ligation mixture, integration may occur by the formation of bridge structures involving linear ligation products (Young, 1983). Strain CL104 trpC2 cat was obtained by inserting a 5.6 kpb EcoRI-BamHI fragment of p1949 into the chromosome using a purified 5.7 kbp fragment of B. subtilis DNA with transforming activity against pheA1 and nic-38 recipients to direct the integration (Young, 1983). Strain SA108 trpC2 cat was isolated by P. Brazier in my laboratory. The 5.6 kpb EcoRI-BamHI fragment of p1949 was ligated with B. subtilis DNA from the hisA region of the chromosome. This plasmid was transformed into B. subtilis 168 and a representative Cm^r transformant (strain SA108) was retained. Both strains CL104 and SA108 were isolated using media supplemented with 5 μg chloramphenicol per ml.

III. LOCATION OF THE CM^R DETERMINANT IN STRAINS CL104 AND SA108

The chromosomal location of the Cm^r determinant in both strains was suspected from the finding that DNA isolated from the strains was unable to transform E. coli to chloramphenicol-resistance. Also, physical analysis failed to reveal the presence of plasmid DNA. This supposition was confirmed by the demonstration that the Cm^r marker was linked to nearby chromosomal markers using PBS1-mediated transduction (57% cotransduction with leu-8 in strain CL104; 80% cotransduction with hisA1 in strain SA108). No linkage was found to any of a wide range of markers from other origins of this chromosome in these experiments.

IV. TANDEMLY DUPLICATED INSERTIONS IN STRAINS CL104 AND SA108

In experiments described elsewhere (Young, 1983) it has been established by genetic analysis that strain CL104 contains at least two copies of the pheA and nic genes. Since the fragment used to direct the insertion of the Cm^r determinant in SA108 carries no known genetic marker, it has not been possible to carry out experiments of a similar nature with this strain. Southern hybridization experiments with both strains have confirmed that they harbor multiple copies of the inserted sequences. The data in Figure 1 show the patterns of hybridization of a nick-translated sample of the 5.7 kbp phe-nic fragment to DNA from strains 168 and CL104 that have been digested with a variety of restriction endonucleases. Equivalent amounts of DNA from the two strains were used in these experiments. Inspection of the figure shows that most of the fragments in the restriction digests of strain 168 DNA to which hybridization occurred are also present in the restriction digests of strain CL104 DNA. However, the lanes containing CL104 DNA have additional bands to which more intense hybridization has occurred. In the EcoRI, BamHI and SalGI digestions the extra band comprises about 11 kbp of DNA; it represents the 5.7 kbp fragment of p1949. Comparison of the patterns of hybridization to the HindIII-digested samples reveals a 3.0 kbp fragment from within the phe-nic fragment to which enhanced hybridization has occurred, as well as new fragments at 6.0 kbp and 1.9 kbp that contain both B. subtilis and p1949 sequences. Collectively these fragments comprise the 11 kbp fragment seen in the EcoRI-, BamHI- and SalGI-digested DNA from strain CL104. The border fragments at 2.9 kbp and 1.4 kbp hybridized at approximately equivalent intensity in the restriction digests of DNA from both strains CL104 and 168. The 5.6 kbp phe-nic fragment has at least 5 PstI sites (data not shown) and cleavage generates several very small fragments. The autoradiogram shows the two border fragments of about 7 kbp and 3.5 kbp that hybridize at approximately equivalent intensities in the restriction digests of DNA

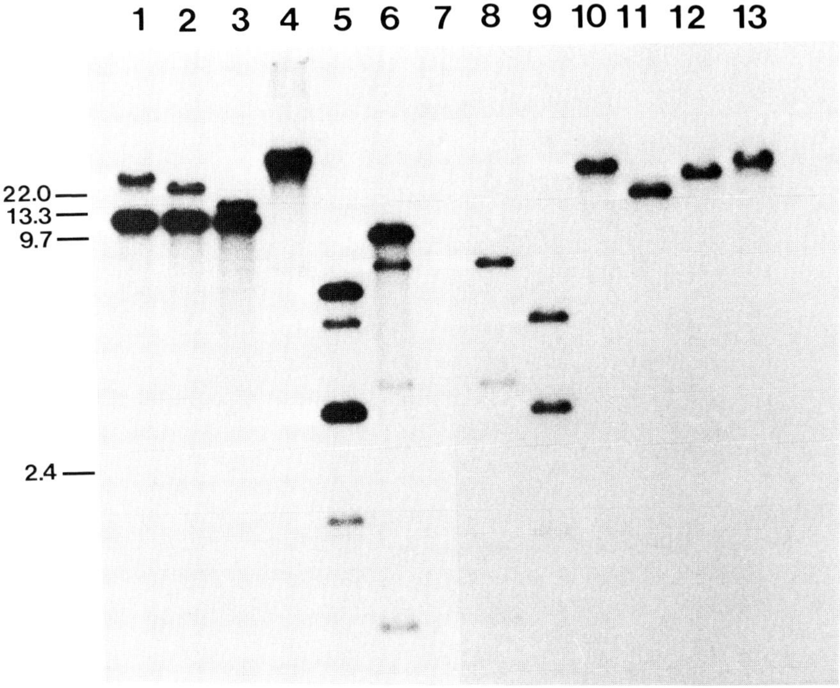

Figure 1. Southern hybridization of DNA from strains CL104 and 168 using the 5.7 kbp phe-nic fragment as a probe. Equivalent amounts of DNA were loaded in each well. The samples were as follows: 0.7% agarose gel. Lanes 1 to 6, strain CL104 DNA digested with SalGI, BamHI, EcoRI, BglII, HindIII, PstI; lane 7, λ BglII; lanes 8 to 13, strain 168 DNA digested with PstI, HindIII, BglII, EcoRI, BamHI, SalG1. The sizes (kbp) and mobilities of the DNA fragments in lane 7 are given on the left hand side.

from the two strains. A smaller internal fragment at about 0.9 kbp shows an enhanced intensity of hybridization in the PstI-cleaved CL104 DNA and the new band of about 9 kbp represents the entire p1949 sequences flanked by sequences of B. subtilis DNA derived from the phe-nic fragment (representing about 1.1 kbp of DNA) have run off the gel. Finally, the enzyme BglII, which cuts neither the 5.6 kbp p1949 sequences, nor the 5.7 kbp phe-nic fragment, releases a fragment of about 25 kbp from strain 168 DNA to which the phe-nic fragment hybridizes. This fragment is replaced in BglII-digested DNA from strain CL104 by a band at about 50 kbp.

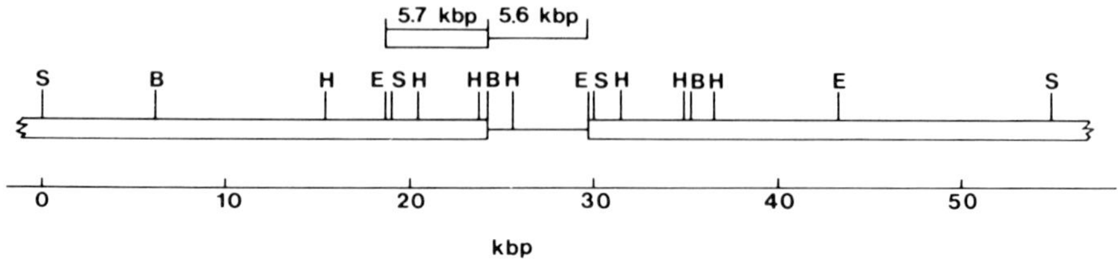

Figure 2. Restriction map of the tandemly duplicated region of the chromosome in strain CL104. The map was constructed using the data in Figure 1. The heterologous p1949 DNA carrying the Cm^r *determinant is represented by the single line. The 5.7 kbp EcoRI-BamHI fragment that lies on either side of it contains the* nic *gene and part of the* pheA *gene at the EcoRI end (Young, 1983). There are, on the average, between 8 and 9 tandemly repeated copies of the exogenote (shown above the map) in the genome; for clarity, only one copy is shown.*

An interpretaion of these data is given in Figure 2. The hybridization probe that was used in this experiment was the 5.7 kbp phe-nic fragment. There is, therefore, no question of hybridization occurring to the p1949 sequences uniquely present in strain CL104. The new bands seen in restriction endonuclease-digested samples of CL104 DNA must, therefore, comprise p1949 sequences covalently joined to B. subtilis DNA. Moreover, it may be deduced that the different intensities of hybridization to the different restriction fragments seen in this experiment reflect the presence of different numbers of copies of the sequences concerned, relative to each other. This finding is considered in quantitative terms later. It also may be concluded that the multiple copies of the inserted DNA lie in a 'head to tail' arrangement in the chromosome; i.e. they are tandemly duplicated. The data cannot be explained by proposing that the exogenote has integrated into the bacterial chromosome at several different points.

Further evidence that the inserted sequences are tandemly duplicated was obtained by using a low percentage (0.35%) agarose gel to enhance the separation of high m.w. restriction fragments from each other. The data in Figure 3 show a clear difference between the sizes of the BglII restriction fragments of DNA from strains CL104 and

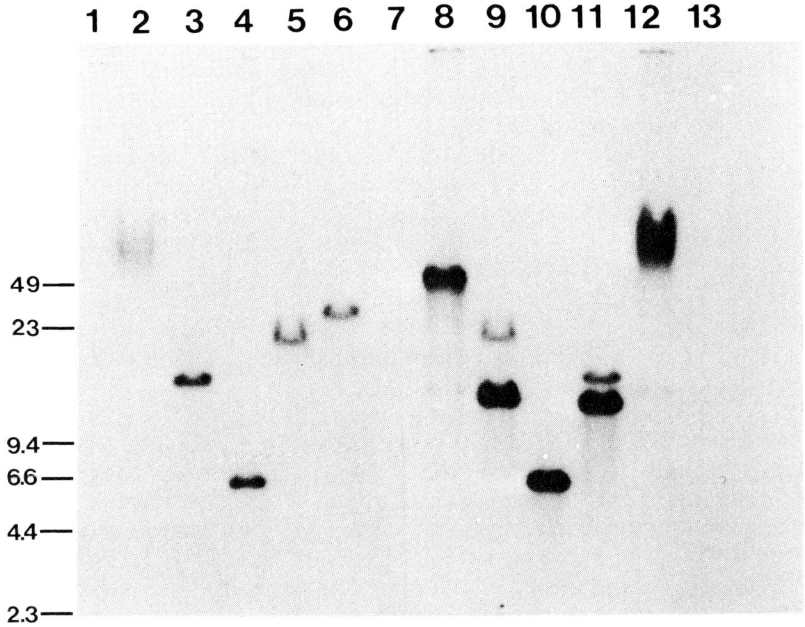

Figure 3. Southern hybridization of DNA from strains CL104 and 168 using the 5.7 kbp phe-nic *fragment as a probe. Equivalent amounts of DNA were loaded in each well. The samples were as follows: 0.35% agarose gel. Lane 1, λ EcoRI; lane 2, undigested DNA from strain 168; lanes 3 to 6, strain 168 DNA digested with EcoRI, EcoRI + BamHI, BamHI, BglII; lane 7, undigested λ DNA; lanes 8 to 11, strain CL104 DNA digested with BglII, BamHI, EcoRI + BamHI, EcoRI; lane 12, undigested DNA from strain CL104; lane 13, λ HindIII. The sizes (kbp) and mobilities of the DNA fragments in lanes 7 and 13 are given on the left hand side.*

168 to which the 5.7 kbp phe-nic fragment hybridizes (lanes 6 and 8). The fact that multiple copies of sequences complementary to the radioactively-labeled probe are present in CL104 DNA is also evident. Compare for example the intensities of hybridization to the EcoRI + BamHI-digested samples in lanes 4 and 10 - this treatment releases a 5.7 kbp fragment from the DNA of both strains that corresponds to the radiolabeled probe.

Similar experiments with strain SA108 using the 0.5 kbp EcoRI-BamHI fragment of pPB11 as probe (data not shown) indicate that in this strain also, tandemly repeated copies of the exogenote are integrated into the bacterial chromosome. This phenomenon does not seem to depend on the provenance of either the heterologous or the homologous portions of the incoming DNA segment. Evidence of similar behavior has been obtained by Saito et al. (1982) who used a fragment from the hisA region incorporated into pUB110. Data obtained by Ferrari et al. (1982) concerning a fragment from the metC-citL region incorporated into pJH101, and Wilson et al. (1981) concerning a fragment from the recG-abrB region incorporated into pCS540 (a chimera between pSC101 and pC194), point clearly to the presence of multiple copies of exogenotic DNA in their experiments.

V. EXCISION OF REPEATED SEQUENCES FROM THE CHROMOSOME

Strains CL104 and SA108 segregated Cm^S progeny at frequencies of 14.3% (30/210) and 1.4% (5/360) after overnight growth in nutrient broth in the absence of chloramphenicol. This behavior suggests that both strains are merodiploid for the segment of B. subtilis DNA that was used to direct insertion of the plasmid sequences into the chromosome. The greater stability of strain SA108 might result from the presence of a smaller duplicated segment in this strain than in strain CL104 since this may reduce the tendency for excision to occur. DNA was prepared from seven Cm^S segregants of strain CL104 and BamHI-restricted samples were hybridized against the radioactively labeled 5.7 kbp phe-nic fragment. In every case the 11 kbp fragment seen in BamHI-digested samples of strain CL104, DNA had been lost to leave only the 18 kbp fragment also seen in BamHI-digested samples of strain 168 DNA. Thus, growth in the absence of chloramphenicol resulted in spontaneous loss of the exogenote from the strains.

VI. AMPLIFICATION OF THE REPEATED SEQUENCES IN STRAINS CL104 AND SA108

The fact that the exogenote could be lost from the strains when selective pressure was removed raised the possibility that selection for resistance to enhanced concentrations of chloramphenicol might lead to amplification of the number of copies of the exogenote per cell. Strains CL104 and SA108 were subcultured onto nutrient agar containing a range of concentrations of chloramphenicol. The first subculture resulted in growth at all concentrations up to and including 20 μg chloramphenicol per ml, but no growth occurred at higher concentrations. Thereafter, the bacteria were subcultured from medium containing the highest concentration of chloramphenicol at which growth had occurred onto media containing successively higher concentrations of the antibiotic. After several subcultures, derivatives of strains CL104 and SA108 were obtained that grow on media containing a range of concentrations of chloramphenicol up to 75 μg/ml DNA was prepared from these derived strains and Southern hybridization analysis of BamHI-digested samples (data not given) showed that growth at successively higher concentrations of chloramphenicol resulted in increasing quantities of the amplified 11 kbp exogenote. Interestingly, unrestricted DNA samples from strains growing at very high chloramphenicol concentrations showed relatively weak hybridization to a band that ran ahead of the undigested band of chromosomal DNA. This band probably represents the product of spontaneous excision of the 11 kbp exogenote (or multiples thereof) which would remain in the population as a circular, nonreplicating element (see Figure 1B where a faint band running just behind the 11 kbp amplified sequences can be seen on close inspection of lanes 8 and 12).

VII. ESTIMATION OF THE NUMBER OF COPIES OF THE AMPLIFIED SEQUENCES

The restriction map in Figure 2 shows that cleavage of CL104 DNA with either EcoRI or BamHI releases a large fragment present as a single copy per chromosome and a smaller 11 kbp fragment comprising the reiterated exogenote. The number of copies of the exogenote per chromosome can therefore be estimated by comparing the intensity of hybridization of the 5.7 kbp phe-nic probe to these two fragments. Since the probe has complete homology with both fragments there was little possibility of the occurrence of a "scaffolding" effect whereby multiple copies of the probe could associate with each other and remain bound to the filter through the agency of one partially hybridized molecule of the probe. BamHI digestion was used in these experiments because there was good separation of the single copy (18 kbp) and multicopy (11 kbp) bands on 0.35% agarose - see Figure 3. After the position of the radioactively-labeled fragments on the nitrocellulose filter had been located by autoradiography, the appropriate regions were cut out and counted using a Beckman liquid scintillation spectrometer. This method is more reliable than scanning of the autoradiograms since the density of the image obtained depends on the

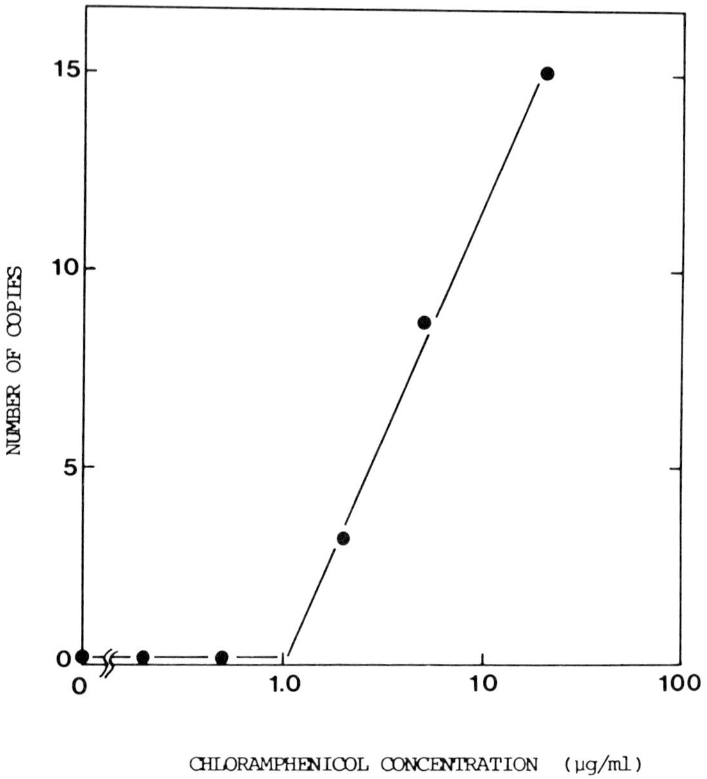

Figure 4. Amplification of the exogenote in derivatives of stain CL104 after growth at elevated concentrations of chloramphenicol, DNA was isolated from the bacteria and the number of copies of the exogenote per genome was determined as described in the text.

extent to which the film has been prefogged (Laskey, 1980) and it is only directly related to the radioactivity present over a relatively narrow range. The results of this experiment show that amplification of the exogenote occurs with increasing concentrations of chloramphenicol, to give an average number of about 15 copies per genome after growth on media containing 20 μg Cm per ml. At a concentration of 5 μg Cm per ml an average number of 8 to 9 copies per genome are present (Figure 4). Visual inspection of the data in Figure 1 might have suggested greater amplification than this. B. subtilis 168 will grow on nutrient agar containing 2 μg Cm per ml. There appears to be some selective advantage in retaining a few (about 3) copies of the exogenote per genome at this concentration of chloramphenicol, but at concentrations below 1 μg Cm/ml the exogenote is lost.

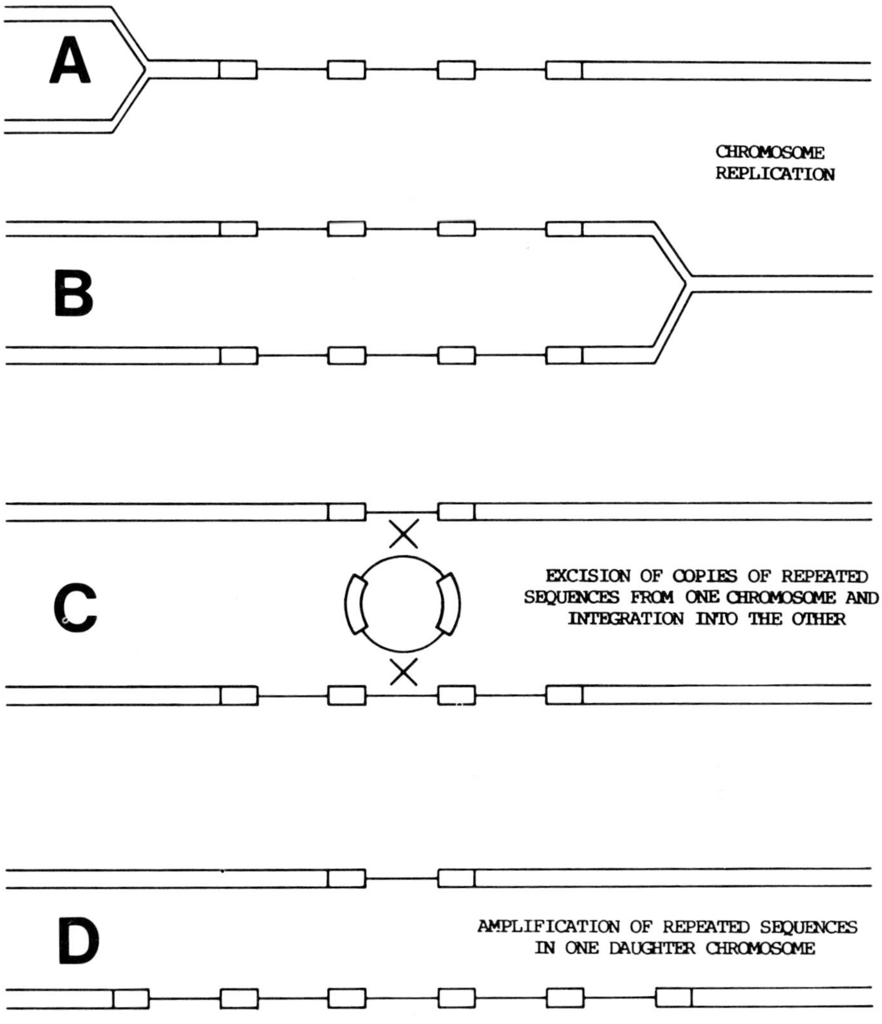

Figure 5. A model for gene amplification in B. subtilis. The model shows the spontaneous excision of two tandemly repeated elements from one daughter chromosome followed by their integration into the other daughter chromosome. Segregation at division will result in one daughter cell with enhanced chloramphenicol tolerance.

A simple model that seeks to explain the amplification of the exogenote is given in Figure 5. It is envisaged that during bacterial growth the excision of one or more copies of the exogenote can occur from one chromosome or from one arm of a partly replicated chromosome (evidence that this occurs has been given previously). If this is followed by reintegration of the exogenote into another chromosome also present in the cell before division occurs, then this will give rise to two dissimilar daughters. One will have lost some or all of the copies of the exogenote that it once harbored; the other will contain an increased number of copies. Thus, in response to elevated concentrations of chloramphenicol, strains with enhanced chloramphenicol tolerance may arise in the population in a gradual stepwise manner.

VIII. GENE AMPLIFICATION IS POTENTIALLY USEFUL FOR MOLECULAR CLONING IN BACILLUS SUBTILIS

Investigators wishing to use B. subtilis as a host for the expression of foreign genes are bedeviled by the well known problem of plasmid instability in this organism. Since the B. subtilis chromosome only very rarely undergoes rearrangements (see, for example, Schneider and Anagnostopoulos, 1981), it seems worthwhile to consider the possibility of using the bacterial chromosome as the "cloning vector" in this organism. The results described here and elsewhere (Haldenwang et al., 1980; Wilson et al., 1981; Young, 1983) indicate that foreign DNA can be inserted into the chromosome provided that a region of sequence homology exists on the exogenote. Moreover, antibiotic selection can be used to amplify the number of copies of the exogenote to form a tandemly-repeated array in the chromosome. For optimum amplification the exogenote should contain a fragment of B. subtilis DNA that will direct insertion near the replication origin. The physiological amplification that occurs at rapid growth rates as a result of dichotomous chromosome replication can thus be exploited.

As an added refinement we are currently investigating the possibility that transfer of the recE4 mutation into amplified strains might enhance stability to an extent that will permit the amplified sequences to be perpetuated in the absence of antibiotic (Cm) selection. This is an attractive possibility since the cost of maintaining selection for the perpetuation of antibiotic-resistant plasmids on a large, industrial scale is significant.

The prospects for the use of the bacterial chromosome as 'vector' in primary cloning experiments remain to be properly assessed. We have been unable to recover the 11 kbp reiterated sequence of strain CL104 as an autonomous plasmid after transforming a variety of strains of E. coli with DNA from strain CL104 that had been digested with either BamHI or EcoRI and then ligated at a low concentration of DNA (Young, 1983). However, we also have been unable to generate this recombinant plasmid in vitro after ligating a purified sample of the 5.7 kbp phe-nic fragment to a purified sample of the 5.6 kbp EcoRI-BamHI fragment of pl949 and then transforming E. coli. The rare Cm^r recombinants of E. coli that have been obtained using either procedure prove to be small, extensively deleted plasmids that do not retain restriction sites for either EcoRI or BamHI. The conclusion that the recombinant plasmid we seek cannot be perpetuated in E. coli seems inescapable. Preliminary experiments with DNA from strain SA108 look more promising. Indeed, it is likely that the excised exogenotes that seem to appear in highly amplified Rec^+ strains (see above) can be used directly to transfer cloned fragments to E. coli.

ACKNOWLEDGMENTS

I thank Patrick Brazier for access to his unpublished data, Graham Price for patient technical assistance and Sian Evans for typing the manuscript.

REFERENCES

Alt, F.W., Kellems, R., Bertino, J. and Schimke, R.T. (1978). **J. Biol. Chem. 253**, 1357.

Chandler, M., Boy de la Tour, E., Williams, D. and Caro, L. (1979). **Molec. Gen. Genet. 176**, 221.

Chisholm. R. (1982). **TIBS 7**, 162.

Ferrari, F. A., Ferrari, E. and Hoch, J.A. (1982). **J. Bacteriol. 152**, 780.

Glover, D., Zaha, A., Stocker, A., Santelli, R., Pueyo, M., Toledo, S. and Lara, F. (1982). **Proc. Natl. Acad. Sci. USA 79**, 2947.

Haldenwang, W.G., Banner, C.D.B., Ollington, J.F., Losick, R., Hoch, J.A., O'connor, M.B. and Sonenshein, A.L. (1980). **J. Bacteriol. 142**, 90.

Hood, L., Campbell, J. and Elgin, S. (1975). **Ann. Rev. Genet. 9**, 305.

Laskey, R.A. (1980). In Methods in Enzymology, Vol. 65 (L. Grossman and K. Moldave, eds.) p. 363, Academic Press, New York.

Loughney, K., Lund, E. and Dahlberg, J.E. (1982). **Nucl. Acids Res. 10**, 1607.

Roberts, J.M., Buck, L.B. and Axel, R. (1983). **Cell 33**, 53.
Saito, H., Anzai, H. and Kawamura, F. (1982). Proceedings of the Fourth International Symposium on Genetics of Industrial Microorganisms, Kyoto.
Schimke, R.T. (1982). Gene Amplification, Cold Spring Harbor Laboratories, Cold Spring Harbor, New York.
Schneider, A.-M. and Anagnostopoulos, C. (1981). **J. Gen. Microbiol. 125**, 241.
Spralding, A.C. and Mahowald, A.P. (1981). **Cell 27**, 203.
Stewart, G.S., Wilson, F.E. and Bott, K.F. (1982). **Gene 19**, 153.
Vasseghi, H. and Claverys, J.-P. (1983). **Gene 21**, 285.
Wilson, F.E., Hoch, J.A. and Bott, K. (1981). **J. Bacteriol. 148**, 624.
Young, M. (1983). **J. Gen. Microbiol. 129**, 1497.

NEW GENETIC METHODS, MOLECULAR CLONING STRATEGIES AND GENE FUSION TECHNIQUES FOR BACILLUS SUBTILIS WHICH TAKE ADVANTAGE OF Tn917 INSERTIONAL MUTAGENESIS[1]

Philip Youngman
John B. Perkins
Kathleen Sandman

Department of Cellular and Developmental Biology
The Biological Laboratories
Harvard University
Cambridge, Massachusetts

I. INTRODUCTION

Tn917, a 5.4 kb transposon identified originally in Streptococcus faecalis (Tomich et al., 1980), was recently introduced into Bacillus subtilis and demonstrated to transpose efficiently (Youngman et al., 1983). A selection system for recovering Tn917 insertions into the B. subtilis chromosome was described which involved the use of a temperature-sensitive plasmid called pTV1 (Figure 1). Insertions at many chromosomal locations were characterized, including insertions that caused auxotrophic and spo (sporulation-defective) mutations.

The present work describes several derivatives of Tn917 and pTV1 that were constructed to take advantage of such insertional mutations to facilitate both in vitro and in vivo studies of the mutated genes. We describe a novel strategy for cloning genes inactivated by transposon

[1]*This work was carried out in the laboratory of R. Losick at Harvard University and was supported by National Science Foundation Grant PCM-8208349 to R. Losick and P.Y., a postdoctoral fellowship to J.B.P. from the National Institutes of Health and a predoctoral fellowship to K.S. from the National Science Foundation.*

ISBN 0-12-274160-9

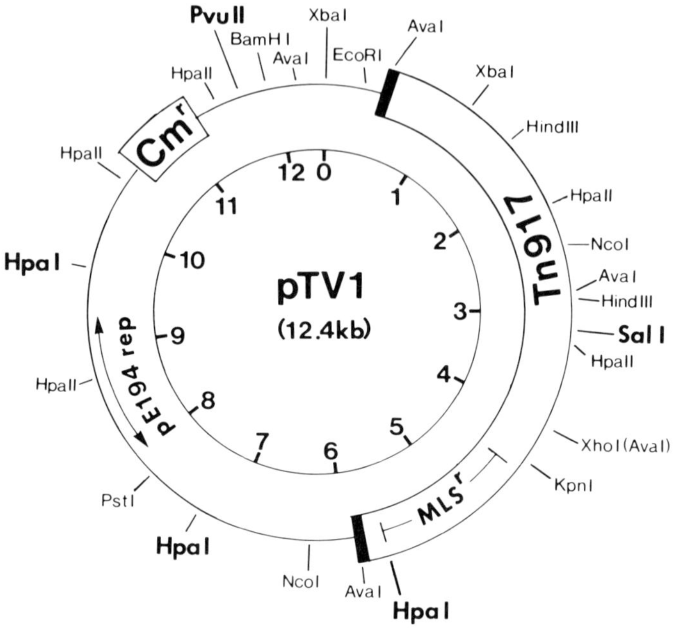

Figure 1. A restriction map of pTV1, a temperature-sensitive Tn917-containing replicon, the construction of which was described previously (Youngman et al., 1983).

insertion, and we describe a derivative of the transposon that carries a promoterless lacZ gene very near one of its ends, which can thus automatically generate a lacZ transcriptional fusion as a consequence of insertion into a gene. In addition, we describe derivatives of Tn917 that carry various drug-resistance genes, including a Staphylococcus chloramphenicol-resistance gene and a Streptomyces thiostrepton-resistance gene, constructed for the purpose of testing whether the transposon might be useful for insertional mutagenesis in other Gram-positive bacteria.

II. RESULTS AND DISCUSSION

A. New spo Loci Identified by Insertional Mutagenesis

In previous studies (Youngman et al., 1983), it was demonstrated that B. subtilis cultures consisting almost entirely of cells that have received chromosomal inserts of Tn917 can be prepared by diluting 33°C cultures of pTV1-

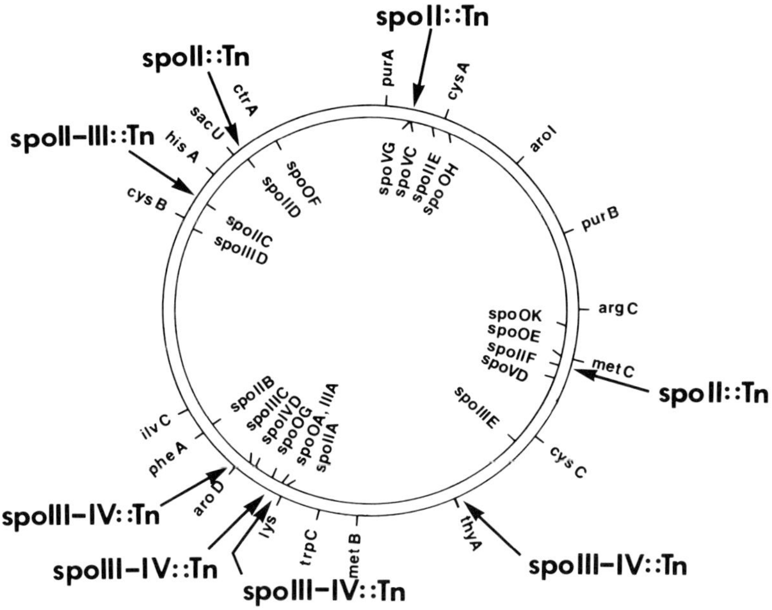

Figure 2. A genetic map of the B. subtilis chromosome showing the location of eight insertional spo mutations relative to various "landmark" auxotrophic mutations and several known spo loci.

containing bacteria at mid-log phase 1:100 into fresh 48°C broth in the presence of MLS drugs (and absence of Cm), and allowing growth (overnight) to stationary phase. After plating to obtain isolated colonies, such transposition-enriched populations were screened for various mutant types. In most such populations, transposon-linked auxotrophs arose at a frequency of 5 to 8% (to be compared with 1 to 2% obtained in Salmonella, when similar experiments are performed with Tn10 (Kleckner et al., 1975)), and approximately 90% of all auxotrophs were glutamate-requirers, containing a transposon insertion within or near the gltA locus. The remaining 10% (insertional auxotrophs with requirements for supplements other than glutamate) were of several kinds.

Transposition-enriched populations were also screened for spo mutants (sporulation-defective mutants), and these were detected at a frequency of only 0.1% to 0.5%. Including three mutants whose map positions were reported previously (Youngman et al., 1983), a total of eight insertional spo mutations have been mapped, and a partial analysis of their phenotypic properties has been made, the results of which are summarized in Figure 2. Two important findings should be emphasized here: 1) all eight insertional spo mutations are distinct from each other, and 2) at least two of the eight (and perhaps more) have identified genetic loci not previously detected in searches for sporulation mutants.

Because the total number of genes estimated to be specifically required for sporulation in Bacillus is on the same order as the number of genes in which mutations produced an auxotrophic phenotype (Piggot, 1973; Hranueli et al., 1974; Henner and Hoch, 1980), the fact that insertional spo mutations are much less abundant than insertional auxotrophs suggests that no sites of particularly high target preference are present in any spo genes and indicates that the apparent absence of "hotspots" for insertion within spo genes should be interpreted as evidence that only the most preferred target sites (such as the one(s) in gltA) have a significantly nonrandom distribution. If so, it may be hoped that lower preference target sites are distributed with a sufficiently high degree of randomness to allow the recovery of insertions into virtually any nonessential gene of B. subtilis, given an effective phenotypic assay for loss of gene function. In any event, we now know for certain that an extensive collection of different insertional spo mutations can readily be obtained.

B. A Novel Strategy for the Cloning of DNA Adjacent to Transposon Inserts

B. subtilis bacteria in a condition of "competence" for genetic transformation are highly proficient for the uptake of linear DNA fragments and for their incorporation by recombination into homologous sequences in host DNA (Dubnau, 1982). When the transforming DNA contains a discrete insert with no homology to host sequences, the insert may still be incorporated by a "marker-replacement" recombination event, involving crossovers on either side of the insert. We have taken advantage of this property of B. subtilis to develop a cloning strategy based on insertion by marker-replacement recombination of a pBR322-derived replicon directly into existing Tn917-generated insertional mutations. Chromosomal DNA on either side of the transposon may then be cloned into E. coli by simply ligating restriction-cut, insert-containing chromosomal DNA at a dilute DNA concentration, and transforming $CaCl_2$-treated E. coli bacteria with a selection for ampicillin-resistance (Ap^r).

A pair of plasmids called pTV20 and pTV21 (Figure 3) were constructed (P. Youngman and J. Perkins, unpublished

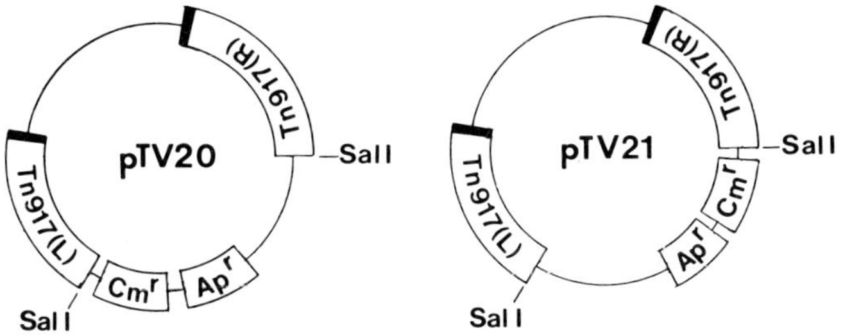

Figure 3. Plasmids resulting from the insertion of pHW9 in two different orientations into a SalI site near the middle of Tn917. Tn917 (L) and Tn917 (R) refer to the left and right arms of Tn917 when the transposon is viewed as having the MLS^r gene on the left.

results) by insertion of the pBR322-derived replicon pHW9 (Horinouchi and Weisblum, 1982) into a SalI restriction site near the middle of Tn917 (see Figure 1). pHW9 has a unique SalI site and carries a Cm^r gene of Gram-positive origin (selectable in B. subtilis) in addition to the Ap^r gene normally carried by pBR322. pTV20 and pTV21 simply represent the two possible orientations for insertion of pHW9 into the middle of Tn917.

Linear monomers of plasmid DNA are unable to establish themselves as autonomous replicons after transformation in B. subtilis (Contente and Dubnau, 1979). Thus, when pTV20 or pTV21 are linearized by digestion with a restriction enzyme that cuts outside the transposon sequence, and are used to transform a competent B. subtilis recipient strain that contains a Tn917 insert at some chromosomal site, a marker-replacement recombination event, of the kind depicted in Figure 4, which inserts pHW9 sequences into the chromosomal copy of Tn917, is the only way in which Cm^r transformants can be obtained. Because pTV20 and pTV21 carry pHW9 sequences in two different orientations with respect to the transposon arms, a single restriction enzyme may be used to separately "clone out" from the two recombinants' chromosomal DNA sequences adjacent to either side of the transposon. In actual practice, less than 1 μg of insert-containing chromosomal DNA is normally required to generate a set of 10 to 20 clones.

Procedures of this kind result in the cloning of gene fragments, of course, and cannot be used to obtain an intact cloned copy of the insertionally mutated gene in a single step. This is not a disadvantage for many kinds of in vitro gene regulation studies, however, where regulatory sequences

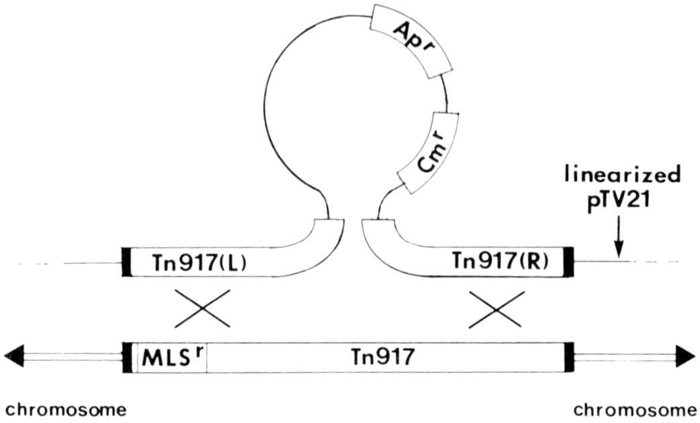

Figure 4. A schematic representation of the kind of marker-replacement recombination event required to generate Cm^r *transformants when an insertional mutant is transformed with linearized pTV21 DNA.*

(such as promoters) "upstream" from the gene's coding sequence are the subjects of interest, and it should be apparent that having cloned fragments of a gene makes isolation of an intact gene sequence a very simple matter.

C. Tn917-Mediated Transcriptional Fusions to lacZ

Casadaban and Cohen (1979) were the first to demonstrate one of the most powerful ways in which transposon insertions may be exploited for the study of gene activity in vivo: when the promoterless coding sequence of a gene, such as the lacZ gene of E. coli, whose product (β-galactosidase) is easy to detect and quantitate, is inserted near the end of a transposon, insertion of the transposon into a gene can automatically generate a transcriptional fusion, placing expression of lacZ under regulation of the promoter for the insertionally inactivated gene. This, of course, greatly simplifies measurement of promoter activity in vivo, and at the same time provides a sensitive way of screening colonies for variants or mutants altered in gene expression, when a chromogenic substrate (like X-gal) is included in the medium.

Construction of such a fusion-generating transposon required the identification of a restriction site near an end of the element where foreign DNA may be inserted without affecting transposition. After verifying that the HpaI site in Tn917 (approximately 200 bp from one end) was suitable in

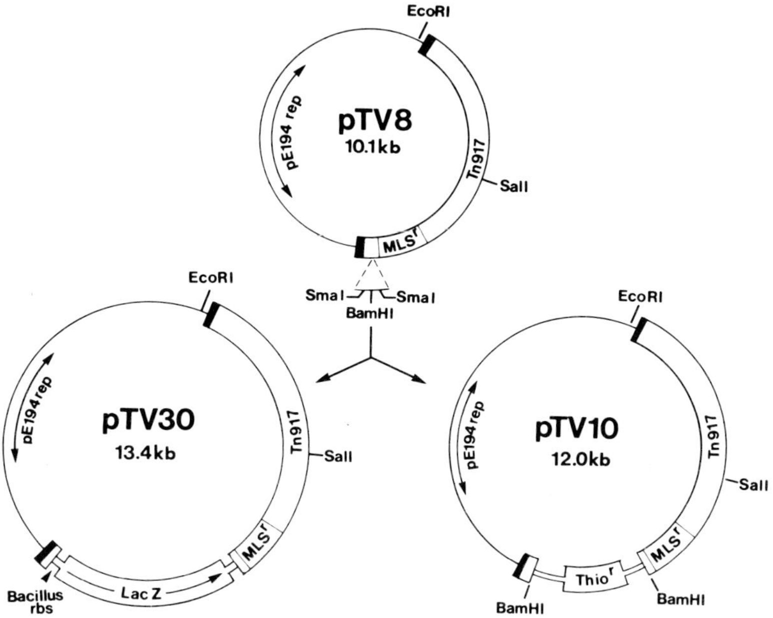

Figure 5. Structural features of pTV8, pTV10 and pTV30 (see text).

these respects (see Figure 1), this site was "replaced" by a 30 bp fragment containing a BamHI restriction site flanked very closely by SmaI sites on either side (P. Youngman and J. Perkins, unpublished results). In the plasmid pTV8, shown in Figure 5, the BamHI and SmaI sites contained within this 30 bp fragment are the only such sites in the plasmid. After partial digestion of pTV8 with SmaI, a lacZ-bearing restriction fragment from plasmid pZΔ326 (P. Zuber and R. Losick, unpublished results) was inserted by ligation, resulting in a plasmid called pTV30 (Figure 5). The fragment from pZΔ326 carries no promoter for the lacZ gene, and its orientation in pTV30 is such that transcription must come from the end of Tn917 for proper expression of the gene. A special feature of this construction is that the lacZ gene derived from pZΔ326 is substituted with a strong Bacillus ribosome-binding site (P. Zuber and R. Losick, unpublished results).

When pTV30 was used to generate transpositions (as described above for pTV1), approximately 85% of insert-containing colonies were white on X-gal plates, and the remaining 15% displayed variable degrees of blueness, with 1 to 2% giving an intensely blue reaction, indicating that an appropriate percentage of insertions can activate the transposon-borne lacZ gene for expression. Work is in progress to determine whether activation in these instances is actually a consequence of transposon-mediated fusion of the lacZ coding sequence to an interrupted transcriptional unit in the B. subtilis chromosome, as would appear to be the most likely explanation.

D. Derivatives of Tn917 Substituted with Additional Drug-Resistance Genes

The knowledge that foreign DNA may be inserted into the BamHI and SmaI sites of pTV8 without inhibiting transposition may readily be put to use for the construction of derivatives of Tn917 that confer other drug resistances in addition to MLS^r. This has the potential of enhancing the usefulness of Tn917 in Bacillus species, and creates the possibility of testing the transposon for activity in other Gram-positive genera, such as Streptomyces, where MLS^r is not ordinarily a convenient selection. For example, pTV8 was used to construct a derivative of Tn917, shown in Figure 5, containing a thiostrepton-resistance gene (tsr) from Streptomyces azureus (Thompson et al., 1980), and work is in progress to devise a selection capable of detecting whether such constructions can transpose in a Streptomyces host. Similar derivatives that carry a Cm^r gene of Staphylococcus origin have also been constructed (P. Youngman and J. Perkins, unpublished results), and it may be hoped that such novel elements will further extend the useful species host range of Tn917, and permit techniques such as those described here to be applied to the study of gene regulation in a broad range of Gram-positive species.

ACKNOWLEDGMENTS

We thank S. Zahler, B. Weisblum, D. Dubnau, D. Clewell and M. Igo for generous gifts of strains and plasmids.

REFERENCES

Casadaban, M.J. and Cohen, S.N. (1979). **Proc. Natl. Acad. Sci. USA** 76, 4530.
Contente, S. and Dubnau, D. (1979). **Molec. Gen. Genet.** 167, 251.

Dubnau, D. (1982). In The Molecular Biology of the Bacilli (D. Dubnau, ed.), p. 147, Academic Press, New York.
Henner, D.J. and Hoch, J.A. (1980). **Microbiol. Rev. 44**, 57.
Hranueli, D., Piggot, P.J. and Mandelstam, J. (1974). **J. Bacteriol. 119**, 684.
Horinouchi, S. and Weisblum, B. (1982). **J. Bacteriol. 150**, 815.
Kleckner, N., Chan, R.K., Tye, B.K. and Botstein, D. (1975). **J. Mol. Biol. 94**, 561.
Piggot, P.J. (1973). **J. Bacteriol. 114**, 1241.
Thompson, C.J., Ward, J.M. and Hopwood, D.A. (1980). **Nature 286**, 525.
Tomich, P.K., An, F.Y. and Clewell, D.B. (1980). **J. Bacteriol. 141**, 1366.
Youngman, P.J., Perkins, J.B. and Losick, R. (1983). **Proc. Natl. Acad. Sci. USA 80**, 2305.

THE SUCROSE SYSTEM AS A MODEL OF GENETIC REGULATION IN BACILLUS SUBTILIS[1]

Agnès Fouet
Elisabeth Aubert
Maryvonne Arnaud
André Klier
Georges Rapoport

Institut Pasteur
Paris, France

Dominique Le Coq

Institut Jacques Monod
Paris, France

I. INTRODUCTION

In our laboratory, the sucrose metabolic system of Bacillus subtilis 168 has been studied for the past two decades with the purpose of elucidating the regulatory mechanisms which control the synthesis of the enzymes involved in this pathway. Biochemical and genetic studies have been carried out on this system, which comprises at least eight loci which have been mapped on the B. subtilis chromosome (Lepesant et al., 1972; 1976; Kunst et al., 1974a). It included two inducible saccharolytic enzymes: an endocellular sucrase and an excreted levansucrase coded by the two genes sacA and sacB, respectively. A third structural gene sacP codes for a membrane (Lepesant et al., 1972; Kunst et al., 1974b; Lepesant et al., 1974) component of the PEP-

[1]*This work was supported by grants from the C.N.R.S. (A.T.P. Microbiologie 1981), I.N.S.E.R.M. (no. 72 79 104) and the Fondation pour la Recherche Médicale.*

ISBN 0-12-274160-9

dependent phosphotransferase system (PTS) of sucrose transport (Lepesant et al., 1976). Sucrase has been purified and has a molecular weight of 55,000 daltons (Kunst et al., 1974b), whereas levansucrase, the primary structure of which has been recently determined, has a molecular weight of 50,000 daltons (Delfour, 1981).

The characterization of mutations affecting the regulation of sucrase and levansucrase synthesis led to the identification of five regulatory loci. Two of them, sacR and sacT, control specifically the expression of sacB and sacA (Lepesant et al., 1976). The sacS locus is defined by three classes of mutations affecting the synthesis of either levansucrase alone or both saccharolytic enzymes. The sacS locus is linked to the sacA, sacP and sacT group in PBS1 transduction, but is completely separated from this group (Lepesant et al., 1972; 1976).

The systematic isolation of mutants affecting the synthesis of levansucrase led to the characterization of two other genes, sacQ and sacU (Lepesant et al, 1972; Kunst et al., 1974a; Steinmetz et al., 1976). The sacU gene was originally defined by two series of mutants referred to as $sacU^h$ and $sacU^-$ and exhibited a hyperproduction (Lvs^h phenotype) and a hypoproduction (Lvs^- phenotype) of levansucrase, respectively. So far, a single sacQ mutant has been isolated; it displays a Lvs^h phenotype. The sacU and sacQ genes were at first regarded as the regulatory genes which play a specific role in the control of expression of the sacB gene exclusively. However, the strains carrying the sacU and sacQ mutations are affected in the production of other extracellular enzymes (α-amylase, protease), and also in their motility and their transformability by exogenous DNA (Kunst et al., 1974a; Steinmetz et al., 1976).

Here we describe the identification of recombinant clones, isolated from different B. subtilis DNA banks, carrying the structural genes sacA and sacB and the regulatory gene sacU. Expression of the corresponding proteins was obtained in a minicell-producing strain of Escherichia coli. The existence of a precursor of levansucrase is demonstrated and the sequence of the signal peptide determined. Regulation by the product of the sacU gene at a posttranscriptional level is also proposed.

II. RESULTS

A. Cloning and Expression of the sacA Gene

A collection of 1,000 clones containing recombinant cosmids representative of the B. subtilis strain 168 genome already has been constructed in the E. coli strain HB101 using a shuttle cosmid vector (pQB79-1) derived from pHC79 (Aubert et al., 1982). Pools of 48 clones were made and the recombinant cosmids from each pool were used to transform competent cells of B. subtilis strain QB666 (sacA321 hisA1 leuA8 thr5). Two groups were found to complement the sacA321 mutation and one particular recombinant cosmid, pBS11G8, was identified and used for further study (Fouet et al., 1982). As it was shown previously that the sacA and sacP loci mapped in the same region of the chromosome, the presence of the sacP gene was looked for in the same recombinant cosmid. Complementation was obtained for the sacP401 mutation of strain QB209, but not for the sacP1 mutation of strain QB200, and it was concluded that the cosmid pBS11G8 does not contain the entire sacP gene. The regulatory locus, sacT, which is located near the sacA and sacP loci, also was not found in pBS11G8 by the complementation test.

The size of the cosmid was estimated to be only 16 kb and thought to contain an insert DNA fragment of about 9 kb (Figure 1). Further analysis showed that part of the cosmid vector pQB79-1 corresponding to the major part of the pC194 fragment (2.7 kb) was lost in the recombinant cosmid. The sacA and sacP sequences were located using labeled RNA extracted from a constitutive high producing strain (QB79 satT, Suc^{c}). Hybridization was performed in the presence of

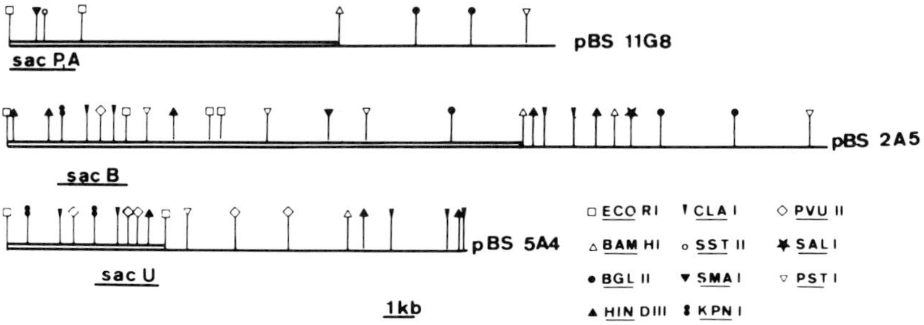

Figure 1. Restriction maps of the recombinant cosmids pBS11G8, pBS2A5 and pBS5A4 containing the sequences of the following loci: sacP, sacA, sacB and sacU, respectively.

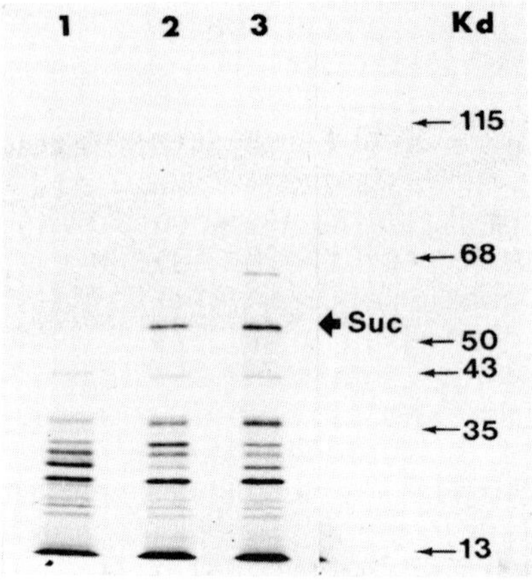

Figure 2. Analysis of the polypeptides coded by the recombinant plasmids pBSG8-1 and pBSG8-2 containing the <u>*sacA*</u> *gene in E. coli AR1062. After purification of the minicells and incorporation of [^{35}S]L-methionine (Fouet et al., 1982), the polypeptides synthesized were analyzed by SDS-PAGE (7.5% to 15% exponential gradient). Lane 1, AR1062 (pHV33); lane 2, AR1062 (pBSG8-1); and lane 3, AR1062 (pBSG8-2). The arrows indicate the migration of authentic sucrase.*

a large excess of nonlabeled RNA extracted from noninduced cells of B. subtilis 168 used as competitors. An EcoRI fragment of about 2 kb located at one end of the insert was shown to contain at least part of the sucrase gene. Since saccharolytic activity was detected in extracts from E. coli cells harboring pBS11G, we concluded that the sacA gene was included entirely in the DNA insert and that a B. subtilis gene can be efficiently expressed in E. coli.

The 2 kb EcoRI fragment was further subcloned into the EcoRI site of the bifunctional vector pHV33 (Rapoport et al., 1979). Two kinds of plasmids were obtained: pBSG8-1 and pBSG8-2, corresponding to both orientations of the inserted sequence. Both plasmids were able to transform the B. subtilis strains QB666 and IS194 (sacA321 sacB91 sacU100 recE4) and all the Cm^r transformants were also Suc^+ indicating that complementation can occur in trans, at least for sacA. It is concluded also that the structural gene sacA has been cloned with its own promoter.

The plasmids pBSG8-1 and pBSG8-2 were introduced by transformation into the minicell producing strain of E. coli, AR1062 (Rambach and Hogness, 1971), and the proteins were analyzed by SDS-PAGE after incorporation of [^{35}S]L-methionine. The autoradiogram is shown in Figure 2. One major additional band was observed in both extracts when compared to the pattern observed for the cells harboring the plasmid pHV33 alone. Its m.w. was estimated to be 55,000 daltons, which is identical to that of authentic sucrase. Immunoprecipitation of the E. coli extracts using specific antibodies confirmed the presence of sucrase and revealed that it represented about 5 to 10% of the total proteins synthesized.

The presence of an active form of the enzyme was sought in E. coli cells carrying the recombinant plasmids. The results clearly indicated that sucrase was synthesized constitutively in E. coli and that the level of expression depended upon the orientation of the 2 kb EcoRI fragment. However, the existence of an active sucrase in E. coli did not allow the cells to grow on sucrose as the sole carbon source, even at a concentration of 1%. It was therefore concluded that sucrase from B. subtilis is expressed in E. coli as a cryptic enzyme.

B. Cloning and Expression of the sacB Gene

Direct selection by transformation for sacB was not possible and we used a biochemical approach to search the sacB gene in the plasmid bank already established with the vector pHV33 (Rapoport et al., 1979). The clones of the bank were hybridized with labeled RNA extracted from strain QB118 (sacR2 sacU32 trpC2 Lvs^c LVS^h) in the presence of nonlabeled RNA from strain QB974 (sacU32 trpC2 Lvs$^+$) under nonlabeled conditions. A single clone, pBS22-61, was isolated from the 2400 clones in the bank. The insert DNA was estimated to be about 1.4 kb and only one sacB mutation (sacB204) was complemented by the plasmid, suggesting that the sacB gene was not entirely included in the insert.

Part of the insert, which reacted strongly with the mRNA probe, was used to screen the cosmid bank (Aubert et al., 1982). One clone gave a positive signal and it was shown that the corresponding cosmid pBS2A5 was able to complement the different sacB mutations isolated in the laboratory. The size of the cosmid pBS2A5 was about 24 kb and its restriction map was established (Figure 1). The localization of the coding sequence of sacB was determined at one end of the DNA insert by hybridization with the plasmid pBS22-61. The localization was confirmed by comparison of the different restriction sites obtained with those reported by Gay et al. (1983) and those deduced from the known amino acid sequence of the protein (the computer compilation was performed by G. Roizes).

```
                                   -29
ACACAGTACA TAAAAAAGGA GACATGAACG ATG AAC ACT AAA AAG TTT GCA AAA
                                 fMet Asn Thr Lys Lys Phe Ala Lys

CAA GCA ACA GTA TTA ACC TTT ACT ACC GCA CTG CTG GCA GGA GGC GCA
Gln Ala Thr Val Leu Thr Phe Thr Thr Ala Leu Leu Ala Gly Gly Ala
                 -1   +1
ACT CAA GCG TTT GCG|AAA GAA ACG AAC CAA AAG CCA TAT AAG GAA ACA
Thr Gln Ala Phe Ala|Lys Glu Thr Asn Gln Lys Pro Tyr Lys Glu Thr

TAC GGC ATT TCC CAT ATT ACA CGC CAT GAT ATG CTG CAA ATC CCC GAA
Tyr Gly Ile Ser His Ile Thr Arg His Asp Met Leu Gln Ile Pro Glu

CAG CAA AAA AAT GAA AAG
Gln Gln Lys Asn Glu Lys
```

Figure 3. DNA and amino acid sequences in the NH_2-terminal region of levansucrase. Nucleotide sequence was determined according to Maxam and Gilbert (1980) after labeling the EcoRI site of the 450 bp EcoRI - TaqI fragment mentioned in the text. The NH_2-terminal Lys of the mature levansucrase was taken as amino acid +1. The cleavage site between the signal sequence and the mature protein is indicated by a vertical bar.

However, the cosmid pBS2A5 was unable to complement the sacB211 mutations of the recE4 strain, QB977, indicating that it did not contain the entire sacB gene. This was confirmed by the difference of the restriction sites of the flanking regions obtained for the cloned sacB gene with those described by Gay et al. (1983). We assumed that during the construction of the cosmid bank two independent EcoRI fragments had been ligated together leading to the cosmid pBS2A5. From these results, it is clear that a small part of the sacB gene encoding the N-terminal end of the protein was not cloned in pBS2A5.

Another E. coli library available in the laboratory was screened for the presence of an intact sacB gene. The colony bank was constructed by inserting a sized partial Sau3A1 digest of DNA from strain QB2010 (sacA321 sacR37 sacU32 thr5) into the BamHI site of the vector λEMBL3 using E. coli strain KH802 as a recipient. A 0.9 kb EcoRI - KpnI fragment of the cosmid pBS2A5 corresponding to the major part of the sacB gene was used as a probe to screen this new bank. About ten phage reacted strongly with the probe and one of them was studied in more detail. An EcoRI - TaqI fragment of about 450 bp, which overlaps the NH_2-terminal sequence of the protein and its putative signal sequence, was subcloned into the large EcoRI - ClaI fragment of pBR322. Preliminary results of the nucleotide sequence are reported in Figure 3. Upstream from the sequence corresponding to the amino-terminal portion of the mature levansucrase there is an open reading frame of 29 amino acids which is characterized by the presence of a hydrophilic region followed by a hydrophobic stretch of about 20 amino acid residues with an Ala in position n-1. This kind of signal peptide has been described already in other bacilli (Petit-Glatron and Chambert, 1981; Kroyer and Chang, 1981; Takkinen et al., 1983; Yang et al., 1983). It is interesting to note that 2 codons upstream from the beginning of the coding sequence there is a TGA stop codon in the same reading frame.

The existence of a precursor of levansucrase was looked for in the minicell producing strain of E. coli, AR1062, after introduction into pBR325 of the recombinant plasmid pLS8 which contains the entire sacB gene. This plasmid was constructed by D. Le Coq from a library of B. subtilis DNA cloned in phage λ Charon 4A by Ferrari et al. (1981). Very few recombinants were obtained and the majority of them had lost the inserted fragment. Two recombinant clones possessing the Lvs^+ phenotype detected directly on the plate (Lepesant et al., 1972) were picked and further analyzed. The presence of an active levansucrase was confirmed by enzymatic assays on the sonicated extracts (the specific activity found was about 0.1 U/mg bacterial protein). Furthermore, one of the clones recovered (clone L) contained a plasmid with a DNA insert of about 800 bp, which probably corresponds to IS1 in the HindIII fragment located at the end of the sacB locus. The other one (clone B) harbored a plasmid identical to the original plasmid pLS8. A bacterial extract of clone B was subjected to SDS-PAGE after labeling with [^{35}S]L-methionine as reported earlier (Fouet et al., 1982) (Figure 4A, lane 2). Additional bands were detected when compared to the pattern obtained for the extract of the cells containing the vector alone (lane 1). One of them has a m.w. which corresponds to that of authentic levansucrase (50,000 daltons), and another one has a m.w. of about 53,000 daltons. These two bands reacted with antibodies directed against mature levansucrase (Figure 4B), suggesting that the lower polypeptide is the mature form and the larger one a precursor form of the enzyme. It is worth noting that in the supernatant of the labeled minicells, only the mature form can be detected (Figure 4A, lane 4). The presence of mature β-lactamase (28,000 daltons) was not observed in this case (compare lane 4 with lane 2 of Figure 4A). This result may be considered an argument for the excretion of mature levansucrase in E. coli minicells.

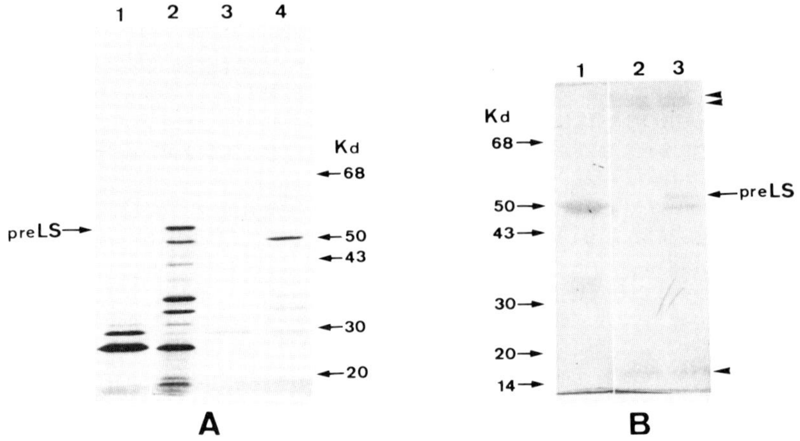

Figure 4. [A]. Analysis of the polypeptides coded by the plasmid pLS8 containing the <u>*sacB*</u> *gene in E. coli AR1062. Experimental procedures were carried out under the same conditions described in Figure 2. Lane 1, AR1062 (pBR325); lane 2, AR1062 (pLS8); lanes 3 and 4, supernatants of the minicells analyzed in lanes 1 and 2, respectively. [B]. Immunodetection of mature levansucrase and precursor of levansucrase (pre LS) after protein blotting. The polypeptides separated as in [A] were transferred to a nitrocellulose filter and treated with antibodies directed against mature levansucrase and then with [^{125}I] protein A from Staphylococcus aureus. Lane 1, authentic levansucrase (2 µg); lane 2, AR1062 (pBR325); and lane 3, AR1062 (pLS8). Arrowheads indicate the presence of nonspecific polypeptides.*

C. Cloning and Expression of the <u>sacU</u> Gene

The <u>sacU</u> gene was originally defined by two kinds of mutations which changed the level of levansucrase synthesis. The <u>sacU</u>$^-$ mutation leads to a reduced synthesis while the <u>sacU</u>^{h} mutation promotes a high level of synthesis of the protein. The <u>sacU</u> gene was searched for among the E. coli recombinant cosmids by complementing a <u>sacU</u>$^-$ mutation of B. subtilis for the Lvs$^+$ phenotype. Lvs$^+$ colonies were screened among the transformants selected by congression with an unlinked auxotrophic marker. A competent culture of strain QB254 SacU$^-$ (<u>sacA321</u> <u>sacU42</u> <u>hisA1</u> <u>trpC2</u>) was exposed to a saturating amount of DNA from strain QB501 SacU$^-$ (<u>sacA321</u> <u>sacU42</u> <u>trpC2</u>) in the presence of cosmid DNAs extracted from the 22 pools of the DNA bank. Among the His$^+$ transformants, Lvs$^+$ colonies were found with recombinant DNAs from one pool. Under the same conditions it was also possible to transform the strain QB136 SacU^h (sacU32 leuA8 trpC2), which has the Lvs^h phenotype, to the wild-type phenotype Lvs$^+$. The cosmid was identified among the individual clones from the positive pool and was referred to as pBS5A4. Its restriction map is shown in Figure 1; it contains a small DNA insert of 6 kb with two KpnI sites.

The cosmid pBS5A4 was introduced by transformation into the minicell producing strain AR1062 and an extract of the transformants was subjected to SDS-PAGE (Figure 5A). A very strong band corresponding to a m.w. of about 46,000 daltons was detected in extract from cells harboring pBS5A4; this polypeptide was missing in the extract containing the cosmid vector alone. A cosmid derivative obtained by elimination of the 1.3 kb KpnI fragment gave similar results, suggesting that the sacU gene is located on the left part of the DNA insert (Figure 1).

Until now, no evidence had been obtained on the nature and the role at the molecular level of the sacU gene product. However, since the sacU mutations affect the level of excretion of some enzymes and also modify the properties of the membrane (Steinmetz et al, 1976), we analyzed the membrane proteins from cells belonging to the two classes of sacU mutants (Figure 5B). Two major polypeptides of 36,000 and 46,000 daltons were characterized in the membrane of the wild-type strain of B. subtilis 168. The lower m.w. component was absent in the membrane fraction from the strain QB136 carrying the sacU^h mutation, whereas the larger one disappeared in strain QB254 harboring the sacU$^-$ mutation. It was shown by use of specific antibodies that the 36,000 dalton polypeptide corresponds to the flagellin, the major protein of the flagella (Simon et al., 1977), which is absent in sacU^h mutants. The 46,000 dalton polypeptide has the same electrophoretic mobility as the major polypeptide synthesized in E. coli minicells harboring pBS5A4. We may assume that these polypeptides are identical.

It has been postulated that the increase of extracellular enzyme synthesis in sacU^h strains is a consequence of a higher transcription of the corresponding genes. To verify such an assumption, total RNAs from strains having the phenotype SacU$^-$, SacU$^+$ and SacU^h, respectively, were extracted and spotted on nitrocellulose filters. The filters were hybridized with the 0.9 kb EcoRI - KpnI DNA fragment of the cosmid pBS2A5. This fragment contains the internal part of the levansucrase gene. The result of such an experiment is shown in Figure 6. The amount of mRNA coding for levansucrase is roughly the same for the dif-

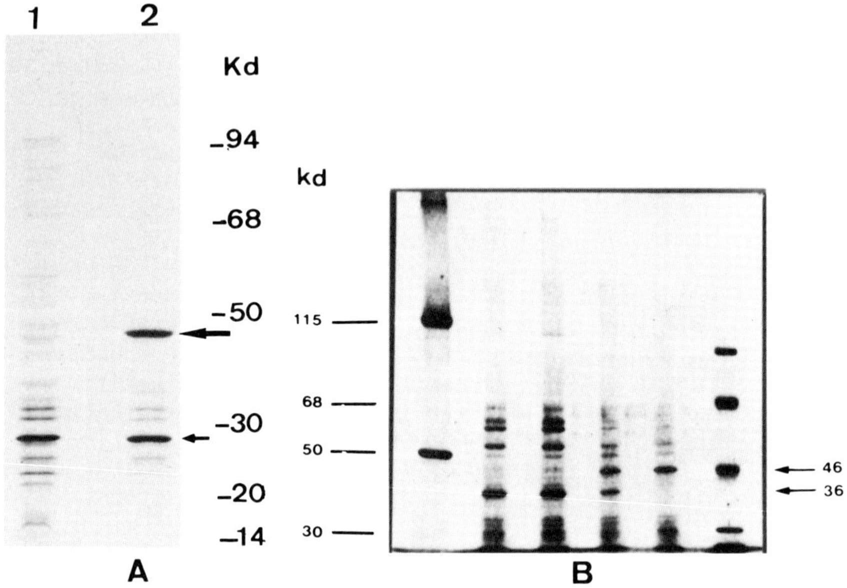

Figure 5. [A]. Analysis of the polypeptides coded by the cosmid pBS5A4 containing the sacU gene in E. coli AR1062. Experimental procedures were carried out under the same conditions described in Figure 2. Lane 1, AR1062 (pQB79-1) and lane 2, AR1062 (pBS5A4). The main arrow indicates the position of the sacU gene product. The small arrow shows the position of the mature β-lactamase encoded by the vector. [B]. Analysis by SDS-PAGE of membrane extracts from strains of B. subtilis carrying sacU mutations. Staining was done with Coomassie blue. Lanes 2 and 3, membrane extract of strain QB254 (SacU$^-$) at two concentrations; lane 4, membrane extract of the wild-type strain 168 (SacU$^+$); lane 5, membrane extract of strain QB136 (SacU^h); and lanes 1 and 6, m.w. markers.

ferent RNAs. Degradation of RNA can be reasonably excluded since agarose gel electrophoresis revealed the presence of intact rRNA, 5S RNA and tRNA species. Therefore, it is unlikely that the increase of levansucrase synthesis in sacU^h mutants is due to an increase in the amount of the levansucrase messenger RNA. Moreover, as it has been reported earlier that the stability of the mRNA of levansucrase is not increased in sacU^h mutants (Petit-Glatron and Chambert, 1981), we can assume that the regulation of levansucrase synthesis takes place at a posttranscriptional level in the sacU^h mutants. The accumulation of the protein may

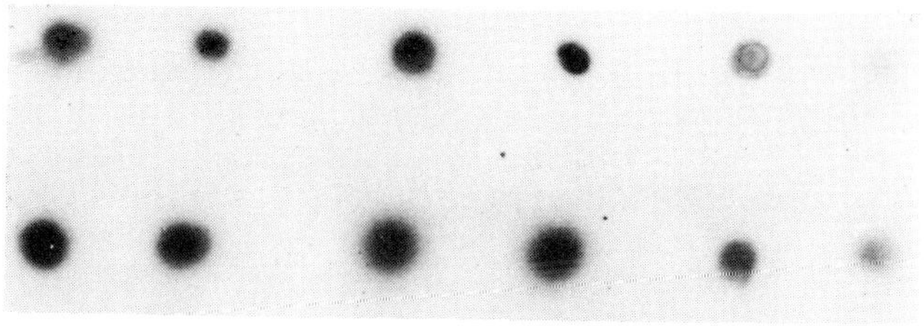

Figure 6. Dot blot of RNAs extracted from strains of B. subtilis carrying <u>*sacU*</u> *mutations. Duplicate experiments were performed at two RNA concentrations (upper line, 7.5 µg total RNA; lower line, 15 µg total RNA). Hybridization was carried out using the [^{32}P]-labeled 0.9 kb EcoRI - KpnI fragment of cosmid pBS2A5 containing part of the levansucrase gene as a probe.*

be a consequence of a better translation linked to an active secretory process mediated by the 46,000 dalton polypeptide described above.

III. DISCUSSION

The use of libraries of B. subtilis DNA constructed with a cosmid or phage λ vectors allowed us to isolate DNA fragments which include the structural genes for sucrase (<u>sacA</u>), levansucrase (<u>sacB</u>) and the regulatory locus, <u>sacU</u>. The recombinant cosmids are relatively small in regard to the theoritical size values needed for in vitro packaging in λ capsid, but it is possible that extensive deletion occurred in the original cosmid after subcultivation, even in selective pressure conditions due to the presence of antibiotics. The <u>sacA</u> gene has been efficiently expressed in E. coli. The gene product which is synthesized has the same size as that of sucrase found in B. subtilis and it is produced in an active form. The amount of the enzyme depends upon the orientation of the gene, suggesting that in one case the promoter of the <u>sacA</u> gene was used whereas in the other orientation a promoter of the plasmid vector was used. It has been previously shown that the order of the markers on the genetic map of B. subtilis is the following: <u>sacT</u> <u>sacP</u> <u>sacA</u> and also it has been suggested that <u>sacT</u> is the promoter of both the structural genes, <u>sacA</u> and <u>sacP</u>

(Lepesant et al., 1976). From the results obtained since then indicating that the sacA gene is expressed in the absence of sacT, it now appears that the three genes do not belong to an operon.

Heterospecific expression of the sacB gene has been difficult to obtain. It seems that the presence of the cloned levansucrase gene has a deleterious effect in E. coli. This is supported by the absence of the complete and functional gene in the plasmid and cosmid banks constructed earlier, and also by the very low number of clones containing an active gene product in the minicell producing strains recovered after subcloning of the sacB gene from a recombinant λ. The few cells, which contain the intact recombinant plasmid, produced among other polypeptides are two components of 53,000 and 50,000 daltons. The larger one is probably the precursor of the mature levansucrase, which is excreted in B. subtilis. In this case, the signal peptide must be about 30 amino acids long and is likely to contain a stretch of hydrophobic amino acids. The supernatant of the minicells contained only the mature form of levansucrase and we may assume, therefore, that the protein is excreted in this system. Integrality of the cells is indicated by the absence of mature β-lactamase found under these conditions. The mature form of levansucrase has the same m.w. as the enzyme purified from the supernatant of the B. subtilis cultures, indicating that the recognition sites for the processing of the precursor are similar in E. coli and in B. subtilis. The sequence of the cloned sacB gene has been determined and the amino acid sequence of the signal peptide deduced. It contains 29 amino acid residues and is characterized by the presence of a hydrophilic portion with 3 Lys residues followed by a hydrophobic sequence with and Ala residue in the n-1 position as it was reported for other exocellular enzymes (Kroyer and Chang, 1981; Takkinen et al., 1983; Ohmura et al, 1983; Yang et al, 1983). However, the signal peptide of levansucrase appears smaller than that found for α-amylase, another excreted protein of B. subtilis which contains a Glu residue in position n-1 (Ohumra et al., 1983; Yang et al., 1983). The sequence of the NH_2-terminal portion of the mature levansucrase is in complete agreement with the results obtained by A. Delfour (1981) by amino acid sequencing, except for 2 glutamine instead of glutamic acid out of 33 amino acid residues analyzed.

The knowledge of the leader sequence will allow us to use the signal peptide of levansucrase to construct a secretion vector in B. subtilis. Such a host-vector system will be promising to promote the synthesis and excretion of heterologous proteins during the vegetative phase of this organism.

The sacU gene also has been cloned and expressed in E. coli. The major polypeptide coded by the sacU gene has a m.w. of 46,000 daltons which is the same size as that found for a major component of the membrane of B. subtilis. This polypeptide was detected in $SacU^+$ and $SacU^h$ strains and is absent in $sacU^-$ mutants.

The cloned sacU gene has been used as a probe for identifying, in the λEMBL3 DNA bank, recombinants which contain the $sacU^h$ allele (unpublished results). It will be interesting to know whether the gene product is the same as that found for the wild-type gene.

From the results described in this paper it seems, unexpectedly, that the $sacU^h$ mutations do not affect the level of expression of the levansucrase mRNA. The hypothesis of a posttranscriptional regulation in B. subtilis is, therefore, very attractive and a model in which a membrane protein component facilitates the translation and the simultaneous secretion of the exocellular enzyme is postulated. In the absence of this protein, we propose that translation and excretion occur with a very low efficiency, even in the presence of intact transcription products. This is consistent with the model of the "signal recognition particle" postulated in eukaryotes (Walter and Blobel, 1981) and extended more recently to E. coli (Oliver and Beckwith, 1982; Hall et al., 1983). Such a hypothesis needs further experimental support in B. subtilis.

ACKNOWLEDGMENTS

We wish to thank R. Dedonder in whose laboratory this work has been carried out. The authors are grateful to I. Smith for providing the B. subtilis strain IS194, and to F. Le Hegarat and L. Hirschbein for supplying the flagellin antiserum. They are indebted to P. Cossart and C. Parsot for advice concerning nucleotide sequencing techniques. We wish also to thank Ms. D. Lefevre for typing this manuscript.

REFERENCES

Aubert, E., Fargette, F., Fouet, A., Klier, A. and Rapoport, G. (1982). In Molecular Cloning and Gene Regulation in Bacilli (A.T. Ganesan, S. Chang and J.A. Hoch, eds.), p. 11, Academic Press, New York.

Delfour, A. (1982). These de Doctorate d'Etat, Universite Paris VII.

Ferrari, E., Henner, D.J. and Hoch, J.A. (1981). **J. Bacteriol. 146**, 430.

Fouet, A., Klier, A. and Rapoport, G. (1982). **Molec. Gen. Genet. 186**, 399.

Gay, P., Le Coq, D., Steinmetz, M., Ferrari, E. and Hoch, J.A. (1981). **J. Bacteriol. 153**, 1424.

Hall, M.H., Gabay, J. and Schwartz, M. (1983). **EMBO J. 2**, 15.

Kroyer, J. and Chang, S. (1981). **Gene 15**, 343.

Kunst, F., Pascal, M., Lepesant-Kejzlarove, J., Lepesant, J-A., Billault, A. and Dedonder, R. (1974a). **Biochimie 56**, 1481.

Kunst, F., Pascal, M., Lepesant, J-A., Walle, J. and Dedonder, R. (1974b). **Eur. J. Biochem. 42**, 611.

Lepesant, J-A., Kunst, F., Lepesant-Kejzlarova, J. and Dedonder, R. (1972). **Molec. Gen. Genet. 118**, 135.

Lepesant, J-A., Kunst, F., Pascal, M., Lipesant-Kejzlarova, J., Steinmetz, M. and Dedonder, R. (1976). In Microbiology, 1976 (D. Schlessinger, ed.) p. 58, American Society for Microbiology, Washington, DC.

Lepesant, J-A., Lepesant-Kejzlarove, J., Pascal, M., Kunst, F., Billault, A. and Dedonder, R. (1974). **Molec. Gen. Genet. 128**, 213.

Maxam, A.M. and Gilbert. W. (1980). **Methods Enzymol. 65**, 499.

Ohmura, K., Yamazaki, H., Takeichi, Yl, Nakayama, A., Otozai, K., Yamane, K., Yamasaki, M. and Tamura, G. (1983). **Biochem. Biophys. Res. Commun. 112**, 678.

Oliver, D.B. and Beckwith, J. (1982). **Cell 30**, 311.

Petit-Glatron, M-F. and Chambert, R. (1981). **Eur. J. Biochem. 119**, 603.

Rambach, A. and Hogness, D.S. (1971). **Proc. Natl. Acad. Sci. USA 74**, 5041.

Rapoport, G., Klier, A., Billault, A., Fargette, F. and Dedonder, R. (1979). **Molec. Gen. Genet. 176**, 239.

Simon, M.I., Emerson, S.U., Shaper, J.H., Bernard, P.D. and Glazer, A.N. (1977). **J. Bacteriol. 130**, 200.

Steinmetz, M., Kunst, F. and Dedonder, R. (1976). **Molec. Gen. Genet. 148**, 281.

Takkinen, K., Petterson, R.F., Kalkkinen, N., Palva, I., Söderlund, H. and Käärïäinen, L. (1983). **Nucl. Acids Res. 11**, 237.

Walter, P. and Blobel, G. (1981). **J. Cell. Biol. 91**, 557.

Yang, M., Galizzi, A. and Henner, D. (1983). **Nucl. Acids Res. 11**, 237.

Session II: Secretion

β-LACTAMASES OF BACILLI: NATURE AND PROCESSING[1]

J. Oliver Lampen
Wu Wang
Peter S. F. Mézes
Yue-Qin Yang

Waksman Institute of Microbiology
Rutgers - The State University of New Jersey
Piscataway, New Jersey

I. TYPES OF β-LACTAMASES IN BACILLI

The synthesis and secretion of enzymes by Bacilli have long attracted intensive study, largely because proteins are released into the culture medium rather than being retained inside the barrier of the outer membrane as in Gram-negative cells. The penicillinases (β-lactamases) have proven to be useful examples for examining the nature of the secretion process. They are highly active enzymes of medium size, relatively stable to proteases, and frequently renaturable. In addition, they are related structurally to penicillin binding proteins (PBPs) of Gram-positive and Gram-negative organisms, many of which are enzymes functioning in cell wall synthesis and are themselves targets of penicillin action (Ambler, 1980; Waxman and Strominger, 1980). The major penicillinases whose structure has been investigated are listed in Table 1. The largest group (class A) are related in amino acid sequence, size and substrate specificity (penicillinases) and cross-react to varying degrees. Some have lipoprotein membrane forms which can be intermediates in production of the extracellular enzyme. All members of this class have a serine residue at the active site which undergoes acylation during the catalytic process.

[1]*Supported by grants from the National Science Foundation (PCM81-16888), Charles and Johanna Busch Memorial Fund and Miles Laboratories, Inc.*

ISBN 0-12-274160-9

Table 1. Characteristics of β-Lactamases

Class[a]		*β-Lactamase*
A	*Penicillinases; exoenzymes, 30 kd* *Related to PBPs* *Some have lipoprotein form* *Ser enzymes*[c]	*B. licheniformis* *B. cereus I* *B. cereus III (γ)*[b] *S. aureus* *E. coli* R_{TEM}
B	*Cephalosporinase; exoenzyme, 23 kd* *Metallothioprotein* (Zn^{++}) *No membrane form*	*B. cereus II*
C	*Cephalosporinase; exoenzyme, 40 kd* *Ser enzyme*[c] *No membrane form*	*E. coli ampC* *P. aeruginosa*

[a]*Ambler (1980).*

[b]*Classification tentative. Sequence not determined.*

[c]*Ser residue at active center. Sequence around Ser is different in Class A and Class C.*

There is a single example of class B, the β-lactamase II of Bacillus cereus. This enzyme is preferentially active on cephalosporins, is smaller than the other β-lactamases and is a metallothioprotein. No membrane form has been detected. Class C is typified by the chromosomal β-lactamase of Escherichia coli. It is preferentially active on cephalosporins and somewhat larger than the exoenzymes of classes A and B. There is a serine residue at the active site, but the adjacent sequence is unrelated to that of class A enzymes (Jaurin and Grundstrom, 1981).

II. LIPOPROTEIN FORMS OF β-LACTAMASES

A culture of Bacillus licheniformis 749 contains three forms of penicillinase: exo-small (29.5 kd), exo-large (31 kd) which carries eight additional residues at the N-terminus and is the first form detected in the medium, and a lipophilic membrane-bound enzyme (32 kd) which carries an additional eight residues. Its N-terminal cysteine is modified by a diglyceride in thioether linkage and an additional fatty acid is attached to the NH_2 group (Nielsen et al., 1981). This structure is identical to that of the major outer membrane lipoprotein of E. coli. Prepenicillinase, as produced in vitro, contains 34 residues beyond the N-terminus of exo-large (Chang et al., 1982). In vivo, lipophilic modification occurs first and 26 residues are then removed by a lipoprotein-specific signal peptidase (Hussain et al., 1982; Tokunaga et al., 1982) making the modified cysteine residue N-terminal. This cysteine is part of a conserved sequence Leu-Ala-Gly↓Cys-a-Ser-Asn where a is an uncharged polar residue and the site of cleavage is shown by the arrow (↓). The Cys residue is characteristically near the junction of the hydrophobic segment and the hydrophilic stretch that precedes the mature enzyme. These segments may orient the residue at the surface of the membrane in such a way that it is accessible to the enzyme which transfers the glycerol unit. A similar lipoprotein penicillinase with the thioether linkage to a diacyl glyceride is present in B. licheniformis 6346 (Nielsen et al., 1981), a strain which produces the other (related) type of B. licheniformis β-lactamase. Staphylococcus aureus also appears to produce a membrane lipoprotein form as well as exopenicillinase (Nielsen and Lampen, 1982a).

B. cereus 569 is unusual in that it can synthesize three β-lactamases. β-lactamase I is produced in large amounts and does not appear to exist as a stable membrane-bound form. The latter is true for β-lactamase II as well. A membrane-bound lipoprotein enzyme is present in strain 569, and this was initially thought to correspond to the β-lactamase I exoenzyme. However, the membrane enzyme has been purified (Connolly and Waley, 1983; Nielsen and Lampen, 1983) and shown to be the γ-penicillinase which was described by Pollock (1956) but whose existence had been questioned. It is immunologically distinct from the β-lactamase I of B. cereus 569 and seems most closely related to penicillinase of B. licheniformis 749. Growth in a medium high in amino acids (to repress protease formation) led to accumulation of a related hydrophilic exo-form. This enzyme is now termed β-lactamase III and is tentatively considered a class A enzyme.

Four lipoprotein β-lactamases have now been identified in B. licheniformis, B. cereus and S. aureus. A number of other cysteine-glyceride lipoproteins are present in these three organisms (Nielsen and Lampen, 1982b), but none have yet been identified.

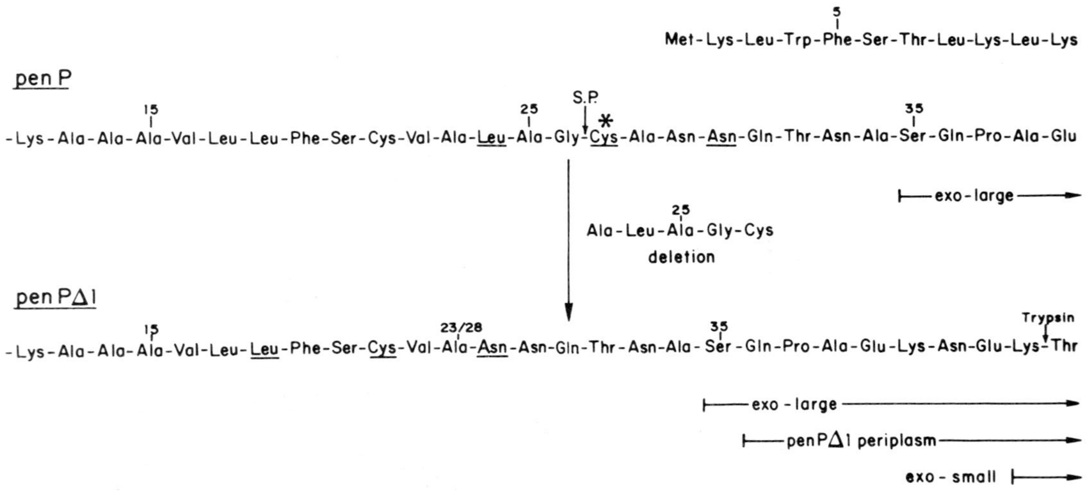

Figure 1. *The signal sequence regions of penicillinases from* penP *and* penPΔ1. *The asterisk denotes the Cys residue that undergoes lipophilic modification and becomes the N-terminus after the cleavage by signal peptidase (S.P.). The underlined residues, Leu24, Cys27, and Asn30, are the most highly conserved in the consensus sequence for lipoprotein formation. The processed forms and the site of cleavage by trypsin are indicated.*

A. Role of Lipophilic Modification in Secretion

The membrane-bound penicillinases of the bacilli probably have considerable protective value for the organism, but they are not necessarily intermediates in formation of the exocellular enzymes. To assess the role of the lipoprotein form, we deleted from the signal sequence of B. licheniformis 749/C penP gene 15 base pairs which encode 5 amino acid residues (Ala-Leu-Ala-Gly-Cys) that include the cysteine residue that undergoes lipophilic modification (Figure 1) and the site of cleavage by signal peptidase (Mezes et al., 1983). The modified gene (penPΔ1) has been cloned in E. coli and B. subtilis. In each case, the production of penicillinase is at least as great as that obtained with the original penP gene. In E. coli all of the product is transferred across the membrane. About three-fourths of it was the size of the in vitro translation product (33 kd) and one-fourth had been processed to a 31 kd periplasmic form one residue shorter than the exo-large enzyme produced in B. licheniformis (Figure 1). Although a potential site for lipophilic modification had been produced in the penPΔ1 product (residues Leu 18 through Asn 29 (Figure 1)) very little formation of lipoprotein occurred, certainly not enough to be physiologically significant.

Genes penP and penPΔ1 were cloned in Pseudomonas aeruginosa (Nielsen et al., 1983). Pseudomonas species are known to export a number of proteins to the extracellular fluid, and we wondered whether there was a fundamental difference between processing of exported proteins in Pseudomonas and in non-secretory Gram-negative organisms. No important differences were found in the production and distribution of the penicillinase in P. aeruginosa or E. coli, thus we were unable to obtain evidence for a difference in their general secretory systems. There may be special mechanisms for the transport of individual extracellular proteins in Gram-negative organisms (Coleman et al., 1983; Goebel and Hedgpeth, 1983).

Cultures of B. subtilis carrying penP or penPΔ1 and of B. licheniformis 749/C growing in 2% casein hydrolysate/salts medium were compared (Mezes et al., 1983a). The total amount of penicillinase was similar in the three cultures, although synthesis lagged behind growth in the plasmid-bearing cells. Release into the medium was also delayed, but most of the penicillinase was in the culture fluid, as exo-small, by late stationary phase. Exo-large was the initial extracellular product with the penP clone but was not detected in penPΔ1 clones unless the cells were lysed. We infer that accessibility of the cleavage site to the appropriate processing enzyme (membrane-bound) is limited by steric features. This may be a result of the shortened signal sequence.

In the B. subtilis penP clone, the cell bound penicillinase was the lipoprotein located on the outer surface of the plasma membrane, but with the penPΔ1 clone rupture of the cells released three penicillinases. The largest was the size of the in vitro translation product (34 kd). The other two had been processed but were still larger than the lipoprotein penicillinase. The penP lipoprotein was readily labeled with [^{3}H]palmitate whereas the penPΔ1 products were not labeled to a significant extent. An unusual feature of the penPΔ1 cells was that only 55 to 60% of the total penicillinase was on the outer surface of the plasma membrane. The remainder was released on mild osmotic lysis and appeared to be present in the cytoplasm or weakly bound to the inner face of the plasma membrane. From these results we conclude that the lipophilic modification is not essential for translocation, but it can enhance processing and secretion.

III. β-LACTAMASES OF BACILLUS CEREUS

B. cereus 569 has attracted considerable attention because the regulation of penicillinase synthesis has several unusual features (Abraham and Waley, 1979) and the strain produces three different β-lactamases. The β-lactamase I is very similar to the B. licheniformis 749 enzyme, but has no detectable membrane-bound form. We have compared the signal sequences of these two enzymes to obtain some indication why the protein is almost completely secreted. The β-lactamase I structural gene (penPC) was obtained as a 4.3 kb EcoRI fragment in pRW33 in E. coli RR1. It was shortened to 1.8 kb and cloned into the ClaI site of pRW33 to yield pRWY22 (6.4 kb). Our best clones produce 1,000 U of penicillinase/mg cells, all of which were cell bound. The single product (ca. 32 kd) was distributed between the membrane fraction and the periplasm in a ratio of about 3:1. No palmitate-labeled enzyme was detected. The prepenicillinase produced in a coupled transcription-translation system with pRWY22 as template had an apparent size of 36 kd (larger than the prepenicillinase of B. licheniformis 746/C). Presumably this pre-β-lactamase I is processed in E. coli to a single form about 1.3 kd larger than the exoenzyme. The precise size of the processed form is being determined.

10
<u>Met</u>-<u>Met</u>-Ile-<u>Leu</u>-Lys^{+}-Asn-Lys^{+}-Arg^{+}-Met-Leu-Lys^{+} ———

20
Ile-Gly-Ile-Cys-Val-Gly-Ile-Leu-Gly-Leu-Ser-Ile-Thr-Ser-Leu-

30 40
Glu^{-}-Ala-Phe-Thr-Gly-Glu^{-}-Ser-Leu-Gln-Val-Glu^{-}-Ala-Lys^{+}-Glu^{-}

-Lys^{+}-Thr-Gly-Gln-Val-/Lys^{+}/His^{+}/Lys^{+}·······COOH

├——— exoenzyme ———→

Figure 2. Signal sequence of B. cereus 569/H β-lactamase I. The three segments are illustrated: the N-terminal positively charged residues (1-11), the hydrophobic residues (12-26) and the charged polar stretch which precedes the mature form. The slanted lines indicate the known N-termini of the exoenzyme. The possible sites of initiation are Met1, Met2 and Leu4; the corresponding DNA triplets are ATG, ATG, and TTG.

We have cloned the penPC gene for β-lactamase I in B. subtilis on vector pRW103 (Mezes et al., 1983b). Essentially all of the product is secreted into the medium.

The sequence of the major portion of the <u>penPC</u> gene has been established. The deduced amino acid sequence of the signal peptide is shown in Figure 2. Our results confirmed the multiple N-termini of the mature forms, Lys/His/Lys/Asn-, and the trypsin peptide known to include the Ser residue in the active center: Phe-Ala-Phe-Ala-Ser-Thr-Tyr-Lys (Knott-Hunziker et al., 1979; Loosemore et al., 1980).

The sequence of the β-lactamase I (<u>penPC</u>) signal peptide accounts for its lack of a lipoprotein form despite its strong homology to the B. licheniformis enzyme. Both sequences contain an N-terminal segment with four positively charged residues, a hydrophobic stretch of 15 or 16 residues, and a long polar region which probably contains the processing sites. The signal sequence of 42 to 48 residues is consistent with the apparent difference of 5 kd between the 36 kd in vitro translation product and the 31 kd exoenzyme. The pre-β-lactamase I of B. cereus 569/H does contain a Cys residue in its signal sequence, but this is not in the characteristic consensus arrangement. Furthermore, the Cys is in the middle of the hydrophobic stretch rather than near where it joins the polar region. We suspect that this Cys is buried in the membrane bilayer and unavailable for lipid modification (Lampen et al., 1983).

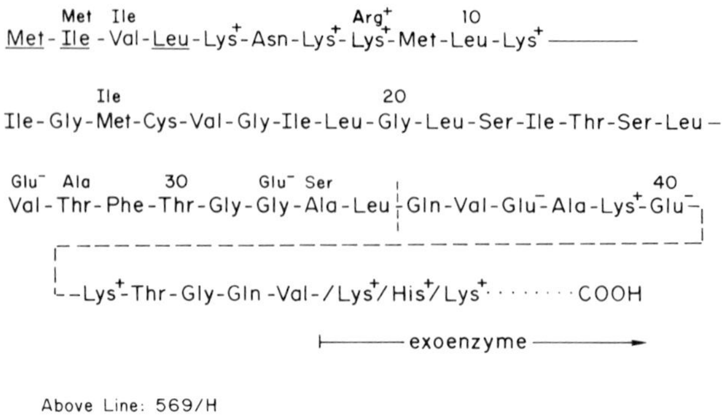

Figure 3. Signal sequence of the β-lactamase I of B. cereus 5B and its comparison with the 569/H enzyme. The sequence is presented as in Figure 2 to show the similarity. The vertical dashed line denotes the end of the extended hydrophobic stretch.

The site of initiation of translation in the penPC gene is not clear. A probable Shine-Dalgarno sequence is located immediately before the ATG codons for the first two Met residues (Figure 2). The TTG at the fourth position is only nine nucleotides away and could well be the site of initiation as it is in the PC1 β-lactamase (McLaughlin et al., 1981) and A protein (Lofdahl et al., 1983) of S. aureus.

A. β-Lactamase I of Bacillus cereus 5B

B. cereus strain 5B produces a β-lactamase I which is similar to that of strain 569/H, but appears to be somewhat larger on SDS polyacrylamide gel electrophoresis (J. Nielsen and J. Lampen, unpublished results) or by ultracentrifugation (Kogut et al., 1956). No cell-bound enzyme has been detected. Because the enzyme is produced in large quantities, we have cloned the 5B gene on pRW33 in E. coli RR1 and determined its sequence to provide additional information concerning the nature of Gram-positive signal peptides. Expression is poor, about 200 U of penicillinase/mg cells, but adequate for detection of the cloned gene. No enzyme has been detected in the culture fluid. The deduced amino acid sequence of the signal region is presented in Figure 3. The main line represents the residues of the 5B enzyme arranged to show the three segments of the sequence as for the 569/H enzyme in Figure 2. The residues above the line are the corresponding residues that are different in the 569/H pre-β-lactamase I. The sequences are generally quite

Table 2. Positively-Charged N-Terminal Segments of Gram-Positive Signal Sequences

	N-Terminus	Reference
B. licheniformis 749/C penicillinase	$M-L-K^+-L-W-F-S-T-L-K^+-L-K^+-K^+-$[a]	Neugebauer et al., 1981
B. cereus 569/H penicillinase	$M-M-I-(L)-K^+-N-K^+-R^+-M-L-K^+-$	This paper
B. cereus 5B penicillinase	$M-I-V-(L)-K^+-N-K^+-K^+-M-L-K^+-$	This paper
S. aureus PC1 penicillinase	$M-K^+-K^+-$	McLaughlin et al., 1981
S. aureus nuclease	$M-A-I-S-N-V-S-K^+-G-Q-Y-A-K^+-R^+-$	Shortle, 1983
S. aureus A protein	$(L)-K^+-K^+-K^+-N-I-Y-S-I-R^+-K^+-$	Lofdahl et al., 1983
B. subtilis α-amylase	$M-F-A-K^+-R^+-F-K^+-$	Yang et al., 1983
B. amyloliquefaciens α-amylase	$M-F-Q-K^+-R^+-K^+-R^+-T-V-S-F-R^+-$	Palva et al., 1982

[a] A, Ala; C, Cys; F, Phe; G, Gly; I, Ile; K, Lys; L, Leu; M, Met; N, Asn; Q, Gln; R, Arg; S, Ser; T, Thr; V, Val; W, Trp; Y, Tyr. (L), DNA triplet is TTG; may be site of initiation of translation.

similar. The differences do not affect the overall character of the signal region, except that the lack of charged residues at positions 27 and 32 gives the 5B sequence an unusually long hydrophobic stretch of 23 residues. This does not interfere with transport; the 5B enzyme is secreted at least as effectively as that in 569/H. The signal sequence of the 5B pre-β-lactamase I resembles the signal sequences of other Gram-positive secreted proteins in that it has relatively long positively charged N-terminal and hydrophobic segments and a charged polar segment preceding the exoenzyme.

IV. N-TERMINI OF GRAM-POSITIVE SIGNAL SEQUENCES

The signal sequences of proteins secreted by Gram-negative bacteria or eukaryotic cells characteristically possess a charged N-terminal sequence that is short and usually does not include more than two positively charged residues (cf. Vlasuk et al., 1983). Occasionally, a negatively charged residue is present. Comparable segments of Gram-positive signal sequences are almost always longer and frequently contain three or four charged residues. Table 2 presents the N-termini of those Gram-positive proteins whose signal sequence has been reported. The S. aureus PC1 pre-β-lactamase is the exception in that this segment contains only the initiator Met and two Lys residues. The prevalence of complex, charged segments suggests that binding of the N-terminus to plasma membrane is a more crucial feature in transport of the protein through the membrane of the Gram-positive cell than it is in Gram-negative cells.

REFERENCES

Abraham, E.P. and Waley, S.G. (1979). In Beta-Lactamases (J.M.T. Hamilton-Miller and J.T. Smith, eds.) p. 311, Academic Press, London.

Ambler, R.P. (1980). **Philos. Trans. R. Soc., London Ser.B Biol. Sci. 289**, 321.

Chang, C.N., Nielsen, J.B.K., Izui, K., Blobel, G. and Lampen, J.O. (1982). **J. Biol. Chem. 257**, 4340.

Coleman, K., Dougan, G. and Arbuthnott, J.P. (1983). **J. Bacteriol. 153**, 909.

Connolly, A.K. and Waley, S.G. (1983). **Biochemistry 22**, 000.

Goebel, W. and Hedgpeth, J. (1982). **J. Bacteriol. 151**, 1290.

Hussain, M., Ichihara, S. and Mizushima, S. (1982). **J. Biol. Chem. 257**, 5177.

Juarin, B. and Grundström, T. (1981). **Proc. Natl. Acad. Sci. USA 78**, 4897.

Kogut, M., Pollock, M.R. and Tridgell, E.J. (1956). **Biochem. J. 62**, 391.

Knott-Hunziker, V., Waley, S.G., Orlek, B.S. and Sammes, P.G. (1979). **FEBS Lett. 99**, 59.

Lampen, J.O., Mezes, P.S.F., Wang, W., Yang, Y.Q., Yeh, E.C.H. and Nielsen, J.B.K (1983). In Protein Transport and Secretion (D. Oxender, ed.) p. xxx, Alan R. Liss, New York.

Lofdahl, S., Guss, B., Uhlen, M., Phillipson, L. and Lindberg, M. (1983). **Proc. Natl. Acad. Sci. USA 80**, 697.

Loosemore, M.J., Cohen, S.A. and Pratt, R.F. (1980). **Biochemistry 19**, 3990.

McLaughlin, J.R., Murray, C.L. and Rabinowitz, J.C. (1981). **J. Biol. Chem. 256**, 11283.

Mezes, P.S.F., Wang, W., Yeh, E.C.H. and Lampen, J.O. (1983a). **J. Biol. Chem. 258**, 000.

Mezes, P.S.F., Yang, Y.Q., Hussain, M. and Lampen, J.O. (1983b). **FEBS Lett.**, in press.

Nielsen, J.B.K, Caulfield, M.P. and Lampen, J.O. (1981). **Proc. Natl. Acad. Sci. USA 78**, 3511.

Nielsen, J.B.K. and Lampen, J.O. (1982a). **J. Biol. Chem. 257**, 4490.

Nielsen, J.B.K. and Lampen, J.O. (1982b). **J. Bacteriol. 152**, 315.

Nielsen, J.B.K. and Lampen, J.O. (1983). **Biochemistry 22**, 000.

Nielsen, J.B.K., Mezes, P.S.F. and Lampen, J.O. (1983). **J. Bacteriol.**, in press.

Palva, I., Sarvas, M., Lehtovaara, P., Sibakov, M. and Kääriäinen, L. (1982). **Proc. Natl. Acad. Sci. USA 79**, 5282.

Pollock, M.R. (1956). **J. Gen. Microbiol. 15**, 154.

Shortle, D. (1983). **Gene 22**, 181.

Tokunaga, M., Loranger, J.M., Wolfe, P.B. and Wu, H.C. (1983). **J. Biol. Chem. 257**, 9922.

Vlasuk, G.P., Inouye, S., Ito, H., Itakura, K. and Inouye, M. (1983). **J. Biol. Chem. 258**, 7141.

Waxman, D.J. and Strominger, J.L. (1980). **J. Biol. Chem. 255**, 3964.

Yang, M., Galizzi, A. and Henner, D. (1983). **Nucl. Acids Res. 11**, 237.

A GENETIC APPROACH TO LEVANSUCRASE SECRETION IN BACILLUS SUBTILIS[1]

Dominique Le Coq
Pascal Ratet
Michel Steinmetz
Philippe Gay

Laboratoire Génétique et Membranes
Institut Jacques Monod
CNRS et Université Paris
Paris, France

I. INTRODUCTION

The successful experiments of Palva and coworkers (1983), who obtained α_2-interferon production and secretion in Bacillus subtilis by fusion of the INFα_2 gene with the sequence of the α-amylase gene encoding the signal peptide, emphasize the importance of the secretion processes in the biotechnology of bacilli.

Gene fusion has been used for some years as a genetic tool in an approach to protein export in Escherichia coli. By this technique, Talmage et al. (1980) demonstrated that the β-lactamase signal peptide of the plasmid pBR322 was able to promote the secretion of rat proinsulin in bacteria. Fusions of the lamB gene with lacZ showed that a signal sequence is necessary but not sufficient to ensure the secretion of a given protein (Moreno et al., 1980; Hall et al., 1982). Such fusions of lacZ with substantial parts of lamB resulted in lethal products, presumably by blocking the secretory apparatus (Bassford and Beckwith, 1979; Emr and Silhavy, 1980). Similar interpretation was made for lethal effects due to overproduction of secreted proteins in E.

[1]*This work was supported by a grant from Mission des biotechnologies, Ministre de la Recherche et de l'Industrie.*

ISBN 0-12-274160-9

coli (Bremmer et al., 1980; Willemot and Cornelis, 1983). This lethality had been utilized to select resistant mutants which were found to be affected by mutations that prevent interactions between the proteins to be exported and the secretory apparatus. Thus these mutations belong to two major classes, they affect either the signal sequences (Emr and Silhavy, 1980) or the secretory apparatus (Oliver et al., 1982).

We described elsewhere the cloning and the expression in E. coli of the structural gene sacB coding for B. subtilis levansucrase (Gay et al., 1983). Levansucrase (EC.2.4.1.10) catalyzes transfructorylation from sucrose to various acceptors, which results in two main physiological reactions, levan synthesis, and sucrose hydrolysis. We have found that E. coli cells which synthesize active levansucrase are poisoned by the presence of sucrose in the culture medium. This property allowed the isolation of plasmids bearing mutations in the cloned sacB gene. Genetics of sacB was developed in E. coli and B. subtilis, including the utilization of deletions mapping in B. subtilis (Steinmetz et al., 1983).

We describe here the isolation of two classes of mutants that should allow a genetic approach of levansucrase secretion. The first class consists of nonsense mutations identified with E. coli nonsense suppressors. The second class consists in missense mutations that seem to affect the secretion of the protein. The study of the two classes of mutations brings genetic evidence concerning the involvement of a prelevansucrase in enzyme secretion. This preprotein is characterized in an accompanying paper (Fouet et al., 1983).

II. MATERIALS AND METHODS

A. Bacterial Strains and Plasmids

Bacterial strains and plasmids used are listed in Table 1. The pLS deletion kit is a collection of plasmid derivatives of pJH101 (Ferrari et al., 1982) which were obtained by cloning partially deleted sacB material (Steinmetz et al., 1983). Lvs^+/Lvs^- stands for the expression of either wild-type or mutant levansucrase in both E. coli and B. subtilis. New sacB mutations were numbered according to the number of the plasmid in which they appeared. Suc^r/Suc^s stands for sucrose resistance versus sensitivity.

Table 1. Plasmids and Bacterial Strains

	Genotype and comments	Origin
Plasmids		
pLS50	pJH101 derivative (Ferrari et al., 1982)	This laboratory
pLS deletion kit	see Figure 2	This laboratory
pLS 102 to 134	pLS50 derivatives carrying, respectively, sacB 102 to 134	This paper
B. subtilis		
QB165	sacA321 $sacS^{c}2$ trpC2 hisA1	S.A. Lepesant
QB174	sacA321 $sacS^{c}2$ trpC2	S.A. Lepesant
CS102-134	sacA321 $sacS^{c}2$ trpC2 sacB102-134	This paper
E. coli		
CG4446	gal1 gal2 str^{r}	O. Huisman
CA165 (CGSC 4980)	thi1 relA1 lacI22 lacz13 spoT1 supB69	B. Bachmann
CA167 (CGSC 5401)	thi1 relA1 lacI22 lacz13 spoT1 supC70	B. Bachmann
AB2300 (CGSC 2300)	ilvD188 argH1 purF1 xyl7 supL2 supE44	
CR34 (CGSC 3642)	thr1 leuB6 thyA6 thi1 deoC1 lacY1 strA67 tonA21 λ^{-} supE44	
MX536 (CGSC 5351)	trp46 his90 arg47 recA1 lacZ53 relA1 nalA20 λ^{-}, F14-13 ilvE supU argH	

B. Media

As described previously, SG stands for solid Spizizen medium supplemented with 2% sucrose and 0.1% glucose. SGHCM stands for the same medium supplemented with additional casein hydrolysate : 500 mg/l and chloramphenicol : 5 mg/l. (This concentration of chloramphenicol was retained to select either Cm^r E. coli or B. subtilis bearing the pC194 chloramphenicol resistance gene [Ferrari et al., 1982]).

C. Genetic Procedures and Levansucrase Assays

The genetic procedures were as described previously. Levansucrase production by B. subtilis colonies was identified by the accumulation of levan around the colonies grown in SG or SGHCM. Enzyme production by E. coli colonies grown in MM glycerol solid medium was identified by a colored test which reveals glucose originating from levansucrase acting on sucrose. After a lysozyme treatment of the colonies (one 10 µl drop of 10 mg/ml lysozyme in 10^{-3} EDTA), sucrose 50% was added and the plates incubated at 37°C. Glucose is revealed by addition of a drop of GOD jewel reagent (Boehringer). Levansucrase assay in toluenized bacteria. Bacteria (E. coli or B. subtilis) are harvested by centrifugation, washed twice by K phosphate buffer (0.1 M, pH 6) and resuspended in the same buffer in the presence of sucrose, 0.25 M and 2% toluene. The suspension is vortexed for 2 minutes and then incubated at 37°C. Glucose is assayed with GOD perid reagents (Boehringer) after removal of the cells by centrifugation.

D. Expression of Cloned Genes in Minicells

The first experiments were carried out in collaboration with Dr. G. Rapoport who gave us the AR1062 strain and the techniques (derived from Rambach and Hogness, 1977), described in the accompanying paper (Fouet et al., 1983). [^{35}S]methionine 10^3 Ci/mmole was from NEN (ref. NEG 009T).

III. RESULTS

A. Isolation of Mutations in the Cloned sacB Gene

E. coli hosts of pLS50 or pLS8 are Lvs$^+$, that is they synthesize active levansucrase. When sucrose is added to the culture medium, the cells undergo lysis within less than one hour. We showed previously (Steinmetz et al., 1983) that survivors are affected either by chromosomal mutations which also result in a loss of ampicillin resistance or by plasmid mutations located within the sacB gene. Plasmid pLS50 (Figure 1) DNA was subjected to hydroxylamine mutagenesis according to Hashimoto and Sekiguchi (1976). After 24 hours of treatment at 37°C, salts were removed by Sephadex G50 chromatography. The treated DNA was used to transform strain CG4446 (devoid of any known suppressor mutation, O. Huisman, personal communication). The Cm^R colonies were patched and replica plated onto LB CM medium containing 60 mM sucrose. Sucrose resistant mutants were isolated. They usually represented approximately 4% of the Cm^R colonies. Fifteen independent mutants were isolated from separate transformation experiments. Plasmid DNA was then extracted from each mutant and was used to transform the original host CG4446. In all the cases, the Cm^R transformants thus obtained were sucrose resistant (Suc^R), indicating that the mutations were borne by the plasmids. Tested in solid medium for levansucrase activity, 9 mutants were found to be strictly negative and 6 gave a weak response. Restriction analysis did not allow us to find any

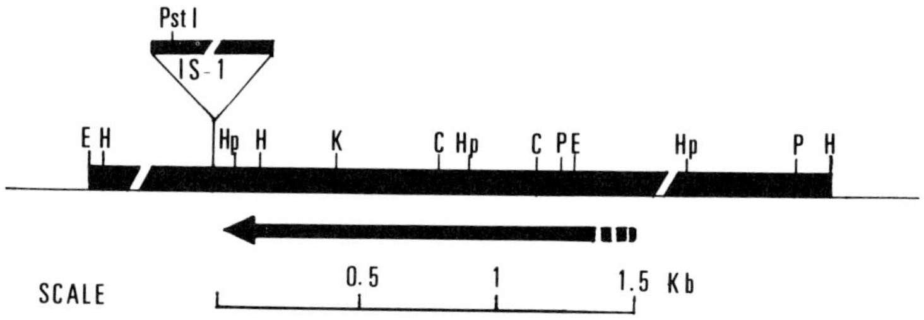

Figure 1. Physical map of plasmid pLS50 insert. C, E, H, Hp, K, P and Pst stand respectively for ClaI, EcoRI, HpaI, KpnI, PvuII and PstI restriction sites. The insertion of IS-1 is responsible for tet gene reactivation. The sequence encoding levansucrase is outlined by the arrow. The dotted end of the arrow indicates the sequence encoding the amino terminus signal peptide.

difference between the mutant plasmids and the original pLS50 DNA. These results indicated that in all the mutants sucrose resistance very likely originated from point mutations induced by the hydroxylamine treatment and located in the sacB gene.

B. Introduction of the Mutation in B. subtilis Genetic Mapping

Mutations were introduced in B. subtilis by congression. Strain QB165 was transformed by each mutant plasmid, the DNA of which was mixed with DNA from strain QB174 (a His^+ derivative of QB165). Each mutant plasmid allowed the isolation of His^+ Lev^- Cm^S colonies, thus giving rise to 15 new sacB mutants in B. subtilis.

The localization of the mutations sacB 101, 102, 111, 113, 115, 118, 122 and 134 was obtained by deletion mapping as previously reported (Steinmetz et al., 1983). The mutant B. subtilis strains were transformed to chloramphenicol resistance by the plasmids of the deletion kit illustrated in Figure 2 which all derived from pJH101 (Ferrari et al., 1982). The simultaneous transformation to the Lvs^+ phenotype indicate that the integrated plasmid bears the wild-type sequence corresponding to the mutation. Figure 2 gives the localization of all the known sacB mutations. It is noteworthy that most mutations except sacB113 map in the

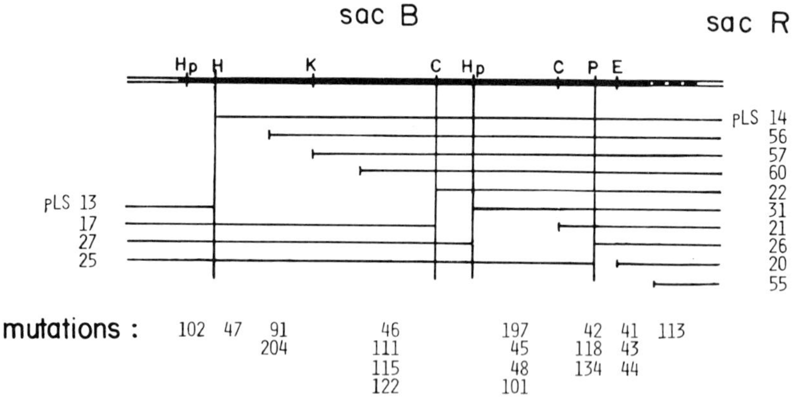

Figure 2. Genetic map of sacB. This map includes all the known alleles. It was established by deletion mapping using the plasmids indicated. Their insertion is represented by a line (Steinmetz et al., 1983).

sequence encoding the mature enzyme. sacB113 is located within a 100 base pair segment upstream and may be in the signal sequence.

C. Identification of Nonsense Mutations

Suppression of potential nonsense mutations in the cloned sacB gene was tested by introduction of the mutant plasmids in various E. coli suppressor strains. Hydroxylamine mutagenesis is supposed to be specific and to cause GC/AT transitions. Then amber mutations (UAG) or ochre mutations (UAA) must originate either from CAG (glutamine), UGG (tryptophan) or CAA (glutamine). On the basis of this specificity, regardless of the level of the potential suppression (Bossi and Roth, 1980) wild-type enzyme has to be recovered either by ochre glutamine or by amber tryptophan suppressors. Strain CA165 (supB, ochre glutamine) and strain MX536 (supU, amber tryptophan) were transformed by the mutant plasmids (leaky mutants were not tested). Among 9 mutants tested, 6 were suppressed. Table 2 presents an extended study of the suppression pattern of these 6 mutations. It indicates clearly that sacB 101, 113, 115 and 134 which are suppressed by supB but not by supE are ochre mutants likely originating from CAA codons.

Table 2. Suppression Pattern of Six sacB Mutants

Supressor	*sacB mutation*					
	101	*102*	*113*	*115*	*118*	*134*
supB (UAA, glu)	+(±)	−(+)	+(+)	+(+)	+(−)	+(+)
supC (UAA, tyr)	−(−)	−(−)	+(±)	±(−)	±(−)	±(−)
supL (UAA, lys)	−(−)	−(+)	−(−)	±(−)	−(−)	±(±)
supE (UAG, glu)	−(−)	−(−)	−(−)	−(−)	−(−)	−(−)
supU (UAG, trp)	−(−)	−(+)	−(−)	−(−)	−(−)	−(−)

The activity of levan sucrase was tested on the colonies. + indicates a strong suppression while ± indicates a very low level. The sign between the brackets gives a rough estimation of the activity tested in toluenized bacteria: + stands for wild-type level; ±, at least one order of magnitude lower than +; −, no activity detected.

D. Characterization of Cryptic Levansucrase in Mutants

Toluene treatment in bacteria is known to destroy the permeability barriers and allow the assay of intracellular enzymes without destroying the cells. We verified that in Lvs^+ E. coli the specific activity of levansucrase is approximately the same when measured either in crude extracts or in toluenized cells (approximately 0.7 to 0.9 U/mg of bacterial protein).

In Table 2 we indicated between brackets a rough estimation of the activity measured in toluenized bacteria. No activity was found in sacB118 suppressed by supB, while suppression seems very efficient on the plates. This indicates that the suppressed enzyme is sensitive to toluenization, which means that the suppressor tested did not restore the wild-type sequence of the protein. In the case of sacB102 an opposite result was found. A weak activity was revealed in toluenized bacteria while nothing could be detected on the colonies. Such a result should reflect a higher sensitivity of the toluene assay. Nevertheless, a similar, but more clear-cut result was observed with two missense mutations, sacB111 and sacB122. These mutations had been classified as leaky since we had detected very low activity on solid medium. Toluenized bacteria, however, exhibited nearly the same activity as the Lvs^+ control. Such a result should suggest that these mutations affect the secretion process. Since they are localized in the second half of the gene, thus far from the signal sequence, they should be of great interest.

E. Expression of the Mutant Plasmids in Minicells

The plasmids bearing the nonsense mutations, as well as plasmids pLS111 and pLS122, were introduced in strain AR1062 which segregates minicells at 37°C. Minicells were isolated by either sucrose or glycerol gradient centrifugation and allowed to incorporate [^{35}S]-labeled methionine. Extracts were subjected to electrophoresis in slab acrylamide gels followed by autoradiography. Figure 3 compares the electrophoresis pattern of extracts obtained respectively from Lvs^+ minicells (AR1062 [pLS50]) or from nonsense sacB115 minicells (AR1062 [pLS115]). Two bands are clearly lacking in the sacB115 mutant due to a simple nonsense mutation. This can be easily explained if we assume that these bands represent both levansucrase and prelevansucrase including an amino terminal signal sequence. This assumption was verified by DNA sequencing (see accompanying paper by Fouet et al., 1983). Lane 1 shows an extract of Lvs^+ minicells which

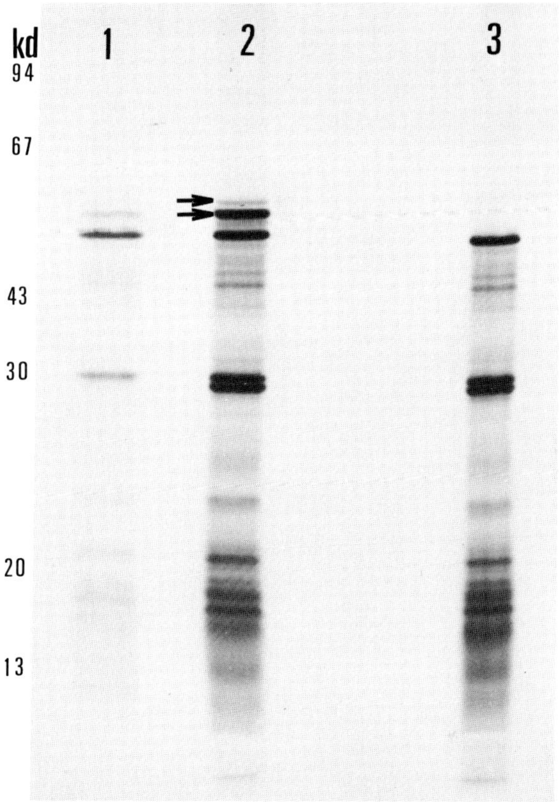

Figure 3. Genetic evidence for the existence of pre-levansucrase. This figure is an autoradiography of a 10% acrylamide slab gel. Molecular weight markers and added unlabeled levansucrse were revealed by Coomassie blue staining. Lane 1, extract from Lvs$^+$ minicells isolated by sucrose gradient centrifugation; lane 2, extract from Lvs$^+$ minicells isolated by glycerol gradient centrifugation; lane 3, extract from sacB115 *minicells. The arrows point to m.w. markers: 94,000; 67,000; 50,000 (levansucrase); 30,000; 20,100 and 14,400. β-lactamase and pre-β-lactamase appear as heavy bands at the level of the 30,000 dalton marker.*

has been purified in a sucrose gradient. It is interesting to note that these minicells did not retain mature β-lactamase while they retain mature levansucrase. Since the incubation of Lvs$^+$ E. coli in the presence of sucrose likely results in membrane fragility, we may assume that the visualized proteins are either intracellular or membrane bound.

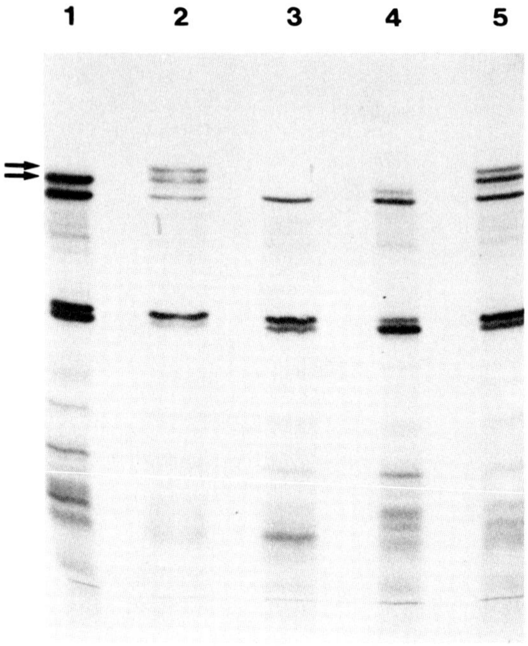

1: pLS50

2: pLS50 -(ethanol)

3: pLS134

4: pLS113

5: pLS111

Figure 4. Expression of various mutants in minicells. Lane 1, Lvs^{+} extract; lane 2, Lvs^{+} minicells' extract after incorporation of [^{35}S]methionine in the presence of 9% ethanol; and lanes 3, 4 and 5, extracts from <u>*sacB134*</u>*,* <u>*sacB113*</u> *and* <u>*sacB111*</u>*, respectively. The arrows point to prelevansucrase and levansucrase.*

This should be consistent with previous results showing that osmotive shock releases only part of the enzyme in the shock fluid (Gay et al., 1983).

Ethanol is known to be a membrane effector that interferes with signal proteolysis (Daniels et al., 1981; Enequist et al., 1981). Figure 4 (lanes 1 and 2) shows that the addition of ethanol 9% in the incorporation mixture of Lvs^{+} minicells strongly enhance the intensity of both pre-β-lactamase and prelevansucrase bands. An extract from <u>sacB111</u> minicells is analyzed in lane 5. The pattern looks very similar to lane 2 just as if the sacB111 mutation was affecting the processing of prelevansucrase thus resulting in a secretory mutation.

IV. DISCUSSION

As stated in the introduction, some hybrid proteins resulting from gene fusions such as leuB - lacZ are lethal for E. coli and allow the screening of secretion mutants (Emr and Silhavy, 1980; Oliver et al., 1982). These mutations affect mainly the interaction of the signal peptide with a so-called secretory apparatus and then prevent what can be regarded as an initiation step in protein secretion.

Sucrose sensitivity in Lvs$^+$ E. coli is only due to the presence of active levansucrase within the periplasmic space. It allows the screening of mutants that have either lost enzyme activity or lost enzyme secretability whatever this concept may include. One may imagine secretory mutants affected in steps other than the initiation of secretion. Wu et al. (1983) reported recently the characterization of a mutation in a λ2 immunoglobulin gene, located outside and downstream from the signal sequence which results in intracellular accumulation of the protein. We describe here the isolation of a missense mutation localized in the middle of the sacB gene which results in enzyme crypticity and in an unusual processing of prelevansucrase. Careful biochemical investigation is needed to confirm the secretory nature of the mutation which cannot be easily predicted in a model involving cotranslational secretion (Smith et al., 1980).

Genetics of nonsense mutations in B. subtilis has always been limited due to the low number of suppressors available (Palva et al., 1983) and to the lack of biochemical information concerning these suppressors. The expression of sacB in E. coli and the easy screening of the negative mutants allowed the characterization of nonsense mutants utilizing E. coli suppressor mutations. Further comparisons between the suppression patterns of the mutations in E. coli and B. subtilis should bring additional information concerning B. subtilis nonsense suppressors.

Nonsense mutations in sacB resulted in the loss of two proteins in minicell extracts, levansucrase and prelevansucrase. They have also resulted in the appearance of new products: the aminoterminus peptides resulting from the interruption of the levansucrase chain. We did not yet characterize these peptides which we like to use to study the processing of the signal peptide.

Action of suppressors on nonsense mutations may result either in a wild-type protein, or in missense mutations. Various substitutions of amino acids can be tested as well defined sites of the protein. We have seen in Table 2 that these substitutions may modulate enzyme activity. Any similar modulation of secretability should be of great interest.

REFERENCES

Bassford, P. and Beckwith, J. (1979). **Nature 277**, 538.

Bossi, L. and Roth, J.R. (1980). **Nature 286**, 123.

Bremer, E., Beck, E., Hindennach, I., Sonntag, I. and Henning, V. (1980). **Mol. Gen. Genet. 179**, 13.

Daniels, C.J., Bole, D.G., Quay, S.C. and Oxenderd, L. (1981). **Proc. Natl. Acad. Sci. USA 78**, 5396.

Emr, S.D. and Silhavy, T.J. (1980). **J. Mol. Biol. 141**, 63.

Enequist, H.G., Hirst, T., Harayama, S., Hardy, S.J.S. and Randall, L.L. (1981). **Eur. J. Biochem. 116**, 227.

Ferrari, F., Ferrari, E. and Hoch, J.A. (1982). **J. Bacteriol. 152**, 780.

Fouet, A., Aubert, E., Arnaud, M., Le Coq, D., Klier, A. and Rapoport. (1983). This issue.

Gay, P., Le Coq, D., Steinmetz, M., Ferrari, E. and Hoch, J.A. (1983). **J. Bacteriol. 153**, 1424.

Hall, M.N, Schwartz, M. and Silhavy, T.J. (1982). **J. Mol. Biol. 156**, 93.

Hashimoto, T. and Sekiguchi, M. (1976). **J. Bacteriol. 127**, 1561.

Mellando, R.P., Vineula, E. and Salas, M. (1976). **Eur. J. Biochem. 65**, 213.

Moreno, F., Fowler, A.V., Hall, M., Silhavy, T.J., Zabin, I. and Schwartz, M. (1980). **Nature 286**, 356.

Oliver, D.B., Kumamoto, C., Quinlan, M. and Beckwith, J. (1982). **Ann. Microbiol. Institut Pasteur 133A**, 105.

Palva, I., Lehtovaara, P., Käärïänen, L., Sibakov, M., Cantell, K., Schein, C.H., Kashinagi, K. and Weissmann, C. (1983). **Gene 22**, 229.

Rambach, A. and Hogness, D.S. (1977). **Proc. Natl. Acad. Sci. USA 74**, 5041.

Steinmetz, M., Le Coq, D., Bendjemia, H. and Gay, P. (1983). **Molec. Gen. Genet**, in press.

Smith, W.P., Tai, P.C., Murphy J.R. and Davis, B.D. (1980). **J. Bacteriol. 141**, 184.

Talmadge, K., Stahl, S. and Gilbert, W. (1980). **Proc. Natl. Acad. Sci. USA 77**, 3369.

Willemot, K. and Cornelis, P. (1983). **J. Gen. Microbiol. 129**, 311.

Wu, G.D., Hozumi, N. and Murialdo, H. (1983). **Cell 33**, 77.

SECRETION OF FOREIGN GENE PRODUCTS BY THE AID OF A BACILLUS SECRETION VECTOR

M. Sibakov
P. Lehtovaara
R. Pettersson
K. Lundström
N. Kalkkinen
I. Ulmanen
K. Takkinen
L. Kääriäinen
I. Palva

Recombinant DNA Laboratory
University of Helsinki
Helsinki, Finland

M. Sarvas

National Public Health Institute
Helsinki, Finland

I. INTRODUCTION

A derivative of the plasmid pUB110, containing the promoter and signal sequence region of the α-amylase gene was constructed to be used as a general expression and secretion vector for foreign products in Bacillus subtilis. The applicability of the vector was studied with TEM β-lactamase, human α2 interferon and some viral membrane proteins. All of them were expressed, but with a much lower efficienty than α-amylase. The secretory proteins were accurately processed and secreted whereas the membrane proteins appeared to be mainly cell-associated. Possible reasons for the significant differences in the yields of foreign proteins are discussed.

ISBN 0-12-274160-9

II. CONSTRUCTION OF A SECRETION VECTOR

Cloning of the α-amylase gene from B. amyloliquefaciens was done by the direct shotgun procedure using pUB110 plasmid as a vector (Palva, 1982). This resulted in a hybrid plasmid pKTH10, bearing a 2.3 kb insert. When it was transformed into IH6064, a B. subtilis host, α-amylase was found in the supernatant at all stages of growth. Under optimal conditions up to 5 g/l of α-amylase were obtained. The stability of the clone was studied by growing it in a large volume without antibiotic pressure. The synthesis continued for 45 hours and no loss of plasmids was detected.

To further increase the amount of α-amylase produced and secreted, a set of B. subtilis hybrids was constructed in which the synthesis of indigenous α-amylase was enhanced by the presence of various combinations of amyR, amyS, papS and pap-9 alleles. These alleles are known to enhance the basic level of secretion. However, when the plasmid pKTH10 was introduced into these hybrids, none of them secreted more α-amylase than the wild-type parent IH6064 harboring the same plasmid (Sibakov et al., 1983).

A restriction map of pKTH10 was constructed and the α-amylase gene was sequenced together with its flanking sequences (Palva et al., 1981; Takkinen et al., 1983). It coded for a protein with a molecular weight of 54,778. Before and after the gene, hair-pin loop structures like typical prokaryotic termination signals were found. The structure preceding the gene suggested that α-amylase was translated from a monocistronic messenger (Takkinen et al., 1983). The length of the messenger RNA has been determined and it confirms the above data.

An unusually long signal sequence with 31 amino acid residues was identified. It was shown that B. amyloliquefaciens α-amylase was correctly cleaved after the C-terminal alanine of the signal sequence in B. subtilis also (Takkinen et al., 1983).

The nucleotide sequence revealed a very strong Shine-Dalgarno sequence showing extensive homology to the 3' end of 16S rRNA. Also, stretches showing homology to the proposed -35 and -10 regions recognized by RNA polymerase $E\sigma^{55}$ were found.

The knowledge of the structure of the promoter and signal sequence region of the α-amylase gene, that of an efficiently expressed and secreted protein gave us a good basis to construct a secretion vector. Plasmid pKTH29 containing the signal sequence region of the α-amylase gene together with 65 first N-terminal amino acid residues from the secreted enzyme was used for modifications. Since there

```
         -31     -29                                                          +37
         Met Phe Gly ---------------------------------------------- Ile Thr Ala
pKTH37   ATG ATT CAA ---------------------------------------------- ATC ACT GCC C[GG AAT TCC]

         -31     -29                                          +30
         Met Phe Gly -------------------------------- Glu His Leu
pKTH38   ATG ATT CAA -------------------------------- GAA CAT TTA TC[G GAA TTCC]

         -31     -29                            +17
         Met Phe Gly ---------------------- Asn Asp Gly
pKTH87   ATG ATT CAA ---------------------- AAC GAC GGC C[GG AAT TCC]

         -31     -29                   +13
         Met Phe Glu -------------- Trp Tyr Thr
pKTH88   ATG ATT CAA -------------- TGG TAT ACG CC[G GAA TTCC]

         -31     -29         -26
         Met Phe Gly Lys Arg Lys
pKTH39   ATG ATT CAA AAA CGA AAG C[GG AAT TCC]
```

Figure 1. The nucleotide sequences of the 3′ ends of the modified α-amylase gene with EcoRI sites. Most of the structural part of the α-amylase gene was removed by E. coli exonuclease III and S1 nuclease, and EcoRI linker (boxed sequence) was added to the 3′ end (Palva, 1983).

were no unique restriction sites within the stretch of 65 amino acids ExoIII-SI and Bal31 digestions were used to remove the extra amino acids. These treatments created a series of plasmids (Figure 1). Because it was not known whether cleavage specificity would be the same, if the amino acid following the C-terminal alanine was changed from the original valine, we wanted to have plasmids coding for a few amino acids in addition to the signal sequence. Plasmids were provided with DNA linkers and 30 of them were sequenced.

To improve the secretion vector for the study of truncated proteins devoid of their natural translation stop signals, a universal stop codon, TGA, in all three reading frames was constructed (Pettersson et al., 1983). This synthetic oligonucleotide was joined to two modified vectors so that any gene could be inserted between the α-amylase signal sequence and the stop codon.

III. EXPRESSION AND SECRETION OF FOREIGN PROTEINS

A. TEM β-Lactamase

As a first example to test the secretion vector, TEM β-lactamase was chosen. For joining of the β-lactamase gene, its own signal sequence was removed with ExoIII-SI digestion. This yielded plasmid pKTH33 devoid of the whole signal suquence and the first amino acid from the N-terminus of β-lactamase (Figure 2). After adding linkers to the modified gene, it was ligated with the secretion vector pool (Palva et al., 1982). Four positive transformants were partially sequenced. Hybrids pKTH78 and pKTH83 containing the full signal sequence of α-amylase secreted β-lactamase so efficiently that over 95% of the enzyme was found in the supernatant at all growth phases. pKTH84 having 14 extra amino acids from the soluble α-amylase also secreted β-lactamase but with a surprisingly low efficiency. On the other hand, pKTH86 which had a truncated signal sequence with 7 amino acids missing from the C-terminus of the α-amylase signal sequence yielded a cell-bound enzyme (Table 1).

The exact signal sequence cleavage site was determined from the purified hybrid proteins by amino acid sequencing. In the construction of pHTH83, where the original cleavage site of alanine-valine was retained, all molecules were correctly cleaved. In the construction of pKTH78, which had the full signal-sequence but the cleavage site was altered from alanine-valine to alanine-glutamic acid, all molecules

```
                   -23        -20             -16                                                                  -1  +1         +4
β -lactamase Met Ser Ile Gln His Phe Arg Val Ala Leu Ile Pro Phe Phe Ala Ala Phe Cys Leu Pro Val Phe Ala His Pro Glu Thr
             5'ATG AGT ATT CAA CAT TTC CGT GTC GCC CTT ATT CCC TTT TTT GCG GCA TTT TGG CTT CCT GTT TTT GCT CAC CCA GAA ACG
                                                                                              EcoRI linker  Pro Glu Thr
pKTH 33                                                                                      5'GGA ATT CCC CCA GAA ACG
```

Figure 2. The nucleotide sequence of the 5' end of the modified β-lactamase gene with EcoRI linkers and the signal sequence of the β-lactamase gene (Palva, 1983).

Table 1. Secretion of β-Lactamase in B. subtilis After Joining to Different Secretion Vector Constructions

Construction	*IU/ml β-lactamase*		*Processing*
	Cells	*Supernatant*	
+14 (pKTH84)	*35*	*450*	*inaccurate*
+ 4 (pKTH83)	*75*	*1850*	*accurate (100%)*
- 1 (pKTH78)	*80*	*2000*	*accurate (70%)*
- 7 (pKTH86)	*220*	*30*	*---*

were correctly or almost correctly (within two amino acids) processed. The construction of pKTH84 bearing the 14 extra amino acids from the soluble α-amylase yielded three subpopulations, none of which was correctly processed (Table 1).

Our experiments with TEM-β-lactamase confirmed the original hypothesis that the signal sequence alone is sufficient to translocate a protein from the cell. Also, it showed that the amino acid following the C-terminal alanine can, at least in this case, be altered from the original valine to glutamic acid without altering the specificity of cleavage. Finally, it confirmed the indispensable role of the first seven proximal amino acids of the signal sequence in the processing of the product.

B. Human α2 Interferon

We also studied the expression and secretion of human α2 interferon when joined to the secretion vector (Palva et al., 1983). The mature IFN-α2 had been cloned in pBR322 and was obtained from Professor C. Weissmann. After joining the modified gene to the appropriate vectors, the two constructions were further characterized: pKTH68 contained six extra amino acids after the C-terminal alinine retaining the natural cleavage site. pKTH93 has only one additional amino acid (from HindIII-linker) and the cleavage site is altered from alanine-valine to alanine-alanine. When grown in liquid cultures both constructions expressed and secreted IFN-α2 at all growth phases. Over 90% was found in the supernatant and in both cases the signal sequence was correctly cleaved (Table 2). These findings further confirmed

Table 2. Secretion of Interferon Synthesized in Transformed B. subtilis

Construction	*Interferon Activity IU/ml Original Culture*		*Secreted Products*
	Cells	*Supernatant*	
pKTH68 (+ 4)	*6000*	*200,000*	*6 extra N-terminal amino acids*
pKTH93 (- 1)	*6000*	*100,000*	*1 extra N-terminal amino acid*

the results obtained with β-lactamase: it seems possible to change the amino acid following the C-terminal alanine without changing the processing specificity.

C. Viral Membrane Proteins

As an example of membrane proteins, we have studied some viral glycoproteins which serve as possible models for vaccine production. Many of these proteins are anchored to the membrane via a C-terminal hydrophobic sequence which most likely ought to be removed in order to get a secreted product in B. subtilis. This may result in the loss of natural stop signals. Therefore, we studied the expression and secretion of Vesicular Stomatitis Virus G protein and Semliki Fores Virus E1 and E2 proteins in a secretion vector containing the stop oligonucleotide. The size of the proteins in the immunoblotting analysis indicated that Bacillus recognizes the universal stop codon. All of the proteins tested were expressed, but the product remained mainly cell-associated. Nothing can be said about the signal sequence cleavage at this stage.

IV. DISCUSSION

Our studies indicate that foreign proteins can be expressed with a Bacillus promoter and secreted with a Bacillus signal sequence. However, the level of expression of foreign proteins was significantly lower than that of α-

Table 3. Expression and Secretion of Foreign Proteins in *Bacillus subtilis*

Protein	Source	Relative Yield[a]	Secretion %[a]	Stability of Product
Secretory proteins				
α-amylase	*B. amyloliquefaciens*	100	100	+++
TEM-β-lactamase	*E. coli*	10	>95	++
α2 interferon	human	1	>95	+
Membrane proteins				
G	Vesicular Stomatitis Virus	0.1	<1	-
E1	Semliki Forest Virus	0.1	<1	-
E2	Semliki Forest Virus	0.1	<1	-

[a]Measured in liquid cultures at 5 hours beyond midlogarithmic growth phase

Table 4. Protease Activity of Bacillus subtilis Hosts

	Relative Protease Activity[a]	
Strain[b]	Serine-	Metallo-
IH6064[c]	25	75
IH6135[c]	25	-
IH6140[c]	<1	-

[a]Protease activities were measured according to Rinderknecht et al. (1968).

[b]All strains are B. subtilis Marburg derivatives.

[c]Strain constructions as described elsewhere (Sibakov, in preparation).

amylase (Table 3). The kinetics of α-amylase, β-lactamase and interferon in B. subtilis compare well until the late stationary phase of growth. After that the α-amylase is further synthesized up to 45 hours, whereas the accumulation of foreign proteins cease and the activity slowly disappears, most likely due to Bacillus exoproteases (Table 3). To get rid of the proteases we constructed a B. subtilis strain with a greatly reduced level of total exoproteases (Table 4). Most of our studies have been carried out with IH6140 having only residual serine protease activity. However, even this low amount of the enzyme appears to be enough to degrade the more sensitive foreign proteins. Whether proteases alone can explain the substantial differences in the yields needs further clarification.

Our data on the amount of mRNA with α-amylase, β-lactamase and E2-protein show that differences at the protein level cannot be explained by differences in the amount of messenger produced. Also, the amount of plasmid DNA obtained from the different hybrids is roughly equal (unpublished observation) and the codon usage for α-amylase appears to be random (Takkinen et al., 1983). However, to test the validity of Bacillus subtilis as a cloning host more data on the kinetics of the system is needed. In addition, the behavior of protease resistant proteins ought to be studied and finally more effort put in the construction of a protease deficient host.

REFERENCES

Palva, I. (1982). **Gene 19**, 81.
Palva, I. (1983). Ph.D. Thesis, University of Helsinki, Finland.
Palva, I., Lehtovaara, P., Kääriäinen, L., Sibakov, M., Cantell, K., Schein, C., Kashiwaga, K. and Weissmann, C. (1983). **Gene 22**, 229.
Palva, I., Pettersson, R.F., Kalkkinen, N., Lehtovaara, P., Sarvas, M., Söderlund, H., Takkinen, K. and Kääriäinen, L. (1981). **Gene 15**, 43.
Palva, I., Sarvas, M., Lehtovaara, P., Sibakov, M. and Kääriäinen, L. (1982). **Proc. Natl. Acad. Sci. USA** 79, 5582.
Pettersson, R.F., Lundström, K, Chattopadhyaya, J.B., Josephson, S., Philipson, L., Kääriäinen, L. and Palva, I. (1983). **Gene**, in press.
Rinderknecht, H., Geokas, M.C., Silverman, P. and Havebrack, B.J. (1968). **Clin. Chim. Acta 21**, 197.
Sibakov, M., Sarvas, M. and Palva, I. (1983). **FEMS Lett. 17**, 81
Takkinen, K., Pettersson, R.F., Kalkkinen, N., Palva, I., Söderlund, H. and Kääriäinen, L. (1983). **J. Biol. Chem. 258**, 1007.

CLONING OF A SERINE PROTEASE GENE FROM BACILLUS AMYLOLIQUEFACIENS AND ITS EXPRESSION IN BACILLUS SUBTILIS

N. Vasantha
Craig S. Rhodes
Leo D. Thompson
Carl D. B. Banner

Department of Molecular Genetics
Genex Corporation
Gaithersburg, Maryland

David Filpula

Department of DNA Chemistry
Genex Corporation
Gaithersburg, Maryland

I. INTRODUCTION

Proteases are a major class of exoenzymes secreted by bacilli at the end of exponential growth (Ingle and Boyer, 1976). In general, most of the extracellular protease activity produced by bacilli consists of two enzymes, an alkaline protease (serine protease or subtilisin) and a neutral protease (metalloprotease). These proteases have been used industrially for a long time, and their biochemical properties have been well characterized. In contrast, the process by which proteases are secreted is not understood. In order to study the molecular mechanism of protease secretion we isolated the gene coding for the serine protease (subtilisin N, E.C.3.4.21.14) from Bacillus amyloliquefaciens. This organism secretes high levels of serine protease, and the amino acid sequence of this protein has been determined (Ingle and Boyer, 1976; Smith et al., 1968).

ISBN 0-12-274160-9

In this paper we report the isolation of apr[Bam],[1] the gene for the serine protease of B. amyloliquefaciens, by marker rescue transformation in Bacillus subtilis (Gryczan et al., 1980a). B. subtilis strains bearing a recombinant plasmid carrying apr[Bam] hyper-produce serine protease. A partial amino acid sequence deduced from the DNA sequence of the cloned gene showed extensive homology to the published amino acid sequence of subtilisin N.

II. MATERIALS AND METHODS

A. Bacterial Strains and Plasmids

B. subtilis strain BR151 (metB10 trpC2 lys3) and B. amyloliquefaciens strain ATCC 23844 were used. Plasmids pBD64 and pUB110 have been described (Gryczan et al., 1980b). Bacteria were grown in Penassay broth (Difco) at 37°C. Kanamycin and chloramphenicol were used at 10 μg/ml and 5 μg/ml, respectively.

B. DNA Isolation and Plasmid Construction

B. amyloliquefaciens cellular DNA was isolated as described by Saito and Miura (1965). It was partially digested with MboI (768 units of enzyme/mg DNA for 7 minutes at 37°C) and ligated to BamHI-digested pBD64 at a weight ratio of 1:1 for 60 minutes at 25°C at a total DNA concentration of 200 μg/ml. The ligated DNA was used to transform competent cells of a derivative of BR151 containing pUB110 (Gryczan and Dubnau, 1978). The transformants were plated on skim milk agar (Luria broth + 1.1% agar + 3% skim milk powder + 10 μg/ml chloramphenicol).

Plasmid DNA was isolated by the method of Holmes and Quigley (1981) with the following modification: after boiling, the samples were treated with proteinase K (50 μg/ml) for 15 minutes at 37°C, and heated at 70°C for 10 minutes (to inactivate the proteinase K) and DNA was precipitated with isopropanol. Restriction digests were performed according to standard procedure.

[1] *We are using a genotypic designation in which the gene is indicated with a standard three letter code followed by a three letter symbol in brackets which indicates genus and the species of origin (in a manner analogous to naming of restriction endonuclease).*

For determination of the DNA sequence, plasmid DNA was digested with ClaI or ClaI plus BglI and ligated to M13 mp8 DNA digested with AccI or AccI plus BamHI (Messing and Vieira, 1982). Single-stranded template was prepared from colorless plaques and used for sequence determination by the method of Messing et al. (1981) and Spanger et al. (1977).

C. Protease Assay

Cultures were centrifuged in an Eppendorf microfuge and the protease activity in the supernatant was assayed using hide powder azure as the substrate (Vasantha and Freese, 1980). One unit of activity was defined as the release of one A_{595} nm unit per ml per hour at 37°C. In order to distinguish between serine protease and neutral protease activities, samples were preincubated with 1 mM PMSF (phenylmethylsulfonyl fluoride) or 1 mM EDTA for 15 minutes at 37°C. The activity that was inhibited by PMSF and not by EDTA was defined as serine protease; the activity that was inhibited by EDTA and not by PMSF was defined as neutral protease.

III. RESULTS

B. subtilis strain BR151 containing the plasmid pUB110 was transformed with B. amyloliquefaciens chromosomal DNA which had been partially digested with MboI and ligated to the BamHI-digested vector pBD64. Transformed cells were incubated for one hour in Penassay broth at 37°C to allow the expression of drug resistance and the transformants were then selected on skim milk plates containing chloramphenicol. After 17 hours of incubation at 37°C, zones of clearing of the precipitated milk protein were observed around nine colonies; these represented about 0.01% of the Cm^r transformants. The time of observation was important. By 24 hours, proteases from the recipient strain had completely cleared the milk on the entire plate.

Colonies from the center of each of the zones of clearing were isolated. In order to separate the chimeric plasmid from the resident pUB110 (Gryczan et al., 1980a), the plasmid DNA from the isolated colonies was extracted and used to transform BR151 (plasmid-free). In each of the nine cases, the ability to hyper-produce protease could be cotransformed with Cm^r. The plasmid in one of these hyper-protease producers was designated as pGX2110.

Table 1. Protease Activity in Culture Supernatant

Strain	Activity (ΔA_{595} per ml per hour)			Percent	
	Complete	PMSF	EDTA	Alkaline	Neutral
B. subtilis BR151	1.5	0.850	0.740	47	53
B. amyloliquefaciens	117.0	52.6	48.0	48	52
B. subtilis BR151 (pBX2110)	220.0	1.76	195.0	99	1

The extracellular protease activity produced by the various strains in Penassay broth was measured 45 hours after the end of exponential growth as outlined in Materials and Methods. The cell density of the various strains was approximately the same at the time of assay.

Extracellular protease activity was measured in a culture of BR151 (pGX2110), and compared with the activity in cultures of each of the parent strains, (BR151 and B. amyloliquefaciens [Table 1]). BR151(pGX2110) had 150- to 200-times as much total protease BR151 and 2- to 3-times as much as B. amyloliquefaciens. The extracellular protease activity in both B. amyloliquefaciens and BR151 consisted of approximately equal amounts of serine protease (as shown by inhibition by PMSF) and neutral protease (as shown by inhibition by EDTA). In contrast, 99% of the protease activity of BR151(pGX2110) was inhibited by PMSF, thus showing that this strain produced serine protease almost exclusively. The fact that the cloned DNA determined only a single protease suggested that it carried the structural gene for serine protease, since most regulatory mutations which are known to affect the level of serine protease coordinately affect that of neutral protease as well.

Restriction analysis of pGX2110 showed that the plasmid consisted of pBD64 plus a 4.8 kb insert (Figure 1). To define the genetic determinant of the hyper-protease phenotype in this insert, several in vitro mutagenesis experiments were done. First, SalI octanucleotide linkers were inserted at either the unique SmaI site or BglII site of this insert. In neither case was the level of expression of protease altered. In contrast, deletion of the 1.5 kb ClaI fragment running from 1.75 to 3.25 on the map (Figure 1) resulted in loss of the ability to hyper-produce protease,

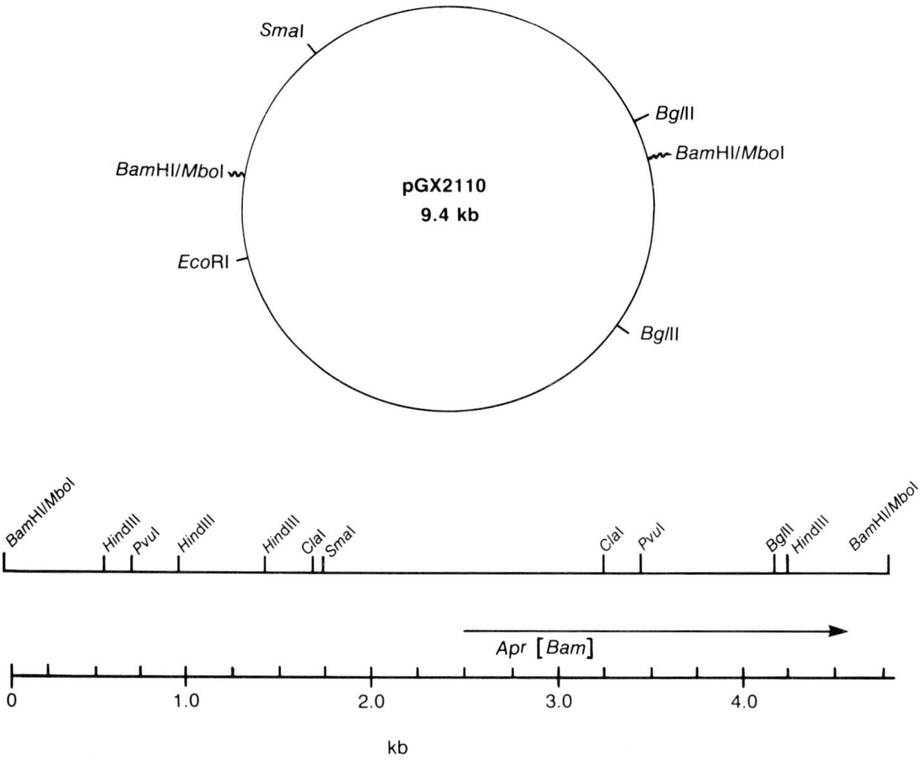

Figure 1. Restriction endonuclease cleavage site map of plasmid pGX2110. The isolation of pGX2110 is described in the text. The cloned B. amyloliquefaciens DNA is located between the two hybrid BamHI/MboI restriction sites and includes the unique SmaI site of the plasmid. A more detailed restriction map of the B. amyloliquefaciens DNA is shown in the lower part of the figure.

indicating that the genetic determinant of this phenotype overlaps at least one of the ClaI sites. Since one of the ClaI sites maps very close to the SmaI site, the nucleotide sequence around the other ClaI site (right) was determined (Figure 2).

Translation of the DNA sequence thus determined showed a large open coding region in one of the three reading frames. The deduced protein sequence showed extensive homology with the amino acid sequence of B. amyloliquefaciens subtilisin (Figure 2). This demonstrates that the structural gene (apr[Bam]) of subtilisin is present on pGX2110. However, there are a few mismatches (inversion) in the apr[Bam] sequence when compared with the amino acid sequence of

```
                1               5                  10                  15
                |               |                   |                   |
              Ala Gln Ser Val Pro Tyr Gly Val Ser Gln Ile Lys Ala Pro Ala
APR4C         GCC CAG TCC GTG CCT TAC GGC GTA TCA CAA ATT AAA GCC CCT GCT

SUBS N        Ala Gln Ser Val Pro Tyr Gly Val Ser Gln Ile Lys Ala Pro Ala


               16              20                  25                  30
                |               |                   |                   |
              Leu His Ser Gln Gly Tyr Thr Gly Ser Asn Val Lys Val Ala Val
APR4C         CTG CAC TCT CAA GGC TAC ACT GGA TCA AAT GTT AAA GTA GCG GTT

SUBS N        Leu His Ser Gln Gly Tyr Thr Gly Ser Asn Val Lys Val Ala Val


                                ClaI
                              -------
                              |     |
               31              35                  40                  45
                |               |                   |                   |
              Ile Asp Ser Gly Ile Asp Ser Ser His Pro Asp Leu Lys Val Ala
APR4C         ATC GAC AGC GGT ATC GAT TCT TCT CAT CCT GAT TTA AAG GTA GCA

SUBS N        Ile Asp Ser Gly Ile Asp Ser Ser His Pro Asp Leu Lys Val Ala


               46              50                  55                  60
                :               |                   :                   |
              Gly Gly Ala Ser Met Val Pro Ser Glu Thr Asn Pro Phe Gln Asp
APR4C         GGC GGA GCC AGC ATG GTT CCT TCT GAA ACA AAT CCT TTC CAA GAC
                                                      *** ***
SUBS N        Gly Gly Ala Ser Met Val Pro Ser Glu Thr Pro Asn Phe Gln Asp


               61              65                  70                  75
                |               |                   |                   |
              Asn Asn Ser His Gly Thr His Val Ala Gly Thr Val Ala Ala Leu
APR4C         AAC AAC TCT CAC GGA ACT CAC GTT GCC GGC ACA GTT GCG GCT CTT
              ***
SUBS N        Asp Asn Ser His Gly Thr His Val Ala Gly Thr Val Ala Ala Leu


               76              80                  85                  90
                |               :                   :                   :
              Asn Asn Ser Ile Gly Val Leu Gly Val Ala Pro Ser Ala Ser Leu
APR4C         AAT AAC TCA ATC GGT GTA TTA GGC GTT GCG CCA AGC GCA TCA CTT
                                                              *** ***
SUBS N        Asn Asn Ser Ile Gly Val Leu Gly Val Ala Pro Ser Ser Ala Leu
```

```
             91                  95                       100                      105
              :                   :                        :                        :
             Tyr Ala Val Lys Val Leu Gly Ala Asp Gly Ser Gly Gln Tyr Ser
APR4C        TAC GCT GTA AAA GTT CTC GGT GCT GAC GGT TCC GGC CAA TAC AGC
                                     *** ***
SUBS N       Tyr Ala Val Lys Val Leu Gly Asp Ala Gly Ser Gly Gln Tyr Ser

                                                   PvuI
                                                 -------
                                                 :     :
             106                110                  115                      120
              :                   :                   :                        :
             Trp Ile Ile Asn Gly Ile Glu Trp Ala Ile Ala Asn Asn Met Asp
APR4C        TGG ATC ATT AAC GGA ATC GAG TGG GCG ATC GCA AAC AAT ATG GAC

SUBS N       Trp Ile Ile Asn Gly Ile Glu Trp Ala Ile Ala Asn Asn Met Asp


             121                125
              :                   :
             Val Ile Asn Met Ser Leu
APR4C        GTT ATT AAC ATG AGC CTC

SUBS N       Val Ile Asn Met Ser Leu
```

Figure 2. Comparison of the amino acid sequence of apr[BAM] deduced from the DNA sequence of plasmid pGX2110 with the amino acid sequence of subtilisin N (Smith et al., 1966). APR4C=pGX2110; SUBS N=subtilisin N (subtilisin from B. amyloliquefaciens). The ClaI and PvuI sites indicated correspond to those at about 3.2 and 3.4 kb on the map of the pGX2110 insert in Figure 1. Asterisks denote region of mismatch. The residue (amino acid) number is that of subtilisin N from Smith et al., 1966.

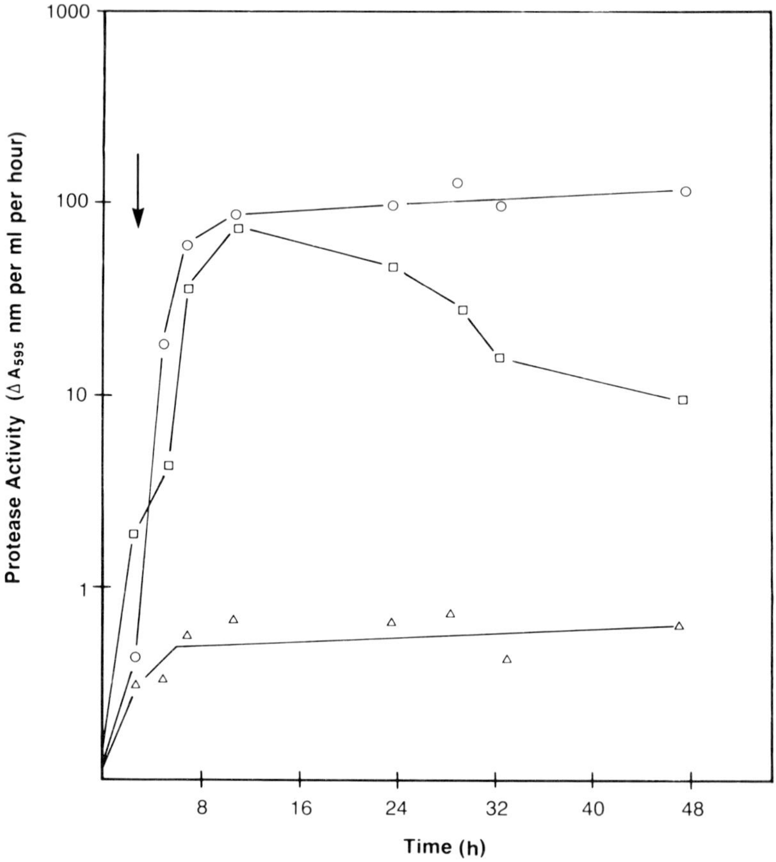

Figure 3. Kinetics of the extracellular protease production. BR151(pBD64) (Δ), B. amyloliquefaciens (□), and BR151(pGX2110 (O) were grown in Penassay broth at 37°C. Extracellular protease activity was assayed as described in Materials and Methods. ↓ denotes the end of exponential growth.

subtilisin. These mismatches could be due to possible strain differences and/or errors in the protein sequence.

The kinetics of extracellular protease production by BR151(pGX2110) was compared with BR151(pBD64) and B. amyloliquefaciens. Each strain was grown in Penassay broth; exponential growth ceased after 3.5 hours. The extracellular protease activity in the BR151(pBD64) culture was extremely low and it increased only 2-fold over a period of 48 hours after the end of exponential growth (Figure 3). The extracellular protease activity of B. amyloliquefaciens was higher than that of BR151(pBD64) during exponential growth. Furthermore, during a period of 9 hours after exponential growth ceased, the protease activity of B. amyloliquefaciens increased 30-fold; later it decreased about 10-fold. In contrast to both of these results, the protease activity produced by BR151(pGX2110) increased approximately 100-fold over a period of 8.5 hours after the end of exponential growth and no subsequent decrease was observed.

IV. DISCUSSION

The gene coding for serine protease (apr[Bam]) from B. amyloliquefaciens has been isolated in B. subtilis using a multicopy plasmid vector. The high efficiency of the marker rescue transformation and the high activity of the B. amyloliquefaciens protease obviated the need for a protease-negative strain as a recipient in the isolation of the gene. Thus, this method may be useful in the cloning of proteases from various bacilli and other Gram-positive bacteria. Indeed, we have also cloned the neutral protease gene (npr[Bam]) from B. amyloliquefaciens using this technique (unpublished data).

Another approach to the cloning of genes for serine proteases from bacteria could be based on the observation that extensive homology in the amino acid sequence exists among the various serine proteases from bacilli (Strongin et al., 1978). Thus the cloned serine protease gene for B. amyloliquefaciens could be used as probe to identify clones carrying protease genes from various Bacillus species. The cloned gene could also be used to isolate protease-deficient mutants directly by insertional inactivation. Protease-deficient mutants which result from mutations in the structural gene would not only be useful hosts for the secretion of heterologous proteins but also to study the role of the various proteases in the physiology of the cell (e.g. in sporulation).

apr[Bam] is stably maintained on the multicopy plasmid pBD64 (data not shown). Although there may be approximately 50 copies of the same protease gene in B. subtilis, the level of alkaline protease expressed is only 6- to 8-times higher than that of B. amyloliquefaciens. There could be many reasons for this apparent lack of a simple correlation between gene number and enzyme level. A similar observation was made in the case of a cloned α-amylase gene from B. amyloliquefaciens on a multicopy plasmid in B. subtilis (Palva, 1980).

Preliminary analysis of the DNA sequence of the apr[Bam] region shows the existence of a large open coding region upstream from the start of the mature protein (data not shown). The region appears to be different from the corresponding region of the genes for exoproteins studied so far in Gram-positive organisms. A typical signal sequence immediately adjacent to the sequence encoding the mature exoprotein can not be inferred from the DNA sequence (Nielsen and Lampen, 1982; Palva, 1982). Further analysis of this region is in progress.

ACKNOWLEDGMENTS

We thank Mark Guyer for his suggestions and criticisms during the course of this work and during the preparation of this manuscript. We thank Steve Fahnestock, Ethel Jackson and Charlie Saunders for critical discussions.

REFERENCES

Gryczan, T., Contente, S., and Dubnau, D. (1980a). **Molec. Gen. Genet 177**, 459.

Gryczan, T., Shivakumar, A.G. and Dubnau, D. (1980b). **J. Bacteriol. 141**, 246.

Holmes, D.S. and Quigley, M. (1981). **Anal. Biochem. 114**, 193.

Ingle, M.B. and Boyer, E.W. (1976). In Microbiology, 1976 (D. Schlessinger, ed.) p. 420, American Society for Microbiology, Washington, DC.

Messing, J., Crea, R. and Seeburg, P.H. (1981). **Nucl. Acids Res. 9**, 309.

Messing, J. and Vieira, J. (1982). **Gene 19**, 269.

Nielsen, J.B.K. and Lampen, J.O. (1982). **J. Biol. Chem. 257**, 4490.

Palva, I. (1982). **Gene 19**, 81.

Saito, H. and Miuva, I. (1963). **Biochim. Biophys. Acta 72**, 619.

Sanger, F., Nickleson, S. and Coulson, A.R. (1977). **Proc. Natl. Acad. Sci. USA 74**, 5463.

Smith, E.L., Delange, R.J., Evans, W.H., London, M. and Maokland, F.S. (1966). **J. Biol. Chem. 243**, 2814.

Strongin, S., Ya, A., Izohoua, I.S., Abramov, Z.T., Gotodetsky, D.I., Eranakova, L.M., Beylanova, L.D. and Stepnov, V.M. (1978). **J. Bacteriol.** 133, 1401.

Vasantha, N. and Freese, E. (1980). **J. Bacteriol. 144**, 1119.

CLONING AND SEQUENCING OF A REGION CONTROLLING EFFICIENT EXPRESSION OF SUBTILISIN FROM BACILLUS AMYLOLIQUEFACIENS[1]

James A. Wells
Eugenio Ferrari
Mark L. Stahl

Biocatalysis Department
Genentech, Inc.
South San Francisco, California

Dennis J. Henner
Ellson Y. Chen

Molecular Biology Department
Genentech, Inc.
South San Francisco, California

I. INTRODUCTION

Subtilisin is a serine class endoprotease secreted in large quantities by many species of Bacillus (Markland and Smith, 1971). The enzyme is produced at the onset of sporulation (Millet, 1970), however, the role of subtilisin in promoting Bacillus sporulation is unclear. Among several possibilities, it may serve to scavenge extracellular protein to replenish amino acid pools. Subtilisin may also assist in cell lysis allowing spore release. Cloning the gene for subtilisin should allow the generation of structural gene mutants so that the importance of subtilisin in spore development may be clarified. Furthermore, the subtilisin gene should contain sequences which are specifically recognized by sporulation-specific σ-factors (Losick

[1]*Funding for this research was generously provided by Genencor, Inc.*

ISBN 0-12-274160-9

and Pero, 1981). Herein, we describe the cloning and expression of the subtilisin gene from Bacillus amyloliquefaciens. Deletion analysis of the cloned gene has defined a 31 bp region at the 5' end necessary for efficient expression of subtilisin.

II. CLONING OF SUBTILISIN

A Sau3A partial digest of B. amyloliquefaciens DNA [ATCC 23844] was ligated into the Escherichia coli/Bacillus subtilis shuttle vector, pBS42 (D. Yansura and D. Henner, unpublished results). A library was constructed in E. coli and probed with a mixture of eight oligonucleotides which were fourteen bases in length. The oligonucleotide probes were synthesized in two pools of four and were designated to cover all nucleotide ambiguity predicted from the published protein sequence at positions 117 to 121 (Markland and Smith, 1967). Colonies which hybridized strongly with the mixture of probe pools (Grunstein and Hogness, 1975) were purified and probed with the separated probe pools as shown in Figure 1.

III. EXPRESSION OF CLONED SUBTILISIN

One of the hybridization positive clones, called pS4, when transformed into B. subtilis I-168 was found to over-express subtilisin-like activity in the culture supernatant by greater than 200-fold. As expected, the activity was sensitive to pMSF yet resistant to EDTA. Furthermore, a prominent protein migrating in SDS gels near the position of authentic subtilisin was found in pBS42 culture supernatants.

The time course of expression of subtilisin activity in B. subtilis I-168 has been compared with the over-expression of subtilisin from pS4. Figure 2 shows that the expression

---

nitrocellulose filters. Panel A: Replica nitrocellulose filter of purified positive colonies probed with probe pool 1. Panel B: The same as A except a separate replica was probed with probe pool 2. The number above the columns designated the original positive colony from which the arrayed clones were derived.

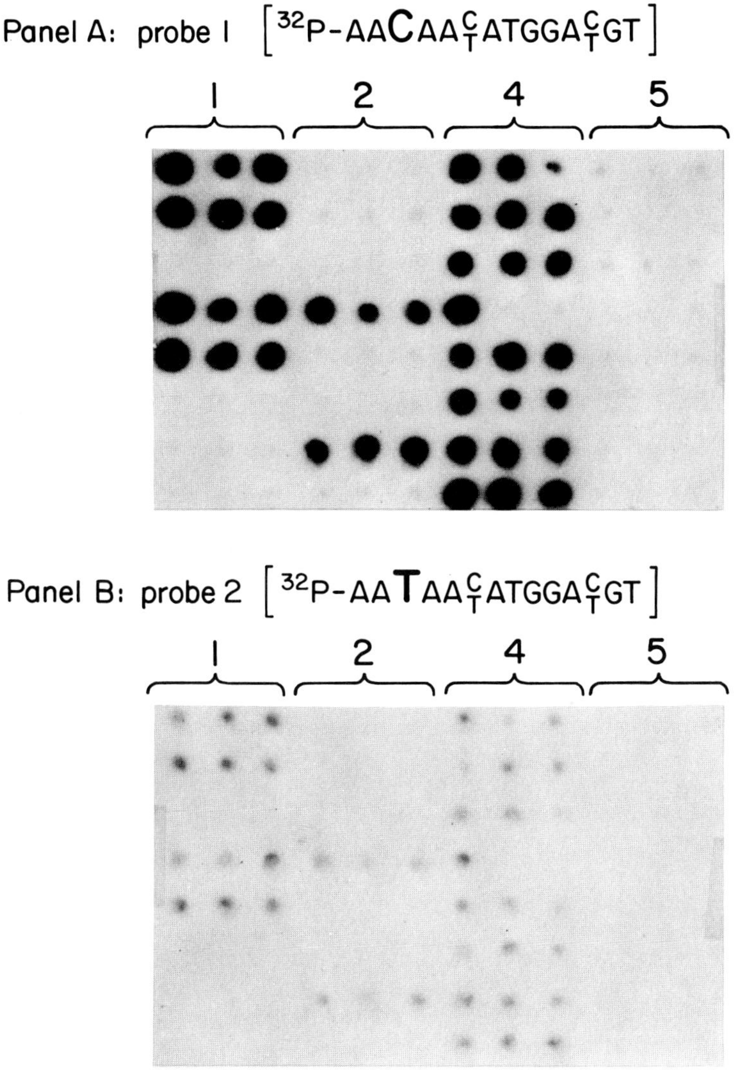

Figure 1. Colony hybridization of E. coli 294 containing Sau3A partial digest of B. amyloliquefaciens DNA in pBS242. E. coli was transformed with the Sau3A pBS42 B. amyloliquefaciens DNA library and replica plated onto nitrocellulose filters. Filters were probed with a mixture of oligonucleotide probe pool 1 [^{32}P-AACAA[C/T] ATGGA[C/T]GT] and pool 2 [^{32}P-AATAA[C/T]ATGGA[C/T]GT]. Positive colonies were purified by diluting into LB media and plating at low cell density. Individual clones were arrayed onto two replica

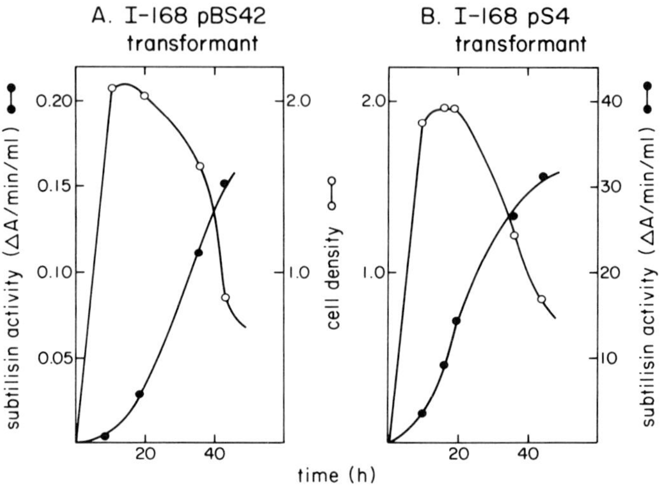

Figure 2. Cell growth and expression of subtilisin activity versus time for B. subtilis I-168 containing either the parent vector, pBS42 (Panel A) or the cloned B. amyloliquefaciens subtilisin gene, pS4 (Panel B). Single cloned colonies were used to innoculate 50 mL of minimal culture medium supplemented with 25 µg/ml L-tryptophan, 0.1% casein hydrolyzed amino acids and 7.5 µg/ml chloramphenicol. Cultures were grown in a shaker flask and sampled at indicated times. Subtilisin activity of the culture supernatants was measured by monitoring the change in absorbance at 412 nm per minute upon incubation with 0.2 mg/ml succinyl [-L-ala-L-ala-L-pro-L-phe-] p-nitroanilide in 0.1 M sodium phosphate (pH 8) at 25°C.

of subtilisin still appears to be under sporulation control despite the large difference in expression levels between the two cultures. The time-course shows the typical lag in subtilisin expression until the cells reach stationary phase and begin to sporulate. The optical density of the culture then decreases during sporulation while subtilisin production continues to rise.

IV. CHARACTERIZATION OF THE CLONED SUBTILISIN GENE

The location of the subtilisin gene (ca. 1.3 kb) within the cloned insert DNA (ca. 4.4 kb) was determined by Southern blotting using probe pool 1. A BamHI to PvuII fragment which hybridized to the oligonucleotide probe pool was sequenced and this directed the sequence of the rest of the gene. The entire mature coding sequence (275 amino acids) is present, however without a signal-like peptide sequence located at the immediate N-terminus. In fact, the closest in-frame initiation codon (GTG) which shows a downstream signal-like peptide sequence and an upstream ribosome binding site is located 107 codons upstream from the mature N-terminus. The nucleotide sequence of the cloned B. subtilis I-168 subtilisin gene (M. Stahl, unpublished results) is 85% homologous to the B. amyloliquefaciens gene and contains a putative GTG initiation codon and similar leader sequence. The coding sequence of these leaders suggests that subtilisin is made as a preproprotease similar in functional structure to the pancreatic serine proteases (Neurath, 1975). Although the sequences suggest subtilisin is made as a larger precursor, direct biochemical evidence is necessary to confirm that subtilisin is made as a preproprotease. We have not yet detected any larger precursors to subtilisin by SDS acrylamide gels either in the supernatant or cell pellets at early or late times of cell culturing.

V. IDENTIFICATION OF THE SUBTILISIN PROMOTER REGION

To define the 5' end of the subtilisin gene, Bal31 deletions were made in the DNA insert in pS4 as described in Figure 3. The sequence for pBS42 is located between the BamHI site and the next clockwise EcoRI site as shown in Figure 3. The subtilisin gene sequence is shown by the shaded box in Figure 3 with its 3' end located closest to the the BamHI site . In separate experiments, deletion of DNA insert sequences between the XmaIII site and the EcoRI site at the end of the vector had no effect on subtilisin expression. Bal31 endonuclease deletions were initiated at the XmaIII site which was presumed close to the 5' end of the subtilisin gene. Following exonuclease treatment, synthetic EcoRI linkers were ligated to the blunt ends to facilitate sequence analysis of the deletion mutants. The mutants were characterized by determining the size of the EcoRI/ClaI fragment from E. coli mini-plasmid preparations. Expression of subtilisin was monitored in a protease deficient derivative of a <u>spoOA</u> mutant, BG-84 (E. Ferrari, unpublished results). Colonies continuing to express subtilisin were identified on skim milk plates by the halos created by proteolysis of casein. Three clones were chosen for further sequence analysis. One of these, clone 5, contained the

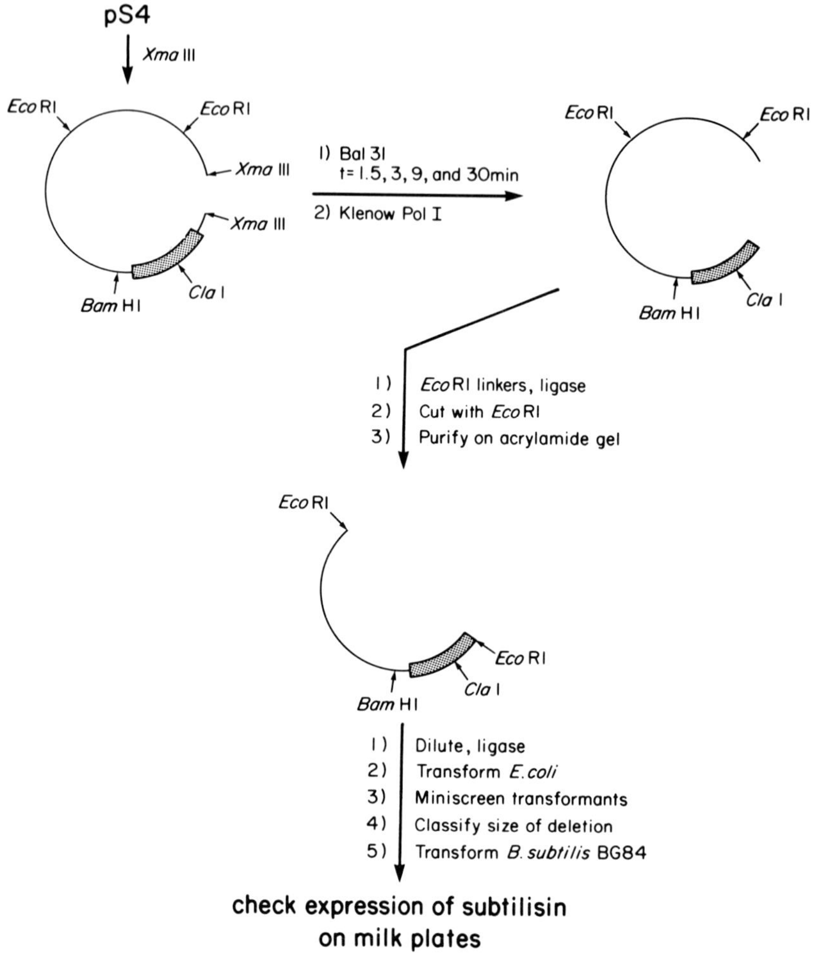

Figure 3. Bal31 exonuclease deletions from the XmaIII site in pS4. pS4 was cleaved at the unique XmaIII site and digested with Bal31 for 1.5, 3, 9 and 30 minutes to generate a set of deletions. DNA from each point was treated with the Klenow fragment of E. coli DNA polymerase I and dNTP's to generate blunt ends. EcoRI linkers were ligated to the blunt ends. The DNA was treated with EcoRI to cleave poly linkers and the two internal EcoRI sites. The large EcoRI fragments containing only the essential portions of pBS42 and the subtilisin gene were purified by polyacrylamide gel electrophoresis. The fragments were self-ligated and used to transform E. coli. Miniplasmid preparations from E. coli transformants were screened for the size of exonuclease deletion by EcoRI/ClaI restriction mapping.

smallest DNA insert which continued to express subtilisin. Clones 3 and 4 had the largest inserts but were greatly diminished in subtilisin expression. The nucleotide sequence of the coding strand between the EcoRI site of clone 5 and clone 4 is shown below.

```
 (5)                             (3)                             (4)
5'↓                               ↓                               ↓3'
 GGTCTACTAAAATATTATTCCATACTATACAATTAATACACAGAATAATCTGTCTAT
```

The fact that clone 5 expressed subtilisin whereas clone 3 did not strongly suggests part or all of the promoter for subtilisin is in the 31 bp sequence between clone 5 and clone 3. The fact that each Bal31 deletion mutant was ligated to the same fixed point in the vector (i.e. the EcoRI site) indicated that the loss in subtilisin expression is not due to the juxtaposition of an adventitious repressor sequence. The sequence underlined in the 31 bp region shares some homology with the -35 and -10 regions of the *spoVC* promoter (Moran et al., 1981). If the promoter is located as shown it would suggest the subtilisin gene might be transcribed by σ^{37} RNA polymerase molecules in B. subtilis. However, S-1 nuclease mapping and/or in vitro transcription studies are necessary to confirm the exact location and σ-factor specificity of the promoter. There are 38 nucleotides from the beginning of clone 4 to the putative GTG initiation codon. Details of the gene sequence and the experimental methods will be published elsewhere.

Cloning and expression of the subtilisin gene should provide a useful tool for studying its role in sporulation. Furthermore, subtilisin is a good model system for studying protein secretion during sporulation.

ACKNOWLEDGMENTS

We are indebted to Doug Smith, Mark Vasser, Peter Ng for technical assistance, and Pam Sherwood and John Adelman for technical advice. We wish to thank Dan Yansura for providing the pBS42-B. amyloliquefaciens gene bank and Dave Powers and Dr. Rey Gomez for helpful discussions. Special thanks to Dr. David Estell for stimulating ideas.

REFERENCES

Grunstein, M. and Hogness, D. (1975). **Proc. Natl. Acad. Sci. USA 72**, 3961.

Losick, R. and Pero, J. (1981). **Cell 25**, 582.

Markland, F.S. and Smith, E.L. (1967). **J. Biol. Chem. 242**, 5198.

Markland, F.S. and Smith, E.L. (1971). In The Enzymes, Vol III (P.D. Boyer, ed.) p. 561, Academic Press, New York.

Millet, J. (1970). **J. Appl. Bacteriol. 33**, 207.

Moran, C.P., Jr., Lang, N., Banner, C.D.B., Haldenwang, W.G. and Losick, R. (1981). **Cell 25**, 783.

Neurath, H. (1975). In Proteases and Biological Control, p. 55, Cold Spring Harbor Laboratory, Cold Spring Harbor, New York,

SECRETION VECTOR OF BACILLUS SUBTILIS CONSTRUCTED FROM THE BACILLUS SUBTILIS α-AMYLASE PROMOTER AND SIGNAL PEPTIDE CODING REGION[1]

Kunio Yamane
Kiyotaka Otozai
Kazutaka Ohmura
Akira Nakayama
Hisato Yamazaki

Institute of Biological Sciences
University of Tsukuba
Sakura, Ibaraki-Ken
Japan

Makari Yamasaki
Gakuzo Tamura

Department of Agricultural Chemistry
The University of Tokyo
Bunkyo-ku, Tokyo
Japan

I. INTRODUCTION

α-amylase is one of the major extracellular enzymes of Bacillus subtilis. The structural gene for this enzyme (amyE$^+$) maps near the aroI locus on the chromosome according to genetic analysis of α-amylase-deficient mutants (Yamaguchi et al., 1974; Yuki, 1975). The gene order around amyE$^+$ is lin2 - tmrA - amyR - amyE - tmrB - aroI (Nomura et al., 1978).

[1]*This work was supported in part by Grants-in-Aid from the Ministry of Education, Science and Culture of Japan.*

ISBN 0-12-274160-9

Many regulatory genes, causing hyperproduction of α-amylase, have been obtained from mutants and naturally occuring strains with hyperproductivity of α-amylase. When we combined the regulatory genes in one cell by DNA-mediated transformation, they showed a clear synergistic effect on the production of α-amyulase. Based on this finding, an extrahyper α-amylase producing strain, T2N26, was constructed through the stepwise introduction of six regulatory genes by DNA-mediated transformation and mutation. The enzyme production increased more than 1,500 times as much as the original strain, B. subtilis 6160, a derivative of B. subtilis Marburg 168 (Hitotsuyanagi et al., 1979; Yamane, 1980). This highly active secretion system in B. subtilis α-amylase seems to be an ideal system to apply to the production of many useful materials in gene engineering.

We cloned a regulatory gene, amyR2, and $amyE^+$ from an α-amylase hyperproducing strain, B. subtilis NA64, into the plasmid pUB110 (Takeichi et al., 1983; Yamazaki et al., submitted for publication). A secretion vector in B. subtilis was constructed from the B. subtilis α-amylase promoter and signal sequence coding region of the cloned DNA. To test this vector, we fused an Escherichia coli β-lactamase gene which was derived from the E. coli plasmid pBR322 but which lacked its own promoter and signal sequence coding region (Palva et al., 1982). The fused E. coli β-lactamase gene was expressed and secreted active β-lactamase by B. subtilis (Ohmura et al., submitted for publication).

II. CONSTRUCTION OF THE PLASMID pTUB4 CONTAINING amyR2 AND $amyE^+$

A DNA fragment containing amyR2 - $amyE^+$ - $aroI^+$, which was derived from the chromosomal DNA of B. subtilis NA64, was integrated into the B. subtilis temperate phage ρ11 genome (Nomura et al., 1979) by the prophage transformation method (Kawamura et al., 1979). The phage was further reconstructed and a specialized transducing phage, ρ11-AA18 (ρ11d amyR2 $amyE^+$ tmrB $aroI^+$) was prepared (Yamazaki et al., submitted for publication). ρ11-AA18 DNA was partially digested by a restriction enzyme Sau3A, and was ligated to the plasmid pUB110 after it was cleaved by BamH1. The constructed plasmid was then transferred into B. subtilis 207-25 (hsrM recE4 amyE07 aroI906 leuA8 metB5 lys21 ery-r) by the method of protoplast transformation (Chang and Cohen, 1979). One of the kanamycin-resistant (Km^r) and amylase-positive transformants harbored a 6.8 kb plasmid, into which a 2.3 kb fragment had been inserted. The plasmid was desig-

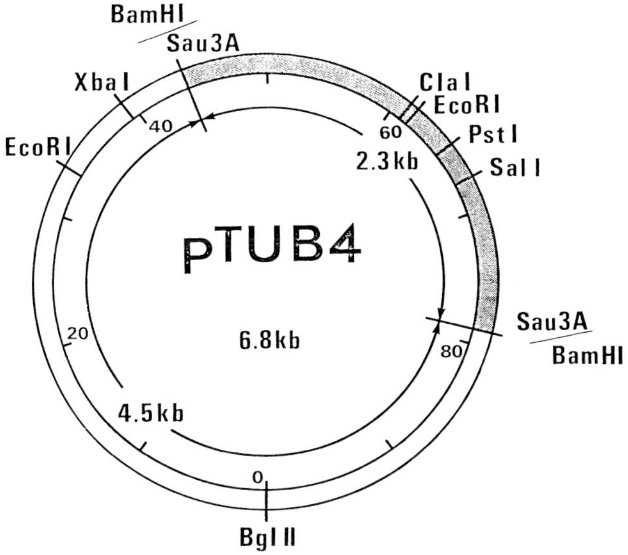

Figure 1. Endonuclease restriction map of the plasmid pTUB4 DNA. The 2.3 kb fragment carrying the amyR2 and amyE+ genes of an α-amylase hyperproducing strain, B. subtilis NA64, was inserted into the plasmid vector pUB110.

nated pTUB4 (Takeichi et al., 1983). The order of the restriction sites in the inserted DNA was ClaI - EcoRI - PstI - SalI - SmaI from the XbaI site to the BglII site of the plasmid. From genetic analysis and comparisons of restriction sites in ρ11-AA18 and pTUB4, it was indicated that the DNA fragment from the XbaI site to the ClaI site, approximately 1.43 kb, contained the regulatory gene, amyR2, and the NH_2-terminal region of amyE$^+$ and that the ClaI - BglII fragment, approximately 2.8 kb, contained the COOH-terminal region of amyE$^+$. After DNA nucleotide sequence analysis, it was revealed that two PstI sites were located in the 2.3 kb insert (Yamazaki et al., submitted for publication) (Figure 1).

III. DNA NUCLEOTIDE SEQUENCE OF amyR2 and amyE$^+$ IN pTUB4

A DNA nucleotide sequence of about 2,600 bp in the amyR2 and amyE$^+$ region was determined by the method of Maxam and Gilbert (1980). A big open reading frame from the initiation codon, ATG (+1 to +3), to termination codon, TAA (+1777 to +1779) was found in the sequence. The twelve amino acid sequence (Leu-Thr-Ala-Pro-Ser-Ile-Lys-Ser-Gly-Thr-Ile-Leu) of the NH_2-terminal region of B. subtilis α-amylase was reported by Mäntsälä and Zalkin (1979). The same amino acid sequence of 12 residues was deduced from the DNA nucleotide sequence (+124 to +159). It was revealed that the precursor protein of α-amylase had an NH_2-terminal extension of 41 amino acid residues. If this sequence is a so-called signal peptide, it is much longer than signal peptides found in other exported proteins in prokaryotes and eukaryotes (Kreil, 1981). Possibly only a part of this sequence forms the signal peptide. For this reason, we suggested that the precursor protein of α-amylase would be cleaved twice to make the mature extracellular enzyme, as reported for the formation of exopenicillinase of B. licheniformis (Nielsen and Lampen, 1982) and Staphylococcus aureus (McLaughlin et al., 1981).

Within the DNA nucleotide sequence from +1 to +1779, the first 1674 bp for the signal peptide and the NH_2-terminal side of amyE$^+$ is almost coincident with the sequence of the α-amylase structural gene from B. subtilis 168 which was cloned using E. coli vector systems (Yang et al., 1983). The nucleotide sequence from +1674 to +1779 was coincident with that of the 3' side of the BamH1 site in pUB110. This result indicated that 34 amino acid residues of the COOH terminal region of α-amylase from pTUB4 was encoded in the plasmid pUB110 DNA used as the vector.

The nucleotide sequence at the 5' side of the structural gene for the mature α-amylase contains the typical sequences for the regulatory signals of gene expression in prokaryotes. The structure of this region containing the promoter and signal sequence coding region of the α-amylase gene is schematically shown in Figure 2.

A Shine-Dalgarno sequence (AAGGAG) for a ribosome binding sequence is found 8 bp upstream of the initiator ATG codon (Ohmura et al., 1983). For the initiation of transcription, two sequences, TTGATAGAGTGATTGTGATAATTTAAAAT and TTGAAAGGAGGAAGCGGAAGAATGAAGTAA, seem to be possible. In the former sequence, the distance from TTGATA to TAAAAT is 17 bp which corresponds to the consensus distance from the RNA polymerase recognition sites to the Pribnow boxes in other transcriptional initiation sites of proteins in B. subtilis (Moran et al., 1982). Furthermore the sequence, TAAAAT, is

---

Figure 2. Schematic drawing of a possible hairpin structure of the inverted repeat sequence, the potential RNA polymerase recognition sites, the potential Pribnow boxes, the Shine-Dalgarno sequence and the signal sequence for secretion in the upstream and promoter region of amyE$^+$.

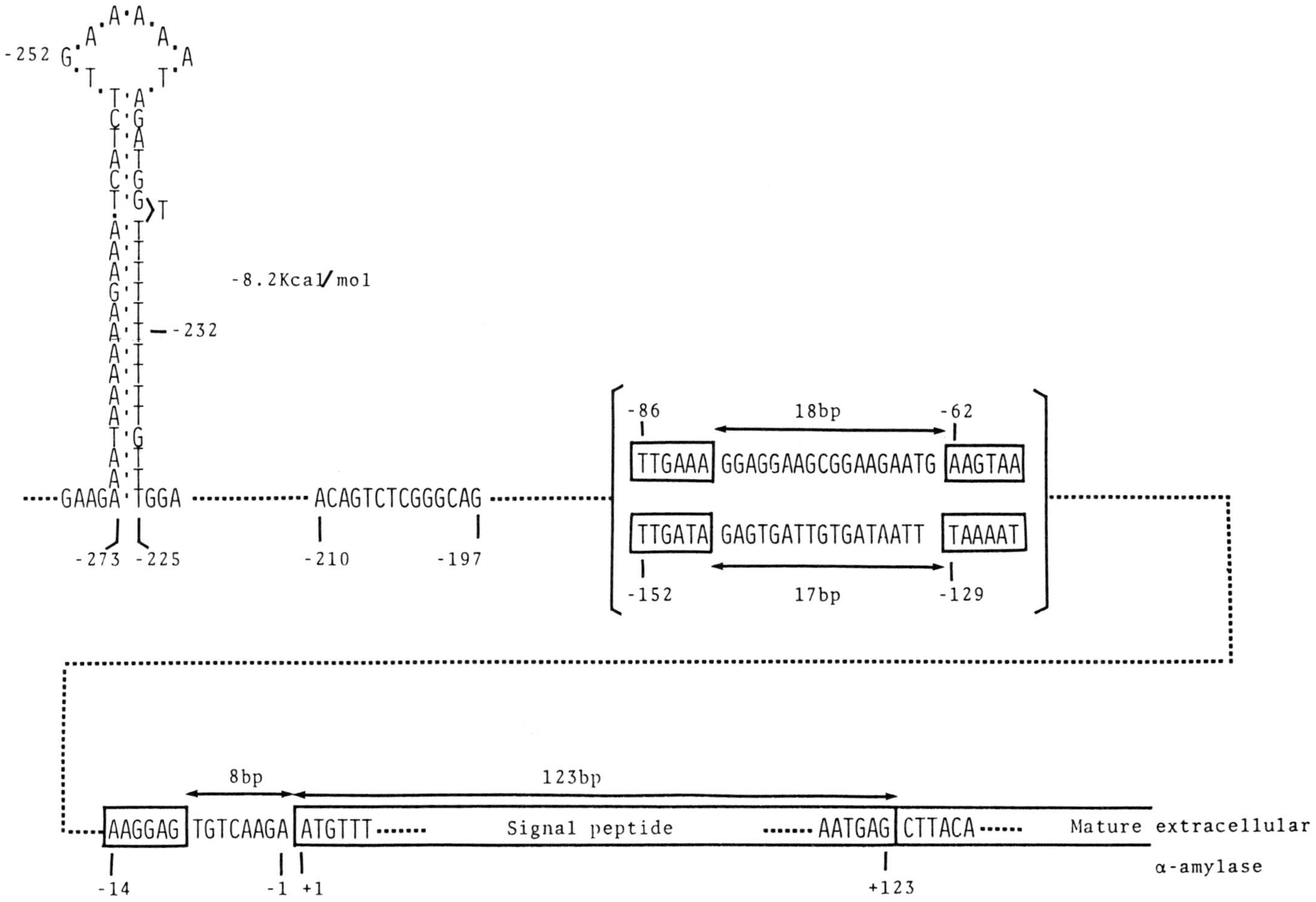
-252
-8.2Kcal/mol
-232
GAAGA
TGGA
-273
-225
ACAGTCTCGGGCAG
-210
-197
-86
18bp
-62
TTGAAA
GGAGGAAGCGGAAGAATG
AAGTAA
TTGATA
GAGTGATTGTGATAATT
TAAAAT
-152
17bp
-129
8bp
123bp
AAGGAG
TGTCAAGA
ATGTTT
Signal peptide
AATGAG
CTTACA
Mature extracellular
α-amylase
-14
-1
+1
+123

similar to the consensus sequence, TATAAT, in Pribnow boxes. We are now investigating which sequence is the actual RNA polymerase recognition site and Pribnow box.

B. subtilis NA64 carries a regulatory gene, amyR2, for the hyperproduction of α-amylase. The DNA nucleotide sequence analysis clarified that there is one inverted repeat structure (-273 to -225), composed almost entirely (41/49) of A and T polymers, in the upstream of the promoter region. The DNA sequence from -273 to -196 seems to correspond to the amyR2 region, because the sequence in this region was quite different from that of the B. subtilis 168 α-amylase gene which was cloned in E. coli vector systems (Yang et al., 1983).

In the promoter and signal sequence coding region of the plasmid pTUB4, one of the AluI restriction sites (GAGCTT) coincided with the protein cleavage site between the signal peptide and the mature extracellular α-amylase. Furthermore, the sequences for the regulatory signals of gene expression were included on one DNA fragment (424 bp) which was generated by the AluI-digestion (Yamazaki et al., submitted for publication).

IV. CONSTRUCTION OF THE SECRETION VECTOR IN B. SUBTILIS

The 424 bp DNA fragment generated by the AluI-digestion was utilized to construct a secretion vector in B. subtilis. The plasmid pTUB4 contains two EcoRI sites. The 4.9 kb and 1.9 kb fragments, generated by EcoRI-digestion, were separated by agarose gel electrophoresis. The cohesive ends of the 4.9 kb fragment were filled in, and the resulting fragment was ligated to HindIII linkers. The 1.9 kb fragment was redigested with AluI and the 424 bp fragment was isolated and then ligated to HindIII linkers. The plasmids, pTUB217 and pTUB218, were constructed from the 4.9 kb and the 424 bp fragment using HindIII linkers. The two plasmids were used as the secretion vectors in B. subtilis (Ohmura et al., submitted for publication).

V. PRODUCTION AND SECRETION OF E. COLI β-LACTAMASE BY THE B. SUBTILIS SECRETION VECTOR

To test the secretion vector, we fused the E. coli β-lactamase gene, which lacked its own promoter and signal peptide coding region and which contained HindIII termini (Palva et al., 1982), to the secretion vectors. The plasmid pKTH74, which was kindly supplied by Dr. I. Palva, Finland, was digested by HindIII. The 1.4 kb fragment generated was isolated and ligated to pTUB217 and pTUB218 after they were digested by HindIII. The constructed plasmid was transferred into B. subtilis 207-25 by the method of protoplast transformation (Chang and Cohen, 1979). The transformants were screened on plates for the expression of β-lactamase activity and Km^r. Several β-lactamase-positive transformants were detected from about 1,000 Km^r transformants. pTUB226 from pTUB217 and pTUB228 from pTUB218 were isolated from two of the transformants. The molecular size of the two plasmids were estimated to be equally 6.7 kb. They produced three DNA fragments (4.9 kb, 1.4 kb and 0.45 kb) by HindIII-digestion.

DNA nucleotide sequences in pTUB226 and pTUB228 at and near the junctions of the α-amylase signal sequence coding region of the α-amylase gene and the E. coli β-lactamase structural gene were analyzed (Figure 3). The nucleotide sequences at the 5' side of the linker region in pTUB226 and pTUB228 were coincident with that of the α-amylase signal sequence coding region. The nucleotide sequence of the 3' side contained the structural gene for the E. coli β-lactamase starting from the cytosine residue at position 3 of the mature enzyme. The linker construction codes for an additional tetrapeptide, Glu-Ala-Cys-Pro, proceeding β-lactamase proper. By the addition of this tetrapeptide, the amino acid sequence of the fused β-lactamase at the junction region is different from those of the NH_2-terminal regions of both α-amylase and β-lactamase. The cleavage site between the signal peptide and mature β-lactamase in the fused enzyme is now being investigated.

B. subtilis 207-25 strains harboring pTUB226 and pTUB228 were grown in LG-medium. β-lactamase activity in the culture supernatants and in the sonicated cells were measured after different periods of culture (Figure 4). The production of the extracellular E. coli β-lactamase by B. subtilis was started in the mid log phase of growth and the maximum amount of enzyme activity was obtained 5 to 7 hours after inoculation. These results indicate that the E. coli β-lactamase gene was expressed in B. subtilis through the aid of the promoter and the signal sequence of B. subtilis α-amylase resulting in more than 95% of the β-lactamase being secreted. However the activity in the culture medium disappeared after 10 hours in culture.

The activity of E. coli β-lactamase secreted into the culture medium from B. subtilis cells was inhibited by rabbit antiserum raised against E. coli β-lactamase as well as E. coli β-lactamase from the plasmid pBR322 (Ohmura et al., submitted for publication).

```
                              -41                                                    -29
                              Met Phe Ala Lys Arg Phe Lys Thr Ser Leu Leu Pro Leu
pTUB4                         ATG TTT GCA AAA CGA TTC AAA ACC TCT TTA CTG CCG TTA

        -28                                                                           -9
        Phe Ala Gly Phe Leu Leu Leu Phe Tyr Leu Val Leu Ala Gly Pro Ala Ala Ala Ser Ala
        TTC GCT GGA TTT TTA TTG CTG TTT TAT TTG GTT CTG GCA GGA CCG GCG GCT GCG AGT GCT
                                       A
        -8                          -1 | +1                                          +12
        Glu Thr Ala Asn Lys Ser Asn Glu|Leu Thr Ala Pro Ser Ile Lys Ser Gly Thr Ile Leu
        GAA ACG GCG AAC AAA TCG AAT GAG CTT ACA GCA CCG TCG ATC AAA AGC GGA ACC ATT CTT

         B.subtilis α-amylase gene
        ------------------------------>|
        -8                          -1                  +2                           +9
        Glu Thr Ala Asn Lys Ser Asn Glu [Gln Ala Cys Pro] Pro Glu Thr Leu Val Lys Val Lys
pTUB226 GAA ACG GCG AAC AAA TCG AAT GAG [CAA GCT TGC CC]C CCA GAA ACG CTG GTG AAA GTA AAA

        -8                          -1                  +2                           +9
        Glu Thr Ala Asn Lys Ser Asn Glu [Gln Ala Cys Pro] Pro Glu Thr Leu Val Lys Val Lys
pTUB228 GAA ACG GCG AAC AAA TCG AAT GAG [CAA GCT TGC CC]C CCA GAA ACG CTG GTG AAA GTA AAA

                                                     E.coli β-lactamase gene
                                               B   |------------------------------->
              -8                            -1 | +1                                  +9
              Ala Phe Cys Leu Pro Val Phe Ala|His Pro Glu Thr Leu Val Lys Val Lys
              GCA TTT TGC CTT CCT GTT TTT GCT CAC CCA GAA ACG CTG GTG AAA GTA AAA

        -23                                                   -9
        Met Ser Ile Gln His Phe Arg Val Ala Leu Ile Pro Phe Phe Ala
pBR322  ATG AGT ATT CAA CAT TTC CGT GTC GCC CTT ATT CCC TTT TTT GCG
```

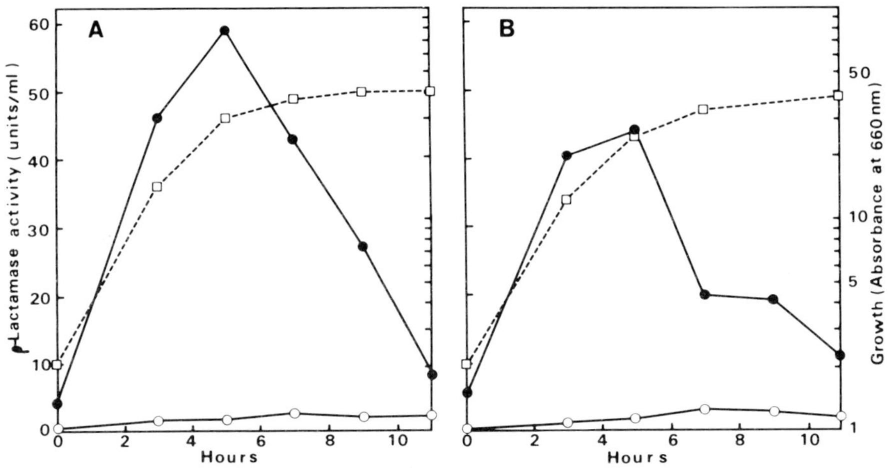

Figure 4. Extracellular production of E. coli β-lactamase by B. subtilis carrying pTUB226 [A] and pTUB228 [B]. The cells were grown in LG-medium containing 10 μg/ml of kanamycin at 37°C. —●—, β-lactamase activity; —O—, β-lactamase activity in the sonicated cells; and ---□---, growth measured by absorbance at 660 nm.

Figure 3. The DNA nucleotide sequences and amino acid sequences deduced from the nucleotide sequences of the junction regions of the B. subtilis α-amylase gene and the E. coli β-lactamase gene in the hybrid plasmids pTUB226 and pTUB228. The nucleotides of the linkers are encased (CAAGCTTGC is the HindIII linker and CC is a part of the EcoRI linker (Palva et al., 1982)). The complete signal sequence (-41 to -1 amino acid residues) and codons for the 12 amino acid residues in the NH_2-terminal region of the mature α-amylase are given in the upper part of the figure. For comparison, nucleotide and amino acid sequences of the signal peptide and the NH_2-terminal region of the E. coli β-lactamase from the plasmid pGR322 are given at the bottom of the figure. The cleavage site between the signal sequence and the extracellular mature α-amylase is indicated by the arrow A, and the site between the signal peptide and the mature E. coli β-lactamase of pBR322 is by the arrow B.

VI. DISCUSSION

We constructed a secretion vector in B. subtilis from the promoter and signal sequence coding region of the B. subtilis α-amylase gene. Then the E. coli β-lactamase structural gene, lacking its own promoter and signal peptide coding region, was introduced into the secretion vector using HindIII linkers. The E. coli β-lactamase gene was expressed in B. subtilis through the aid of the promoter and signal sequence of B. subtilis α-amylase. Furthermore, 95% of β-lactamase synthesized was secreted into the culture medium. However the activity was decreased after 7 hours in culture and not accumulated in contrast to α-amylase. This destruction of the β-lactamase activity in the medium was probably due to attack by extracellular proteases, because the culture period, coinciding with the disappearance of the β-lactamase activity, was the beginning of the stationary phase of growth at which point synthesis and secretion of extracellular proteases occurred. Therefore, it is clear that the isolation of the extracellular protease-deficient mutants is the first problem to which the secretion vector can be applied for practical utilization.

ACKNOWLEDGMENTS

We thank Professor H. Saito and Dr. F. Kawamura, Institute of Applied Microbiology, The University of Tokyo, for their helpful discussions, Dr. I. Palva, The Central Public Health Laboratory, Mannerheimintie 166, SF-00280, Helsinki 28, Finland, for his kind supply of plasmid pKTH74, and Dr. M. Inoue, School of Medicine, Gunma University, Maehashi, Japan, for his kind supply of rabbit antiserum raised against E. coli β-lactamase. We also thank Yuichi Hirata, Kouji Nakamura, Kiyoshi Nakazawa, Kenzaburo Suzuki, Naoyuki Tashiro, Takashi Furusato and Cheng-guangli for their help with these experiments.

REFERENCES

Chang, S. and Cohen, S.N. (1979). **Molec. Gen. Genet. 168,** 111.

Hitotsuyanagi, K., Yamane, K. and Maruo, B. (1979). **Agric. Biol. Chem. 43,** 2343.

Kawamura, F., Saito, H. and Ikeda, Y. (1979). **Gene 5,** 87.

Kreil, G. (1981). **Annu. Rev. Biochem. 50**, 317.
Maxam, A.M. and Gilbert, W. (1980). **Methods Enzymol. 65**, 499.
Mäntsälä, P. and Zalkin, H. (1979). **Meth. Enzymol. 65**, 499.
McLaughlin, J.R., Murray, C.L. and Rabinowitz, J.C. (1981). **J. Biol. Chem. 256**, 11283.
Moran, C.P., Jr., Lang, N., LeGrice, S.F.J., Len, G., Stephens, M., Sonenshein, A.L., Pero, J. and Losick, R. (1982). **Molec. Gen. Genet. 186**, 339.
Nielsen, J.B.K. and Lampen, J.O. (1982). **J. Biol. Chem. 257**, 4490.
Nomura, S., Yamane, K., Masuda, T. Kawamura, F., Mizukami, T., Saito, H., Takatsuki, A., Yamasaki, M., Tamura, G. and Maruo, B. (1979). **Agric. Biol. Chem. 43**, 2367.
Nomura, S., Yamane, K., Sasaki, T., Yamasaki, M., Tamura, G. and Maruo, B. (1978). **J. Bacteriol. 136**, 8.
Ohmura, K., Shiroza, T., Nakamura, K., Nakayama, A., Yamane, K., Yoda, K., Yamasaki, M. and Tamura, G., submitted for publication.
Ohmura, K., Yamazaki, H., Takeichi, Y., Nakayama, A., Otozai, Kl, Yamane, K., Yamanasaki, M. and Tamura, G. (1983). **Biochem. Biophys. Res. Commun. 112**, 678.
Palva, I., Sarvas, M., Lehtovaara, Ph., Kibakov, M. and Kääriäinen, L. (1982). **Proc. Natl. Acad. Sci. USA 78**, 5582.
Takeichi, Y., Ohmura, K., Nakayama, A., Otozai, K. and Yamane, K. (1983). **Agric. Biol. Chem. 47**, 159.
Yamaguchi, K., Nagata, Y. and Maruo, B. (1974). **J. Bacteriol. 119**, 416.
Yamane, K. (1980). **J. Agric. Chem. Soc. Jpn. 54**, 877.
Yamazaki, H., Ohmura, K., Nakayama, A., Takeichi, Y., Otozai, K., Yamasaki, J., Tamura, G. and Yamane, K., submitted for publication.
Yang, M., Galizzi, A. and Henner, D. (1983). **Nucl. Acids Res. 11**, 327.
Yuki, S. (1975). **Jpn. J. Genet. 50**, 155.

Session III: Transcription

IN VITRO TRANSCRIPTION OF BACTERIOPHAGE Ø29 DNA[1]

Margarita Salas
Rafael P. Mellado
Jose M. Lazaro
Jose M. Sogo[2]

Centro de Biologiz Molecular (CSIC-UAM)
Universidad Autonoma, Canto Blanco
Madrid, Spain

I. INTRODUCTION

Bacillus subtilis phage Ø29 contains a linear, double-stranded DNA of 18,000 base pairs (Sogo et al., 1979) with a viral protein, p3, covalently linked at the two 5' ends (Salas et al, 1978; Harding et al., 1978; Ito, 1978; Yehle, 1978). In vivo early RNA is synthesized by the host RNA polymerase from the light (L) Ø29 DNA strand since the direction of transcription is from right to left and late RNA is made from the heavy (H) DNA strain, from left to right (Schachtele et al., 1973; Carrascosa et al., 1976). Late transcription requires the product of the early gene 4 (Sogo et al, 1979). Early transcription in vivo takes place from the two end regions of Ø29 DNA and late transcription occurs from the middle region of the genome, in agreement with the location of early and late genes, respectively. In

[1]*This investigation has been aided by grant GM 27242 from the National Institutes of Health and by grants from Comision Asesora para el Desarrollo de la Investigacion Cientifica y Tencica and Fondo de Investigaciones Sanitarias. R.P.M. was the recipient of a senior fellowship from the Ministerio de Educacion y Ciencia.*

[2]*Present address: ETH. Institut für Zellbiologie, Hönggerberg, CH-8093 Zürich, Switzerland.*

ISBN 0-12-274160-9

addition, symmetric transcription (at early times from the DNA L strand and at late times from the DNA H strand) exists in a region at the middle of the genome (Sogo et al., 1979).

The analysis under the electron microscope of the interaction of B. subtilis RNA polymerase with Ø29 DNA showed the existence of seven specific binding sites named A1, A2, A3, B1, B2, C1 and C2, located at 1.7, 25.5, 26.7, 59.4, 79.3, 91.3 and 99.3 DNA length units (Sogo et al., 1979).

When the in vitro transcription of Ø29 DNA with the B. subtilis RNA polymerase was analyzed using the R-loop technique (Brack, 1979), eight transcripts were obtained. The initiation position of six of them correlated well with the B. subtilis RNA polymerase binding sites (Sogo et al., submitted).

To study how the gene 4 product controls Ø29 DNA late transcription, a Ø29 DNA fragment containing the complete sequence of gene 4, has been cloned under the control of the P_L promoter of the phage λ. After activation of the promoter, protein p4 was synthesized, accounting for about 30% of the de novo produced protein (Mellado and Salas, 1982). When extracts from E. coli transformed with the gene 4-containing recombinant plasmid were added to the B. subtilis RNA polymerase, transcription from the middle of Ø29 DNA, corresponding to the late region, was obtained.

II. RESULTS AND DISUCSSION

A. In vitro Transcription of Ø29 DNA with B. subtilis RNA Polymerase

Ø29 DNA was transcribed with the B. subtilis RNA polymerase and the hybrid DNA-RNA molecules were analyzed by electron microscopy (Sogo et al., submitted) using the R-loop technique (Brack, 1979). Figure 1A shows a micrograph from the molecule transcribed for 0.75 minutes containing one R-loop. The histogram for this transcription time (Figure 2A) shows one major peak, with the sharp side at position 25.4, that corresponds to the initiation of transcription from the A2 binding site, going from right to left, as expected for early transcription. After 1.5 minutes of tanscription the histogram is similar (Figure 2B) except that there is more transcription from the right end than at a shorter time. Figure 1B shows a molecule transcribed for 1.5 minutes, with two R-loops. After 5 minutes of transcription the pattern changed drastically (Figure 3A). Five main R-loops were obtained, located between 13.7 to 25.6, 28.0 to 43.0, 59.0 to 70.2, 72.1 to

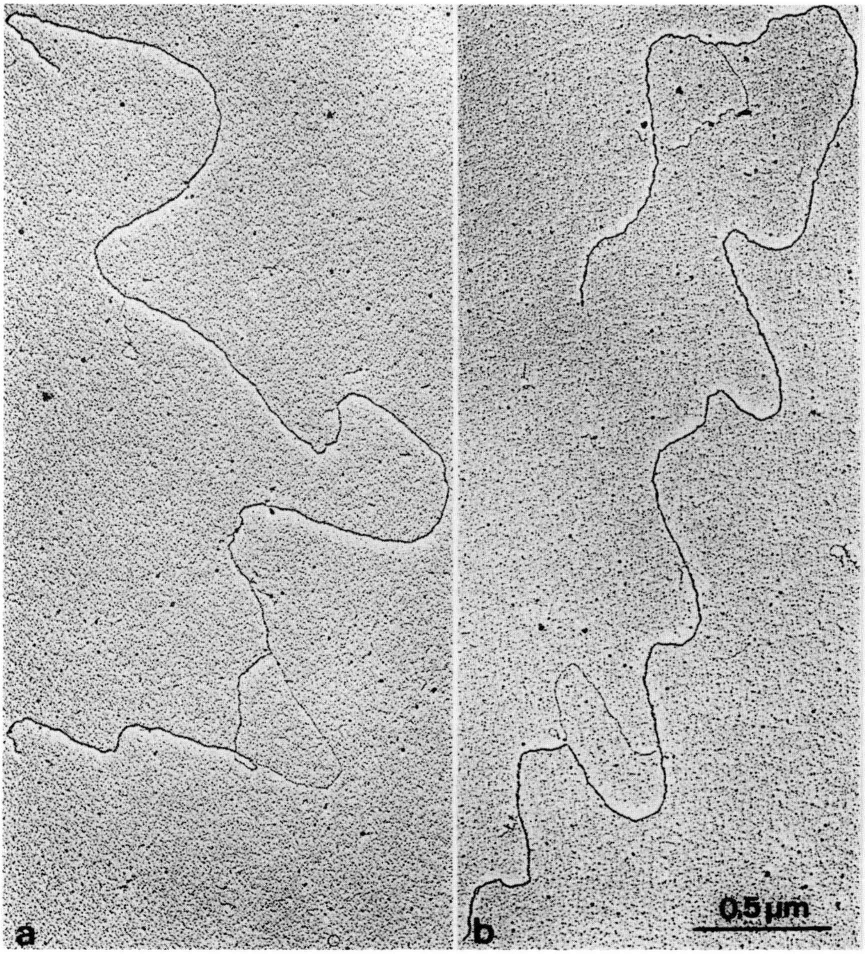

Figure 1. Electron micrographs of transcription R-loop molecules obtained with B. subtilis RNA polymerase on Ø29 DNA. Ø29 DNA was transcribed with B. subtilis RNA polymerase for 0.75 minutes [A] or 1.5 minutes [B] at 37 °C and the samples were prepared for electron microscopy as described by Sogo et al. (submitted).

91.4 and 92.7 to 99.0 length units. Transcription is initiated at positions 25.6, 28.0, 70.2, 91.4 and 99.0 (see later) and therefore occurs from right to left, except for that starting at position 28.0 which takes place from left to right. A small R-loop, probably starting at position 1.6 and moving to the left was also observed.

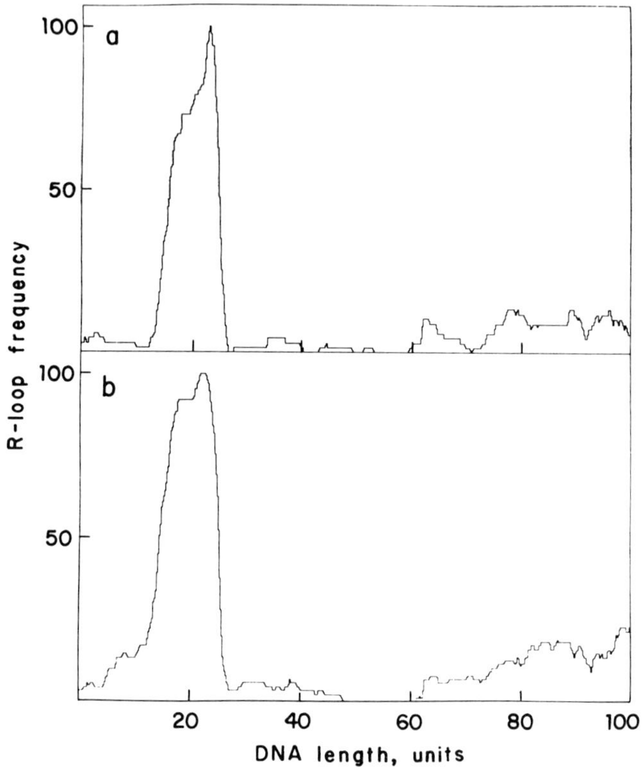

Figure 2. Histogram of transcription R-loop molecules obtained with B. subtilis RNA polymerase on Ø29 DNA. Ø29 DNA was transcribed with B. subtilis RNA polymerase for 0.75 minutes [A] or 1.5 minutes [B] at 37 °C and the samples were prepared for electron microscopy as described by Sogo et al. (submitted). 95 DNA molecules with 124 R-loops were analyzed in [A] and 98 DNA molecules with 145 R-loops in [B].

To confirm both the correct orientation of the DNA-RNA hybrid molecules as well as the direction of transcription, fragments HpaI A and EcoRI B (see Figure 7) were transcribed. Figure 3B shows the histogram obtained with fragment HpaI A, located at the left of the genome. The two large R-loops starting at positions 27.5 and 29.0 were seen, the transcription taking place from right to left and from left to right, respectively. The small R-loop at position 1.6 was also observed. The histogram obtained with fragment EcoRI B (Figure 3C) showed two peaks with the starting positions at 68.3 and 79.1, the direction of transcription

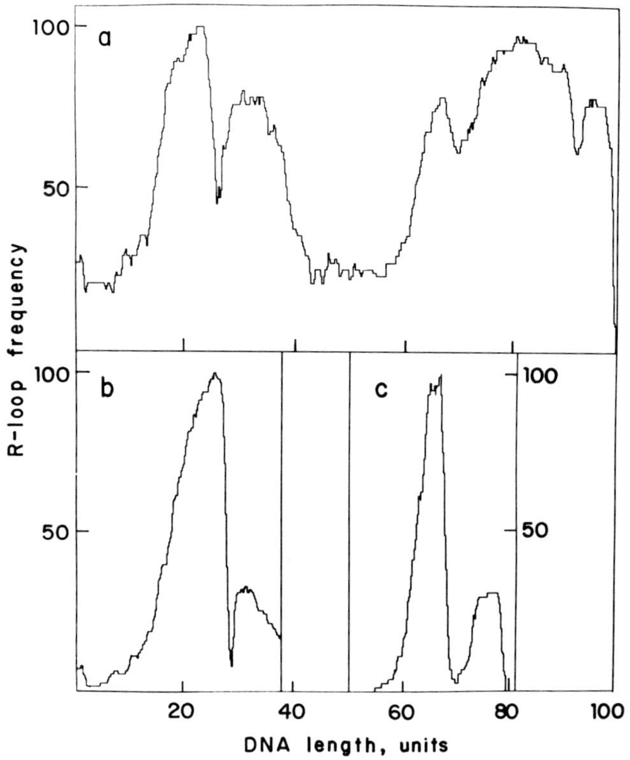

Figure 3. Histogram of transcription R-loop molecules obtained with B. subtilis RNA polymerase on Ø29 DNA and fragments HpaI A and EcoRI B. Ø29 DNA [A] or fragments HpaI A [B] or EcoRI B [C] were incubated at 37 °C with B. subtilis RNA polymerase for 5 minutes in the case of the intact DNA and for 2.5 minutes in the case of the fragments and the samples were prepared for electron microscopy as described by Sogo et al. (submitted). 60 DNA molecules with 193 R-loops were analyzed in [A], 112 molecules with 146 R-loops in [B] and 96 molecules with 101 R-loops in [C]. From Sogo et al. (1983).

being from right to left. Comparison of the histograms obtained with the whole DNA and with fragments HpaI A and EcoRI B (Figure 3) shows the existence of a good correlation and that the broad peak at position 72.1 to 91.4 (Figure 3A) overlaps another small peak at 72.5 to 79.1 length units (Figure 3C). In addition to all of the above peaks a new one appeared after 10 minutes of transcription, between 1.8 and 10.3 units, probably transcribing from right to left (Sogo et al., submitted).

From the above results we can conclude that at short incubation times of Ø29 DNA with the B. subtilis RNA polymerase there is one major transcript starting at position 25.6 and going from right to left. Later on, new transcripts appear going from the right end to position 62. Finally, at longer incubation times eight transcripts are seen starting at positions 1.6, 10.3, 25.6, 68.3, 79.1, 91.4 and 99.0 and going from right to left, and one starting at position 28.0 and transcribing from left to right. The transcripts that start at positions 1.6, 25.6, 79.1, 91.4 and 99.0 correspond to the binding sites A1, A2, B2, C1 and C2 found with the B. subtilis RNA polymerase (Sogo et al, 1979) and those starting at 10.3 and 68.3 correspond to the binding sites A1III and B1I found only with the Escherichia coli enzyme (Sogo et al., submitted). All of these are early transcripts. The transcript that starts at position 28 and goes from left to right up to position 43 corresponds to the binding site A3 and probably represents late transcription. This transcript appears after longer incubation times and is not seen at high salt (Sogo et al., submitted. See Figure 7 for a summary of the transcription map of Ø29 DNA with the B. subtilis RNA polymerase as compared with the in vivo transcription map.

B. Cloning of Gene 4 Under the Control of the P_L Promoter of Phage λ

The Ø29 DNA fragment HindIII G contains 1150 bp (Escarmis and Salas, 1982; Yoshikawa and Ito, 1982) and is located in an early region transcribed from right to left (Sogo et al., 1979) (see Figure 7). In this fragment there are two partially overlapping reading frames; one with a coding capacity for a polypeptide of 125 amino acids which was shown to be protein p4 (Mellado and Salas, 1982; Escarmis and Salas, 1982) involved the control of late transcription (Sogo et al., 1979), and the other, coding for all but the last five carboxy terminal amino acids of the terminal protein p3, which has a total of 266 amino acids (Escarmis and Salas, 1982).

The HindIII G fragment was cloned first in the HindIII site of plasmid pBR322 (Bolivar et al., 1977) to provide a

---

Figure 4. Recombinant plasmids containing the Ø29 DNA fragment HindIII G from wild-type Ø29 DNA with respect to the P_L promoter. Plasmids pRMw51 and pRMs463 contained the HindIII G fragment from wild-type Ø29 DNA and from mutant sus4(56) (Moreno et al., 1974), respectively. From Mellado et al. (1982).

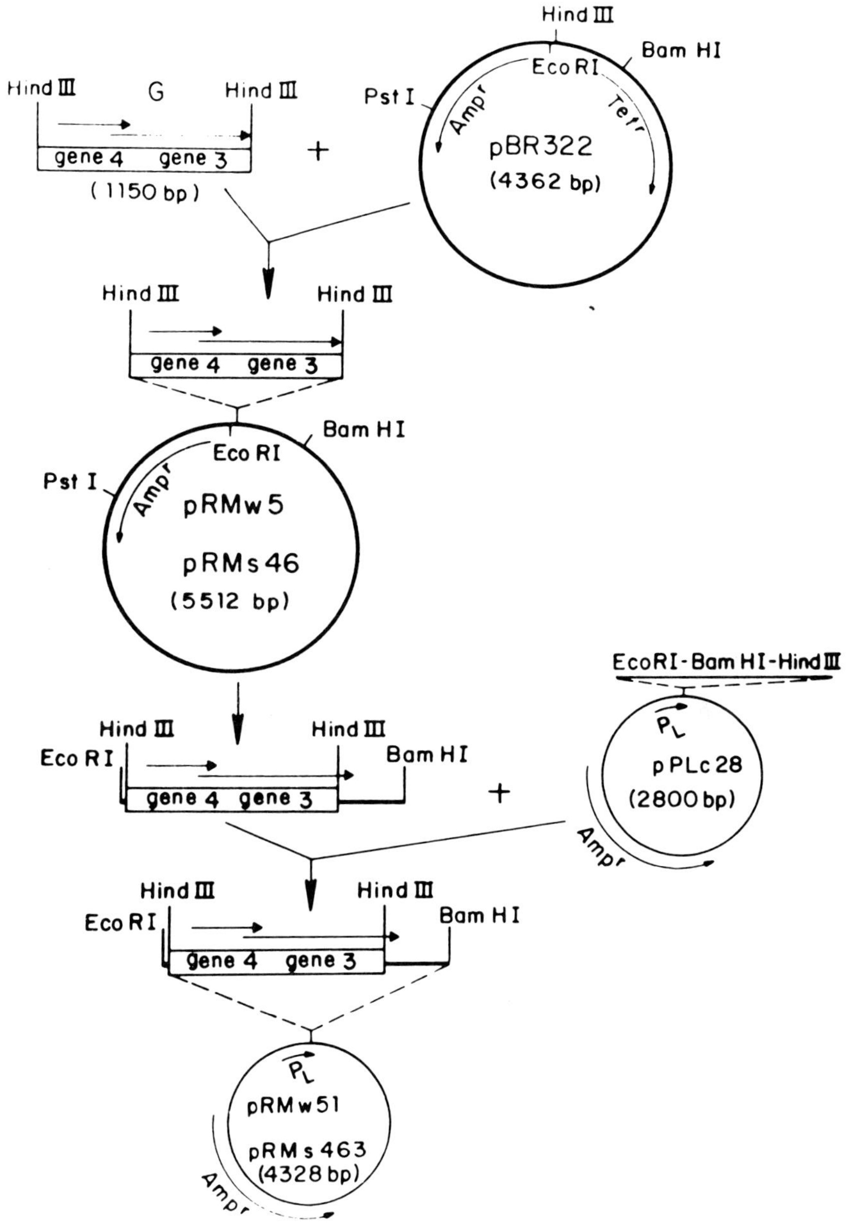
Hind III
G
Hind III
gene 4 gene 3
(1150 bp)
+
Hind III
Bam HI
Eco RI
Pst I
Ampr
Tetr
pBR322
(4362 bp)
Hind III
Hind III
gene 4 gene 3
Bam HI
Eco RI
Pst I
Ampr
pRMw5
pRMs46
(5512 bp)
Hind III
Hind III
Eco RI
Bam HI
gene 4 gene 3
+
EcoRI-Bam HI-Hind III
PL
pPLc28
(2800 bp)
Ampr
Hind III
Hind III
Eco RI
Bam HI
gene 4 gene 3
PL
pRMw51
pRMs463
(4328 bp)
Ampr

translation termination signal (Sutcliffe, 1978) so that the sequence coding for the last five amino acids of protein p3 would be replaced by another one adding nine new amino acids (protein p3'). To overproduce proteins p4 and p3' the recombinant plasmids were cut with EcoRI and BamHI and the resulting fragments were ligated to plasmid pPLc28 (Remaut et al., 1981) digested with the same enzymes, to place genes 4 and 3 under the control of the P_L promoter of phage λ present in plasmid pPLc28. The new recombinant plasmids obtained, pRMw51 and pRMs463 with the HindIII G fragment from wild type Ø29 DNA or from mutant sus4(56), respectively, are shown in Figure 4 (Mellado and Salas, 1982).

C. Inducible Synthesis of Proteins p4 and p3'

E. coli K-12ΔH1Δtrp, containing a λ lysogen with the ts repressor CI857, and harboring the vector pPLc28 or the recombinant plasmids pRMw51 or pRMs463, was incubated as described (Mellado and Salas, 1982), shifted at 42°C and labeled with ^{35}S-methionine for 10 minutes at various times after the shift. As a control, samples from the cultures kept at 30°C were labeled at zero time and the latest time. Shortly after incubation the rate of synthesis of three polypeptides with apparent molecular weights of 27,500, 15,000 and 12,500 increased markedly in the case of plasmid pRM251 (Figure 5, lanes g to i). The three polypeptides were missing when the vector without insert was used (Figure 5, lanes b to d). The protein of 12,500 daltons was not synthesized when the recombinant carried the DNA fragment from mutnat sus4(56) (plasmid pRMs463) being the other two polypeptides synthesized normally (Figure 5, lanes l to n). These results clearly identify the 12,500 daltons polypeptide as the gene 4 product, protein p4. The 27,500 daltons polypeptide is a modified protein p3 (p3') and the 15,000 daltons polypeptide corresponds to a fusion protein (Mellado and Salas, 1982).

Figure 5. Induced synthesis of protein p4 directed by the recombinant plasmid pRMw51. Bacterial cultures harboring the vector pPLc28 or the recombinant plasmids pRMw51 or pRMs463 were grown, labeled with ^{35}S-methionine and subjected to SDS-polyacrylamide gel electrophoresis as described (Mellado and Salas, 1982). ^{3}H-concanavalin A peptides of known molecular weight (Wang et al., 1971) were used as markers (The Radiochemical Centre, Amersham). The starting time of each labeling period (in minutes) and the temperature of incubation are indicated above the lanes. From Mellado et al. (1982).

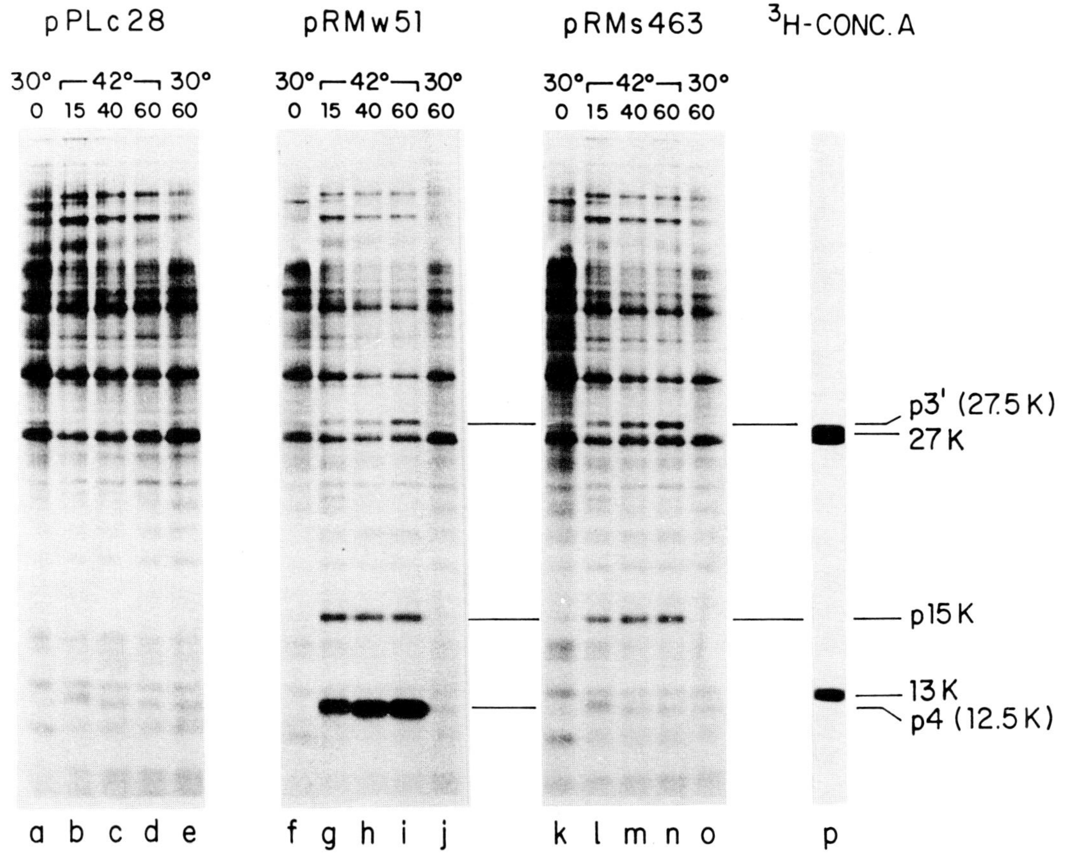
pPLc28
pRMw51
pRMs463
³H-CONC. A
30° ┌─42°─┐ 30°
0 15 40 60 60
p3' (27.5 K)
27 K
p15 K
13 K
p4 (12.5 K)
a b c d e
f g h i j
k l m n o
p

To determine the level of synthesis of protein p4 coded for by plasmid pRMw51, the cultures were incubated at 42°C and labeled with ^{35}S-methionine at different times. Even at 4 hours after heat induction the synthesis of protein p4 was still taking place at maximal rate. Densitometry of the labeled proteins indicated that the highest level of synthesis, reached at 90 to 120 minutes after induction, was 30% of the de novo synthesized protein (Mellado and Salas, 1982). Protein p4 synthesized in E. coli was stable for at least 210 minutes as shown by a pulse and chase experiment (Mellado and Salas, 1982).

D. In vitro Transcription of Ø29 DNA by the B. subtilis RNA Polymerase in the Presence of Extracts Containing Protein p4

To determine the effect of protein p4 on the in vitro transcription, Ø29 DNA was incubated with the B. subtilis RNA polymerase in the presence of extracts from E. coli harboring the control plasmid pPLc28 or the gene 4-containing recombinant plasmid, from wild-type phage or from mutant sus4(56), and the DNA-RNA hybrid molecules were analyzed by electron microscopy as previously described. When Ø29 DNA was transcribed for 5 minutes with the B. subtilis RNA polymerase in the presence of extracts from E. coli harboring the control plasmid pPLc28 transcription took place mainly at the two end regions and very little at the middle of the DNA (Figure 6A). Addition of extracts from E. coli harboring the gene 4-containing recombinant plasmid from wild-type Ø29 DNA gave rise to transcription from the middle of the DNA, from position 28 to 60, that corresponds to late genes (Figures 6B and 7). As a control, addition of extracts from E. coli containing the sus4-recombinant plasmid did not give rise to any transcription from the middle region of Ø29 DNA (Figure 6C).

---

described by Sogo et al. (submitted). 103 DNA molecules with 142 R-loops were analyzed in [A], 168 DNA molecules with 330 R-loopes in [B] and 127 DNA molecules with 155 R-loops in [C].

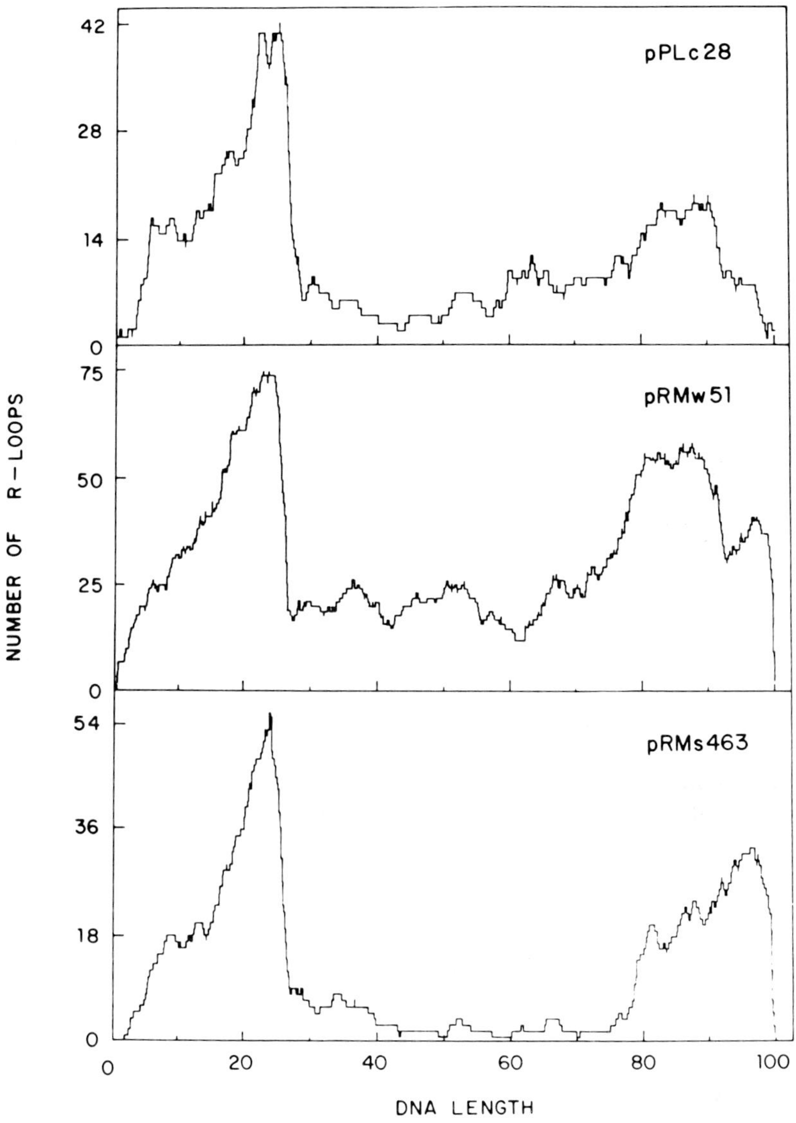

Figure 6. Histogram of transcription R-loop molecules obtained with B. subtilis RNA polymerase of Ø29 DNA in the presence of extracts containing protein p4. Ø29 DNA was transcribed for 2 minutes at 37 °C with B. subtilis RNA polymerase in the presence of extracts from E. coli harboring the control plasmid [A] , the wild-type gene 4-containing plasmid [B] or the sus4-containing plasmid [C] and the samples were prepared for electron microscopy as

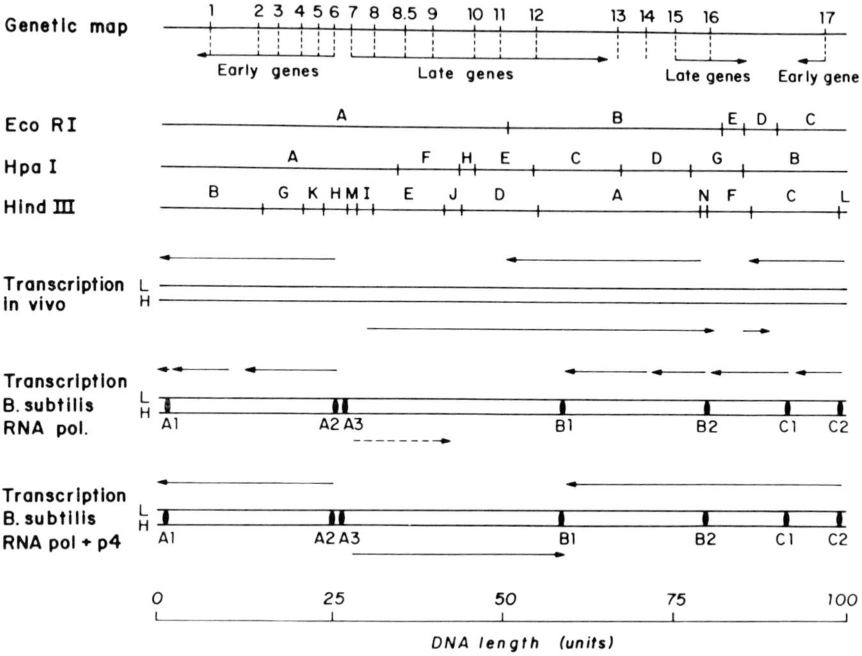

Figure 7. Transcription map of Ø29 DNA. The genetic map of Ø29 was taken from Sogo et al. (submitted). The numbers indicate genes and the lines with the arrows below the genes indicate direction of transcription. The EcoRI, HpaI and HindIII map cleavage sites were taken from Inciarte et al., (1976) and Yoshikawa and Ito (1982). The in vivo transcription map of Ø29 DNA was taken from Sogo et al. (1979). The lines in the middle represent the light (L) and heavy (H) DNA strands. The lines with the arrows indicate direction and extent of early or late transcription from the L or H DNA strand, respectively. The in vitro transcription map of Ø29 DNA with B. subtilis RNA polymerase was taken from Sogo et al. (submitted). The binding sites (Sogo et al., 1979) are indicated in the middle of the DNA strands. The solid lines with arrows indicate direction and extent of transcription from the DNA L strand and the discontinuous line with arrow represents transcription from the DNA H strand which takes place long after incubation times. In the case of the the transcription of Ø29 DNA with B. subtilis RNA polymerase in the presence of protein p4, the solid lines with arrows indicate direction and extent of transcription from the L and H DNA strand, respectively.

To study further the mechanism of action of protein p4 in the control of late transcription we have undertaken the purification of the protein from the E. coli extracts harboring the gene 4-containing recombinant plasmid. A partially purified preparation of protein p4, when added to the core RNA polymerase, stimulates specifically the in vitro synthesis of RNA that hybridizes to the late DNA strand from the HindIII D fragment (see physical map in Figure 7) (R. P. Mellado, J. M. Lazaro and M. Salas, unpublished results). This result suggests that protein p4 may act as a sigma-like factor. Further purification of the protein to study how it promotes late transcription and to determine the structure of late promoters in Ø29 DNA is under way.

REFERENCES

Bolivar, F., Rodriguez, R.L., Green, P.Y., Betlach, M.C., Heynecker, H.L., Boyer, H.W., Crosa, Y.H. and Falkow, S. (1977). **Gene 2**, 95.

Brack, C. (1979). **Proc. Natl. Acad. Sci. USA 76**, 3164.

Carrascosa, J.L., Camacho, A., Moreno, F., Jimenez, F., Mellado, R.P., Vinuela, E. and Salas, M. (1976). **Eur. J. Biochem. 66**, 229.

Escarmis, C. and Salas, M. (1982). **Nucl. Acids Res. 10**, 5785.

Harding, N., Ito, J. and David, G.S. (1978). **Virology 84**, 279.

Inciarte, R.M., Lazaro, J.M., Salas, M. and Vinuela, E. (1976). **Virology 74**, 314.

Ito, J. (1978). **J. Virol. 82**, 895.

Mellado, R.P. and Salas, M. (1982). **Nucl. Acids Res. 10**, 5773.

Moreno, F., Camacho, A., Vinuela, E. and Salas, M. (1974). **Virology 62**, 1.

Remaut, E., Stanssens, P. and Fiers, W. (1981). **Gene 51**, 81.

Salas, M., Mellado, R.P., Vinuela, E. and Sogo, J.M. (1978). **J. Mol. Biol. 119**, 269.

Schachtele, C.F., De Sain, C.B. and Anderson, D.L. (1973). **J. Virol. 11**, 9.

Sogo, J.M., Inciarte, M.R., Corral, J., Vinuela, E. and Salas, M. (1979). **J. Mol. Biol. 127**, 411.

Sogo, J.M., Lozano, M. and Salas, M. (1983). Submitted for publication.

Sutcliffe, J.G. (1978). **Cold Spring Harbor Symp. Quant. Biol. 43**, 77.

Wang, J.L., Cunningham, B.A. and Edelman, G.M. (1971). **Proc. Natl. Acad. Sci.** USA **68**, 1130.
Yehle, D.c. (1978). **J. Virol. 27**, 776.
Yoshikawa, H. and Ito, J. (1982). **Gene 17**, 323.

STRUCTURE, REGULATION AND GENETIC LOCUS OF A TEMPORALLY EXPRESSED PROMOTER OF BACILLUS SUBTILIS[1]

Sui-Lam Wong
David S. Goldfarb
Chester W. Price
Roy H. Doi

Department of Biochemistry and Biophysics
University of California
Davis, California

I. INTRODUCTION

Temporally regulated genes of Bacillus subtilis are expressed at least partly in response to nutrient depletion in the growth medium. The products of these genes mediate a number of post-exponential phase functions and include catabolite controlled intracellular and extracellular enzymes (Priest, 1977) and developmental enzymes directly involved in the sporulation process. Thus it is fundamental for both the efficient commercial use of the organism and to model sporulation regulatory systems that we understand the mechanisms controlling gene expression during the exponential and stationary phases of growth.

Losick and Pero (1981) proposed a model for transcriptional regulation based on the observation of multiple RNA polymerase holoenzymes in sporulating B. subtilis. They suggested that a cascade of sigma factors conferred changing promoter specificity on the RNA polymerase core enzyme and controlled the sequential expression of genes involved in the sporulation process. Data from several laboratories now indicate that at least five RNA polymerase holoenzymes are

[1]*This research was supported in part by National Science Foundation Grant PCM 79-24872 and National Institute of General Medical Sciences Grant GM 19673.*

ISBN 0-12-274160-9

present in vegetative and sporulating cells (see Doi, 1982 for review). The vegetative cell contains in addition to the major holoenzyme $E\sigma^{55}$ (E = core enzyme; σ^{55} - sigma factor with molecular mass of 55,000 daltons), several minor holoenzymes including $E\sigma^{37}$ (Haldenwang and Losick, 1980), $E\sigma^{32}$ (Johnson et al., 1983), and $E\sigma^{29}$ (Wiggs et al., 1981). Sporulating cells contain $E\sigma^{55}$, $E\sigma^{37}$, and a sporulation-specific $E\sigma^{29}$ (Haldenwang et al., 1981). Additional core-associated polypeptides have been identified but not fully characterized (Wong and Doi, 1982; Fukuda and Doi, 1977). These five holoenzymes have different promoter specificities in vitro (Losick and Pero, 1981; Johnson et al., 1983). Thus the sequential functioning of sigma factors could conceivably result in a temporally regulated expression of genes during sporulation.

In order to test the model of multiple RNA polymerase holoenzymes as controlling factors in gene expression, it was of interest to us to isolate a temporally regulated gene. We could then study the role of minor RNA polymerase holoenzymes(s) and other regulatory elements on the expression of such a gene and perhaps explain its expression during stationary phase and its repression during growth. By use of the expression probe plasmid, pGR71 (Goldfarb et al., 1981), we have isolated a B. subtilis DNA fragment containing a gene expressed only during the stationary phase and transcribed in vitro only by $E\sigma^{37}$ promoters. The promoter recognized by $E\sigma^{37}$ has a sequence similar to that reported for two other σ^{37} promoters (Moran et al., 1981), contains a region of dyad symmetry which overlaps the promoter, and controls a gene which may encode an extracellular protein.

II. RESTRICTION AND TRANSCRIPTION MAPS OF THE S FRAGMENT

We isolated a B. subtilis DNA fragment containing a temporally regulated promoter by use of the expression-probe plasmid, pGR71 (Goldfarb et al., 1981). This 1,250 bp HindIII fragment (S fragment) contains a promoter which expresses the promoterless chloramphenicol acetyltransferase (CAT) gene of pGR71 only during the stationary phase of growth; no CAT activity was observed during the exponential phase.

In order to determine the promoter site and holoenzyme which transcribes this temporally regulated gene, we used the purified S fragment as a template for in vitro transcription mapping with $E\sigma^{55}$, $E\sigma^{37}$ and $E\sigma^{29}$. To our surprise, the relatively small DNA fragment contained four

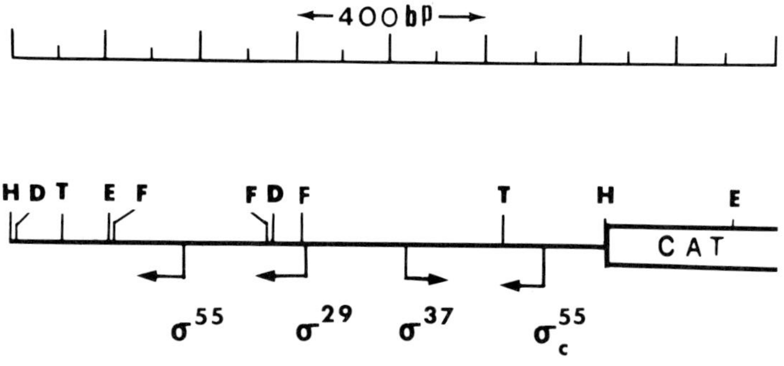

Figure 1. Transcription map and promoter sites on the S Fragment. The location of the promoters for $E\sigma^{55}$, $E\sigma^{37}$ and $E\sigma^{29}$ were determined by analysis of run-off transcripts from the S fragment and S fragment shortened by cleavage with restriction enzymes.

promoter sites, as shown in Figure 1. There are two promoter sites for $E\sigma^{55}$, one for $E\sigma^{29}$ and one for $E\sigma^{37}$, which was the only promoter which read towards the CAT gene. We found a high degree of promoter specificity in our transcription studies, with each promoter recognized **only** by its cognate holoenzyme.

III. IN VIVO ANALYSIS OF THE PROMOTERS ON THE S FRAGMENT

The in vitro transcription analyses indicated the location of four promoters on the S fragment. In order to verify the existence of promoters at these locations, we subcloned each putative promoter site into a promoter probe plasmid which contained a promoterless selective gene. Putative promoter regions from the S fragment were inserted first into the E. coli plasmid pK01 (McKinney et al., 1981). The insertion of S fragment promoter regions **in the correct orientation** gave pK01 galactokinase gene expression. We estimated the relative strength of the promoters in E. coli using the amount of galactokinase synthesized as a direct measure of promoter efficiency. The results illustrated that the subcloned regions indeed did contain promoters

Table 1. Promoters Inserted Into the pK01 Plasmid

Promoter	*Source of Promoter*	*Galactokinase Units*[a]
None		*17*
E. coli <u>*rrnP*</u>$_1P_2$		*2,800*
E. coli <u>*gal*</u>		*650*
E. coli <u>*lac*</u>		*520*
E. coli <u>*ara*</u>		*210*
B. subtilis σ^{37}	*pGR71-S*	*65*
B. subtilis σ^{29}	*pGR71-S*	*147*
B. subtilis σ^{55}	*pGR71-S*	*72*
B. subtilis σc^{55}	*pGR71-S*	*192*

[a]*Galactokinase units are expressed as nmoles of galactose phosphorylated per minute per* OD_{650}*. The data for E. coli promoters are from McKenney et al. (1981).*

utilized by E. coli RNA polymerase. The more surprising aspect of the results was that all the B. subtilis promoters inserted into pK01 -- including those recognized only by the minor forms of the B. subtilis RNA polymerase -- were recognized by the E. coli enzyme (Table 1). Although the B. subtilis promoters were used with relatively low efficiency, there was significant utilization of all the promoters. This suggests that the E. coli RNA polymerase, which exists as a single holoenzyme form, is able to recognize a wide spectrum of promoter sequences.

We verified temporal expression of the σ^{37} promoter region by placing it ahead of the promoterless trpBA-lacZ fusion of plasmid pCED6 (furnished kindly by A. L. Sonenshein), allowing expession of the lacZ gene by transcriptional and translational read-through. With the ^{37} promoter in pCED6, B. subtilis did not synthesize β-galactosidase until the cells had reached the stationary phase of growth (Figure 2). Thus the expression of the lacZ gene in this plasmid was controlled by the σ^{37} promoter during growth.

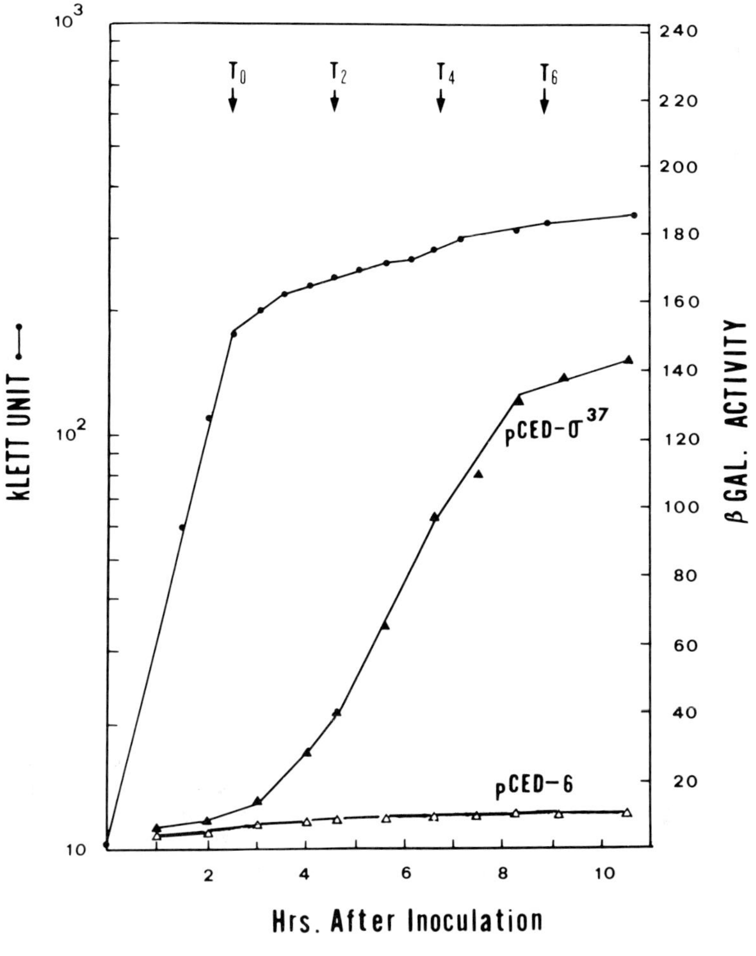

Figure 2. Expression of the σ^{37} promoter from S fragment after insertion into the promoter probe plasmid pCED6. pCED6 was kindly provided by A.L. Sonenshein. The β-galactosidase activity is expressed as:

$$\frac{1000 \times OD_{420}}{vol(ml) \times time(min) \times Klett\ Unit}$$

The closed and open triangles represent β-galactosidase activity in pCED6 with the σ^{37} promoter and pCED6 alone, respectively.

SpoVG	AGGATTTCA	GAAAAAATCGTG	GAATTGATACACTAA
SpoVC	AGGTTTAAA	TCCTTATCGTTATGG	GTATTGTTTGTAATA
S-σ^{37}	AGTCTTTTA	AGTAAGTCTACTC	GAATTTTTTAAAAG
	AGg-TTt-A	← 12-15 bp →	GaATTgtT

Figure 3. Comparison of the promoters recognized by $E\sigma^{37}$. The sequences for *spoVG* *and* *spoVC* *genes are from Moran et al. (1981). The lowest line represents the consensus sequence derived from the 3 sequences with the large letters representing 3/3 and the lower letters 2/3.*

```
                                        HO-UC        CA U G----16s rRNA
                                             UUUCCUC  C  A
                                              |||||||  | |
     -35                    -10                                    Met
GAATAGTCTTTTAAGTAAGTCTACTCTGAATTTTTTAAAAGGAGAGGGTAAAGAGTG
        -------  -- -  -     -  - --  -------

    AGGXTT                  GGXATTGXT      ΔG' = -13.5 kcal/mol
```

Figure 4. The regulatory region for the σ^{37} promoter in the S fragment. The -10 and -35 regions are underlined as well as the translation initiation codon GTG. The region of dyad symmetry is indicated by the dashed line with the center of symmetry indicated by a dot. The ribosomal binding site of the gene with the σ^{37} promoter is also illustrated.

IV. BASE SQUENCE ANALYSIS OF THE S FRAGMENT

We used the Maxam-Gilbert (1977) technique to determine the base sequence of most of the S fragment. The sequence of the σ^{37} promoter (Figure 3) is similar to the σ^{37} promoters reported previously by Moran et al. (1981). The -10 and -35 regions and the distance between these two sites are conserved in all these examples.

A significant feature of the sequence is the 35 bp region of dyad symmetry overlapping the promoter sequence for $E\sigma^{37}$ (Figure 4). This region of symmetry is the same length as the symmetrical operator region for the lac operon in E. coli (Barkley and Bourgeois, 1978). Although the presence of this symmetrical region may be coincidental, it may define a protein binding region which regulates gene expression during exponential and stationary phase.

Another region of interest is the ribosomal binding site of the gene (Figure 4). The open reading frame starting at a GTG codon extends 460 bp to the end of the S fragment. The ribosome binding site preceding the GTG codon (Figure 4) has a free energy of base pairing of -13.5 kcal/mol, which is at the low end of values (-14 to -23 kcal/mol) reported for other B. subtilis Shine-Dalgarno binding sites (Murray and Rabinowitz, 1982; Moran et al., 1982). Thus, although the GGAGG sequence is important for mRNA-30S ribosome interaction, the absence of this sequence in our σ^{37} gene suggests that other factors besides a 5 bp sequence complementarity to the Shine-Dalgarno site play an important role in the initiation process.

The sequence data have revealed another intriguing aspect of this cryptic gene transcribed by $E\sigma^{37}$. As shown in Figure 5, the N-terminal amino acid sequence predicted from the base sequence can be divided into a hydrophilic and hydrophobic region resembling the signal peptides of proteins excreted by B. subtilis, E. coli and eukaryotes. The signal peptidase usually cleaves the proprotein on the carboxy terminal side of an uncharged, relatively small amino acid such as ala, gly or ser in the signal peptide (Austen, 1979). The cryptic protein encoded by the σ^{37} gene has an AlaGlnAlaAla sequence identical to the cleavage site of the E. coli OmpA protein (Movva et al., 1980). Cleavage at this site would produce a signal peptide of about 30 amino acid residues, a size similar to the signal peptide of pro-β-lactamase of B. licheniformis (Kroyer and Chang, 1981; Neugebauer et al., 1981).

V. GENETIC LOCUS OF THE S FRAGMENT

We determined the chromosomal locus of the S fragment as a possible means of identifying the functions of the genes it contains. We first moved the S fragment from PGR71-S to pCP112, an integrative mapping plasmid (Price et al., 1983). On transformation of a 168<u>trpC2</u> strain to chloramphenicol resistance (Cm^r), this plasmid inserted a Cm^r element at the site of the S fragment in the B. subtilis chromosome. We used a PBS1 lysate of the Cm^r strain to transduce to prototrophy each of the mapping kit strains of Dedonder et al. (1977) and found the Cm^r marker 77% linked to the glyB locus. Data from additional two and three factor transductional crosses (with the Cm^r strain as donor and Bacillus Genetic Stock Center strain 1A122 tre12 thiA78

B. subtilis cryptic gene (σ^{37})		Ref.*
	MetArgSerLysLys LeuTrpIleSerLeuLeuPheAlaLeuThrLeuIlePheThrMetAlaPheSerAsnMetSerAlaGlnAlaAla	
E. coli OmpA protein		
	MetLysLys ThrAlaIleAlaIleAlaValAlaLeuAlaGlyPheAlaThrValAlaGlnAla↓Ala	1
Rat Preproinsulin		
	MetAlaLeuTrpMetArg PheLeuProLeuLeuAlaLeuLeuValLeuTrpGluProLysProAlaGlnAla↓Phe	2

*(1) Movva et al., 1980, Beck and Bremer, 1980; (2) Chan et al., 1976.

Figure 5. The signal peptide sequence of the cryptic gene with a σ^{37} promoter. The arrow indicates the postulated site of cleavage by the signal peptidase. The other sequences are shown for comparison. The arrow points to known sites of signal peptidase cleavage for these signal peptides.

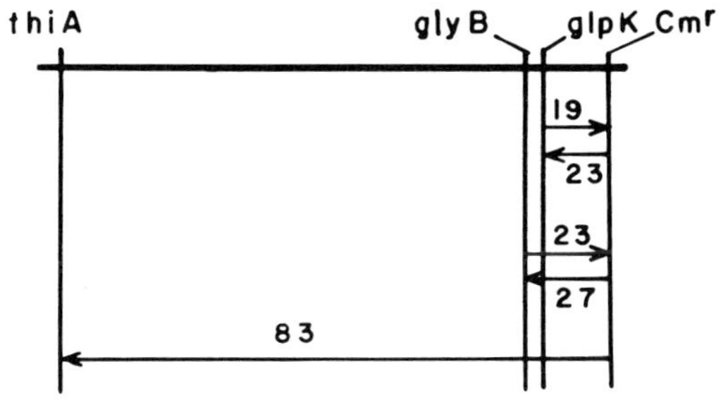

Figure 6. Genetic map of the glyB region constructed by two and three factor transductional crosses. The genetic distances represent 100% -- the % cotransduction, with the tail of the arrow indicating the selected marker.

glyB133 glpK21 as recipient) were used to construct the map shown in Figure 6. The marker order suggested by these crosses is thiA-glyB-glpK-Cmr^r.

The S fragment lies near no know sporulation genes (Henner and Hoch, 1980), but in the region containing gtaC, which encodes phosphoglucomutase, a cell wall enzyme (Young et al., 1969). Crosses in progress will order the S fragment locus relative to gtaC.

VI. TRANSLATION STOP-START DURING EXPRESSION OF THE CAT GENE FROM THE σ^{37} PROMOTER IN THE S FRAGMENT

Usually the expression of the CAT gene in the pGR71 plasmid occurs from a B. subtilis ribosome binding site (rbs) introduced with the B. subtilis promoter (Goldfarb et al., 1982). This results in the production of a fusion protein containing an N-terminal peptide from B. subtilis fused to the CAT enzyme by translation through the CAT leader region. The E. coli rbs in the CAT leader region is not generally used. These results indicate that part of the barrier for expression of E. coli genes in B. subtilis is the result of poor utilization of the E. coli rbs by the B. subtilis translation system. Thus it was unexpected to find that the CAT enzyme made under the control of our σ^{37} promoter was not a fusion protein, but native-sized (Figure 7).

The sequence analysis of the S fragment has provided a possible explanation for the apparent utilization of the E. coli CAT gene rbs. There is an open reading frame of 460 bp which begins near the σ^{37} promoter and continues throughout

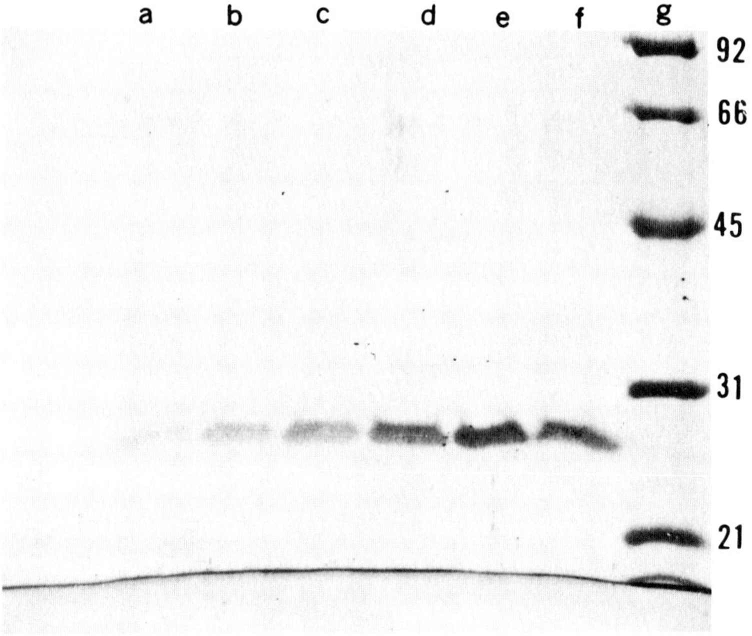

Figure 7. SDS-polyacrylamide gel electrophoresis patterns of the CAT product made form pGR71-S. Lanes A to D contained different amounts of chloramphenicol acetyltransferase (CAT) purified from B. subtilis BD630 carrying pGR71-S plasmid. Cells were harvested at T_6 (6 hours after stationary phase) for enzyme purification. Lanes E to F show the authentic CAT purified from E. coli HB101 carrying pBR328 plasmid by affinity chromatographic analyses using a chloramphenicol-Sepharose column (lane E) and coenzyme A-Sepharose column (lane F). Lane G shows the molecular standards X 10^{-3} daltons.

the S fragment into the leader region of the CAT gene (unpublished data). However, in the CAT leader region, the open reading frame ends at a stop condon (Figure 8). The stop codon resides within the E. coli rbs of the CAT leader region and upon translation termination, the ribosome is in direct contact with the CAT rbs. Although typically the CAT rbs is not efficiently utilized by the B. subtilis translation system, in this special case, a B. subtilis ribosome which stops within an E. coli rbs may be able to initiate translation and produce a native-sized CAT protein.

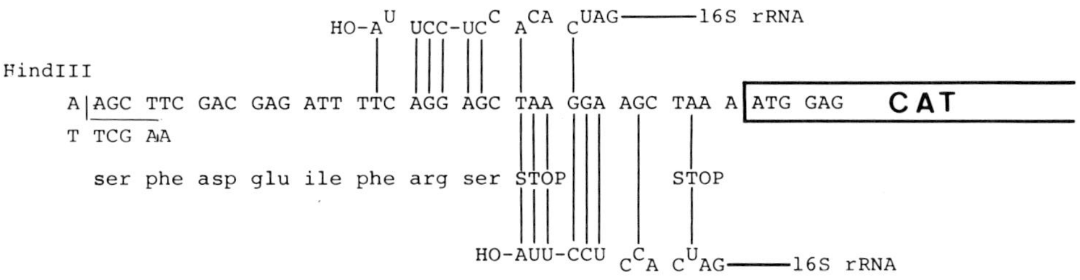

Figure 8. Sequence of the CAT gene leader region showing the translation stop signals and ribosomal binding sites. The amino acid sequence represents the C-terminal end of the 19,000 dalton product encoded by the gene transcripted by Eσ^{37} in pGR71-S. Note that the translation stop codon is within the ribosome binding site of the CAT gene. We propose that the ribosome which stops translation at the termination codon also initiates translation of the CAT gene which results in the synthesis of a native-sized CAT product.

VII. DISCUSSION

The DNA sequence data have been particularly revealing as to the properties of the gene containing a σ^{37} promoter: a) the conserved nature of the -10 and -35 region of the promoter; b) the presence of a region of dyad symmetry overlapping the promoter; c) the occurrence of an rbs without a "strong" complementarity to the Shine-Dalgarno sequence; and d) the possible presence of a signal peptide suggesting that this gene encodes an extracellular protein.

We interpret these preliminary data as follows: this temporally expressed gene has a promoter recognized by Eσ^{37} and is transcribed after the cell has reached the stationary phase of growth. Gene expression is repressed during growth by a protein factor which recognizes the region of dyad symmetry which overlaps the promoter region. The signal peptide sequence suggests that this gene codes for an extracellular protein, since many extracellular proteins are produced after the exponential phase of growth of B. subtilis. We are now testing these conjectures by additional genetic and biochemical analyses.

The absence of a strong complementarity between the mRNA and the Shine-Dalgarno sequence also demonstrates that not all B. subtilis mRNA will have a canonical GGAGG sequence and that other initiation factors must be involved for translation. Furthermore, the apparent utilization of

E. coli rbs by the B. subtilis translation system (Figure 8) demonstrates that under particular situations, a weak mRNA-rRNA interaction can be overcome. We postulate that termination of translation directly in a rbs site facilitates the utilization of that rbs site for initiation by the stalled ribosome. This could be significant in the translation of internal cistrons in a polycistronic mRNA, since efficient utilization of the ribosomes would occur and coordinate synthesis of proteins would result.

Our results on this regulated promoter point to other phenomena which can be investigated. These include a) the determination of the factors which control expression of the gene transcribed from the σ^{37} promoter; b) the consequence of inactivation of this gene; c) the identification of the gene product; d) the relationship of this gene to the sporulation process; e) the relationship of this gene to the divergent gene transcribed by $E\sigma^{29}$ and the covergent gene transcribed by $E\sigma^{55}$; and f) a general understanding of the requirements for transcription and translation in B. subtilis. An understanding of these phenomena should lead to a model not only of temporal expression of this gene, but for the general mechanisms regulating metabolism and development of this organism.

REFERENCES

Austen, B.M. (1981). **FEBS Letters 103**, 308.

Barkley, M.D. and Bourgeois, S. (1978). In The Operon (J.H. Miller and W.S. Resnikoff, eds.), p. 177, Cold Spring Harbor Laboratories, New York.

Beck, E. and Bremer, E. (1980). **Nucl. Acids Res. 8**, 3011.

Chan, S.J., Keim, P. and Steiner, D.F. (1976). **Proc. Natl. Acad. Sci. USA 73**, 1968.

Dedonder, R.A., Lepesant, J.-A., Lepesant-Kejzlarova, J., Billault, A., Steinmetz, M. and Kunst, F. (1977). **Appl. Environ. Microbiol. 33**, 989.

Doi, R.H. (1982). **Arch. Biochem. Biophys. 214**, 662.

Fukuda, R. and Doi, R.H. (1977). **J. Bacteriol. 129**, 422.

Goldfarb, D.S., Doi, R.H. and Rodruguez, R.L. (1981). **Nature 293**, 309.

Goldfarb, D.S., Doi, R.H. and Rodriguez, R.L. (1982). **Proc. Natl. Acad. Sci. USA 79**, 5886.

Haldenwang, W.G., Lang, N. and Losick, R. (1981). **Cell 23**, 615.

Haldenwang, W.G. and Losick, R. (1980). **Proc. Natl. Acad. Sci. USA 77**, 7000.

Henner, D.J. and Hoch, J.A. (1980). **Microbiol. Rev. 44**, 57.

Johnson, W.C., Moran, C.P., Jr. and Losick, R. (1983). **Nature 302**, 800.

Kroyer, J. and Chang, S. (1981). **Gene 15**, 343.

Losick, R. and Pero, J. (1981). **Cell 25**, 582.

Maxam, A.M. and Gilbert, W. (1977). **Proc. Natl. Acad. Sci. USA 74**, 560.

McKenney, K., Shimatake, H., Court, D., Schmeissner, U., Brady, C. and Rosenberg, M. (1981). In Gene Amplification and Analyses, Vol. 2, Structural Analysis of Nucleic Acids (J.G. Chirikjian and T.S. Papes, eds.), p. 383, Elsevier/North Holland.

Moran, C.P., Lang, N., LeGrice, S.F.J., Lee, G., Stephens, M., Sonenshein, A.L., Pero, J. and Losick, R. (1982). **Molec. Gen. Genet. 186**, 339.

Moran, C.P., Jr., Lang, N. and Losick, R. (1981). **Nucl. Acids Res. 9**, 5979.

Movva, R.N., Nakamura, K. and Inouye, M. (1980). **J. Biol. Chem. 225**, 27.

Murray, C.L. and Rabinowitz, J.C. (1982). **J. Biol. Chem. 257**, 1053.

Price, C.W., Gitt, M.A. and Doi, R.H. (1983). **Proc. Natl. Acad. Sci. USA 80**, 4074.

Priest, F.G. (1977). **Bacteriol. Rev.** 41, 711.

Wiggs, J.L., Gilman, M.Z. and Chamberlin, M.J. (1981). **Proc. Natl. Acad. Sci. USA** 78, 2762.

Wong, S.-L. and Doi, R.H. (1982). **J. Biol. Chem. 257**, 11932.

Young, F.E., Smith, C. and Reilly, B.E. (1969). **J. Bacteriol. 98**, 1087.

INHIBITION BY LIPIARMYCIN OF BACILLUS SUBTILIS RNA POLYMERASE[1]

Stuart F. J. LeGrice
Hannah Alexander[2]
Stephan Miller[3]
Abraham L. Sonenshein

Department of Molecular Biology and Microbiology
Tufts University
Schools of Medicine, Veterinary Medicine and Dental Medicine
and
Sackler School of Graduate Biomedical Sciences
Boston, Massachusetts

I. INTRODUCTION

The use of drugs that inhibit DNA-dependent RNA polymerase has been important in dissecting the mechanism of RNA synthesis and in understanding the roles of individual subunits of RNA polymerase (Krakow et al., 1975). One of these drugs, lipiarmycin, has the interesting property of inhibiting preferentially the holoenzyme (sigma subunit containing) form of the enzyme (Sonenshein et al., 1977). It does so because it binds more rapidly or more tightly to holoenzyme than it does to core enzyme (Sonenshein and Alexander, 1979).

Holoenzyme that has been exposed to lipiarmycin cannot initiate RNA synthesis although the enzyme can still bind to DNA; once RNA polymerase has bound to DNA, however, it is

[1]*Supported by research grants from the USPHS (GM30408) and the National Science Foundation (PCM 79-00944)*
[2]*Present address: Scripps Clinic and Research Foundation, La Jolla, California*
[3]*Present address: Harvard School of Public Health, Cambridge, Massachusetts*

ISBN 0-12-274160-9

immune to the action of the drug (Sonenshein and Alexander, 1979). These observations suggest that lipiarmycin binds to free RNA polymerase but does not interfere with subsequent binding to DNA, the first step in RNA synthesis. It was not clear from previous experiments, however, that RNA polymerase that has been exposed to lipiarmycin binds correctly to DNA. That is, the failure to initiate might be due to binding at sites other than promoter sites. In the present communication we show that binding of lipiarmycin-inactivated RNA polymerase to DNA occurs exclusively at promoter sites.

The preference of lipiarmycin for the sigma-containing form of RNA polymerase may be explained if the sigma subunit is the lipiarmycin binding site or is part of that site. Alternatively, association of sigma with the core enzyme may lead to a conformational change that exposes the lipiarmycin binding site. Here we show that inactivation of RNA polymerase by lipiarmycin is temperature-dependent, as though its binding causes or is dependent upon some conformational change.

II. MATERIALS AND METHODS

A. Bacterial Growth and RNA Polymerase Extraction

Two wild-type strains of Bacillus subtilis, 3610 and W168, were used for isolation of RNA polymerase. Cells were grown in either 121A medium (Sonenshein and Roscoe, 1969) or the very rich medium of Halling et al. (1977). RNA polymerase was purified by high speed centrifugation, ammonium sulfate fractionation, DEAE-cellulose chromatography and DNA affinity chromatography as described previously (Sonenshein and Alexander, 1979; LeGrice and Sonenshein, 1982). Core and sigma fractions were separated by chromatography on phosphocellulose or Bio-Rex70 (Sonenshein and Alexander, 1979). Only the major vegetative form ($E\sigma^{55}$) of B. subtilis RNA polymerase was used.

B. Transcription Assays

RNA polymerase activity was routinely measured by the method of Losick and Sonenshein (1969), except that the specific activity of 8-^{14}C-ATP was 4 mCi/mmole. The initiation reaction was monitored as synthesis of the dinucleotide pApU using phage Øe DNA was template and α^{32}P-UTP and AMP as substrates (Sonenshein and Alexander, 1979).

To measure synthesis of <u>tms</u> RNA, the reaction mixture (50 μl) contained 40 mM Tris-HCl, pH 7.9, 10 mM $MgCl_2$, 0.1 mM DTT, 0.1 mM EDTA, 10% (v/v) glycerol, 150 μM ATP, GTP and CTP, 10 μM ^{3}H-UTP (1 μCi/mmole), 0.2 pmoles tms promoter fragment (a 1030 bp PstI-HindIII fragment of pLS5ΔRI) and 0.5 pmoles RNA polymerase holoenzyme.

After 10 minutes incubation at 37°C, reactions were terminated by addition of 60 μl water and extracted with 100 μl Tris-saturated phenol (50 mM Tris-HCl, pH 8). The aqueous phase was extracted three times with ether, dried of excess ether and thereafter processed as described by Maxam and Gilbert (1980). Dried pellets were resuspended in half strength "urea dyes" solution of Maxam and Gilbert, without NaOH, and electrophoresed through 5% polyacrylamide gels containing 8 M urea (LeGrice and Sonenshein, 1982). Following electrophoresis, gels were prepared for fluorography as described by Bonner and Laskey (1974).

C. Exonuclease III Protection Experiments

Protection of the <u>tms</u> promoter from exonuclease III digestion in the presence of native or lipiarmycin-inactivated RNA polymerase was performed in the following manner: reaction mixtures (50 μl) contained 40 mM Tris-HCl, pH 7.9, 10 mM $MgCl_2$, 0.1 mM DTT, 0.05 pmole ^{32}P-labeled DNA containing the <u>tms</u> promoter (a 280 bp HindIII/EcoRI fragment of plasmid pLS5ΔRI labeled at the EcoRI or HindIII end by polynucleotide kinase and γ-^{32}P-ATP (LeGrice and Sonenshein, 1982)) and amounts of RNA polymerase indicated in the text. Following RNA polymerase addition and incubation at 37°C for 10 minutes, 25 units of Exonuclease III were added and incubation allowed to proceed for a further 5 minutes at 37°C. Reactions were terminated by addition of an equal volume of 0.2 M EDTA, pH 7, and the samples thereafter processed as described by Maxam and Gilbert (1980) for DNA sequencing reactions. The reaction products were fractionated by electrophoresis through 6% polyacrylamide gels containing 8 M urea, and subsequent autoradiography utilized Kodak X-Omat XAR-5 film and Du Pont "Lightning-Plus" intensification screens.

D. Template DNAs

DNA of phage Øe and SP01 was extracted as described previously (Brevet and Sonenshein, 1972). Fragments containing the tms promoter were isolated from plasmid pLS5ΔR1 (Donnelly and Sonenshein, 1982) after restriction enzyme cleavage and sucrose gradient centrifugation (LeGrice and Sonenshein, 1982).

E. Enzymes and Chemicals

Restriction enzymes and Exonuclease III were obtained from New England Biolabs or Bethesda Research Laboratories. ^{3}H-UTP and α-^{32}P-UTP were from ICN and New England Nuclear, respectively. Lipiarmycin was the kind gift of Dr. G. C. Lancini, Gruppo Lepetit.

III. RESULTS

A. Effect of Lpm on Binding of RNA Polymerase to Promoter Sites

In previous work on the mechanism of action of Lpm we have shown that the drug preferentially inhibits the activity of the σ-containing form of RNA polymerase, that it inhibits the initiation step in RNA synthesis, and that it does so without seeming to reduce the rate, extent, or stability of binding of RNA polymerase to DNA (Sonenshein and Alexander, 1979). These results suggest that the specificity of the drug for holoenzyme is a reflection of the nature of the target of Lpm (e.g., σ might be part of the target) rather than a reflection of inhibition of a σ function (i.e. stimulation of binding of RNA polymerse to promoter sites). These experiments, with whole phage DNA, left open the possibility that Lpm had an effect on RNA polymerase-DNA interaction too subtle to be noticed by the methods employed. We have therefore examined in more detail the effect of Lpm on binding of RNA polymerase to promoter sites.

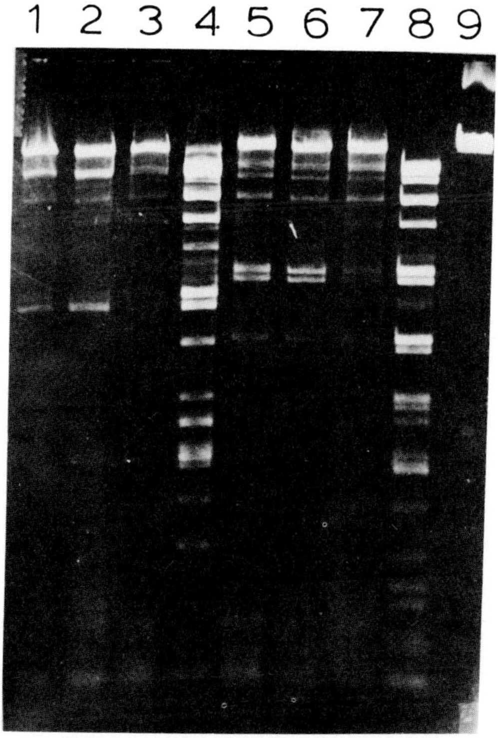

Figure 1. Effect of lipiarmycin on retention of RNA polymerase-DNA complexes on nitrocellulose filters. DNA of phages SP01 and Øe were cleaved with restriction enzyme EcoRI and fragments produced were tested for binding to RNA polymerse as described by Talkington and Pero (1978). The RNA polymerase was pre-incubated for 3 minutes at 37 °C with or without lipiarmycin (2.5 μg/ml), as indicated. Binding to B. subtilis phage DNA fragments was during a 10 minute incubation at 37 °C. Subsequently, an excess of Coliphage λ DNA was added (100 μg/ml) and incubation was extended a further 10 minues to reduce non-specific binding of RNA polymerase to fragmented DNA. Complexes were collected by slow filtration, disrupted with SDS and subjected to electrophoresis in 0.7% agarose. Lane 1, SP01 fragments bound by RNA polymerase in the absence of lipiarmycin; lane 2, SP01 fragments bound in the presence of lipiarmycin; lane 3, SP01 fragments retained without RNA polymerase; lane 4, total EcoRI* cleavage products of SP01 DNA; lane 5, Øe fragments bound by RNA polymerase in the absence of lipiarmycin; lane 6, Øe fragments bound in the presence of lipiarmycin; lane 7, Øe fragments retained without RNA polymerase; lane 8, total EcoRI* cleavage products of Øe DNA; lane 9, λ DNA.*

Cleavage of phage SP01 DNA with restriction endonuclease EcoRI* yields 26 fragments of which 4 have been shown to interact with host holoenzyme in a filter-binding assay (Talkington and Pero, 1978 and Figure 1). We have shown that the related phage Øe is cleaved into about 23 fragments of which 3 are retained on a nitrocellulose filter after incubation with host RNA polymerase (Figure 1). Preincubation of RNA polymerase with Lpm (2.5 μg/ml; 3 minutes at 37°C) had no effect on the pattern of fragments retained after a subsequent incubation with cleaved DNA (Figure 1). Since such treatment with Lpm reduces transcriptional activity by more than 90%, we conclude that the drug neither inhibits the binding of RNA polymerase to promoter-containing DNA nor enhances its binding to random DNA sequences.

This experiment, however, does not rule out the possibility that RNA polymerase inactivated by Lpm binds near but not exactly at the promoter site. We have tested this possibility by examining the pattern of protection against various nucleases that is afforded by RNA polymerase bound to a bacterial promoter called tms (Haldenwang et al., 1981). In work to be published elsewhere (S. LeGrice and A. Sonenshein, manuscript in preparation) we have analyzed the contacts between RNA polymerase and various bases in the promoter sequence. For instance, binding of RNA polymerase to tms-containing DNA gives at least partial protection against DNase I cleavage of 30 to 40 nucleotides in the promoter region. In the same region, bound RNA polymerase enhances cleavage at some sites. Pretreatment of RNA polymerase with Lpm had no effect on this protection and enhancement pattern (data not shown) even though transcriptional activity was completely abolished by such treatment (see Figure 2).

Binding of RNA polymerase to tms DNA also protects the DNA against exonucleolytic attack. Exo III, the nuclease used here, normally degrades double-stranded DNA in the 3'-->5' direction until the mid-point of the DNA is reached. For the tms promoter fragment used, its 280 bp length was reduced to single strands of about 140 bp (Figure 3D, 3H). When RNA polymerase was bound to the tms DNA that was 5' labeled at the EcoRI stie, ExoIII digestion yielded single-strands of about 190 bases (Figure 3 E to G). This corresponds to protection of the DNA starting from a point located very close to the RNA synthesis initiation site and extending upstream. Inactivation of RNA polymerse by Lpm had no effect on the pattern of ExoIII digestion (Figure 3 A to C). We conclude therefore that, to within the accuracy of the methods employed (±1 to 5 bp), Lpm inhibits the initiation of RNA synthesis without interfering with binding

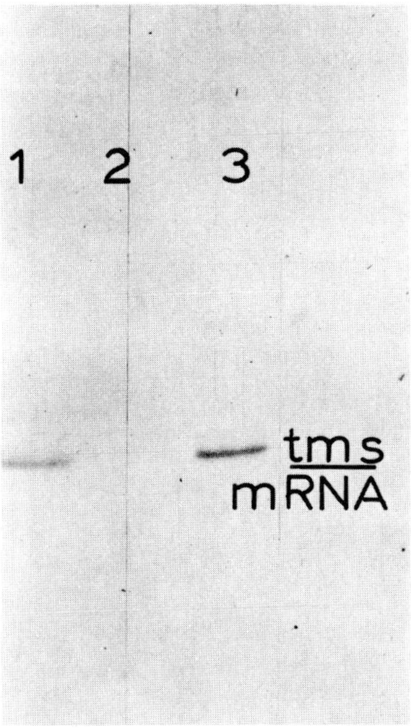

Figure 2. Effect of lipiarmycin on binding of RNA polymerase to tms *promoter. The effect of lipiarmycin on in vitro transcription from the* tms *promoter was measured as described under Materials and Methods. Lane 1, complete reaction mix without lipiarmycin; lane 2, reaction mix containing RNA polymerase that had been pre-incubated with lipiarmycin (1.5 μg/ml; 5 minutes at 37°C); lane 3, reaction mix containing RNA polymerase that had been pre-incubated with an amount of ethanol (2%) equivalent to that used to dissolve the lipiarmycin used in lane 2.*

of RNA polymerase to promoter sites and therefore must do so without inhibiting any known function of the σ subunit.

B. Lack of Competition between Nucleoside Triphosphates and Lipiarmycin for Binding to RNA Polymerase

The remaining steps in the initiation of RNA synthesis that might be sensitive to Lpm are binding of nucleoside triphosphates and catalysis of phosphodiester bond formation. We attempted to assay the former by studying the kinetics of inhibition as a function of substrate concentra-

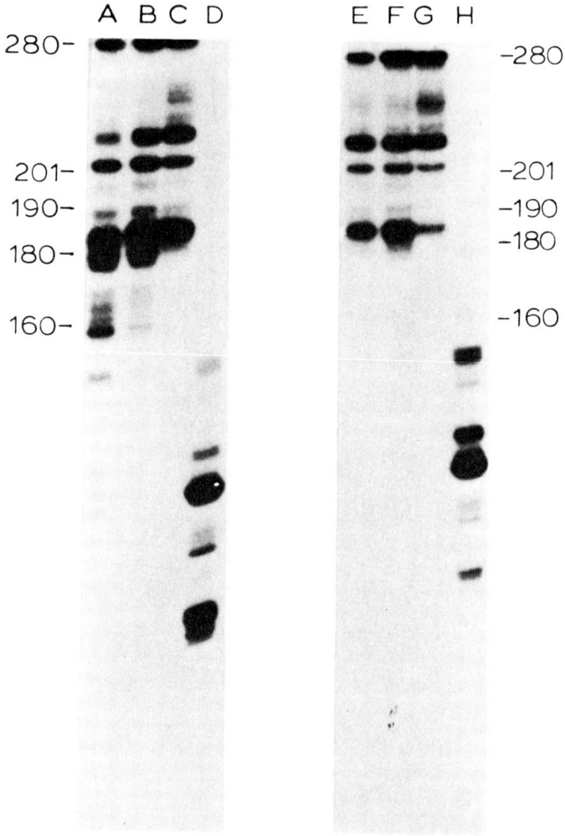

Figure 3. Protection of the tms promoter against digestion by Exonuclease III was measured as described under Materials and Methods. A 280-bp tms promoter fragment was labeled by polynucleotide kinase at the EcoRI site located about 90 bases downstream from the transcription start point. Labeled DNA was mixed with increasing amounts of RNA polymerase that had been pretreated with lipiarmycin (1.5 μg/ml; 5 minutes at 37°C) (lanes A to C) or with untreated RNA polymerase (lanes E to G). After binding, complexes were challenged with Exo III. Control DNA samples incubated with (lane D) or without (lane H) lipiarmycin were tested for susceptibility to Exo III in the absence of RNA polymerase.

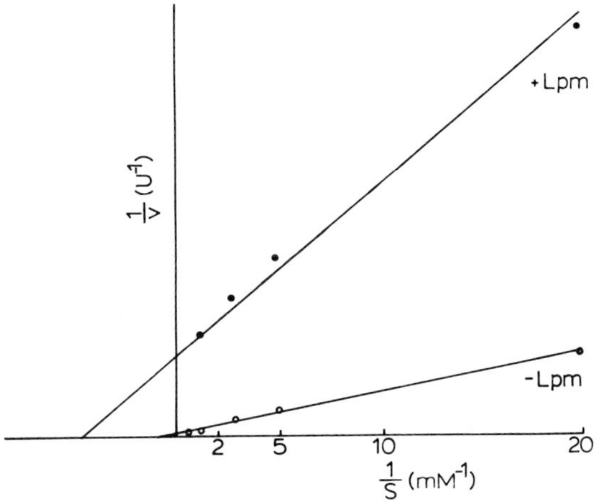

Figure 4. Effect of lipiarmycin on the substrate dependence of RNA polymerase. Synthesis of pApU, as described under Materials and Methods, was assayed at various concentrations of AMP (α-^{32}P-UTP was constant) using untreated RNA polymerase or RNA polymerase that had been pretreated with lipiarmycin (1 μg/ml; 2 minutes at 37 °C). AMP was present during this preincubation, as well as during subsequent synthesis of pApU. One unit of activity led to incorporation of 20,000 cpm of UMP in 60 minutes at 37 °C.

tion. If competitive kinetics were found, one could conclude that Lpm acts by occupying the nucleoside triphosphate binding site. Using phage Øe DNA as template we measured synthesis of the initiating dinucleotide pApU in the presence and absence of Lpm and at varying concentrations of AMP or UTP. As shown in Figure 4, variation of the AMP concentration showed typical Michaelis-Menten kinetics for enzyme activity; addition of Lpm to parallel reactions showed neither competitive inhibition nor classical non-competitive inhibition (i.e. both the V_{max} and apparent K_m were altered). Analogous experiments in which the UTP concentration was varied gave similar results, as did experiments in which long chain RNA synthesis was measured (data not shown). Failure to find competitive kinetics does not necessarily mean the Lpm has no effect on nucleoside triphosphate binding, however. The fact that Lpm inactivates RNA polymerase nearly irreversibly (Sonenshein and Alexander, 1979) means that non-competetive kinetics would be obtained no matter what the true mechanism of inhibition is (Segel, 1975).

C. Why Does Lipiarmycin Preferentially Inhibit Holoenzyme?

Previous studies indicated that free core enzyme interacts with lipiarmycin (Sonenshein and Alexander, 1979). Moreover, mutant studies led to the conclusion that the Lpm^r phenotypes of several mutants were associated with the core fraction of RNA polymerase and not with the sigma fraction (Sonenshein et al., 1977). The mutations in question mapped in the rfm-std (rpoB-rpoC) locus (Halling et al., 1977) further implicating the core enzyme as the target of the drug. More recent experiments indicated that Lpm^r mutant RNA polymerases are inactivated by lipiarmycin at a much slower rate than is wild-type RNA polymerase (H. Alexander and A. Sonenshein, unpublished), suggesting again that the core enzyme contains the binding site for the drug. How then can one explain the preferential inihibition of holoenzyme by lipiarmycin?

Wu et al. (1976), working with E. coli RNA polymerase, have shown that association of sigma factor with core enzyme leads to a conformational change in the core. We have considered the possibility that such a conformational change exposes the binding site for the drug. This was tested by analyzing the rate of inactivation of RNA polymerase by lipiarmycin at various temperatures (Figure 5). Taking the rate of inactivation as a measure of the second order rate constant of lipiarmycin binding, we found that the rate of binding was 25- to 30-fold lower at 0°C than it was at 37°C. Assuming that association between drug and enzyme is noncovalent and that any temperature dependence observed is due to conformational changes, we conclude that conformational change in RNA polymerase is required for lipiarmycin binding. Such a conformational change, if verified by further experiments, could represent association of sigma and core or could be induced by the drug itself.

IV. DISCUSSION

Lipiarmycin inhibits the initiation of RNA synthesis by holoenzyme but does not interfere with binding of RNA polymerase to promoter sites. Thus lipiarmycin preferentially inhibits the sigma-containing form of RNA polymerase but does not inhibit the only reaction known to be catalyzed by sigma (stable complex formation at promoter sites). In other words, this drug has the property of binding to a form of RNA polymerase produced by interaction of core and sigma but only inhibits the activity of the core component.

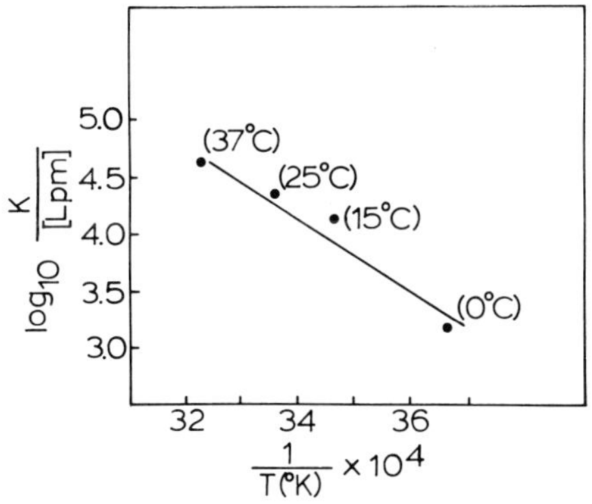

Figure 5. Rate of inactivation of RNA polymerase by lipiarmycin at different temperatures. RNA polymerase and lipiarmycin were mixed at the indicated temperature and incubated for 0 to 5 minutes. Samples withdrawn at various times were assayed for residual transcriptional activity using the standard assay (Materials and Methods) and phage Øe DNA as template. For each temperature, a rate of inactivation of RNA polymerase was calculated (K) and converted to a second-order rate constant by division by the concentration of lipiarmycin (K/[Lpm]). The results are plotted versus temperature (°K; 0°C = 273°K). For each temperature, the rate of inactivation was corrected for the spontaneous rate of decay of RNA polymerase at that temperature.

The exact reaction inhibited by lipiarmycin remains a mystery. Attempts to assay effects on substrate binding have given mixed results. Lipiarmycin gives neither competitive nor non-competitive kinetics of inhibition with respect to substrate concentration. Preliminary experiments with radioactive ATP have suggested that association of ATP and RNA polymerase is inhibited by lipiarmycin (Miller and Sonenshein, unpublished). However, this should be confirmed by affinity labeling (using azido ATP, for example) before strong conclusions are drawn.

Lipiarmycin has proven to be useful in assaying the role of host RNA polymerase after phage infection (Osburne and Sonenshein, 1980) and in separating the DNA binding and initiation steps in RNA synthesis. Its greatest potential usefulness is to facilitate isolation and characterization of sigma mutants. This has not yet been possible using simple, straightforward selections. More sophisticated approaches remain to be tried.

ACKNOWLEDGMENT

We thank Dr. G. C. Lancini for the gift of lipiarmycin.

REFERENCES

Bonner, W.H. and Laskey, R.A. (1974). **Eur. J. Biochem. 46**, 83.
Brevet, J. and Sonenshein, A.L. (1972). **J. Bacteriol. 112**, 1270.
Donnelly, C.D. and Sonenshein, A.L. (1982). In Molecular Cloning and Gene Regulation in Bacilli (A.T. Ganesan, S. Chang and J.A. Hoch, eds.), p. 63, Academic Press, New York.
Haldenwang, W.G., Lang, N. and Losick, R. (1981). **Cell 23**, 615.
Halling, S.H., Burtis, K.C. and Doi, R.H. (1977). **J. Biol. Chem. 252**, 9024.
Krakow, J.S., Rhodes, G. and Jovin, T.M. (1975). In RNA Polymerase (R. Losick and M. Chamberlin, eds.), p. 127, Cold Spring Harbor Laboratories, New York.
LeGrice, S.F.J. and Sonenshein, A.L. (1982). **J. Mol. Biol. 162**, 551.
Losick, R. and Sonenshein, A.L. (1969). **Nature (London) 224**, 35.
Maxam, A. and Gilbert, W. (1980). In Methods in Enzymology, Vol. 68 (L. Grossman and K. Moldave, eds.), p. 499, Academic Press, New York.
Osburne, M.S. and Sonenshein, A.L. (1980). **J. Virology 33**, 945.
Segel, I.H. (1975). Enzyme Kinetics: Behavior and Analysis of Rapid Equilibrium and Steady-State System. John Wiley and Sons, Inc., New York.
Sonenshein, A.L. and Alexander, H. (1979). **J. Mol. Biol. 127**, 55.
Sonenshein, A.L., Alexander, H.B., Rothstein, D.M. and Fisher, S.H. (1977). **J. Bacteriol. 132**, 73.
Sonenshein, A.L. and Roscoe, D.H. (1969). **Virology 39**, 265.
Talkington, C. and Pero, J. (1978). **Proc. Natl. Acad. Sci. USA 75**, 1185.
Wu, F.Y.-H., Yarbrough, L.R. and Wu, C.-W. (1976). **Biochemistry 15**, 945.

CLONING USING BACTERIOPHAGE SPP1v AS THE VECTOR: VECTOR DEVELOPMENT, STABILITY AND EXPRESSION[1]

Aline I. Desmyter
Jacqueline B. Rice
John N. Reeve

Department of Microbiology
Ohio State University
Columbus, Ohio

I. INTRODUCTION

Bacteriophage SPP1v is a derivative of the virulent phage SPP1 developed as a cloning vector (Heilmann and Reeve, 1982). Cloning is accomplished by insertion of DNA into the single BamHI site of the vector. Digestion of SPP1v vector DNA by BamHI reduces the frequency of transfection of competent cells of Bacillus subtilis by approximately 1,000-fold. Cloning of restriction fragments generated by the enzymes BglII or BclI into the BamHI site of SPP1v creates recombinant molecules which, if the cloned DNA fragment does not itself contain an internal BamHI site, are not inactivated in transfection by exposure to BamHI. This provides a mechanism to selectively isolate recombinant phage from a ligation mixture; exposure of the ligation mixture to BamHI, following ligation and before transfection, prevents transfection by reconstituted SPP1v vector phage. Cloning in SPP1v does not require expression of cloned DNA in infected B. subtilis cells nor does it require any homology between cloned DNA sequences and the B.

[1]*This research was supported by National Science Foundation Grant PCM 7912019 and contract 81-0087 from the Air Force Office of Scientific Research. J.N.R. is the recipient of Research Career Development Award AG 00108 from the National Institutes of Health.*

ISBN 0-12-274160-9

subtilis chromosome. SPP1v cloning is, in these respects, directly comparable to cloning in E. coli using a virulent λ-based vector and, as with λ, it is also possible to use plaque-hybridization procedures to directly identify recombinant phage carrying desired sequences. Plaque hybridization is particularly useful as a selection mechanism if BamHI treatment of the ligation mixture is inappropriate, e.g. if BamHI fragments themselves are to be cloned. Plaque hybridization was used, for example, to identify recombinant phage in which plasmid pUB110 had been cloned in SPP1v by ligation of BamHI digested SPP1v to BamHI digested pUB110 (Heilmann and Reeve, 1982). In this report, we describe construction of a derivative of SPP1v with increased cloning capacity, some unusual recombinants obtained in cloning using SPP1v and infection of minicells of B. subtilis to analyze the expression of SPP1v recombinant phages.

II. CONSTRUCTION OF SPP1vm

SPP1v was constructed by in vitro insertion of a unique BamHI site into a viable deletion mutant, ΔX, of SPP1 (Heilmann and Reeve, 1982). The BamHI site was placed within a region of the SPP1 genome known to be nonessential for phage growth, directly adjacent to the region of the genome deleted by ΔX. A novel deletion mutant of SPP1, ΔM, was recently isolated in the laboratory of T. A. Trautner and generously provided to us for use in SPP1 vector constructions. This deletion removes approximately 1 kbp of DNA and, in so doing, deletes the thirteenth smallest EcoRI fragment of SPP1 and fuses the eighth and tenth smallest EcoRI fragments (Figure 1). We have introduced ΔM into SPP1v to create SPP1vm. DNA from SPP1ΔM was digested with BglI and ligated to the smallest BglI fragment of SPP1v prepared by extraction from an agarose gel following BglI digestion of SPP1v. This BglI fragment of SPP1v contains the BamHI cloning site of SPP1v (indicated by the large arrowhead in Figure 1) and ΔX. The presence of ΔX in an SPP1 genome results in a distinctive plaque morphology so that, following ligation and transfection with the mixture of SPP1ΔM DNA and the BglI fragment of SPP1v, phage from plaques with the ΔX morphology were isolated. The structures of the genomes of these phage were analyzed by agarose gel electrophoresis. The patterns of EcoRI restriction fragments of SPP1w.t. (wild-type), SPP1ΔM, SPP1v and SPP1vm are shown in Figure 1. It can be seen that SPP1vm contains both ΔX (reducing the size of EcoRI fragment 1) and ΔM (fusing EcoRI fragments 8 and 10 and deleting EcoRI frag-

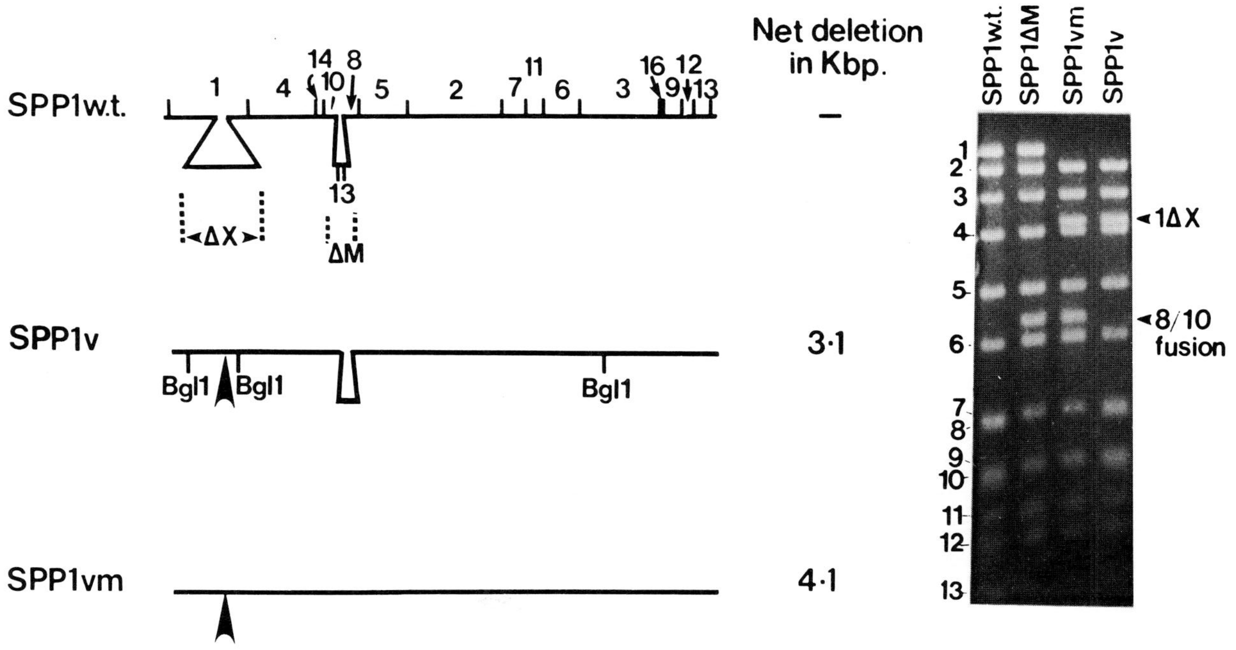

Figure 1. Construction of SPP1vm.

ment 13). The net deletion of DNA in SPP1vm is approximately 4.1 kbp. SPP1w.t. phage particles normally package approximately 1.8 Kbp of terminally redundant DNA. There should therefore be sufficient space in SPP1vm to allow the cloning of at least 5.9 kbp of foreign DNA into the BamHI site of this vector. All procedures developed for use with SPP1v are equally applicable to SPP1vm and the presence of ΔM provides a physical location marker for orientation and measurement of molecules formed in DNA:DNA heteroduplex experiments.

III. DELETIONS OBSERVED IN CLONING WITH SPP1v

During the development of SPP1v and in subsequent use of SPP1v to clone specific DNA fragments we have frequently isolated recombinant phage which do not contain precisely the fragment of DNA introduced into the ligation reaction. Many recombinant phage appear to have suffered major deletions and, in some cases, the vector has undergone major genomic reorganizations (A. Desmyter, H. Heilmann, J. Reeve, G. Morelli and T. Trautner, in preparation). Similar anomalous results have also been reported by Behrens et al. (1983) using the cloning vehicle SPP1vic which is very similar to SPP1v but contains a unique Pst1 cloning site rather than a BamHI site. We have undertaken a series of experiments to investigate further this phenomenon. A recombinant plasmid, pET407 which consists of DNA from the methanogenic microorganism Methanobrevibacter smithii and most of the sequences of plasmid pBR322 (Hamilton and Reeve, 1984), was used as the test substrate for cloning into SPP1v. The location and origin of DNA in recombinant phage, which had originally been part of pET407, were determined by restriction enzyme analyses and by Southern blot analyses. Radioactive probes specific for either the methanogen- or pBR322-derived DNA sequences were used. Results from one series of experiments are shown in Figure 2. SPP1v and pET407 were digested with BamHI, ligated together, and following transfection phage were isolated from plaques which gave a positive signal using ^{32}P-labeled pET407 as the probe in a plaque hybridization screen. Recombinants were not found which contained the complete sequence of pET407. Analyses identified phage in which deletions had occurred either in the vector and/or in the pET407 sequences. In some cases more than one phage was present in the preparation and by repeated plaque purification it was possible to show that a larger recombinant phage was continuously giving rise to a smaller phage by deletion. An example is shown in

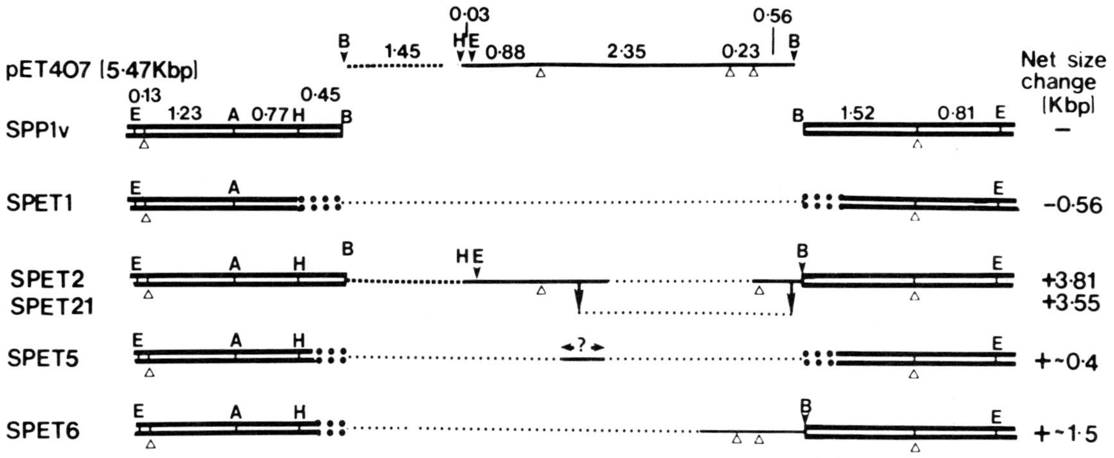

Figure 2. *Physical structure of the DNA of recombinant phage obtained in cloning pET407 in SPP1v. The top line in the diagram depicts pET407 linearized by BamHI digestion. The broken line is M. smithii DNA and the solid line is pBR322 DNA (Hamilton and Reeve, 1984). A restriction map of the DNA adjacent to the BamHI site in SPP1v, also cleaved at the BamHI site, is shown directly below the pET407 map. The physical structure of a series of recombinant phage, designated SPET1, SPET2, etc. obtained in an attempt to clone pET407 into SPP1v are shown below SPP1v. Deleted areas of the vector are indicated by large dots and deleted areas of pET407 by small dots. SPET21 arose spontaneously during growth of SPET2 in B. subtilis MCB. SPET5 contains a small but undefined fragment of pBR322 DNA as shown by Southern blotting. Sites for the enzymes EcoRI, BamHI, AvaII, HindIII and BglI are indicated by the symbols E, B, A, H, and Δ, respectively. There are no differences in the regions of the genomes of the phages which are not shown in the Figure.*

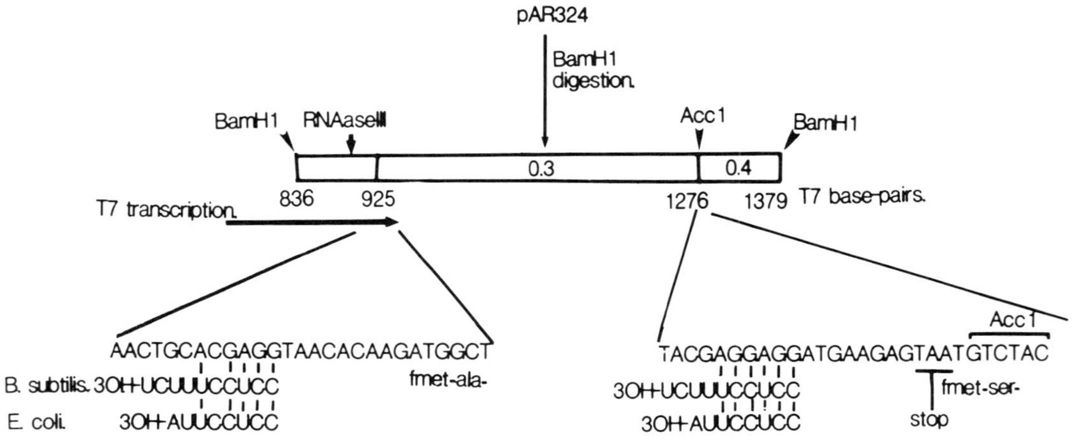

Figure 3. Structure of the T7 DNA, containing the T7 0.3 gene, cloned in SPP1v. Plasmid pAR324 (Studier and Rosenberg, 1981) consists of pBR322 plus the fragment of T7 DNA shown in the diagram. The T7 fragment was cloned in the BamHI restriction site of pBR322 using BamHI linkers. Figures below the DNA fragment are the location of that particular base pair in the T7 genome designating the extreme left end of T7 as 0. All details of T7 in the figure are based on the results presented by Dunn and Studier (1981).

Figure 2 in which phage SPET21 was routinely produced by growth of SPET2 in B. subtilis. Many phage were isolated which, even though they gave an initial positive reaction to the pET407 hybridization probe, were subsequently found to be identical to SPP1v (not shown in Figure 2). Construction of SPP1v created a situation in which cloned fragments are flanked by a directly repeated DNA sequence at least 10 base pairs in length (Heilmann and Reeve, 1982). Excision of cloned fragments may be occurring by recombination at the BamHI sites at each end of a cloned fragment facilitated by the extensive regions of homology extending from these BamHI sites.

Experiments to date have necessarily employed recombination proficient strains of B. subtilis because SPP1 transfection of competent cells requires Rec^+ cells (Trautner and Spatz, 1973). Experiments are currently in progress to determine if the frequency of deletion occurrence is less using transfection of either Rec^+ or Rec^- protoplasts. Unfortunately SPP1 does not form plaques on lawns of B. subtilis grown on the standard medium used for protoplast regeneration and this technical problem must first be resolved. The results typified by the SPET2--->SPET21 observations (Figure 2) do demonstrate, however, that not all of the deletions observed following transfection of competent cells are directly attributable to the processing that DNA undergoes during transfection. As previously observed for plasmid-based recombinant molecules in B. subtilis (Kreft et al., 1982), there also appear to be preferred sites for deletion events to occur inSPP1v-based recombinant molecules during their replication in B. subtilis cells.

IV. CLONING THE 0.3 GENE OF COLIPHAGE T7 IN SPP1v

We are currently investigating the fidelity of synthesis of the product of the 0.3 gene of coliphage T7 in infected cells of E. coli by determining the frequency of misincorporation of ^{35}S-cysteine into this protein which normally does not contain cysteine residues (J. Rice, R. Libby and J. Reeve, manuscript submitted for publication). To extend this work to the fidelity of 0.3 protein synthesis in B. subtilis, it was necessary to clone the 0.3 gene in SPP1v. Several previous attempts to clone the intact early region of T7, either in E. coli (Studier and Rosenberg, 1981) or B. subtilis (Scherzinger et al., 1980), have been unsuccessful. We were also unable to clone the complete early region of the T7 genome into SPP1v (H. Heilmann, A. Desmyter and J.

Reeve, unpublished results). We therefore cloned the 0.3 gene into SPP1v starting from the plasmid, pAR324 (provided by F.W. Studier (Studier and Rosenberg, 1981)), which consists of the 0.3 gene cloned in the BamHI site of pBR322. BamHI digested SPP1v was ligated to the fragment of DNA containing the 0.3 gene isolated by agarose gel electrophoresis from a BamHI digest of pAR324. Following transfection, ^{32}P-labeled pAR324 DNA was used as a hybridization probe to identify plaques containing SPP1v::0.3 recombinant phage. Phage were obtained with the T7 0.3 gene sequence in either orientation. Phage with the 0.3 gene in the correct orientation for transcription starting from the SPP1 promoter 2 (Stüber et al., 1981) (opposite to the normal orientation for T7 transcription) were designated SPP1v::0.3+ and those with the incorrect orientation for transcription were designated SPP1v::0.3-. Figure 3 shows the details of the 543 bp fragment of the T7 genome cloned into SPP1v. The asymmetric AccI site was used to determine the orientation of cloning. This site may, itself, be useful in cloning as it is located immediately following the initiation ATG codon for the T7 0.4 gene and is preceded by translation stop signals and an apparently good ribosome binding sequence (Dunn and Studier, 1981). The diagram illustrates that there are sequences preceding the 0.3 and 0.4 genes, 5 and 6 bases in length respectively, which as mRNAs should hybridize to the 16S rRNA of both E. coli and B. subtilis ribosomes.

V. EXPRESSION OF SPP1v RECOMBINANT PHAGE IN INFECTED MINICELLS

Minicells of B. subtilis were infected with recombinant phage and allowed to incorporate ^{35}S-methionine. Radioactively labeled polypeptides, synthesized in infected minicells, were analyzed by fluorography following polyacrylamide gel electrophoresis as previously described for analysis of SPP1 gene products (Mertens et al., 1979). We were unable to detect differences between the polypeptides synthesized in SPP1v infected minicells and those synthesized in minicells infected by a variety of SPP1v recombinant phage. There were SPP1-encoded polypeptides which migrated, during electrophoresis, to approximately the same location as the 0.3 protein. We therefore used rabbit anti-0.3 antiserum in attempts to precipitate radioactively labeled 0.3 protein from SPP1v::0.3+ infected minicells to ensure that co-migration of polypeptides was not preventing detection of 0.3 protein synthesis. The antiserum did not

Table 1. Hybridization of ^{3}H-RNA Synthesized in SPP1v::0.3+ Infected Minicells to Filter-Bound DNA[a]

DNA on filter (5 μg DNA/filter)	^{3}H-RNA hybridized (c.p.m.)	% of input radioactivity bound
---	209	1.4
SPP1v	6454	44.2
pAR324	217	1.5
pBR322	192	1.3

[a]Minicells (4 x 10^{10}) from B. subtilis CU403 thyA thyB metB divIVB1 (Reeve et al, 1973) were infected (input m.o.i.=1) with SPP1v::0.3+ as described by Mertens et al. (1979). The infected minicells were allowed to incorporate [5,6-^{3}H]uridine (150 μCi/ml; 47 Ci/mmole; Amersham Corp., IL, 60005) for 30 minutes at 37°C. Radioactively labeled RNA was prepared and DNA:RNA hybridization carried out exactly as described by Miller (1982).

The fragment of T7 DNA cloned in SPP1v::0.3+ is approximately 1% of the total size of this genome. Assuming that all the genome were transcribed equally, transcription of the 0.3 sequence should have been clearly detectable by comparing the amount of ^{3}H-RNA bound to pBR322 with the amount bound to pAR324. These plasmids differ only by the presence of the fragment of T7 DNA in pAR324 (see Figure 3 and Studier and Rosenberg, (1981)).

precipitate radioactively labeled 0.3 protein confirming that this protein is not synthesized in detectable amounts in SPP1v::0.3+ minicells of B. subtilis. Minicells infected with SPP1v::0.3+ were allowed to incorporate [5,6-^{3}H]uridine to label mRNA. The labeled mRNA was used in RNA:DNA filter binding hybridization experiments. As shown in Table 1, very few, if any, transcripts of the 0.3 gene were present in the RNA preparation. It must therefore be concluded that the cloned 0.3 gene is not efficiently transcribed in infected minicells even though the gene is cloned in a region of the SPP1 genome which is heavily transcribed in SPP1 infected cells (Stüber et al., 1981) and which was previously shown to be expressed in infected minicells (Mertens et al., 1979). We are currently determining whether the 0.3 gene is expressed in SPP1v::0.3+ infected nucleated cells of B. subtilis.

VI. CONCLUSIONS

SPP1v and SPP1vm can be used to clone and amplify specific fragments of DNA in B. subtilis without the need for gene expression. As with plasmid cloning in B. subtilis, there are frequent problems of instability of recombinant genomes when SPP1v is used as the vector, but as shown by the cloning of the T7 0.3 gene, it is also not difficult to obtain desired recombinants. SPP1v, SPP1vm and SPP1vic (Behrens et al., 1983) are virulent phages and as such are not ideal for use as expression systems. Phage infection of minicells may be used to investigate encoded mRNAs and polypeptides (Reeve, 1979). There are, however, significant differences between SPP1 expression in nucleated cells and in minicells (Mertens et al., 1979) and there are most probably major differences in the quantitative expression of genes cloned in SPP1 vectors in infected cells and in infected minicells. The methyl transferase gene cloned by Behrens et al. (1983) in SPP1vic is clearly functionally expressed in infected B. subtilis cells but there is no discernible difference between the polypeptides synthesized in minicells infected by the vector, SPP1vic, and the polypeptides synthesized in minicells infected by the SPP1vic-methyl transferase encoding recombinant (J. Reeve and T. Trautner, 1983; unpublished results). Phage infection does offer the opportunity of introducing recombinant DNA molecules into B. subtilis cells without the need for either competent cells or protoplasts. Infection can therefore be used to study immediate effects of cloned genes on actively growing, physiologically normal cells. Incorporation of appropriate mutations into the viral vector genome should create a situation in which viral genes are not expressed and infected cells are therefore not immediately killed.

All phage described in this report have been deposited in the Bacillus Genetics Stock Center for general distribution.

REFERENCES

Behrens, B., Pawlek, B., Morelli, G. and Trautner, T.A. (1983). **Molec. Gen. Genet. 189**, 10

Dunn, J.J. and Studier, F.W. (1981). **J. Mol. Biol. 148**, 303.

Hamilton, P.T. and Reeve, J.N. (1984). In Microbial Chemoautotrophy (W.R. Strohl and O.H. Tuovinen, eds.), Ohio State Press, Columbus, Ohio, in press.

Heilmann, H. and Reeve, J.N. (1982). **Gene 17**, 91.
Kreft, J., Parrisius, J., Burger, K.J. and Goebel, W. (1982). In Molecular Cloning and Gene Regulation in Bacilli (A.T. Ganesan, S. Chang and J.A. Hoch, eds.), p. 145, Academic Press, New York.
Mertens, G., Amann, E. and Reeve, J.N. (1979). **Molec. Gen. Genet. 172**, 271.
Miller, J.H. (1982). Experiments in Molecular Genetics, p. 328, Cold Spring Harbor Laboratory Press, New York.
Reeve, J.N., Mendelson, N.H., Coyne, S.I., Hallock, L.L. and Cole, R.M. (1973). **J. Bacteriol. 114**, 860.
Scherzinger, E., Laupper, H.-F., Voll, N. and Wauke, M. (1980). **Nucl. Acids Res. 8**, 1287.
Stüber, D., Morelli, G., Bujard, H., Montenegro, M.A. and Trautner, T.A. (1981). **Molec. Gen. Genet. 181**, 518.
Studier, F.W. and Rosenberg, A.H. (1981). **J. Molec. Biol. 153**, 503.
Trautner, T.A. and Spatz, H.Ch. (1973). **Topics Microbiol. Immunol. 62**, 61.

Session IV: Cloning

DEVELOPMENT OF AN INDUCIBLE PROMOTER FOR CONTROLLED GENE EXPRESSION IN BACILLUS SUBTILIS

Daniel G. Yansura
Dennis J. Henner

Departments of Vaccine Development and Molecular Biology
Genentech, Inc.
South San Francisco, California

I. INTRODUCTION

A major problem in the study of gene expression in Bacillus subtilis has been the lack of a well characterized control system that allows the experimenter to easily and rapidly repress or derepress any desired gene product. Without a doubt, such easily manipulated systems as the lac, trp and lambda P-L promoter have been extremely useful in Esherichia coli for expressing both foreign and native gene products. Very useful features of these systems are that they are readily available, have been engineered in a number of ways to ease the placement of other genes under their control and can be induced by simple methods such as temperature shifts or media manipulations.

We decided to attempt to construct an analogous system in B. subtilis that would have the advantages of the systems described above for E. coli. Since no well characterized systems exist that are native to B. subtilis, we decided to use one of the E. coli systems and transfer it in a functional state to B. subtilis. The system we chose to use was the lac system. A number of reasons dictated this choice. All the components of the system had been cloned and were readily available. Another important factor was that previously contructed hybrid promoters which contained the lac operator had been demonstrated to be controllable by the lac repressor (de Boer et al., 1983b). We also were confident that we couldexpress the lac repressor in B. subtilis by giving it a Bacillus promoter and ribosome binding site.

GENETICS AND BIOTECHNOLOGY
OF BACILLI

ISBN 0-12-274160-9

In this report we will describe the contruction of hybrid promoters containing RNA polymerase recognition sites derived from Bacillus promoters and the operator from the lac promoter. Also we will describe the expression of the lac repressor in B. subtilis. We will show that genes placed under the control of such hybrid promoters can be controlled by expressing them in the same cell that also expresses the lac repressor. This control is easily mediated through the addition of isopropyl-B-thiogalactoside (IPTG)

II. CONSTRUCTION OF HYBRID PROMOTERS

The pac-I promoter is a derivative of the promoter of the penicillinase gene of B. licheniformis 749C (Neugebauer et al., 1981; Gray and Chang, 1981; Imanaka et al., 1981). For ease of manipulation of the penicillinase gene, a HpaII site approximately 40 bp upstream of the promoter was converted to an EcoRI site, and a PvuII site approximately 600 bp 3' to the end of the gene converted to a BamHI site

---

Figure 1. Consruction of the pac-I promoter. The pac-I promoter was constructed and placed in front of the penicillinase gene as diagrammed. The parent plasmid, pBSA42, is the shuttle vector pBS42 (Band and Henner, 1983) which contains the penicillinase gene of B. licheniformis (Neugebauer et al., 1981; Gray and Chang, 1981; Imanaka et al., 1981). For convenience, a HhaI site approximately 40 bp upstream of the promoter was converted to an EcoRI site and a PvuII site downstream of the gene was converted to a BamHI site (data not shown). The sequence of primer 1 was:

5'-GAAAGTATTAC-3'

and the sequence of primer 2 was:

5'-AATTGTGAGCGG-3'.

The sequence of the synthetic lac operator with BamHI linkers was:

5'-GGATCCAATTGTGAGCGGATAACAATTCCGGATCC-3'.

"Primer repairs" were preformed as previously described (Goeddel et al., 1980). Plasmid pBSA80 was constructed in strain MM294, with selection for Amp resistance on X-gal indicator plates. Blue colonies were chosen for screening. Plasmid pBSA105 was constructed in strain D1210 (lacI^q), with selection for Amp resistance. Symbols: Ppcn, penicillinase; lac Op, lac operator.

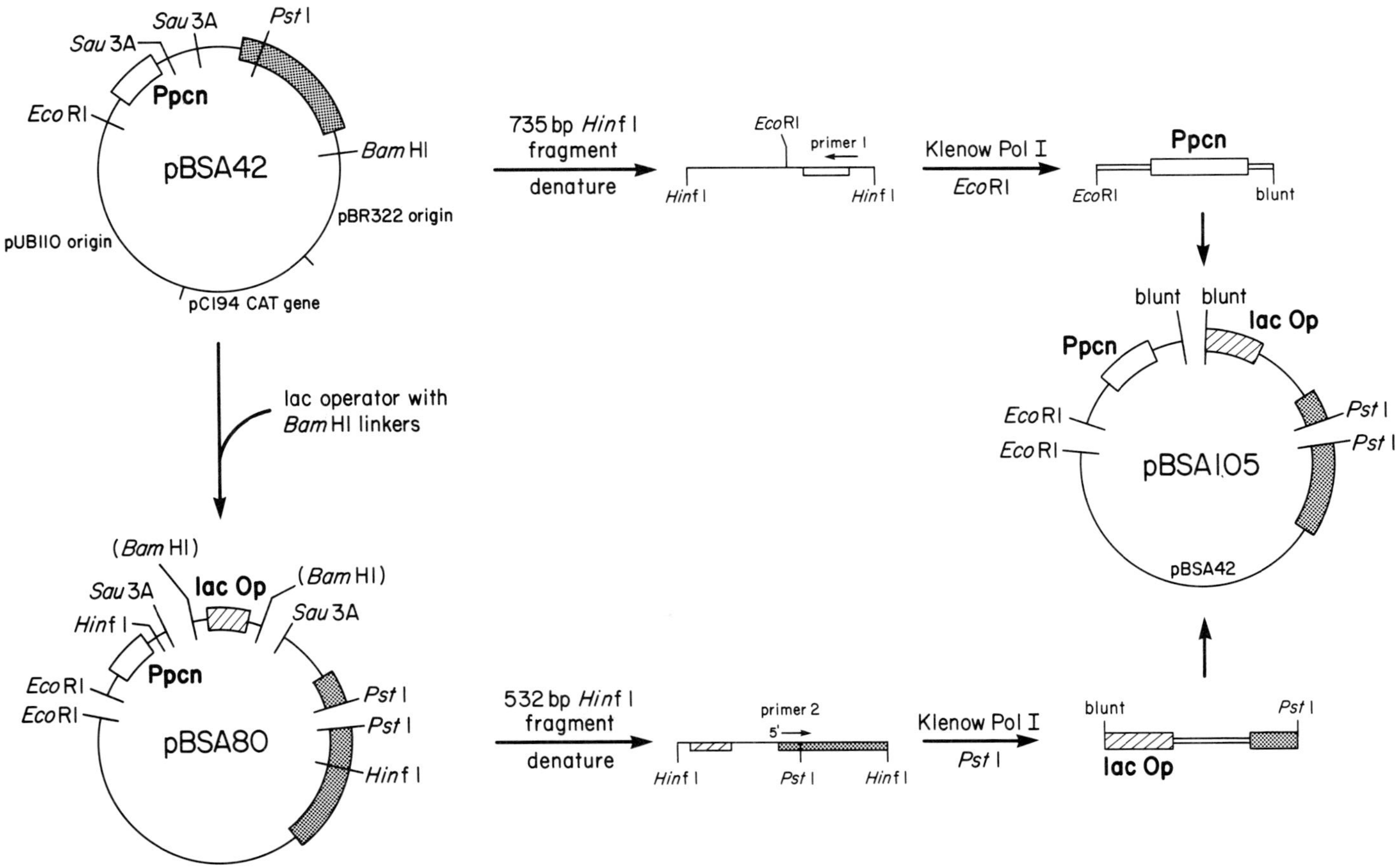
Sau 3A
Sau 3A
Pst I
Eco RI
Ppcn
pBSA42
Bam HI
pBR322 origin
pUB110 origin
pC194 CAT gene
735 bp Hinf I
fragment
denature
EcoRI
primer 1
Hinf I
Hinf I
Klenow Pol I
EcoRI
Ppcn
EcoRI
blunt
blunt
blunt
lac Op
Ppcn
Eco RI
Eco RI
Pst I
Pst I
pBSA105
pBSA42
lac operator with
Bam HI linkers
(Bam HI)
lac Op
(Bam HI)
Sau 3A
Sau 3A
Hinf I
Ppcn
Eco RI
Eco RI
Pst I
Pst I
Hinf I
pBSA80
532 bp Hinf I
fragment
denature
primer 2
5'
Hinf I
Pst I
Hinf I
Klenow Pol I
Pst I
blunt
Pst I
lac Op

(data not shown). The entire penicillinase gene contained on the EcoRI - BamHI fragment was subcloned onto a shuttle vector, pBS42, which can replicate in both E. coli and B. subtilis, expressing chloramphenicol resistance in both organisms (Band and Henner, 1983). The shuttle vector containing the penicillinase gene was designated pBSA42. The contruction of the pac-I derivative of the penicillinase promoter is outlined in Figure 1. An 80 bp Sau3A fragment between the promoter and ribosome binding site was removed and replaced by a synthetic lac operator bounded by BamHI linkers. The orientation of the operator with respect to the promoter was checked by using a synthetic DNA fragment to prime a DNA polymerase "runoff" reaction using the 532 bp HinfI fragment as a template. The operators in the correct orientation showed a 509 bp band, while those in the incorrect orientation showed a 39 bp band (data not shown). One of those in the correct orientation was designated pBSA80 and used for subsequent constructions. A synthetic DNA fragment was used in a "primer repair" reaction to create a segment of DNA containing the penicillinase promoter, bounded by an EcoRI site and a blunt end 6 bp downstream of the -10 region. Similarly, a "primer repair" reaction was used to create a segment of DNA having a blunt end at the beginning of the lac operator and a PstI site at the other end. Ligation of these fragments together into a vector plasmid created the plasmid pBSA105, containing the pac-I promoter. The sequence of the pac-I promoter is shown in Figure 3.

The spac-I promoter is a derivative of a promoter of the lytic B. subtilis bacteriophage SP01. The promoter has previously been sequenced and is contained on a 1.1 kpb EcoRI* fragment (Lee et al., 1980). The construction of the spac-I derivative of this promoter is outlined in Figure 3. Basically, the promoter was cloned as three separate fragments, which were then assembled into the final spac-I promoter. A 250 bp HincII - EcoRI fragment was subcloned directly from SP01 DNA. The HincII site on this fragment interrupts the -35 region of the promoter, while the EcoRI site lies on the 5' (upstream) side of the promoter. A fragment extending from the HincII site in the -35 region to

---

which create an XbaI overhang, and which contains the lac operator and a portion of the -10 region. The vectors used for the constructions were pBR322 and two derivatives of pBR32, pR2 and PIAΔ7Δ4-5, which were chosen for their convenient restriction sites. All ligation mixtures were transformed into strain MM294, with selection for Amp resistance (pBR322 and PIAΔ7Δ4-5) or Tet resistance (pR2). Symbols: -35, -35 region; -10, -10 region; lac Op, lac operator.

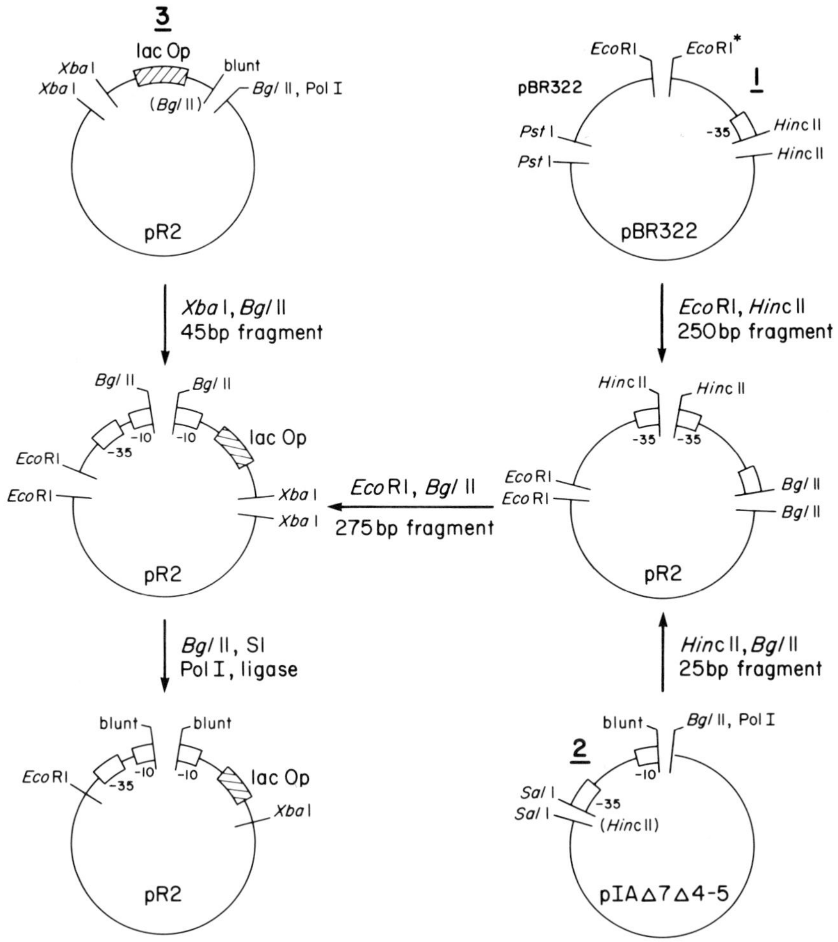

Figure 2. Consruction of the spac-I promoter. The spac-I promoter was constructed in a series of steps as diagrammed. Fragments that did not originate from the constructions diagrammed on the figure are numbered and their derivation is as follows: 1- 250 bp EcoRI - HincII fragment derived from the 1,100 bp EcoRI fragment 26 of SPO1, containing a portion of the -35 region of the promoter; 2- synthetic complementary fragments:*

5'-TCGACTTTATCTACAAGGTGTGGCA-3' and

5'-TGCCACACCTTGTAGATAAAG-3'

which create a SalI overhang, and which contain a portion of the -35 region and a portion of the -10 region; 3- synthetic complementary fragments:

5'-TAATGTGTGGAATTGTGAGCGGATAACAATTAAGCTTAGGAT-3' and

5'-CTAGATCCTAAGCTTAATTGTTATCCGCTCACAATTCCACACATTA-3'

```
EcoRI
GAATTCGGTG GAAACGAGGT CATCATTTCC TTCCGAAAAA ACGGTTGCAT TTAAATCTTA CATATGTAAT

      <<<< <<  lac Op  >>>>>>    Sau3A                   *****             met
ACTTTCAATT GTGAGCGGAT AACAATTCCG GATCAATCAA ATATTCAAAC GGAGGGAGAC GATTTTGATG
      ---- ---------- ----------
```

```
EcoRI
GAATTCTACA CAGCCCAGTC CAGACTATTC GGCACTGAAA TTATGGGTGA AGTGGTCAAG ACCTCACTAG

GCACCTTAAA AATAGCGCAC CCTGAAGAAG ATTTATTTGA GGTAGCCCTT GCCTACCTAG CTTCCAAGAA

AGATATCCTA ACAGCACAAG AGCGGAAAGA TGTTTTGTTC TACATCCAGA ACAACCTCTG CTAAAATTCC

                                                                <<< <<< lac Op
TGAAAAATTT TGCAAAAAGT TGTTGACTTT ATCTACAAGG TGTGGCATAA TGTGTGGAAT TGTGAGCGGA
                                                       ---------  ----------

  >>>>>>HindIII  **** *    XbaI EcoRI met
TAACAATTAA GCTTAAGGAG GTGTATCTAG AATTCATG
---------- ---------- ---------- --------
```

*Figure 3. Sequences of hybrid promoters pac-I and spac-I. The nucleotide sequences of the pac-I (above) and spac-I promoters are shown. The -35 and -10 regions of the promoters are overlined, probable ribosome binding sites are indicated by *'s, the palindromic sequences of the lac operator are indicated by << >>, and the initiation codons are indicated by "met". Sequences which are not derived from the parent promoter are underlined.*

the middle of the -10 region was synthesized and subcloned in such a way as to recreate the HincII site in the -35 region and a BglII site in the -10 region. A third synthetic fragment extended from the middle of the -10 region, through the lac operator, and to convenient HindIII and XbaI sites. This fragment was subcloned in such a way as to recreat a BglII site in the -10 region, and the XbaI site past the lac operator. The promoter was then assembled in three steps as outlined in Figure 2. The sequence of this hybrid promoter is shown in Figure 3.

III. EXPRESSION OF THE LAC REPRESSOR IN BACILLUS SUBTILIS

In order to express the lac repressor in B. subtilis, we placed it behind a promoter and ribosome binding site that should function in B. subtilis. The promoter and ribosome binding site that we chose was that for the B. licheniformis penicillinase gene. An exact replacement of the natural promoter and ribosome binding site of the repressor gene with the penicillinase promoter and ribosome binding site was accomplished in such a manner that no changes in the sequence or the spacing of the penicillinase promoter and ribosome binding site were made. The details of this construction will be reported elsewhere.

IV. CONTROL OF GENE EXPRESSION IN BACILLUS SUBTILIS

In order to determine whether the components of the system described above could function in B. subtilis, it was necessary to put them together in the same cell and attempt to demonstrate induction. Figure 4 shows the construction of a plasmid which contains the penicillinase gene under the control of the pac-I promoter and the lac repressor under the control of the penicillinase promoter. This plasmid was designated pAIQ25. When pAIQ25 was transformed into B. subtilis, chloramphenicol resistant colonies were obtained. In order to demonstrate whether these transformants expressed penicillinase, they were patched onto plates containing polyvinyl alcohol (PVA) and stained for penicilliianse activity with iodine (Sherratt and Collins, 1973). Duplicate plates with and without 1 mM IPTG were used to see whether any noticeable modulation of the penicillinase expression occurred. Figure 5 shows such plates and it was readily apparent that the transformants expressed penicillinase and that the expression could be induced by the addition of IPTG. Quantitative measurements of the amount of penicillinase expressed in liquid cultures of pAIQ25 transformants showed that the addition of 1 mM IPTG caused a hundred-fold increase in the levels of penicillinase.

The spac-I promoter was used to demonstrate the controlled expression of leukocyte interferon A in B. subtilis. Figure 6 shows the construction of a plasmid which is analogous to pAIQ25, designated pLIQ-1. This plasmid contains the spac-I promoter linked to the interferon gene and the lac repressor gene on a neomycin resistant shuttle vector pBS7. After transformation of pLIQ-1 into B. subtilis, transformants were picked and assayed for interferon production using a bio-assay procedure (Stewart, 1979). Cultures of pLIQ-1 transformants showed levels of 2,000 U/ml/OD when grown in the absence of IPTG, while the addition of IPTG increased the expession levels to 100,000 U/ml/OD.

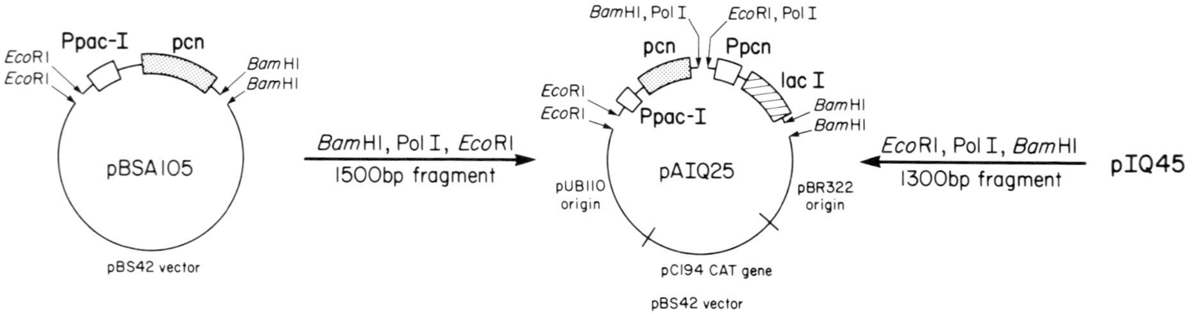

Figure 4. Construction of pAIQ25. The construction of a plasmid carrying the lac repressor and the penicillinase gene under the control of the pac-I promoter is diagrammed. Plasmid pAIQ25 was constructed by ligating three fragments, one was the pBS42 vector, the second contained the penicillinase gene and the third contained the lac repressor gene. Plasmid pAIQ25 was constructed in strain MM294 with selection for Amp resistance. Symbols: Ppac-I, pac-I promoter; Ppcn, penicillinase promoter; pcn, penicillinase coding region; lacI, lac repressor coding region.

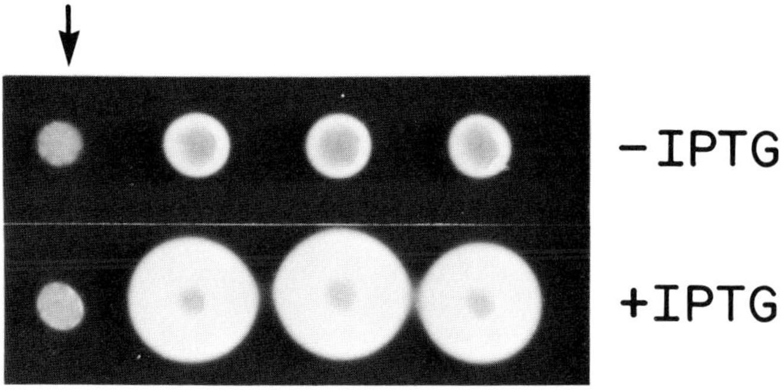

Figure 5. Assay for pennicillinase activity on PVA plates. B. subtilis colonies carrying the plasmid pAIQ25 were plated on LB plates containing 0.8% PVA and 10 μg/ml cmp. The plates were stained and developed as previously described (Sherratt and Collins, 1973). The arrow indicated colonies carrying the parent plasmid pBS42.

V. USE OF THE SPAC-I PROMOTER TO ALTER THE RIBOSOME BINDING SITE

The spac-I promoter has the useful feature of having the Shine-Dalgarno region surrounded by two unique restriction sites (see Figure 3). We took advantage of this feature to explore the effects on expression caused by changes in the sequence of the Shine-Dalgarno region. Figure 7 shows the construction of a series of plasmids which are altered in only the sequence of the Shine-Dalgarno region. Table 1 shows the sequences of the various regions used and the expression levels in both E. coli and B. subtilis. It is obvious that drastic changes in the expression levels are caused by the sequence alterations shown. Most noticeably, pSFIF-I expresses interferon in E. coli, but does not express detectable levels of interferon in B. subtilis. Only when the degree of complementarity of the Shine-Dalgarno region for the end of 16S rRNA is raised can interferon expression in B. subtilis be detected. These results also seem to suggest that the sequence of the region surrounding the Shine-Dalgarno sequence has more severe effects on expression levels in B. subtilis than in E. coli (compare pSFIF IV-VII).

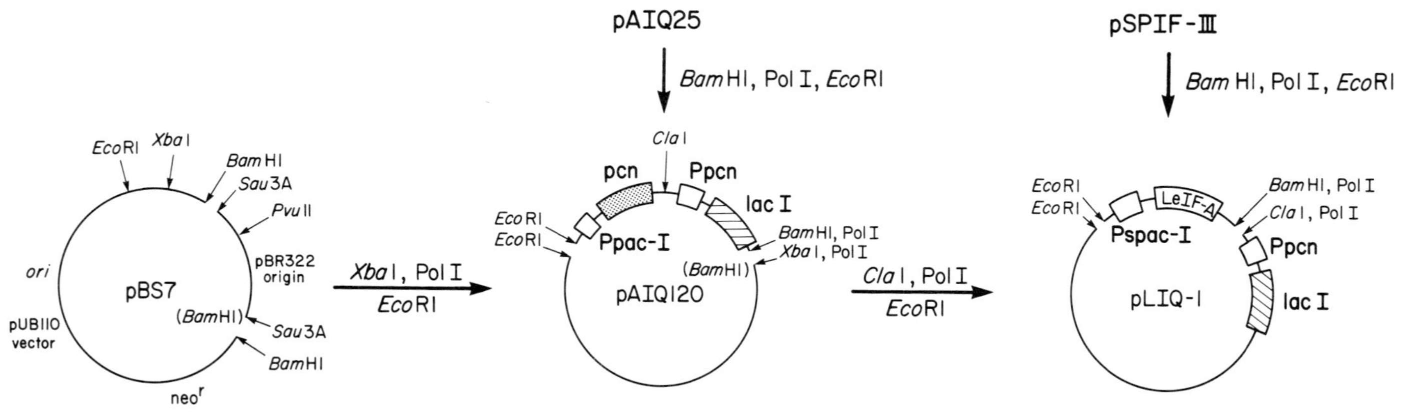

Figure 6. Construction of pLIQ1. The parent of pLIQ1 was AIQ120, a neomycin resistant analogue of pAIQ25 described above. pAIQ120 was constructed by ligating the EcoRI - BamHI fragment of pAIQ25 containing the penicillinase gene and the lac repressor gene into the shuttle vector pBS7 whose derivation is shown. The penicillinase gene of pAIQ120 was replaced with a leukocyte interferon gene under the control of the spac-I promoter. The construction of pSFIF-III is outlined in Figure 7. Symbols: Pspac-I, spac-I promoter; Ppac-I, pac-I promoter; Ppcn, penicillinase promoter; pcn, penicillinase coding region; lacI, lac repressor coding region; leIF-A, leukocyte interferon A coding sequence.

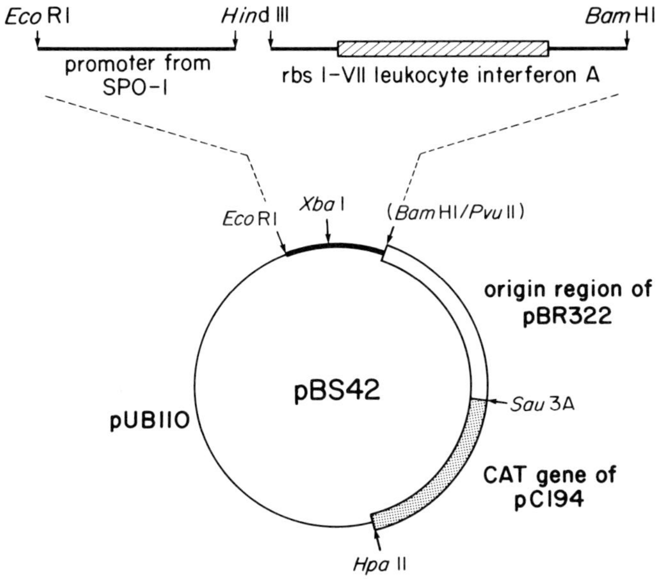

Figure 7. Construction of a series of expression plasmids with varied Shine-Dalgarno sequences. The vector for these constructions is pBS42 (Band and Henner, 1983). The spac-I promoter on an EcoRI - HindIII fragment was ligated to each of a series of HindIII - BamHI fragments which contained the leukocyte interferon A gene preceded by various Shine-Dalgarno regions (de Boer et al., 1983a). The sequences preceding the leukocyte interferon gene are detailed in Table 1.

VI. DISCUSSION

These results demonstrate clearly that we have constructed a control system that can be used to modulate gene expression in B. subtilis. Both a secreted gene product (penicillinase) and an intercellular gene product (interferon) have been expressed in B. subtilis and the level of expression increased significantly upon the addition of IPTG. The demonstration of controlled expression indicates that, first, the hybrid promoters function in B. subtilis and are capable of binding the lac repressor, second, the lac repressor is expressed in B. subtilis and is capable of assembling into a functional multimer, and third, IPTG enters the cell in sufficient quantity to induce the system.

Table 1. Interferon Activity in Crude Extracts of B. subtilis

Plasmid	PSDR sequence[a]	LeIF A(U/ml)	
		B. subtilis	E. coli
pBS42	-------------	<800	ND
pSPIF-I	AAGCTTAGGATCTAGAATTCATG	<800	26,500 (1.8)
pSFIF-II	AAGCTTAAGGAGGATCTAGAATTCATG	200,000 (0.6)	4,000 (0.3)
pSFIF-III	AAGCTTAAGGAGGTGATCTAGAATTCATG	330,000 (1.0)	14,500 (1.0)
pSPIF-IV	AAGCTTGGAGGTTTTAATTCATG	150,000 (0.5)	40,500 (2.8)
pSPIF-V	AAGCTTGGAGGAAAAAATTCATG	75,000 (0.2)	46,500 (3.2)
pSPIF-VI	AAGCTTGGAGGCCCCAATTCATG	10,000 (0.03)	65,000 (4.5)
pSPIF-VII	AAGCTTGGAGGGGGGAATTCATG	3,200 (0.01)	8,000 (0.6)

B. subtilis I168 (trpC2) or *E. coli* (F^-, $lacI^q$, gal^-, pro^-, leu^-, thi^-, thi^-, $endoI^-$, hsm, hsr, RecA, rpsL) cells carrying the indicated plasmids were grown to a density at OD 600 of 1.0 in L-broth supplemented with 10 μg/ml of chloramphenicol and 0.5% glucose. Triplicate one ml aliquots of each culture were harvested by centrifugation in an Eppendorf microfuge for 4 minutes. The *B. subtilis* pellets were suspended in 0.1 ml of a solution of 10 mg/ml lysozyme in 10 mM Tris, 1 mM EDTA, pH 8, and incubated at 37°C for 15 minutes. The suspension was then dissolved in 0.9 ml of 0.1% SDS and these samples were diluted 50- to 200-fold in phosphate buffered saline containing 1 mg/ml bovine serum albumin (PBS-A). the *E. coli* pellets were suspended in 0.3 ml of a solution of 150 μg/ml lysozyme in 100 mM Tris, 20% sucrose, 20 mM EDTA, pH 8, and incubated on ice for 30 minutes. 0.1 ml of 0.25 M EDTA was added, followed by 0.6 ml of a solution of 0.3% Triton X-100, 150 mM Tris, 0.2 mM EDTA, 1 mM PMSF, pH 8. The cell debris was removed by centrifugation in an Eppendorf microfuge for 10 minutes and the supernatants were diluted 10- to 50-fold in PBS-A. Interferon levels were determined in a competitive ELISA assay and also in an interferon bioassay by the cytopathic effect inhibition of vesicular stomatitis virus on MDBK cells. Since the assays gave almost identical results, only the bioassay data is presented. The relative expression levels shown in parentheses were computed by assigning the expression level for pSFIF-III a relative value of 1.0.

[a]The sequence of the relevant part of the PSDR for each plasmid is presented and the bases that are complementary to the 3' end of *B. subtilis* 16S rRNA are indicated with a ".". The initiation codon of the leukocyte interferon gene is overlined. The sequence of the 3' end of *B. subtilis* 16S rRNA is 3'-UCUUUCCUCCACUAG-5' (cited in de Boer et al., 1983a). The sequence of the 3' end of *E. coli* 16S rRNA is 3'-AUUCCUCCACUAG-5'.

This control system should be useful in the expression of both native and foreign genes in B. subtilis. It has already demonstrated its utility by allowing us to introduce the B. licheniformis penicillinase gene into B. subtilis on a high copy plasmid, which we and others had previously been unable to do (unpublished; Gray and Chang, 1981). Studies on the effect of induction of the penicillinase gene might enable us to determine why the gene might not be introduced in a constitutive form on a high copy plasmid.

The spac-I promoter should have additional benefits besides the ability to be controlled by the lac repressor. It has a number of useful restriction sites that allow facile construction of various expression vectors. The fact that the Shine-Dalgarno region is flanked by unique restriction sites should allow an even more thorough investigation of the effects of sequence changes in this region on gene expression. Also, if desired, the Shine-Dalgarno region might be removed entirely at the HindIII site and the spac-I promoter placed in front of a native Shine-Dalgarno region.

In conclusion, we feel that we have reached our goal of building a versatile and simple transcriptionally controlled promoter system, and we hope that it will enable us to rapidly move forward with an understanding of the important factors in the control of gene expression in B. subtilis.

ACKNOWLEDGMENTS

We would like to thank Herman de Boer, who made available to us the series of plasmids containing the leukocyte interferon gene preceded by a variety of Shine-Dalgarno regions. We would also like to thank the Organic Synthesis group without whose dependable DNA synthesis the above work would not have been possible.

REFERENCES

Band, L. and Henner, D.J. (1983). **Nature**, submitted.

de Boer, H.A., Comstock, L.J., Hui, A., Wong, E. and Vasser, M. (1983a). In Gene Amplification and Analysis, Vol. 3 (T.S. Papas, M. Rosenberg and J.G. Chirikjian, eds.), Elsevier Science Publishing Company, New York, in press.

de Boer, H.A., Comstock, L.J. and Vasser, M. (1983b). **Proc. Natl. Acad. Sci. USA 80**, 21.

Goeddel, D.V., Shepard, H.M., Yelverton, E.Y., Leung, D. and Crea, R. (1980). **Nucl. Acids Res. 8**, 4057.

Gray, O. and Chang, S. (1981). **J. Bacteriol. 145,** 422.
Imanaka, T., Tanaka, T., Tsunekawa, H. and Aiba, S. (1981). **J. Bacteriol. 147,** 776.
Lee, G., Talkington, C. and Pero, J. (1980). **Molec. Gen. Genet. 180,** 57.
Neugebauer, K., Sprengel, R. and Schaller, H. (1981). **Nucl. Acids Res. 9,** 2577.
Sherratt, D.J. and Collins, J.F. (1973). **J. Gen. Microbiol. 76,** 217.
Stewart, W.I., II (1979). The Interferon System, Springer, Berlin.

CLONING AND CHARACTERIZATION OF THE GENE FOR A THIOL-ACTIVATED CYTOLYSIN IN BACILLUS SUBTILIS[1]

Jürgen Kreft
Michael S. Gilmore
Bodo Müller
Gerhard Weidinger
Werner Goebel

Institut für Genetik and Mikrobiologie
Würzburg, West Germany

I. INTRODUCTION

Extracellular proteins with hemolytic or cytolytic activity are produced by many bacteria (Smyth and Duncan, 1978) and are often found associated with pathogenic forms. In constast to Escherichia coli, where the genetics of hemolysin are studied thoroughly (Berger et al., 1982; Goebel and Hedgpeth, 1982) the genetics of the SH-activated cytolysins from Gram-positive bacteria are poorly understood. One member of this interesting group of cytolytic toxins, which share some common biochemical and immunological properties, is cereolysin. In the following communication cloning and partial characterization of the cereolysin gene will be described.

II. MATERIALS AND METHODS

The donor strain Bacillus cereus GP4 is a natural isolate from our laboratory. The cosmid vector pJC74 and the shuttle vector pJKK3-1 have been previously described (Collins and Brüning, 1978; Kreft and Hughes, 1982), as well

[1]*This work was supported by a grant from the Deutsche Forschungsgemeinschaft (SFB 105 - A12).*

ISBN 0-12-274160-9

as the common procedures for chromosomal DNA and plasmid isolation, cleavage and ligation of DNA, and transformation of E. coli and B. subtilis. All other experimental details will be described elsewhere (Kreft et al., 1983; M. Gilmore, manuscript in preparation).

III. RESULTS AND DISCUSSION

A. Cloning of the Cereolysin Determinant in E. coli and B. subtilis

B. cereus GP4 carries the cereolysin gene(s) on its chromosome. Therefore a gene bank of this strain was constructed in E. coli using the BamHI digested cosmid vector pJC74 which was ligated with partially Sau3A-digested chromosomal DNA of B. cereus GP4. Among several thousand cosmid clones a few were found which showed faint hemolysis on erythrocyte agar after 2 to 3 days of incubation at 37°C. The recombinant cosmid with the smallest insert of foreign DNA was isolated and it was shown, by Southern hybridization, that the inserted DNA originated from the donor strain B. cereus GP4 (results not shown).

The weak expression of the cloned hemolysin determinant in E. coli did not allow a biochemical characterization of the gene product. Therefore a PstI fragment of the recombinant cosmid pJC74 hly1 was recloned into the shuttle vector pJKK3-1. Besides the recombinant plasmid pJKK3-1 hly2 which contained the complete PstI fragment from pJC74 hly1 with the hemolysin determinant, the smaller plasmid pJKK3-1 hly1 was found in E. coli. This plasmid showed a deletion of about 1 kb in the recloned PstI fragment from pJC74 hly1 which did not affect hemolysin production.

After transformation of B. subtilis BR151 with pJKK3-1 hly1 all Tc^r transformants expressed strong hemolytic activity comparable to that of the donor B. ceresu GP4. The cloning and recloning procedure is shown in Figure 1.

B. Biochemical Characterization of the Hemolysin Expressed by pJKK3-1 hly1

As already mentioned, E. coli with pJC74 hly1 expressed only weak hemolysis on erythrocyte agar plates after prolonged incubation. This is most likely due to the inability of E. coli to secrete this hemolysin into the medium, and therefore presumably it is released only after (partial) lysis of cells. In contrast, B. subtilis with pJKK3-1 hly1

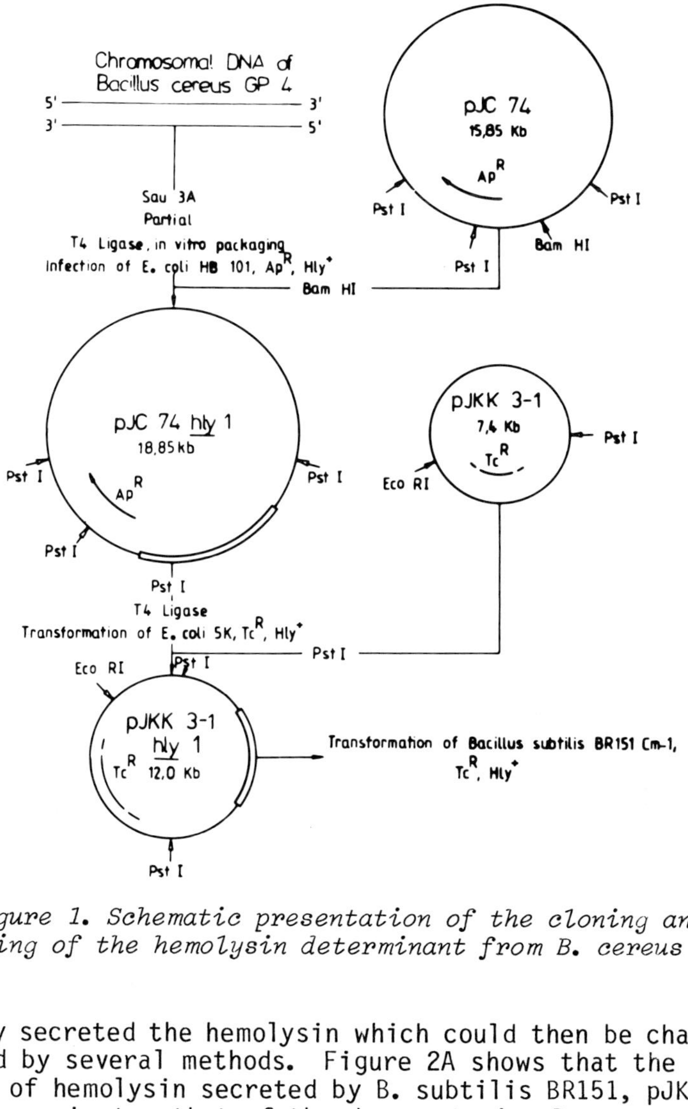

Figure 1. Schematic presentation of the cloning and recloning of the hemolysin determinant from B. cereus GP4.

readily secreted the hemolysin which could then be characterized by several methods. Figure 2A shows that the total amount of hemolysin secreted by B. subtilis BR151, pJKK3-1 hly1 approximates that of the donor strain, B. cereus GP4.

Cereolysin is inhibited by cholesterol (Cowell et al., 1976) and Figure 2B shows that incubation of culture supernatants with increasing amounts of cholesterol prior to assay of hemolytic acitivity also inhibited the hemolysin produced by B. subtilis BR151, pJKK3-1 hly1 to the same extent as the cereolysin from B. cereus GP4. Another property of cereolysin (and related cytolysins) is its activation by SH-reagents (Smyth and Duncan, 1978), and Figure 2C shows that addition of dithiothreitol (DTT) to the

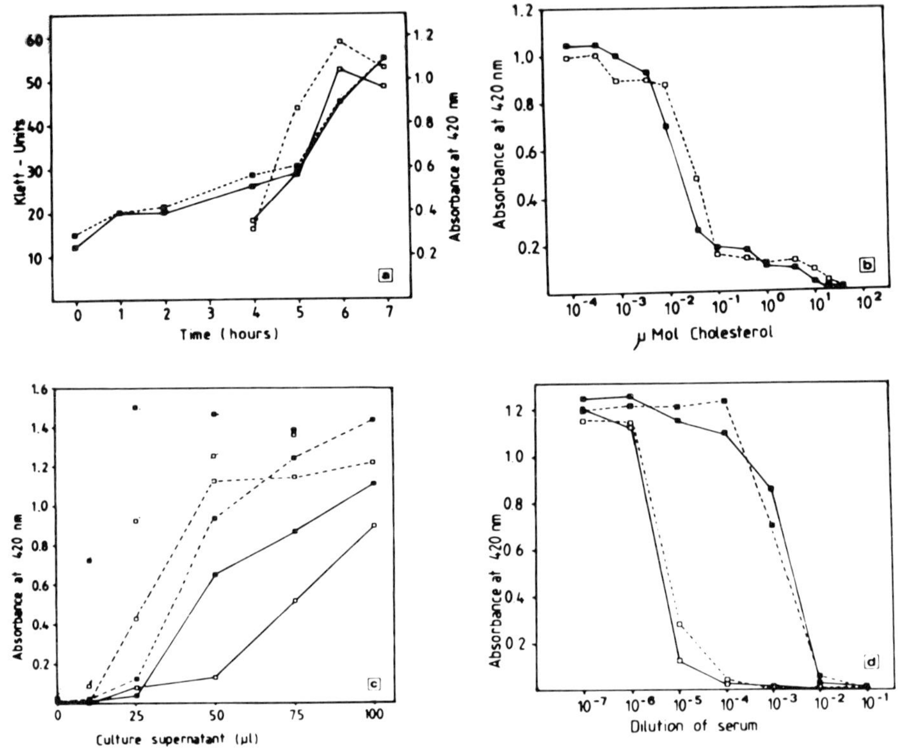

Figure 2. Comparison of hemolysin from B. subtilis BR151CM with pJKK3-1hly1 and cerolysin from B. cereus GP4. [A] Growth curve (B. subtilis ■---■, B. cereus ■——■) and hemolytic activity in culture supernatants (B. subtilis □---□, B. cereus □——□). [B] Inhibition of hemolytic activity after preincubation (10 minutes, room temperature) of culture supernatant with increasing amounts of cholesterol (B. subtilis □---□, B. cereus ■——■). [C] Activation of hemolytic activity after preincubation (10 minutes, room temperature) of culture supernatants with two different concentrations of DTT (B. subtilis, no DTT □——□; 0.5 mM DTT □---□; 1.25 mM DTT □···□; B. cereus, no DTT ■——■; 0.5 mM DTT ■---■; 1.25 mM DTT ■···■). [D] Neutralization of hemolytic activity after preincubation (10 minutes, room temperature) of culture supernatants with increasing amounts of normal serum or antiserum raised against cereolysin (B. subtilis, normal serum ■---■; antiserum □---□; B. cereus, normal serum ■——■; antiserum □——□).

culture supernatant of B. subtilis BR151, pJKK3-1 hly1 stimulated its hemolytic activity to the same extent as the hemolytic activity of the B. cereus GP4 supernatant. Finally, the culture supernatants of both strains were preincubated with antiserum raised against cerolysin from B. cereus GP4. Figure 2D shows that preincubation of culture supernatants inhibits hemolysis with both strains at the same dilution of antiserum. The inhibition observed with 1,000 times higher concentrations of serum from nonimmunized animals is due to cholesterol inevitably present in sera. These experiments clearly show that the hemolysin synthesized by B. subtilis BR151 carrying pJKK3-1 hly1 has the same specific biochemical properties as the authentic cereolysin from B. ceresu GP4.

C. Lack of Hybridization of the Cloned Cerolysin Gene to DNA from Listeria monocytogenes and Streptococcus pyogenes

Since cereolysin has some common properties with listeriolysin (from L. monocytogenes) and also streptolysin O (from Strep. pyogenes), we tested to see if the cloned cereolysin gene from B. cereus GP4 has homology to genes for the latter cytolysins. For this, chromosomal DNA from L. monocytogenes NCTC 10527 and ATCC 19119 (listeriolysin producers) or Strep. pyogenes 203 U (a streptolysin O producer), respectively, was digested with EcoRI, electrophoresed in an agarose gel and the fragments were transferred to nitrocellulose filters. PstI digested pJC74 hly1 DNA was also transferred to the filters and served as a control. [^{32}P]-labeled pJC74 hly1 was used as a probe and hybridized to the filter bound fragments. Figure 3 shows that no hybridization of the cereolysin gene probed with Streptococcus or listeria DNA was observed under conditions which in a similar experiment gave strong hybridization with DNA from B. cereus GP4 (data not shown). This demonstrates that there is no detectable homology between the cerolysin gene and the genes for listeriolysin and streptolysin O despite the similar biochemical properties of these toxins.

D. Mapping of the Cloned Cerolysin Gene and Partial DNA Sequence Analysis

The recombinant plasmid pJKK3-1 hly1 has been mapped with several restriction enzymes as shown in Figure 4. To further characterize the cloned cerolysin determinant several derivatives of pJKK3-1 hly1 have been constructed

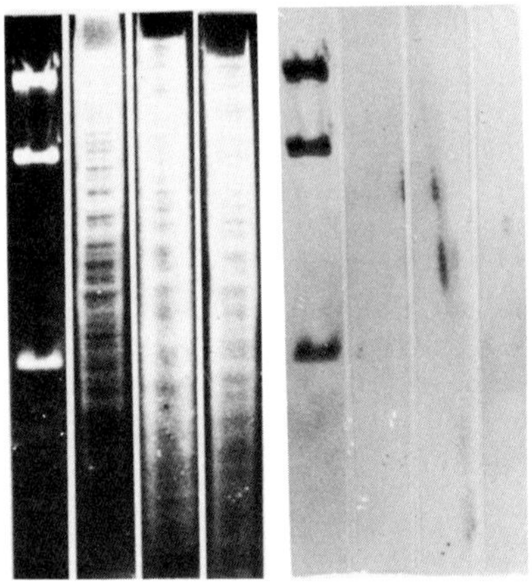

Figure 3. Gel electrophoresis and hybridization of chromosomal DNA from Strep. pyogenes and L. monocytogenes. Lane a, pJC74 hly1 digested with PstI; lane b, Strep. pyogenes 203 U DNA digested with EcoRI; lane c, L. monocytogenes NCTC 10527 digested with EcoRI; lane d, L. monocytogenes ATCC 19119 DNA digested with EcoRI; and lanes e to h, autoradiogram after hybridization with [^{32}P]-labeled pJC74 hly1 DNA.

and a partial DNA sequence has been established. These results will be described in detail elsewhere (M. Gilmore, manuscript in preparation).

In order to localize the cereolysin gene(s) more precisely on the 4.6 kb insert of pJKK3-1 hly1, deletion derivatives of this plasmid were constructed in vitro by digestion of the plasmid with appropriate restriction enzymes and subsequent religation of the digestion products followed by transformation of B. subtilis. Figure 5 shows that a deletion terminating at the left side BamH1 site (see Figure 4) does not affect cereolysin production, whereas the DNA sequence surrounding the nearby EcoRI site seems to be essential. By similar methods, the terminus on the right side of the insert was mapped to within about 100 bp beyond the second BamH1 site in the middle of the cloned fragment. By this approach the length of the fragment sufficient for full expression of cereolysin could be limited to a size of about 2.1 kb. This matches well the size of a DNA fragment needed for the expression of the cereolysin protein with an estimated molecular mass of about 60,000 daltons (Smyth and

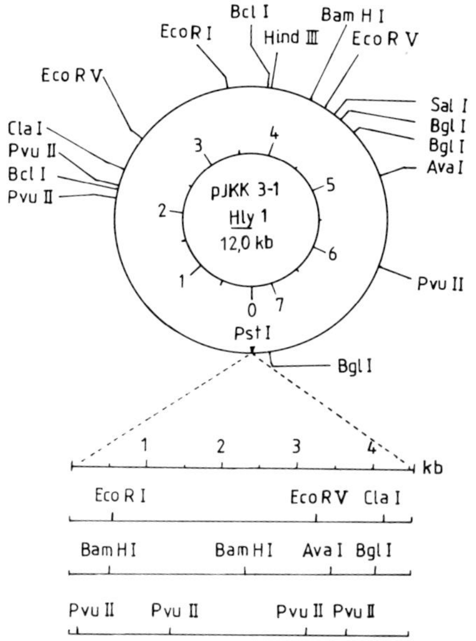

Figure 4. Restriction map of pJKK3-1 hly1. The PstI fragment derived from pJC71 hly1 is shown in linar form.

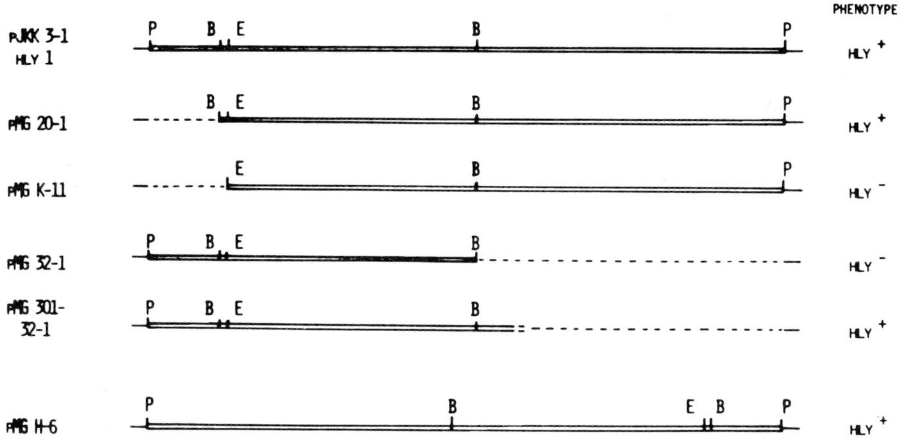

Figure 5. Influence of deletions and inversion of the cloned fragment on cereolysin production. pMG20-1, K-11, 32-1 and 301-32 are deleted derivatives of pJKK3-1 hly1. The broken lines indicate the deleted part of pKJJ3-1 hly1; E, EcoRI; B, BamHI; and P, PstI. In pMG H-6 the PstI fragment from pJC74 hly1 with the cereolysin gene has been inverted relative to its original orientation in the vector pJKK3-1.

Duncan, 1978) as well as additional coding capacity for regulatory regions and a presumptive signal peptide. Figure 5 also shows that inversion of the whole recombinant PstI fragment does not influence the Hly^+ phenotype. This evidence demonstrates that the cloned fragment is transcribed from the cereolysin promoter.

The small (201 bp) fragment between the left BamHI and EcoRI sites has been shown above to be essential for cereolysin expression. Therefore this fragment was cloned into M13 mp9 and subsequently sequenced. Figure 6 shows the preliminary DNA sequence of this fragment. In the part proximal to the EcoRI site, a sequence with good homology to the consensus sequences for B. subtilis vegetative -35 and -10 promoter regions (Losick and Pero, 1981) can be identified. Further toward the EcoRI site a putative ribosome binding (SD) site can be identified which is complementary to 8 of 10 consecutive bases on the B. subtilis 16S rRNA (Murray and Rabinowitz, 1982). In vivo promoter activity of this fragment in E. coli has been demonstrated by subcloning it into a promoter detection system (McKenney et al., 1981) and observing expression of the galK gene. Further experiments will be performed to demonstrate conclusively whether this promoter is responsible for transcription of the cereolysin gene itself.

Interestingly, we have observed partial expression of lacZ α-complementation peptide in M13 mp9 clones carrying the BamHI/EcoRI insertion in the proper orientation. Examination of the sequence of the 201 bp insert fused with the lacZ peptide reveals multiple stop codons in every reading frame prior to the GTG codon one base pair beyond the putative ribosome binding site, thereby preventing read through. Beyond this GTG codon into the lacZ sequence, there are no further triplets for over 100 base pairs in frame which are known to initiate translation. Similarly, this GTG codon initiates the only open reading frame of the sequenced portion of the cereolysin insert, and is not followed by another initiation codon for 45 bp. Use of the GTG codon as a start codon for cereolysin gene expression, and the small window between the ribosome binding site and this start codon may explain, in part, the poor expression of the cloned insert in E. coli. We are currently attempting to determine the effect of point mutations resulting in GTG--->ATG transitions as well as inserts expanding the window between the ribosome binding site and the GTG codon on the expression of cereolysin in alternate hosts. Such an approach will allow us to dissect the relative contributions of transcription, translation and posttranslational processing in the expression of extracellular proteins from

```
G G A T C C T T A A C A A A A T G T T T A C A A T A A T T C
A A T T A T A A A A A T G C A G C A T T T T A T A T G A A A A
A G A A A G T A C T T G C T T T A C G G C A G C T A T T A C
A T T A G T T G C T C C A T T G A C A A A G T G T T G C A T
T T G C T C A T G A A A A T G A T G G G G G A C A G A G A T
T T G G A G T T A T T C C G C G C T G G T C T G C T G A A G
A T A A A C A T A A A G A A G G C G T G A A T T C
```

Figure 6. Preliminary DNA sequence of the 201 bp BamH1/EcoRI fragment from pJKK3-1 hly1. The putative promoter (-35 and -10) and ribosome binding (SD) regions are boxed. Translational stop codons preceeding the putative promoter region are underlined.

more, characterization of the cereolysin gene at the DNA sequence level will allow future detailed comparison with similar genes encoding SH-activated cytolysins from pathogenic Streptococcus and Lysteria species.

ACKNOWLEDGMENTS

The authors wish to thank H. Berger and M. Härtlein for performing the initial cosmid cloning and for preparation of antisera, respectively. B. Frank is thanked for expert technical assistance, J. van Emdem for providing chromsomal DNA from Strep. pyogenes and H. Seeliger for the Listeria strains.

REFERENCES

Berger, H., Hacker, J., Juarez, A., Hughes, C. and Goebel, W. (1982). **J. Bacteriol. 152**, 1241.

Collins, J. and Brüning, H. (1978). **Gene 4**, 85.

Cowell, J.L., Grushoff-Kosyk, P.S. and Bernheimer, A.W. (1976). **Inf. Immunol. 14**, 144.

Goebel, W. and Hedgpeth, J. (1982). **J. Bacteriol. 151**, 1290.

Kreft, J. and Hughes, C. (1982). **Curr. Topics Microbiol. Immunol. 96**, 1.

Kreft, J., Berger, H., Härtlein, M., Müller, B., Weidinger, G. and Goebel, W. (1983). **J. Bacteriol.**, in press.

Losick, R. and Pero, J. (1981). **Cell 25**, 582.
McKenney, K., Shimatake, H., Court, D. Schmeissner, U., Brady, C. and Rosenberg, M. (1981). In Gene Amplification and Analysis, Vol. II, (J.C. Chirikjian and S. Papas, eds.) p. 383, Elsevier/North Holland.
Murray, C.L. and Rabinowitz, J.C. (1982). In Molecular Cloning and Gene Regulation in Bacilli (A.T. Ganesan, S. Chang and J.S. Hoch, eds.) p. 271, Academic Press, New York.
Smyth, C.J. and Duncan, J.L. (1978). In Bacterial Toxins and Cell membranes (J. Jeljaszewicz and T. Wadström, eds.) p. 129, Academic Press, London.

CHLORAMPHENICOL INDUCIBILITY OF FOREIGN GENE EXPRESSION IN BACILLUS SUBTILIS

P. S. Lovett
D. M. Williams
E. J. Duvall
S. Mongkolsuk

Department of Biological Sciences
University of Maryland Baltimore County
Catonsville, Maryland

I. INTRODUCTION

Control of gene expression in Bacillus subtilis has been most extensively studied at the level of transcriptional regulation. RNA polymerase can be modified by the addition of any of several sigma-like subunits that change the promoter-recognition specificity of the enzyme (Losick and Pero, 1981). Recently, however, a novel posttranscriptional regulatory mechanism was suggested to explain the inducible expression of an erythromycin-resistance (Ery^r determinant that is present on a plasmid that is capable of replication in Staphylococcus aureus and B. subtilis (Horinouchi and Weisblum, 1980; Shivakumar et al., 1980). The model focuses on controlling the availability to 16S rRNA of the ribosome binding site sequence in the mRNA for a structural gene by changes in the secondary structure of the RNA. The inducer, erythromycin, was suggested to control gene expession by indirectly causing destabilization of a stem-loop in mRNA that sequesters the ribosome binding site for the erythromycin-resistance determinant.

cat genes specify the enzyme chloramphenicol acetyltransferase (CAT), and have been identified in a variety of Gram-positive and Gram-negative bacteria (Shaw, 1975). The expression of cat genes from Gram-positive bacteria is inducible by chloramphenicol (Cm) whereas expression of cat determinants from Gram-negative seems unaffected by the

GENETICS AND BIOTECHNOLOGY
OF BACILLI

ISBN 0-12-274160-9

antibiotic (Winshell and Shaw, 1969). We have identified Cm-inducible cat genes in strains of the Gram-positive organism B. pumilis, and have used one such gene cat-86, to develop a promoter-cloning and expression plasmid for B. subtilis (Williams et al., 1981a; 1981b; Schoner et al., 1983; Mongkolsuk et al., 1983). The useful pattern of restriction-enzyme sensitive sites within and preceding cat-86 has allowed localization of the region essential to Cm-inducibility. Evidence is presented suggesting that the Cm-inducibility of cat-86 may represent a form of posttranscriptional regulation.

II. RESULTS

A. Plasmid Constructions

Figure 1 shows a diagram of plasmid pPL703. The plasmid consists of a 0.9 kb PstI-BglII fragment of DNA cloned from B. pumilus NCIB 8600 inserted between the EcoRI and BamHI sites of pUB110 with the aid of a 21 bp EcoRI-PstI linker. The linker contains internal BamHI and SalI sensitive sites (Messing et al., 1981). pPL703 specificies neomycin-resistance (Neo^r) due to the pUB110 gene for neomycin/kanamycin nucleotidyl transferase (Sadaie et al., 1980). The cat-86 gene present on the cloned B. pumilus DNA is essentially unexpressed in this plasmid. Promoter-containing fragments inserted into the unique EcoRI, BamHI, SalI, or PstI site activate expression of cat-86 so that the derivative plasmids specify Cm^r in B. subtilis. The level of expression of cat-86 promoted by a 284 bp EcoRI fragment from phage SP02, plasmid pPL708, is shown in Figure 2. The cat-86 gene encodes a protein of about 30,000 daltons as inferred from the nucleotide sequence of the gene (Harwood et al., 1983). Analysis of pPL703 and pPL708 in a B. subtilis maxicell system (Kobayashi and Saito, 1983) demonstrates that pPL708 specificies a 28,000 dalton protein whose appearance is promoter-dependent and Cm-inducible (Figure 2).

Plasmid pPL708, and a parent pPL608, permit expression of inserted heterologous genes in B. subtilis (Williams et al., 1981b). Insertion of a HindIII E. coli DNA fragment spanning the trpC gene into cat-86 allowed Cm-inducible expression of the trpC gene product indoleglycerolphosphate synthetase (Williams et al., 1981b). Nucleotide sequence analysis indicates that the trpC-containing fragment is inserted into cat-86 in the correct reading frame (Harwood et al., 1983). By contrast, heterologous genes such as the

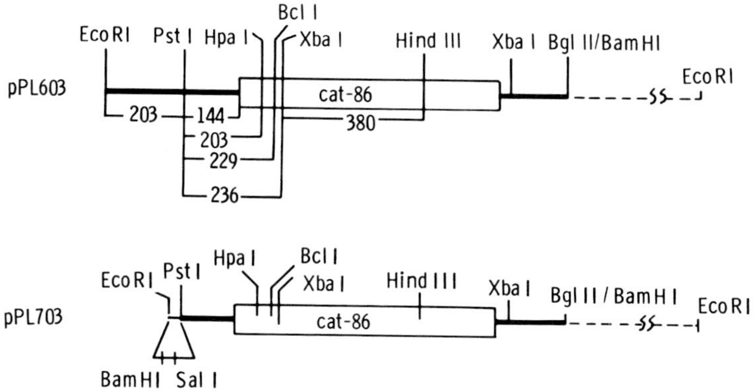

Figure 1. Diagram of pPL603 and pPL703. pPL703 was derived from pPL603 by replacing a 203 bp EcoRI-PstI fragment with a 21 bp adapter from M13mp7 (Messing et al., 1981). The adapter contains internal BamHI and SalI sensitive sites (Messing et al., 1981).

mouse DHFR gene or the Tn9 cat gene inserted into the unique PstI site of pPL608 are expressed but this expression is not Cm-inducible (Schoner et al., 1983; P. Lovett, in press). In order to more precisely locate the region essential to Cm-inducibility, the 1.5 kb fragment containing the mouse DHFR gene was inserted into two locations in pPL708 and the Cm-inducibility phenotype was tested (Figure 3). The insertion at PstI (pPL708-TR1) resulted in DHFR expression that was not Cm-inducible (Table 1). However, the insertion at the BclI site, located in codon 29 of cat-86, resulted in Cm-inducible expression of DHFR (pPL708-TR2; Table 1). The DHFR gene was chosen for these experiments because the sequence preceeding the coding region contains three inframe translation termination codons (C. Simonsen, personal communication) making it unlikely that the active gene product would be synthesized as a fusion protein. Although DHFR expression in pPL708-TR2 is Cm-inducible, the level of induction is clearly less than is seen in the induction of cat-86 in pPL708 (Table 1). The B. pumilus DNA sequence 3' to the BclI site was unessential to the Cm-induction of DHFR, since transfer of a region composed of the promoter fragment through the coding sequence of DHFR to the first BglII site (EcoRI-BglII fragment) to the EcoRI-BamHI sites of pUB110 permitted Cm inducible expression of DHFR (pPL708-TR2b; Table 1).

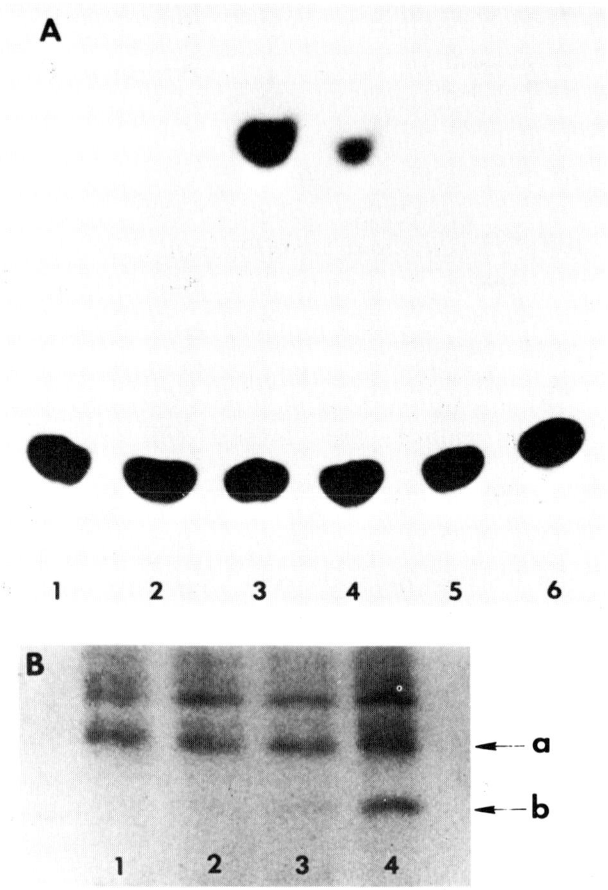

Figure 2. Autoradiograms demonstrating [A] acetylation of ^{14}C-Cm by extracts of pPL708-containing cells and [B] promoter-dependence and Cm-inducibility of a 28,000 dalton protein specified by pPL708. [A] Reactions were run and chromatography done in solvent C (as described in Shaw, 1967). Incubations of the reaction mixtures were at 37 °C for 15 minutes. Crude extracts of BR151 harboring either pPL703 or pPL708 (cells grown in 4.5 mg/ml of Cm) were the source of CAT specified by these plasmids. The crude extracts were diluted to 0.1 mg/ml. Well 1, complete mix minus enzyme; well 2, complete mix plus protein from BR151 (pPL703); well 3, complete mix plus CAT purchased from Sigma; well 4, complete mix plus protein from BR151 (pPL708); wells 5 and 6, same as wells 3 and 4 except acetyl CoA was omitted. [B] Autoradiogram demonstrating that pPL708 directs the synthesis of a Cm-inducible 28,000 protein as detected by maxicell analysis (Kobayashi and Saito,

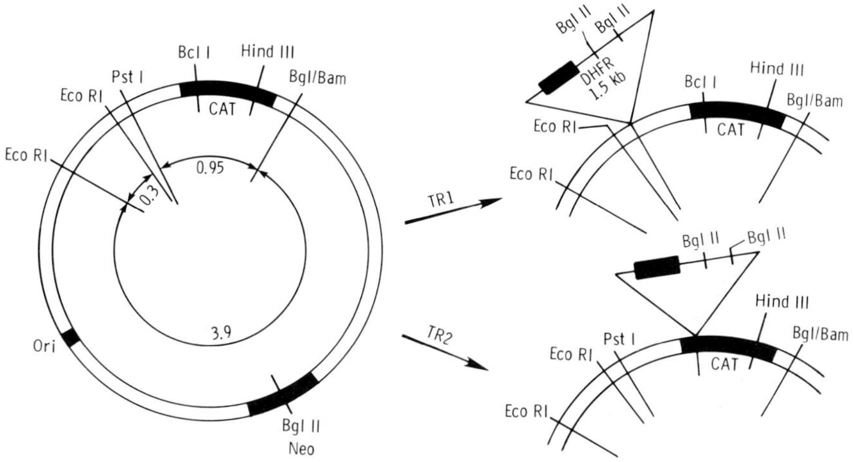

Figure 3. Construction of pPL708-TR1 and pPL708-TR2. The methods used are described in Duvall et al., (1983).

1983). Well 1, extracts of cells harboring pPL703; well 2, extract of cells harboring pPL703 grown in 0.5 μg/ml of Cm; well 3, extract of cells harboring pPL708 grown without Cm; well 4, extract of cells harboring pPL708 grown in Cm. Non-radioactive molecular weight markers were run in parallel and were used to estimate the molecular weight of the Cm-inducible protein. Only a portion of the autoradiogram is shown. a = Neomycin/kanamycin nucleotidyl transferase (Sadaie et al., 1980); b = CAT.

Table 1. Plasmid-Specified Enzyme Activities in B. subtilis

Plasmid	Specific Activity: DHFR +Cm	DHFR −Cm	CAT +Cm	CAT −Cm
pPL708	-	-	3.2	0.10
pPL708-TR1	0.83	0.71	2.8	0.08
pPL708-TR2	0.90	0.12	-	-
pPL708-TR2B	1.27	0.16	-	-

Plasmids were in B. subtilis BGSCIS53. Extracts were prepared from cells grown for 2 hours at 37°C in Penassay broth containing 0.5 μg/ml Cm or no drug. DHFR specific activity is expressed as nmoles of folate reduced per minute per mg protein. CAT specific activity is expressed as μmol of Cm acetylated per minutes per mg protein (Duvall et al., 1983).

B. The cat-86 Ribosome Binding Site Is Predicted to Exist in a Stem-Loop Configuration in RNA

The nucleotide sequence of the 234 bp PstI-BclI region which is essential to Cm-inducible expression of DHFR demonstrates that the fragment contains the first 29 codons of cat-86, and that the translation initiation codon for the cat gene, which is TTG, is preceded by the ribosome binding site sequence AGGAGG (Duvall et al., 1983). Further upstream are a series of 10 translation termination codons with at least two in each of the three reading frames (Duvall et al., 1983). Examination of the nucleotide sequence spanning the ribosome binding site sequence demonstrates that AGGAGG is part of a 14 bp sequence that is repeated in the inverted form 14 bp upstream. Thus, transcription of this region into RNA should sequester the cat-86 ribosome binding site in a stable stem-loop configuration (Figure 4).

Plasmid pC194 contains a cat gene whose expression is also Cm-inducible (Horinouchi and Weisblum, 1982). The nucleotide sequence (data derived from Horinouchi and Weisblum, 1982) surrounding the cat ribosome binding site sequence contains terminal inverted repeat regions. It is

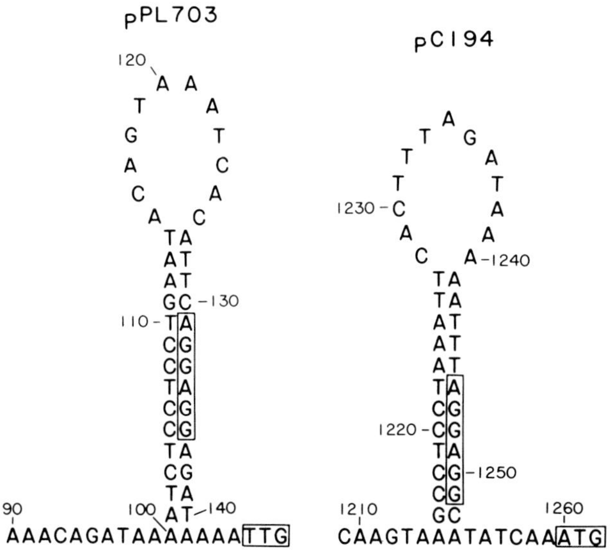

Figure 4. Nucleotide sequence of the antisense strand in the vicinity of the cat ribosome binding site in pPL703 and pC194 shown in stem-loop configuration (from Duvall et al., 1983; Horinouchi and Weisblum, 1982).

therefore likely that in the corresponding RNA, the cat ribosome binding site will be sequestered in a stem-loop configuration (Figure 4).

C. Detection of pPL708 Specified cat-86 mRNA in the Absence of Cm

A direct approach to distinguishing between transcriptional versus posttranscriptional control of cat-86 expression by Cm is to assay for cat-86 mRNA in the presence and absence of the antibiotic. Hybridization of a radioactively labeled probe cloned from within the cat-86 gene to RNA from cells grown in the presence or absence of Cm indicates no detectable difference in cat mRNA levels (manuscript in preparation). Thus, cat-86 transcripts are synthesized from pPL708 in the absence of the inducer, Cm.

III. DISCUSSION

The mechanisms that might be used to regulate the Cm-inducible expression of cat-86 are variations of two basic control systems: control of transcription of the gene or control of translation of the corresponding RNA. The available evidence does not completely eliminate either system, although the following observations suggest that cat-86 induction may be a posttranscriptional regulatory event. First, heterologous promoter fragments that activate cat-86 expression promote Cm-inducible expression of the gene. It is unlikely the Cm regulates these foreign promoters. Second, cat-86 is a foreign gene in B. subtilis. Transcriptional control of Cm-inducibility requires a regulatory molecule encoded either by the host (B. subtilis) or by the cloned fragment. Presently, we have not eliminated host contribution to the regulation. However, products encoded by the cloned 234 bp fragment would seem unlikely as regulatory elements: the first 29 amino acids of CAT and a theoretical peptide consisting of 11 amino acids encoded by a short open reading frame within the 234 bp fragment (Duvall et al., 1983). Lastly, Northern blot experiments show no difference in the level of cat-86 mRNA in cells grown in the presence or absence of Cm.

If the key regulatory event in the induction of cat-86 involves destabilization of the stem-loop that sequesters the ribosome binding site, how might this occur? Direct extrapolation of the pE194 regulatory model cannot be made since there appears to be no alternative regions for intramolecular base pair formation within the 234 bp region. An alternative is that Cm (or a derivative metabolite) induces a conformational or functional change in the ribosomes that mediates the CAT stem-loop destabilization. In this regard it is interesting to note the occurrence of sequences in the stem base and the loop regions of pPL703 (positions 94 to 99 and 117 to 122) and pC194 (1211 to 1215 and 1234 to 1239) (Figure 4) that show partial homology to bases at the 3' end of 16S rRNA of B. subtilis, 3'UCUUUCUCC... (Kroyer and Chang, 1981). Whether such sequences play a role in associating the stem-loop regions with ribosomes is presently unknown.

REFERENCES

Duvall, E.J., Williams, D.M., Lovett, P.S., Rudolph, C., Vasantha, N. and Guyer, M. (1983). **Gene**, in press.
Harwood, C.R., Williams D.M. and Lovett, P.S. (1983). **Gene**, in press.
Horinouchi, S. and Weisblum, B. (1980). **Proc. Natl. Acad. Sci. USA 77**, 7079.
Horinouchi, S. and Weisblum, B. (1982). **J. Bacteriol. 150**, 815.
Kobayashi, Y. and Saito, H. (1983). **Proc. Natl. Acad. Sci. USA 80**, 658.
Kroyer, J. and Chang, S. (1981). **Gene 15**, 343.
Losick, R. and Pero, J. (1981). **Cell 25**, 582.
Messing, J., Crea, R. and Seeburg, P.H. (1981). **Nucl. Acids Res. 9**, 309.
Mongkolsuk, S., Chiang, Y.-W., Reynolds, R.G. and Lovett, P.S. (1983). **J. Bacteriol.**, in press.
Sadaie, Y., Burtis, K.C. and Doi, R.H. (1980). **J. Bacteriol. 141**, 1178.
Shaw, W.V. (1967). **J. Biol. Chem. 242**, 687.
Shaw, W.V. (1975). **Methods Enzymol. 43**, 737.
Shivakumar, A.G., Hahn, J., Grandi, G., Kozlov, Y. and Dubnau, D. (1980). **Proc. Natl. Acad. Sci. USA 77**, 3903.
Schoner, R.G., Williams, D.M. and Lovett, P.S. (1983). **Gene 22**, 47.
Williams, D.M., Duvall, E.J. and Lovett, P.S. (1981a). **J. Bacteriol. 146**, 1162.
Williams, D.M., Schoner, R.G., Duvall, E.J., Preis, L.H. and Lovett, P.S. (1981b). **Gene 16**, 199.
Winshell, E. and Shaw, W.V. (1969). **J. Bacteriol. 98**, 1248.

PARAMETERS AFFECTING THE STABILITY OF RECOMBINANT BIFUNCTIONAL PLASMID TRANSFER FROM ESCHERICHIA COLI TO BACILLUS SUBTILIS

G. R. Ostroff

Department of Pharmacology
University of Massachusetts Medical School
Worcester, Massachusetts

J. J. Pène

School of Life and Health Sciences
University of Delaware
Neward, Delaware

I. INTRODUCTION

Work from several laboratories has recently attempted to develop Bacillus subtilis as a cloning system (Ehrlich, 1978; Gryzcan et al., 1978; Keggins et al., 1978; Kawamura et al., 1979; Gryzcan et al., 1980; Tanaka and Kawano, 1980; Hoch et al., 1982). Although several plasmids originally isolated in Staphylococcus aureus can be propagated in B. subtilis (Ehrlich, 1977; Gryczan et al., 1978), attempts to clone DNA sequences with these vehicles have met with limited success as a result of the requirement for plasmid multimers for efficient transformation of B. subtilis (Canosi et al., 1978).

To overcome the requirement for plasmid multimers, Rapoport et al. (1979) first cloned B. subtilis DNA with a bifunctional vector in Escherichia coli. Chimeric plasmid multimers spontaneously generated in E. coli were then used to transform competent B. subtilis recipients. Following the same approach, we have cloned B. subtilis BamHI and SalI fragments, and bacteriophage Ø29 HindIII fragments via the bifunctional vectors pDH5060 and pLP1201 in E. coli (Ostroff

GENETICS AND BIOTECHNOLOGY
OF BACILLI

ISBN 0-12-274160-9

and Pène, 1983a; 1983b). However, E. coli-propagated chimeric plasmid DNA was unstable and transformed with reduced efficiency when returned to B. subtilis.

There have been a number of reports of unstable chimeric plasmid DNA transfer and propagation in B. subtilis (Ehrlich, 1978; Goebel et al., 1978; Kreft et al., 1978). For example, Unlen and coworkers (1981) described the instability of pHV14 chimeras containing Ø105 EcoRI E and F fragments when transferred from E. coli to B. subtilis. The reason for this chimeric plasmid instability is unknown and diminishes the potential use of B. subtilis as a cloning host.

In this communication, we examine the parameters affecting the stability of individual homologous and heterologous cloned DNA sequences returned to B. subtilis from an E. coli background. In addition, we report the isolation and partial characterization of a spontaneous mutant of B. subtilis which overcomes some of the problems involved in gene transfer between these two species when used as a transformation recipient.

II. MATERIALS AND METHODS

A. Bacteria, Plasmids and Growth Conditions

Strains of B. subtilis (MI112 r^-m^-, recE4, and PSL1 r^-m^-, stp, recE4) and E. coli (SK2267 recA1, sbcB15, endA1, hsrR4, hsrM, and C600SF8 recBC, hsrBC, hsrR4, hsrM) were grown and competent cells prepared as previously decribed (Ostroff and Pène, 1983a). The bifunctional plasmid vectors pDH5060 (constructed by S. Chang, Cetus Corporation) and pLP1201, and hybrid plasmids containing homologous B. subtilis BamHI inserts: pDH-BSB-1.7, pDH-BSB-2.9, pDH-BSB-3.9, pDH-BSB-9.5, and heterologous bacteriophage Ø29 HindIII inserts: pLP-H3Ø29A and pLP-H3Ø29E were constructed and isolated as previously described (Ostroff and Pène, 1983a; 1983b). For analytical purposes, CCC-plasmid DNA was purified from 5 to 10 ml of stationary B. subtilis cultures by a previously described miniprep procedure (Ostroff and Pène, 1983b).

B. Restriction Nuclease Reactions and Agarose Gel Electrophoresis

Restriction endonucleases were purchased from Bethesda Research Laboratories or New England Biolabs and used as suggested by the suppliers or in the core buffer described by O'Farrell (1980). Plasmid deletions were characterized by double digestion with appropriate restriction enzymes in O'Farrell core buffer. DNA fragments were resolved on 0.8% to 1.5% vertical agarose gels as previously described (Ostroff and Pène, 1983a).

C. Characterization of the Physical Integrity of Plasmid DNA Incubated with Competent B. subtilis Cells

Competent cultures were incubated with 1 to 2 μg/ml (α^{32}P)dCTP labeled plasmid DNA (diluted to specific activity of 5 x 10^5 cpm/μg) at 37°C. At various times, 0.5 ml samples were chilled and EDTA was added at a final concentration of 50 mM. After centrifugation for 5 minutes (12,000 x g, 4°C), total and TCA-soluble radioactivity of the extracellular DNA in the supernatant solutions were determined. Radioactivity was counted with a Beckman LS8000 scintillation spectrophotometer in TT-21 aqueous scintillant (Yorktown Research, Hackensack, NJ) for 10 minutes and corrected for quenching. Duplicate samples (100 μl) of the extracellular supernatants of [^{32}P]-labeled pDH-BSB-1.7 and pLP-H3Ø29A DNA incubated for various times with competent B. subtilis cells were concentrated by ethanol precipitation and plasmid DNA size analyzed by agarose gel electrophoresis and autoradiography.

III. RESULTS

A. Transformation Frequency and Stability of Individual E. coli-Propagated Chimeras in B. subtilis

To study the problems of reduced transformation frequency and stability of hybrid plasmid DNA transferred from E. coli to B. subtilis, we examined the fate of individual cloned homologous and heterologous inserts in pDH5060 and pLP1201 in a restriction and recombination deficient B. subtilis strain (MI112). In all cases examined (Table 1), plasmids containg homologous or heterologous inserts transform B. subtilis MI112 at low efficiency (0.02 to 5% of vector DNA). In addition, as measured by deletion formation, chimeras propagated in E. coli are unstable when returned to B. subtilis, and the frequency of deletions is proportional to the insert size (Table 1). The majority of the deletions of E. coli-propagated chimeras appear to result from damage directed toward cloned insert sequences

Table 1. Transformation Frequency and Stability of pDH5060 and Individual Chimeras in B. subtilis MI112

Plasmid	Transformation[a] Frequency	Stability[b]	N[c]
pDH5060	5.5×10^4	100	24
pDH-BSB-1.7	5.0×10^2	51	12
pDH-BSB-2.9	3.3×10^2	43	12
pDH-BSB-3.9	1.7×10^2	32	12
pDH-BSB-9.5	1.1×10^1	0	10
pLP-H3Ø2.9A	2.3×10^2	35	20
pLP-H3Ø29E	2.8×10^3	48	12

[a]*Transformation is reported as Cm^r-transformants per μg DNA per ml cells.*

[b]*Stability is expressed as a percentage of the total number of transformants examined which contained intact chimeric plasmid DNA.*

[c]*Number of individual Cm^r-transformants examined.*

during early events in the transformation process of competent B. subtilis recipients. This conclusion is based on the following observations: 1) the vectors pDH5060 and pLP1201 are stably transferred from E. coli to B. subtilis, 2) in all cases examined, the deletion includes all or a portion of the cloned insert, and 3) only a single form of plasmid DNA (intact or deleted) was observed in several hundred individual Cm^r-colonies examined within 25 generations after transformation with hybrid plasmid DNA isolated from E. coli (Ostroff and Pène, 1983b).

B. The Origin of Chimeric Plasmid DNA Affects Transformation Frequency and Stability

To determine if chimeric plasmid instability resulted from propagation through E. coli, chimeras which escaped deletion damage after transformation and propagation in strain MI112 were isolated. These chimeras were propagated either in B. subtilis or in E. coli, and their physical integrity was reexamined after transformation of strain MI112. When reisolated from E. coli, chimeras which were

Table 2. Effect of DNA Source on Chimeric Plasmid DNA Transformants in B. subtilis strain MI112

Plasmid	Transformation Frequency[a]		Stability[b]	
	E. coli	*B. subtilis*	*E. coli*	*B. subtilis*
pDH5060	2.6×10^4	3.0×10^4	100 (10)	100 (10)
pDH-BSB-1.7	5.2×10^2	2.8×10^4	50 (24)	100 (28)
pDH-BSB-2.9	1.3×10^2	1.8×10^4	45 (20)	95 (20)
pDH-BSB-9.5	5	1.4×10^4	0 (5)	58 (24)
pPL-H3Ø29A	21	2.4×10^4	20 (20)	96 (24)

The transformation frequency and stability of plasmid DNA isolated from B. subtilis strain MI112 were compared to identical DNA isolated from E. coli strain SK2267. Chimeric plasmid DNA isolated from MI112 was shown to be intact by restriction endonuclease mapping.

[a] *Transformation frequency is reported as Cm^r-transformants per µg DNA per ml cells.*

[b] *Stability is expressed as a percentage of the total number of transformants examined (shown in parentheses) which contained intact chimeric plasmid DNA.*

initially undamaged suffered deletions when returned to B. subtilis and transformed with reduced efficiency (Table 2). However, identical chimeras isolated from B. subtilis transformed MI112 55- to 5,000-fold greater than the same chimeric plasmid DNA isolated from E. coli. In addition, the source of DNA increased the frequency of stable chimeras isolated in MI112 from 0 to 50% when isolated from E. coli to 60 to 100% when isolated from B. subtilis.

The simplest explanation which accounts for the inefficient and unstable transfer of chimeric plasmid DNA between E. coli and B. subtilis is restriction of heterologously propagated insert sequences. The observation that plasmid pDH5060 transfer is unaffected by propagation in E. coli suggests that this vector lacks recognition sequences for B. subtilis restriction systems. Since strain MI112 is both phenotypically restriction deficient for hsrR and hsrM (Tanaka, 1979), our data suggest that a restriction system other than $hsrR^+$ and $hsrM^+$ is responsible for the instability of heterologously propagated chimeric plasmid DNA in

B. subtilis. Such a restriction system may not have been observed previously, since the effect of restriction on chimeric plasmid DNA transfer between E. coli and B. subtilis has not been examined.

C. Isolation of a Chimeric Plasmid DNA Transformation-Proficient Mutant

We reasoned that the occurrence of stable Cm^r-transformants could result from either random escape from restriction or from a genotypic change in the recipient. To distinguish between these two possibilities five hundred MI112 transformants were examined to detect intact chimeric plasmid DNA. Twenty MI112 Cm^r-transformants containing intact plasmid or hybrid plasmid DNA were chosen and spontaneously cured of plasmid DNA by growth in the absence of chloramphenicol. These cured Cm^s-colonies were confirmed to be free of plasmid DNA by miniprep gel analysis, made competent and retransformed with pDH5060, pDH-BSB-1.7 and pLP-H3Ø29A DNA. Two classes of cured Cm^s-strains were observed. Class I strains (19/20) were similar to the parental strain MI112: 1) they were poorly transformed to Cm^r with heterologous propagated hybrid plasmid DNA, 2) transformants contained deleted hybrid plasmid molecules at high frequency and 3) they were all transformed at high efficiency with pDH5060 vector DNA. The single Class II strain, PSL1, differed phenotypically from the parental strain MI112 as evidenced by efficient stable transformation by both pDH5060 vector DNA and pDH-BSB-1.7 and pLP-H3Ø29A hybrid plasmid DNA.

D. Characterization of the Transformation Phenotype of PSL1

The chimeric plasmid transformation efficiency of PSL1 was compared to the parent strain MI112 with native pDH5060, pDH5060 homologous and pLP1201 heterologous chimeras propagated in E. coli (Table 3). PSL1 and MI112 were transformed at a similar efficiency with the vector pDH5060. However, chimeras isolated from E. coli transformed PSL1 at frequencies 5- to 110-fold higher than its parental strain MI112 (Table 3). The greatest increase in transformation efficiency was observed with chimeras containing inserts of 4 Kbp and larger; hybrid plasmids containing these large inserts transformed strain MI112 poorly (see Table 3).

The phenotype of strain PSL1 also resulted in increased stability of chimeric plasmid DNA transferred from E. coli (Table 3). This increase in stability was up to 100% for plasmids containing inserts 1.7 to 4.2 kbp in length, but

Table 3. Comparison of Transformation Frequency and Stability of pDH5060 and Chimeras in B. subtilis MI112 and PSL1

Plasmid	Transformation Frequency[a]		Stability[b]	
	MI112	PSL1	MI112	PSL1
pDH5060	2.8×10^4	3.1×10^4	100 (10)	100 (10)
pDHBSB-1.7	3.1×10^3	2.5×10^4	51 (17)	100 (10)
pDH-BSB-2.9	2.1×10^3	1.9×10^4	42 (8)	100 (10)
pDH-BSB-3.9	1.1×10^3	3.0×10^4	5 (10)	94 (10)
pDH-BSB-9.5	2.5×10^2	2.8×10^4	0 (5)	21 (22)
pLP-H3Ø29A	2.0×10^3	3.1×10^4	30 (14)	100 (10)

Parental strain MI112 and the mutant PSL1 were transformed to Cm^r with the indicated plasmid and hybrid plasmid DNA isolated from E. coli.

[a]Relative transformation frequency was calculated by normalizing chimeric plasmid transformation frequency to pDH5060 vector transformation frequency.

[b]Stability is expressed as the percentage of the total number of transformants examined (total number examined) containing intact chimeric plasmid DNA.

was reduced to 25% for the transfer of the large chimera containing a B. subtilis 9.5 kbp insert. In addition, PSL1 was transformed at efficiencies 20- to 100-fold higher than MI112 with clone pools of pDH5060 and pLP1202 chimeras propagated in E. coli. Thus, PSL1 is a highly transformable recE4 strain of B. subtilis which allows stable transfer of individual recombinant plasmid DNA molecules and clone pools containing inserts up to at least 4 kbp in length from E. coli to B. subtilis.

E. Preliminary Characterization of the Basis of the PSL1 Phenotype

We have been unable to detect any differences in plasmid DNA uptake and intracellular stability of E. coli-propagated chimeric plasmid DNA during transformation of MI112 and PSL1 (data not shown). In addition, analysis of extracellular

DNA showed that there was no difference in the amount of acid-soluble radioactivity (up to 5.6% of the input) of E. coli or B. subtilis-propagated [^{32}P]-labeled extracellular plasmid DNA after incubation with competent cultures of MI112 or PSL1 (data not shown). However, agarose gel analysis of [^{32}P]-labeled plasmid DNA size in supernatants of transforming cultures revealed that DNA propagated in E. coli was endonucleolytically degraded by competent MI112 cells (Figure 1). This degradation was detected 30 to 60 minutes after incubation of competent MI112 cells with E. coli-propagated DNA, but was not observed with B. subtilis-propagated DNA. Moreover, chimeric plasmid DNA from E. coli was not substantially degraded after 60 minutes exposure to competent PSL1 cells. Thus, increased transformation efficiency and stability of E. coli-propagated chimeric plasmid DNA transformed in PSL1 appears to result from reduced extracellular endonucleolytic damage.

IV. DISCUSSION

E. coli-propagated chimeric plasmid DNA cloned via the bifunctional vectors pDH5060 and pLP1201 is unstable and transforms with reduced efficiency when returned to B. subtilis. Characterization of the transfer of individual E. coli-propagated chimeras to competent B. subtilis recipients suggests that these problems are mediated by restriction of insert sequences during transformation. We propose that competent B. subtilis strains are able to recognize and damage heterologously propagated DNA sequences since low stable transfer frequency of E. coli-propagated hybrid plasmids is observed even in restriction-deficient (hsrM and hsrR) strains. The evidence to support this conclusion is the following: 1) deletions are targeted toward insert sequences; 2) only single forms of plasmid DNA (intact or deleted) are found in individual transformants; and 3) identical chimeras isolated from E. coli, but not from B. subtilis, are damaged during transformation.

To improve the transfer efficiency of pDH5060 chimeras from E. coli to B. subtilis, we have isolated a highly transformable spontaneous mutant of B. subtilis strain MI112 (hsrM, hsrR, recE4). The spontaneous mutant, PSL1, a cured derivative of a stable pDH-BSB-1.7 MI112 transformant differs phenotypically from the parent strain MI112 as shown by 1) stable transformation by individual recombinant bifunctional plasmids from E. coli, 2) increased stable transfer

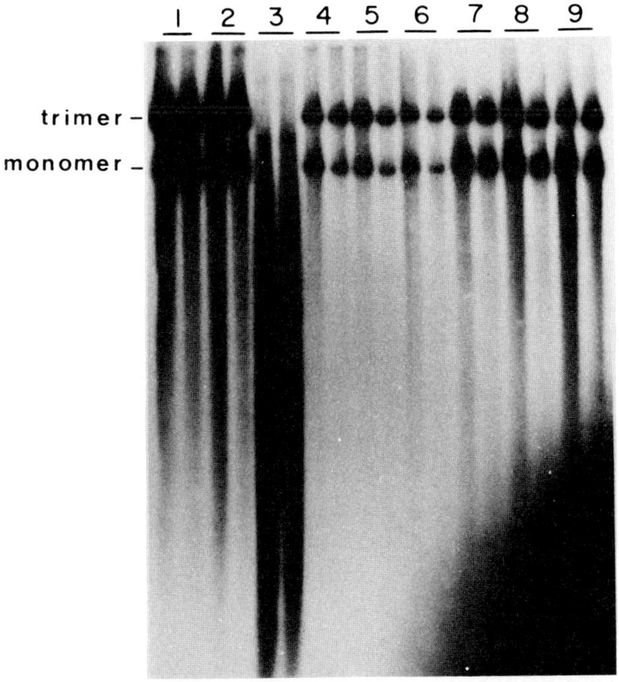

Figure 1. Physical integrity of pDH-BSB-1.7 DNA incubated with competent B. subtilis cells: effect of DNA source and mutant strain PSL1. Duplicate samples (100 μl) of [^{32}P]-labeled pDH-BSB-1.7 and pLPH3Ø29A DNA incubated for various times with competent B. subtilis cells, as described in Materials and Methods, were concentrated by ethanol precipitation and analyzed by agarose gel electrophoresis and autoradiography. Wells 1 to 3, pDH-BSB-1.7 DNA isolated from E. coli and incubated with competent B. subtilis MI112 cells for 5 minutes, 1; 30 minutes, 2; and 60 minutes, 3. Wells 4 to 6, pDH-BSB-1.7 DNA isolated from B. subtilis and incubated with competent B. subtilis MI112 cells for 5 minutes, 4; 30 minutes, 5; and 60 minutes, 6. Wells 7 to 9, pDH-BSB-1.7 DNA isolated from E. coli and incubated with competent B. subtilis PSL1 cells for 5 minutes. 7; 30 minutes, 8; and 60 minutes, 9. The positions of monomeric and multimeric (trimer) ccc-plasmid DNA are indicated.

of pDH5060 clone pools from E. coli, and 3) reduced endonucleolytic degradation of extracellular heterologously propagated chimeric plasmid DNA.

Analysis of the physical integrity of plasmid DNA incubated with competent cells shows that in strain MI112, E. coli propagated plasmid DNA is endonucleolytically degraded outside the cell (Figure 1). This degradation is reduced when B. subtilis propagated chimeric DNA is incubated with competent MI112 cells. In addition, chimeric plasmid DNA from either E. coli or B. subtilis is not substantially degraded during incubation with competent PSL1 cells. Thus, on the basis of the observation that reduced endonucleolytic damage to B. subtilis propagated chimeric plasmid DNA is correlated with increased transformation acitivty in MI112, we concluded that reduced damage to E. coli propagated plasmid DNA contributes to the highly transformable phenotype of the mutant PSL1. This suggests that an endonuclease activity capable of selective cleavage of heterologously propagated chimeric plasmid DNA is reduced or absent in the mutant PSL1. The mechanism of recognition of E. coli-propagated chimeric plasmid DNA is unclear, but could operate through cleavage of unmodified sites in cloned fragments during transient interaction with the cell surface.

The mutant strain, PSL1, should prove useful as a recipient for the stable transfer of recombinant bifunctional plasmid DNA from E. coli to B. subtilis. However, use of PSL1 does not completely overcome the problem of plasmid instability in B. subtilis, since preliminary data show that some chimeras which can be stably transferred from E. coli to B. subtilis are unstable during long-term propagation in strain PSL1. Thus additional work will be required to elucidate the mechanism(s) leading to chimeric plasmid instability during long-term propagation in B. subtilis.

REFERENCES

Canosi, U., Morelli, G. and Trautner, J.A. (1978). **Molec. Gen. Genet. 166**, 259.

Contente, S. and Dubnau, D. (1979). **Molec. Gen. Genet. 167**, 251.

Ehrlich, S.D. (1977). **Proc. Natl. Acad. Sci. USA 74**, 1620.

Ehrlich, S.D. (1978). **Proc. Natl. Acad. Sci. USA 75**, 1433.

Ehrlich, S.D., Jupp, S., Niadet, B. and Goze, A. (1978). _In_ Genetic Engineering (H.W. Boyer and S. Nicosia, eds.) p. 25, Elsevier/North Holland, Amsterdam.

Goebel, W., Kreft, J., Bernhard, K., Schremph, H. and Weidinger, G. (1978). In Genetic Engineering (H.W. Boyer and S. Nicosia, eds.) p. 47, Elseveir/North Holland, Amsterdam.

Gryczan, T.J., Contente, S. and Dubnau, D. (1978). **J. Bacteriol. 134,** 318.

Gryczan, T.J., Contente, S. and Dubnau, D. (1980). **Molec. Gen. Genet. 177,** 459.

Hoch, J., Nguyen, A. and Ferrari, E. (1982). In Genetic Engineering of Microorganisms for Chemicals (A. Hollaender, ed.) p. 163, Plenum Press, New York.

Kawamura, F., Saito, H. and Ikeda, Y. (1979). **Gene 5,** 87.

Keggins, K.M., Lovett, P.S. and Duvall, E.J. (1978). **Proc. Natl. Acad. Sci. USA 75,** 1423.

Kreft, J., Bernhard, K. and Goebel, W. (1978). **Molec. Gen. Genet. 162,** 59.

O'Farrell, P.H., Kulter, E and Nakanishi, M. (1980). **Molec. Gen. Genet. 179,** 421.

Ostroff, G.R. and Pène, J.J. (1983a). **Molec. Gen. Genet.,** in press.

Ostroff, G.R. and Pène, J.J. (1983b). **Molec. Gen. Genet.,** in press.

Rapoport, G., Klier, A., Billault, F., Fargette, F. and Dedonder, R. (1979). **Molec. Gen. Genet. 176,** 239.

Tanaka, T. (1979). **Molec. Gen. Genet. 175,** 235.

Tanaka, T. and Kawano, N. (1980). **Gene 10,** 131.

Ullen, M., Flock, J.I. and Philipson, L. (1981). **Plasmid 6,** 161.

CLONING OF GENETIC MATERIAL IN BACILLI

P. M. Rabinovich
Yu. V. Yomantas
M. Ya. Haykinson
A. I. Stepanov

Institute of Genetics
and Selection of Industrial Microorganisms
Moscow, U.S.S.R.

The mechanism of genetic transformation in Bacilli (Dubnau, 1976; Canosi et al., 1978) accounts for the peculiarities of DNA cloning in Bacillus subtilis. At present, there is no doubt that the efficiency of cloning in bacilli depends on the DNA structure of the DNA vector molecule. Canosi et al. (1978) demonstrated the significance of the structure of plasmid DNA for successful transformation in bacilli. These cells are transformed with oligomeric but not monomeric DNAs of staphylococcal plasmids. Transformation with monomers is only obtained when the DNA contains direct repeats, or regions homologous to DNA from the recipient cells (Michel et al., 1980; Canosi et al., 1981). Monomeric DNA, however, is capable of transforming B. subtilis cell protoplasts (Chang and Cohen, 1979).

We have studied the effect of direct and inverted internal repeats of plasmid DNA on transformation of bacilli. We utilized a vector containing the cloned riboflavin operon of B. subtilis (Bresler et al., 1973; Bresler et al., 1978). This operon has been cloned in Escherichia coli cells in RSF2124 and pBR322 vectors (Rabinovich et al., 1978; Panina et al., 1983). The molecular weight of the cloned EcoRI fragment containing the riboflavin operon (Figure 1), consisting of seven genes (Bresler et al., 1973; Bresler et al., 1978) is 6.3 Md (Panina et al., 1983). At least some of them are expressed in E. coli (Rabinovich et al., 1978). Our original attempts to clone the entire EcoRI fragment into B. subtilis ribB110 recE4 using the staphylococcal pUB110 plasmid were unsuccessful. We then tried using plas

ISBN 0-12-274160-9

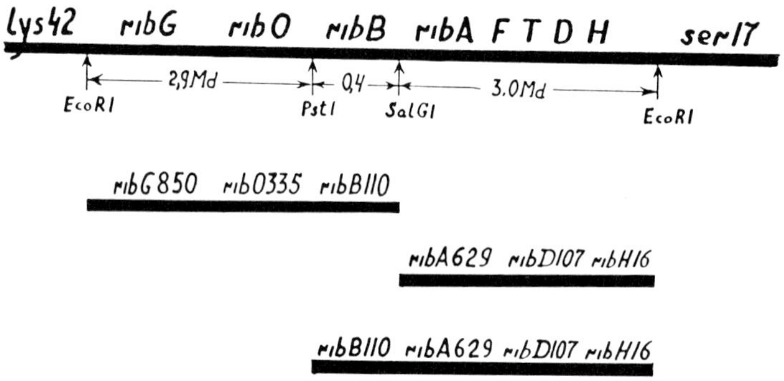

Figure 1. The structure of B. subtilis riboflavin operon.

mids capable of replicating both in E. coli and B. subtilis. A series of shuttle plasmids composed of pBR322 and pUB110, or pC194, pSA2100, pSA501 DNA (Yomantas et al., 1979) were constructed. Hybrid plasmids with the riboflavin operon or a portion of it on PstI DNA fragments were obtained in E. coli using the shuttle vector pJJ10 (pBR322-pUB110) (Yomantas et al., 1979) (Figure 2). Transformation of B. subtilis ribB110 recE4 with these clones did not result in the isolation of clones containing the riboflavin operon insert; only plasmids identical to the pJJ10 vector were obtained.

We then tried to transform plasmids containing the entire riboflavin operon or part of it into B. subtilis cells with the help of the "marker rescue" technique (Gryczan et al., 1980). In this case, the bi-replicon pJJ10 vector served as helper plasmid (Figure 2). Since the riboflavin operon is homologous to the corresponding chromosomal region of the recipient strain, we utilized a strain with the recE4 mutation as a recipient (Yomantas et al., 1980). We discovered that the system of "marker rescue" can also function in the recE4 mutant, although its efficiency is decreased in comparison with $recE4^{+}$ cells. The efficiency of the rescue in recE4 cells is dependent on the size of the homologous region for donor and resident plasmid DNA and, in addition, on the concentration of donor DNA (Figure 3).

Thus, we were able to isolate B. subtilis ribB110 recE4 transformants bearing the pJJ101 hybrid plasmid with a portion of the riboflavin operon genes (Yomanatas et al., 1980). However, we failed to transform the entire riboflavin operon which lies on the 6.3 Md EcoRI fragment.

We have now succeeded in cloning the entire riboflavin operon into B. subtilis by means of a specially developed technique of "step-by-step joining" of the homologous

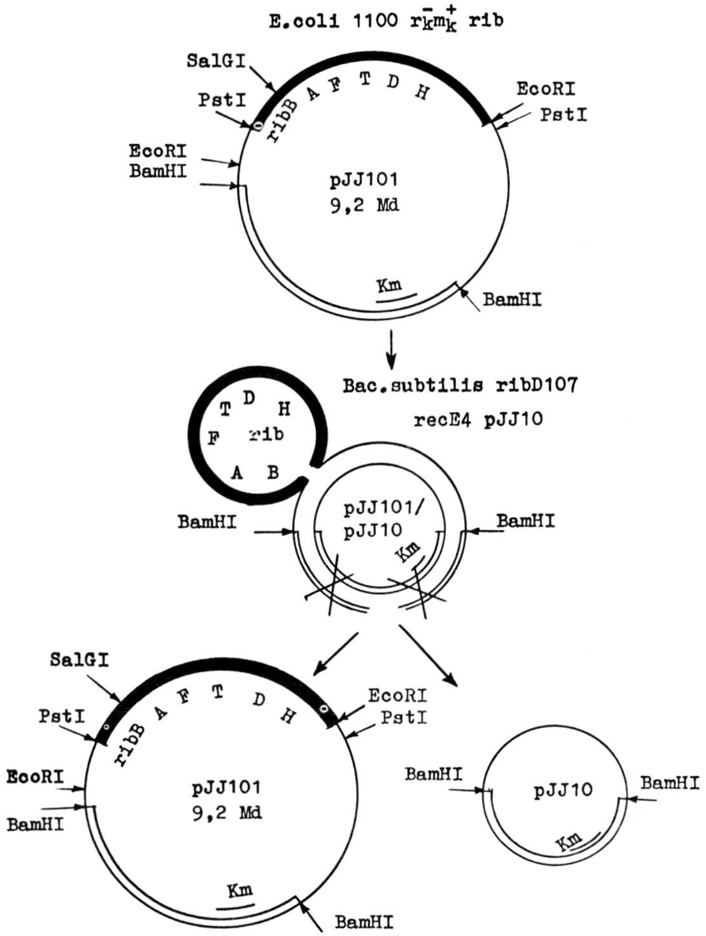

Figure 2. The scheme for cloning a portion of the riboflavin operon according to the "marker rescue" technique in recE4 recipient. pBR322 (├──┤), PUB110 (▭), rib (▬).

genetic material in vivo (Yomantas et al, 1982). We used the "marker rescue" method in recE4 cells described above. pJJ108 containing a distal part of the rib operon was employed as a helper plasmid. This plasmid is analogous to pJJ101, but the fragment with the rib genes has an opposite orientation. The proximal part of the operon, with the region of homology to the resident plasmid within the region of the ribB gene, has been introduced into B. subtilis ribG850 recE4 cells by means of pJJ105 propagated in E. coli (Figure 4). The rescue of the pJJ105 plasmid, due to

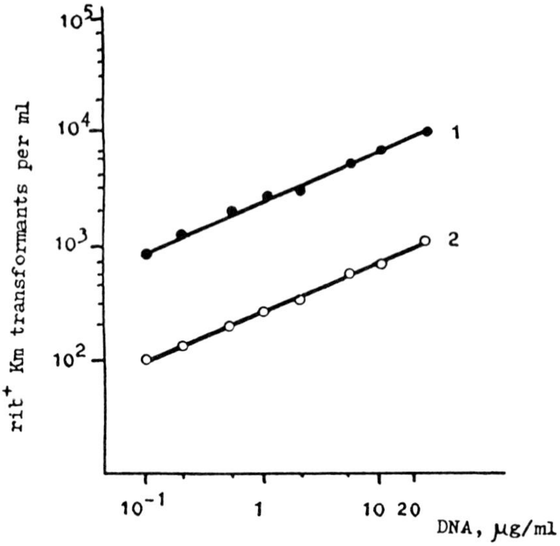

Figure 3. Efficiency of recE4 ribD107/pJJ10 strain transformation with plasmids: 1) pJJ101 (pJJ10 rib) and 2) pJJ104 (pBR322 rib).

homology in the region of the ribB gene and pBR322 DNA, resulted in the formation of a pJJ110 hybrid having all the gene of the riboflavin operon on the EcoRI fragment of 6.3 Md. Thus, the technique of "step-by-step" joining makes it possible to construct hybrid plasmids in vivo. This technique could be used for creating a library of overlapping bacilli genes.

Considering the effectiveness of bacilli transformation with oligomeric plasmid DNAs, the role of internal direct and inverted repeats in cell transformation using monomers was studied. A hybrid plasmid pMX1 consisting of the EcoRI fragment with the riboflavin operon, pBR322, and two genomes of pUB110 plasmid, as direct repeats, was obtained in E. coli rib8-2 recA cells (Figure 5). Monomeric forms of this plasmid were capable of transforming B. subtilis recE4. The plasmid pMX1 segregates after transformation, producing plasmids similar in size to pUB110 and pJJ101 (Figure 5) (Haykinson et al. 1982). Thus, a plasmid similar to pJJ101 with a single copy of pUB110 arises from the pMX1 hybrid having direct repeats of pUB110 DNA. Consequently, unlike the pJJ101 plasmid which contains one pUB110 copy, monomeric forms of pMX1 plasmid with two pUB110 DNA copies in direct repeats are able to transform B. subtilis.

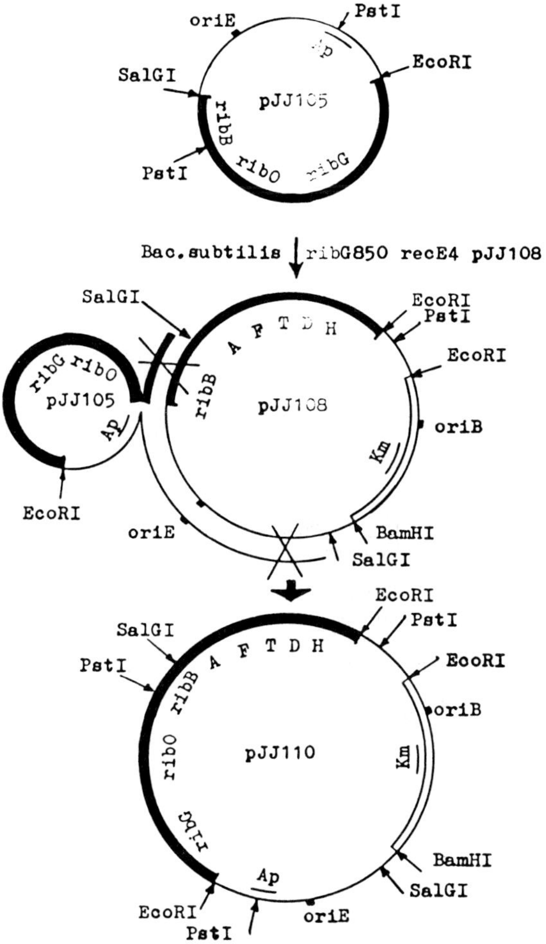

Figure 4. The scheme for cloning the riboflavin operon by joining homologous DNA regions. pBR322 ( ), pUB110 ( ), rib ( ).

The major part of the riboflavin operon within pMX1 was deleted by restriction with XbaI, subsequent ligation, and transformation of E. coli recA cells. The deletion plasmid pMX20, with a molecular mass of 8.75 Md, was obtained which contained the pUB110 duplication and had lost the region of homology with the B. subtilis chromosome (Figure 6). Monomeric forms of pMX20 can transform recE4 and $recE4^{+}$ cells and, after transformation, segregant plasmids pMX10 and pMX29 are formed (Figure 6). The formation of these plas-

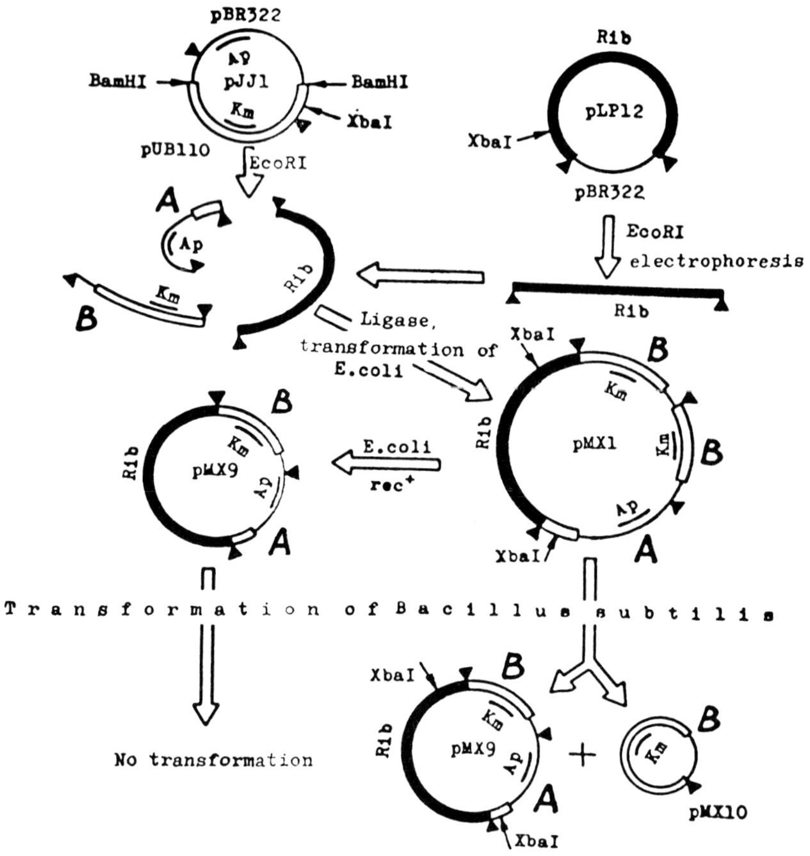

Figure 5. Construction of pMXI plasmid containing direct DNA repeats. EcoRI sites (▲), A, B - EcoRI fragments of pJJ1 plasmid.

mids, as previously described for the pMX1 hybrid, probably is a result of intramolecular recombination between the direct repeats of pUB110 DNA.

Transformation of B. subtilis with the pMX20 plasmid linearized with PstI endonuclease outside of the regions of direct repeats also led to the formation of a plasmid with the size of pUB110 (Figure 5). The mechanism of this formation possibly is associated also with recombination alongside direct repeats.

B. subtilis cells can also be transformed efficiently with a hybrid plasmid consisting of pUB110 DNA and direct repeats of pBR322 DNA. Thus, the existence of direct repeats makes it possible to clone DNA fragments of a rela-

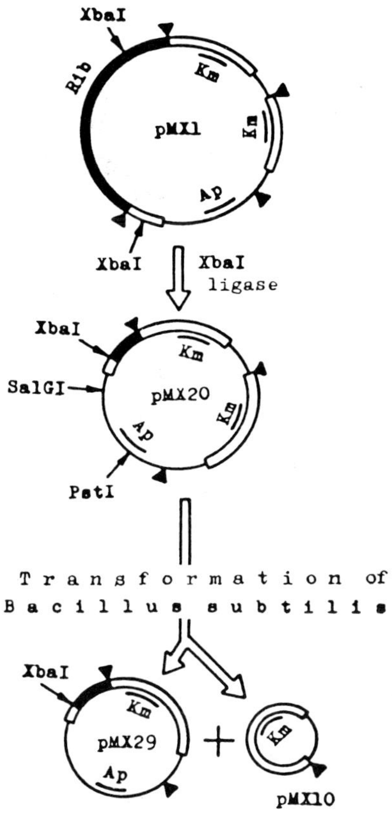

Figure 6. Construction of pMX20 vector plasmid containing direct DNA repeats. EcoRI sites (▲).

tively high molecular mass in B. subtilis. It is likely that the size of monomeric hybrid plasmids, in this case, corresponds to that of DNA constrained according to B. subtilis transformation mechanism.

A disadvantage of this system is that it required a preliminary propagation of hybrid plasmids within E. coli cells, since direct repeats are unstable in B. subtilis recE4 and $recE4^+$ strains. Therefore, we explored the possibility of using vectors with inverted repeats to clone DNA into B. subtilis cells. We used the plasmid pSM19035, isolated from Streptococcus sanguis by Behnke et al. (1979). This plasmid can transform B. subtilis cells and it specifies inducible resistance to erythromycin. It contains two inverted repeats of 7 Md each (Figure 7). The low copy number of pSM19035 plasmid in B. subtilis cells somewhat complicates its isolation and analysis. We isolated a dele-

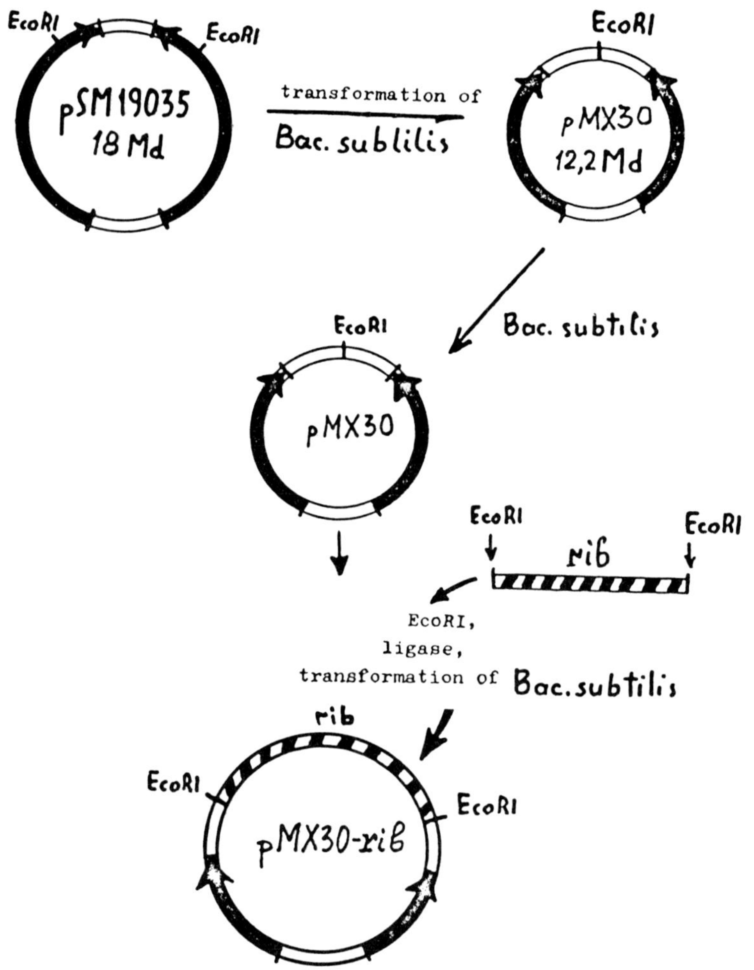

Figure 7. Construction of pMX30 plasmid with inverted repeats and its use for cloning rib operon of B. subtilis into bacilli cells.

tion mutant, pMX30, with a molecular mass of about 12 Md. The mutant contains inverted repeats of 2 Md. The pMX30 plasmid can transform B. subtilis as a monomer, with a high efficiency, retaining the initial structure. Monomers of a pMX30-rib hybrid plasmid containing the EcoRI fragment with the riboflavin operon can also transform B. subtilis recE4 (Figure 7). This hybrid plasmid is stable and its structure does not change after transformation of $recE4^{+}$ cells of B. subtilis (Haykinson et al., 1982). Linearization of pMX30

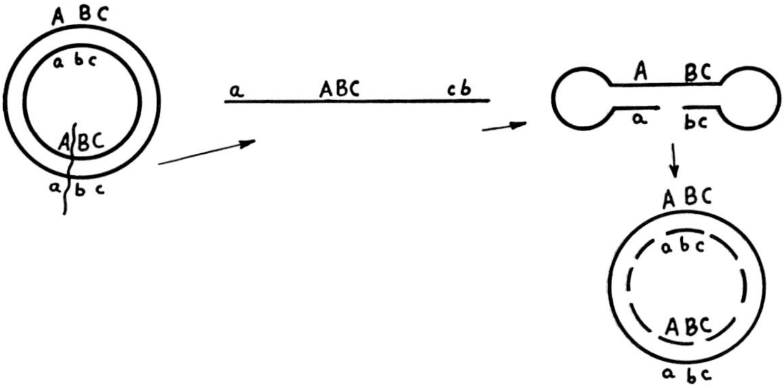

Figure 8. A model on B. subtilis transformation with plasmids containing inverted repeats.

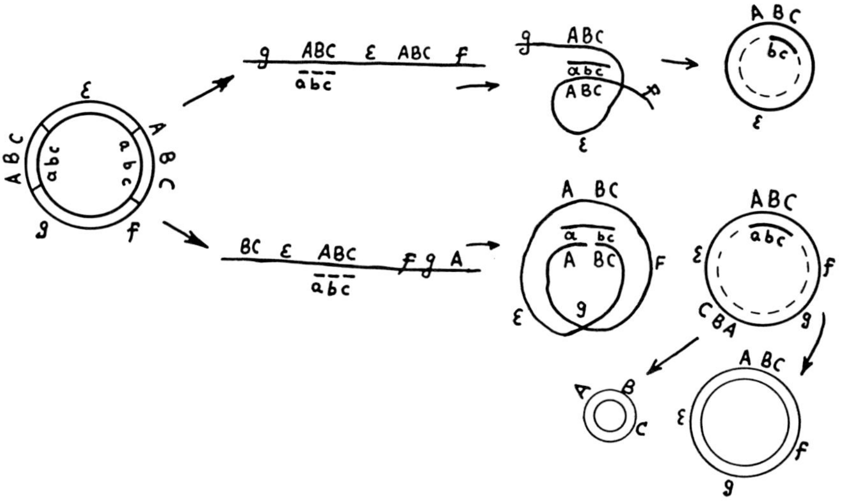

Figure 9. A model describing B. subtilis transformation with plasmids containing direct DNA repeats.

plasmid at the unique EcoRI site situated beyond the inverted repeats leads to the loss of its transforming activity (Figure 7).

Based on the general view concerning the mechanism of transformation in bacilli, the following scheme of B. subtilis transformation by a plasmid having inverted DNA repeats could be proposed: cutting of the plasmid DNA molecule within one of the repeats, insertion into a cell of single-stranded linear DNA, formation of a "dumb-bell" structure, repair, correction of a break, replication and formation of the initial double-stranded circular structure (Figure 8) (Haykinson et al., 1982).

For plasmids with direct repeats, the transformation model would be analogous to the scheme proposed by Canosi et al. (1981). This model was developed to account for the transformation of B. subtilis with plasmids carrying DNA fragments homologous to chromosomal DNA. The only difference is the fact that transformation of cells with plasmids having direct repeats does not require recE gene functions (Figure 9).

Figure 10 depicts the models for plasmid transformation of B. subtilis using as a basis the model proposed for transformation of B. subtilis with chromosomal DNA. The first three stages - adsorption, fragmentation and entry of single-stranded DNA - are similar for all kinds of DNA. The fourth stage - synapsis - differs depending on the structure of the transforming DNA. Transformation resulting from the intermolecular interaction (A, B, C) is strictly dependent on recE functions, but transformation resulting from the intramolecular interaction (D, E, F) is independent of recE functions. The further fate of DNA after synapsis (Figure 10, column 5) may include rearrangements of plasmid DNA resulting from the exchange of genetic information in the region of synapsis between donor and recipient DNA (A, B, C). When transformation with plasmids having direct repeats (D, E) takes place, recombination of donor DNA within these repeats is observed. In the case of transformation with plasmids containing inverted repeats (F), no changes in the plasmid structure occur.

Thus, it may be seen in the scheme presented that the products of transformation are determined by the structure of plasmid DNA, since this structure determines the type of synapsis.

The pMX39 vector, a cointegrant of plasmids pMX30 and pBR322 at the EcoRI site, was used to clone several genes into B. subtilis, in particular the gene of B. amyloliquefaciens controlling α-amylase synthesis.

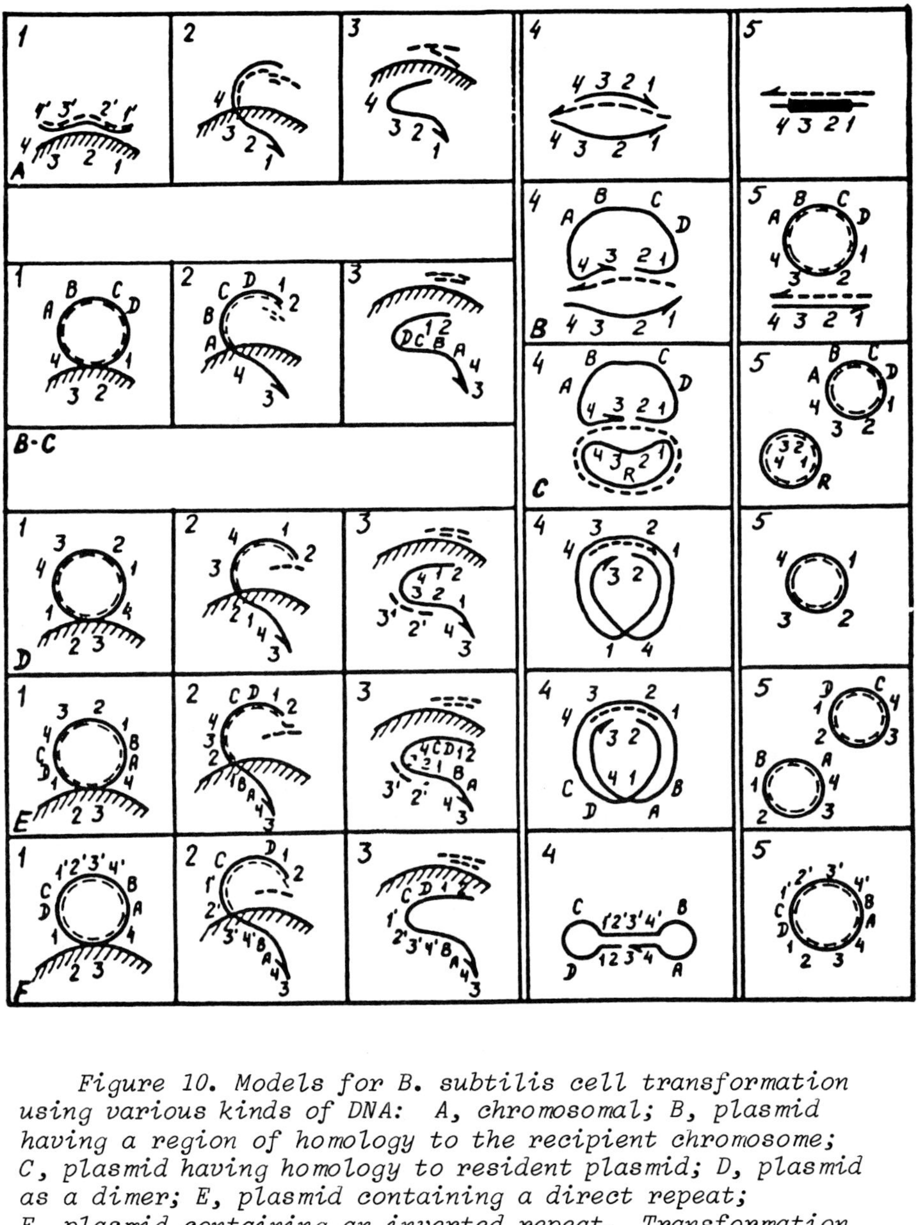

Figure 10. Models for B. subtilis cell transformation using various kinds of DNA: A, chromosomal; B, plasmid having a region of homology to the recipient chromosome; C, plasmid having homology to resident plasmid; D, plasmid as a dimer; E, plasmid containing a direct repeat; F, plasmid containing an inverted repeat. Transformation stages: 1, DNA adsorption; 2, 3, DNA entry into the cell; 4, synapsis; 5, completion of transformation. Designations on DNA: 1,2,3,4, and 1',2',3',4', complementary DNA sites within synapsis region; A,B,C,D,R, DNA sites beyond synapsis region.

REFERENCES

Behnke, D., Golubkov, V.I., Malke, N., Boitsov, A.S. and Totolian, A.A. (1979). **FEMS Microbiol. Lett. 6**, 5.

Bresler, S.E., Glazunov, E.A., Gorinchuk, G.F., Chernik, T.P. and Perumov, D.a. (1978). **Genetika 14**, 1530.

Bresler, S.E., Vyacheslavov, L.G., Kalinin, V.L., Kreneva, R.A., Kushev, V.V., Lanzov, V.A., Mosevitsky, M.I., Perumov, D.A., Rybchin, V.N. (1973). In Elementary Genetic Processes, p. 211, Nauka, Lenigrad.

Canosi, U., Iglesias, A. and Trautner, T.A. (1981). **Molec. Gen. Genet. 181**, 434.

Canosi, U., Morelli, G. and Trautner, T.A. (1978). **Molec. Gen. Genet. 166**, 259.

Chang, S. and Cohen, S. (1979). **Molec. Gen. Genet. 168**, 111.

Dubnau, D. (1976). In Microbiology - 1976 (D. Schlesinger, ed.), p. 14, American Society for Microbiology, Washington, D.C.

Gryczan, T., Contente, S. and Dubnau, D. (1980). **Molec. Gen. Genet. 177**, 459.

Haykinson, M.Ya., Rabinovich, P.M. and Stepanov, A.I. (1982a). **Dolk. AN SSSR 265**, 975.

Haykinson, M.Ya., Rabinovich, P.M. and Stepanov, A.I. (1982b). **Dolk. AN SSSR 265**, 1264.

Michel, B., Polla, E. and Ehrlich, S.D. (1980). In Abstracts of the 5th European Meeting of Bacterial Transformation and Transfection, Florence, p. 19.

Panina, L.I., Yomantas, Yu.V., Haykinson, M.Ya. and Rabinovich, P.M. (1983). **Genetica 19**, 174.

Rabinovich, P.M., Beburov, M.,Yu., Linevich, Z.K. and Stepanov, A.I. (1978). **Genetika 14**, 1696.

Yomantas, Yu.V., Rabinovich, P.M., Bandrin, S.V., Demianova, N.G., Kozlov, Yu.I. and Stepanov, A.I. (1979). **Dokl. AN SSSR 244**, 993.

Yomantas, Yu.V., Rabinovich, P.M., Rebentish, B.A. and Stepanov, A.I. (1980). **Dokl. AN SSSR 254**, 493.

Yomantas, Yu.V., Rabinovich, P.M. and Stepanov, A.I. (1982). **Dolk AN SSSR 265**, 482.

CHROMOGENIC DETECTION OF GENETIC REGULATORY SIGNALS CLONED IN BACILLUS SUBTILIS

Mark M. Zukowski
Denis Speck
Muriel Kauffmann
Jean-Pierre Lecocq

Transgene S.A.
Strasbourg, France

I. INTRODUCTION

Expression of heterospecific genes in Bacillus subtilis is of paramount importance in establishing this Gram-positive microorganism as an efficient alternative to Escherichia coli for applications in recombinant DNA technology. To express plasmid-borne genes in B. subtilis, genetic regulatory signals that differ from those of E. coli are normally required. In E. coli, plasmid vectors suitable for cloning fragments of DNA that carry transcriptional promoter or termination signals, as well as translational initiation sequences, are now well characterized. Detection in these systems is based on expression of genes that encode β-galactosidase (Casadaban and Cohen, 1980; Casadaban et al., 1980; Gentz et al., 1981) or confer antibiotic resistance to host cells (West et al., 1979; An and Friesen, 1979). For B. subtilis, insertional activation of a chloramphenicol acetyltransferase gene originating from Bacillus pumilus or the transposable genetic element Tn9 has been successfully employed as the basis of a 'promoter-probe' plasmid vector (Williams et al., 1981; Goldfarb et al., 1981, respectively). Recently, we introduced a unique promoter-probe system, a chromogenic method whereby fragments of DNA that promote gene expression in B. subtilis are rapidly detected by a change of color of bacterial colonies (Zukowski et al., 1983). The system is based upon the production of catechol 2,3-oxygenase (C23O) in B. subtilis by insertional activa-

GENETICS AND BIOTECHNOLOGY
OF BACILLI

ISBN 0-12-274160-9

tion of the Pseudomonas putida gene, xylE, which was transferred from the TOL plasmid to a B. subtilis/E. coli shuttle vector to construct the promoter-detection plasmid, pTG402. Although xylE is functionally expressed in E. coli, C230 is not detected in B. subtilis unless a fragment of DNA capable of promoting gene expression is ligated into a cleavage site on pTG402 upstream from xylE. A special feature of the system is the method of detection : colonies of cells that express xylE become yellow within seconds after selection plates are sprayed with catechol, a colorless substrate that is converted by C230 to the yellow product, 2-hydroxymuconic semialdehyde.

Here, we briefly recount the construction of pTG402, then describe derivative plasmids and potential applications of a chromogenic method which offers an approach to develop plasmid gene expression vectors for a wide variety of host organisms.

II. RESULTS

A. Construction of the Promoter-Detection Plasmid pTG402

The xylE gene, wholly contained within a BamHI/XhoI subfragment of the XhoI-I fragment of the TOL plasmid pWWO (Downing and Broda, 1979; Nakazawa et al., 1980; Franklin et al., 1981), was first transferred to pBR322 (Bolivar et al., 1977) to construct pTG206. Since xylE does not carry its own promoter on the BamHI/XhoI fragment, expression of the gene is dependent upon a transcriptional promoter resident on the vector plasmid (e.g. the tet promoter in the case of pTG206). The xylE-containing fragment was next transferred from pTG206 to pHV33, the latter plasmid vector capable of replicating in E. coli or B. subtilis (Primrose and Ehrlich, 1981). The newly constructed plasmid, pTG402 (Figure 1) was selected in E. coli by spraying ampicillin-resistant (Ap^r), chlroamphenicol-resistant (Cm^r), tetracycline-sensitive (Tc^s) colonies with a 0.5 M solution of catechol. Yellow colonies, due to the presence of 2-hydroxymuconic semialdehyde (Figure 1), indicated that the xylE gene was present and functionally expressed. The plasmid was then introduced into B. subtilis by transformation of competent cells. Cm^r transformants were sprayed with catechol, but yellow coloration failed to develop.

To determine whether rearrangement or deletion of the xylE gene was responsible for lack of expression in the Gram-positive host, pTG402 was isolated from B. subtilis and re-introduced into E. coli. All Ap^r Cm^r Tc^s transformants

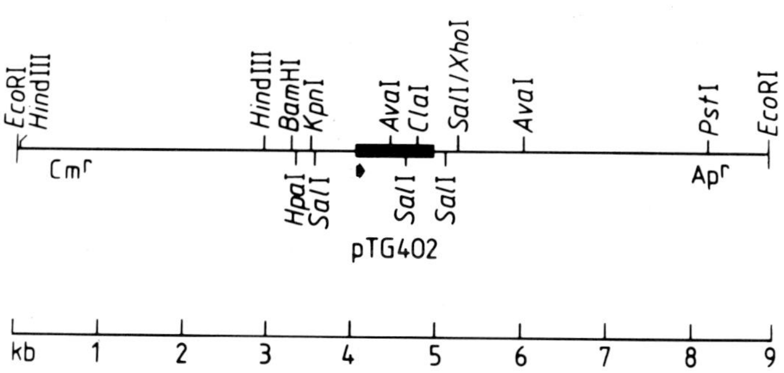

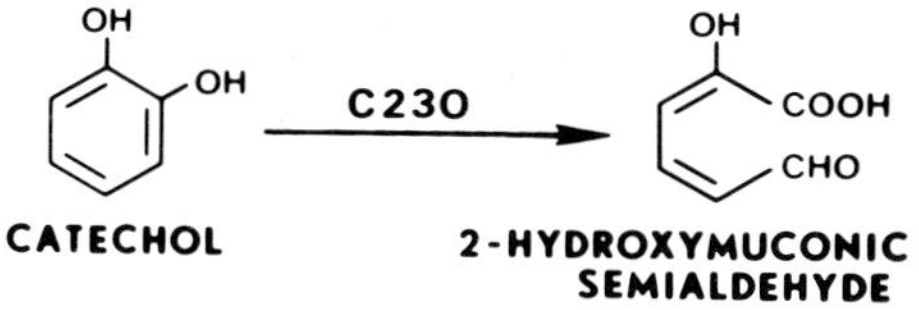

Figure 1. Top - Partial restriction endonuclease map of pTG402. Heavy line represents xylE; arrow indicates direction of mRNA transcription. The xylE gene on pTG402 is expressed in E. coli but not in B. subtilis until a sequence of DNA that promotes expression is inserted into a cleavage site, such as BamHI, HpaI or KpnI upstream from the structural gene. Bottom - Conversion of catechol to 2-hydroxymuconic semialdehyde by catechol 2,3-oxygenase [C230, catechol: oxygen 2,3-oxidoreductase (decyclizing) EC1.13.11.2] encoded by the xylE gene.

rapidly became yellow when sprayed with catechol. This demonstrated that xylE had remained intact in the B. subtilis host in which gene expression was not detected. It suggested that a transcriptional and/or translational block to heterospecific gene expression was responsible for the lack of xylE activity in B. subtilis, but further experimental results soon indicated that the problem was at the level of transcription.

B. Expression of the xylE Gene in B. subtilis

Sequences of DNA that promote expression of the xylE gene in B. subtilis were isolated in the following manner. B. subtilis chromosomal DNA was digested to completion with the Sau3A restriction endonuclease. Resulting fragments were ligated to pTG402 which was previously digested at the unique BamHI site which lies approximately 800 base pairs (bp) upstream of xylE. The ligation mixture was introduced into B. subtilis either through transformation first in E. coli and subsequently in B. subtilis or preferably, by direct transformation of B. subtilis protoplasts (Chang and Cohen, 1979). When Cm^r plasmid-bearing B. subtilis transformants were sprayed with catechol, yellow colonies were observed at a frequency of 2.8×10^{-3} of total transformants. This indicated that the xylE gene was functionally expressed in B. subtilis under the control of a genetic regulatory signal present on the insert.

To examine whether fragments of DNA from other species might also promote expression of xylE, chromosomal DNA from Bacillus licheniformis, Bacillus pumilus and E. coli was digested with Sau3A and fragments ligated to the BamHI site of pTG402. In all instances, yellow colonies were observed after Cm^r transformants were sprayed with catechol. The frequency of plasmids that expressed xylE under the control of E. coli DNA was, however, at least 10-fold lower (ca. 2×10^{-4}) than those of the Bacilli (ca. 2×10^{-3}). In related experiments, we observed that Sau3A fragments of DNA from B. subtilis bacteriophage Ø29 and a BamHI/BglII fragment of plasmid pUB110 (Gryczan et al., 1978) also promote expression of xylE, but attempts to express the gene in B. subtilis under the control of DNA from E. coli bacteriophage lambda were unsuccessful.

C. C230 Produced in B. subtilis

Plasmids from several transformants that expressed xylE were examined for DNA insert size and the specific activity of the C230 produced in B. subtilis (Table 1). Enzyme activities varied broadly, but no correlation between the size of the insert and C230 activity was observed. The levels of C230 produced in B. subtilis compared favorably, in most instances, with that of the uninduced enzyme in P. putida mt-2, but were appreciably lower than that observed from E. coli cells harboring pTG402 (approximately 12,000 mU/mg specific activity).

Analysis of C230 produced in B. subtilis revealed that the enzyme shares identical characteristics to that produced in P. putida or E. coli. The following criteria were used in the determination. 1) Partially purified cell-free extracts from each organism were resolved on a polyacrylamide gel using non-denaturing conditions. C230 was identified by spraying the gel with catechol after electrophoresis was terminated. Yellow bands appeared at coincident loca-

Table 1. Representative C230 Specific Activities in B. subtilis

Source of insert[a]	*Plasmid*	*Insert Size*[b] *(bp)*	*Specific Activity*[c] *(mU/mg)*
-	*None*	-	*0*
-	*pTG402*	-	*0*
-	*pWWO*[d]	-	*160*
B. subtilis	*pTG403*	*500*	*238*
	pTG405	*575*	*1,703*
	pTG409	*900*	*170*
	pTG413	*500*	*14*
	pTG414	*1,500*	*288*
	pTG416	*1,100*	*2,011*
B. pumilus	*pTG435*	*200*	*1,794*
	pTG436	*550*	*327*
	pTG437	*1,800*	*725*
B. licheniformis	*pTG438*	*700*	*555*
	pTG440	*600*	*1,018*
	pTG441	*500*	*2,727*
E. coli	*pTG432*	*600*	*42*
	pTG433	*500*	*324*
pUB110	*pTG431*	*1,550*	*1,473*
Ø29	*pTG447*	*300*	*1,853*

[a]*For chromosomal DNAs and Ø29, Sau3A fragments were ligated to the BamHI site of pTG402. For pUB110, a 1.55 kb fragment resulting from double digestion with BamHI and BglII was ligated to the BamHI site of pTG402.*

[b]*Insert sizes were determined by agarose gel electrophoresis of plasmids digested with ClaI, HindIII and AvaI, or BamHI and ClaI. Bacteriophage λ cI857Sam7 DNA digested with HindIII or EcoRI and HindIII was used as the standard for molecular weight determinations.*

[c]*Method of Sala-Trepat and Evans (1971). One milliunit (mU) corresponds to the formation at 30°C of 1 nmole of 2-hydroxy-muconic semialdehyde per minute. Protein concentrations were measured by the method of Lowry et al. (1951) using bovine serum albumin as reference.*

[d]*Host cells, P. putida, mt-2. In all other cases, host cells were B. subtilis MI112.*

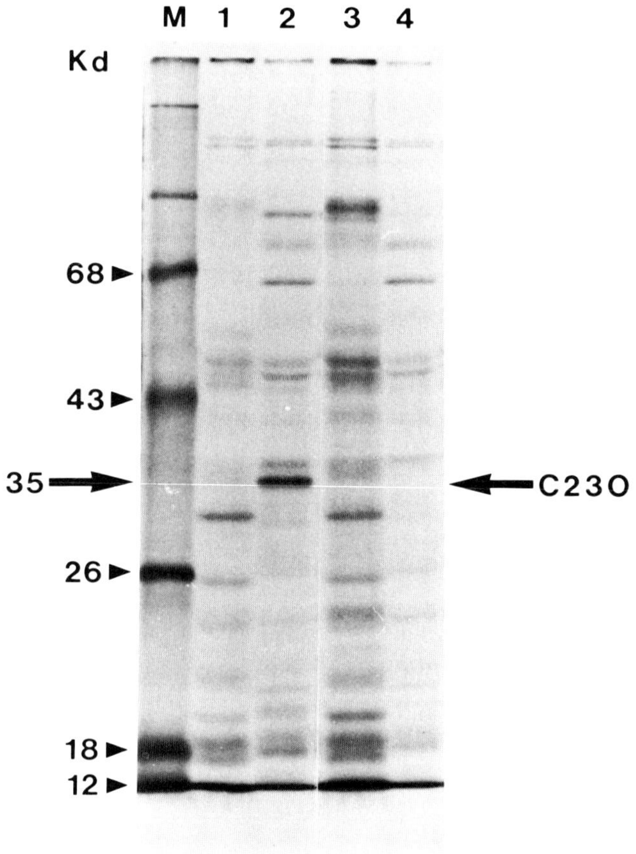

Figure 2. Immunoprecipitation of C23O produced by B. subtilis (method of Pavirani et al., 1982). Molecular weight markers, lane M. Radiolabeled (^{35}S-methionine) proteins from MI112/pTG447 immunoprecipitated with non-immune serum, lane 1 or with anti-C23O antiserum, lane 2. Radiolabeled proteins from control cells in which xylE is not functionally expressed, immunoprecipitated with non-immune serum, lane 3 or with anti-C23O antiserum, lane 4. Kd, Kilodaltons.

tions in the gel for all extracts except that of the B. subtilis strain harboring pTG402 without a functional promoter (see Zukowski et al., 1983). 2) Crude antiserum prepared from a rabbit injected with C23O purified from E. coli reacted with C23O from B. subtilis, P. putida and E. coli in a double-diffusion Ouchterlony test. The antiserum did not react with an extract prepared from a B. subtilis strain

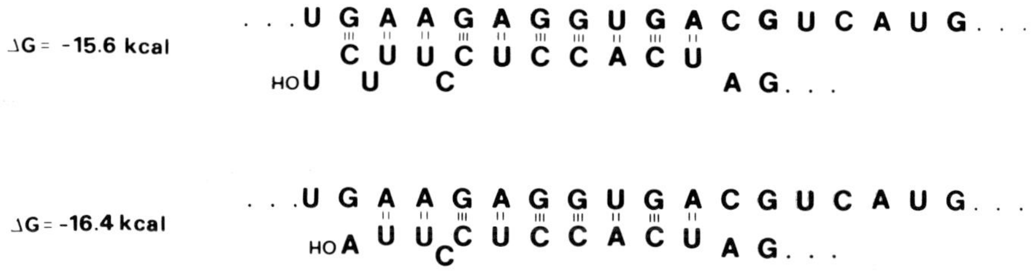

Figure 3. Putative ribosome binding site of xylE mRNA and interaction between the site and 16S rRNA from B. subtilis (top) and E. coli (bottom). The free energy of base pairing, ΔG, calculated after Tinoco et al. (1973).

harboring pTG402 without a functional promoter (data not shown). 3) Immunoprecipitation of C230 prepared from a B. subtilis strain harboring plasmid pTG447, which expresses xylE from a Ø29 Sau3A fragment of DNA, revealed a sharp band corresponding to a molecular weight of 35,000 daltons (Figure 2), consistent with the mass of the C230 subunit (Nozaki, 1979; Zukowski et al., 1983). 4) Examination of the nucleotide sequence immediately upstream of the AUG initiation codon of xylE (Figure 3) reveals a putative ribosome binding site (Shine and Dalgarno, 1975) where extensive complementarity between the site and the 3' region of 16S rRNA is evident. The distance between the site and the initiation codon is calculated to be 9 bases (criteria of Moran et al., 1982). Furthermore, there exist 2 termination codons (both UGA ant positions -13 to -15 and -28 to -30 relative to AUG) immediately upstream and in-phase with the AUG initiation codon. Taken together, these data clearly suggest that translational initiation of xylE mRNA in B. subtilis commences at the same initiation codon as that in P. putida and E. coli.

D. Construction of Derivative Plasmids of pTG402

In an effort to reduce the distance between the unique BamHI site of pTG402 and the xylE gene, and to decrease the size of pTG402 itself, the following manipulations were employed. Plasmid pTG431, which contains a 1.55 kb BamHI/BglII fragment of pUB110 on pTG402, was linearized with BamHI, then treated successively with exonuclease III and nuclease S1 (Davidson et al., 1980). Unphosphorylated BamHI linkers [5'd(CGGATCCG); Amersham] were attached with T4 DNA ligase and the resulting plasmids were used to trans-

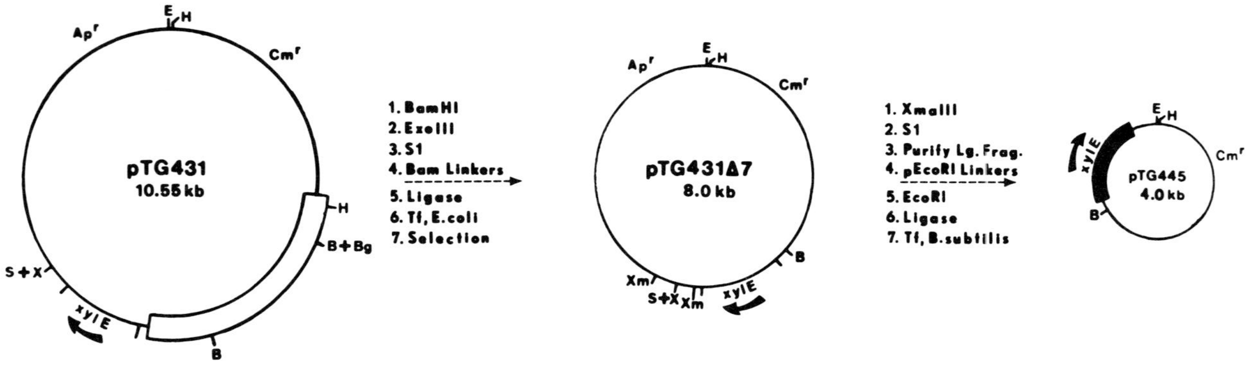

Figure 4. *Construction of promoter-detection plasmids pTG431Δ7 and pTG455, as described in the text. Enlarged area on pTG431 represents portion of plasmid deleted during construction of pTG431Δ7. Restriction endonucleases: B, BamHI; Bg, BglII; E, EcoRI; H, HindIII; S, SalI; X, XhoI; Xm, XmaIII. Tf = transformation.*

form E. coli. Ap^r Cm^r transformants were sprayed with catechol, and plasmids from several yellow colonies were analyzed. Plasmid pTG431Δ7 (Figure 4), a derivative of pTG431 from which 2.5 kb of DNA had been asymmetrically deleted, was shown to have a BamHI site approximately 150 bp upstream of the xylE gene. pTG431Δ7 was then digested with XmaIII, the protruding 5' termini were eliminated with S1 nuclease, and the large resulting fragment purified from an agarose gel. Phosphorylated EcoRI linkers [5'd(pGGAATTCC); Collaborative Research, Inc.] were ligated to the fragment with T4 DNA ligase, and this was followed by extensive digestion with EcoRI restriction endonuclease. Fragments were diluted, recircularized by the addition of T4 DNA ligase, and finally introduced into B. subtilis by protoplast transformation. The resulting plasmid, pTG445 (Figure 4), contains a unique BamHI site approximately 150 bp upstream of xylE, a unique EcoRI site approximately 200 bp 3' to the UGA termination codon of xylE, a unique HindIII site 29 bp proximal to the EcoRI site, and the chloramphenicol acetyltransferase gene of pC194 (Horinouchi and Weisblum, 1982) which renders host cells resistent to Cm. The small size of the promoter-detection plasmid pTG445 is more convenient than pTG402 for cloning larger fragments of DNA in B. subtilis and may contribute to increased plasmid stability. Furthermore, we have recently introduced a transcriptional termination region in the unique HindIII site of pTG445 (Zukowski et al., in preparation) and this will most likely be effective for cloning particularly strong promoters (Gentz et al., 1981).

III. DISCUSSION

We have described the construction, characterization and modifications of a system in which fragments of DNA that promote heterospecific gene expression in B. subtilis are detected by a simple color assay. This chromogenic method offers several advantages. 1) Specially prepared indicator plates are not necessary to monitor xylE gene expression. 2) Yellow coloration is observed only for those cells that express xylE; background coloration is not observed for the cells in which xylE is present but remains unexpressed. 3) The intensity of the color or the time of its appearance after spraying colonies is directly related to the specific activity of C23O. Visual inspections are confirmed by using a simple spectrophotometric assay to more accurately estimate C23O specific activities. 4) The C23O substrate, catechol, is very inexpensive as compared with the chromogenic β-galactosidase substrate, 5-bromo-4-chloro-3-indoyl β-D-galactosidase (X-gal) needed to measure very low levels of lacZ gene expression in an analogous system for E. coli. 5) Translation of xylE mRNA has been demonstrated in P. putida, E. coli and B. subtilis. The expression of the xylE gene in the yeast Saccharomyces cerevisiae (Aigle et al., manuscript in preparation) indicates that our chromogenic assay encompasses a broad host range.

In addition to these advantages, several applications of the chromogenic detection system might be envisioned. 1) Fragments of DNA that promote regulated expression of the xylE gene can be monitored rather easily. Comparison of yellow and white colonies on minimal media either supplemented or not with various carbohydrates or amino acids, or on sporulation medium, could indicate the presence of positively, or negatively-controlled promoters or sporulation-specific promoters. 2) For plasmids that express xylE, construction of other recombinant plasmids can be rapidly identified after a fragment of DNA is cloned in a site within the xylE gene (e.g. AvaI, SalI, ClaI, EcoRV). This would result in insertional inactivation of xylE, in which case colonies would remain white after spraying with catechol. 3) Likewise, cloning of a foreign gene in-phase with a segment of xylE corresponding to the amino-terminus of C230 might result in a fusion polypeptide which is functionally active. 4) Transcriptional terminators can be isolated by cloning in a site between an active promoter and the xylE gene. Efficient termination should result in pale yellow or white colonies. 5) Stability of plasmid DNA, in the autonomously replicating or chromosomally-integrated state, under non-selective conditions, can be followed by coloration of colonies. 6) Because the xylE gene can be expressed in many different hosts, the chromogenic assay can serve as the basis for developing gene expression vectors for a wide variety of organisms.

REFERENCES

An, G. and Friesen, J.D. (1979). **J. Bacteriol. 140**, 400.

Bolivar, F., Rodriguez, R.L., Greene, P.J., Betlach, M.C., Heynecker, H.L., Boyer, H.W., Crosa, J.H. and Falcow, S. (1977). **Gene 2**, 95.

Casadaban, M.J., Chou, J. and Cohen, S.N. (1980). **J. Bacteriol. 143**, 971.

Casadaban, J.J. and Cohen, S.N. (1980). **J. Mol. Biol.** 138, 179.

Chang, S. and Cohen, S.N. (1979). **Molec. Gen. Genet. 168**, 111.
Davison, B.L., Murray, C.L. and Rabinowitz, J.C. (1980). **J. Biol. Chem. 255**, 8819.
Downing, R. and Broda, P. (1979). **Molec. Gen. Genet. 168**, 189.
Franklin, F.C.H., Bagdasarian, M., Bagdasarian, M.M. and Timmis, K.N. (1981). **Proc. Natl. Acad. Sci. USA 78**, 7458.
Gentz, R., Langner, A., Chang, A.C.Y., Cohen, S.N. and Bujard, H. (1981). **Proc. Natl. Acad. Sci. USA 78**, 4936.
Goldfarb, D.S., Doi, R.H. and Rodriques, R.L. (1981). **Nature 293**, 309.
Gryczan, T.J., Contente, S. and Dubnau, D. (1978). **J. Bacteriol. 134**, 318.
Horinouchi, S. and Weisblum, B. (1982). **J. Bacteriol. 150**, 815.
Lowry, O.H., Rosebrough, N.J., Farr, A.L. and Randall, R.J. (1951). **J. Biol. Chem. 193**, 265.
Moran, C.P., Lang, N., Le Grice, S.F.J., Lee, G., Stephens, M., Sonenshein, A.L., Pero, J. and Losick, R. (1982). **Molec. Gen. Genet. 186**, 339.
Nakazawa, T., Inouye, S. and Nakazawa, A. (1980). **J. Bacteriol. 144**, 222.
Nozaki, M. (1979). **Topics Curr. Chem. 78**, 145.
Pavirani, A., Mage, R. and Fitzmaurice, L. (1982). **Eur. J. Immunol. 12**, 485.
Primrose, S.B. and Ehrlich, S.D. (1981). **Plasmid 6**, 193.
Sala-Trepat, J.M. and Evans, W.C. (1971). **Eur. J. Biochem. 20**, 400.
Shine, J. and Delgarno, L. (1975). **Nature 256**, 232.
Tinoco, I., Borer, P.N., Dengler, B., Levine, M.D., Ulenbeck, O.C., Crothers, D.M. and Gralla, J. (1973). **Nature New Biol. 246**, 40.
West, R.W., Neve, R.L. and Rodriguez, R.L. (1979). **Gene 7**, 271.
Williams, D.M., Duvall, E.J. and Lovett, P.S. (1981). **J. Bacteriol. 146**, 1162.
Zukowski, M.M., Gaffney, D.F., Speck, D., Kauffmann, M., Findeli, A., Wisecup, A. and Lecocq, J.P. (1983). **Proc. Natl. Acad. Sci. USA 80**, 1101.

Session V: Synthesis of Sporulation Associated Products

CLONING AND SEQUENCE ANALYSIS OF THE <u>spoOA</u> LOCUS OF BACILLUS SUBTILIS[1]

Franco Ferrari[2]
Kathleen Trach
Jean Spence[3]
Eugenio Ferrari[4]
James Hoch

Division of Cellular Biology
Department of Basic and Clinical Research
Research Institute of Scripps Clinic
La Jolla, California

I. INTRODUCTION

The hallmark of the initiation of the sporulation process in bacteria is the placement of a septum at one end rather than in the middle of the cell. This asymmetric septum subsequently grows by invagination of the membrane yielding a cell within a cell called a forespore. Subsequent stages in sporulation involve maturation of this forespore to a spore. This laboratory has been interested for some time in the regulatory mechanisms that control the initiation of sporulation. Our approach to the initiation of sporulation has been to isolate mutants defective in the

[1]*This research was supported in part by NIH Research Grant GM 19416.*
[2]*On leave of absence from the Department of Pediatrics, University of Pavia, Pavia, Italy; present address: Syntro Corporation, San Diego, California.*
[3]*Syntro Corporation; present address: Department of Biology, University of Utah, Salt Lake City, Utah.*
[4]*Present address: Genentech, Inc., South San Francisco, California.*

ISBN 0-12-274160-9

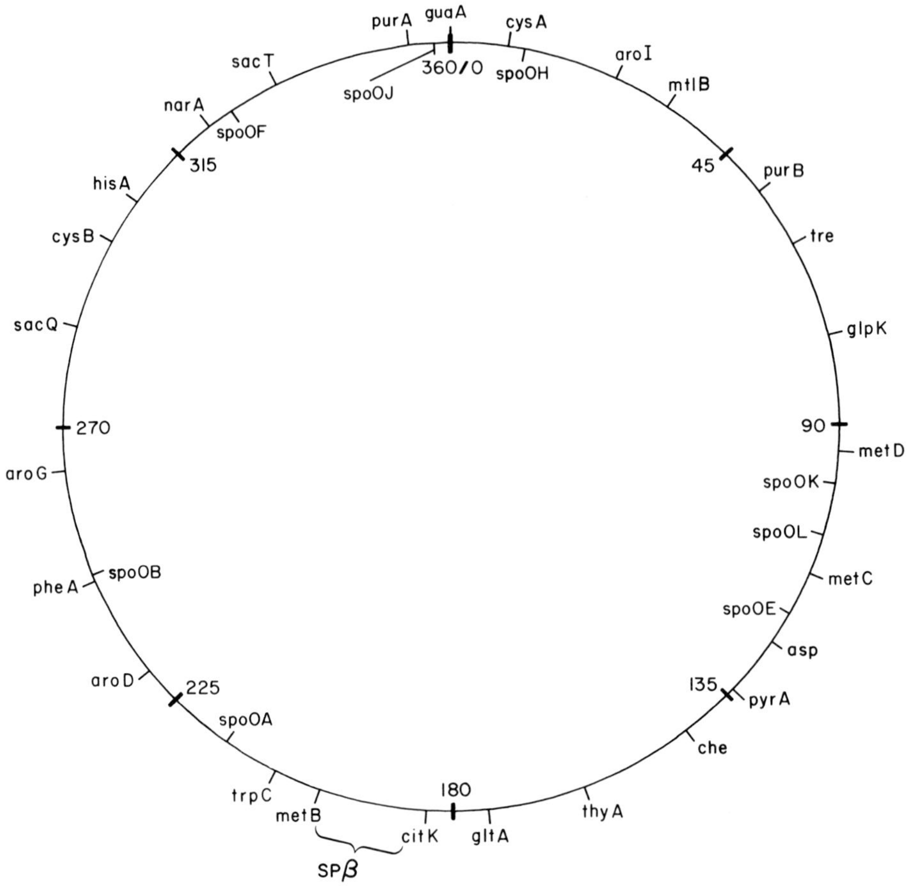

Figure 1. Abbreviated genetic map of Bacillus subtilis.

initiation process. These mutants are the stage 0 mutants and the mutations are designated by the genotypic symbol spo0. Nine genes have been found among several hundred mutations blocked in this process and they have been designated spo0A, spo0B, etc. (Hoch, 1976; Piggot and Coote, 1976). The majority of the stage 0 mutations map in five loci that are unlinked on the Bacillus subtilis chromosome (Figure 1). Stage 0 mutants may be blocked in any one of the processes leading to the initiation of development: the formation of intracellular metabolic signal, the mechanisms by which this signal is associated with the switch mechanism or in the transmission of a metabolic signal to the transcription machinery. In any case it is clear that all of the stage 0 mutants have gross pleiotropic effects on the synthesis of a wide variety of gene products associated with the sporulation process (Hoch, 1979). The most pleiotropic of the stage 0 mutations occur in the spoOA locus. In this report we describe the cloning and sequencing of the spoOA locus.

II. RESULTS

A. Cloning of the spoOA Locus in Bacteriophage λ

DNA containing the spoOA locus was isolated from a library of Bacillus subtilis DNA prepared in the Charon 4A lambda vector (Ferrari et al., 1981). Bacteriophage containing the spoOA locus were identified by their ability to transform spoOA mutants to prototrophy. Extensive restriction enzyme analyses of the inserts contained within one of these phage identified two EcoRI fragments that contained all of the known spoOA mutations. Cloning of subfragments of these two EcoRI fragments in the vector pJH101 (Ferrari et al., 1983) and subsequent transformation experiments allowed us to identify the regions of these EcoRI fragments that contained transforming activity for spoOA mutations. The results of these analyses are shown in Figure 2. The top of the figure shows a partial genetic fine structure map constructed by transformation before the locus had been cloned. All of the alleles at the left end of the locus are contained within the deletion 204. The EcoRI site at 1100 bp separates the majority of the spoOA mutations from two mutations, spoOA9v and spoOA153. These latter mutations are contained within an immediately adjacent EcoRI to HincII fragment of 660 bp. The spoOA9v allele is the allele which defines the spoOC locus. Transformation of the spoOA alleles with plasmids containing the indicated subfragments of this region allowed us to locate them to a HincII to EcoRI fragment of 840 bp. None of the mutations were found to be to the left of the HincII site as shown in Figure 2.

B. Sequence Analysis of the spoOA Locus

Nucleotide sequence analysis of the DNA encompassing the spoOA locus and its flanking regions was undertaken using the Maxam and Gilbert technique (Maxam and Gilbert, 1980). The potential open reading frames derived from this sequence are shown in Figure 3. A large open reading frame extending from the HincII site through the EcoRI site, from left to right as shown in the figure, is present. There were no other open reading frames of any substantial size in this

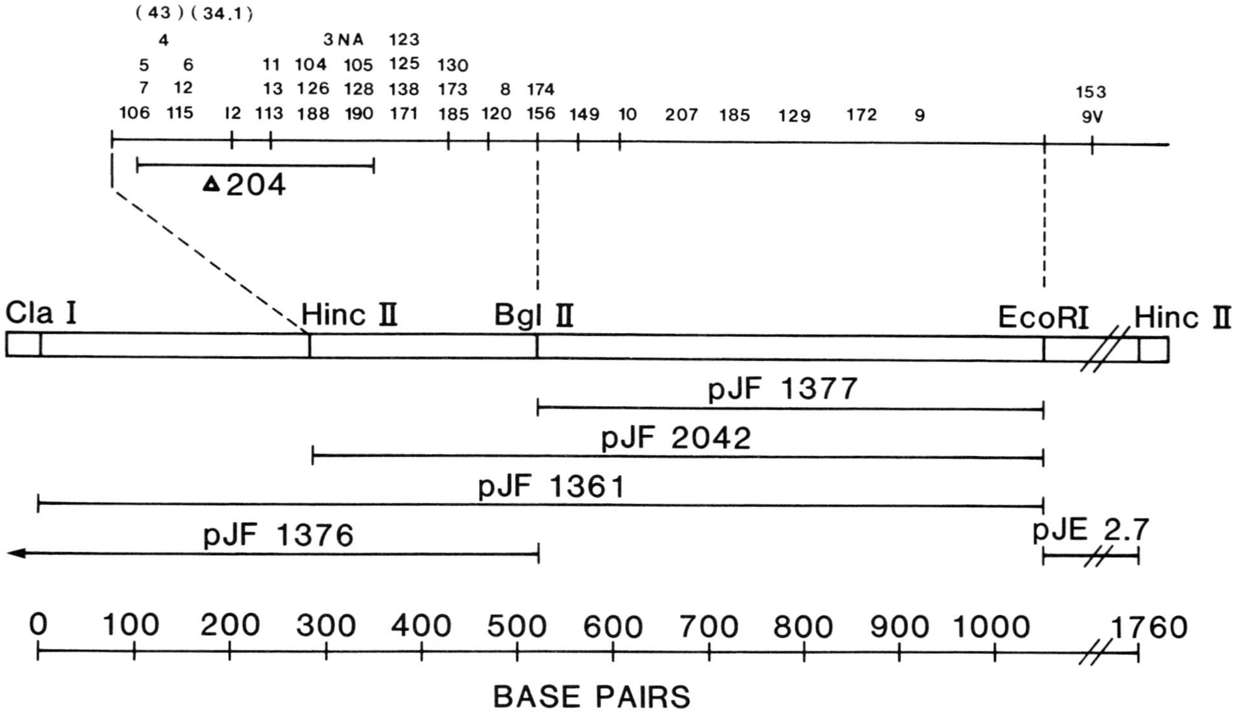

Figure 2. *Genetic and physical map of the* *spo0A* *locus. The top of the figure is a genetic fine structure map of the* *spo0A* *locus constructed by three factor transformation crosses. Those alleles represented by hash marks on the line were used as reference markers in the crosses. The extent of the restriction fragments, cloned in pJH101, used to determine the location of each allele on the physical map is shown below the physical map.*

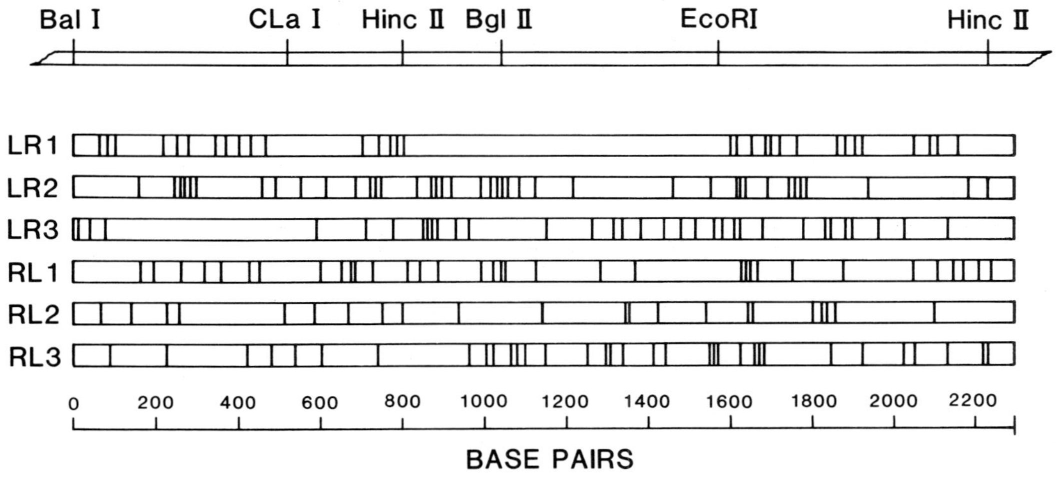

Figure 3. Location of open reading frames in the spo0A locus. The complete nucleotide sequence of the DNA comprising the spo0A locus was determined by Maxam and Gilbert (1980) sequence analyses. Both strands were sequenced. Each line in the boxed areas below the physical map indicates a translational stop codon. LR and RL indicate the frame from left to right or right to left, respectively.

```
GTAAGCCTGTTAATGGAATATATAGAAGGACAGGAAGAC ATG GAA GTG ATC GGC GTT GCT TAT AAC CGA CAG GAA TGC
                                        MET GLU VAL ILE GLY VAL ALA TYR ASN ARG GLN GLU CYS

CTG TCG CTG TTT AAA GAA AAA GAT CCC GAT GTG CTC GTA TTA GAT ATT ATT ATG CCG CAT CTA GAC GGA
LEU SER LEU PHE LYS GLU LYS ASP PRO ASP VAL LEU VAL LEU ASP ILE ILE MET PRO HIS LEU ASP GLY

CTT GCG GTT TTA GAG AGG CTG AGG GAA TCA GAT CTG AAA AAA CAG CCG AAT GTC ATT ATG CTG ACA GCC
LEU ALA VAL LEU GLU ARG LEU ARG GLU SER ASP LEU LYS LYS GLN PRO ASN VAL ILE MET LEU THR ALA

TTT GGG CAG GAA GAT GTC ACG AAA AAG GCC GTC GAT TTA GGC GCG TCC TAC TTT ATT CTC AAA CCG TTT
PHE GLY GLN GLU ASP VAL THR LYS LYS ALA VAL ASP LEU GLY ALA SER TYR PHE ILE LEU LYS PRO PHE

GAT ATG GAA AAC CTT GTC GGC CAT ATC CGC CAG GTC AGC GGA AAT GCC AGC AGT GTG ACG CAT CGT GCG
ASP MET GLU ASN LEU VAL GLY HIS ILE ARG GLN VAL SER GLY ASN ALA SER SER VAL THR HIS ARG ALA

CCA TCA TCG CAA AGC AGT ATT ATA CGC AGC AGC CAG CCT GAA CCA AAG AAG AAA AAT CTC GAC GCG AGC
PRO SER SER GLN SER SER ILE ILE ARG SER SER GLN PRO GLU PRO LYS LYS LYS ASN LEU ASP ALA SER

ATC ACA AGC ATT ATC CAT GAA ATC GGC GTC CCA GCC CAT ATT AAA GGC TAT CTC TAT CTG CGC GAA GCA
ILE THR SER ILE ILE HIS GLU ILE GLY VAL PRO ALA HIS ILE LYS GLY TYR LEU TYR LEU ARG GLU ALA

ATC TCA ATG GTA TAC AAT GAC ATC GAA TTG CTC GGC AGC ATT ACA AAA GTC CTC TAT CCG GAC ATC GCC
ILE SER MET VAL TYR ASN ASP ILE GLU LEU LEU GLY SER ILE THR LYS VAL LEU TYR PRO ASP ILE ALA

AAA AAA TTT AAC ACA ACC GCA AGC CGT GTA GAA AGA GCG ATC CGC CAT GCA ATT GAA GTG GCA TGG AGC
LYS LYS PHE ASN THR THR ALA SER ARG VAL GLU ARG ALA ILE ARG HIS ALA ILE GLU VAL ALA TRP SER

AGA GGA AAC ATT GAT TCC ATT TCC TCG TTG TTT GGT TAT ACT GTC AGC ATG ACA AAA GCT AAA CCT ACC
ARG GLY ASN ILE ASP SER ILE SER SER LEU PHE GLY TYR THR VAL SER MET THR LYS ALA LYS PRO THR

AAC AGT GAA TTC CAT TGC AAT GGT TGC GGA TAA GCTGAGGTTAGAGCATAA
ASN SER GLU PHE HIS TYR ASN GLY CYS GLY ###
```

Figure 4. Amino acid sequence of the putative spo0A gene product.

Figure 5. Nucleotide sequence of the ribosome binding site preceding the putative start of the spoOA gene product. Potential ribosome binding sites are indicated below the sequence. The extent of the palindrome is indicated above the sequence.

region. Since all of the spoOA mutations are to the right of the HincII restriction site in this region, we conclude that this major open reading frame must encompass the spoOA locus. In the region between the EcoRI site and the HincII site, downstream from this open reading frame, there are no open reading frames of any substantial size. Since this region contains the alleles spoOA9v and spoOA153 it seems likely that these alleles are mutations in the open reading frame that extends past EcoRI. In addition, one sizable open reading frame was uncovered in the same left to right direction immediately after the BalI restriction site and stopping just after the ClaI site.

In order to determine the start position of translation of the spoOA gene within the reading frame, the sequence was analyzed for a potential start codon preceded by a reasonable ribosome binding site. In this analysis all of the potential start codons (ATG, TTG, GTG and CTG) were examined in detail. The most likely candidate for a start codon is the ATG located at position 910 of the sequence (Figure 4). If the spoOA protein begins at this site, the protein would consist of 230 amino acids or a protein of about 25,600 kilodaltons (K.D.) in size. Examination of the sequence of the protein (Figure 4) reveals a potential protein of average amino acid composition and containing no particularly distinctive regions of structure.

The ribosome binding site preceding the start codon at BP 910 is unusual (Figure 5). There are two overlapping regions of homology to 16S ribosomal RNA. In addition, these ribosome binding sites are contained within a 15 base pair palindromic structure. Whether this type of structure has regulatory significance for translation of the spoOA messenger RNA is unknown at this time.

III. DISCUSSION

With the completion of the nucleotide sequence of the spoOA locus, three of the stage 0 loci have been cloned and sequenced. The spoOF locus has been cloned and shown to code for a protein of approximately 20,000 in K.D. (Shimotsu, 1982). The spoOH locus has been cloned and shown to code for a protein of approximately 29,000 K.D. (Dubnau et al., 1981). The spoOB locus has been cloned also and although the sequence of this gene is not yet done, it appears that the locus codes for a protein of approximately 24,000 K.D. (Hirochika et al., 1982; Ferrari et al., 1982). Thus, we will soon have a detailed picture of the molecular structure of the proteins encoded by genes controlling the initiation of sporulation.

The sequence of the spoOA locus may have resolved one longstanding problem as to whether the locus consisted of one or two genes. The spoOA9v allele has many phenotypic properties different from the other spoOA mutations. This mutation was found to have much less effect on the transcription of the 0.4 gene than mutations in the other portion of the spoOA locus (Ollington et al., 1982). For this reason it was thought that the spoOA9v allele defined another additional locus. The sequencing results presented here suggest that all of the alleles are part of a single gene because there is no obvious unique open reading frame in the region that the spoOA9v allele maps. Further genetic studies will have to be undertaken to prove that the spoOA9v allele is actually part of the upstream open reading frame that comprises spoOA.

Although the putative product of the spoOA locus is a protein of approximately 26,000 K.D., we have not yet proven this region actually codes for a protein of this size. Part of the reason for this is because we have never been able to successfully maintain clones containing the entire locus, that is fragments containing both the left and the right side of the sequenced region, in E. coli. We have some evidence that the product of the spoOA locus is made in very low quantities in the cell. Gene fusions which fuse the proximal portion of the spoOA locus at the BglII site to β-galactosidase produce extremely low levels of β-galactosidase when introduced into Bacillus subtilis. The present data suggests that the copy number of this protein in the cell is less than 10 per cell.

Now that the means are becoming available to identify the products of the spoO loci and obtain these products in pure form it will be of particular interest to determine how these gene products are able to control transcription from a wide variety of genes.

ACKNOWLEDGMENTS

We thank Syntro Corporation for help in the early portions of the sequence analysis. This is publication number 3320-BCR from the Research Institute of Scripps Clinic.

REFERENCES

Dubnau, E., Ramakrishna, N., Cabane, K. and Smith, I. (1981). **J. Bacteriol. 147**, 622.

Ferrari, E., Henner, D.J. and Hoch, J.A. (1981). **J. Bacteriol. 146**, 430.

Ferrari, F.A., Lang, D., Ferrari, E. and Hoch, J.A. (1982). **J. Bacteriol. 152**, 809.

Ferrari, F.A., Nguyen, A., Lang, D. and Hoch, J.A. (1983). **J. Bacteriol. 154**, 1513.

Hirochika, H., Kobayashi, Y., Kawamura, F. and Saito, H. (1981). **J. Bacteriol. 146**, 494.

Hoch, J.A. (1976). In Advances in Genetics (E. M. Caspari, ed.), Vol. 18, p. 69, Academic Press, New York.

Hoch, J.A. (1978). In Spores VII (G. Chambliss and J. C. Vary, eds.), p. 119, American Society for Microbiology, Washington, D.C.

Maxam, A.M. and Gilbert, W. (1980). **Methods Enzymol. 65**, 499.

Ollington, J.F. Haldenwang, W.G., Huynh, T.V. and Losick, R. (1981). **J. Bacteriol. 147**, 432.

Piggot, P.J. and Coote, J.G. (1976). **Bacteriol. Rev. 40**, 908.

Shimotsu, H., Kawamura, F., Kobayashi, Y. and Saito, H. (1983). **Proc. Natl. Acad. Sci. USA 80**, 658.

AMPLIFICATION OF SPORULATION GENES AND ITS EFFECT ON DIFFERENTIATION

Yasuo Kobayashi
Hiroyuki Anaguchi
Masanao Oda
Masaji Okamoto
Hitoshi Ayaki
Hidetoshi Yamada

Department of Applied Biochemistry
Hiroshima University
Fukuyama, Japan

Fujio Kawamura
Hidenori Shimotsu
Huiga Saito

Institute of Applied Microbiology
University of Tokyo
Bunkyo-ku, Tokyo, Japan

Hirohiko Hirochika

Institute for Plant Virus Research
Tsukuba Science City
Yatabe, Ibaraki, Japan

Sporulation of Bacillus subtilis is one of the typical model systems of unicellular differentiation. Many sporulation mutants have been isolated and characterized, and about 40 sporulation genes have been identified (Piggot and Coote, 1976; Henner and Hoch, 1980). However, the structure and function of these sporulation genes were not studied in detail, since the isolation of sporulation genes and their products was almost impossible.

ISBN 0-12-274160-9

Recently, several sporulation genes have been cloned with the development of gene cloning strategies (Segall and Losick, 1977; Kawamura et al., 1980; Dubnau et al., 1981; Ferrari et al., 1981; Liu et al, 1982; Bonamy and Suzlmajster, 1982; Ikeuchi et al., 1983). We have succeeded in the construction of five specialized transducing phage carrying sporulation genes spo0B, spo0F, spoIIC, spoIIG, and spoVE, respectively, by the prophage transformation method with the restriction endonuclease EcoRI (Kawamura et al., 1979). To characterize the structure and function of these sporulation genes, the EcoRI fragments carrying each sporulation gene were recloned from the transducing phage to plasmid pUB110 (Gryczan et al., 1978). The present paper describes the characterization of these specialized transducing phage, identification of the gene products, and the effect of the recombinant plasmids harboring sporulation genes on the sporulation of B. subtilis.

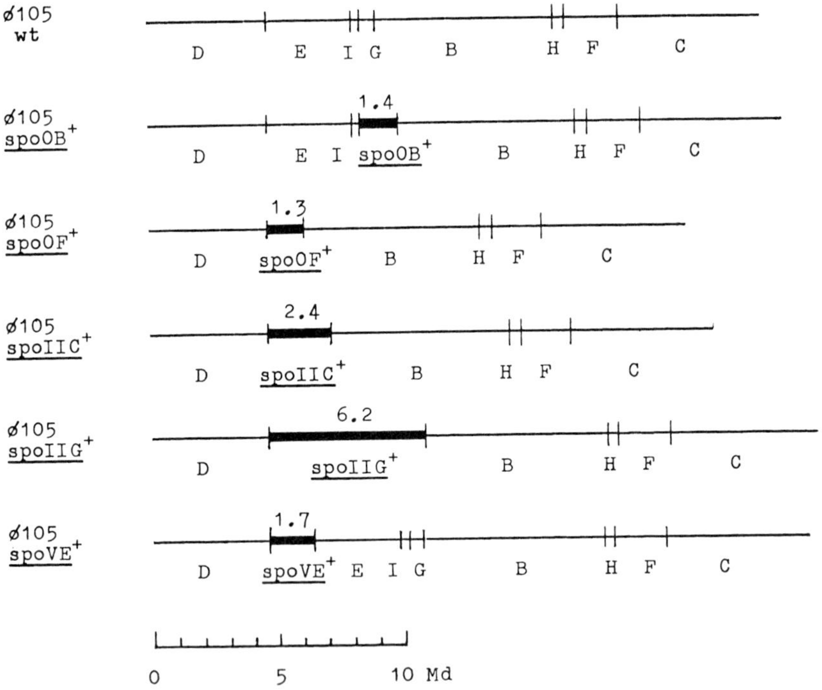

Figure 1. EcoRI restriction maps of Ø105 genomes carrying B. subtilis spo+ genes.

I. CHARACTERIZATION OF THE SPECIALIZED TRANSDUCING PHAGE CARRYING SPORULATION GENES

Specialized transducing phage Ø105spoOB, Ø105spoOF, Ø105spoIIC, Ø105spoIIG, and Ø105spoVE were constructed using restriction endonuclease EcoRI by prophage transformation method (Kawamura et al., 1979). Figure 1 shows the EcoRI restriction maps of these transducing phage genomes. Ø105spoOB lacks the EcoRI G fragment of Ø105 which is replaced by a 1.4 Md fragment derived from B. subtilis chromosomal DNA (Hirochika et al., 1982). Ø105spoVE has no deletion of the EcoRI fragments of Ø105 and a 1.7 Md chromosomal fragment is inserted between the EcoRI fragments D and E of Ø105 (H. Yamada and Y. Kobayashi, in preparation). In the other three transducing phage, Ø105spoOF (Hirochika et al., 1982) Ø105spoIIC (H. Anaguchi and Y. Kobayashi, in preparation), and Ø105spoIIG (H. Ayaki and Y. Kobayashi, in preparation), the cloned fragment replaces the EcoRI E, I, and G fragments of Ø105.

The transducing phage restore effectively the sporulation of the respective sporulation mutants. For example, sporulation efficiency of strain 1S43 (spoIIC298 trpC2) lysogenic for Ø105spoIIC is comparable to that of the wild-type strain (10^8 spores/ml), indicating that the cloned spoIIC gene functions normally in the lysogen. All of the transducing phage can multiply upon induction, but neither

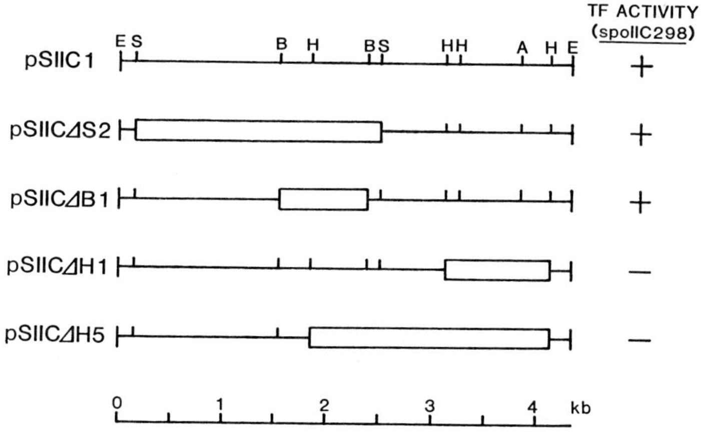

Figure 2. Restriction maps of the spoIIC EcoRI fragment and transforming activity (TF) of pSIIC and its deletion derivatives. The activity of these DNAs in transforming spoIIC298 to spo$^+$ is shown by +. Symbols for the restriction enzymes used are: A, AvaI; B, BclI; E, EcoRI; H, HindIII; S, SalI.

lysogenize nor form plaques without helper phage Ø105. These results suggest that the genes on the EcoRI E, I, and G fragments are not essential for phage multiplication, but are necessary for lysogenization and plaque formation. So far, the maximum size of the EcoRI fragment inserted in the Ø105 specialized transducing phage is 6.2 Md which corresponds to about 26% of the parental phage genome.

Figure 3. Autoradiograms of plasmid-specified polypeptides synthesized in minicells containing pUBSB derivatives [A] and pSIIC derivatives [B]. Minicells were purified by the procedure of Reeve et al. (1973). B. subtilis strain 1A292 (divIVB1, metB5, thyA, thyB) with or without the recombinant plasmid was grown at 30°C with shaking in Spizizen minimal medium containing 0.5% glucose, 0.1 mM $CaCl_2$, 0.01% casamino acids, 100 μg each of thymine and methionine/ml to the early stationary phase; one hour [A] or 30 minutes [B] after the end of logarithmic growth phase. The minicells were separated by 5 to 30% linear sucrose density gradient centrifugation. The purified minicells obtained were finally suspended in minimal medium containing 10% glycerol. The purified minicells (100 μl) were labeled with 1.5 μCi of [^{14}C]-amino acid mixture at 37°C for 30 minutes in the presence of 20 μg each of valine and isoleucine/ml. The samples for SDS-polyacrylamide gel electrophoresis were prepared by the method of Shivakumar et al. (1979). The samples containing about 36,000 dpm [A] or 64,000 dpm [B] were subjected to SDS-polyacrylamide gel electrophoresis as described by Laemmli and Favre (1973). After electrophoresis, the gel was processed for fluorography (Chamberlain, 1979). The molecular weight standards are indicated by numbers in kilodaltons. OB and IIC indicate the product of spoOB and spoIIC, respectively. K1, K2 and K5 are the pUB110-coded proteins (Shivakumar et al., 1979). The lower part of the Figure shows the spo^+ transforming activity of each plasmid. The plasmids present in the minicell preparation are: [A] (1) and (10) no plasmid; (2) and (9) pUB110; (3) pUBSB35; (4) pUBSBΔAva-125; (5) pUBSBΔBgc1; (6) pUBSBΔBgc3; (7) pUBSBΔBca1; (8) pUBSB19. Detailed description of the plasmids will be published elsewhere (M. Oda and Y. Kobayashi, in preparation). [B] (1) and (8) no plasmid; (2) and (7) pUB110; (3) pSIIC-1; (4) pSIICΔS2; (5) pSIIC-2; (6) pSIICΔH1.

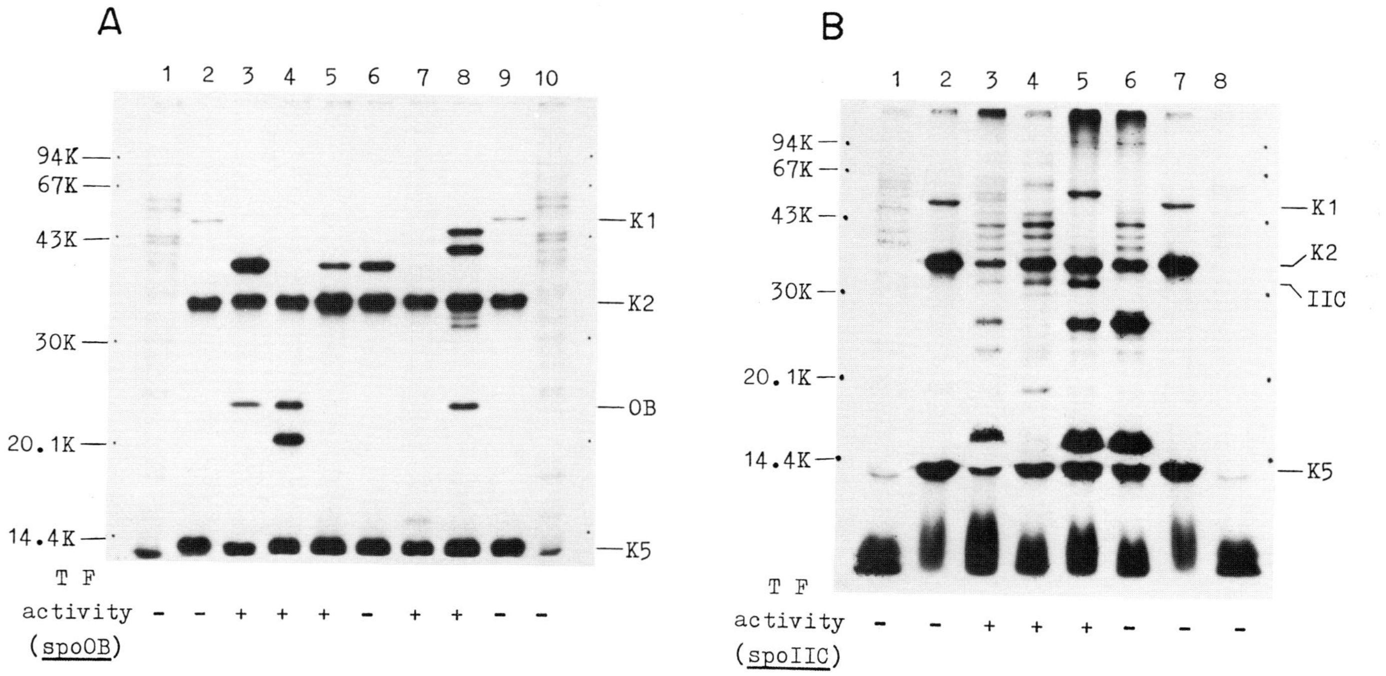

A
1 2 3 4 5 6 7 8 9 10
94K
67K
43K
30K
20.1K
14.4K
K1
K2
0B
K5
T F
activity - - + + + - + + - -
(spo0B)
B
1 2 3 4 5 6 7 8
94K
67K
43K
30K
20.1K
14.4K
K1
K2
IIC
K5
T F
activity - - + + + - - -
(spoIIC)

II. CHARACTERIZATION OF THE RECOMBINANT PLASMIDS HARBORING SPORULATION GENE

To characterize further the sporulation genes, the spo^+ chromosomal DNA fragment cloned in each transducing phage was transferred to plasmid pUB110 using endonuclease EcoRI and T4 DNA ligase. The plasmids obtained were designated pUBSB, pUBSF, pSIIC, pSIIG and pSVE (Kawamura et al., 1981; Y. Kobayashi et al., in preparation). These plasmids carry spo0B, spo0F, spoIIC, spoIIG, and spoVE genes, respectively.

To identify the location of the sporulation gene in the spo^+ fragments, deletion plasmids were constructed in vitro using restriction endonucleases. For example, the $spoIIC^+$ fragment has two SalI-, two BclI-, and four HindIII-restriction sites, but pUB110 does not have any of these sites. Therefore, the deletion plasmids were constructed by completely or partially digesting pSIIC DNA with SalI, BclI, or HindIII and religating the restricted fragments. The ligated DNA mixture was used to transform the B. subtilis strain to kanamycin resistance (Km^r) and the deletion plasmids were screened by size from these Km^r transformants. Figure 2 shows the restriction maps of the $spoIIC^+$ fragment and the spo^+ transforming activity (TF) of pSIIC and its deletion plasmids. The result suggests that the spoIIC298 mutation resides on the right end of the fragment. Similarly, deletion plasmids of pUBSB, pUBSF, pSIIG, and pSVE were constructed and the spo^+ transforming activity of these plasmids were examined and the location of spo markers on the cloned fragment was determined (details will be published elsewhere).

Using these plasmids, we have succeeded in the identification of the products of spo0B, spo0F, and spoIIC genes. As shown in Figure 3, spo0B and spoIIC gene products were

---

described by Laemmli and Favre (1973). The gel was processed for fluorography with EN³HANCE (New England Nuclear). Samples in lanes 1 to 8 contain 13,000, 47,000, 50,000, 54,000, 42,000, 42,000, 54,000 and 55,000 dpm, respectively. OF is the product of spo0F gene. K1, K2 and K5 are the pBU110-coded proteins. Plasmids are described by Shimotsu et al. (1983). The lower part of the figure shows the spo^+ transforming activity of each plasmid. Lane 1, no plasmid; 2 and 3, pUB110; 4, pUBSF13; 5, pUBSFΔB; 6, pUBSFΔH; 7, pUB110, and 8, pUBSF13. Lanes 1 to 6, proteins synthesized in vitro; lanes 7 and 8, proteins synthesized in maxicells.

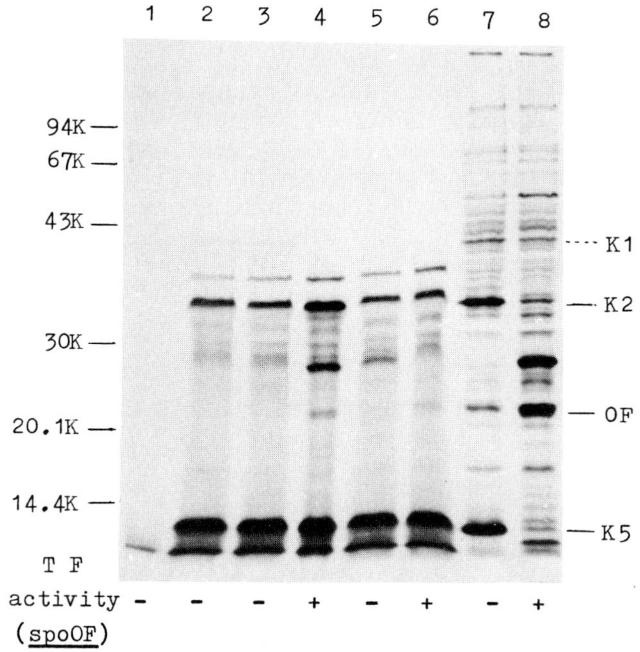

Figure 4. Autoradiograms of pUBSF13 DNA-directed proteins synthesized in vivo and in vitro. In vivo: Maxicell samples were prepared as described by Shimotsu et al. (1983) from B. subtilis strain 4309 (metB5 nonB RecE4) harboring pUB110 and UOT0397 (metB5 hisA1 recE4 pUBSF13). In vitro: Cell extracts from an in vitro DNA-directed protein-synthesizing system were prepared from B. subtilis strain JH642 (trpC2 pheA1) according to Shibuya and Kaziro (1979) with some modifications. Reaction mixture contained 50 mM Tris-HCl, pH 7.8, 40 mM ammonium acetate, 16.5 mM magnesium acetate, 2 mM dithiothreitol, 3% (w/w) PEG-6000, 45 μM folinic acid, 6 mM ATP, 0.5 mM each of GTP, CTP, UTP, 20 mM PEP-3Na, 6.6 μM of [^{14}C]-leucine (334 μCi/μmole), 3.4 μM of [^{14}C]-phenylalanine (553 μCi/μmole), 0.1 mM each of other 18 amino acids, 2.5 mg of PEG-treated S-30 proteins/ml, 30 A_{260} units of preincubated ribosomes/ml, 200 μg of B. subtilis tRNA/ml, and 20 μg of template DNA/ml. After the reaction mixture was incubated at 37°C for 90 minutes, 1/10 vol. of 2.2 N NaOH was added and the mixture was incubated at 37°C for 15 minutes. Proteins were precipitated by the addition of 5% trichloroacetic acid, washed with 0.5% trichloroacetic acid and ethylether, and dissolved in sample buffer. The samples from the maxicells and the in vitro system were subjected to SDS-polyacrylamide gel electrophoresis as

identified by minicell method (Reeve et al., 1973; M. Oda and Y. Kobayashi, in preparation). The spo0F gene product was identified by maxicell method (Shimotsu et al., 1983) and by a in vitro transcription-translation coupled system (Figure 4; M. Okamoto and Y. Kobayashi, in preparation). The sporulation gene-specific band was identified by the coincidence of the spo^+ transforming activity of the plasmid and the presence of the unique band on the autoradiograms. Thus, proteins 24K (M_r, 24,000), 22K (M_r, 22,000) and 32K (M_r, 32,000) were identified as the products of spo0B, spo0F and spoIIC genes, respectively.

III. EFFECT OF THE RECOMBINANT PLASMID ON SPORULATION

We have previously reported the inhibition of sporulation of a wild-type strain (spo^+ recE4) by pUBSF (Kawamura et al., 1981). To determine whether the other recombinant plasmids possess a similar effect, the sporulation of a wild-type strain harboring recombinant plasmid was examined and an example is shown in Table 1. The upper half of the table shows the inhibition of sporulation by pSIIC and its derivatives. The recombinant plasmids pSIIC-1 and pSIIC-2 (the direction of the inserted $spoIIC^+$ fragment is opposite to that of pSIIC-1) exhibited a slight inhibition of sporulation. The deletion plasmids, pSIIΔS2 and pSIICΔB1, also exhibited inhibition, but others, pSIICΔH1 and pSIICΔH5, as well as pUB110, did not inhibit sporulation.

The lower half of the table shows the restoration of sporulation of strain 4305 (spoIIC298 recE4) by recombinant plasmids. Strain 4305 harboring pSIICΔS2 or pSIICΔB1 recovered sporulation at the level of the strain carrying pSIIC-1 or pSIIC-2, but neither pSIICΔH1 nor pSIICΔH5 restore sporulation. Since both pSIIC-1 and pSIIC-2 have the sporulation restoring activity, the $spoIIC^+$ fragment may have its own promoter. Similar experiments were carried out using other recombinant plasmids and hosts and the results were summarized in Table 2.

IV. DISCUSSION

The present paper shows that the recombinant plasmids harboring sporulation genes affect the sporulation of the wild-type strain. They can be classified into three types according to their effect on sporulation. Type I plasmid

Table 1. Sporulation of Strains 4309 and 4305 Harboring pSIIC Derivatives

Host cell	*Plasmid*	*Viable cells/ml*	*Spores/ml*
4309	*none*	2.85×10^8	2.76×10^8
(spo+ recE4)	*pUB110*	2.33×10^8	2.16×10^8
	pSIIC-1	2.21×10^8	5.95×10^7
	pSIIC-2	2.45×10^8	5.90×10^7
	pSIICΔS2	1.66×10^8	6.30×10^7
	pSIICΔB1	2.53×10^8	3.23×10^7
	pSIICΔH1	2.05×10^8	1.78×10^8
	pSIICΔH5	1.85×10^8	1.98×10^8
4305	*none*	1.70×10^8	<10
(spoIIC298 recE4)	*pUB110*	2.26×10^8	<10
	pSIIC-1	1.29×10^8	4.08×10^7
	pSIIC-2	1.85×10^8	3.29×10^7
	pSIICΔS2	1.43×10^8	6.02×10^7
	pSIICΔB1	2.41×10^8	5.10×10^7
	pSIICΔH1	1.24×10^8	<10
	pSIICΔH5	1.78×10^8	<10

Cells were grown in Schaeffer's medium (per liter: 8 g of Difco nutrient broth, 0.25 g of $MgSO_4 \cdot 7H_2O$, 1 g of KCl, 10^{-6} M $Ca(NO_3)_2$, and 10^{-5} M $MnCl_2$, pH 7.0) at 36°C with shaking for 24 hours. Viable cells were counted on NB plates (per liter: 8 g of Difco nutrient broth and 15 g of agar). Heat resistant spores were counted on NB plates after heating the cells for 10 minutes at 90°C.

has no inhibitory effect on sporulation. Type II has a slight inhibition, and Type III inhibits sporulation severely. pUBSB is a Type I plasmid. This plasmid does not inhibit the sporulation of the wild-type strain and restores the sporulation of UQT0436 (spo0B136 recE4) to the level of wild-type strain (10^8 spores/ml). pSIIC is a type II plasmid. It inhibits slightly the sporulation of the wild-type strain and restores sporulation of strain 4305 (spoIIC298 recE4) to the level of 10^7 spores/ml. Plasmids pUBSF, pSIIG and pSVE are Type III. They inhibit severely both the sporulation of the wild-type strain and restoration of the asporogenic strains (10^3 to 10^4 spores/ml).

Table 2. Effect of Recombinant Plasmid on Sporulation

Plasmid	*Sporulation of spo$^+$ strain^a (spores/ml)*	*Sporulation of spo$^-$ strain^b (spores/ml)*
none	10^8	<10
pUB110	10^8	<10
pUBSB(spo0B$^+$)	10^8	10^8
pUBSF(spo0F$^+$)	10^3	ND
pSIIC(spoIIC$^+$)	10^7	10^7
pSIIG(spoIIG$^+$)	10^3	10^4
pSVE(spoVE$^+$)	10^4	10^3

[a]*Strain 4309 (spo$^+$ recE4) was used as a host strain for plasmids.*

[b]*Asporogenous strains UOT0436 (spo0B136 recE4), UOT0294 (spo0F221 recE4), 4305 (spoIIC298 recE4), HU1002 (spoIIG41 recE4) and 5205 (spoVE85 recE4) were used as host strains for plasmids pUBSB, pUBSF, pSIIC, pSIIG, and pSVE, respectively. Cell cultivation and spore counting were carried out as described in Table 1. Detailed analysis of the effect of the recombinant plasmids on sporulation will be published elsewhere.*

When the specialized transducing phage Ø105spo0F, Ø105spoIIG, or Ø105spoVE is lysogenized in a respective sporulation mutant, the lysogen sporulates normally (10^8 spores/ml). This fact suggests that the inhibition of the sporulation does not occur by a single copy of the spo$^+$ fragment. Therefore, it is important to note that some sporulation genes will not be able to be cloned by complementation and with the multicopy plasmid vector, although they will be able to be cloned with the phage vector.

There are several possibilities on the mechanism of the sporulation inhibition caused by the recombinant plasmid. 1) Excess production of the gene product synthesized by the multicopy plasmid interferes with the delicate sporulation process, 2) the fused abnormal protein produced by the cloned chromosomal DNA and the plasmid DNA or a polypeptide produced from an unknown gene adjacent to the cloned sporulation gene may inhibit the sporulation, or 3) a specific regulatory protein might be titrated by the amplified sporulation gene.

To clarify the inhibitory effect on sporulation by the recombinant plasmid, further analysis will be required. Especially, it will be necessary to carry out a detailed analysis of the promoter region of the sporulation gene and the purification and characterization of the gene product. Experiments are in progress to determine the nucleotide sequence of the cloned <u>spo</u>$^+$ fragments.

REFERENCES

Bonamy, C. and Suzlmajster, J. (1982). **Molec. Gen. Genet. 188**, 202.

Chamberlain, J.P. (1979). **Anal. Biochem. 98**, 132.

Dubnau, E., Ramakrishna, N., Cabane, K. and Smith, I. (1981). **J. Bacteriol. 147**, 622.

Ferrari, E., Henner, D.J. and Hoch, J.A. (1981). **J. Bacteriol. 146**, 430.

Gryczan, T.J., Contente, S. and Dubnau, D. (1978). **J. Bacteriol. 134**, 318.

Henner, D.J. and Hoch, J.A. (1980). **Microbiol. Rev. 44**, 57.

Hirochika, H., Kobayashi, Y., Kawamura, F. and Saito, H. (1982). **J. Gen. Appl. Microbiol.** 28, 225.

Ikeuchi, T., Kudoh, J. and Kurashi, K. (1983). **J. Bacteriol. 154**, 988.

Kawamura, F., Saito, H., Hirochika, H. and Kobayashi, Y. (1980). **J. Gen. Appl. Microbiol. 26**, 345.

Kawamura, F., Shimotsu, H., Saito, H., Hirochika, H. and Kobayashi, Y. (1981). <u>In</u> Sporulation and Germination (H.S. Levinson, A.L. Sonenshein and D.J. Tipper, eds.) p. 109, American Society for Microbiology, Washington, DC.

Laemmli, U.K and Favre, M. (1973). **J. Mol. Biol. 80**, 575.

Liu, H.-M., Chak, K.F. and Piggot, P.J. (19820). **J. Gen. Microbiol. 128**, 2805.

Piggot, P.J. and Coote, J.G. (1976). **Bacteriol. Rev. 40**, 908.

Reeve, J.N., Mendelson, N.H., Coyne, S.I., Hallock, L.L. and Cole, R.M. (1973). **J. Bacteriol. 114**, 860.

Segall, J. and Losick, R. (1977). **Cell 11**, 751.

Shibuya, M. and Kaziro, Y. (1979). **J. Biochem. 86**, 403.

Shimotsu, H., Kawamura, F., Kobayashi, Y. and Saito, H. (1983). **Proc. Natl. Acad. Sci.** USA **80**, 658.

Shivakumar, A.G., Hahn, J. and Dubnau, D. (1979). **Plasmid 2**, 279.

GENETIC AND BIOCHEMICAL STUDY OF BACILLUS THURINGIENSIS

V. G. Debabov
R. R. Azizbekyan
V. M. Stepanov
G. G. Chestukhina

Institute of Genetics
and Selection of Industrial Microorganisms
Moscow, U.S.S.R

I. INTRODUCTION

Bacillus thuringiensis is the only species of bacteria which is employed in large-scale in the insecticide industry. The preparations have different commercial designations in a number of countries: Dipel (USA), Turicid (Switzerland), entomobacterine and dendrobacillin (USSR). Various subspecies or serotypes of B. thuringiensis have a distinct, specific action on various insects, mainly, from Lepidoptera, with the exception of B. thuringiensis subsp. israelensis which has proved active against mosquitoes and flies, i.e. the insects from Diptera.

The insecticidal activity of preparations obtained using B. thuringiensis is mainly associated with the crystalline proteinaceous material formed in bacteria in the process of sporulation and designated crystal, parasporal crystal, parasporal body or Δ-endotoxin. Actually, the crystal is a protoxin which dissolves, is activated and converts into "true toxin", after being digested within the intestine gut of insect larvae (Lecadet and Martouret, 1967).

Further development of application of biological preparations toxic for pest insects necessitates a decrease in the cost of their manufacturing and augmentation of their efficiency. It is preferable to construct bacilli strains having: 1) an elevated pathogenicity for insects; 2) a modified spectrum of action; 3) an increased resistance to UV and other environmental factors; 4) the ability to grow

ISBN 0-12-274160-9

utilizing simple media, in submerged cultures; 5) resistance to bacteriophage; and 6) retained security for man and animals.

To resolve the above mentioned tasks, one should elucidate the molecular basis of Δ-endotoxin action and elaborate a means for genetic manipulations with the bacilli of this species.

In the present communication, a brief review of the work conducted in the Institute of Genetics and Selection of Industrial Microorganisms is presented concerning both studies on structural organization of proteins of Δ-endotoxins and the development of particular genetics of B. thuringiensis.

II. PROTEINS OF Δ-ENDOTOXIN

Physical and chemical studies of Δ-endotoxin proteins involve some problems, such as a necessity to provide rigid conditions for dissolution of proteins, their tendency to aggregation and stable association with crystal inclusions of intracellular proteinases of B. thuringiensis.

The detailed studies of several years developed in our institute (Zalunin et al., 1979; Chestukhina et al., 1980) demonstrate that the crystals formed by the majority of serotypes, with the exception of several strains belonging to V serotype, contain one protein. Molecular weights of the proteins are presented in Table 1. The presence of the single protein within Δ-endotoxin was confirmed in several laboratories (Tyrell et al., 1981; Huber et al., 1981). However, we revealed, though minor, still quite reliable differences between proteins of crystals from various strains. These differences are clearly seen when electrophoretic samples are run simultaneously (Figure 1), and they should not be neglected, especially, when we are to explain differences in the biological spectrum of action of various B. thuringiensis serotypes, on the basis of chemical alterations in the structure of Δ-endotoxin proteins.

Limited proteolysis of protein protoxin with different proteinases, such as trypsin, chymotrypsin, subtilisin BPN', pronase E, B. thuringiensis extracellular serine proteinase, intracellular serine proteinase of B. thuringiensis and B. amyloliquefaciens, and a mixture of proteinases from Galleria melonella larvae gut, gives the similar result - a stable product of proteolysis is formed which is the N-terminal protein domain (Chestukhina et al., 1982). This is based on determination of N-terminal amino acid in native proteins and domains resistant to proteolysis.

Table 1. Molecular Weights of Proteins Forming Crystals of Different B. thuringiensis Strains

Molecular Weights				
145,000	135,000	130,000	135,000 130,000	135,000 130,000 65,000
var. *thuringiensis*(I) strain 1223(I) var. *insectus* strain 1217 strain 199	var. *alesti*(III) strain 1225 var. *kenyal* strain 1228 var. *dendrolimus* strain 1277 var. *morrisoni* strain 1252 var. *darmstadi-ensis* strain 1154	var. *finitmus*(II) strain 1162 var. *kurstaki* strain 1226 var. *galleriae*(V) strain 1167 var. *tolworthi* strain 1253 var. *thompsoni* strain 1166	var. *galleriae*(V) strain 696 strain 449 strain 273 strain 220 strain 561 strain 16 strain 73	var. *galleriae*(V) strain 612 strain 614 strain 615 strain 650 strain 223

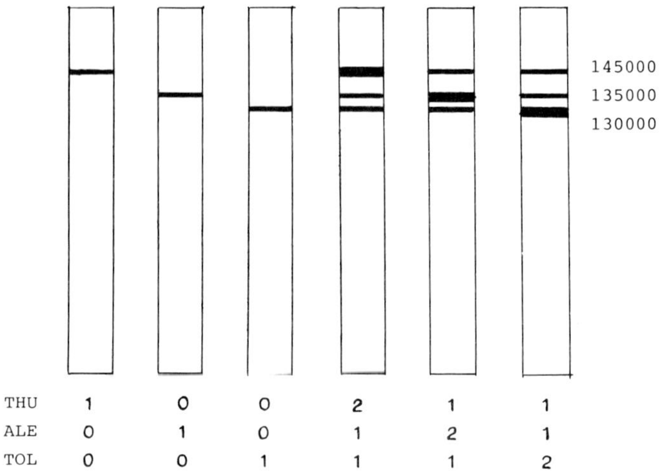

Figure 1. Molecular weight of Δ-endotoxins from various B. thuringiensis variants. SDS-PAGE (in 5% gel) in the presence of 8 M Urea. Symbols: variant thuringiensus (THU), alesti (ALE) and galleriae (GAL). Crystals dissolved in 8 M urea solution, 1% SDS, 10^{-3} M DTE, pH9.0 at 100°C, 5 minutes. Protein solutions mixed using different ratios prior to sampling.

Table 2. Molecular Weight of Crystal-Forming Proteins and Their Stable N-Terminal Domains

Variant	Serotype	Strain	Molecular Weights	
			Protein	N-Terminal Domain
insectus	I	1217	145,000	80,000
alesti	III	1225	135,000	70,000
galleriae	V	1167	130,000	65,000

In all cases, methionine is discovered to occupy the N-terminal position. It should be noted that the values of N-terminal domain retain the differences characteristic of native proteins, whereas the degrading C-terminal half of the molecule is likely to have the similar size in different proteins (Table 2). Similar results were obtained by Bulla et al. (1981); when studying proteolysis of Δ-endotoxin from var. kurstaki (serotype III), they reported the m.w. of the N-terminal domain to be 68,000.

There is good reason to believe that the stable N-terminal domains correspond to the literature-described "true" toxins of crystals formed in intestines of larvae. In contrast to protoxin, toxin kills larvae when directly introduced into hollow body escaping intestines. All N-terminal domains proved toxic when introduced into the hemocoel.

Analysis of intermediates of proteolysis makes it possible to conclude that Δ-endotoxins of all serotypes are built similarly and that the non-stable C-terminal domain is degraded stepwise under the action of proteases, according to the following scheme:

Serotype III protoxin 70,000 - 15,000 - 15,000 - 35,000
Serotype V protoxin 65,000 - 15,000 - 15,000 - 35,000

The above scheme, though yielding no strong evidence, still allows a search for differences in biological specificity among N-terminal domains.

The question arises, whether the whole N-terminal fragment is toxic, or whether smaller fragments may be derived which retain the biological activity. We recently succeeded in the isolation of a fragment of about 10,000 m.w. (crystals of var. alesti and tolworthi were degraded), after treatment of crystals with subtilisin or thiol-dependent B. thuringiensis protease. The fragment (var. alesti) retained entomocidal activity against larvae of the silk worm at the same level as the N-terminal domain. The fragment was isolated by ultrafiltration of the total hydrolysate through PM-30 membrane, followed by gel filtration on a Sephadex G-75 column equilibrated with 0.05 M sodium carbonate buffer, pH 8.5, containing 4 M urea, 1% sodium dodecyl sulfate and 10^{-3} M dithioerythrite. Amino acid composition of protoxin, N-terminal domain and the fragment obtained is presented in Table 3. As shown in the table, amino acid composition is similar in the domain and the fragment, differing from that of protoxin by a decreased lysine content. These results suggest the presence of repetitions in the primary structure of endotoxin.

Thus, Δ-endotoxins from all B. thuringiensis variants have the same structure, and similar, though not identical, proteins. The toxic character is localized within a small protein fragment equal to 8% of its mass.

Table 3. Amino Acid Composition of Crystal-Forming Protein (Protoxin) of N-Terminal Stable Domain (Toxin) and of a Low Molecular Weight, Biologically-Active Fragment of Δ-Endotoxin of B. thuringiensis subsp. alesti

Amino Acid	Protoxin		Toxin		Fragment	
	Residues	Mol %	Residues	Mol %	Residues	Mol %
1/2 Cys	13	1.1	6.4	1.0	1	0.2
Asp	139	11.6	69	10.9	9	9.7
Thr	78	6.5	40	6.3	6	6.4
Ser	98	8.1	60	9.4	8	8.4
Glu	143	11.9	69	10.9	10	10.9
Pro	56	4.6	36	5.7	5	5.9
Gly	95	7.9	51	8.0	8	9.4
Ala	66	5.5	36	5.7	5	6.1
Val	72	6.0	46.5	7.3	7	7.3
Ile	62	5.2	40	6.3	6	7.0
Leu	106	8.8	62	9.8	8	9.1
Tyr	54	4.5	20	3.1	4	4.1
Phe	59	4.9	38	6.0	5	5.1
His	26	2.2	13	2.1	1	1.4
Lys	36	3.0	6	1.0	1	0.9
Arg	74	6.2	32	5.0	7	7.3
Met	8	0.7	6	0.85	1	1.4
Trp	14	1.2	4	0.5	1	0.3

Degradation by CNBr followed by subsequent analysis of fragments points to some differences in distribution of methionine residues in N-terminal domains of various serotypes (Figure 2). Solubility of domains is different, for example the domain of serotype III is not dissolved in 2 M NaCl, while domains of serotypes IX and V are soluble. Also, resistance of domains to proteolysis is not similar (Figure 3). Taking these differences into account, it is suggested that the difference in toxicity for a given insect species may depend not on differences of the acting polypeptide but rather on its availability (solubility, the ability to be degraded by proteases, etc.) within the insect gut.

It cannot be excluded that in addition to proteases of larvae gut, intracellular proteases may also participate in increasing or decreasing the activity and, possibly, cause a change in the action spectrum of a preparation. In strains

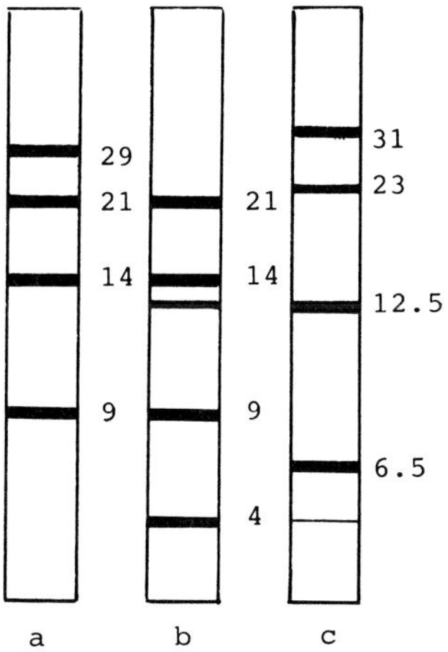

Figure 2. The separation of CNBr fragments obtained from N-terminal domains of protoxins from various serotypes by SDS-Page (in 10% gel): (a) serotype IX; (b) serotype III; (c) serotype V.

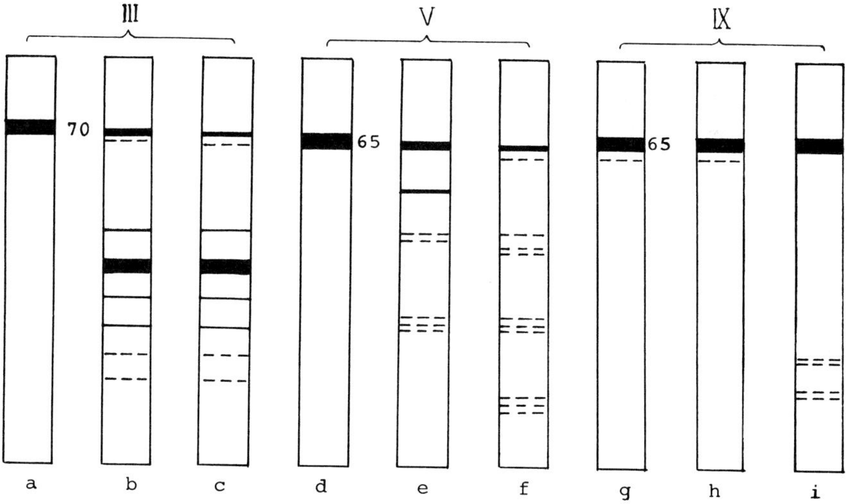

Figure 3. Subtilisin hydrolysis of N-terminal domains of B. thuringiensis Δ-endotoxin (II, V, IX serotypes). Electrophoresis performed in SDS-PAGE (10% gel). Hydrolysis for 60 min at enzyme-protein ratio 0:100 (a,d,g); 1:100 (b,e,h); 4:100 (c,f,i).

Table 4. Comparison of Auxotrophs of B. thuringiensis and B. subtilis

Mutants of *Bacillus thuringiensis* No.	Designation	Growth requirements needed on synthetic medium	Possible analogy to *B. subtilis* mutations
10, 48	Pur⁻	adenine, guanine, hypoxanthine	purB
53, 56	Pur⁻ T	guanine strictly needed	
59	Arg⁻ A	arginine strictly needed	argA
9	Arg⁻ °O	arginine could be replaced by ornithine	argO
50	Arg⁻ C	arginine could be replaced by citrulline	argC
14, 35	Arg⁻ T	arginine could be replaced by ornithine but not citrulline	
2, 3, 4, 3, 10, 11, 14, 35	Thr⁻	threonine needed but could be replaced by homoserine	thr
6, 54, 55, 57	IlvB, C or D	valine and isoleucine	ilvB, C, or D
58	Val⁻ T	valine	
7, 9, 14, 30, 34, 35, 36, 37	Met⁻ C or D	methionine needed but replaced by homocysteine	metC or D
33, 51	His⁻	histidine needed	not analyzed

belonging to galleriae var. which were chosen for their increased virulence, a true toxin of 65,000 m.w. has been frequently detected, along with the protoxin (Table 1). Thus, selection of strains having an altered activity of intracellular proteases may be regarded as a promising line of the selection work with B. thuringiensis.

V. M. Stepanov with coworkers (Stepanov et al., 1981; Chestukhina et al., 1982) demonstrated that serine proteinases of B. thuringiensis and related B. cereus belong to the subclass of thiol proteinases, i.e. contain an SH group essential for the activity expression. B. thuringiensis and related B. cereus differ in this respect from many other bacilli studied. A striking structural resemblance of extracellular serine proteinases of B. thuringiensis to those of taxonomically remote Thermoactinomyces vulgaris was discovered (Stepanov et al., 1981).

III. PARTICULAR GENETICS OF B. THURINGIENSIS

A. Mutations

Considering that strains of var. galleriae (serotype 5a-5b) are employed in the USSR as producers of entomobacterine, a great deal of attention was given to the study of genetic peculiarities of this serotype and also to the examination of phage preferentially lysing these strains.

One of the main tasks in genetic studies of microorganisms is creation of a collection of marked strains. Auxotrophic mutants were obtained in B. thuringienis var. galleriae using treatment of vegetative cells with nitrosoguanidine or spores with diethylsulfante. The mutants isolated were auxotyped and assigned to 12 types, 8 of them being analogous to the corresponding B. subtilis mutants (Table 4). A collection of mutations with a low frequence of reversions (10^{-8} to 10^{-9}), suitable for further work, were obtained.

B. Transduction

Previously, transduction was demonstrated in strains belonging to I and III serotypes of B. thuringiensis (Barjac, 1970; Thorne, 1978). In the present work, using marked strains this method was applied to galleriae, dendrolimus and israelensis serotypes (Pogosbekova and Azizbekyan, 1981; Pogosbekova and Azizbekyan, 1983; Stepanova and Asisbekyan, 1983). Summarized data on intra- and intervariant transduction are given in Table 5. As seen in Table 5, the frequency of transfer of various markers is nearly equal, which indicates the generalized nature of transduction brought about by various phage. The similarity of frequency values in intra- and intervariant transduction suggests a homology among DNA sequences.

Table 5. Transduction in B. thuringiensis

Phage	*Serotype*		*Transduced marker*	*Transduction frequency*[a]
	Donor	*Recipient*		
Tg13	*Gal*[b]	*Gal*	Thy^+	2.5×10^{-5}
			Ade^+	3.7×10^{-6}
			Gua^+	5.8×10^{-6}
			Ura^+	1.6×10^{-6}
			Trp^+	9.2×10^{-6}
			Tet^r	2.0×10^{-6}
Tg13	*Gal*	*Den*	Trp^+	6.0×10^{-7}
Tg13	*Den*	*Gal*	Gua^+	5.2×10^{-7}
Tg18	*Gal*	*Gal*	Thy^+	4.1×10^{-7}
			Ade^+	3.2×10^{-7}
			Gua^+	1.8×10^{-7}
CP55	*Gal*	*Gal*	Thy^+	7.0×10^{-7}
			Gua^+	2.0×10^{-7}
			Str^r	1.5×10^{-7}
CP55	*Isr*	*Isr*	Trp^+	1.0×10^{-6}
CP55	*Isr*	*Gal*	Ery^r	4.0×10^{-6}
CP55	*Gal*	*Isr*	Str^r	5.0×10^{-6}

[a]*Reversion frequency of mutations used less than* 10^{-8}

[b]*Serotypes: Gal, galleriae; Den, dendrolimus; Isr, israelensus*

C. Protoplast Fusion

This technique was adapted to B. thuringiensis var. galleriae and studied using multiply marked strains (Belykh et al., 1979; Azizbekyan and Belykh, 1981). UV irradiation of protoplast mixtures has been shown to increase recombination frequency. The frequency of appearance of "primary" colonies on selective media was 10^{-4} to 10^{-5}. Clonal analysis of "primary" colonies revealed the following classes: 1) mixed clones with recombinants maintained nonstably in a number of generations; 2) clones consisting of mixed populations of stable forms (parental or recombinant); and 3) clones yielding stable recombinants (Grigoryevan and Azizbekyan, 1980; Azizbekyan et al., 1982). This method can be used, for example, for obtaining useful forms based on interspecies recombinants. We used B. thuringiensis var. galleriae 48(351) Rif^r Str^r and B. cereus

Table 6. Phage Sensitivity of Recombinants Obtained in Protoplast fusion of B. cereus x B. thuringiensis

Strain		Efficiency of phage plating[a]				
		Tg4	Tg12	Tg13	Td14	Td15
B. thuringiensis 48S		1	1	1	1	1
B. thuringiensis 56R		$<10^{-4}$	1	1	1	1
B. cereus CP7(pBC16)		$<10^{-6}$	10^{-4}	$<10^{-7}$	10^{-7}	$<5 \cdot 10^{-7}$
Recombinants	1		$5 \cdot 10^{-2}$	$<10^{-7}$		
	2	$<10^{-6}$	$4 \cdot 10^{-4}$	$<10^{-7}$		
B. thuringiensis	5	$<10^{-6}$	$5 \cdot 10^{-2}$	$<10^{-7}$		
48S x *B. cereus*	9	$<10^{-6}$	$4 \cdot 10^{-3}$	$<10^{-7}$		
GP-7 (pBC16)	10	$<10^{-6}$	$4 \cdot 10^{-3}$	$<10^{-7}$		
	20	$<10^{-6}$	10^{-3}	$6 \cdot 10^{-4}$		
	29		$2 \cdot 10^{-5}$		$5 \cdot 10^{-3}$	$<5 \cdot 10^{-7}$
	35	$<10^{-6}$	10^{-4}		$5 \cdot 10^{-2}$	$<5 \cdot 10^{-7}$
	44	$<10^{-6}$	$2 \cdot 10^{-2}$	$<10^{-7}$		
	65		10^{-4}		10^{-2}	$<5 \cdot 10^{-7}$
	68	$<10^{-6}$	10^{-1}	$<10^{-7}$		
	70	$<10^{-6}$	$2 \cdot 10^{-2}$	$8 \cdot 10^{-4}$		
Recombinants	51	$<10^{-4}$	1	1		
B. thuringiensis	52	$<10^{-4}$	1	1		
56R x *B. cereus* GP-7						

[a]*Phage titer on B. thuringiensis 48S strains is given as 1*

GP7 (pBC16) strains (Belykh et al., 1983). The plasmid pBC16 specifies resistance to tetracycline. The frequency of Rif^r Tc^r clones occurrence was 10^{-5} to 10^{-6}. In these clones plasmid pBC16 was physically identified. Changes in phage sensitivity of recombinants are regarded as evidence for the transfer of other markers, in addition to pBC16 (Table 6). The plasmid pBC16 itself does not lead to a change in phage sensitivity. However, an incidence of the plasmid changing cell sensitivity to phage has been recorded. Phage sensitivity of cells responsible for chloramphenicol resistance was changed after transformation of protoplasts with pC194 plasmid (Table 7).

A decrease in efficiency of phage propagation is not associated with the change in absorption, as shown in model experiments, and cannot be explained by modification, since

Table 7. Phage Sensitivity of Tc^r and Cm^r Transformants

Indicator strain	Efficiency of Phage Plating		
	Tg4	Tg13	Tg27
69-6	1	1	1
69-6 Tc^r(pBC16)	1	1	1
69-6 Cm^r(pC194)	1	10^{-2} to 10^{-3}	10^{-3}
69-C Cm^s[(a)]	1	1	1

[(a)] Strain 69-C Cm^s obtained after curing the plasmid containing 69-6 Cm^r(pC194) strain

Tg13 and Tg27 phage grown on Cm^r transductants still had a limited efficiency of plating on a strain bearing pC194 plasmid.

This does not mean that B. thuringiensis bacteria lack restriction and modification systems. An impact of the previous host could be traced in the course of plasmid transformaion and phage infection. At present, a restriction enzyme belonging to class II has been isolated and purified.

IV. SOME PERSPECTIVES

Success in strain construction is based nowadays on the state of our knowledge of the genetics of a microbe and availability of cloning systems. B. thuringiensis bacteria are approaching this stage. A set of markered strains and systems of genetic transfer, such as transduction, protoplast fusion, plasmid transformation, conjugation-like processes, are available.

Unraveling of the molecular basis of the toxic action of crystalline proteins and revealing of the structural organization of Δ-endotoxins are a near possibility. We are aware that a large set of multicopied, stably-inherited plasmids exist in B. thuringiensis. So, what could be done in the field of applied science on the basis of these achievements?

It seems unlikely to augment Δ-endotoxin yield, since it already amounts to 30% of the cell weight. Still, it may be possible to alter its quality. In B. thuringiensis var. galleriae one crystal is formed by two proteins. In this way strains having a widened spectrum of action could be constructed. It seems worthwhile to elucidate the role of bacilli proteases and to obtain strains having an optimal level of yield, which could lead to an increase in toxicity for insects or even to change the action spectrum. One can utilize nonsporulating variants, this probably being congenial for the environment (Noshiitsutsuji-uwo et al., 1975).

Cryptic plasmids may present a basis for stable vectors, provided that genes for resistance to antibiotics (or other selectable markers) are introduced into these plasmids. The latter may also serve as a source of par genes which stabilize the inheritance of heterologous plasmids.

Since B. thuringiensis var. kurstaki has a long history of large scale application, it is quite feasible that the shortest way of obtaining preparations, on the basis of toxins of israelensis or of B. sphaericus, is transfer of corresponding toxins into B. thuringiensis var. kurstaki.

REFERENCES

Azizbekyan, R.R. and Belykh, R.A. (1981). **Genetika 17,** 1936.

Azizbekyan, R.R., Belykh, R.A and Stepanova, T.V. (1982). **Dokl AN SSSR 262,** 226.

de Barjac, H. (1970). **C.r. Acad. Sci. 270D,** 2227.

Belykh, R.A., Stepanova, T.V. and Azizbekyan, R.R. (1983). In press.

Belykh, R.A., Yakubova, P.M. and Azizbekyan, R.R. (1979). **Genetika 15, N 5,** 837.

Bulla, L.A. Jr., Kramer, K.J., Cox, D.J., Jones, B.L., Davidson, L.I. and Lookhart, G.L. (1981). **J. Biol. Chem. 256,** 3000.

Chestukhina, G.G., Ephremyan, A.S., Gaida, A.B., Osterman, A.L., Khodova, O.M. and Stepanov., V.M. (1982). **Bioorganich. Biokhimiya 8,** 1649.

Chestukhina, G.G., Kostina, L.I., Mikhailova, A.L., Tyurin, S.A., Klepikova, F.S. and Stepanov, V.M. (1982). **Arch. Microbiol. 132,** 159.

Chestukhina, G.G., Zalunin, I.A., Kostina, L.I., Kotova, T.S., Katrukha, S.P. and Stepanov, V.M. (1980). **Biochem. J. 187,** 457.

Grigoryeva, T.M. and Azizbekyan, R.R. (1980). **Genetika 16,** 1786.

Huber, H.E., Lüthy, P., Ebersold, H.-R. and Cordier, J.-L. (1981). **Arch. Microbiol. 129,** 14.

LeCadet, M.M. and Martouret, D. (1967). **J. Invert. Pathol. 9,** 322.

Nishiitsutsuji-uwo, J. Wakisaka, Y. and Mamoru, E. (1975). **J. Invert. Pathol. 25**, 255.

Pogosbekove, M.R. and Azizbekyan, R.R. (1981). **Genetika 17**, 609.

Pogosbekova, M.R. and Azizbekyan, R.R. (1983). In press.

Stepanov, V.M., Chestukhina, g.g., Rudenskaya, G.N., Epremyan, A.S., Osterman, A.L., Khodova, O.M. and Belyanova, L.P. (1981). **Biochem. Biophys. Res. Commun. 100**, 1680.

Stepanova, T.V. and Azizbekyan, R.R. (1983). **Dokl. AN SSSR**, in press.

Thorne, C. (1978). **Appl. Environ. Microbiol. 35**, 1109.

Tyrrell, D.J., Bulla, L.A., Jr., Andrews, R.E., Jr., Kramer, K.J., Davidson, L.J. and Nordin, P.H. (1981). **J. Bacteriol. 145**, 1052.

Zalunin, I.A., Chestukhina, G.g. and Stepanov, V.M. (1979). **Biokhimya 44**, 693.

REGULATION OF BACILLUS THURINGIENSIS PROTOXIN PRODUCTION[1]

Arthur I. Aronson
William Beckman
Scott A. Minnich

Department of Biological Sciences
Purdue University
West Lafayette, Indiana

I. INTRODUCTION

The formation of a parasporal body or crystalline inclusion in Bacillus thuringiensis subspecies generally occurs 2 to 3 hours after the end of exponential growth, i.e. after completion of the forespore septum (Young and Fitz-James, 1959; Somerville, 1971; Aronson and Fitz-James, 1976). Immunological studies of subspecies kurstaki confirmed the microscopic studies (Monro, 1961a; 1961b; Andrews et al., 1981). The one exception to date is Bacillus medusa which forms an inclusion commencing at the end of exponential growth (Aronson and Fitz-James, 1976). In order to synthesize the amount of protoxin protein found in these crystals (assuming one molecular species), about 25 to 30% of the protein synthetic activity at the time of formation must be devoted to the synthesis of this one protein species. Clearly the cell requires elaborate regulatory signals to ensure production of the protoxin at a defined time and in quantities necessary to form the inclusion.

During the study of plasmid curing of B. thuringiensis subspecies kurstaki (HD-1), J. González and B. Carlton (personal communication) found a derivative, HD1-9, that did not form crystals when cultured at 30°C even though a plasmid of

[1]*This research was supported by a grant from the National Science Foundation and Showalter Fund at Purdue University.*

ISBN 0-12-274160-9

29 Md implicated in protoxin synthesis (Held et al., 1982) was present. We have continued studies of this strain and found protoxin production to be conditional. This phenotype could be transferred from any HD-1 strain to Bacillus cereus by cell mating (González et al., 1982) and appeared to be dependent on the transfer of a 29 Md plasmid. The ability to transfer this phenotype to naturally acrystalliferous B. cereus permitted further study of the role of plasmid genes in the regulation of protoxin synthesis.

II. MATERIALS AND METHODS

More lab Techniques

In Table 1 are listed bacterial strains. Bacteria were grown and sporulation achieved in an enriched G-Tris (Aronson et al., 1971) or a minimal medium. The latter was G-Tris medium with the yeast extract replaced by 0.2% (w/v) sodium glutamate (Nickerson and Bulla, 1975). Spores and crystals were usually formed on solid media with plates incubated for 36 hours at 30°C or 32°C and 4 to 5 days at 25°C. They were scrapped off in distilled water, washed once with 1 M NaCl and 4 to 5 times with water. Dilutions of the final suspensions were counted in a Petroff Hauser chamber and equal numbers of spores (5×10^8 to 10^9) were pelleted in a microfuge. The pellets were equilibrated with 20 to 30 µl UDS buffer: 0.05 M cyclohexylaminoethane sulfonic acid (CHES), 6 M urea, 1% sodium dodecyl sulfate (SDS), 50 mM dithioerythritol, 2 mM phenylmethylsulfonyl fluoride (PMSF) pH 9.6, suspended in 20 µl UDS, placed in boiling water for 2 minutes and then at 37°C for 45 minutes. After centrifugation for 5 minutes in a microfuge, the pellets were resuspended in 15 µl UDS and placed at 37°C for 40 minutes. The supernatants were pooled and aliquots run on 5 to 20% linear gradient SDS-polyacrylamide gels at 35 mA for 16 hours with circulating buffer (Aronson et al., 1982). Gels were either stained or prepared for transfer to nitrocellulose (Towbin et al., 1979) and treatment with antibody plus ^{125}I protein A.

Either spores plus crystals per se or extracts were also directly spotted (10^5 to 5×10^5 spores) on Whatman no. 1 discs, placed on a filter soaked with 0.1 N NaOH for 10 minutes at 25°C, then to a filter with 0.1 M Tris, pH 8.0, and finally equilibrated with 0.05 M sodium phosphate, pH 8.5. The filter papers were blotted and treated with antibody and finally ^{125}I protein A or ^{125}I rabbit anti-mouse serum. Rabbit antibodies were prepared against purified crystals (Aronson et al., 1982) of HD73 or kurstaki or crystal proteins solubilized by titrating to pH 12 with

Table 1. Bacterial Strains

Strain	Phenotype	Plasmids (Md)	Source
B. thuringiensis subsp. *kurstaki*, HD-1	Cry^+	125, 100, 52/51, 44, 29, 9.3, 5.4/5, 2/4.9	B. Carlton, University of Georgia
B. thuringiensis subsp. *kurstaki*, HD-7	Cry^+	110, 52, 44, 19, 5.2/4.9	B. Carlton, University of Georgia
B. thuringiensis subsp. *kurstaki*, HD1-9	Cry^+/25°C Cry^-/30°C	52, 44, 29, 5.2/4.9	B. Carlton, University of Georgia
B. cereus 569	Cry^-	150, 8	C. Thorne, University of Massachusetts
B. cereus 569K	Cry^-, Trp, Str^R	150, 8	EMS treatment of *B. cereus* 569 Str^R spores[a]
B. thuringiensis HD73	Cry^+	50, 7.5, 5.4/5.2/4.9	Bacillus Genetics Culture Center

[a]Ito and Spizizen, 1971

1 M NaOH (Bulla et al., 1981) and then dialyzing against 0.05 M sodium phosphate, pH 8.0. Antisera were purified by DEAE-chromatography (Fahey, 1967) followed by precipitation in 50% saturation $(NH_4)_2SO_4$ and stored in small vials at -10°C.

Monoclonal antibodies to kurstaki crystal suspensions were prepared in Balb/c mice. Clones were injected into the peritoneal cavity of mice, tapped periodically and the fluid was stored at -10°C. The latter preparations reacted with the 134,000 protoxin and to some extent with the 65,000 toxin (detected with ^{125}I rabbit anti-mouse serum) and were highly specific in that there was no cross reaction with protoxin extracted from the closely related B. thuringiensis HD73 crystals (Krywienczyk et al., 1978) in contrast to the kurstaki rabbit antibody. The HD73 crystal rabbit antibody reacted strongly with HD73 crystal extracts and less well with kurstaki crystal extracts.

Plasmid screening was done by growing cells overnight on LB agar, transferring to 3 ml LB broth and incubating for 3 to 4 hours at 30°C until early- to mid-exponential growth. Protoplasts were prepared and lysed on agarose gels as described by Gonzalez et al. (1982) except that 0.6% gels were used. After photographing, some gels were treated with 0.1 N HCl for 5 minutes, transferred to nitrocellulose and probed with a ^{32}P-labeled EcoRI fragment containing coding sequences for the kurstaki chromosomal protoxin gene (Held et al., 1982).

III. RESULTS

A. Conditional Expression of Protoxin in kurstaki Derivatives

Protoxin genes in B. thuringiensis subsp. kurstaki are present in a 29 Md plasmid as well as chromosomal DNA (Held et al., 1982). González and Carlton (personal communication) isolated, through a series of steps involving plasmid loss (spontaneous and growth at 42°C), a kurstaki derivative, HD1-9, that was acrystalliferous even though the 29 Md plasmid was present. The parental strain, HD1-7, differed only in the presence of a 110 Md plasmid (Table 1 and Figure 1) implicating that size class in protoxin synthesis. We initially confirmed the presence of two copies of the protoxin gene in both strains. As previously described (Held et al., 1982) there is a single PvuII fragment from the plasmids and two PvuII fragments from the chromosomal gene that reacted with the probe.

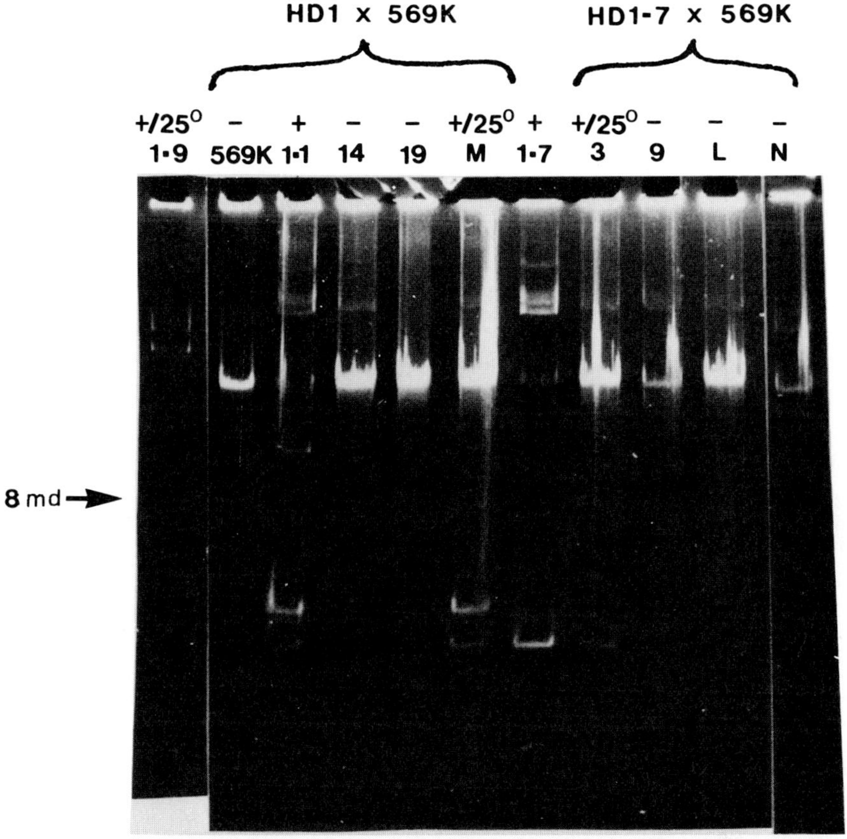

Figure 1. Agarose gel electrophoresis of plasmid mini-preps, prepared as described in Materials and Methods, of B. thuringiensis subsp. kurstaki variants and various transcipients as indicated on the figure (also see Table 2). + indicates crystal formation by the strain at either 25°C or 30°C; - indicates no crystals seen in the phase microscope at either temperature or in any antibody tests as in Figure 5; +/25 indicates crystal formation only when cultures were incubated at 25°C. In all cases, the transcipients produced less protoxin than the parental strains (see Figure 4). Lanes labeled 1-9 and N were from separate gels.

Protoxin synthesis was found in HD1-9 by treating a Western transfer of extracts of sporulating cells grown at 30°C with antibody to kurstaki crystals but the amount was less than the parental strains, HD1-7 or HD1 (unpublished results). Conditional expression was therefore suspected

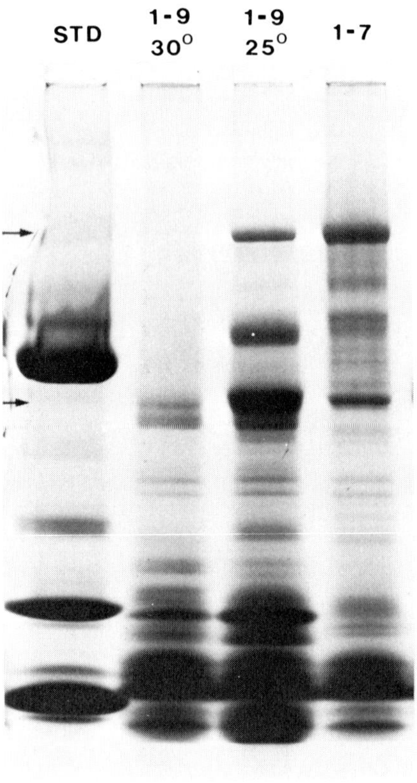

Figure 2. Electrophoretic profile of the proteins in extracts of spores plus crystals of B. thuringiensis subsp. kurstaki derivatives grown at 25°C or 30°C. Spores plus crystals were formed on G-Tris agar and were washed, counted and extracted as described in Materials and Methods. Top arrow indicates position of 134,000 protoxin polypeptide; lower arrow is position of ca. 60,000 degradation product of protoxin. Standards from top to bottom are bovine serum albumin (67,000), chymotrypsinogen (25,000) and cytochrome c (12,700). The profile for strain HD1-7 is for a 30°C preparation; essentially identical results were obtained for spores and crystals formed at 25°C.

and it was indeed found that when cells were incubated at 25°C rather than 30 to 32°C, crystals were seen in the phase microscope and a protein band of ca. 134,000 (reacting with kurstaki protoxin antibody) was detected in SDS-acrylamide gels (Figure 2). This band was seen only in cells grown at 25°C in contrast to the parental strain, HD1-7. Assuming that the only difference between HD1-7 and HD1-9 was the absence of a 110 Md plasmid from the latter, a role for this plasmid in the control of protoxin synthesis was implied. Unfortunately, it is not yet feasible to isolate this large plasmid and reintroduce it into cells or protoplasts.

Fortuitously, it was also found that the conditional phenotype of HD1-9 was suppressed in a cycloserine resistant derivative if the medium contained cycloserine. The growth rate at 30°C in the presence of cycloserine was somewhat less than without the antibiotic so some "catabolic" effect may be involved.

The loss of the 110 Md plasmid appeared to unmask the conditional phenotype implying that some property of the protoxin gene (regulatory or structural regions) or another 29 Md-encoded function was required for protoxin expression. Plasmids were transferred therefore by cell mating (González et al., 1982) from various kurstaki derivatives to B. cereus 569 (Table 2), a strain known to lack either copy of the protoxin gene (W. Beckman, unpublished results). It was found that the frequency of plasmid transfer from kurstaki was very low, however, so it was not feasible to detect transcipients by randomly picking B. cereus colonies from G-Tris-streptomycin plates. Plasmid-containing transcipients could be readily detected by using a B. cereus 569 auxotroph in the mating and selecting for B. cereus prototrophs on minimal agar containing streptomycin. Almost every prototroph contained one or more plasmids but transfer of chromosomal genes must also take place. The latter is not a necessary condition for plasmid transfer since in some mating (i.e. HD73 x B. cereus 569K) there is a high frequency (30-60%) of plasmid transfer without restoration of prototrophy. In the experiments summarized in Table 2, however, transferred chromosomal genes may play a role in the expression of the protoxin gene.

In all cases, whether the donor strains were conditional or not, the transcipients only produced protoxin at 25°C, if at all. The conditional property was not due to the recipient strain, B. cereus 569, since transfer of protoxin synthesis from B. thuringiensis HD73 into B. cereus 569 wild-type (or two different auxotrophs) resulted in protoxin synthesis at both 25°C and 30°C (Table 2 and Figure 3).

The transfer of the 29 Md plasmid appeared to be a necessary but not sufficient condition for protoxin synthesis (Table 2 and Figure 1). Strains that contained only the 29 Md plasmid (9,14,19,L,K_{11}) or this one plus the 44 Md plasmid (N) produced few if any crystals. Protoxin was synthesized at 25°C if both the 29 Md and one or more small plasmids of 4 to 6 Md were present (M,3,K_4 in Table 2) but

Table 2. Conditional Production of Protoxin in Transcipients

Transcipients	Growth conditions G/25°C	G/30°C	Profile of plasmids transferred to B. cereus (Md)
B. cereus 569K	-	-	see Table 1
HD-1 x B. cereus 569K			
14	-	-	29
19	-	-	29
M	+	-	29, ca. 5
HD1-1	++	++	see Table 1
HD1-7 x B. cereus 569K			
L, 9	±	-	29
N	±	-	44, 29
3	+	-	29, ca. 5
HD1-7	++	++	see Table 1
HD1-9 x B. cereus 569K			
K_4	+	-	44, 29, ca. 5
K_{11}	-	-	29
HD1-9	++	-	see Table 1
HD73 x B. cereus 569K			
B_4	+	-	50
C_{1-4}	+	+	50, ca. 5
HD73	++	++	see Table 1

+, -, see legend to Figure 1; ++, numerous crystals in phase microscope, strong staining bands on gels; ±, occasional crystals in phase microscope, barely detectable staining band on gels when extracts from 10^9 spores were fractionated.

in all cases, the transcipients produced much less protoxin than the parental strains, for example HD1-7 and transcipient 3 (Figure 4). In no case was the total array of HD1 plasmids transferred so the function of other plasmids in protoxin synthesis is not known but at least the small ones appeared to have a role in the amount produced.

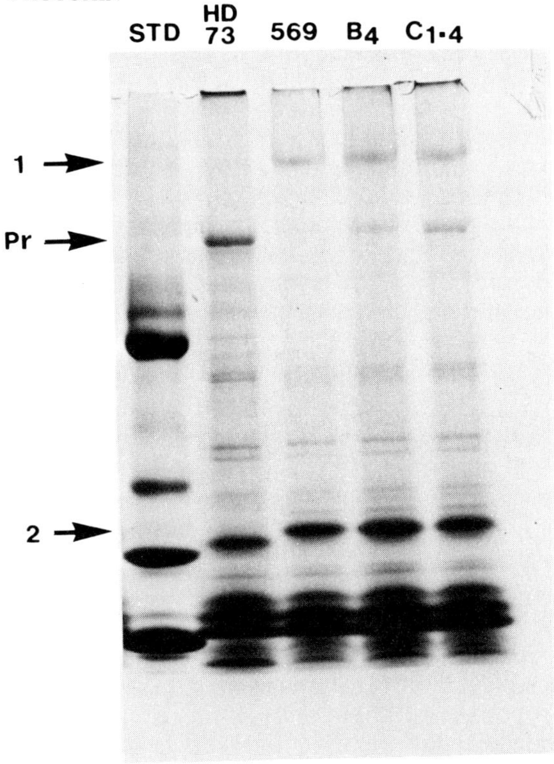

Figure 3. Gel electrophoresis of spore and crystal extracts of B. thuringiensis HD73, B. cereus 569 and two transcipients, B4 and C_{1-4}. B_4 received only the 50 Md plasmid from HD73, whereas C_{1-4} received the 50 Md and 2 plasmids of ca. 5 Md. The spores plus crystals were scrapped from G-Tris plates incubated at 30°C and were washed, counted and extracted as described in Materials and Methods. Arrow labeled 1 indicates position of B. cereus exosporial protein band; arrow Pr indicates position of 134,000 protoxin protein; arrow 2 indicates position of ca. 26,000 spore coat protein not found in HD73 extracts. Other major low molecular weight bands are spore coat polypeptides.

The fact that similar results were obtained whether nonconditional strains such as HD1 or HD1-7 or a conditional strain, HD1-9, were mated with B. cereus indicated that temperature sensitivity was probably an inherent property of the 29 Md plasmid (unless a chromosomal gene was involved and was always transferred). The lack of temperature sensitivity in kurstaki is thus due to other properties of the strain, possibly one or more cryptic plasmids.

experiment, samples (10^5 to 5×10^5 spores) were spotted on Whatman no. 1 filters and probed with kurstaki crystal antibody plus ^{125}I protein A to confirm the other measurements of protoxin synthesis. A shift to 32°C any time after mid-exponential growth phase permitted crystal formation at 32°C. In all cases, protoxin synthesis commenced several hours after the end of exponential growth. In a shift down, protoxin synthesis occurred as long as the shift was well before the normal time of synthesis. The later the shift, the fewer the number and smaller the size of the crystals.

The temperature sensitive "regulator" appeared to accumulate continuously during growth and sporulation. Apparently cells could synthesize enough prior to the final one to two doublings in this medium to function as a positive regulator (inducer) and permit protoxin synthesis at 32°C.

C. Protoxin Expression in HD73 Is Not Conditional and Appears to Require Only the 50 Md Plasmid

B. thuringiensis HD73 is very closely related to kurstaki in toxicity profile, antigenic cross reactivity of the protoxin polypeptide (Krywienczyk et al., 1978) and hybridization of a digest of total DNA with a 4.6 kb EcoRI fragment from kurstaki containing the protoxin gene. In this case, transfer of the 50 Md plasmid to B. cereus 569 was sufficient for protoxin synthesis (Table 2 and Figure 3) at either 25°C or 30°C. The plasmid transfer frequency was sufficiently high that it was not necessary to select prototrophs so the extent of chromosome transfer, if any, is not known.

In some cases, small plasmids of ca. 5 Md were also transferred but there was no effect on the amount of protoxin synthesized (Figure 3). In addition, strain B4 containing only the 50 Md plasmid from HD73 (plus >100 Md and 8 Md plasmids indigenous to B. cereus 569) was again mated with HD73. Transcipients now containing 1 or 2 plasmids of ca. 5 Md in addition to the 50 Md plasmid were found but there was no affect on protoxin synthesis (unpublished results). In all cases, however, the amount of protoxin produced by these transcipients was less than that formed by the parental strain HD73 (confirmed by bioassay on Manduca sexta larvae in collaboration with Dr. Peter Dunn).

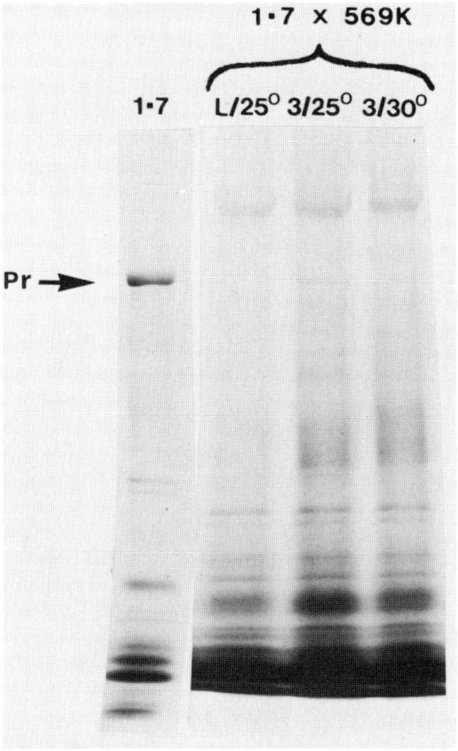

Figure 4. Gel electrophoresis profile of proteins in extracts of 6 x 10^8 spores (plus crystals) of B. thuringiensis subsp. kurstaki HD1-7 and various trancipients from the mating of HD1-7 and B. cereus 569K (see Table 2). Cells were grown and sporulated on G-Tris agar plates incubated at 25 °C or 30 °C. Spores were suspended in distilled water, washed, counted and extracted as described in Materials and Methods. Arrow Pr indicates position of 134,000 protoxin polypeptide.

B. Control of Conditional Synthesis of Protoxin is Expressed During Exponential Growth

Strain HD1-9 was incubated in G-Tris medium in a side arm flask at either 25°C or 32°C. At various times, 5 ml were removed to flasks for a shift up or down and these flasks were incubated until sporulation was complete. Protoxin synthesis was scored by examination for crystals in the phase microscope and by electrophoresis of spore plus crystal extracts on SDS-acrylamide gels. In a duplicate

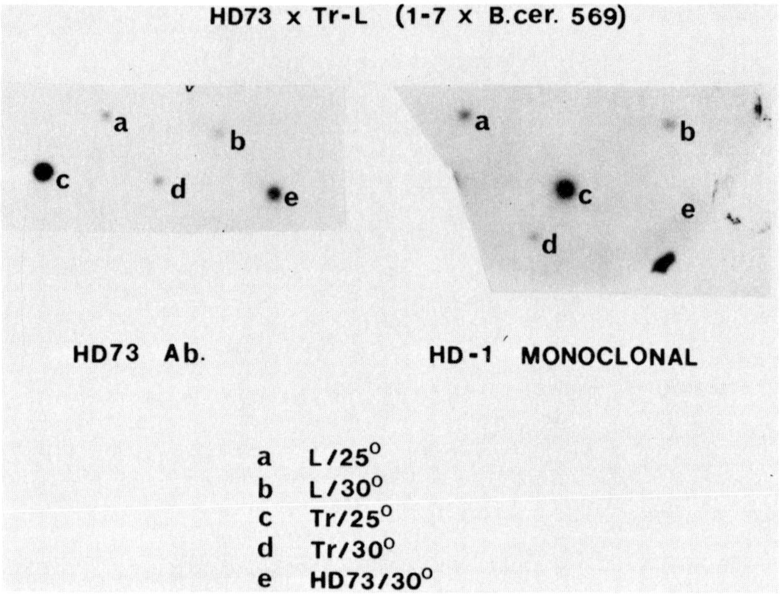

Figure 5. Conditional expression of protoxin antigen in B. cereus transcipient (Tr) from a mating of B. thuringiensis HD73 with B. cereus transcipient 1-7L (see Table 2). Spores and crystals were formed on G-Tris agar plates incubated at 25°C and 30°C. Portions of the suspensions were washed twice with distilled water, the spores counted in a Petroff Hauser chamber and 2 x 10^5 spores (plus crystals) of each spotted on Whatman no. 1 filter paper. The papers were treated as described in Materials and Methods, incubated either with HD73 crystal antibody or monoclonal antibody to kurstaki protoxin and then with ^{125}I protein A or ^{125}I rabbit anti-mouse serum.

D. Regulation of Conditional Expression in kurstaki is Trans-Acting and Dominant

It was possible to distinguish parasporal protein produced by the closely related kurstaki and HD73 strains (Krywienczyk et al., 1978). Kurstaki monoclonal antibodies did not react with HD73 parasporal protein while HD73 parasporal antibody reacted much better with the homologous preparation than with kurstaki (Figure 5). In this case, HD73 was mated with a kurstaki HD1-7 transcipient, L in Table 2, i.e. a B. cereus strain containing the 29 Md plasmid from HD1-7. Transcipients were found that could produce both HD73 and kurstaki protoxin antigens but again only at 25°C (Figure 5).

B. cereus subsp. israelensis produced a parasporal body unique in structure (Charles and de Barjac, 1982), size of polypeptides (Aronson et al., 1982) and toxicity specific to Dipteran larvae. There was no cross reactivity of antibody to israelensis parasporal proteins with kurstaki protoxin nor vice versa. The capacity to synthesize israelensis parasporal antigen was transferred to a kurstaki HD1-9 auxotroph and both antigens were produced by the transcipient but only at 25°C.

Is likely, therefore, that the factor controlling conditional protoxin synthesis was encoded by the 29 Md plasmid, was trans-acting and was "dominant" over presumptive regulatory factors produced by HD73 or B. cereus subsp. israelensis plasmids.

IV. DISCUSSION

The uncovering of the conditional phenotype in B. thuringiensis subsp. kurstaki and the ability to transfer the capacity for protoxin synthesis to B. cereus has enabled us to unravel regulatory features of protoxin synthesis. Kurstaki derivatives appeared to contain a latent conditional phenotype that was unmasked either by loss of the 110 Md plasmid in deriving HD1-9 from HD1-7 or by transfer of the 29 Md plasmid to B. cereus 569. A role for at least some of the cryptic plasmids in regulating protoxin synthesis is supported by a) the uncovering of a conditional phenotype by loss of a 110 Md plasmid in HD1-9 and b) the increased synthesis of protoxin in transcipients containing 1 or 2, 5 to 6 Md plasmids in addition to the 29 Md protoxin-encoding plasmid. In contrast, the small plasmids in HD73 did not seem to have a function in protoxin production. The results with kurstaki, however, imply that plasmid curing experiments, per se, may be misleading as to whether or not a specific plasmid that was lost contained the protoxin gene (Gonzáles et al., 1981; Faust et al., 1983). A direct demonstration of the absence of the coding sequences is required.

Conditional expression in kurstaki seemed to be dependent on both the "catabolic" properties of the cell and a function encoded by the 29 Md plasmid. The former is implied by a) the uncovering of temperature sensitivity in HD1-9 by loss of a 110 Md plasmid from HD1-7 and b) the suppression of the conditional phenotype in an HD1-9 cycloserine resistant mutant. The mutant grew somewhat slower at

30°C in the presence of cycloserine and an altered catabolic state of the cell may be important in overcoming the conditional phenotype.

The 29 Md plasmid also appeared to be involved in regulation since all transcipients were conditional, not only for the kurstaki protoxin but for synthesis of non-temperature sensitive protoxin produced by other strains. For the present, we have assumed that the chromosomal genes that were also transferred to B. cereus (no evidence for transfer of the chromosomal protoxin gene) have no role in the conditional synthesis of protoxin. The factor encoded by the kurstaki 29 Md plasmid would thus be trans-acting and dominant not unlike some mutant lac repressors (Jobe et al., 1972). The shift up experiments would best fit these results by assuming constitutive synthesis of an inducer by the 29 Md plasmid. Accumulation of sufficient inducer by growth at 25°C until mid-exponential phase would permit protoxin synthesis at 32°C much later during sporulation. A second assumption is that the inducer once synthesized is stable at 32°C, perhaps by formation of oligomers.

One puzzling result is the inability of all transcipients to produce as much protoxin in B. cereus as in the parental strain, although HD73 transcipients produced amounts much closer to the parental strain than did kurstaki transcipients. These B. thuringiensis strains are very closely related to B. cereus and it is unlikely that they differ markedly in catabolic properties. Differences in expression may be due to the number of plasmid copies of the protoxin gene and/or the presence of a chromosomal protoxin gene copy in kurstaki and HD73. This latter gene differed from the plasmid gene in restriction enzyme profile (W. Beckman, unpublished results) and extent of expression in E. coli (W. Beckman and P. Dunn, unpublished results). The chromosomal gene was apparently not sufficient since many mutants containing only this gene but devoid of the 29 Md plasmid (and most other kurstaki plasmids) failed to produce measurable amounts of protoxin (Stahly et al., 1978) but this chromosomal gene cloned into an E. coli vector was functional (Held et al., 1982). Obviously, further studies are required to explore the possible interaction of the two protoxin genes, the importance of gene copy number and catabolic factors.

ACKNOWLEDGMENTS

Dr. Peter Dunn of the Department of Entomology performed all toxicity tests; Ms. Patricia Hillman provided very able technical assistance. We especially thank Mr. José González and Dr. B. Carlton of the University of Georgia for providing their HD-1 derivatives with pertinent data.

REFERENCES

Andrews, R.E., Jr., Bechtel, D.B., Campbell, B.J., Davidson, L.I. and Bulla, L.A., Jr. (1981). In Sporulation and Germination (H.S. Levinson, A.L. Sonenshein and D.J. Tipper, eds.) p. 174, American Society for Microbiology, Washington, DC.

Aronson, A.I., Angelo, N. and Holt, S.C. (1971). **J. Bacteriol. 106**, 1016.

Aronson, A.I. and Fitz-James, P. (1976). **Bacteriol. Rev. 40**, 360.

Aronson, A.I., Tyrell, D.J., Fitz-James, P.C. and Bulla, L.A., Jr. (1982). **J. Bacteriol. 151**, 399.

Bulla, L.A., Jr., Kramer, K.J., Cox, D.J., Jones, B.L., Davidson, L.I. and Lookhart, G.L. (1981). **J. Biol. Chem. 256**, 3000.

Charles, J.F. and de Barjac, H. (1982). **Ann. Microbiol.** (Inst. Pasteur) **113A**, 425.

Fahey, J.L. (1967). In Methods in Immunology and Immunochemistry, Vol. I (C.A. Williams and M.W. Chase, eds.) p. 321, Academic Press, New York.

Faust, R.M., Abe, K., Held, G.A., Iizuka, T., Bulla, L.A., Jr. and Meyers, C.L. (1983). **Plasmid 9**, 98.

González, J.M., Dulmage, H.T. and Carlton, B.C. (1981). **Plasmid 5**, 351.

González, J.M., Jr., Brown, B.J. and Carlton, B.C. (1982). **Proc. Natl. Acad. Sci. USA 79**, 6591.

Held, G.A., Bulla, L.A., Jr., Ferrari, E., Hoch, J.A., Aronson, A.I. and Minnich, S.A. (1982). **Proc. Natl. Acad. Sci. USA** 79, 6065.

Ito, J. and Spizizen, J. (1971). **Mutat. Res. 13**, 93.

Jobe, A., Riggs, A.D. and Bourgeois, S. (1972). **J. Mol. Biol. 64**, 181.

Krywienczyk, J., Dulmage, H.T. and Fast, P.G. (1978). **J. Invert. Pathol. 31**, 372.

Monro, R.E. (1961a). **J. Biophys. Biochem. Cytol.** 11, 329.

Monro, R.E. (1961b). **Biochem. J. 81**, 225.

Nickerson, K.W. and Bulla, L.A., Jr. (1975). **J. Bacteriol. 23,** 598.
Somerville, H.J. (1971). **Eur. J. Biochem. 18,** 226.
Stahly, D.P., Dingman, D.W., Bulla, L.A., Jr. and Aronson, A.I. (1978). **Biochem. Biophys. Res. Commun. 84,** 581.
Towbin, H., Staehlin, T. and Gordon, J. (1979). **Proc. Natl. Acad. Sci. USA 76,** 4350.
Young, I.E. and Fitz-James, P.D. (1959). **J. Biophys. Biochem. Cytol. 6,** 483.

STRUCTURAL AND REGULATORY ANALYSIS OF A CLONED BACILLUS THURINGIENSIS CRYSTAL PROTEIN GENE[1]

H. R. Whiteley
H. E. Schnepf
J. W. Kronstad
H. C. Wong

Department of Microbiology and Immunology
University of Washington
Seattle, Washington

I. INTRODUCTION

During sporulation, cells of Bacillus thuringiensis synthesize a large parasporal crystal which contains one or more polypeptides of ca. M_r 135,000. The crystal protein (δ-endotoxin) is lethal to many lepidopteran larvae and is used commerically as a pesticide. We have cloned a gene coding for a crystal protein from a large plasmid of B. thuringiensis subspecies kurstaki (Schnepf and Whiteley, 1981) and have determined the DNA sequence of the promoter region (Wong et al., 1983). An intragenic probe derived from the cloned gene has been used to survey twenty-two strains of B. thuringiensis to determine the location of the gene (Kronstad et al., 1983).

This paper describes the sequence structure of the promoter region for the crystal protein gene, the amino acid composition deduced from the DNA sequence for the entire gene, and the distribution of hydrophilic and hydrophobic amino acids in the protein. Data are also presented that

[1]*This research was supported by USPHS grants GM-20784 and GM-26100 from the National Institute of General Medical Science and by a grant from the Cetus Corporation. H.R.W. is a recipient of Research Career Award K5-GM-442 from the National Institute of General Medical Sciences.*

ISBN 0-12-274160-9

some strains contain more than one crystal protein gene or more than one of three related crystal protein genes.

II. METHODS

Growth of cultures, preparation of plasmids, techniques used in hybridization and the preparation of hybridization probes, immunoblotting, digestion with restriction endonucleases and the electrophoretic separation of plasmids and peptides have been described (Schnepf and Whiteley, 1981; Kronstad et al., 1983). The strain used for cloning the first crystal protein gene was obtained from L. A. Bulla (University of Idaho, Moscow, Idaho) and was first designated B. thuringiensis subspecies kurstaki HD-1 (Schnepf and Whiteley, 1981); this strain had been isolated from a commercial pesticide named "Dipel". Subsequent experiments (Kronstad et al., 1983) showed that this strain has a different complement of plasmids than an HD-1 strain received from H. T. Dulmage (U.S. Cotton Insects Lab, U.S.D.A., Brownsville, Texas). To differentiate between the two strains, the strain used in the first cloning experiments was renamed "HD-1-Dipel". All genes were cloned into pBR322 of Escherichia coli using essentially the same methods as those described by Schnepf and Whiteley (1981). Methods used for the DNA sequence analyses and S1 nuclease mapping have been given by Wong et al. (1983). The hydropathy analysis was performed according to Kyte and Doolittle (1982).

III. RESULTS AND DISCUSSION

A. Gene Structure and Transcription

Detailed electron microscopic studies (Bechtel and Bulla, 1976) showed that deposition of crystals in subspecies kurstaki begins at about stage III of sporulation and that a large, well-defined crystal is produced by about stage IV to stage V. A gene coding for the crystal protein from B. thuringiensis subspecies kurstaki HD-1-Dipel has been cloned (Schnepf and Whiteley, 1981) and used to assay for crystal protein mRNA in a series of samples isolated from sporulating cultures (Wong et al., 1983). The presence of the crystal protein in these samples was monitored by immunoblotting using antibodies specific to a ca. M_r 135,000 peptide isolated from solubilized crystals from the same strain; the amounts of antigen were estimated by ELISA tests. These experiments showed that the crystal protein mRNA appeared 1.5 hours after the onset of the stationary phase and then increased in amount. The synthesis of the crystal protein antigen followed the same kinetics, indicating that expression of this gene is regulated primarily at the level of transcription.

In order to investigate the regulation of transcription in greater detail, we determined the DNA sequence of the gene and the promoter region (Wong et al., 1983; H. E. Schnepf, H. C. Wong and H. R. Whiteley, manuscript in preparation). S1 nuclease mapping using RNAs extracted from B. thuringiensis at various times during sporulation revealed that transcription begins from two adjacent start sites. Synthesis of RNA from the first site ("Bt I") begins 1.5 hours after the onset of stationary phase, increases for the next 2.5 hours and then decreases to virtually zero by 7.5 hours. The second start site ("Bt II") is activated abruptly and strongly at 5.5 hours and transcription continues from this site through the last sampling interval at 7.5 hours. In contrast, transcription of the gene in the recombinant E. coli strain occurs from a separate start site located between Bt I and II and the gene is expressed equally well at all stages of growth.

At present, there is no information concerning the structure of vegetative B. thuringiensis promoters. However, several promoters recognized by the σ^{55}-RNA polymerase from vegetative cells of B. subtilis have been sequenced and a consensus sequence for the -10 and -35 regions has been proposed (Moran et al., 1982). Not surprisingly, the latter are completely different from the -10 and -35 regions corresponding to the two crystal protein start sites. However, some homologies between Bt I and II promoter regions and two B. subtilis sporulation genes (spoVC and spoVG, Moran et al., 1981a; 1981b) have been noted (Wong et al., 1983) and the sequence for an additional sporulation gene (0.3 Kb gene) is now available (M. A. Stephens, N. Lang and R. Losick, personal communication). Comparison of the DNA sequences upstream from Bt I and II with the comparable sequence for spoVG (Moran et al., 1981a) and the 0.3 Kb gene are shown in Figure 1.

Both the B. thuringiensis crystal protein gene and the B. subtilis sporulation genes contain A-T rich sequences upstream from the initiation sites. The spoVG gene also resembles the crystal protein gene in that it contains two overlapping promoters; however, both of these promoters are activated at the same time (1 to 2 hours after the onset of stationary phase) and each is recognized by a different polymerase (Johnson et al., 1983). In contrast, transcrip-

```
-50       -40       -30       -20       -10
AATTAGTTGCACTTTGTGCATTTTTTCATAAGATGAGTCATATGTTTTAAATT  Bt I
ACGAGCAGGATTTCAGAAAAAATCGTGGAATTGATACACTAATGCTTTTATAT  spoVG

-50       -40       -30       -20       -10
AAAATTGATATTTAGTAAAATTAGTTGCACTTTGTGCATTTTTTCATAAGATGAGTCATATGTTTAAATT  Bt II
GGTTTCCAATAATTTTAACGAAAGTTCCATCTGATTTAACAAAAGATAAAAC AGTCACATATTATCGTG  0.3 Kb gene
```

Figure 1. Comparison of crystal protein promoters with two B. subtilis sporulation promoters. The arrows show the start site and direction of transcription. The sequences in spoVG and the 0.3 kb genes that match the Bt I and II sequences have been underlined.

tion of the 0.3 Kb gene occurs after 4 to 5 hours in the stationary phase and apparently requires either a polymerase containing a new sigma factor or the particpiation of another sporulation-specific regulatory peptide(s) (M. A. Stephens, N. Lang and R. Losick, personal communication). As shown in Figure 1, a few of the bases immediately preceding the Bt I and downstream spoVG start sites match; however, there is little or no homology in the rest of the sequence. A greater degree of homology is seen in comparing the Bt II and the 0.3 kb promoters: matching sequences occur around -6 and -30 and also at the start of transcription (Figure 1).

It would be interesting to determine if matching sequences could be found between Bt I and other sporulation genes activated at 1 to 2 hours and between Bt II and sporulating genes transcribed at ca. 5 hours into stationary phase. Possibly, classes of genes possessing similar promoter structures are activated at specific times during sporulation by virtue of the synthesis of sigma subunits which impart different transcriptional specificities to the polymerase. This type of mechanism - i.e., the turning on of transcription of classes of genes by synthesis of new sigma subunits - is known to regulate the development of B. subtilis phages SP82 and SP01 (Lawrie et al., 1977; Talkington and Pero, 1979; Lee and Pero, 1981).

Another related question concerns the structures of the B. thuringiensis RNA polymerases which transcribe the crystal protein gene from the Bt I and II start sites. Since the promoter structures of Bt I and II differ so markedly from the consensus B. subtilis promoter and polymerases from vegetative cells of B. thuringiensis and B. subtilis do not transcribe the cloned gene (J. W. Kronstad and H. R. Whiteley, unpublished observations), it seems clear that sporulation-specific polymerases must be involved. This proposal receives support from the finding that expression of a cloned crystal protein gene in B. subtilis (Klier et al., 1982) occurs only during sporulation. The latter observation also indicates that similar polymerases are present in sporulating cells of these two bacilli.

The 3' terminus of transcription was also determined by S1 nuclease mapping (H. E. Schnepf, H. C. Wong and H. R. Whiteley, manuscript in preparation); the terminus was found to coincide with an inverted repeat sequence which could assume a very stable stem loop structure similar to those reported at the 3' ends of other prokaryotic mRNAs. Based on the S1 mapping and the position of this stem and loop, the size of the crystal protein mRNA is calculated to be 3730 bases. Preliminary analysis of the transcribed sequence does not indicate extensive secondary RNA structure.

B. Amino Acid Composition

The sequenced DNA (4221 bp) includes 3528 bp of coding region flanked by 80 to 90 untranslated bases at the 5' end and by 134 untranslated bases at the 3' end (H. E. Schnepf, H. C. Wong and H. R. Whiteley, manuscript in preparation). The deduced amino acid composition for the crystal protein is given in Table 1 and compared with data obtained by Tyrell et al. (1981) by chemical analysis of purified crystals from a kurstaki strain. In general, there is good agreement between the sets of data. The deduced amino acid sequences gives an M_r of 133,500 for this crystal protein.

It is known (Angus, 1954; Bulla et al., 1979) that the crystal protein is a protoxin which is proteolytically cleaved in the gut of susceptible insects to a toxin of ca. M_r 68,000. We have studied the synthesis of antigenic peptides and the toxicity of extracts in a series of mutants containing Tn5 inserts (Schnepf et al., in preparation). These experiments indicate that the toxic peptide is located in the NH_2-terminal portion of the M_r 135,000 protoxin. A similar conclusion was reached by Chestukhina et al. (1982) on the basis of analyses for the N-terminal methionine.

Figure 2 presents an analysis of the hydropathy (Kyte and Doolittle, 1982) of the crystal protein based on the deduced amino acid sequence. There are two interesting features in the complex pattern generated for this large protein. The first is a hydrophobic region near the NH_2-

Table 1. Amino Acid Composition of Bacillus thruingiensis Subspecies kurstaki Crystal Proteins

	Moles/100 Moles Amino Acids	
	Deduced from nucleotide sequences	Chemically determined[a]
Asp	12.0[b]	13.5
Thr	6.3	6.2
Ser	7.3	8.3
Glu	12.0[c]	12.2
Pro	4.8	4.4
Gly	6.8	7.2
Ala	5.4	5.4
1/2Cys	1.5	2.0
Val	6.9	6.2
Met	0.8	1.0
Ile	6.0	4.9
Leu	8.7	8.2
Tyr	4.4	4.9
Phe	4.6	5.2
Lys	2.8	2.8
His	1.9	1.8
Arg	6.4	6.7
Trp	1.5	0

[a]Tyrell et al., 1981; [b]sum of asp and asn; [c]sum of glu and gln.

terminus (residues 35 to 70) which could be significant if the toxin's mode of action involves cell membrane proteins. A second interesting feature of Figure 2 is the extensive hydrophilic region (residues 650 to 715) near the center of the protoxin -- i.e., near the presumed site of proteolytic cleavage. It would be expected that cleavage would occur at an exteriorly oriented hydrophilic region, accessible to proteases. On the whole, the COOH-terminal half of the molecule, which is ultimately degraded to smaller peptides, contains more hydrophilic regions than the NH_2-terminal half. Additional work on the chemistry of the protein will be required to relate these regions to the secondary and tertiary structure of the protein, to the sites of cleavage to smaller molecular weight peptides and to the possible mechanisms of toxicity of the toxic portion.

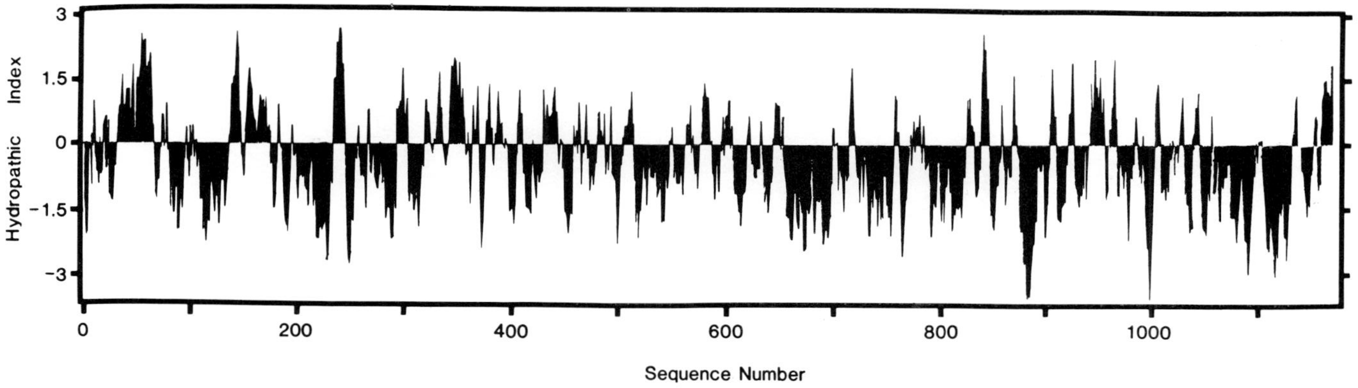

Figure 2. Analysis of hydropathy of the deduced amino acid sequence. The hydropathy index was calculated according to Kyte and Doolittle, 1982, by averaging the values for each 7 amino acids along the sequence. Positive values are hydrophobic and negative values are hydrophilic.

C. Multiple Genes Coding for the Crystal Protein

Several lines of evidence (cloning, curing experiments and plasmid transfer) indicate that the crystal protein genes in various subspecies of B. thuringiensis are located on plasmids (Schnepf and Whiteley, 1981; Held et al., 1982; Klier et al., 1982; Stahley et al., 1978; Gonzalez et al, 1981; 1982). We used an intragenic probe to determine the location of the gene in 22 strains of B. thuringiensis (Kronstad et al., 1983). Hybridization was found predominantly to plasmid DNA (in 17 out of the 18 strains which gave a positive reaction with our probe). Unexpectedly, we found that more than one plasmid hybridized in at least 7 strains. When our intragenic probe was hybridized to HindIII digests of plasmid DNA from 3 strains of subspecies kurstaki and 3 strains of subspecies thuringiensis, we found that one to three restriction fragments hybridized, depending on the strain. These results, as well as the presence of the gene on two or more plasmids in the same strain, suggested that some strains either contain related genes or they contain multiple copies of the same gene. The sizes of the hybridized HindIII restriction fragments and the plasmids in these 6 strains are shown in Table 2. For reasons given below, this group has been provisionally designated as the "A genes".

To investigate the relationship of the genes and the peptides which they encode in the kurstaki and thuringiensis strains, we cloned the "6.6 gene" from the 50 md plasmid

Table 2. "A Genes": HindIII Restriction Fragments and Plasmids that Hybridize with an Intragenic Probe

Strain	*HindIII fragments, Kb*				*Plasmids, Mdal*	
kurstaki,						
HD-1	*6.6*	*5.3*	*4.5*		*~150,**	*44*
HD-1-Dipel	*6.6*		*4.5*		*~150 **	
HD-73	*6.6*					*50*
thuringiensis,						
berliner 1715		*5.3*	*4.5*	*2.3*	*~150,*	*60, 55*
HD-290		*5.3*	*4.5*		*~150,*	*57*
HD-2		*5.3*				*57**

*The cloned genes and the plasmids from which they were derived have been underlined; * indicates a doublet.*

present in strain HD-73 and two "5.3 genes": one from the 44 md plasmid in strain HD-1 and the other from the 57 md plasmid doublet of strain HD-2 (J. W. Kronstad and H. R. Whiteley, manuscript in preparation). The "4.5 gene" was cloned earlier (Schnepf and Whiteley, 1981); this is the gene whose DNA sequence is discussed in the preceding sections. Preliminary results from restriction mapping of recombinant plasmids containing the 4.5, 5.3 and 6.6 "genes" show that although the maps are not identical, many of the HindIII, EcoRI and PvuII sites are the same. A more precise assessment of the degree of relatedness can be obtained by heteroduplex mapping.

On the other hand, electrophoretic separation followed by immunoblotting showed that recombinant E. coli strains containing the "5.3 gene" produced a slightly smaller antigenic peptide than strains containing the "4.5 gene" and the "6.6 gene"; the products of the latter two genes appear to be similar in size. Parallel experiments using solubilized preparations of crystals demonstrated that HD-2 (a source of one of the "5.3 genes") contains a slightly smaller peptide than HD-1-Dipel (4.5 and 6.6 "genes") or HD-73 ("6.6 gene"). In agreement with Calabrese et al. (1980), two peptides were seen in stained gels of solubilized crystals from strain HD-1. The smaller of the two corresponded in mobility to the "5.3 gene" product whereas the larger corresponded to the 4.5 and 6.6 "gene" products; it is not known if both of the latter are expressed in strain HD-1. The presence of more than one peptide in crystals has been noted earlier for other strains as well (Herbert et al., 1971; Calabrese et al, 1980; Yamamoto and McLaughlin, 1981; Chestukhina et al., 1982). Overall, these studies suggest that the three cloned "A genes" are closely related, that at least one may code for a smaller peptide and that more than one gene may be expressed in a single strain.

More direct evidence concerning the latter point comes from experiments using antibodies prepared against purified crystals from subspecies thuringiensis HD-2. These experiments revealed the presence of another crystal protein gene in strain HD-2 (J. W. Kronstad and H. R. Whiteley, manuscript in preparation). This gene, provisionally designated as "B gene", was cloned from the 57 md plasmid doublet. Preliminary analyses of the cloned gene indicate that the restriction map is completely different from that of the three "A genes". Furthermore, the peptide produced by the recombinant E. coli strain containing the cloned "B gene" reacts with the HD-2 antibody preparation but not with the antibodies to the "A gene" crystal proteins and is larger than the peptides produced by the recombinant strains containing "A genes". When crystals from HD-2 were solubilized, electrophoresed and stained with Coomassie blue, two peptides of ca. M_r 130,000 and 145,000 were found. Comparisons with the peptides synthesized by the various recombinant strains suggest that the "5.3 gene" cloned from HD-2 codes for the lower molecular weight peptide and the "B gene" codes for the higher molecular weight peptide. This implies that the second peptide seen in solubilized HD-2 crystals did not arise by degradation but that each peptide is the product of a separate gene and that both genes are expressed.

These observations support the idea that there are at least two types of genes ("A" and "B") which code for proteins of different antigenicity and electrophoretic mobility. There seem to be several related variants of the "A gene" and at least one (the "5.3 gene") codes for a peptide of slightly lower molecular weight. It is interesting that a single strain may have one, two or three of these related genes either on different plasmids or even on the same plasmid. For example, as stated above, we cloned a "5.3 gene" from a 44 md plasmid from strain kurstaki HD-1. However, hybridization experiments with plasmids isolated by sucrose gradient sedimentation showed that the "6.6 gene" and the "4.5 gene" present in this strain were both located on one of the two ca. 150 md plasmids. Also, the 57 md plasmid doublet of subspecies thuringiensis apparently contains the "5.3 gene" as well as the "B gene". It is possible that one member of the doublet may contain both genes. Although the "A genes" seem to be widely distributed among the sample of strains we have studied (the distribution of the "B gene" has not yet been determined), it seems likely that additional genes could be present, at least in those strains whose crystals contain more than one peptide. Furthermore, in some strains, the gene is located only on the chromosome and cloning experiments (Klier et al., 1982; Held et al., 1982) indicate that in other strains, the gene is located both on the chromosome and on a plasmid. The diversity in the locations of the gene, the multiplicity of related genes and the possibility that there are several different crystal protein genes indicates an unexpectedly complex genetic situation. Clearly, additional experiments will be needed to establish which genes are expressed in different subspecies and to correlate the various genes with particular peptides and their toxicities.

ACKNOWLEDGMENTS

We wish to thank Dr. Richard Losick for making the sequence of the 0.3 kb gene available to us prior to publication and Dr. Doug Nicoll for providing computer programs.

REFERENCES

Angus, T.A. (1954). **Nature 173**, 545.
Bechtel, D.B. and Bulla, L.A. (1976). **J. Bacteriol. 172**, 1472.
Bulla, L.A., Davidson, L.I., Kramer, K.J. and Jones, B.L. (1979). **Biochem. Biophys. Res. Commun. 91**, 1123.
Calabrese, D.M., Nickerson, K.W. and Lane, L. C. (1980). **Canad. J. Micro. 26**, 1006.
Chestukhina, G.G., Kostina, L.I., Mikhailova, A.L., Tyurin, S.A., Klepikova, F.S. and Stepanov, V.M. (1982). **Arch. Microbiol. 132**, 159.
Gonzalez, J.M., Dulmage, H.T. and Carlton, B.C. (1981). **Plasmid 5**, 351.
Gonzalez, J.M., Brown, B.J. and Carlton, B.C. (1982). **Proc. Natl. Acad. Sci. USA 79**, 6951.
Held, G.A., Bulla, L.A., Ferrari, E., Hoch, J., Aronson, A.I., Aronson, A.I. and Minnich, S.A. (1982). **Proc. Natl. Acad. Sci. USA 79**, 6065.
Herbert, B.N., Gould, H.J. and Chain, E.B. (1971). **Eur. J. Biochem. 24**, 366.
Johnson, W.C., Moran, C.P. and Losick, R. (1983). **Nature 302**, 800.
Klier, A., Fargette, F., Ribier, J. and Rapoport, G. (1982). **EMBO J. 7**, 791.
Kronstad, J.W., Schnepf, H.E. and Whiteley, H.R. (1983). **J. Bacteriol. 154**, 419.
Kyte, J. and Doolittle, R.F. (1982). **J. Mol. biol. 157**, 105.
Lawrie, J.M., Spiegelman, G.B. and Whiteley, H.R. (1977). **Gene 2**, 251.
Lee, G. and Pero, J. (1981). **J. Mol. Biol. 152**, 247.
Moran, C.P., Lang, N. and Losick, R. (1981a). **Nucl. Acids Res. 9**, 5979.
Moran, C.P., Lang, N., Banner, C.D.B., Haldenwang, W.G. and Losick, R. (1981b). **Cell 25**, 783.
Moran, C.P., Lang, N., LeGrice, S.F.J., Lee, G., Stephens, M., Sonenshein, A., Pero, J. and Losick, R. (1982). **Mol. Gen. Genet. 186**, 339.

Schnepf, H.E. and Whiteley, H.R. (1981). **Proc. Natl. Acad. Sci. USA 78**, 2893.
Stahley, D.P., Dingman, D.W., Bulla, L.A. and Aronson, A.I. (1981). **Biochem. Biophys. Res. Commun. 84**, 581.
Talkington, C. and Pero, J. (1979). **Proc. Natl. Acad. Sci. USA 76**, 5465.
Tyrell, D.J., bulla, L.A., Andrews, R.E., Kramer, K.J., Davidson, L.I. and Nordin, P. (1981). **J. Bacteriol. 145**, 1052.
Wong, H.C., Schnepf, H.E. and Whiteley, H.R. (1983). **J. Biol. Chem. 258**, 1960.
Yamamoto, T. and McLaughlin, R.E. (1981). **Biochem. Biophys. Res. Commun. 103**, 414.

PLASMID-ASSOCIATED DELTA-ENDOTOXIN PRODUCTION IN BACILLUS THURINGIENSIS[1]

Bruce C. Carlton
José M. González, Jr.

Department of Molecular and Population Genetics
University of Georgia
Athens, Georgia

I. INTRODUCTION

Bacillus thuringiensis (Bt) is a Gram-positive sporulating bacterium which is distinguished taxonomically from its close relative Bacillus cereus, and is of commercial importance because its sporulating cells produce a high molecular weight proteinaceous crystal (the parasporal body) which is highly toxic to larvae of many lepidopteran and some dipteran insects (Dulmage, 1979; Dulmage et al., 1981). The large number of natural strains isolated differ in their flagellar antigens (de Barjac, 1981), immunological properties of the δ-endotoxin (parasporal body toxin) protein (Krywienczyk and Angus, 1967), and insecticidal activities (Dulmage et al., 1981). Some 20 or 21 different Bt subspecies, classified by their flagellar (H) serotypes, are presently recognized (de Barjac, 1981, and personal communication).

Little information was known about the genetics of the δ-endotoxin genes in the various subspecies until recently, when a number of laboratories, including our own, began investigating the possible relationship between extrachromosomal plasmid elements (which are ubiquitous in Bt) and δ-endotoxin production. Our approach to the genetics of δ-endotoxin inheritance has focused on two major techniques. The first involved plasmid curing analyses, generally by random screening of cultures for the occurrence of sponta-

[1]*This work was supported by a research grant from Shell Development Company, Modesto, California.*

ISBN 0-12-274160-9

neous crystal-negative (Cry^-) variants, as well as of strains which lack one or more plasmids but are still crystal-producing (Cry^+). Using this approach, we correlated crystalline-toxin production with specific high-molecular weight plasmids in several different subspecies of Bt (González et al., 1981). The second approach used was that of plasmid transfer. This phenomenon, a natural plasmid-exchange process occurring in Bt strains (González and Carlton, 1982), was used to demonstrate that the transfer of crystal-producing ability always correlates with transfer of the same donor-strain plasmid previously implicated in curing studies. Further, the crystals produced by Cry^+ "transcipients" (recipient cells that have acquired plasmid DNA from a donor strain) have been shown to exhibit the immunological and insecticidal properties of the donor strain, not of the recipient (González et al., 1982). These two complementary approaches have led us to conclude that the δ-endotoxin genes in different strains of Bt are encoded on high-molecular weight plasmids of different sizes. In this report we extend these analyses to a number of additional natural strains. We also report the isolation of certain "unusual" variants in which the toxin-coding plasmid is no longer detectable as CCC (closed covalent circular) DNA.

Tech. used to study the δ-crystal toxin plasmid

II. MATERIALS AND METHODS

Prototype strains of Bt were kindly provided by Dr. H. T. Dulmage, Cotton Insects Research, U.S.D.A. - A.R.S., Brownsville, Texas; the number, flagellar serotype, and variety of each is listed in Table 1. B. cereus NRRL 569 was obtained from Dr. K. Bernhard. B. cereus T was from our Bacillus stock collection. Cultures were routinely grown at 30°C and classified as Cry^+ or Cry^- by phase-constrast microscopy after sporulation on nutrient agar (Difco Laboratories, Detroit, Michigan). Generation of plasmid patterns on 0.5% agarose gels and the isolation and purification of plasmid DNA were as described previously (González and Carlton, 1980; González et al., 1982). Labeling of DNA by nick translation and the Southern blotting procedure were done according to Maniatis et al. (1982). Partially-cured variants, both Cry^+ and Cry^-, were isolated as previously described (González et al., 1981; González and Carlton, 1983). Transfer of plasmids between strains growing in mixed culture was carried out as described earlier (González et al., 1982).

III. RESULTS AND DISCUSSION

A. Evidence for Plasmid-Toxin Association by Comparison of Cry$^+$ and Cry$^-$ Variants of Several Strains

Our first evidence implicating specific plasmids in toxin production involved the isolation of Cry$^-$ mutants of five Cry$^+$ Bt prototype strains (HD-1, HD-2, HD-4, HD-8 and HD-73) and the comparison of their plasmid patterns with those of their Cry$^+$ parental strains (González et al., 1981). Loss of toxin production was correlated with the loss of single plasmids in strains HD-2, HD-4 and HD-73. More recently (González and Carlton, 1983), a single plasmid was similarly implicated in toxin production in strain HD-567.

Figure 1 shows the type of plasmid curing data obtained with strains HD-2, HD-567, HD-4 and HD-73. The prototype HD-2 strain, HD2-1, lost its 75 Md plasmid in Cry$^-$ mutants such as HD2-2. The HD-567 prototype, HD567-1, lost its 75 Md plasmid to give Cry$^-$ mutants such as HD567-42 (the similarity in size to the HD-2 plasmid is fortuitous). Cry$^-$ mutants of HD-4, such as HD4-2, lost the ca. 105- Md plasmid present in HD4-1. Prototype strain HD73-1 lost a 50 Md plasmid to give Cry$^-$ mutants such as HD73-17. The less intense 50 Md plasmid band still visible in HD73-17 is due to a plasmid which comigrates with the toxin plasmid (González et al., 1981). Bioassay of Cry$^-$ mutants of HD-2, HD-567, HD-4 and HD-73 showed them to be non-toxic (González et al., 1981; González and Carlton, 1983).

Occasionally a culture received from the Dulmage collection contained some Cry$^-$ cells. Isolation of such Cry$^-$ variants and comparison of their plasmid patterns with those of the Cry$^+$ majority cells implicated a 55 Md plasmid in toxin production in strain HD-74 (Figure 1) and aided in the preliminary work with HD-500 and HD-567. Sometimes two separate cultures of the same serotype and variety, one Cry$^+$, the other Cry$^-$, generated identical plasmid patterns except for the absence of a single plasmid in the Cry$^-$ culture. A 68 Md plasmid was thus linked with crystal production in the H-8ac strain HD-536 (Cry$^+$) by comparison with a Cry$^-$ H-8ac culture, HD-501 (Figure 1). Similarly, an ca. 100 Md plasmid was implicated in toxin production in the H-12 Cry$^+$ strain HD-542 by comparison with a Cry$^-$ H-12 culture, HD-543 (patterns not shown).

In strain HD-8 a single Cry$^-$ mutant was isolated (González et al., 1981) in which an ca. 130 Md plasmid had undergone apparent deletion, generating a smaller plasmid of ca. 90 Md (patterns not shown). In a single Cry$^-$ mutant of

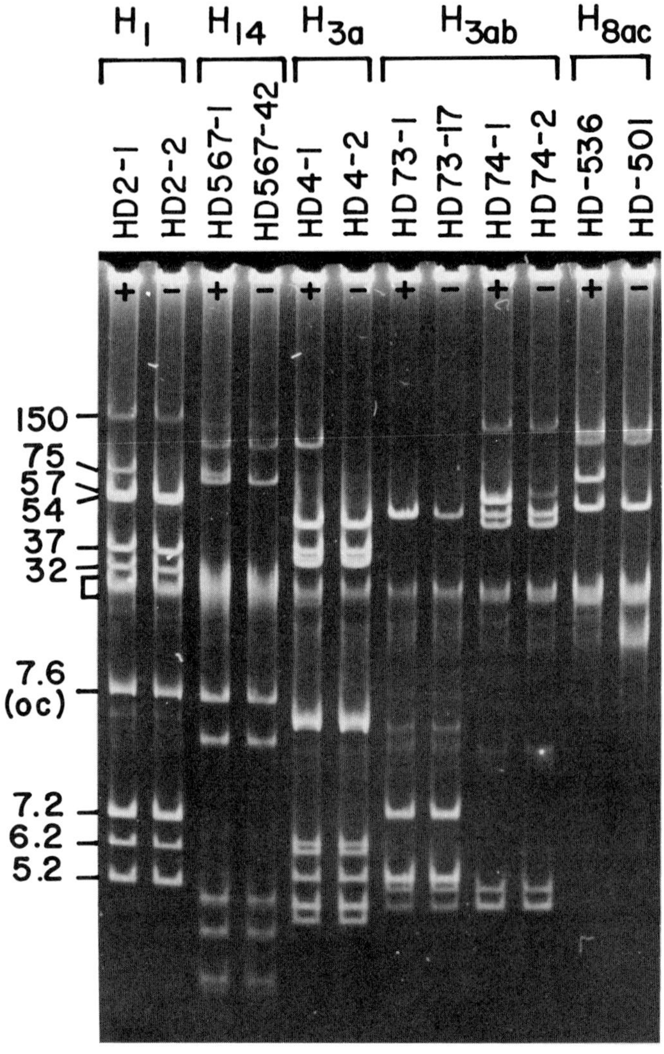

Figure 1. Modified Eckhardt lysate-electrophoresis on 0.5% agarose of the plasmids of five Cry$^+$/Cry$^-$ pairs of B. thuringiensis strains, showing that each Cry$^-$ variant lacks only one of the plasmids of its Cry$^+$ counterpart. In this and in the following figures, strain numbers are listed above each lane, flagellar serotypes are written above the strain numbers; the symbol (+) equals Cry$^+$ and (-) equals Cry$^-$. The bracket marks the position of the linear fragment smears derived from chromosomal DNA (most of which remains

strain HD-1, the strain used commercially, a 29 Md plasmid acquired an insertion of 4 to 5 Md (González et al., 1981). However, futher analyses have led us to conclude that this insertion was fortuitous; curing studies have shown that a plasmid of ca. 110 Md is probably involved in toxin production in HD-1 (unpublished results).

B. Unusual Mutants of H-14 Strains

The closely related H-14 strains, HD-567 and HD-500, are nearly identical in plasmid content; HD-500 lacks the 4.9 Md plasmid and has an ca. 125 Md plasmid not present in HD-567 (see Figure 3A). A 75 Md plasmid was implicated in toxin production in both strains by its absence in all Cry^- mutants (see Figures 1 and 3A) and its presence in Cry^+ variants lacking other plasmids. However, two unusual Cry^+ variants, HD567-26 and HD500-5, seemed exceptions in that agarose gels showed no detectable CCC 75 Md plasmid, and yet active toxin was produced.

Figure 2A summarizes the origin and properties of HD567-26 and several derivatives. All variants pictured arose spontaneously. HD567-11 arose from the prototype HD567-1 (Figure 1) by loss of the LDE (linear DNA element), an extrachromosomal DNA molecule detected only as the linear form (González and Carlton, 1983) and similar or identical in size to the LDE previously detected in HD-1 (González et al., 1981). HD567-11 lost the 68 Md plasmid to give HD567-25, which lost the 75 Md plasmid to give a typical Cry^- mutant, HD567-33. However, HD567-25 also underwent apparent curing of the 75 Md plasmid to give the unusual Cry^+ variant HD567-26. HD567-26 lost the 10.6 Md plasmid to give HD567-32, which then generated two Cry^+ variants, HD567-40 and HD567-39, each of which had one new plasmid. The arrowheads (<) point to the new 49 Md plasmid in HD567-40 and to the new 32 Md plasmid in HD567-39 (obscured in this gel by the linear fragment smear). Cry^- mutants derived from HD567-40 (such as HD567-49) and from HD567-39 (such as HD567-73) lost the new plasmids.

The DNA from the gel in Figure 2A was transferred to nitrocellulose and probed using purified HD-567 75 Md plasmid labeled with ^{32}P. The autoradiograph of the resulting

---

at the top of the gel) and from degraded large plasmids. The molecular masses of the HD-2 plasmids (in megadaltons, Md) are listed on the left margin as a size reference.

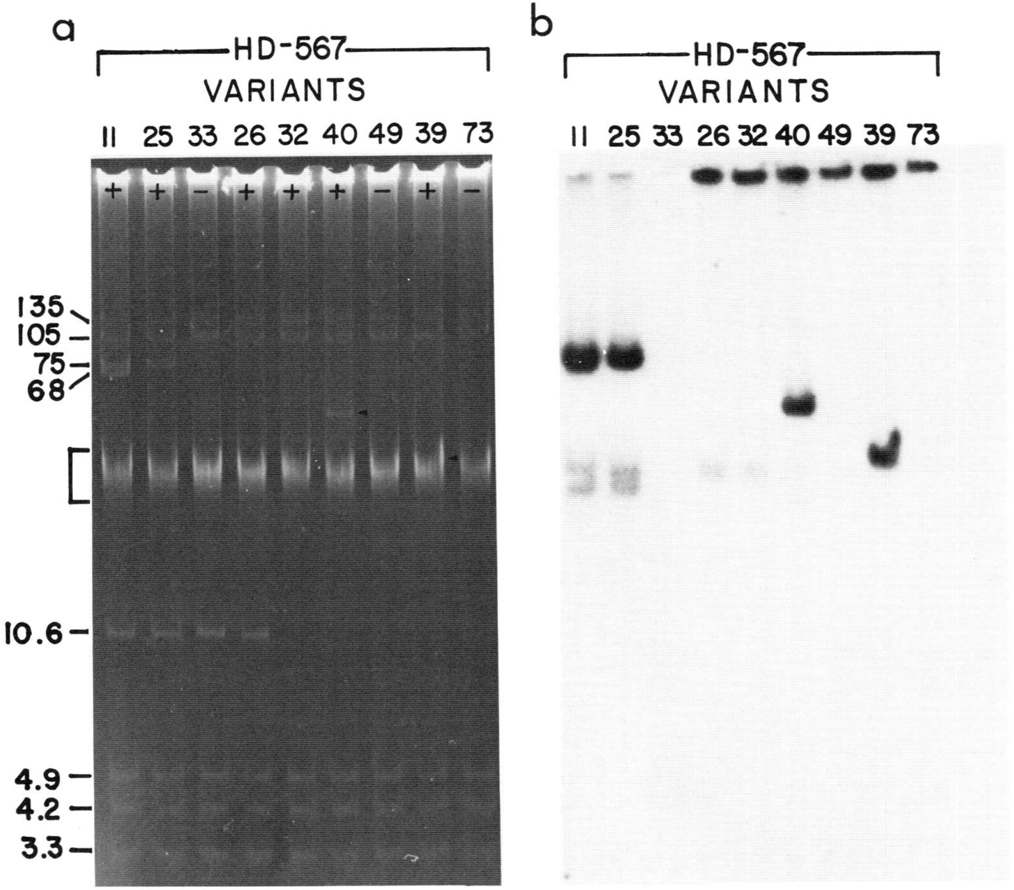

Figure 2. [A] Agarose gel plasmid patterns of several HD-567 variants showing both apparent and true curing of the 75 Md plasmid as well as the generation of new plasmids involved in toxin production. Molecular masses (in Md) of the HD567-11 plasmids are listed in the left margin as a size reference. The arrowheads (<) indicate the new 49 Md and 32 Md plasmids present in HD567-40 and -39, respectively (the 32 Md plasmid is obscured by the linear fragment smear). [B] Southern blot hybridization of the plasmids in [A], after transfer of the DNA to nitrocellulose. The probe was 75 md plasmid DNA from HD-567, labeled with ^{32}P.

blot (Figure 2B) shows strong hybridization to the CCC 75 Md plasmid bands of HD567-11 and -25. The lane containing cells of the typical Cry⁻ mutant HD567-33, shows no hybridization; this variant is truly cured of the 75 Md plasmid. The lanes containing cells of HD567-26 and -32, however, show strong hybridization at the top of the gel, indicating that the 75 Md (or part of it) is present in these variants, although it does not enter the gel. The new 49 Md and 32 Md plasmids in HD567-40 and -39 also hybridize to the probe, showing them to be derived from the 75 Md plasmid. The variants cured of the new plasmids (HD567-49 and -73) still show strong hybridization at the top of the gel, indicating that these Cry⁻ mutants still retain part of the 75 Md plasmid.

The results in Figure 2 may indicate integration of the 75 Md plasmid into the chromosome in HD567-26 and its partial excision in HD567-32 to generate the two new plasmids seen in HD567-40 and -39. The intense hybridization at the top of the HD567-40, -49, -39 and -73 lanes would be due to portions of the 75 Md plasmid remaining in the chromosome after these excision events and which are retained even after the new plasmids are lost (HD567-49 and -73). A similar phenomenon has been observed in the unrelated H-3ab strain HD-1, where a mutant analogous to HD567-26 has been isolated in which the presumptive toxin plasmid is undetectable, but which gives rise to derivatives containing new plasmids (unpublished results).

Figure 3A shows the properties of six spontaneous variants of strain HD-500. The prototype, HD500-1 (not shown), lost the LDE to generate HD500-3. HD500-3 lost the ca. 125 Md plasmid to give HD500-4, which then lost the 75 Md plasmid to generate HD500-8 which is Cry⁻. HD500-4 also gave rise to the unusual Cry^+ mutant HD500-5, in which no 75 Md plasmid is detectable. HD500-5 in turn gave rise to the Cry^- mutant HD500-7 (no change in plasmid pattern) and to the Cry^+ mutant HD500-6, lacking the 68 Md plasmid. Figure 3B shows the results of transfer of the DNA from the gel in Figure 3A to nitrocellulose and Southern blot hybridization. The probe was the same ^{32}P-labeled 75 Md plasmid DNA from HD-567 used in Figure 2B. Strong hybridization to the 75 Md plasmid CCC band is observed in HD500-3 and -4, as well as weaker hybridization to what is probably its OC (open circular) form at the top of these lanes and to its linear form in the middle of the figure. Lesser but significant hybridization to the 68 Md plasmid is also seen in HD500-5, -7, and -8, where it is not masked by hybridization to the 75 Md plasmid band. However, in the lanes containing cells of HD500-5 and -6, strong hybridization is detectable to a broad band of linear fragments in the middle of the

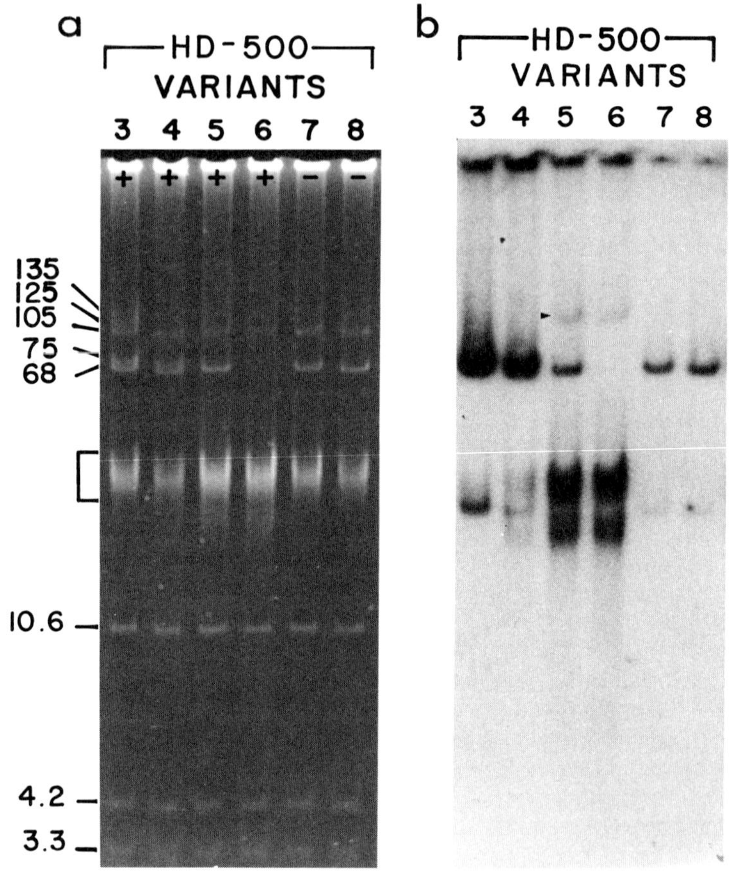

Figure 3. [A] Agarose gel plasmid patterns of several variants of strain HD-500, showing both apparent and true curing of the 75 Md plasmid. Molecular masses (in Md) of the plasmids of HD500-3 are listed in the left-hand margin. [B] Southern blot hybridization of the gel in [A], using ^{32}P-labeled 75 md plasmid DNA from HD-567 as a probe. The arrowhead (>) indicates the faint band (possibly a dimer of the 75 md plasmid) detectable in HD500-5 and -6.

figure as well as to the top of the gel (possibly to an OC form). A faintly hybridizing band is also visible in HD500-5 and -6 whose mobility places it in the range of 120 to 150 Md (this band is not visible in Figure 3A). In the Cry$^-$ strains HD500-7 and -8, only the CCC form of the 68 Md plasmid hybridized significantly, showing that the 75 Md plasmid sequences detected in HD500-4 (which generated HD500-8) and HD-500-5 (which generated HD500-7) have been lost.

Figures 2 and 3 demonstrate that there is more than one possible manner in which a plasmid can be present in a strain but undetectable on agarose gels. The two variants HD567-26 and HD500-5 are clearly not analogous, since chromosomal integration of plasmid DNA does not explain the results shown in Figure 3B. Possibly the 75 Md plasmid has mutated to a dimeric form in HD500-5 which forms large amounts of linear fragments during cell lysis, leading to a faint CCC dimeric band (Figure 3B, arrow) and an intensely hybridizing linear smear. Loss of the 75 Md plasmid (whether in its normal or its dimeric form) would then produce mutants such as HD500-7 and -8 which are truly "cured".

C. Transfer of Toxin Plasmids Among Strains of B. thuringiensis and B. cereus

Transfer of Bt plasmids from Bt donor strains into Bt and B. cereus recipient strains (González and Carlton, 1982) was used to demonstrate the transmission of four toxin-coding plasmids (González et al., 1982; Gonzáles and Carlton, 1983). The usual protocol involved mixing vegetative cells of a Cry$^+$Str^s Bt donor strain and a Cry$^-$Str^r Bt or B. cereus recipient strain and selecting for Str^r cells after a period of mixed growth. Whenever Cry$^+$Str^r transcipients were detected, their agarose gel plasmid patterns demonstrated that the same donor plasmid was always acquired and was the plasmid previously implicated in toxin production from curing studies. The toxin plasmids of HD-2, HD-73 and HD-263 were transmitted to Cry$^-$Str^r recipients derived from HD-2 and HD-73 (Gonzáles et al., 1982; this work). Cry$^+$ HD-2 transcipients carrying toxin plasmids from HD-73 or HD-263 were shown by immunological tests to be hybrid strains, having H-1 flagella (that is, like HD-2) but producing crystals of the kurstaki type (i.e., same as the plasmid donor strains HD-73 and HD-263); likewise, B. cereus recipients that had acquired any of these toxin plasmids produced crystals that were immunologically related to those of the donor strain (González et al., 1982).

Figure 4 shows a representative sample of Cry$^+$ transcipients. The five prototype strains show the original donor plasmid background for reference; the donor used was often not the prototype shown, but a derivative with a plasmid array altered by curing or deletion (González et al., 1982). Four Cry$^-$Str^r recipient strains are shown:

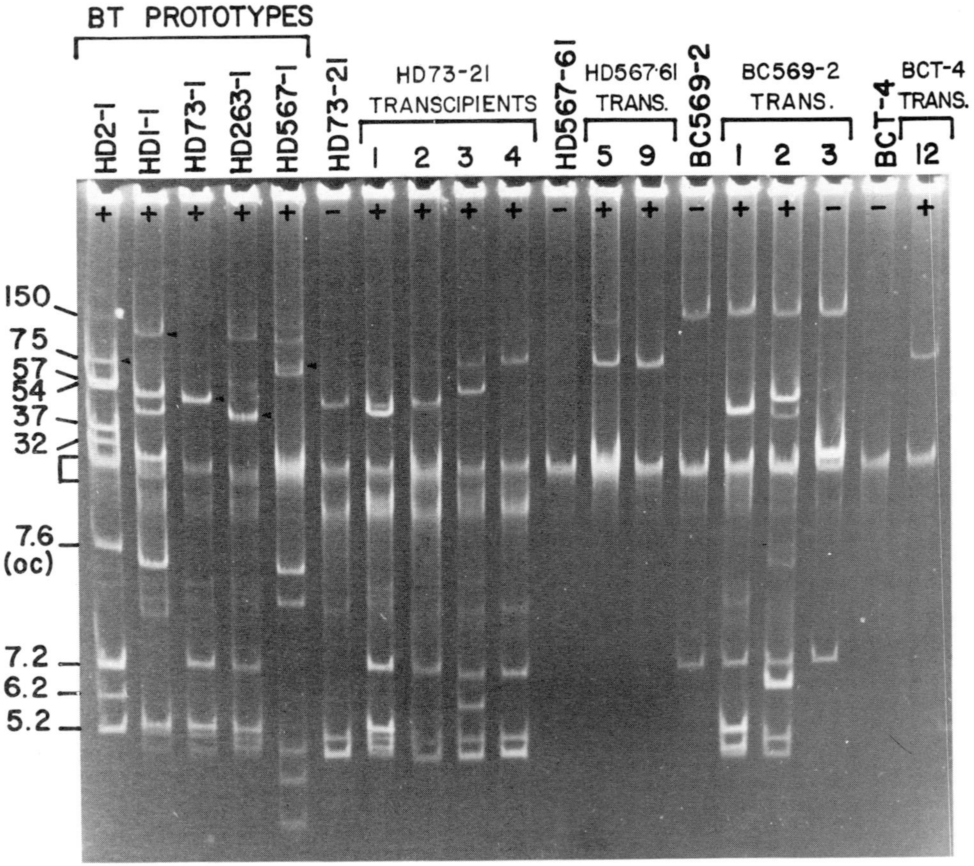

Figure 4. Agarose gel plasmid patterns of Cry^+ prototype strains, Cry^- recipient strains, and representative transcient strains (both Cry^+ and Cry^-) showing transfer of Bt plasmids into Bt and B. cereus strains. The arrowheads (<) point to the prototype strain plasmid implicated in toxin production. The molecular masses of the plasmids of HD-2 are listed on the left margin as size references. HD1-1 and HD263-1 both contain a 1.4 md plasmid that ran off the gel.

HD73-21, BC569-2, BCT-4 and HD567-61. These were derived from HD73-1, BC569-1, BCT-1 and HD567-1 (González et al., 1982; González and Carlton, 1983).

Figure 4 shows that HD-2, HD-73 and HD-263 can transmit their toxin-coding (and other) plasmids into HD73-21. Transcipient HD73-21-1 has acquired the 44 Md (toxin) and three small plasmids from HD263-1. HD73-21-2 has acquired the 50 Md (toxin) and the 7.5 Md plasmids from an HD-73 donor. The next two transcipients, HD73-21-3 and -4, show the transfer of the 75 Md toxin plasmid from HD-2 into HD-73. The absence in both of these transcipients of the 47 Md resident plasmid suggests that it may be incompatible with the acquired 75 Md plasmid.

Figure 4 also shows transfer of the HD-73 and HD-263 toxin-coding plasmids into BC569-2. BC569-2-1 acquired the 44 Md (toxin), and three small plasmids from an HD-73 donor (the 43 Md plasmid is a deleted derivative of the 50 Md/47 Md plasmid present in HD73-17 and HD73-21). The DH-2 toxin plasmid did not transfer into BC569-2 but did transfer into BCT-4, to generate the transcipient BCT-4-12. Conversely, the toxin plasmids of HD-73 and HD-263 did not transfer into BCT-4, while they transferred into BC569-2 with ease.

HD-1 did not transfer the putative ca. 110 Md toxin plasmid into the recipients used (of HD-2, HD-73, BC-569 and BC-T origin). Transfer of the 29 Md plasmid into BC569-2 gave the Cry^- transcipient BC569-2-3, further indicating that this is not a toxin-coding plasmid.

Toxin-producing ability did not transfer from strain HD-567 into HD-2, HD-73 BC-569 or BC-T recipients. When the plasmidless recipient HD-567-61 was used, however, we obtained Cry^+ transcipients such as HD567-61-5 (Figure 4), which has only the 75 Md (toxin) and ca. 135 Md plasmids (González and Carlton, 1983). HD567-61-5 was cured of the ca. 135 Md plasmid by growth at 42°C, generating HD567-61-9, which contains only the 75 Md plasmid and still produces a visible and toxic crystal. Pure plasmid DNA from HD567-61-9 was used as a probe in the Southern blots shown in Figures 2B and 3B.

These experiments have reinforced the assignment of toxin-coding genes to specific plasmids by showing that the same plasmid implicated by plasmid curing experiments is involved in transfer of crystal-producing ability. The fact that Cry^+ transcipients of Cry^- recipient cells produced toxin crystals with the immunological and insecticidal properties of the donor strains argues that the δ-endotoxin structural genes reside on the implicated plasmids.

Table 1. Correlations Between Specific Plasmids and Delta-Endotoxin Production in Various Strains of B. thuringiensis

Prototype Strain Number[a]	H-serotype and Variety Name	Number of Plasmids	Size of Plasmid Implicated in Toxin Production	Type of Implicating Evidence[b]	Reference
HD-2	1, thuringiensis	10	75 md	A,T	González et al., 1981; González et al., 1982; this work
HD-73	3ab, kurstaki	6	50 md	A,T	González et al., 1981; González et al., 1982
HD-74	3ab, kurstaki	7	55 md	A	This work
HD-1	3ab, kurstaki	12	ca. 110 md	A,D	This work
HD-263	3ab, kurstaki	11	44 md	T	González et al., 1982
HD-4	3a, alesti	10	ca. 105 md	A	González et al., 1981
HD-8	5ab, galleriae	4	ca. 130 md	D	González et al., 1981
HD-536	8ac, ostriniae	4	68 md	A	This work
HD-542	12, thompsoni	4	ca. 100 md	A	This work
HD-567	14, israelensis	9	75 md	A,T	González and Carlton, 1983
HD-500	14, israelensis	9	75 md	A	This work

[a]Refer to number in the strain collection of H.T. Dulmage; [b]A = absence of the plasmid in Cry^- variant(s); D = deleted form of the plasmid detected in Cry^- variant(s); T = transfer of the plasmid into a Cry^- Bt or B. cereus recipient converted it to Cry^+

IV. CONCLUDING REMARKS

Table 1 summarizes our work correlating certain Bt plasmids with crystalline toxin production. The assignments of toxin genes to specific plasmids by curing studies were confirmed in HD-2, HD-73 and HD-567 by transmission of the implicated plasmids into Cry⁻ recipients, converting them into toxin producers. The presumptive toxin-coding plasmid is of a different size in each strain examined, even in related strains. For example, while the four strains of var. kurstaki studied show similarities in their small plasmids, their toxin plasmids are 50, 55, ca. 110, and 44 Md in size. The spontaneous changes observed in plasmid sizes (Figure 2; González et al., 1981) may account for this variability. The two H-14 strains HD-500 and HD-567 both have toxin plasmids of 75 Md, probably bacause they are descended from the same isolate (D. Dean, personal communication) of Goldberg and Margalit (1977). All plasmids implicated in toxin production in our work are large in size (44 to ca. 110 Md). A survey of 40 to 50 crystal-producing strains of Bt, comprising 20 serotypes and 25 varieties, showed that some strains lacked small plasmids but all contained at least one large plasmid greater than ca. 20 Md (unpublished results). The evidence to date suggests that toxin genes only reside on large plasmids. Our curing and plasmid transfer studies suggest that crystal production, the principal taxonomic criterion used to separate the B. thuringiensis/B. cereus group into two distinct species, is inconstant, since Bt strains can lose their toxin plasmids to become Cry⁻ (i.e., B. cereus-like) and B. cereus strains can acquire toxin plasmids and thereby become Cry⁺ (i.e., Bt-like).

The recent successes in assigning toxin genes and transmissibility functions to Bt plasmids, as well as the cloning in other laboratories of toxin genes from several Bt strains and serotypes, suggest that detailed genetic analysis and manipulation of B. thuringiensis and B. cereus strains may soon become a reality.

REFERENCES

de Barjac, H. (1981). In Microbial Control of Pests and Plant Diseases, 1970-1980 (H.D. Burges, ed.) p. 35, Academic Press, New York.

Dulmage, H.T. (1979). In Genetics in Relation to Insect Management (M.A. Hoy and J.J. McKelvey, Jr., eds.) p. 116, Rockefeller Foundation, New York.
Dulmage, H.T. and Cooperators (1981). In Microbial Control of Pests and Plant Diseases, 1970-1980 (H.D. Burges, ed.), p. 193, Academic Press, New York.
González, J.M., Jr. and Carlton, B.C. (1980). **Plasmid 3**, 92.
González, J.M., Jr., Dulmage, H.T. and Carlton, B.C. (1981). **Plasmid 5**, 351.

González, J.M., Jr. and Carlton, B.C. (1982). In Genetic Exchange: A Celebration and a New Generation (U.N. Streips, S.H. Goodgal, W.R. Guild and G.A. Wilson, eds.) p. 85, Marcel Dekker, New York.
González, J.M., Jr., Brown, B.J. and Carlson, B.C. (1982). **Proc. Natl. Acad. Sci. USA 79**, 6951.
González, J.M., Jr. and Carlton, B.C. (1983). **Plasmid**, in press.
Goldberg, L.J. and Margalit, J. (1977). **Mosquito News 37**, 355.
Krywienczyk, J. and Angus, T.A. (1967). **J. Invertebr. Pathol. 9**, 126.
Maniatis, T., Fritsch, E.F. and Sambrook, J. (1982). Molecular Cloning (a laboratory manual), Cold Spring Harbor Laboratories, New York.

Focus Sessions

FOCUS SESSION: PHAGE

Hideo Hirokawa
Sophia University, Tokyo, Japan
"Protein Priming of DNA Replication in Bacillus Small Phage"

Philippe Hoet
University of Lovain, Brussels, Belgium
"Cloning of the Origin of Replication of Bacteriophage 2C"

Robert Marrero
University of Rochester, Rochester, New York
"Cloning of Heterologous DNA into a Non-Essential Region of SP02 Prophage"

Benny Raden
Karolinska Institute, Stockholm, Sweden
"Bacillus subtilis Phage SP02 DNA Polymerase Gene L"

Bernard E. Reilly
University of Minnesota, Minneapolis, Minnesota
"Bacteriophage Ø29 in vitro DNA Encapsidation for Use in Gene Cloning"

Charles Stewart
Rice University, Houston, Texas
"Cloning the SP01 Genome"

Thomas Trautner, Chairman
Max-Planck Institute, Berlin, Germany
"DNA Methyltransferase of Bacillus subtilis and Its Phage"

Many aspects of B. subtilis bacteriophage with an immediately obvious relationship to application in biotechnology were covered during the regular sessions. The Focus Session on phage was slanted toward their basic biology, although also here the general line of the conference was very obvious.

ISBN 0-12-274160-9

DNA replication of "phage" Ø29 and M2 has become increasingly interesting after the demonstration that the protein, covalently bound to both 5' ends of the DNA molecule, mediates priming of DNA replication. H. Hirokawa reported in vitro studies with cell-free extracts of Ø29- or M2-infected cells which would catalyze the formation of a complex between the terminal protein of Ø29 or M2 DNA and [α-^{32}P]dAMP in the presence of dATP, $MgCl_2$ and ATP. Failure of extracts from cells infected with certain sus-mutants of Ø29 or M2 to mediate complex formation identified genes involved in complex formation. Heterologous combinations of M2 or Ø29 DNA with extracts from Ø29 infected cells did not mediate complex formation, pointing to the high specificity of this reaction in spite of many other similarities between Ø29 and M2.

A search for the origin of DNA replication of one of the large, HMU-containing phage, 2C, was reported by P. Hoet. Following the technique of Bott and coworkers, which led to the identification of the origin of replication of pBSX, the authors inserted restriction fragments of C2 DNA into plasmid pSC540 of Cohen and Chang. pSC540, composed of pC194, joined at its unique HpaII site to pSC101, cannot replicate in B. subtilis although its CAT gene can be expressed. Transforming B. subtilis cells with the C2/pSC540 ligation mixture, the authors identified a few Cm-resistant colonies harboring plasmids, which were stably maintained and contained C2 DNA from a region within or near the redundant end of the phage DNA molecule which would represent an origin of DNA replication of C2.

B. Raden and L. Rutberg communicated results on the cloning of gene L of bacteriophage SP02 which codes for the phage-specified DNA polymerase. Partial HindIII or SauA3 digests of SP02 DNA were cloned into pC194 or pHV14. Cells transformed with recombinant plasmids containing the phage polymerase gene on variously sized fragments showed elevated levels of DNA polymerase activity and allowed the growth under nonpermissive conditions of SP02 phages carrying sus-mutations in gene L. SP02 WT recombinants resulted from such infections. The DNA polymerase gene of SP02 was estimated to have a maximal size of 2.4 Kb.

Some 75% of the SP01 genome degraded into EcoRI or XbaI fragments was cloned into pBD64 by J. F. Currand and C. R. Stewart. A number of fragments produced could not be cloned in either E. coli or B. subtilis. As had been observed with other phage DNAs, nonclonability could be associated with the presence of phage promoters in nonclonable fragments. In these cases the generation of lethal transcripts and/or interference with adequate expression of vector functions might cause instability of plasmid or host cell.

The limitation of DNA size in DNA packaging was investigated by R. Marrero with temperate phage SPO2. Cells with an oversized prophage SPO2, into whose unique BglII site had been inserted the E. coli plasmid pRM422 (3.6 Md), could be stably maintained. As a consequence of the expression of the CAT gene of pC194 present in pRM422 the cells were resistant to levels of 10 μg/ml of chloramphenicol. Induction of such cells with mitomycin C yielded low titer lysates (ca. 10^4 PFU/ml) which were not capable of transducing the CAT gene and which contained 10 to 15% of clear-type mutants in addition to other plaque-type mutants. Studies on progeny phage derived from such lysates indicated that all phage had lost the nonessential pRM422 DNA in addition to DNA deleted in the region containing the obviously nonessential phage attachment site.

With Ø29, Bjornste and Anderson in 1981 established the only in vitro packaging system so far available in B. subtilis. This system has now been used to package heterologous DNA. B. Reilly, M. A. Bjornste and D. L. Anderson had ligated random EcoRI fragments of B. subtilis to the terminal Ø29 gp-3 EcoRI fragment required for the initiation of DNA packaging. The ligation mixture was exposed to the packaging reaction and the presence of chimeric Ø29/B. subtilis phage was demonstrated through transducing B. subtilis auxotrophs to prototrophy.

Phage mediated DNA methylation in SPR, SPβ, Ø3T has been studied in Trautner's laboratory over the last years. In all cases investigated, a phage gene specificies one DNA methyltransferase with dual methylation specificity (GG$\overset{+}{C}$C and $\overset{+}{C}\overset{+}{C}$GG in SPR; GG$\overset{+}{C}$C and G$\overset{+}{C}$NGC in SPβ or Ø3T). Methyltransferase genes of SPPR and Ø3T have been cloned and are expressed both in E. coli and B. subtilis. These genes have no homology to corresponding bacterial genes. With the DNA sequence of the SPR methyltransferase established and with the availability of phage mutants affecting specificity of methylation it will be possible to define domains of the methyltransferase controlling various steps of the DNA methylation reaction.

FOCUS SESSION: SPORES

Glenn H. Chambliss
University of Wisconsin, Madison, Wisconsin
"Synthesis of Specific Proteins During Sporulation"

Eugenie Dubnau
Public Health Research Institute, New York, New York
"Regulation and Expression of spoOH Genes"

Allessandro Galizzi
University of Pavia, Pavia Italy
"Bacillus subtilis Genes Involved in Spore Outgrowth"

Charles Johnson
Harvard University, Cambridge, Massachusetts
"spoO Control of Transcription"

Chester Price
University of California, Davis, California
"Physical and Genetic Mapping of the Bacillus subtilis Sigma-55 Gene"

Hans J. Rhaese
University of Frankfurt, Frankfurt, Germany
"Effect of Amplification of Spore Genes on Differentation and Stability of Genetic Information"

Donald J. Tipper, Chairman
University of Masachusetts, Worcester, Massachusetts
"Cloning the Bacillus subtilis 168 spoIIA, spoIVA, and gerJ Loci in Plasmid pHV33"

Michael Vodkin
U. S. Army Medical Research Institute of Infectious Disease
Fort Detrick, Maryland
"Cloning of the PA Gene in Bacillus anthracis"

Michael A. von Tersch
University of Georgia, Athens, Georgia
"Development of a Cloning System in Bacillus megaterium and Its Application for Megacin Immunity and Structural Genes"

ISBN 0-12-274160-9

The "spores" session was not totally devoted to sporulation, and other sessions also contained papers directly relevant to sporulation which are included in this volume. The first group of papers in the "Spores" session concerned the structure and function of specific B. subtilis spo genes.

C. Johnson showed that sigma factor variation during sporulation cannot be the sole control of spo gene expression, at least for the spoVG gene, which is expressed, both in vivo and in vitro, from two alternate transcription initiation sites 10 bp apart. The upstream transcript is produced by Eσ37 and downstream by Eσ32, utilizing overlapping, unique promoter sites. The concentrations of both Eσ37 and Eσ32 are maximal in B. subtilis vegetative cells and fall markedly between T_1 and T_3 (1 and 3 hours from the start of sporulation at 37°C). In frame fusion of the E. coli lacZ gene to the 5' end of the spoVG gene, placing lacZ under control of the promoter, ribosome binding sites (RBS) and N-terminus of the spoVG gene and its product, allowed determination of the level of expression of this gene. When this recombinant gene is inserted (in single copy number) within lysogenic SPβ, β-galactosidase synthesis under spoVG control is enhanced 10- to 50-fold between T_1 and T_3, in contrast to the decrease in Eσ37 and Eσ32 concentrations. This enhancement is under control of spo0B and spo0F, so is not merely related to growth phase. Deletion of a 26 bp, AT-rich sequence 160 bp upstream of the Eσ37 transcription start point is known to markedly reduce expression in vivo. It appears to be a candidate for interaction with additional transcriptional control elements, which must exist.

E. Dubnau used similar lacZ fusions to measure in vivo expression determined by the 5' end of the B. licheniformis spo0H gene when maintained as a plasmid in B. subtilis. The B. licheniformis gene carries its own promoter recognized by Eσ55. Plasmid DNA detects a 1 Kb transcript on Northern gels of RNA from both vegetative and sporulating cells. The gene contains a 168 amino acid open reading frame bracketed by a 230 bp 5' leader and a 260 bp 3' tail in the transcript. The fusion plasmid can replicate in E. coli under ampicillin selection or in B. subtilis under chloramphenicol selection. The B. subtilis transformant gives blue colonies on X-gal plates, indicating a low level of β-galactosidase production. To test function of the fusion gene at single copy number, integration into the chromosome was engineered by transformation into a rec^+ strain in which integration of pE194 (a ts replicon) had been selected by growth at high temperature with chloramphenicol. Integration of the spo0H plasmid occurs at the pE194 site, the only site of homology. In batch culture, production of β-galactosidase occurs in vegetative cells, but at a lower level that was enhanced 8- to 9-fold during post-experimental growth. This increase was not affected by host chromosomal spoOA, spoOB, spoOF, spoOH or spoIIIA mutations, but was repressed by glucose. Thus the B. licheniformis spoOH gene is growth-phase regulated and catabolite repressed, but is not controlled by other spo pathway genes tested. Mutations in these genes also failed to affect catabolite repression of spoOH. A second fusion plasmid with the same orientation and apparent size of spoOH insert, behaved differently. Cells carrying this fusion produced dark blue colonies on X-gal plates and produced vegetative levels of β-galactosidase about equal to the maximal level seen post-exponentially in the former case. These levels were enhanced in the presence of glucose. The explanation of these intriguing observations is unknown at present.

G. Chambliss described the regulation of the B. subtilis α-glucosidase gene. α-glucosidase is induced only by maltose or maltotrisose repressed by glucose and is not inducible by sporulation. It is hyperinducible between T_0 and T_2 in spoIIA mutants or in mutants blocked in "earlier" spo loci such as spoOA. Mutants blocked at spoIIB or later are not inducible, although spoOF is an exception in behaving like a spoIIB mutant. Several clones encoding α-glucosidase activities have been isolated from a B. subtilis gene bank for further analysis.

C. Price has cloned the σ55 gene (rpoD) and shown that it produces the correct protein in E. coli. Sequencing of the rpoD region shows it to be located between two open reading frames, P62 and P17, with P62 read off the same strand. Since the equivalent E. coli gene is part of an operon including ribosomal protein and DNA primase genes, and rpoD maps very close to dnaE, complementation for dnaE on the rpoD clone fragment was sought and found. Identity of dnaE and the p62 gene is being tested.

H. Rhaese described a new method for detecting genome rearrangements in B. subtilis during sporulation. Using a new technique, complete restriction endonuclease digests of vegetative and T_4 chromosomal DNAs are separately fractionated by electrophoresis as horizontal bands, and then blotted at right angles onto each other under hybridization conditions. One DNA is labelled so that a diagonal line of hybridization signals should be produced, if all fragments are unique and identical. Using several restriction endonucleases, Veg X Veg and Spo X Spo controls, it was found Veg X Spo blots showed a significant number of nondiagonal signals potentially indicating fragments of altered size.

A. Galizzi and coworkers have isolated several B. subtilis mutants temperature-sensitive for outgrowth and have now cloned the outB81 gene. Five clones were found with a high frequency of transformation of outB81 mutant cells to ts^+ for spore outgrowth. They turned out to be identical, containing a 14 Kb EcoRI insert which also carries the aroI marker and part of the amyE gene. Restriction endonuclease mapping locates the outB81 gene midway between these two markers. Clones have also been screened for reacting selectively with fragments of RNA from outgrowing spores. Two such clones had an identical 7.8 Kb RI fragment which reacted strongly with the RNA probe. One has been mapped by subcloning on pJH101, which renders B. subtilis resistant to chloramphenicol only by integration. It is linked to gluA by PBS1 transduction.

D. Tipper and coworkers failed to find complementation of lys by DNA in the Ferrari et al. λ libraries or existing plasmid banks, including the bank in cosmid vector pQ79.1 of Aubert. A new bank of partial SauIIIa fragments of B. subtilis DNA in this cosmid vector was created and one E. coli colony was found, DNA from which (cos 12) complemented lys-1 and lys-3 in rec^+ strains, as well as spoIIA markers. spoIIA26, but not spoIIA42 or either of the lys markers, was complementated in a $recE4^-$ background. The clone thus lacks an intact lys gene, and lacks an intact copy of the distal IIA gene but has at least one other intact spoIIA gene proximal to lys. The clone failed to complement spoIIA176 (rec^+) which was located further from lys than spoIIA50, indicating that the clone terminates before this marker. Both of the spoIIA genes identified presumably produce diffusible products. Mutants in them are recessive to wild-type.

M. Vodkin reported on the isolation of clones expressing the PA (protective antigen) gene of B. anthracis toxin. The edema factor (EF) and lethal factor (LF) of this toxin function only in the presence of PA, which apparently mediates their entry into sensitive cells. As its name suggests, antibodies to PA are protective. However, present vaccines, derived from culture supernatants of virulent strains, are far from ideal. Cloning of PA is aimed at producing a better vaccine. Presence of a 168 Kb plasmid in B. anthracis correlates with toxin production. A bank of this plasmid DNA in pBR322 was created in E. coli and screened with anti-PA using peroxidase-labeled antibody. Two positive plasmids were found, producing normal-sized PA in E. coli (Western blot). Assays for the PA-dependent characteristic morphological effect of EF on cultured cells were also positive. The two clones contain the same 6 Kb insert in opposite orientation, indicating that the cloned gene probably carries its own promoter and RBS. Subcloning is in progress.

M. von Tersch described cloning B. megaterium DNA in the homologous host, especially genes for megacins A-216 and A-19213, in a system which will allow selection by the associated immunity functions. Neither B. subtilis nor E. coli is sensitive to megacins.

Plasmid pBC16 (4.6 Kb) encoding tetracycline resistance has been used as a vector for PEG-enhanced transformation of B. megaterium protoplasts. It was found as many as 35% of the Tet^r transformants carried recombinant plasmids. In some cases, the insert DNA was as large as 20 Kb in size. Shotgun cloning of restriction fragments of megacinogenic plasmids pBM309 (48 Kb) and pMB113 (44 Kb) into the XbaI, EcoRI and BamHI sites of pBC16 with immunity selection resulted in clones that expressed immunity alone and others that expressed both the immunity and structural genes for each megacin. All megacin A-216 immune clones contained the XbaI G fragment of pMB309 (3.0 Kb) while two clones that expressed both production and immunity to megacin A-216 contained 3 common XbaI fragments E, G, and H (8.1 Kb total). Clones that expressed immunity to megacin A-19213 contained the EcoRI fragment (2.o Kb) of pMB113. Immune producer clones of megacin A-19213 contained the BglII-A fragment (18.5 Kb).

FOCUS SESSION: GENERAL GENETICS

Juan-Carlos Alonso
Max-Planck Institute, Berlin, Germany
"Requirement for a Plasmid-Coded Product in the Stability of Plasmid pC194"

Linda Anderson
University of North Carolina, Chapel Hill, North Carolina
"Reconstruction of the Defective Phage PBSX"

Tadahiko Ando
Riken Institute, Wako-Shi, Japan
"Site-Specific Endonucleases in Bacillus subtilis: Application of Monoclonal Antibodies to Their Characterization"

Majorie H. Barnes
University of Massachusetts, Worcester, Massachusetts
"Cloning of the Structural Gene for Polymerase III of Bacillus subtilis"

Manuel Espinosa
Brookhaven National Laboratory, Upton, New York
"Expression of Amylomaltase by the Pneumococcal Recombinant Plasmid pL69 in Bacillus subtilis"

Donald M. Green
University of New Hampshire, Durham, New Hampshire
"Two-dimensional Zymogram Analysis of Bacillus subtilis Nucleases"

George Ordal
University of Illinois, Urbana, Illinois
"Bacillus subtilis Genes Specifying Chemotactic Functions"

Gerard Venema
University of Groningen, Haren, Netherlands
"The Bacillus subtilis recE Product and Cloning Expression of the Escherichia coli RecA Gene in Bacillus subtilis"

ISBN 0-12-274160-9

Ronald Yasbin, Chairman
University of Rochester, Rochester, New York
"recE: What's It All About?"

Several interesting contributions were made in this focus session. J.-C. Alonso reported on a mutant of plasmid pC194, termed pC194-1 which cannot be stably maintained during cell division in Bacillus subtilis and makes the cell sensitive to MMS in the presence of a selective marker. However it could be stabilized in TRANS by the presence of other unrelated plasmids in the host cell. The segment necessary for stabilization was located within a 0.51 kb segment outside of the replication origin. This segment might specify a gene product of 2.7 Kd. Deletion of the part of this region in pC194 WT generated the phenotype of the unstable plasmid pC194-1.

Aspects of reconstruction of the genome of defective phage PBSX was discussed by L. Anderson. It was shown earlier that a fragment from the PBSX-metC region of the B. subtilis chromosome can rescue a nonreplicative vector. Now evidence was presented for the existence of the origin of phage DNA replication and perhaps a gene for phage related protein on this fragment. This fragment containing oriP has been used as a physical probe to identify the neighboring chromosomal fragments of DNA. Twenty-two Kb of contiguous chromosomal DNA has been isolated to date. None of the known phage mutations can be rescued by any of the fragments tested, but a map relating physical to biological characteristics of this region has been constructed.

T. Ando discussed the isolation and characterization of a number of site-specific endonucleases in Bacillus strains. The genes for these enzymes from related strains have been introduced into the Marburg strain by transformation. The genetic loci of five restriction-modification systems were determined and the hsrR, hsrC and hsrF (genes of BsuR, BsuC and BsuF) were strongly suggested to be alleles. B. amyloliquefaciens N produced two site-specific endonucleases, BamNI and BamNX, and strongly restrict the growth of phage NR2 and 1. The phage DNA restriction is mediated by BamNX. Mutant phages NR2rH and 1rH were isolated. Both are immune to restriction by BsuR and BsuC. Mouse monoclonal antibodies were prepared against BsuR to ellucidate the character of BsuR and its allelic enzymes and to purify BsuR and other proteins which interact with BsuR.

The strategy to isolate the polC gene of B. subtilis was outlined by M. Barnes. The gene has been partially cloned into Escherichia coli using the plasmid p1949. This plasmid is a hybrid constructed from plasmids pC194 and pMB9, carries a single EcoRI site, resistance to chloramphenicol and replicates autonomously in E. coli. Its replication in B. subtilis requires its integration into the genome. Using plasmid p1949, one hybrid, p154t, was found to contain a 6.5 Kb fragment of B. subtilis DNA that encompassed two of the three polC markers: azp-12 to ts-6. It was clear that this fragment would serve as a probe to select the complete gene from other B. subtilis libraries.

Expression of the enzyme amylomaltase by the Pneumococcal recombinant plasmid pLS69 introduced into B. subtilis was reported by M. Espinosa. The level of amylomaltase activity was identical to that of induced cells of S. pneumonia but in B. subtilis the enzyme production was constitutive. The presence of pLS69 did not enhance the ability of B. subtilis to grow with maltose, presumbably because the free sugar was not transported into the cell. The proteins specified by the plasmid have been analyzed in a minicell system. In conclusion it was pointed out that in many cases deletions of recombinant plasmids carrying foreign DNA occur after plasmid establishment. The instability of such plasmids in B. subtilis appeared to result from the presence of strong promoters, deletion of which provides a selective advantage to the plasmid.

A very sensitive two-dimensional electrophoretic analysis was used by D. Green to identify the proteins associated with the development of competence in B. subtilis. Eighty-three discrete nuclease activities have been detected in B. subtilis lysates. They were all characterized with respect to monomeric molecular weights, cation activation requirements and preference for double- and single-stranded DNA substrates. Based on these criteria, a mimimun of 16 classes of activities were identified. Thirty-seven polypeptides associated with the development of competence were found along with induction of 4 nucleases and suppression of 6 nucleases. Transformation defective mutants have been identified to have reduced levels of competent associated (17,000 m.w.) nuclease. They are defective in DNA uptake, unable to inactivate exogenous DNA and unable to induce several competence-associated nucleases.

G. Ordal has isolated chemotaxis mutants, a great majority of these mapped in the region between pyrD and thyA, but those having a defect in the chemotactic methyl transferase mapped very close to aroF. Three cloned fragments of B. subtilis DNA from a λ Charon 4A bank have been subcloned in pFH7. These were then integrated into B.

subtilis lysogenic for prophage SPβc2. Each of these clones were introduced by transduction into each mutant and determined which, if any, contained the corresponding wild-type gene. Great difficulty was encountered in introducing mutational alleles onto these phages. Therefore integrated SPc2del-2::Tn917 was integrated into the che region and specialized transducing phage for chemotaxis genes were isolated.

The recA gene containing 1.8 Kb DNA fragment of E. coli, which was originally cloned in pBR328, was recloned into the B. subtilis expression vector pPL608 in a strain of B. subtilis carrying the recE allele (presumed to be similar to the recA gene of E. coli) by G. Venema. The plasmid expressed the $recA^+$ gene product in B. subtilis minicells. The expression was under the control of the phage SP02 promoter present in the plasmid and depended on proper orientation of the gene with respect to the promoter. The $recA^+$ gene product in the recE4 mutant of B. subtilis restored its ability to recombine along with lessening its sensitivity to mitomycin C. As in E. coli, the $recA^+$ protein is induced by UV irradiation in B. subtilis suggesting the similarities of the genetic control. However, these similarities may be superficial as pointed out by R. Yasbin. Specifically the recA mutant of E. coli rapidly degrades DNA and that is due to the normal control the $recA^+$ gene product has over the $recBC^+$ enzyme. Athough similar behavior was noted in recE cells of B. subtilis earlier, a recent careful analysis revealed that the degradation of cellular DNA was promoted by the activity of resident Bacillus prophages. Furthermore, in B. subtilis, unlike in E. coli, the 'SOS' inducible functions can be separated with regard to their dependence on a functional $recE^+$ gene product. As an example, Yasbin stated that filamentation does not require a $recE^+$ gene product whereas W-activation and prophage induction are abolished in the recE mutant strains. Thus extrapolation between the two systems might result in erroneous conclusions.

Index

R